Personnel
Management

Barbara Jarran

Personnel Management
HRM in Action
THIRD EDITION

Derek Torrington and Laura Hall

Prentice Hall

London   New York   Toronto   Sydney   Tokyo   Singapore
Madrid   Mexico City   Munich

First edition published 1987
Second edition published 1991

This third edition first published 1995 by
Prentice Hall International (UK) Limited
Campus 400, Maylands Avenue
Hemel Hempstead
Hertfordshire, HP2 7EZ
A division of
Simon & Schuster International Group

Typeset in 10/12pt Sabon
by Goodfellow and Egan Ltd, Cambridge, UK

Printed and bound in Great Britain by
T. J. Press Ltd, Padstow

Library of Congress Cataloging-in-Publication Data

Torrington, Derek, 1931–

    Personnel management : HRM in action/Derek

Torrington and Laura Hall. — 3rd ed.

      p.   cm.

    Includes bibliographical references and index.

    ISBN 0-13-149543-7 (pbk.)

    1. Personnel management.   I. Hall, Laura,

1952–. II. Title.

HF5549.T675   1995

658.3—dc20   95–3888

                                        CIP

British Library Cataloguing in Publication Data

A catalogue record for this book is available from
the British Library

ISBN 0-13-149543-7

 2 3 4 5   99 98 97 96

Contents

We acknowledge the following permissions:

from the American Academy of Management to use Table 3.1, Figure 24.3 and Table 24.1; from Braybrooke Press Ltd to use Figure 3.2 and Table 10.1; from John Wiley and Sons Inc to use Figure 3.3, Figure 3.4, Figure 10.4 and Figure 20.1; from the Free Press (a division of Simon and Schuster) to use Figure 3.5; from John Wiley and Sons Ltd to use Figure 3.6; from D Guest to use figure 3.7; from the IPD to use Figure 7.1, Figure 8.2, Figure 8.3, Figure 35.2, Table 35.3 and the boxed quote on page 330; from Findlay Publications Ltd to use figure 7.3; D Burn and L Thompson to use Table 8.2; from the Institute of Employment Research to use Figure 10.1; from J Atkinson to use Figure 10.2 and Figure 10.3; from the Human Resource Management Journal to use Table 13.3 and Table 17.1; from McGraw Hill Book Company for Figure 17.1 and 17.2; from Stanley Thornes Publishers to use Figure 18.2; from Idea Group Publishing Ltd to use Figure 19.3; from P Miller to use Table 22.1; from Harcourt Brace to use Figure 25.2; from the Equal Opportunities Commission for Table 20.1; from the Academy of Management Journal for Figure 24.3 and Table 24.1; Ralph Windle for the poem in Chapter 30, and for permission to use some material in Chapter 30, that also appears in their *Personnel Management Handbook (1987)*; from Sage Publications to use the boxed example on p.305.

Preface

The material of this book deals with the personnel processes in and around organisations that can lead to the effective management of human resources, as well as providing an effective management service to resourceful humans. It is the fifth in a series that started with Torrington and Chapman in 1979 and 1983, continuing with Torrington and Hall in 1987 and 1991.

The title remains as *Personnel Management*, first to maintain the continuity and secondly because it describes the contents. The specialist people in the field still mainly retain the badges of 'Personnel Director', 'Personnel Manager' and so forth and the main institutional influences, the Institute of Personnel and Development and the Personnel Standards Lead Body, appear to affirm that 'Personnel' is the appropriate label for those specialising in aspects of human resource management. The subtitle *HRM in Action* acknowledges the main current influence on personnel practice.

The degree of restructuring is greater than in the second edition. We have eight parts, beginning with an introduction and ending with a finale. Each of these parts has a single-word title, aiming to be clear and free from jargon.

The bulk of the book is in Parts II to VII, containing a total of 33 chapters. Each of these six parts begins with strategy and ends with interaction, the opening chapter in each providing a review of the strategic aspects of the function that is the subject of the part. This is in response to the great current interest in strategy and makes the necessary link to the concept of human resource management without becoming involved in its incoherent lack of agenda. After this come the chapters with an operational emphasis. The final chapter in each part is an examination of the skills involved in an interactive episode that lies at the heart of the function that has been explored. The logic of this is that personnel management incorporates more of these face to face skills than any other aspect of management. Parts II to VII therefore all have the overall format of:

strategy – operations – interaction

This seems to be the most effective way of producing a book which remains comprehensive and practical as well as keeping up with current thinking.

We fit all this together with a model of the Personnel and Development Process (Figure 0.1), showing the inputs of business and individual needs, and the outputs of business effectiveness and individual satisfaction.

The structure also echoes all the features of the occupational map and associated national vocational qualifications being produced by the Personnel Standards Lead Body (PSLB). Figure 0.2, which is also in Chapter 1, shows the match between the structure of the book and the PSLB format. There is further material in the Teachers' Manual about the use of the book in connection with PSLB standards.

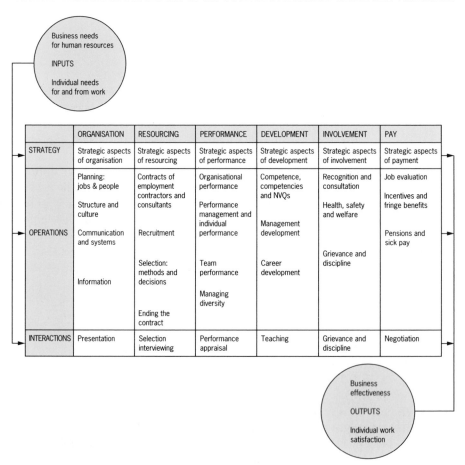

Figure 0.1 Model of the Personnel and Development process

PSLB ACTIVITIES	CHAPTERS IN THIS BOOK
A. Strategy and organisation	
A1 Contribute to organisational strategy	2, 4
A2 Organisational structure and process	6
A3 Culture and values	6
A4 Personnel strategy and plans	3, 5
Resourcing	
B. B1 Resourcing strategy and planning	10
B2 Recruitment of new employees	11, 12, 13
B3 Deployment of the work force	8
B4 Release from the organisation	14
B5 Hire sub-contractors	11, 17
C. Development	
C1 Performance development strategy and planning	16, 22
C2 Performance management	18
C3 Promote training	22
C4 Long term individual development	25
C5 Team development	19
D. Reward	
D1 Reward strategy and plans	32
D2 Levels of reward	33
D3 Benefits	34, 35
D4 Pay	32, 34, 35
E. Relations with employees	
E1 Employee relations strategy and plans	27
E2 Commitment of employees	28
E3 Communication	7
E4 Employee support	29, 30
E5 Health and safety	29
E6 Compliance	–
E7 Negotiations with individuals and groups	36
E8 Equal opportunities	20

Figure 0.2   Match between the structure of this book and the PSLB format

PART I

Introduction

1 The nature of personnel management

Jobs, careers and our whole experience of employment have changed more in the last ten years than in the previous two centuries. The social impact of this change is scarcely recognised and frequently attributed to the temporary hiatus of 'the recession'. The fundamental change is a steady reversal of the trend of the last 200 years, during which the organisation has been not only the central feature of economic activity but also the boundary within which most people work, in which they find their personal security, their career prospects and the means to meet their work-related needs. No more. Organisations are becoming smaller and less reliable. Entrepreneurs are less likely to found a dynasty for their children to inherit and more likely to launch a project to be developed, exploited and then closed down or sold on within two or three years. The movement and availability of investment capital is less at the disposal of the tycoon following a dream with remorseless determination and more disposed of by nine-to-five manipulators of yield ratios yawning in front of computer terminals. Organisations are becoming leaner and smaller. We have de-layering and down-sizing; right-sizing and outplacement; core/periphery workforces; sub-contracting and temporary contracts; a growth in self-employment and part-time working. The organisation as an entity is going out of fashion and the above terms have arrived in the management vocabulary to describe the process of keeping the business as small as possible and the jobs within the business as flexible (and as insecure) as possible.

Because of this development, personnel management is experiencing the biggest change in its history. Many commentators believed that the arrival of human resource management was to be the great change in emphasis, but that was no more than re-thinking the processes inside the organisation; we now have to think beyond the organisation as entity. Personnel management has grown and developed with the increasing size and variety of organisations. It is in the throes of fundamental change because that process has gone into reverse and organisation as *entity* is in decline. We are rediscovering organisation *as a process*.

Consider the following imaginary scenario. There are six people to watch among the crowds thronging Piccadilly Station. First is Charles, Personnel Director, who is on his way to London for yet another strategy meeting; there is the possible closure of the plant in South Korea in order to take advantage of the lower labour costs in Sri Lanka. Then there is the meeting with the executive search consultants to review the candidates for the Chief Executive post in the new subsidiary at Luton before flying out to LA to propose that the design function should be relocated to Rome – they won't like that!

Also walking briskly along to the first class section of the London train is Sam (who may be Samantha or Samuel) a freelance consultant specialising in management development, setting off to run a three-day event for a large company that is rapidly developing its overseas activities and needs Sam's expertise to bring some of the senior executives up to date on European issues. During the journey Sam hopes to do some more work on the distance learning package that the business school have asked for.

On a different platform Sharon has left her commuter train and is hurrying towards the office, hoping that the computer system is working properly, so that she can pull off those reports that are needed for the management meeting later in the day. She is Personnel Administration Manager for her company and is regularly required to produce personnel projections and analyses for meetings. She has just spotted Adrian and has decided to dodge around to the other side of the platform to avoid him. Adrian has been hired on a temporary six-month contract to develop the computer system, but he seems more interested in developing his own career and making sure that his work can not possibly be finished in the time allotted.

John and Mary are some way ahead and exchanging views on what it is like to be a line manager. There used to be quite a lot of expertise in the personnel department to help with such things as absence, discipline, performance management and all the range of matters relating to people at work, but now everything is left to 'the line'. The Chief Executive called it 'empowerment'. John and Mary feel that it is having responsibility dumped on you without really knowing what you are doing and without much reward, either.

Charles, Sam, Sharon, Adrian, John and Mary could well be going to work that day for the same company but specialisation, rationalisation and the emphasis

REVIEW TOPIC 1.2

In the above scenario some roles were assigned explicitly to women or to men, others were gender neutral. What was the significance of this? Were they realistic? Is there any connection between the way those roles were assigned and the decline of organisation as entity?

on market mechanisms mean that there is less emphasis on the company being an organisation of which they are a part, although their individual activities still have to be co-ordinated.

There is a major shift in emphasis for personnel managers. Less and less, they administer the contract of *employment*: more and more they administer the contract for *performance,* and the performance may come from employees, but it is just as likely to come from non-employees. Personnel lead the way from within their own ranks, with the training function being dismantled and the specialist work of developing skills, competences and capacities being contracted out to consultants and specialist suppliers. Other aspects of the personnel function that are increasingly contracted out are recruitment, selection and many aspects of payment. The new activity of outplacement is typically handed to consultants and the even newer con-

Macclesfield, in the north of England, was the centre of silk manufacture from the beginning of the eighteenth century to the middle of the twentieth. The town's heritage museum portrays vividly how people were engaged in making silk buttons, working individually or as small family units in garrets producing buttons to the order of merchandisers and being paid by the piece, as and when there was an order. They were all home workers.

Ten miles away the village of Styal developed around a mill that represented a different mode of working. Instead of work being put out to people, people were brought in to the work. There is an apprentice house, where foundlings were housed and both cared for and exploited during their teenage years. Begun in 1783, the firm employed 2000 people by 1834 (Rose 1986, p. 13). This was the beginning of a trend that was to continue uninterrupted until very recently. The entity of the organisation was the focus for economic activity and it was also the vehicle for our working lives. We became employees, the organisation took over responsibility for our jobs and our livelihood, our training and our security in old age. Welfare officers were invented and later turned into personnel officers. Trade unions developed. We acquired elaborate structures of authority and lines of responsibility.

Today Styal Mill is a textile museum, still surrounded by the village of houses built by the mill owner for his employees. It is owned by the National Trust and visited by thousands of people every year. It is a flourishing, successful business but it employs only a handful of people on a full-time, permanent basis. Many more are temporary, part-time employees or volunteers.

cept of employee assistance programmes are usually regarded as necessarily being contracted out if they are to be credible.

The complex of contemporary personnel management

Personnel management today has several different strands within it. As the function has evolved it has added new dimensions without ever shedding those developed in earlier periods. For years personnel managers tried to disown their welfare officer origins, yet employee welfare remains a central feature of the role. In the 1980s many people claimed that human resource management had replaced personnel management but, except as a label, this was rarely true. If we are to understand personnel management today we need to trace its development, to see how new dimensions have been added progressively to make personnel management the most varied, fascinating and demanding of all management roles.

Although we cannot attribute any particular ideology to a complete group of people at any one time, it is possible, roughly, to show the development of the personnel function by suggesting a general self-image, which obtained at different periods.

The social reformer

Before personnel emerged as a specialist management activity, there were those in the nineteenth century who tried to intervene in industrial affairs to support the position of the severely underprivileged factory workers at the hands of a rapacious employer. The Industrial Revolution had initially helped people to move away from the poverty and harshness of rural life, or from the hopelessness of the orphanage, to the factories and the cities, but the organisation of the work soon degraded human life and dehumanised working people. In the words of William Wordsworth:

> Men, maidens, youths,
> Mothers and little children, boys and girls,
> Enter, and each the wonted task resumes
> Within this temple, where is offered up
> To Gain, the master idol of the realm,
> perpetual sacrifice.

Free enterprise, the survival of the fittest and the ruthless exploitation of the masses were seen as laws of nature, and it was the social reformers such as Lord Shaftesbury and Robert Owen who produced some mitigation of this hardship, mainly by standing outside the organisation and the workplace, offering criticism of employer behaviour within and inducing some changes. This was aided by the more general social commentary of Dickens's novels and the observations of Friedrich Engels.

We need to trace the evolution of personnel management to this type of person, as it was their influence and example that enabled personnel managers to be appointed and provided the first frame of reference for the appointees to work within. It would also be incorrect to say that this type of concern is obsolete. There are regular reports of employees being exploited by employers flouting the law, and the problem of organisational distance between decision-makers and those putting decisions into practice remains a source of alienation from work. In one large company an inscription was printed on a report stating that it should not be bent, twisted or defaced. A group of employees in the same company made a muted complaint about their lack of identity by producing lapel badges saying: 'I am a human being, do not bend, twist or deface'.

The acolyte of benevolence

The first people to be appointed with specific responsibility for improving the lot of employees were usually known as welfare officers; they saw their role as dispensing benefits to the deserving and unfortunate employees. The motivation was the Christian charity of the noble employer who was prepared to provide these comforts, partly because the employees deserved them, but mainly because the employer was disposed to provide them.

The leading examples of this development were the Quaker families of Cadbury and Rowntree, and the Lever Brothers' soap business. All set up progressive schemes of unemployment benefit, sick pay and subsidised housing for their employees during the latter part of the nineteenth century. Although later accused of paternalism, these initiatives marked a fundamental shift of employer philosophy. Seebohm Rowntree became a renowned sociologist as well as being chairman of his company for sixteen years and putting into practice the reforms he advocated in his writings. Cadbury Schweppes and Unilever remain among the most efficient and profitable businesses in the United Kingdom a hundred years after the foundation of the Bournville village and Port Sunlight. In other instances the philosophy was perverted by relatively cheap welfare provisions being offered as a substitute for higher wages, and was used extensively to keep trade unions at bay.

The Institute of Welfare Officers was established in 1913 at a meeting in the Rowntree factory at York and the welfare tradition remains strong in personnel management, although it continually re-emerges in different forms. There is constant comment on the provision of facilities such as childcare and health screening, as well as occasional discussions about business ethics (for example, Pocock 1989). The extent to which contemporary working practices for professional and executive employees make unreasonable demands of time and inconvenience is receiving increasing attention, as is the need for employees of all types to balance work and domestic responsibilities:

> Care-friendly employment practices will be the phenomenon of the future. Only by
> addressing the needs of employees caring for children, dependants with disabilities and

the elderly, will employers be able to attract and retain the non-traditional sectors of the workforce which are forecast to form the workforce of the 1990s. (Worman 1990)

The humane bureaucrat

The first two phases were concerned predominantly with the physical environment of work and the amelioration of hardship among 'the workers'. We now come to the stage where employing organisations were taking a further step in increasing their size and specialisation was emerging in the management levels, as well as on the shopfloor. This led to the growth of personnel work on what is loosely called staffing, with great concern about role specification, careful selection, training and placement. The personnel manager was learning to operate within a bureaucracy, serving organisational rather than paternalist-employer objectives, but still committed to a basically humanitarian role.

For the first time, there was a willingness to look to social science for support. Much of the scientific management philosophy of F. W. Taylor informed personnel thinking:

> First. Develop a science for each element of a man's work, which replaces the old rule-of-thumb method.
>
> Second. Scientifically select and then train, teach, and develop the workman, whereas in the past he chose his own work and trained himself as best he could.
>
> Third. Heartily cooperate with the men so as to insure all of the work being done in accordance with the principles which have been developed.
>
> Fourth. There is an almost equal division of the work and the responsibility between the management and the workmen. The management take over all work for which they are better fitted than workmen, while in the past almost all of the work and the greater part of the responsibility was thrown upon the men. (Taylor 1911, pp. 36–7)

Work was to be made more efficient by analysis of what was required and the careful selection and training of the workman, who would then be supported by the management in a spirit of positive co-operation.

The Frenchman Henri Fayol (1949) considered not the workman but the management process and his analytical framework for management is sometimes known as scientific administration, as his approach had much in common with Taylor's.

The humane bureaucracy stage in the development of personnel thinking was also influenced by the Human Relations school of thought, which was in many ways a reaction against scientific management, or a reaction against the way in which scientific management was being applied. Just as the high ideals of the Cadburys and Rowntrees had been adulterated by some of their imitators, so Taylor found his managerial philosophy was seldom fully appreciated, and scientific management became identified with hyper-specialisation of work and very tight systems of payment.

The human relations approach appealed immediately to those who were concerned about industrial conflict and the apparent dehumanising potential of scientific management. The main advocate was Elton Mayo (1933) and the central idea was to emphasise informal social relationships and employee morale as contributors to organisational efficiency.

It was during this stage of development that personnel managers began to develop a technology as well as an approach, and many of the methods developed at this time remain at the heart of what personnel managers do; the idea of fitting together two sets of requirements is a theme to which we shall return.

The consensus negotiator

Personnel managers next added expertise in bargaining to their repertoire of skills. The acolytes of benevolence had not been numerous or strong enough to satisfy employee aspirations as a result of employer voluntary provision. In the period after the Second World War there was relatively full employment and labour became a scarce resource. Trade unions extended their membership and employers had to change firm, traditional unitarism as the reality of what Allan Flanders, the leading industrial relations analyst of the 1960s, was to call 'the challenge from below' was grudgingly recognised. Where the personnel manager could at best be described as a 'remembrancer' of the empoyees, the trade union official could be their accredited representative.

Trade union assertiveness brought a shift towards bargaining by the employer on at least some matters. There was a growth of joint consultation and the establishment of joint production committees and suggestion schemes. Nationalised industries were set up, with a statutory duty placed on employers to negotiate with unions representing employees. The government encouraged the appointment of personnel officers and set up courses for them to be trained at universities. A personnel manager advisory scheme was set up at the Ministry of Labour, and this still survives as the first A in ACAS (Advisory, Conciliation and Arbitration Service).

The trend began during the early 1940s but received a major boost when the sellers' market of the immediate post-war period began to harden and international competition made more urgent the development of greater productive efficiency and the elimination of restrictive (or protective) practices. The personnel manager acquired bargaining expertise to deploy in search of a lost consensus.

Organisation man

Next came a development of the humane bureaucracy phase into a preoccupation with the effectiveness of the organisation as a whole, with clear objectives and a widespread commitment among organisation members to those objectives. The approach was also characterised by candour between members and a form of operation that supported the integrity of the individual and provided opportunities for personal growth. There was an attempt to understand the interaction of organisational structures between, on the one hand, the people who make up the organisation and, on the other, the surrounding society in which it is set.

This development was most clearly seen in the late 1960s and is most significant because it marks a change of focus among personnel specialists, away from dealing with the rank-and-file employee on behalf of the management towards dealing with the management and integration of managerial activity. Its most recent manifestation has been in programmes of organisation and management development, as companies have sub-contracted much of their routine work to peripheral employees, and concentrated on developing and retaining an elite core of people with specialist expertise on whom the business depends for its future.

Manpower analyst

The last of our historical stereotypes is that of manpower analyst, associated with the term 'management of human resources'. A development of the general management anxiety to quantify decisions has been a move towards regarding people as manpower or human resources. A relatively extreme form of this is human asset accounting, which assigns a value to individual employees in accounting terms and estimates the extent to which that asset will appreciate or depreciate in the future so that eventually everyone is written off, in more ways than one.

More widespread was the use of manpower planning, which is:

> a strategy for the organization, utilization and improvement of an organization's human resources. It comprises three main activities: (a) assessing what manpower of what different grades, categories and skills will be needed in the short term and long term (i.e. manpower demand); (b) deciding what manpower an organization is likely to have in the future, based on current trends and anticipated external circumstances (i.e. manpower supply); and (c) taking action to ensure that supply meets demand (e.g. training, retraining, recruitment). (Message 1974)

Although orginally based on an assumption of organisational expansion, manpower planning was reshaped during the onset of organisational contraction to ensure the closest possible fit between the number of people and skills required and what was available. The activity was boosted by the advent of the computer, which makes possible a range of calculations and measurements that were unrealistic earlier.

Human resource management

The concept of human resource management, or HRM, took the management world by storm during the 1980s and has represented a significant change of direction. The difference needs to be explored, even though the nature and degree of the difference remain largely matters of opinion rather than fact, and the similarities are much greater than the differences.

Personnel management is *workforce-centred*, directed mainly at the organisation's employees; finding and training them, arranging for them to be paid, explaining management's expectations, justifying management's actions, satisfying employees' work-related needs, dealing with their problems and seeking to modify management action that could produce unwelcome employee response. The people who work in the organisation are the starting point, and they are a resource that is relatively inflexible in comparison with other resources such as cash and materials.

Although indisputably a management function, personnel is never totally identified with management interests, as it becomes ineffective when not able to understand and articulate the aspirations and views of the workforce, just as sales representatives have to understand and articulate the aspirations of the customers. There is always some degree of being between the management and the employees, mediating the needs of each to the other. Thomason quotes from both Miller and Spates to express this idea:

> Miller argues that the personnel management role is 'different from other staff jobs in that it has to serve not only the employer, but also act in the interests of employees as individual human beings, and by extension, the interests of society' (Miller 1975). Similarly, Spates finds a conception of the personnel management role which provides a place for the goals and aspirations of workers... For him, the function of personnel administration is concerned with 'organizing and treating individuals at work so that they will get the greatest possible realization of their intrinsic abilities, thus attaining maximum efficiency for themselves and their group and thereby giving to the concern of which they are a part its determining competitive advantage and its optimum results'. (Thomason 1981, p. 38)

HRM is *resource-centred*, directed mainly at management needs for human resources (not necessarily employees) to be provided and deployed. Demand rather than supply is the focus of the activity. There is greater emphasis on planning, monitoring and control, rather than mediation. Problem-solving is undertaken with other members of management on human resource issues rather than directly with employees or their representatives. It is totally identified with management interests, being a general management activity and is relatively distant from the workforce as a whole, as employee interests can only be enhanced through effective overall management.

Underpinning personnel management are the twin ideas that people have a right to proper treatment as dignified human beings while at work, that they are only effective as employees when their job-related personal needs are met, and that this will not happen without personnel management intervention in the everyday manager/subordinate relationships. Personnel managers are involved in a more direct way in the relationship between other managers and their subordinates, because the personnel aspects of management are often perceived by line managers as not central to their role.

Underpinning human resources management is the idea that management of human resources is much the same as any other aspect of management and an integral part of it that cannot be separated out for specialists to handle. People have a right to proper treatment as dignified human beings while at work, and they will be

The rock-hard, steely-eyed film star Clint Eastwood has appeared in several films as tough cop Harry Callaghan, whose approach to law and order is to shoot first and not bother asking too many questions afterwards. On one occasion he had killed rather a lot of people even by his own high standards, so that he was becoming politically embarrassing to the authorities. Something had to be done. The Chief of Police nerved himself and called Harry into his office, taking care that there was a large table between them, and gave him the news that he was being transferred to personnel. There was a moment of electric silence. A nervous tic flickered briefly on Harry Callaghan's right cheek. His jaw locked and those famous cold blue eyes gave the Chief a look that could have penetrated armour plate as he hissed his reply through clenched teeth: 'Personnel is for assholes'. Whereupon he left the room, slamming the door with sufficient vigour to splinter the woodwork in several places.

Being a man of few words Harry Callaghan did not explain further, but we can interpret his view as being the common one that personnel work is typically undertaken by deviant innovators, who have their own 'soft' agenda of being nice to people and who shirk the hard, competitive world of marketing, the precision of finance or the long hours and hard knocks of manufacturing. It is soft, ineffectual and unimportant.

effective when their personal career and competence needs are met within a context of efficient management and a mutually respectful working relationship. The specialist role is directed towards acquiring the deployment of right numbers and skills at the right price, supporting other managers in their people management and contributing to major strategic change.

This is how we interpret the distinction between personnel management and human resources management, but the distinction is one over which there is much debate and uncertainty (see, for example, Guest 1989; Legge 1989; Sisson 1989; Hart 1993; Torrington 1994a). Legge provides the most scrupulous analysis and concludes that there is in fact very little difference between the two, but there are some differences that are important; first, that human resources management concentrates more on what is done to managers rather than on what is done by managers to other employees; secondly, that there is a more proactive role for line managers; and thirdly, that there is a top management responsibility for managing culture. We return to all these matters later in the book.

It would be inaccurate to suggest that one approach has taken over from the other, just as it would be wrong to suggest that one is modern and the other old-fashioned, or that one is right and the other wrong. Both are usually present in one organisation; sometimes in one person. This can cause tension and ambiguity. As an emphasis for the work of personnel specialists there is a tendency for human resources management to increase at the expense of personnel management, and we suggest the following reasons for this change:

1. The devolution of personnel duties to line managers means that more of the mediation and reconciliation of needs associated with personnel management

is being undertaken by line managers, like John and Mary at the opening of this chapter. Managers of all kinds are increasingly their own personnel managers as part of a tendency for all managers to become more general ('all-singing, all-dancing') than specialised in their responsibilities.

2.   With widespread unemployment, much temporary and part-time working, a gradual reduction in normal working hours and a shortening of the working lifetime as a proportion of the total lifetime, the workplace is not quite as significant as a source of personal self-esteem and as an arena for achieving personal objectives as it was 10–15 years ago. When full-time employment is an experience shared by all for most of their adult lives, then it is the source of most opportunities and the means of self-actualisation. Now it is an experience which a significant minority do not share at all and a further significant minority only experience in the 'peripheral workforce'. Even those employed full-time in 'proper jobs' probably spend no more than 20 per cent of their time for half their lifetime at work. In this situation the meeting of personal goals at work is a prospect denied to many and an instrumental orientation to work becomes more common.

REVIEW TOPIC 1.3

Although men are tending to retire well before the retirement age of 65 years, the retirement age for women is being raised from 60 to 65 years. How will this alter the relative experience of employment between men and women?

3.   Personnel specialists have long sought organisational power. Karen Legge (1978, pp. 67–94) described contrasted approaches used by them in this quest. First was *conformist innovation*, whereby personnel specialists identify their activities with the objective of organisational success, emphasising cost benefit and conforming to the criteria of organisational success adopted by managerial colleagues, who usually have greater power. In contrast are the *deviant innovators*, who identify their activities with a set of norms or values that are distinct from, but not necessarily in conflict with, the norms of organisational success. They will emphasise social values rather than cost benefit.

   HRM is a form of conformist innovation: close identification with central management interests; it theoretically provides a repositioning of the personnel function to make it more influential.

4.   There is an ever-increasing range of mini-expertise needed within the personnel area. The range of activities covered by the function has tended to expand and that range of activities requires a wide variety of specialist knowledge. The law is the most obvious of these additions, including the areas of concern that have a dimension based on law, such as equal opportunity, but there has also been growing involvement with organisational change, pensions, statutory and

occupational sick pay, more sophisticated approaches to payment, government initiatives on training and employment and the application of the computer. This leads to an increasing use of external resources, reinforcing the tendency for personnel managers to become deployers of resources and knowledgeable about sources, rather than simply deployers of skills and knowledgeable about people.

5.   The reduced assertiveness of most trade unions has made industrial action less likely and has reduced managerial apprehensiveness about unfavourable employee response.

6.   The prolonged economic recession of the late 1980s stimulated management concern with immediate survival at the expense of longer-term development. Some new companies grew quickly but then declined quickly, emphasising the benefits of working at the here-and-now rather than contemplating the future. This has usually been accompanied by a narrow human resource management approach with a greater emphasis on the present and avoidance of long-term commitments other than to key personnel.

7.   The emphasis of employment legislation has shifted away from employee rights towards union containment, so lessening the degree of management anxiety about this 'frightener'.

8.   There is an increasing need for personnel activities to be justified in cost terms as, for instance, in the direct charging for internal training events, so that the training function operates in the same way as an external supplier, with the same need to constantly justify its activities. The gradual advance in the application of computerisation makes it easier for costs, or notional costs, to be attached to an increasing range of activities that were previously part of general overheads.

The seven stereotypes we have identified have all blended together to make the complex of contemporary personnel management. Although they have emerged roughly in sequence, all are still present to a varying degree in different types of personnel post and the nature of personnel work today can only be understood by an appreciation of its varied components.

REVIEW TOPIC 1.4

Which of those seven stereotypes do you personally find most attractive as describing the sort of job you would like to do? Which one, or combination, of the seven most accurately describes the job you have?

Other personnel management stereotypes

Various other emphases have been seen in personnel management recently, without becoming dominant to the same extent as the seven described.

Social *engineering* is a concern with the social role of work and the use of the workplace to solve social problems. This is a major interest of policy-makers, who connect problems such as urban violence and drug abuse with the quality and availability of employment opportunity. Companies occasionally undertake initiatives to make a contribution in this area and it has been boosted by the concept of corporate responsibility. *Legal wangling* became dominant in the 1970s, when a plethora of legislation protecting the rights of workers and trade unions gave managers a considerable fright: but managerial concern about legislation has much reduced since 1980. Industrial democracy was a heady concept which has also receded, but there are moves towards greater *employee involvement* still proceeding. Now, however, discussion is more of involvement and briefing rather than participation or control. *Labour market analysis* improves the understanding of the setting of the organisation within a structure of society with the influences that society therefore exerts. A whole range of questions stem from the nature of the labour force and the way it is changing, as well as the way in which the employment being offered is changing. Interest in this area has increased considerably, with concern about the changing demographic trends and the implications of the European Community. *Internationalism* remains an enigma. Logically it changes everything, as companies exchange narrow nationalism for exciting internationalism, but as a discrete personnel activity it remains difficult to pin down (Torrington 1944b, pp. 4–9) and personnel management continues to be practised within national economic, legal, linguistic and cultural boundaries. We have a separate chapter on the international dimension at the close of the book.

The Personnel Standards Lead Body

During 1993 and 1994 a unique project drew on the experience and perspective of 1500 personnel specialists to develop an up to date map of the personnel activity. Within the framework of the National Council for Vocational Qualifications, the Personnel Standards Lead Body was a large group of influential and experienced personnel specialists. It was deliberately composed of employers rather than those from education, in order to meet the spirit of the vocational qualification process that is described further in Chapter 23.

The outcome of this work is a set of standards which provide a map of personnel work in five areas that are set out in Table 1.1. There is a close match between the activities identified by the PSLB and the coverage of this book, although we place some activities under different headings and have separate sections on development and performance. Table 1.2 provides a guide to where material related to the PSLB standards is to be found in this book.

Table 1.1 *Personnel activities identified by the Personnel Standards Lead Body*

A.	**Strategy and organisation**
	A1 Contribute to organisational strategy
	A2 Organisation structure and processes
	A3 Culture and values
	A4 Personnel strategy and plans
B.	**Resourcing**
	B1 Resourcing strategy and planning
	B2 Recruitment of new employees
	B3 Deployment of the workforce
	B4 Release from the organisation
	B5 Hire sub-contractors
C.	**Development**
	C1 Performance development strategy and planning
	C2 Performance management
	C3 Promote training
	C4 Long term individual development
	C5 Team development
D.	**Reward**
	D1 Reward strategy and plans
	D2 Levels of reward
	D3 Benefits
	D4 Pay
E.	**Relations with Employees**
	E1 Employee relations strategy and plans
	E2 Commitment of employees
	E3 Communication
	E4 Employee support
	E5 Health and safety
	E6 Compliance
	E7 Negotiations with individuals and groups
	E8 Equal opportunities

Ways of organising the personnel function

Personnel departments vary considerably in size from one person only up to several hundreds. We examined forty-two organisation charts of the personnel function in different establishments and found that in every case jobs were defined on a functional basis (employee relations manager, recruitment officer, management development adviser and so forth) or as general responsibilities, such as personnel manager, factory personnel officer, group personnel manager or manager, human resources. The most significant influence on the organisation of the personnel function seems to be either the degree of centralisation or the degree of attenuation.

The degree of centralisation is an issue affecting only larger organisations. Sisson and Scullion (1985) reported on research in the largest 100 companies in the

Table 1.2 *Match between PSLB standards and chapters in this book*

PSLB activities	Chapters in this book
A. Strategy and organisation	
A1	2,4
A2	6
A3	6
A4	3,5
B. Resourcing	
B1	10
B2	11,12,13
B3	8
B4	14
B5	11,17
C. Development	
C1	16,22
C2	18
C3	22
C4	24,25
C5	19
D. Reward	
D1	32
D2	33
D3	34,35
D4	32,34,35
E. Relations with employees	
E1	27
E2	27,28
E3	7
E4	29,30
E5	29
E6	missing
E7	36
E8	20

United Kingdom to show that some companies have very large corporate personnel departments, others have a small head office team, others have a single executive and others have no corporate personnel activity at all. They explain this in terms of whether or not the management at the centre have retained responsibility for a number of aspects of operating management that are critical as well as discharging responsibility for strategic management. If personnel is a critical function in which a common approach is needed because of the organisation being in a single business, like Marks & Spencer or Ford, then there is likely to be a strong corporate personnel function, although the moves away from national-level bargaining have reduced the imperatives behind this sort of centralisation. In the multidivisional corporation, there is not the same logic behind centralisation.

The degree of attenuation is a more localised issue stemming from making the business leaner and fitter. The organisation retains a senior personnel manager with

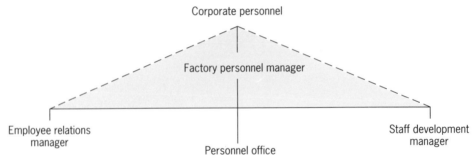

Corporate personnel

Factory personnel manager

Employee relations
manager

Personnel office

Staff development
manager

Figure 1.1   Sample structure of the personnel function in an establishment that is
part of an organization with a strong corporate personnel department

significant rank and responsibility but little specialist support at middle to senior
management levels and a personnel administration manager keeping excellent
records and dealing with a host of routine matters, rather like Charles and Sharon
at the opening of this chapter. The degree of attenuation varies, but the greater it is
the fewer specialist roles there will be. Though there are no standard forms of
organisation, three samples are shown in Figures 1.1, 1.2 and 1.3.

Figure 1.1 shows the situation of a personnel department in a subsidiary of an
organisation with a strong corporate personnel function determining most policy questions and maintaining consistency of practice across a number of different establishments. Figure 1.2 is an establishment of similar size, but Figure 1.3 is a well developed,
independent function in a large, integrated organisation. Notice the dotted lines in
Figure 1.1., indicating split accountability between the local manager and head office.

REVIEW TOPIC 1.5

Sketch a rough organisation chart of the personnel function in your
establishment. Consider the degree of attenuation and centralisation of
personnel activities in the organisation. What effect do they have on the
roles and distribution of responsibility among members of the personnel
function? How would roles and distribution of responsibility change
with a change in the degree of attenuation or centralisation?

Most job holders within the personnel function carry several responsibilities. The
following are some of the most common job titles and the duties attaching to them.

Personnel or HR Manager/Director   This is the general manager in charge of the
personnel function, who acts as its figurehead and main spokesperson, representing personnel issues in all senior management discussions and policy making.
There are usually one or two more specialist responsibilities attaching to the
post. In Figure 1.2, for instance, the personnel manager is responsible for
employee relations and all pay matters. This is the role, together with most of

Figure 1.2 Sample structure of the personnel function in an autonomous establishment

those that follow, for which the Institute of Personnel and Development's membership examinations provide the most appropriate and widely regarded qualification.

Personnel Officer In most establishments this is the title of the person who deals with all personnel issues, being a second type of generalist role. In larger

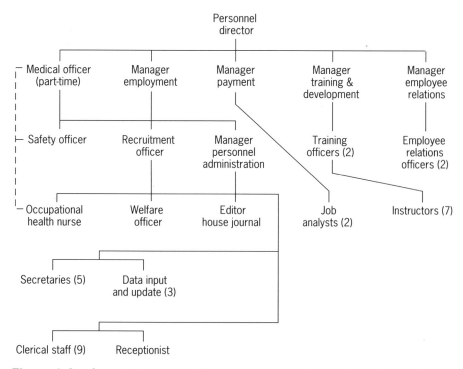

Figure 1.3 Sample structure of the personnel function in a large integrated organization

establishments it is a general title with a specific explanatory responsibility following in brackets. Figure 1.2 again provides an example.

Employee Relations Manager   The most common specialist role is that dealing with the collective relationship between management and employees, especially where this is formalised through union recognition and procedure agreements. It often includes responsibility for pay issues, employee involvement and communication.

Management Development Manager   Another strong tradition is to concentrate responsibility for training and employee development in the hands of a specialist, although there is an increasing tendency to deal with development matters by heavy reliance on outside facilities, such as consultants like Sam. There is also a focus on *management* development rather than on *employee* development to emphasise the managements' responsibility for developing their staff.

Training and Development consultants   Training officers have similar responsibilities to personnel officers in that they may be single trainers with general training duties in an establishment, or they may be charged with specific training tasks, such as operator training. The term 'consultant' is increasingly being used instead of 'officer' to ensure that the work is used as a consultancy by managers to arrange the training *they* want rather than what the training officer has organised. Formal qualifications in organisational or occupational psychology are often held by training specialists, and IPD stage 2 qualifications devote one-third of the total syllabus to this area.

Recruitment and Selection Manager   These posts are not as widespread as they were and usually these duties are the regular part-time responsibility of several people in a personnel department, yet the work remains highly skilled and many large organisations still retain specialist personnel, usually with an occupational psychology background expertise.

Human Resource Planner   This is a much less clear job title with many variations, such as 'manpower analyst', which is used to describe someone whose expertise is basically in manpower planning and statistics, and who will do much of the preliminary work on personnel planning and strategy.

Organisation Development Consultant   This role specialises in enabling the organisation to adapt to its changing environment and its members to develop their roles to meet the new challenges and opportunities that are emerging. It is a job with few administrative features and is usually held by someone with an independent, roving commission.

Safety Officer/Welfare Officer   The area of health, safety and welfare is one where there are strong legal constraints on employer action and the Safety Officer is not always a part of the personnel function at all. Large organisations often have one or more welfare officers to deal with general issues of employee support and there has recently been an increase in employee assistance programmes, which perform part of the welfare function through the use of an outside agency.

Personnel Administration Manager   The final role in this sample list is a long-standing one, which is changing direction. There is some tendency for personnel administration to increase, and a part of the expanding numbers in personnel departments is in the clerical/administrative/keyboard area, with the demands of such tasks as statutory sick pay and the need to maintain a personnel database on the computer. This part of the operation is run by someone who used to be called 'office manager', but who is now more likely to be described as 'personnel administration manager'.

So far this chapter has been devoted to considering the personnel specialism, but the personnel function of management as a whole is equally important. Each manager has inescapable responsibilities and duties of a personnel type, so that personnel management is not only of interest to specialists but to all managers. The degree and nature of the involvement differs, but the need for a philosophy or set of beliefs to underpin one's actions remains the same.

Many organisations do not have personnel specialists at all. The existence of a specialised personnel function is clearly related to size, and the increasing number of small businesses do not need, or cannot afford, this type of specialism. They may use consultants, they may use the advisory resources of university departments, they may use their bank's computer to process the payroll, but there is still a personnel dimension to their management activities.

A philosophy of personnel management

The philosophy of personnel management that is the basis of this book has been only slightly modified since it was first put forward in 1979 (Torrington and Chapman 1979, p. 4). Despite all the changes in the labour market and in the government approach to the economy, this seems to be the most realistic and constructive approach, based on the earlier ideas of Enid Mumford (1972) and McCarthy and Ellis (1973). As it has a further slight development for this edition, it is worth showing how it has changed from 1979 to today. The original was:

> Personnel management is most realistically seen as a series of activities enabling working man and his employing organisation to reach agreement about the nature and objectives of the employment relationship between them, and then to fulfil those agreements. (Torrington and Chapman 1979, p.4)

Our definition for 1995 is:

> Personnel management is a series of activities which: first enable working people and the business which use their skills to agree about the objectives and nature of their working relationship and, secondly, ensures that the agreement is fulfilled.

Only by satisfying the needs of the individual contributor will the business obtain the commitment to organisational objectives that is needed for organisational success, and only by contributing to organisational success will individuals be able to satisfy their personal employment needs. It is when employer and employee – or business and supplier of skills – accept that mutuality and reciprocal dependence that personnel management is exciting, centre-stage and productive of business success. Where the employer is concerned with employees only as factors of production, personnel management is boring and a cost that will always be trimmed. Where employees have no trust in their employer and adopt an entirely instrumental orientation to their work, they will be fed up and will render ineffectual the work of any personnel function.

Personnel managers are great grumblers, and some will react to the last paragraph by saying that they do not get the support they deserve. Personnel decisions are always taken last, never get proper resources and so forth. Sometimes this is correct, but all too often it is a self-fulfilling prophecy, because the personnel people are pursuing the wrong objectives, or carefully keeping out of the way when things get really tough; which was exactly Harry Callaghan's point. Personnel managers are like managers in every other part of the business. They have to make things happen rather than wait for things to happen, and to make things happen they not only have to have the right approach: they also have to know their stuff. Read on!

☐ Summary Propositions

1.1 Personnel management is undergoing its biggest-ever change as organisation-as-entity declines and we rediscover organisation as process.

1.2 The complex of contemporary personnel management work is made up of seven facets, which have been dominant at various times during the evolution of personnel management ideas.

1.3 Personnel management is the work of personnel specialists; the personnel function of management includes work that is undertaken by all managers.

1.4 The philosophy of personnel management in this book is that it is a series of activities which: first, enable working people and the business which use their skills to agree about the objectives and nature of their working relationship and secondly, ensures that the agreement is fulfilled.

References

Fayol, H. (1949), *General and Industrial Management*, London: Pitman.

Guest, D. E. (1989) 'Personnel and HRM – Can you tell the difference?' *Personnel Management*, vol. 21, no. 1, January.

Hart, T. J. (1993), 'Human resource management: time to exorcise the militant tendency', *Employee Relations*, vol. 15, no. 3, pp. 29–36.

Legge, K. (1978), *Power, Innovation and Problem-solving in Personnel Management*, London: McGraw-Hill.

Legge, K. (1989) 'Human Resource Management: a critical analysis'. In J. Storey (ed.) *New Perspectives on Human Resource Management*, London: Routledge.

Mackay, L. E. and Torrington, D. P. (1986), *The Changing Nature of Personnel Management*, London: Institute of Personnel Management.

Mayo E. (1933), *The Human Problems of an Industrial Civilisation*, New York: Macmillan.

McCarthy, W. E. J. and Ellis, N. D. (1973), *Management by Agreement*, London: Hutchinson.

Message, M. C. (1974), 'Manpower planning'. In D. P. Torrington (ed.) *Encyclopaedia of Personnel Management*, Aldershot: Gower.

Mumford, E. (1972), 'Job satisfaction: a method of analysis', *Personnel Review*, vol. 1, no. 3.

Pocock, P. (1989), 'Is business ethics a contradiction in terms?' *Personnel Management*, vol. 21, no. 11, December.

Rose, M. B. (1986), *The Gregs of Quarry Bank Mill*, Cambridge: Cambridge University Press.

Sisson, K. (1989), 'Personnel management in perspective' and 'Personnel management in transition', in *Personnel Management in Britain*, Oxford: Basil Blackwell, pp. 3–40.

Sisson, K. and Scullion, H. (1985), *'Putting the corporate personnel department in its place'*, Personnel Management, December.

Taylor, F. W. (1911), *Scientific Management*, New York: Harper & Row.

Thomason, G. (1981) *A Textbook of Personnel Management (4th edition)*, London: Institute of Personnel Management.

Torrington, D. P. (1994a), 'How dangerous is human resource management? A reply to Tim Hart', *Employee Relations*, vol. 15, no. 5, pp. 40–53.

Torrington, D. P. (1994b), *International Human Resource Management*, Hemel Hempstead; Prentice Hall.

Torrington, D. P. and Chapman, J. B. (1979), *Personnel Management*, Hemel Hempstead: Prentice Hall.

Worman, D. (1990), 'The forgotten carers', *Personnel Management*, vol. 22, no. 1.

2 Organisation strategy

As we saw in chapter one, strategy has become a salient feature of management thinking and action, especially as the business environment has become more unpredictable. Strategy is about developing a vision of what the business is, what it could be, how it could get there, and then setting objectives that are milestones along that particular road through a changing environment. It has been a commonplace idea among marketing specialists for much longer than among personnel people, who have been more familiar with the idea of policy as a general guideline for decision making.

The recent preoccupation with strategy has reduced interest in policy, so that it has become almost a dated, old-fashioned concept. Our definition of policy is a declared mode of action for the future. In everyday conversation we hear people state that honesty is the best policy, or we ask politicians to state their policy on nuclear disarmament or law and order, or we note the claim of an organisation to be an equal opportunity employer. Features of policy we find in business organisations are ways of shaping the implementation of strategy so that the business can work effectively in reaching strategic objectives. There may be a strategic decision to introduce a new product range, followed by a policy decision on whether to manufacture or buy in, whether to locate the new line in plant X or in plant Y. A strategic decision to raise more capital may be followed by a policy decision on the timing of the share issue. The distinction between strategy and policy is seldom clear, although strategy is usually related to planning what is to be achieved, and policy is the framework within which the plans to implement the strategy will be put into operation.

Stoner and Wankel provide contrasted definitions:

[Strategy is] ... the broad program for defining and achieving an organization's objectives; the organization's response to its environment over time. (Stoner and Wankel 1986, p. 695)

A policy is a general guideline for decision-making. It sets up boundaries around decisions, including those that can be made and shutting out those that cannot. In this way it channels the thinking of organization members so that it is consistent with organizational objectives. Some policies deal with very important matters, like those requiring strict sanitary conditions where food or drugs are produced or packaged. Others may be concerned with relatively minor issues, such as the way the employees dress. (p. 91)

Strategy and policy within a framework for management action

We need to set strategy and policy-making in a framework of management action, shown in Figure 2.1.

- *Mission:* What is the organisation for? Where is it going? The general mission of the business is a matter on which the members of the organisation will talk for hours and seldom come to a conclusion, but it is the precursor of policy and depends on an appreciation of both the expertise within the business and the nature of customer or client needs that could be met. It is general and visionary.

  At one time the mission of British American Tobacco was to manufacture and distribute tobacco products, but that broadened and later narrowed once more. Newspaper barons broaden their mission to encompass television interests, and railroad businesses declare themselves to be in transportation. A business may modify its purpose to include manufacturing as well as marketing, or it may drop manufacture to concentrate on marketing.

- *Strategy:* The overriding mission is then continuously implemented by developing a programme of initiatives to define and achieve the organisation's objectives.

- *Policy:* The overall mission and strategy are guided by a series of policies to channel decision and action, shaping the organisation and providing the direction that is needed.

- *Procedures:* Procedures are more familiar to personnel managers than to most management specialists as they form the substance of much employee relations activity, but in our action framework they have the more general meaning of being the drills that implement the policy, so that a policy decision to advertise all vacancies within the organisation before external advertising

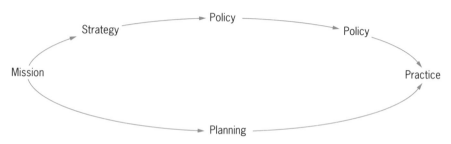

Figure 2.1 A framework for management action

begins is implemented by a procedure to specify who does what, in what order, when and with what authorisation or other trigger to action.

- *Planning:* Strategy, policy and procedures can all be co-ordinated and moved into action by planning. Not only does each stage benefit from planning, but a planning approach can ensure that all three are thought through and put into operation together.

- *Practice:* The final element is what actually happens. No organisation has a procedure for everything, and no procedure is so comprehensive as to rule out the need for interpretation and judgement. Practice is a mixture of implemented procedure, *ad hoc* decisions, reaction to policy, and the ebb and flow of interaction between the organisation and its environment. The effectiveness of policy can only be determined by the practice that ensues. We shall never know how good was Lord Raglan's policy for the Battle of Balaclava because he made a mess of it by sending inaccurate instructions to his troops, who undertook the suicidal Charge of the Light Brigade: the proof of the pudding.

The six elements described have very blurred edges between them. Sometimes there is policy that bears no relationship to mission, sometimes there is a procedure that has been devised without a policy to inform it, and frequently there is practice without procedure, but by identifying these discrete elements we can see more clearly how strategy and policy interact.

The nature of strategy

Until recently the concept of strategy was confined to the conduct of war. It derives from the Greek *strategia*, which was the function of a general in battle. Generals

---

The Crimean War between Russia on the one hand and Britain, France and Turkey on the other raged between 1853 and 1856. It was an attempt by Britain and France to limit Russian expansion into the Balkans and the Mediterranean area. In the course of a generally disastrous campaign, there was a legendary incident of futile heroism that became a massacre because of confusion over orders. Men formed a brigade of six hundred and seven light cavalry, who were ordered to charge down a narrow valley. They were met by concerted enemy artillery fire from all sides and only 198 returned. The British commander, Lord Raglan, had issued the order:

> Advance and take advantage of any opportunity to recover the heights. You will be supported by infantry, which have been ordered to advance on two fronts.

In semaphore transmission the second sentence was distorted so that it read:

> You will be supported by infantry, which have been ordered. Advance on two fronts.

had to lead their troops and before doing that they had to produce a plan of action. That plan might be to advance and win territory, to deliver a city from siege, to destroy the enemy's lines of supply or to defend a position against attack. There is a saying in military folklore that no plan survives its first encounter with the enemy, and strategy always embraces the two aspects of objectives and response to the environment.

A further aspect of strategic thinking that Greek generals had to include was the location of their actions in a varied context. Any army has to maintain a constructive relationship with the citizens and political leaders of the territory in which it is engaged. A military decision to attack may be overtaken by a political decision to hold your fire and a successful military campaign to capture territory may be nullified by a failure to maintain food supplies to the citizens of the newly occupied area.

REVIEW TOPIC 2.1

The Japanese apparently having a saying, 'business is war'. What parallels can you see between a general at war and being a manager running a business? Who is the enemy?

The application of strategic thinking in business developed in the period after World War II, as business grew in size and complexity. Until that time many businesses were based on an assumption that the product would evolve, but rarely change, and that the customers would neither vary nor expect a different form of service. By the 1950s businesses were becoming bigger and with more specialisation and a widening product range, so the management response was policy formulation, providing co-ordinating frameworks defining who could do what, and clear procedures to be followed. The best-known of all business historians, the American Alfred Chandler, showed the inadequacy of that approach and identified the alternative approach of strategy, defined as:

> … the determination of the basic long-term goals and objectives of an enterprise, and the adoption of courses of action and the allocation of resources necessary for carrying out these goals. (Chandler 1962, p. 16)

This definition incorporates the idea of working out what to expect and what a business should try to achieve in advance of deciding the courses of action to be adopted in getting there, as well as how the strategy was formulated. This emphasised that the relationship between a business and its environment was not stable and predictable, but changing and uncertain.

Although Chandler's thesis revolutionised management thinking, it did not include a working through of the role of the individual manager in strategy. In the military analogy it explained the function of the general, but not the role of the officers. This was worked out by Schendel and Hofer (1978) to involve four distinct stages. First was goal-setting, just as Chandler had described. The second was strategy formulation, which is the process of working out a model of how the goals can be reached, a plan of action. The third stage was strategy implementation, which was putting the strategy into operation, making it happen. The fourth stage was strategic control, monitoring progress by obtaining feedback information. That feedback could confirm the effectiveness of the plan, or the effectiveness of the implementation. It could also indicate the likelihood of reaching the goal.

The feedback loop is essential to make strategy effective but it requires excellent judgement, or supreme generalship, to make the right decisions about the information. If things are going wrong, where is action required? Is the goal unobtainable, is the plan of action flawed in some way, or is there something wrong in the way we are trying to make it happen? There will always be a reluctance to abandon a goal because the implications are so great, but the supreme generals will make that decision, if it is inescapable, before it is too late.

Business strategy and personnel management

The formulation and implementation of strategy is in some ways inimical to personnel management. Although personnel managers – like all managers – have cheerfully accepted the importance of strategy, few have really come to terms with its implications. The stock in trade of personnel work is predictability: letting people know where they stand, setting up an appraisal system that will endure rather than being constantly changed, being clear about human resource requirements over the next five years and putting plans into place to ensure their availability, succession planning, career planning, equal opportunity policies, smoking policies, redundancy policies, unequivocal agreements with trade unions about the relationship between management and union. Adapting to strategic realities and developing human resource strategies at the same time as retaining credibility in the eyes of all those who work for the business is a central challenge in an age when the organisation as an entity is in retreat.

There are many advantages of strategic management to effective personnel work. There is a clear sense of direction and focus on where the business is going. From that clear sense of direction can stem specific objectives, the collation of necessary information, the anticipation of problems and the assessment of strengths, weaknesses and opportunities. Because of the emphasis on analysis and precision there is a tendency for strategists to concentrate on economic data and overlook the way in which people and their values can influence the implementation – or failure to implement – a chosen strategy. This is where the personnel specialist can be invaluable because:

> 'economic' analysis of strategy fails to recognise the complex role which people play in the evolution of strategy...strategy is also a product of what people *want* an organisation to do or what they feel the organisation should be like. (Johnson and Scholes 1989, p. 113).

Strategy is only partly determined by scrupulous analysis of statistical and economic data. Again the military analogy helps us to understand this point. Napoleon enjoyed a remarkable series of victories because he was, in a psychological sense, personally driven to conquest; but he also realised that battles were won because people wanted to win them. In reflecting on his Spanish campaign he commented that in warfare only a quarter was a matter of material resources; the important three-quarters was human relations and personal character. Strategy is not only a product of human analysis of objective data, it is also a product of people's dreams and ambitions. Its implementation depends on people's commitment, skill, will and collaboration. This is the very stuff of personnel management. The way the personnel specialists make their input is one of the principle drives behind HRM:

> ... people management decisions ought not to be treated as incidental operational matters ... the HRM 'message' is that decisions about what kind of employee 'stock' one is going to aspire towards, how much is to be invested in it and so on, are issues of crucial top management importance and ought not only to be seen to derive explicitly from the corporate plan, but to constitute a key set of considerations which feed into that plan. (Storey 1992, pp. 26–7)

One of the best-selling management books of all time was that by Peters and Waterman (1982), who included the 7-S model of organisational effectiveness that had been developed earlier within the McKinsey consulting firm. The seven were:

> Strategy, Structure, Systems, and
> Skills, Staff, Style, Shared Values.

They are separated out on two lines because some later commentators have drawn a distinction between the first three – hard – and the other four – soft – Ss. Each of the soft Ss is what personnel managers specialise in and why the personnel manager is a crucial member of any strategy group.

To perform this strategic function personnel managers have to be closely involved with, and exert influence upon, the central management process in all parts of the business. To be effectively involved, they need to speak with authority by having a distinctive and comprehensive range of expertise and skills. They also need to understand their organisational culture and be sensitive to the motivations and concerns of individuals and groups within the business and, to some extent, outside it.

With the increasing number of pressure groups expressing various types of social concern, there are many issues of management strategy that come under public scrutiny, from the dumping of nuclear waste and the use of ozone-friendly materials to the methods of selling timeshare apartments. As those working in organisations become more selective in their employment, management approaches to strategy have to be highly sensitive to matters of public concern, not only to meet customer expectations but also to avoid offending those of their own employees who may well be members of the pressure groups scrutinising the organisation's strategy.

Inside the business the values to constrain strategy are manifested in trade union organisations, in professional groupings and in coalitions of interest which develop, particularly in response to perceived threat. The interest in organisational culture is partly an attempt to get a closer fit between the values of the various stakeholders in the business and the objectives of that business.

In today's changing business environment there is an increasing need for personnel specialists to stop focusing on short-term, tactical 'fire-fighting' and to direct their efforts towards long-term, strategic planning. As Georgiades explains: 'The focus shifts from throwing lifebelts to drowning people, to walking upstream and finding out who is throwing them off the bridge and why' (Georgiades 1990, p. 44). His organisational model emphasises a move on the part of personnel specialists towards organisational interventions, focusing on issues of leadership, human resource management strategy and organisational culture. Such a move is seen as enhancing personnel's ability to contribute directly to corporate goals. Examples of such interventions can be found in Yeandle and Clark (1989) and Carolin and Evans (1988).

Strategic approaches

Most of the approaches to devising strategy have come from marketing specialists. In 1965 Igor Ansoff proposed a series of four strategy areas: market penetration, product development, market development and diversification. Michael Porter (1979) provides a model for structural analysis that is widely adopted, but which is unsuitable for the personnel specialist. It focuses on five environmental forces shaping the competitive position of the business: threats to entry, consumers' bargaining power, suppliers' bargaining power, the threat of substitute products and jockeying for position in crowded markets.

The organisation specialist Henry Mintzberg (1991) has attempted to identify the strategy process in the organisation in general. He has five groupings. First the core business is *located*. Who are we? What are we doing? What do we do best? What could we be doing better than others? What should we strip away, by contracting out, selling on or demerging, to ensure that we have the best possible chance of competitive success? Secondly, the core business is *distinguished* by determining the characteristics that are necessary to enable the business to survive and to achieve the competitive advantage for which an opportunity has been perceived. The core business is then *elaborated* to give it strength and resilience: penetrating existing markets more deeply, promoting existing products in new markets, expanding geographically or developing new products. Extending the core business is the process of taking the business beyond its core by diversifying into a new business or by integrating in the operating chain, as when a manufacturer buys a supplier or a distribution network. *Reconceiving* the core business is putting all of these features together to arrive at some total strategic plan.

Although these approaches deal with considerations that initially seem outside the specialist sphere of personnel people, they need to understand the forces that will influence profoundly whatever personnel initiatives are needed. Without a clear understanding of the strategic approaches of the business, personnel specialists are isolated from strategic decision-making: without a commitment to the strategy of the business, personnel specialists are isolationist. Both are recipes for being ineffective, as there is no place for voices crying in the wilderness.

Strategic methods

How do you develop strategy? What are the practical methods available to help you in developing the appropriate vision without losing discipline? Here are some of the tried and tested methods.

Brainstorming

Brainstorming is a specialised technique for developing a range of new ideas for examination:

> … groups attempt to create a 'freewheeling' atmosphere where any ideas, however absurd, are recorded. Evaluation of the quality of ideas is strictly excluded and is carried out after the idea-generation phase is complete. [The] view is that the flow of ideas in the group will trigger off further ideas whereas the usual evaluative framework will tend to stifle imagination. This may be because group members are concerned not to appear ridiculous in the eyes of others. (Smith 1973, p. 69)

Brainstorming can have a useful place at the creative end of strategy formulation when fresh ideas have to be found and creativity is required.

REVIEW TOPIC 2.3

Try an informal brainstorm the next time you are on a car journey with one or two other people. One or two possible starters are:

(a) Think of different uses for a piece of wood (e.g. 'Christmas dinner for woodworm')
(b) What would make working life tolerable? (e.g. 'Voluntary euthanasia')
(c) What is the greatest show on earth? (e.g. 'The House of Commons – when it's closed')

Patterning

Patterning is a form of *post hoc* rationalisation by putting shape and purpose around something that emerges from practice, either through trial and error or

A drill for brainstorming

You need a flip chart, blackboard or overhead projector and someone who can write quickly and legibly. Before the meeting, decide what its purpose is. Is it:

- to find uses for a new idea;
- to generate a range of new ideas;
- to find a better way of doing something; or
- to find a solution to a problem?

Generating ideas

(a) Appoint a note-taker.
(b) Introduce the purpose of the meeting and ask group members to call out any idea relating to that purpose which comes into their heads.
(c) Write ideas on a flip chart so that all members can see them.
(d) Encourage members to develop the ideas of others ('hitch-hiking') as well as 'sparking' in different directions.
(e) Ban judgement, as all ideas are valid, however bizarre, even if they seem to be repeating what has already been said. Even such subtle judgements as laughter, gasps of disbelief and nods of approval can inhibit or direct thinking. All should be banned at this stage.
(f) Generate momentum, so that the group keeps going.
(g) Reach a target number – say 65 – in 15 to 30 minutes.

Classifying the ideas

(a) Collectively classify the ideas into five or six groups, possibly adding others suggested by the classification.
(b) Ask the group to rank the ideas in each classification against questions such as:

- how new?
- how relevant?
- how feasible?

through simply identifying and describing something so that it becomes a vehicle for future purposeful action.

Initially this sounds like the exact opposite of strategy:

> Strategies that emerge? Managers who acknowledge strategies already formed? Over the years we have met with a good deal of resistance from people upset by what they perceive to be our passive definition of a word so bound up with proactive behaviour and free will. (Mintzberg 1987, p. 108)

The method is the same as that of the acacdemic researcher. First evidence is collected by *chasing trails*. Some of this is predetermined and purposeful, such as collecting the sales figures and checking on the bank position, looking at payroll costs and reports from research and development: the normal monitoring that is part of every manager's role. Other aspects are lateral thinking, looking for diversions and alternative perspectives. There is a great deal of talking to people; not interviewing them but talking to get angles and opinions, fragments of information, encouraging them to talk to you, following their own agenda. You are, however, looking at this information not to control, but to find pieces of a puzzle: a pattern. The second stage is *organising into patterns*. If any manager thinks that looking for strategies which are already there is a passive activity, this is the cure for that misconception. You look at your information and put it together into different shapes and sequences, looking for shape and meaning that was implicit in the information, but which was not apparent until you put it together properly. It is like solving an anagram. The letters REHCAHERAGRAMTTT could be rearranged into THAT GREAT CHARMER, or into the name of a well-known person. Organising into patterns is the same sort of process, as you look at information in different ways and differently organised until it means something that is more than the simple sum of its parts. As with anagrams you may see it at once, or you may not see it at all: you just hope that the penny will drop.

Confirming the pattern is when you develop the crude pattern into one with more detail, colour and strength. The strategy has emerged from an understanding of indicators that were present in current practice. By being understood and clarified it becomes a model for future action that is more purposeful, as there is now a blueprint where previously there was 'happenstance'.

> The genetic code of DNA was cracked by Francis Crick and James Watson at Cambridge in 1953. They knew that it consisted of a chain of sugars and phosphates which were held together by nucleotides. Each nucleotide had a different organic base, but they did not know how the bases fitted together. After countless attempts to find the pattern, they decided to try linking the bases in pairs. Working with cut-out models of the four bases they suddenly saw the pattern: an adenine–thymine pair was exactly the same shape as a guanine–cytosine pair. They had found the key to the genetic code.

SWOT

A simple technique that can be used in working out a strategic response is the SWOT analysis of identifying the strengths, weaknesses, opportunities and threats that exist. This can be done in one of two ways, either as a general form of audit of the people side of the business or as an assessment of the specific capability in relation to one part of the strategy of the business. Figure 2.2 is how the first type of analysis might look.

Strengths	Weaknesses
Highly skilled staff Culture fits strategy Competitive pay rates in most areas	Performance appraisal scheme unpopular and ineffective Shortage of IT staff High level of absence

Opportunities
New product line provides promotion
   prospects
Graduate intake has been doubled this
   year
New flexible payment scheme ready for
   launch soon
	Threats
	Three equal value cases likely to go to tribunal
	Recent 15% hike in pay rates for IT staff
	   at X Co.
	All overseas sales team have been
	   approached with lucrative offers from
	   Danish competitor

Figure 2.2 SWOT analysis

The second type of analysis enables you to line up the human resource considerations to be assessed in relation to a specific proposal such as opening a new plant, relocating a sales team, closing a distribution outlet and so on.

The nature of policy

Much of personnel work is in policy rather than strategy. Part of the *strategy* of a supermarket may be to extend its opening hours. Part of the personnel *policy* may be to target recruitment of new staff at those over the age of 55 years, in the belief that this will be an effective way of meeting the strategic requirement. Businesses regularly make strategic decisions to reduce the number of people employed by some euphemism such as down-sizing, right-sizing, rationalisation or reshaping. There is then a policy question of how this should be done.

The main aspect of all these policy discussions is the concern with the future rather than the past. The objective is to set a framework within which action can be taken, not to analyse what has gone wrong in the past – though that may be a preliminary to the policy formulation. Often people in an organisation await a policy statement before they can make progress with day to day matters, so that the policy is a framework within which other people operate using their own discretion and making their own decisions. It is not the same as an instruction, which is much more precise, allowing scant discretion.

There is not much point in determining a policy as a framework for action by others if the policy is not known to the others, so the other part of our definition is that the policy is declared. Once the policy is known it is likely to be criticised, and may be undermined by opponents, so managers may be reluctant to make statements of policy on certain matters – such as trade union recognition – in order to avoid the arguments and problems that the statement could cause.

The reasons for having policies

Statements of policy produce problems for the policy maker. If your policy does not work very well you are criticised for incompetence. If your policy is disliked you become unpopular and your enemies try to undermine your policy initiative. If your policy is accepted by others, you have very little scope for changing it or trying to forget it. Why do managers bother with policy statements? Would it not be simpler just to make decisions on matters as they arise, 'treating each case on its merits', rather than being bound by the straitjacket of a declared position? Here are six reasons why managers try to use statements of policy.

Clarification

There are always managers who want to make things clear to their colleagues. A manager wishing to encourage senior colleagues to agree an increased departmental budget will have to set out the policy that the budget increase will be used to implement. A wish to spend £50,000 for new equipment will only be supported if there is a convincing case of policy for its use.

A manager wanting to increase the amount of responsibility assumed by subordinates will achieve this most effectively if there are clear guidelines for the delegation of that responsibility. Clarification of policy is one means of making that delegation possible.

Reducing dependence on individuals

The development of a strong (but not inflexible) policy framework makes an organisation less dependent on the knowledge and judgement of individuals. Most readers will have heard something like one of the following:

> If there's anything you want to know about recruitment, ask Charlie. He's got it all at his finger tips.

> We can't make a move on this until we've got the all-clear from the boss.

> Mary really is marvellous at controlling the debtors. She keeps it all in her head and we'd be lost without her.

Splendid individuals are no substitute for sound policies.

Producing consistent management behaviour

Policy provides a discipline for managers as they have to behave in a consistent way, avoiding capricious changes of direction and bewildering their colleagues. It is important to distinguish between policy and precedent. Personnel managers are nearly as keen on precedents as are trade union officials, but this is using as a framework for action what has happened in the past instead of what should happen in the future. Imaginative and realistic policy making is a way of breaking out from the cage of doing things tomorrow in the same way as they were done yesterday, because that is the only security available. Precedents look back; policies look forward.

At first some managers carp about the need to behave consistently because they feel it undermines their authority, but they soon find that the policy framework's limitation on their own whimsicality prevents them wasting energy thinking up new strategies for problems they have already solved and builds a progressively more positive response from their colleagues.

Knowing where we stand

There is a growing expectation among members of organisations to be supplied with information. Much of this relates to security of employment and management intentions. Without statements of management policy, employees will assume adherence to management precedent. Whenever there is a new development, managers want to know where they stand as their individual policy platform will have been affected and they will quickly want to know what repairs and redevelopments are needed.

Responding to legal and other external pressures

Finally, there is the organisational response to changes in the law and similar external influences. When a new piece of legislation appears on the statute book, managers wait for policy guidance on its influence. An example is the 1984 Data Protection Act. This had received extensive media coverage for years prior to its enactment and thousands of managers must have attended one-day conferences about its implications, but for each organisation there was the need for working out a policy to ensure consistent compliance with its provisions.

REVIEW TOPIC 2.4

What is the purpose of your organisation? Is there any value in policy statements that are vague, for example: 'It is our policy to provide attractive terms and conditions of employment for all employees'? Is it necessary for a policy to be written down?

Devising policies

The two most common methods of devising policies are both inadequate. One is to use the policy of another business as a model; the other is to start with a blank piece of paper to produce something that sounds good. Copying from elsewhere usually means that the policy will be at best very vague and at worst inappropriate through having first been devised for a different situation. The inadequacy of starting with a blank piece of paper is that the writing is likely to reflect the values and prejudices of the author rather than the needs of the organisation and its members.

As a policy is only as good as the practice it produces, we offer a three-part rule for policy formulation:

1. Policy does not translate into effective practice without a commitment to both the policy and the measures needed to make it work.
2. Commitment is more likely when the policy develops out of issues in the organisation itself.
3. Where the policy is devised, and later sustained, by the involvement of all those affected by it.

If a policy is adopted independently of issues relevant to the organisation, and not seen as relevant by members of the organisation, then commitment is unlikely and the policy will probably not work. Here is a simple four-step procedure that could be used to devise policies.

● *Identify the topic:*   Individual topics on which policy clarification is needed have to be identified and worked on when the time is ripe. One push will be changes in the law, such as the Data Protection Act mentioned earlier; another will be a management initiative in some other policy framework, such as an intention to double production, or introduce shiftwork, or to use performance appraisal to inform promotion decisions. Other pushes towards policy statements are questions from employees or other managers about where they stand, uncertainties about the future, unexpected change, review of the mission and strategic objectives of the business, or the many organisational muddles.

    In identifying the topic, one has to be sure that it is correctly identified and that a policy statement will be timely. Taking the Data Protection example again, there is little point in developing a policy before the legislative details are clear or at a time when other people are saying that the matter lacks urgency.

● *Selling the idea:*   Closely related to identifying the topic is getting support for the idea of a policy on that topic. This requires at least an expanded headline to show what should be achieved, and then provisional support for the idea is won through preliminary consultation and testing of reaction. This is the beginning of making sure that there will be commitment. The policy deviser will pick with care those to be consulted, mixing together those with political influence in the organisation, so that their support will help produce the necessary political will for the policy to succeed and those with expertise, so that there is an early input of constructive suggestions.

- *Determining the key features:* After the general idea has been accepted and shaped, there will be the key features of the policy to be determined. In the area of trade union recognition or de-recognition, for example, the idea to be sold is whether or not to recognise. If the idea of recognition is accepted, the key features to be determined will be to decide which union to recognise and for what the union will be recognised – individual grievances only, terms and conditions of employment, manning levels or what?

    This stage is also dependent on effective consultation, so that the commitment is not lost and so that the personnel specialist develops the policy in a way that is relevant to real issues in the organisation itself. The person promulgating the policy must at this stage have the nerve to abort the whole exercise or to make a completely fresh start, if general support cannot be sustained.

- *Agree the details:* The last stage is to agree the precise details of the policy statement, with all the implications for later interpretation and implementation. If the key features have been previously determined then the detailed considerations can be carried through without the risk of jeopardising what the policy is intended to achieve, but the importance of the details should not be ignored.

This simple, outline procedure begs two questions: who does the drafting? with whom does that person consult? The first question has a straightforward answer. Devising a policy is a job to be centred on one person, who can not only remain faithful to the original vision, but can also ensure a single style and coherence in the drafting, no matter how many different suggestions and points of view are eventually accommodated. That one person needs to 'own' the drafting of the policy, being seen by all observers as the owner, protecting it from the perils of committee writing when the clarity of the message and the thrust of the policy itself can be lost through the incorporation of unedited chunks from various sources seeking to guard a sectional interest.

Whom one should consult obviously depends on the subject of the policy, but we repeat that the involvement of those affected by the policy will improve its chances of translation into practice.

Implementing policies

There are four steps in putting the final policy into operation.

Publicity

If a policy is to work it must be known to, understood and accepted by those affected. Much of this will have been ensured by devising it properly, but those consultations will mainly have been with representatives of interests only, so there will still be individuals needing to understand and seek answers to their questions. Obviously, it is not sufficient simply to send a copy to all concerned; briefing will be needed and possibly training sessions. Some features of the policy will be unwelcome to some people as it will involve changing aspects of current practice, so that the publicity, briefing and training need to win commitment, just as the stages of devising the policy in the first place have had that objective. Brewster and Richbell (1982) describe the difficulty personnel people face:

> Sometimes it seems as though a great many very talented personnel specialists are wasting an awful lot of time ... they develop sensible, well thought-out policies that would make their company one of the most progressive and highly respected of employers. And then they see their efforts continually frustrated and subverted by a management team that seems determined to ignore most of what the personnel department does. (Brewster and Richbell 1982, p. 38)

Procedures

The procedures needed to implement the policy must be ready and correct. Seldom can a policy operate without some drill to help it along, such as a form to be completed to log personal information held on computer, or a notification of who is empowered to halt a production process because of a health risk. If a policy is being accepted unwillingly, the procedure needs to be as simple and clear as possible to avoid making it even less popular.

Monitoring

Any policy initiative will drift away from the original intention unless its implementation is monitored. First, it has to be monitored for deliberate or accidental breaches. No matter how extensive the consultation and briefing, some managers will forget what they are supposed to do and some may try to avoid it. Secondly, there may be problems about the policy that had not been foreseen, and the first uncertainty will wing its way at high speed back to the person who took the policy initiative. If this type of issue can be spotted and dealt with quickly, the policy will be sustained and strengthened. If the breach is overlooked, there will be many more. If the problems are not resolved by the initiator *ad hoc* and inconsistent strategies will evolve, thereby destroying one of the main intentions of policy formulation. Increasingly, policy effectiveness can be assessed by quantitative means. The Commission for Racial Equality has been advocating for some time that organisations should monitor the racial and ethnic mix of employees to assess the effect of any equal opportunity policy that may be introduced. Although not a popular proposal, it is gradually being adopted and is best done through computerising personnel records. Quantitative assessment is not, however, enough: 'while analytical and quantitative techniques are essential to the development of company employment policies, a qualitative, creative dimension is equally necessary to shape direction and purpose' (Rothwell 1984, p. 30).

Policy effectiveness has to be monitored by discussion, seeing and evaluating the number and type of problems that occur, and by 'walking the job'. We have constantly noticed in our research that the most satisfied, and perhaps the most effective, of the personnel managers with whom we have spoken place great emphasis on getting out of the office for informal walkabouts and chats with people. The computer terminal is no substitute for seeing for oneself and getting into the action.

Tony and Joyce are both Divisional Personnel Managers in a manufacturing company where briefing groups have recently been introduced and are not working very well. There is also a long-running problem about absence, with up to 30 per cent of shop floor personnel missing each day.

Tony explains that the problem lies with the supervisors, who have not understood the briefing process properly and simply will not get on top of the absence issue, despite his clear policy guidelines and many memos sent to the Divisional Operations Managers.

Joyce sees it differently. She's been round to have a chat with each of the supervisors and realises that they do not have the confidence to handle team briefing; they've never had to do that sort of thing before and the 'training' they had from the consultant was way above their heads. Just before last month's briefing she had short rehearsals – coaching, really – with the supervisors working in pairs. When the time for the real briefing came along most of them did it really well, although two of them want to have a further session with her. While she was doing this she acquired a completely fresh understanding of the absence issue. Now that certainly is a problem, but she's got a couple of ideas...

Modifying

The point of monitoring policy is not simply to be sure it is right, but also to modify it where it seems wrong. Though an obvious enough statement, policy modification is not simple. Those who initiate policy are often very reluctant to change it, because of the implied inadequacy of their original formulation. Also, modification requires even more consultation than formulation, as it is not only representatives with whom one must consult, but all those affected.

A further aspect of modifying is that policies become out of date so that policy modification is not only correcting errors, it is also ongoing development of policy to suit changing situations and to create fresh opportunities.

Strategy, policy, formality and chaos

Review topic 2.2 in this chapter raised the question about whether or not policies need to be written down. The value of writing is the ease of implementation, the support for consistency and the basis for consultation. The problem about writing is that it involves the management in declaring a position that it may not wish to publicise, such as a policy decision not to recognise trade unions. Also, there is the problem of change. A written, published policy is much harder to change than the informal understanding or strategy, and often that which is written differs from what is practised. Brewster and Richbell (1982) distinguish between policies that are 'espoused', being officially endorsed and often written, and 'operational' policies, which are the strategies that managers actually follow. The latter may deviate slightly or substantially from the former.

This book opened with the suggestion that personnel work was on the verge of the biggest change ever in its practices because of the decline of the organisational entity. Policy is an instrument of stability: knowing where we stand. Some people now argue that strategy, policy and planning are all ultimately hopeless attempts to visualise and plan the future of the business. This line of thinking comes partly from business experience and the acceleration of change, which is exactly why strategy took over from policy as the mechanism of management control. It is also stimulated by the work of some scientists in developing a theory of chaos to understand a range of natural phenomena that have chaotic dynamics and where new patterns emerge through spontaneous self organisation (for example, Gleick 1987). This leads to a school of thought that emphasises organisational learning as a logical step beyond strategic management, policy making and their concomitant methods devoted to trying to hold all the variables steady until the logic of cause and effect has been demonstrated. The feedback loops are extremely short and the adjustments to the new situation are constant, with all members of the organisation adjusting themselves to the discipline of learning from unfolding events, rather than waiting for the plan and following it to the letter.

> That debate has not, however, focused clearly on the critical unquestioned assumptions upon which the planning approach is based, namely that about the nature of causality ... cause and effect links disappear in innovative human organizations, making it impossible to envision and plan their long-term futures. (Stacey 1993, p. 17)

The concept of the learning organisation is still new and the implications are not easy to grasp, but the argument demonstrates the danger of developing management approaches of strategy, policy and procedure that are too inflexible to match the requirements of the business. If strategy and policy are to be a viable framework for action in the future and not simply a confirmation of precedents from the past, they must deliver not only commitment to the status quo but also a commitment to changing that status quo.

☐ SUMMARY PROPOSITIONS

2.1 Strategic management has four elements: goal-setting, strategy formulation, strategy implementation and strategic control.

2.2 Many personnel managers are not comfortable with strategy, but their participation is essential because strategy is a product of what people *want* an organisation to do or what they feel the organisation should be like.

2.3 Policy is a declared mode of action for the future and part of a framework for management action to translate mission into practice via strategy, policy and procedures all integrated by planning.

2.4 The reasons for having policy are clarification, reducing dependence on individuals, producing consistent managerial behaviour, knowing 'where we stand' and responding to legal and other external pressures.

2.5 A three-part rule for policy formulation is: (1) policy does not translate into effective practice without a commitment to both the policy and the measures needed to make it work; (2) commitment is more likely when the policy develops out of issues in the organisation itself; and (3) where the policy is devised, and later sustained, by the involvement of all those affected by it.

2.6 A procedure for devising policy is: identifying the topic, selling the idea, determining the key features, agreeing the details.

2.7 The four steps to put policy into operation are publicity, procedures, monitoring and modifying.

2.8 Strategy is linked to planning what to do, while policy is the framework for carrying forward everyday affairs.

2.9 Both strategic management and policy formulation are designed to make the future predictable. This is not always possible and an inflexible approach to either can make the business ineffective.

References

Brewster, C. J. and Richbell, S. (1982), 'Getting managers to implement personnel policies', *Personnel Management*, December.

Carolin, B. and Evans, E. (1988), 'Computers as a strategic management tool', *Personnel Management*, July.

Chandler, A. D. (1962), *Strategy and Structure: Chapters in the History of the American Industrial Enterprise*, Cambridge, Massachusetts: MIT Press.

Georgiades, N. (1990), 'A strategic future for personnel?' *Personnel Management*, February.

Gleick, J. E. (1987), *Chaos: Making a New Science*, London: Heinemann.

Mintzberg, H. (1987) 'Crafting strategy', *Harvard Business Review*, July–August.

Mintzberg, H. (1991) 'Generic Strategies', in H. Mintzberg and J. B. Quinn (eds) *The Strategy Process*, Englewood Cliffs, NJ. Prentice Hall.

Peters, T. J. and Waterman, R. H. (1982) *In Search of Excellence*, London: Harper & Row.

Porter, M. E. (1979), 'How Competitive Forces Shape Strategy', *Harvard Business Review*, vol. 57, no. 2.

Rothwell, S. (1984), 'Integrating the Elements of a Company Manpower Policy', *Personnel Management*, November.

Schendel, D. E. and Hofer, C. W. (1978), *Strategic Management: A New View of Business Policy and Planning*, Boston: Little, Brown.

Stacey, R. (1993) 'Strategy as order emerging from chaos', *Long Range Planning*, vol. 26, no. 1, pp. 10–17.

Stoner, J. A. F. and Wankel, C. (1986), *Management* (3rd edition), Englewood Cliffs, NJ: Prentice Hall.

Storey, J. (1992), *Developments in the Management of Human Resources*, Oxford: Basil Blackwell.

Yeandle, D. and Clark, J. (1989), 'Personnel strategy for an automated plant', *Personnel Management*, June.

3 Human resource strategy

We have already seen how interest in strategy has taken personnel management by storm. The rhetoric of strategic involvement is now embedded in 'personnel speak' and the strategy for human resources is a central component of business strategy. The key question for personnel managers is whether or not they are in on the decision making. Storey has described how this presents a dilemma for personnel directors:

> If, in order to win business credibility on the board, they suppressed traditional personnel perspectives, the whole question of their distinctive contribution would be open to question ... If, on the other hand, the personnel director seeks to give a higher profile to the distinctive attributes of a 'personnel view', this may be seen to renege on the 'business primacy' axiom ... (Storey 1992, p. 275)

In this chapter we set out the nature of human resource strategy, its development and integration with organisational strategy.

What is human resource strategy?

Human resource strategy involves a central philosophy of the way that people in the organisation are managed and the translation of this into personnel policies and practices. It requires personnel policies and practices to be integrated so that they make a coherent whole, and also that this whole is integrated with the business or organisational strategy. These themes of integration and a central philosophy of people management have been drawn out by a number of writers, for example Handy *et al.* (1989) and Hendry and Pettigrew (1986). Baird *et al.*, as early as 1983, go one step beyond this and argue that there can be no organisational strategy without the inclusion of human resources. A third theme, identified by Handy *et al.*, is that the above demands a strategic view of the role of personnel management in the organisation. We will come back to these themes later on.

So far we have a definition of what is involved in human resource strategy, but what does one look like? Human resource strategy is generally behaviour based. In

Table 3.1 *Business strategies, and associated employee role behaviour and HRM policies*

Strategy	Employee role behaviour	HRM policies
1. Innovation	A high degree of creative behaviour	Jobs that require close interaction and co-ordination among groups of individuals
	Longer-term focus	Performance appraisals that are more likely to reflect longer-term and group-based achievements
	A relatively high level of co-operative, interdependent behaviour	Jobs that allow employees to develop skills that can be used in other positions in the firm
		Compensation systems that emphasise internal equity rather than external or market-based equity
	A moderate degree of concern for quality	Pay rates that tend to be low, but that allow employees to be stockholders and have more freedom to choose the mix of components that make up their pay package
	A moderate concern for quantity; an equal degree of concern for process and results	Broad career paths to reinforce the development of a broad range of skills
	A greater degree of risk taking; a higher tolerance of ambiguity and unpredictability	
2. Quality enhancement	Relatively repetitive and predictable behaviours;	Relatively fixed and explicit job descriptions
	A more long-term or intermediate focus	High levels of employee participation in decisions relevant to immediate work conditions and the job itself
	A moderate amount of co-operative, interdependent behaviour	A mix of individual and group criteria for performance appraisal that is mostly short term and results orientated
	A high concern for quality	A relatively egalitarian treatment of employees and some guarantees of employment security.
	A modest concern for quantity of output	Extensive and continuous training and development of employees
	High concern for process: low risk-taking activity; commitment to the goals of the organisation	
3. Cost reduction	Relatively repetitive and predictable behaviour	Relatively fixed and explicit job descriptions that allow little room for ambiguity
	A rather short-term focus	Narrowly designed jobs and narrowly defined career paths that encourage specialisation expertise and efficiency
	Primarily autonomous or individual activity;	Short-term results-orientated performance appraisals
	Moderate concern for quality	Close monitoring of market pay levels for use in making compensation decisions
	High concern for quantity of output	Minimal levels of employee training and development
	Primary concern for results; low risk-taking activity; relatively high degree of comfort with stability	

Source: Schuler and Jackson (1987). Reproduced with permission of the Academy of Management.

the traditional ideal model there would be analysis of the types of employee behaviour required to fulfill business objectives, and then an identification of personnel policies and practices which would bring about and reinforce this behaviour. A very good example of this is found in Schuler and Jackson (1987). They used the three business strategies defined by Porter (1985) and for each identified employee role behaviour and HRM policies required. Their conclusions are shown in Table 3.1.

Similar analyses can be found for other approaches to business strategy, for example in relation to the Boston matrix (Purcell 1992) and the developmental stage of the organisation (Kochan and Barocci 1985). Some human resource strategies describe the behaviour of all employees but others have concentrated on the behaviour of Chief Executives and senior managers. The type of strategies described above are at a fairly general level, and there is much more concentration now on tailoring the approach to the particular needs of the specific organisation.

Many human resource strategies aim to target not just behaviour, but through behaviour change to effect a change in the culture of the organisation. The target is therefore to change the common view of 'the way we do things around here' and to attempt to change the beliefs and values of employees. There is much debate as to whether this is achievable.

Before we move on to look at the different degrees to which human resource strategy is and can be integrated with organisational strategy, it is important to consider how human resource strategy relates to human resource planning. Our starting point is with Bramham in 1989 who identified, along with other authors at the time, the difference between manpower planning and human resource planning. His view was that:

> There are particularly important differences in terms of process and purpose. In human resource planning the manager is concerned with motivating people – a process in which costs, numbers, control and systems interact to play a part. In manpower planning the manager is concerned with the numerical elements of forecasting, supply–demand matching and control, in which people are a part. There are therefore important areas of overlap and interconnection but there is a fundamental difference in underlying approach (p. 147)

The emphasis in Bramham's book is on motivating employees to achieve organisational objectives by defining plans and targets that enable the personnel function to manage the culture of the organisation. This appears very little different from our definition of human resource strategy outlined above.

What is the difference then between strategy and planning? A common view has been that they are virtually one and the same – hence the term 'strategic planning'. In an article in the *Harvard Business Review* (February, 1994) Henry Mintzberg gives us his view. He distinguishes between strategic thinking, which is about creating a vision of how things could be, and strategic planning, which is about collecting the relevant data and also programming the vision into what needs to be gone to get there.

> Strategic thinking, in contrast is about synthesis. It involves intuition and creativity. The outcome of strategic thinking is an integrated perspective of the enterprise, a not-too-precisely articulated vision of direction ... (p. 108)

In this chapter we will concentrate on the strategic vision and in Chapter 5 we will concentrate on the planning process.

The degree of integration with organisational strategy

The degree of integration between organisational strategy and human resource strategies varies considerably between different organisations. Figure 3.1 shows a range of possible relationships.

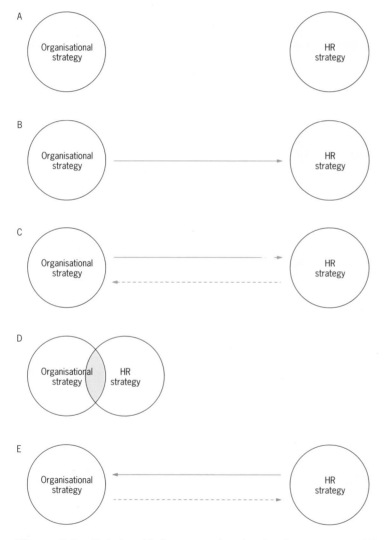

Figure 3.1 Relationship between organisational strategy and HR strategy

In *Approach A* there is no relationship at all, if indeed organisational and human resource strategy *did* exist in an explicit form in the organisation. This is a typical picture of 20 years ago but still exists today, particularly in smaller organisations.

Approach B represents a growing recognition of the importance of people in the achievement of organisational strategy. Employees are seen as key in the implementation of the declared organisational strategy, and human resource strategy is designed to fit the requirements of the organisation's strategy. Some of the early formal models of human resource strategy, particularly that proposed by Fombrun, Tichy and Devanna in 1984, concentrate on how the human resource strategy can be designed to ensure a close fit.

This whole approach depends on a view of strategy formulation as a logical rational process, which remains the view in many organisations. The relationship in Approach B is exemplified by organisations which cascade their business objectives down from the senior management team through functions, through departments, through teams and so on. Functions, for example, have to propose a functional strategy which enables the organisational strategy to be achieved. Departments have to propose a strategy which enables the functional strategy to be achieved, and so on. In this way the personnel function (as with any other) is required to respond to organisational strategy by defining a strategy which meets organisational demands.

Approach C takes the relationship one step further, as it recognises the need for two-way communication and some debate. What is demanded in the organisation's strategy may not be viewed as feasible and alternative possibilities need to be reviewed. The debate, however, is often limited, as shown in the boxed example.

Approaches D and E show a much closer involvement between organisational and human resource strategy. *Approach D* represents the people of the organisation

---

In one large multinational organisation an objectives-setting cascade was put into place. This cascade did allow for a dialogue between the planned organisation strategy and the response of each function. In the organisation's strategy there was some emphasis on people growth and development and job fulfilment. The Personnel Department's response included among other things an emphasis on line management involvement in these areas, which would be supported by consultancy help from the Personnel Department.

The top management team replied to this by asking the Personnel Department to add a strategic objective about employment welfare and support. The Personnel Department strongly argued that this was a line management responsibility, along with coaching, development and so on. The function saw its customers as the managers of the organisation, not the employees. The result of the debate was that the Personnel Function added the strategic objective about employee welfare.

Although the approach in this case appeared two-way – the stronger of the parties was the management team, and they were determined that their vision was the one that would be implemented!

being recognised as the key to competitive advantage rather than just the way of implementing organisational strategy. Human resource strategy therefore becomes critical and, as Baird argued, there can be no strategy without human resource strategy. Organisational and human resource strategy are developed together in an integrated way. It appears that the personnel function has finally made it. The bad news is that in many organisations this is not the case. People issues may count for a lot, but the personnel function still has some way to go. Storey (1989), reporting on a large scale research project, found a clear emphasis on people strategies, for example total quality, but also found that the personnel function had rarely been involved in developing them.

Approach E offers an alternative form, different from integration, which places human resource strategy in prime position. The argument here is that if people are the key to competitive advantage, then we need to build on our people strengths. Logically then, as the potential of our employees will undoubtedly affect the achievement of any planned strategy, it would be sensible to take account of this in developing our strategic direction. Butler (1988) identifies this model as a shift from human resources as the implementors of strategy to human resources as a driving force in the formulation of the strategy. He sees this within the context of a model of emergent strategy, as shown in Figure 3.2.

REVIEW TOPIC 3.1

Which of these approaches to human resource strategy most closely fits your organisation? Why did you come to this decision?
What are the advantages and disadvantages of the approach used?

So far we have considered human resource strategy and its relationship to organisational strategy and have only mentioned in passing the role of the personnel or human resource function in this. We will now explore that role.

The role of the personnel function in strategy

The extent to which the human resource function is involved in both organisational and human resource strategy development is dependent on a range of factors.

Factors influencing the role

The personnel role in the organisation
Involvement in strategy is clearly dependent on the level of regard for the personnel function. There is a variety of ways to describe how the personnel function is seen

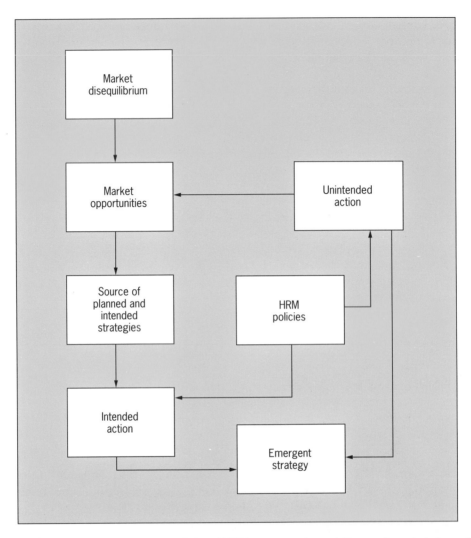

Figure 3.2   Butler's unified model of HRM, strategy formulation and market dynamics (Butler 1988). Reproduced with permission of Braybrooke Press Ltd.

in the organisation, as shown in Chapter 1. One specific way in which this can be viewed is through the role of the most senior personnel person.

There is a greater likelihood of involvement in strategy when the most senior personnel person is at Director level on the main Board. Purcell (1994) in a recent survey found that only 30% of companies in the private sector with 1000 or more employees had such a Director. He found that many more had an executive with the title of Director, but without main Board membership and the influencing potential that is allied with this. The Institute of Personnel Management (IPM) (1992) found two-thirds of personnel functions represented on the top management team and

Brewster and Smith (1990) found the same proportions in large organisations. They also found, however, that a smaller percentage (around half) were involved in strategic planning. Even looking at the most favourable evidence from the research, a picture emerges of limited involvement in strategic matters. The good news is that the IPM's survey found that representation on the top management team was predicted to increase.

Organisational culture

The organisation's view of the importance of people and how they should be treated is inevitably an important factor in personnel involvement. For example, does the organisation see people as a cost or an investment? Buller (1988) found that the degree of integration between organisational and human resource strategy was influenced by its philosophy towards people.

Organisational environment

Buller also found that in organisations placed in a more turbulent environment, the personnel function were more likely to be involved in strategy. If an organisation operates in a stable and comfortable environment there is no pressure to change, whereas a turbulent environment demands that the organisation looks for new approaches and ways of doing things. A major crisis often operates in this way, and often brings with it a new Chief Executive for the organisation. The influence of a Chief Executive is critical regarding personnel involvement. The Chief Executive is the one person who can begin to shake up the traditional culture in the organisation where the personnel function may not have been valued or involved in the past.

These three influences are not particularly easy to manipulate, but what the personnel function *can* do is look for windows of opportunity in these areas and *use* them. In order to do this the function needs to use business and financial language; to describe the rationale for personnel activities in terms of business benefits; to act as a business manager first and a personnel manager second; to appoint line managers into the personnel function; to concentrate on priorities as defined by the business;

Frank Sharp, Head of Human Resources, explains the functional mission statement at Ilford Mobberley as:

> As a team we will...lead the development of Human Resource policies to enable all employees to contribute effectively to the successful achievement of Ilford business and profitability objectives.

The functional goals which the HR team needed to commit to are:

> By 1995 the HR team will be acknowledged by our internal customers and external peers as a professional customer oriented, innovative, progressive, influence in the Imaging Products Division. This will be achieved by establishing a long term successful partnership with line managers to ensure the achievement of the empowerment of all employees on the Mobberley site, thereby contributing to the expectations of customers both internal and external.

and to offer well developed change management skills that can be used immediately. In addition, the function needs to prepare itself by thinking strategically; identifying a functional mission and strategy and involving line management in the development of human resource strategy.

Specific personnel roles in strategy

Specific roles that the personnel function is in a good position to fulfil are those of co-ordinating people issues across the organisation; providing organisational people information; asking questions about the people implications of business strategy; acting as a consultant or facilitator to line managers and the top team on strategy matters; selling the strategy; and acting as a role model for strategic changes.

REVIEW TOPIC 3.2

Which personnel skills are most valued in your organisation, and why?
In what specific ways could you use the ones that Frank Sharp describes?

Frank Sharp from Ilford Mobberley has a clear view on the personnel role in strategy, which is to:

> *Diagnose and analyse* the blocks to the organisation achieving its business mission.
> *Interpret and prioritise* what human resource activities can be used to get over or around those blocks.
> *Develop a concept and vision* of what the organisation could look like with the blocks removed, and then sell this.
> *Lead change* through action, and doing what it's selling.

More specifically, he identifies ongoing skills to use working with managers in the achievement of the strategy as:

> *Remove barriers* – for example, payment systems that get in the way of a new approach, even though our first perspective may be that these things can't be changed.
> *Slay dragons/myths* – for example, talk to opinion leads and ask them what it would be like in an ideal organisation and what would get in the way of achieving it. Having elicited responses such as 'you'll never get the unions to agree to that' go out and demonstrate that it can be done.
> *Facilitate* – meetings and encourage managers to do that.
> *Coach* – managers as we work with them. Identify their inherent strengths and help to develop them.
> *Train* – managers in organisational development and give them a tool kit to use.
> *Recognise* – when they have done something significant.

Formal models of human resource strategy

We will now turn to review some of the formal models of human resource strategy from the academic literature before reviewing some examples of strategies in use. These models have appeared increasingly since 1984 and provide us with both analytical tools to understand how human resource strategy is developed, and some prescriptions of a recommended way to develop strategy. We will review some of the most influential models, but for a more detailed evaluation see Boxall (1992)

Fombrun, Tichy and Devanna's matching model

In their book *Strategic Human Resource Management* (1984) Fombrun *et al.*, based in Michigan USA, proposed the basic framework shown in Figures 3.3 and 3.4 below. Figure 3.3 represents the location of human resource management in relation to organisational strategy, and you should be able to note how Approach B is used. Figure 3.4 shows how activities within human resource management can be unified and designed in order to support the organisation's strategy. The strength of this model is that it provides a simple framework to show how selection, appraisal, development and reward can be mutually geared to produce the required type of employee performance. For example, if an organisation required co-operative team behaviour with mutual sharing of information and support the broad implications would be as follows.

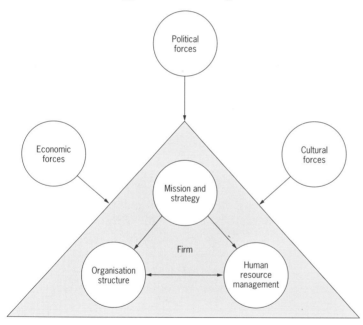

Figure 3.3   Strategic management and environmental pressures (Fombrun, Tlchy and Devanna 1984, p. 35) in *Strategic Human Resource Management*, © John Wiley and Sons Inc. 1984. Reprinted by permission of John Wiley and Sons, Inc.

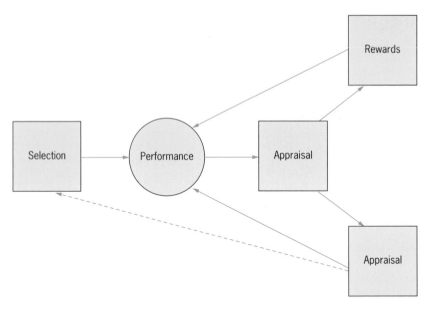

Figure 3.4   The human resource cycle (Fombrun, Tichy and Devanna 1984, p. 41) in *Strategic Human Resource Management,* © John Wiley and Sons Inc. 1984. Reprinted by permission of John Wiley and Sons, Inc.

- *Selection*:   successful experience of team work and sociable, co-operative personality; rather than an independent thinker who likes working alone.
- *Appraisal*:   based on contribution to the team, and support of others; rather than individual outstanding performance.
- *Reward*:   based on team performance and contribution; rather than individual performance and individual effort.

There is little doubt that this type of internal fit is valuable. However, question-marks have been raised over the model due to its simplistic response to organisation strategy. The question 'what if it is not possible to produce a human resource response that enables the required employee behaviour and performance?' is never addressed. So, for example, the distance between now and future performance requirements; the strengths, weaknesses and potential of the workforce; the motivation of the workforce; and employee relations issues are not considered.

This model has also been criticised because of its dependance on a rational strategy formulation rather than on an emergent strategy formation approach; and because of the nature of the one-way relationship with organisational strategy.

The Harvard model

This model produced by Beer *et al.*, also in 1984, is an analytical model rather than a prescriptive one and has been adopted more readily in the United Kingdom. The model, as shown in Figure 3.5, recognises the different stakeholder interests which impact on employee behaviour and performance, and also gives greater emphasis to

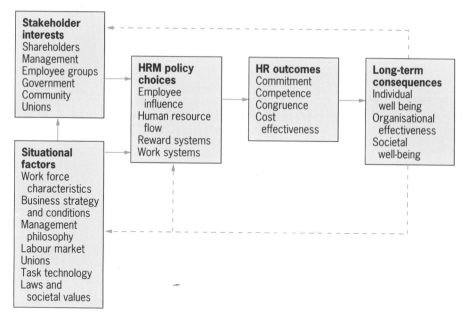

Figure 3.5   The Harvard framework for human resource management. Reprinted with permission of The Free Press, a Division of Simon and Schuster, from *Managing Human Assets* by Michael Beer, Bert Spector, Paul R. Lawrence, D. Quinn Mills, Richard E. Walton. Copyright © 1984 by The Free Press.

factors in the environment which will help to shape human resource strategic choices – identified in the 'Situation factors' box. Poole (1990) also notes that the model has potential for international or other comparative analysis, as it takes into account different sets of philosophies and assumptions which may be operating.

Although Beer *et al.*'s model is primarily analytical there are prescriptive elements leading to some potential confusion. These prescriptive elements are rather different from those in Fombrun *et al.*'s model, which prescribe matching fit with organisational strategy and a process for engaging what are identified as the key human resource activities. The prescription in Beer *et al.*'s model is found in the box 'HR outcomes', where specific outcomes are identified as desirable.

The Warwick model

This model, based on the Harvard model, emanates from the Centre for Strategy and Change at Warwick University. As you will see from Figure 3.6 from Hendry and Pettigrew (1990) the prescriptive elements of the Harvard model are absent and there is a greater emphasis on an analytical approach to human resource strategy. The model gives full recognition to the external context of human resource strategy; and also identifies a two-way rather than a one-way relationship with organisational strategy as explained in approaches C and E earlier in this chapter. There is also important recognition of the impact of the role of the personnel function on the human resource strategy content.

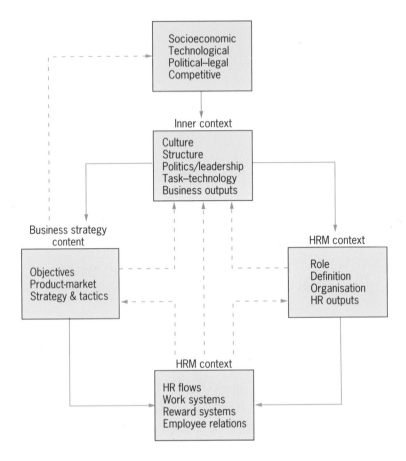

Figure 3.6 Model of strategic change and human resource management (Hendry and Pettigrew 1992, p. 139) in 'Patterns of strategic change in the development of Human Resource Management' in *British Journal of Management*, copyright © 1992 John Wiley and Sons Ltd. Reprinted by permission of John Wiley and Sons Ltd.

In a key statement Hendry and Pettigrew warn against 'treating the design of HRM systems in an overly rational way' and have noted the importance of learning to the formation of strategy. The authors of this model recognise Mintzberg's perspective of emergent strategy rather than a purely rational top-down planned approach.

Guest's model

Guest has adapted the Harvard model in a very different way. His model is a prescriptive one based on the four HR outcomes. He has developed these into four policy goals: strategic integration, commitment, flexibility and quality (1989b). These policy goals are related to HRM policies and expected organisational outcomes as shown in Figure 3.7. He describes the four policy goals as follows.

- *Strategic integration*: ensuring that HRM is fully integrated into strategic

2 A theory of HRM		
HRM policies	**Human resource outcomes**	**Organisational outcomes**
Organisation/ job design		**High** Job performance
Management of change	Strategic integration	**High** Problem-solving Change
Recruitment, selection/ socialisation	Commitment	Innovation
Appraisal, training, development	Flexibility/ adaptability	**High** Cost-effectiveness
Reward systems		
Communication	Quality	**Low** Turnover Absence Grievances
	Leadership/culture/strategy	

Figure 3.7 A theory of HRM (Guest 1989, p.49). Reprinted with permission of the author

planning, that HRM policies are coherent, that line managers use HRM practices as part of their everyday work.

- *Commitment*: ensuring that employees feel bound to the organisation and are committed to high performance via their behaviour.
- *Flexibility*: ensuring an adaptable organisation structure, and functional flexibility based on multiskilling.
- *Quality*: ensuring a high quality of goods and services through high quality, flexible employees.

Guest sees these goals as a package – all need to be achieved to create the desired organisational outcomes.

Clarity of goals gives a certain attractiveness to this model – but this is where the problems also lie. Whipp (1992) questions the extent to which such a shift is possible and Purcell (1991) sees the goals as unattainable. The goals are also an expression of human resource management, as opposed to personnel management, and as such bring us back to the debate about what human resource management really is and the inherent contradictions in the approach (see, for example, Legge 1991). Because of the prescriptive approach bringing with it a set of values, it suggests that there is only one best way and this is it. Although Guest (1987) has argued that there is no best practice, he also encourages the use of the above approach as the route to survival of UK businesses.

Human resource management strategic themes

The range of current human resource strategic themes includes flexibility; quality; customer orientation; empowerment; commitment; team working; leadership and continuous learning. Many of these themes are interlinked and typically each organisation will combine a range of themes appropriate to its needs. We will first look in some more detail at some of the themes and then see how one organisation has used them in practice.

Flexibility is commonly identified as an organisational goal, although Blyton and Morris (1992) argue that there is only limited evidence of it being used strategically as opposed to a short term fix. Flexibility can be defined in a wide variety of different ways; for example, Bramham (1989) identifies eight definitions. Blyton and Morris (1992) concentrate on four key types of flexibility:

- *task or functional flexibility*: where employees may be multiskilled and involved in a wide range of tasks, with fewer boundaries between jobs. This type of flexibility encourages team working practices, and in its ultimate form destroys the distinction between craft and operator jobs and tasks;
- *numerical flexibility*: where the labour supply is made flexible by the use of different types of employment contracts and sub-contracting. For example, Hankin (1990) found some core/periphery strategies;
- *temporal flexibility*: where the number and timing of hours worked can be varied to meet organisational needs, as for example in annual hours contracts;
- *wage flexibility*: where wages offered are individualised rather than standardised by the use, for example, of performance related pay or pay for skills offered rather than tasks allocated.

Although flexibility is high on the agenda, there are potential contradictions with other strategic themes. The use of functional flexibility which decreases the use of specialist skills and the use of sub-contractors to provide numerical flexibility may have undesirable consequences for the achievement of a quality strategy.

Quality is another key theme. The achievement of a quality service or a quality product demands a culture of quality where everyone in the organisation feels responsible for seeking out and solving problems in the production process, and where everyone desires and takes part in continuous improvement. In this way quality is built into the process rather than being checked at the end. To achieve this, responsibility needs to be delegated to the lowest possible level in the organisation, and full participation and involvement of all employees is expected. Individuals are 'empowered' by being given the resources and support to take on this responsibility. Team-based environments are usually operated when the team is given a target and it is up to them how they control themselves and achieve the task. One of the platforms of a quality culture is often the requirement to 'get it right first time'.

Very closely allied with quality is the notion of customer orientation. Quality is often defined in terms of the product being fit for the purpose intended, understanding customer needs and meeting customer expectations (see, for example, Dale and Cooper 1992). This brings with it an emphasis on getting to know the customer and their needs and responding appropriately. In human resource terms this requires a culture which always puts the customer first in everything that is done. This customer orientation does not only apply to external customers of the organisation but internal ones, too. In this way one department or team will be the 'customer' for the work that is produced by another department or team. For example, all line departments will be customers of the training courses and consultancy offered by the training department.

Also closely allied with the achievement of quality is a strategic emphasis on employee commitment. Given this commitment employees can be trusted to take responsibility and make the right decisions. This commitment removes the need for a high level of control. Commitment is seen to flow from involvement and empowerment and also from appropriate leadership. This increased emphasis on leadership underlines the value of vision and the ability to inspire employees rather than traditional management skills.

Continuous learning is a strategic theme which is increasingly apparent, and which we would argue is perhaps the most critical. A learning culture is based on the idea that it's OK to say 'I don't know the answer ... but I'm going to find out'; and where it's OK to get things wrong – as long as we learn something from that. We will look at continuous learning in the next section of this chapter, but it is worth noting at this point that there are some inherent contradictions between a quality strategy based on 'right first time' and a learning strategy based on 'it's OK to get it wrong'.

The following boxed example shows how one organisation has used and adapted some of the strategic themes we have just discussed.

Strategy, learning and change

Learning must be a key theme in human resource strategy. We argue this on two counts:

1. We have noted elsewhere that we live in turbulent times with constant change, and that much of the emphasis in strategy is on providing a coherent view on how to deal with changing demands in the environment. Garratt (1990) argues that for an organisation to survive, learning in the organisation has got to be greater or at least equal to the degree of change.

2. We accept Mintzberg's proposition of emergent strategy, as outlined in Chapter 2, and that strategy formation results from
    > ready–fire–aim–fire–aim–fire–aim
    rather than
    > ready–aim–fire

    We therefore need to act in order to think as well as to think in order to act. This being the case we learn from experimentation (both successful and unsuccessful), with successful experiments gradually converging and becoming the strategy. To benefit from our actions we need an organisation which is open to the potential for learning which is available.

High Performance Teams at Digital, Ayr

In an extremely competitive market the Ayr plant had to demonstrate that they could manufacture specified computer systems at a 'landed cost' competitive with other Digital plants, especially those in the Far East. To do this management had to rapidly introduce a package of changes. They had a strategic focus and a clear vision of the changes (both technical and organisational) required to promote success and they 'sold' this to the employees and corporate management. The high performance team concept they sold had two great advantages – inbuilt quality and flexibility. Supportive policies were put in place – such as a new skill-based pay system. Employment policies in terms of career planning, training and development and other reward policies were also designed to be consistent with and reinforce the initiative.

Management introduced unsupervised autonomous groups called 'high performance teams' with around a dozen members with full 'back to front' responsibility for product assembly, test, fault finding and problem solving, as well as some equipment maintenance. They used flextime without timeclocks and organised their own team discipline. Individuals were encouraged to develop a range of skills and help others in developing their capability. The ten key characteristics of the teams were as follows:

> self-managing, self-organising, self-regulating;
> front to back responsibility for core process;
> negotiated production targets;
> multiskilling – no job titles;
> share skills, knowledge, experience and problems;
> skills-based payment system;
> peer selection, peer review;
> open layout, open communications;
> support staff on the spot;
> commitment to high standards and performance.

Management had to learn to stand back and let the groups reach their own decisions – this approach eventually released considerable management time. A great deal of attention was given to how the transition was managed and this was seen as critical to the success of the approach. Time was taken to ensure maximum formal and informal communication and consultation, and there was a critical mass of key individuals prepared to devote themselves to ensure success. Employees were involved to the fullest extent so that they eventually felt they owned the concepts and techniques which they used. Training covered job skills, problem solving techniques and 'attitude training' in the concepts of high performance organisational design.

Adapted from Buchanan (1982) (used with permission of John Wiley and Sons Ltd) in 'High Performance: new boundaries of acceptability in worker control' in *Job Control and Worker Health*, ed Sauter, S.L., Hurrell Jnr, J.J. and Cooper, C.L. Copyright © 1982 John Wiley and Sons Ltd.

In order to form successful strategy in response to a changing environment it appears critical that the organisation becomes a learning organisation, which as defined by Garratt is:

An organisation which facilitates the learning of all its members and continuously transforms itself.

We have already noted some of the behavioural characteristics of this, which include the acceptability of making mistakes, as long as we learn from them; and being able to admit lack of knowledge or skill and ask for help when needed. Also included would be a free flow of accurate information, decisions being taken at the lowest possible level and continuous self-development for all. We look at the characteristics of learning organisations in much more detail in Chapter 17 on Organisational Performance.

☐ SUMMARY PROPOSITIONS

3.1 Human resource strategy is a central philosophy of the way that people in the organisation should be managed. It requires consistent and mutually reinforcing policies in all areas of personnel management.

3.2 It usually involves descriptions of required employee behaviour, and sometimes of the culture of the organisation.

3.3 In an ideal world the development of human resource strategy would be fully integrated with the development of organisational strategy; in reality this relationship is often of a different nature.

3.4 There are many different academic models of human resource strategy. Some are analytical, some are prescriptive and some combine elements of both.

3.5 Human resource strategy themes currently centre around quality, customer orientation, flexibility, commitment, involvement, leadership, team working and continuous learning.

3.6 We propose that the most critical human resource strategy centres around organisational learning.

References

Baird, L., Meshoulam, I. and De Give, G. (1983), 'Meshing human resources planning with strategic business planning: a model approach.' *Personnel*, Sept/Oct, vol. 60, Pt 5, pp.14–25.

Beer, M., Spector, B., Lawrence, P. R., Quinn Mills, D. and Walton, R. E. (1984), *Managing Human Assets*, New York: Free Press.

Blyton, P. and Morris, J. (1992), 'HRM and the limits of flexibility'. In P. Blyton and J. Turnbull (eds) *Reassessing Human Resources Management*, London: Sage.

Blyton, P. and Turnbull, P. (eds) (1992), *Reassessing Human Resource Management*, Sage.

Boxall, P. F. (1992), 'Strategic human resource management: beginnings of a new theoretical sophistication?', *Human Resource Management Journal*, vol. 2, no. 3.

Bramham, J. (1989), *Human Resource Planning*. London: Institute of Personnel Management

Buchanan, D.A. (1982), 'High performance: new boundaries of acceptability in worker control', *Job Control and Worker Health*, Sauter, S. L., Hurrell, J. J. Jnr. and Cooper, C., Chichester, John Wiley and Sons Ltd, pp. 255–73.

Buller, P.F. (1988), 'Successful partnerships: HR and strategic planning at eight top firms', *Organisational Dynamics*,

Butler, J. (1988/9), 'Human resource management as a driving force in business strategy', *Journal of General Management*, vol. 13, no. 4.

Dale, B. and Cooper, C. (1992), *Total Quality and Human Resources: An Executive Guide*, Blackwell.

Fombrun, C., Tichy, N.M. and Devanna, M. A. (1984), *Strategic Human Resource Management*, New York: Wiley.

Garratt, B. (1990), *Creating a Learning Organisation*, Cambridge: Director Books.

Guest, D. (1987), 'Human resource management and industrial relations', *Journal of Management Studies*, vol. 24, no. 5.

Guest, D. (1989a), 'Human resource management: its implications for industrial relations and Trade Unions'. In J. Storey (ed.) *New Perspectives on Human Resource Management*, London: Routledge.

Guest, D. (1989b), 'Personnel and HRM: can you tell the difference?' *Personnel Management*, January.

Hakim, C. (1990), 'Core and periphery in employers' workforce welfare strategies: evidence from the 1987 ELUS Survey.' *Work, Employment and Society*, vol. 4, no. 2, pp. 157–88.

Handy, L., Barnham, K., Panter, S. and Winhard, A., (1989), 'Beyond the personnel function – the strategic management of human resources', *Journal of European Industrial Training*, vol. 13, no. 1.

Hendry, C. and Pettigrew, A. (1986), 'The practice of strategic human resource management', *Personnel Review*, vol. 13, no. 3.

Hendry, C. and Pettigrew, A. (1990) 'Human resource management: an agenda for the 1990s', *International Journal of Human Resource Management*, vol. 1, no. 1.

Institute of Personnel Management (1992), *Issues in People Management, No. 4, The Emerging Role of the Personnel/HR Manager: A United Kingdom and Irish Perspective*. London: Institute of Personnel Management.

Kochan, T.A. and Barocci, T. A. (1985), *Human Resource Management and Industrial Relations: Text, Readings and Cases*, Boston: Little Brown.

Legge, K. (1991), 'Human resource management: a critical analysis'. In J. Storey (ed.) *New Perspectives on Human Resource Management*, London: Routledge.

Mintzberg, H. (1994), 'The fall and rise of strategic planning', *Harvard Business Review*, February.

Poole, M. (1990), 'Editorial: HRM in an international perspective', *International Journal of Human Resource Management*, vol. 1, no. 1.

Porter, M. (1985), *Competitive Advantage*, New York: Free Press.

Purcell, J. (1991), 'The impact of corporate strategy on human resource management'. In J. Storey (ed) (1989), *New Perspectives on Human Resource Management*, London: Routledge.

Purcell, J. (1994), 'Personnel earns a place on the Board', *Personnel Management*, February.

Salaman, G. *et al.* (ed.) (1992), *Human Resource Strategies*, Sage.

Schuler, R.S. and Jackson, S.E. (1987), 'Linking competitive strategies with human resource management practices', *Academy of Management Executive*, vol. 1, no. 3, August.

Storey, J. (ed.) (1989), *New Perspectives on Human Resource Management*, London: Routledge.

Whipp, R. (1992), 'Human resource management, competition and strategy; some productive tensions.' In P. Blyton and P. Turnbull (eds) *Reassessing Human Resource Management*, London: Sage.

PART II

Organisation

4 Strategic aspects of organisation

Personnel managers have always been involved in the organisation of the business in their operational role. This is why there was the development phase, described in Chapter 1, of the humane bureaucrat, as businesses grew bigger and became more specialised. The interest in organisation development provided a further twist to the tale. In this section of the book we examine several aspects of personnel activities that are linked into both organisation as entity and organisation as process. Structure and culture are largely concerned with the entity; planning, information, communication and presentation are all to do with organisation as a process.

Strategic aspects of organisation are grounded in the simple proposition of Alfred Chandler (1962) that 'structure follows strategy'. Whatever strategy for growth a business pursued, the structure of the business followed and reflected the demands of that strategy. He was, of course, writing at a time when the idea of growth was universally accepted as an automatic objective for any business, but his analysis remains a central feature of understanding business organisations.

Chandler's three stages of business development

After examining the growth of seventy large American businesses, Chandler concluded that they all pass through three stages of development: unit, functional and multidivisional.

Any business begins by being on a single location, with a single product and a single decision maker. It may be Rolls and Royce or Hewlett and Packard rather than Eddie Land or Clive Sinclair, but it is still a single decision-making function with two or three people working very closely together and doing almost everything. The first stage of development into the *unit firm* involves the process of vertical integration, with specialist functions being set up and other people employed as turnover increases, the beginning of hierarchy and attempts to achieve some economies of scale. One further feature of this is to expand forwards or backwards in the operating chain, by acquiring another business, such as a supplier, or raw materials or a retail outlet.

Evolving into a *functional organisation* introduces specialisation as departments are established to deal with different functions such as marketing, personnel and finance. If the business expands still further and diversifies into different industries and products, there is then the final stage of turning into a *multidivisional form*. Chandler observed that the process of transition was usually delayed and often very dissatisfying to the original entrepreneur. His explanation for this was that the entrepreneur/founder was typically brilliant at strategy (otherwise there would not be a continuing business) but rarely interested in, or skilful at, structuring a business, especially as the structuring process put power and decision into other hands.

Chandler's thesis has been examined by a number of researchers in the period since it was first propounded. Three slight modifications are worth mentioning here, particularly in relation to the evolution of the multidivisional form. First Rumelt (1982) showed that the likelihood of a firm having a multidivisional structure was increased as it diversified. Miles and Snow (1984) carried out extensive studies to examine what they called strategic fit: the match between strategy, structure and internal management processes. They demonstrated that businesses need organisation structures and management processes that are appropriate to their strategy, or there is a likelihood that their strategy will fail. Both of these may seem like unsurprising, even obvious, conclusions: their value is to confirm the enduring potency of Chandler's ideas. A more significant modification comes from Peters and Waterman (1980), who suggested that businesses could make temporary structural changes to cope with the more rapidly changing contemporary environment without abandoning its overall structure.

Having a structure that matches the strategy is thus crucial to the success of strategy, and structure (organisation as entity) interrelates closely with the management process (organisation as process).

One of the most remarkable entrepreneurs and technological innovators of the 1970s was Clive Sinclair. The dramatic success of the first pocket calculator was quickly followed by the digital watch and the first home computers, ZX81 and Spectrum. An admiring Prime Minister gave him a knighthood and it seemed that he could do no wrong, but there was no appropriate structure to sustain the strategy. There was a shortage of management skills, especially in marketing and distribution, so there was a retreat. Sir Clive re-established his company to undertake only research and invention. Everything else was sub-contracted, while the handful of people who made up Sinclair Research concentrated on the next technological breakthrough: the electric car. Technically ingenious, the product was a flop. There had been no authoritative marketing guidance to demonstrate that the product would never sell. The strategy could not succeed without the appropriate structure and management processes.

Centralisation and decentralisation

One of the popular ideas of the 1980s was the strategic business unit, which was a method of empowerment, except that it was not an individual manager being empowered but a complete operating unit of the business. The management of a particular unit was given an agreed budget and an agreed set of targets for the forthcoming period. Therafter they had freedom to manage themselves in whatever way they thought fit, provided that they first of all submitted regular reports and secondly that they met the targets and complied with the budget expectations.

This was a form of decentralisation, and many managers in strategic business units made the wry comment that the one thing that was not decentralised was the strategy! What is to be decentralised and what is to remain central or drawn into the centre? Hendry (1990, p. 93) makes the interesting observation that in the process of a business decentralising its operations, personnel often remains one of the last centralising forces. He attributes this to the belief of personnel people and chief executives about issues such as equity, order, consistency and control. The personnel function will relinquish these reluctantly as they see great risks in, for instance, methods of payment being set up on different principles in separate parts of the business. What about coercive comparisons? What about equal value claims if we do not monitor closely from the centre?

The focus of this concern is changing. Control of collective bargaining and pay structures – the traditional strongholds of the personnel director – are being gradually abandoned and decentralised in favour of new power bases such as group contracts, succession planning, management development and graduate recruitment (Hendry 1990, p. 99).

There is, however, a different dimension to the centralisation/decentralisation question. In writing about international companies the American Kobrin (1988) has demonstrated that managers have to centralise and decentralise at the same time. It does not need the international dimension to make this comment valid. Each component part of the business has to have its strengths and knowledge developed and exploited to the full if it is to be effective, and this requires a greater degree of empowerment than most advocates of budget-driven strategic business units acknowledge. At the same time the individual operating unit has to maximise its contribution to group objectives, and that will inevitably lead to occasional profound conflict between unit and group objectives. The strategic role for the personnel people here is not simply to cope with the conflict when it breaks out, but somehow to develop a culture that succeeds in delivering the apparently irreconcilable requirements: enough autonomy for people really to deploy their skills, enthusiasm and commitment, but enough control for group-wide considerations ultimately to prevail, when they have been tested in the furnace of unit aggressive interrogation. The last part is vital.

Personnel people increasingly have as a part of their role those aspects of co-ordination that go beyond budgetary and planning controls. There are two particular suggestions.

Henry was the Managing Director of a growing business with six operating subsidiaries. Fiona was the Financial Director, who had just joined from a rather larger company. One of the six operating subsidiaries was in difficulties and it appeared to Henry, Fiona and their Board colleagues that it would need to be closed. Fiona said she would work out the numbers over the weekend.

On Monday Fiona showed her proposals, including the cost of severance for all employed at the subsidiary, to Henry and Barry, the General Manager. She sighed and said she supposed he would like her to go down and get it done with. Henry asked if she had consulted with the Personnel Director, George. She had not, so George was asked in and a different strategy was agreed: Barry would be called up to Head Office. Barry came, clearly having a shrewd idea of what was afoot. Henry explained the situation and said there really seemed no alternative but to close the plant, but Barry was not to worry; he would be looked after. Barry replied that the plant would only close over his dead body and that they did not know what they were talking about. Fiona produced her analysis and was closely questioned by Barry and strongly challenged on certain of her assumptions. After three hours of vigorous argument Henry called a halt by asking Barry to come back within a week with counter proposals. He still felt that Fiona's analysis was correct and that the plant should close, but if he could produce watertight, convincing alternatives they would be listened to. Fiona complained that her professional judgement was being doubted, but George shepherded Barry out of the room.

Five days later Barry was back with a plan that he had discussed with the General Managers of two other subsidiaries and which they said they could make work by slight variations in the way they worked together. The plan involved a drastic reduction in the workforce, but Barry's plant would remain open, targets would be met and they would be back within budget in six months' time. Now it was the turn of Henry and Fiona to closely question Barry, but eventually they agreed that his proposal was a better strategy for the group as a whole.

The first is *evangelisation*, the process of winning the acceptance throughout the business of a common mission and a shared purpose. This idea of needing to win hearts and minds has been a common thread in management thinking for most of this century, and a specialised example is provided later in this chapter from the work of Hopfl (1993). It takes on particular significance in the decentralised business and it is indeed a remarkable management team who will be able to commit themselves with enthusiasm to closing down their local operation on the grounds that the business as a whole will benefit if an operation elsewhere is developed instead.

Co-ordination through evangelisation works through *shared beliefs*. The beliefs may be interpreted in different ways and may produce varied behaviours, but there is the attempt to promulgate relatively simple doctrines to which members of the organisation subscribe and through which they are energised. Some readers of this book will have learned their catechism as children, or will have studied the thirty-nine articles defining the doctrinal position of the Church of England. Although this may seem inappropriate to the business world, in the 1970s a British company, Vitafoam, was established by a man who required his senior executives to copy out his annual policy statement by hand, three times, before handing it back to him. It is now commonplace for companies to have mission statements, which come close to being unifying articles of faith.

> At the top is the mission statement, a broad goal based on the organization's planning premises, basic assumptions about the organization's purpose, its values, its distinctive competencies, and its place in the world. A mission statement is a relatively permanent part of an organization's identity and can do much to unify and motivate its members. (Stoner & Freeman, 1992, p. 188)

Evangelisation also works through *parables*. Schein (1985, p. 239) identified 'stories and legends' as one of the key mechanisms for articulating and reinforcing the organisation's culture.

The company house magazine helps in circulating the good news about heroic deeds in all parts of the company network. Better are the word of mouth exchanges and accounts of personal experience. Evangelisation can use *apostles*, ambassadors sent out to preach the faith. These are the people – usually in senior positions – who move around the company a great deal. They know the business well and can describe one component to another, explaining company policy, justifying particular decisions and countering parochial thinking. They can also move ideas around ('In Seoul they are wondering about ... what do you think?') and help in the development of individual networks ('Try getting in touch with Oscar Jennings in Pittsburgh ... he had similar problems a few weeks ago.') At times of crisis, apostles are likely to be especially busy, countering rumour and strengthening resolve. It may be important that most of the apostles come from headquarters and have personally met, and can tell stories about, the founder. Anita Roddick's Body Shop is an organisation that grew rapidly on the basis of working in a way that was markedly different from the conventions of the cosmetics industry that it was challenging. Its growth seemed to need people in all parts to identify closely with the vision and personality of the founder:

> The inductresses' eyes seem to light up whenever Anita's name is mentioned. We are told, in semi-joyous terms, the great tale concerning that first humble little shop in Brighton. And ... one of our inductresses uses the phrase, 'And Anita saw what she had done, and it was good'. (Keily 1991, p. 3)

Co-ordination can be improved by the development and promulgation of *standards and norms*. Many companies have sought the accreditation of BS 5750, the British Standard for quality, others claim to be equal opportunity employers. Thinking companies will wish to set standards for many aspects of their operation, especially in personnel matters. The Human Resources Section at Shell centre are charged with developing and maintaining standards relating to alcohol and drug abuse. If standards are adopted throughout a company they become a form of co-ordination. Furthermore, it is not necessary for all of them to be developed at the centre. Decentralised standards formulation can enable different parts of the business to take a lead as a preliminary to universal adoption of the standards they have formulated: an excellent method of integration.

Planning

Just as the concept of strategy has somewhat overwhelmed the use of policy as a management instrument, it has also shaded out the use of planning. Planning had its heyday in management thinking during the 1960s, when the clever ideas of operations research were seen as a means whereby future activities could be forecast with confidence so that plans could then be made deliver that future, 'the past is history ... the future is planning'. The attraction of planning was that you could make the future happen instead of waiting for it happen to you. To be a reactive manager was almost as bad as having a communicable disease.

The trouble was that the future rarely turned out as expected; some completely unforeseen event scuppered the plans. The great example was the use of Programme Evaluation Review Technique (PERT), in planning the development and production of the Polaris missile system. Sapolsky (1972, p. 246) studied its application and decided that as a planning technique it was as effective as rain dancing, and that its obvious success was due not to its technical efficiency but to the mystique of infallibility that its managers were able to promote.

As enthusiasm for change took over from a commitment to planning among managers, there was a tendency to think that all action needed to be spontaneous. Particularly in Britain, the predilection for short-term thinking received an unfortunate boost, with the concomitant difficulties of a reluctance to invest and an unwillingness to make provision – through training, for instance – to a future that might not happen. Peters appeared to dismiss planning altogether, producing less than two pages devoted to the topic in a 560-page tome:

> The long-range strategic plan, of voluminous length, is less useful than before. But a strategic 'mind-set', which focuses on skill/capability building (e.g. adding value to the work force via training to prepare it to respond more flexibly and be more quality-conscious) is more important than ever. (Peters 1989, p. 394)

There we have another clue to the future orientation of personnel management, as we think of organisation as process rather than entity. Peters sees little scope for the strategic plan of the type beloved by the marketing specialists and the MBA graduate, but calls instead for some forward-looking, creative personnel work. This echoes the Japanese concern with the longer term. Holden (1994, p. 125) gives the example of a Japanese computer company with a development plan for all employees that takes 42 years to complete! As will be seen in the next few chapters, personnel work requires an approach to planning that is rather more flexible and imaginative – soft as well as hard – than that of the manpower planning textbooks of the 1970s.

Information and communication

Information is a prerequisite for all decision making, and the handling of information is crucial to all personnel work: aggregated data on numbers, ages, skills, hours, rates of pay and so on, and information relating to individuals.

Communication is a varied process whereby information of the above, specific type is merged with other types of data, understanding, feeling and image to create the process whereby the organisation functions. This requires care with organisational structure, for what is an organisation chart except a statement about responsibilities, status, channels of communication and job titles? It requires an appreciation of organisational culture, an effective set of systems, procedures and drills and it requires personal competence in members of the organisation, especially managers.

One of the main strategic aspects of communication is communicating across national and cultural boundaries, where feedback is especially important both to monitor what is happening and to develop understanding between the operations. Those in country A will inevitably have limited understanding about the situation of those in country B, to say nothing of the cultural and linguistic uncertainties that feedback can help to clarify.

Recently, business expansion has been frequently by acquisition rather than simple growth of what Chandler described as the unit firm. This produces a particularly intense communications problem. Employees in the acquired company will feel a greater sense of community with each other than with those who have acquired them. They will see corporate affairs from their own standpoint and will tend to be cautious in their behaviour and suspicious in their interpretation of what they hear from their new owners. Personnel people can have a crucial part to play in managing the requisite communications and information flow.

When the expansion is by acquisition of businesses in a different country, with a different set of cultural norms, the problems are intensified. Even when initial suspicion begins to unwind, there are still difficulties; for example in terms of rivalry, distorted perceptions and resource allocation.

Rivalry

Whatever is done to develop a shared sense of purpose and a common identity, companies in different countries tend to take pride in their own accomplishments and to disparage the accomplishments of other nationality groups. As long as this stimulates healthy competition rivalry can benefit the company, but it quickly becomes destructive, as in the situation of the car assembly plant in Britain which constantly rejected and returned gearboxes made by a plant of the same company in a different country.

Distorted perceptions

National boundaries produce distorted ideas about the 'other' people, whose achievements are underestimated and undervalued in comparison with the achievements of your own group, which may be overestimated.

Rover Group was the largest car manufacturer in Britain and the last of the major manufacturers that could claim to be British. In view of the tradition of car manufacture this was a point of symbolic significance. When the company developed a technical collaboration with the Japanese Honda company there was considerable discussion and uncertainty, but the collaboration proved fruitful. At the beginning of 1994 a controlling interest in Rover Group was sold to the German company BMW. This produced a very strong reaction and anxiety that the future of the British operation would be blighted. The Honda association was also regarded as being vitiated by this move. Despite many assurances, the management had to engage in unrelenting communication and consultation for months in order to reassure company employees and to avoid uncertainties in the product and financial markets.

Resource allocation

Allocation of resources between competing interests is always problematical, but becomes even more difficult in international comparisons. A company in a vulnerable situation may go as far as to provide disinformation about a rival in order to win additional resources.

Brandt and Hulbert (1976) studied organisational feedback in a number of multinational companies that had their headquarters in Europe, Japan and the United States. They found that the American organisations had many more feedback reports and meetings between headquarters and subsidiaries than their European or Japanese counterparts. In contrast, Pascale (1978) found that Japanese managers in Japan used face-to-face contacts more than American managers as well as more upwards and lateral communication. Japanese managers in America used communication in the same way as Americans.

One of the few values of management jargon is that the jargon quickly becomes universally understood by the experts, no matter what their nationality. JIT (Just in Time), QWL (Quality of Working Life), TQM (Total Quality Management) are understood by managers everywhere, although NVQ (National Vocational Qualification) and IIP (Investors in People) are understood only by a more select audience.

Disseminating information and other messages within the organisation helps to develop corporate culture, a sense of collaboration across national boundaries in order to integrate the business. Members of different units in the business have to understand why a company has been acquired in Korea or Chile, even though it seems to threaten the livelihood of some parts of the parent organisation. Comprehensive communication can raise awareness of the wider market and the opportunities that are waiting to be grasped. Foulds and Mallet (1989, p. 78) suggest the following as purposes of international communication, most of which are just as relevant if one is operating within a single national boundary:

> to reinforce group culture so as to improve the speed and effectiveness of decision taking;

to encourage information exchange in internationally related activities and prevent the 'reinvention of the wheel';

to form the background to the succession planning activity – certain cultures demand certain types of people;

to establish in peoples' minds what is expected of them by the parent company;

to facilitate change in a way acceptable to the parent company;

to undermine the 'not invented here' attitudes and thereby encourage changes;

to improve the attractiveness of the company in the recruitment field – particularly where the subsidiary is small and far from base; and

to encourage small activities, which may be tomorrow's 'cream', and give such activities a perspective within the international activities.

> The problem of communicating across linguistic boundaries is illustrated by this official translation from a government announcement in Prague:
>
> Because Christmas Eve falls on a Thursday, the day has been designated a Saturday for work purposes. Factories will close all day, with stores open a half day only. Friday, December 25 has been designated a Sunday, with both factories and stores open all day. Monday, December 28, will be a Wednesday for work purposes. Wednesday, December 30, will be a business Friday. Saturday, January 2, will be a Sunday, and Sunday, January 3, will be a Monday.

The organisation must operate holistically. It is not the sum of its parts: the whole exists in every part, like the human body. If you are ill a sample of your blood or the taking of your temperature is just as good an indicator to a doctor wherever it comes from. Customers have a holistic view of the organisation because they are interested in what it delivers as a product or service, not in whether the design section is more efficient than the warehouse. Managers cannot work effectively in their part of the business without understanding its simultaneous relationship to the whole. Businesses function holistically and holism is a function of constant, efficient communication, like the bloodstream and the central nervous system.

A major development in information and communication has, of course, been the arrival of personnel management information systems, discussed in Chapters 7 and 8. These enable information to be stored, located, summarised and analysed instantaneously, although one of the leading European experts on the subject feels that progress has been painfully slow:

> ... the development of imaginative CPISs is pathetically slow. Today's CPISs still look very much like those of 10 to 15 years ago. (They) may use a mouse to point arrows at icons, store endless amounts of data, be in technicolour and they may be networked, but the differences in value they offer ... do not represent 15 years of development. (Richards-Carpenter 1994, p. 63)

A strategic issue for personnel specialists is to consider how the potential of this facility can be realised more effectively.

A quite different aspect of communication for the personnel specialist is the need for propaganda or public relations. Delegation of responsibility for aspects of personnel management by empowering the line manager is a theme to which there is frequent reference in this book. This empowerment goes both ways, as managers from other backgrounds bring their perspective more intrusively into what personnel specialists have enjoyed regarding as their own preserve. The public relations approach is a clear example, with many businesses running communications with employees along similar lines to communications with customers. Often privately derided as 'hard-sell gimmicks' these methods are not always popular in the personnel community. Perhaps the best-known of these activities was a series of commitment-raising projects in British Airways. Hopfl (1993) describes the opening of a three day workshop 'Visioning the Future':

> This event requires a level of stage management that would not be unfamiliar to a touring rock band ... One of the trainers stands at the door to ensure that no-one gets in early to 'spoil' the experience. Nine o'clock. The doors to the conference room are opened ... the opening music from 'Also Sprach Zarathustra'...blasts out a triumphal welcome ... The lights dim and the corporate logo appears before them. Three days of management development have begun. (Hopfl 1993, p. 120)

Although this is alien to many personnel people they soon realise that people are so used to slick presentation in all departments of their lives that presentation of information at work needs to use contemporary techniques if it is to have impact.

☐ SUMMARY PROPOSITIONS

4.1 Organisational strategy is inextricably linked with the structure of the business: one can not be changed without changing, or requiring change, in the other.

4.2 One common strategic initiative is to decentralise, using the strategic business unit as the locus of business activity. This requires specific measures to co-ordinate the decentralised fragments.

4.3 The current concern with change has reduced the emphasis on planning that was popular in the 1960s and 1970s.

4.4 Decentralisation has to be accompanied by intensive communication to ensure that the business continues to operate holistically.

References

Brandt, W. K. and Hulbert, J. M. (1976), 'Patterns of communication in the multinational company', *Journal of International Business Studies*, Spring, pp. 57–64.

Chandler, A. D. (1962), *Strategy and Structure*, Cambridge, Mass: MIT Press.

Foulds, J. and Mallet, L. (1989), 'The European and international dimension'. In T. Wilkinson (ed.) *The Communications Challenge*, London: Institute of Personnel Management.

Hendry, C. (1990), 'Corporate management of human resources under conditions of decentralisation', *British Journal of Management*, vol. 1, no. 2, pp. 91–103.

Holden, N. J. (1994), 'International HRM with vision'. In D. P. Torrington, *International Human Resource Management*, Hemel Hempstead: Prentice Hall.

Hopfl, H. (1993), 'Culture and commitment: British Airways'. In D. Gowler, K. Legge and C. Clegg (eds) *Case Studies in Organizational Behaviour*, 2nd edition, London: Paul Chapman.

Keily, D. (1991), 'Body shop blues', *The Sunday Times*, 8 December, p. 3.

Kobrin, S. J. (1988), 'Expatriate reduction and strategic control in American multi-national corporations', *Human Resource Management*, vol. 27, no. 1, pp. 63–75.

Miles, R. E. and Snow, C. E. (1984), 'Fit, failure and the hall of fame', *California Management Review*, vol. 26, no. 3, pp. 10–28.

Pascale, R. T. (1978), 'Communication and decision making across cultures: Japanese and American comparisons', *Administrative Science Quarterly*, March, pp. 91–110.

Peters, T. J. (1989), *Thriving on Chaos*, London: Pan Books.

Richards-Carpenter, C. (1994), 'Why the CPIS is a disappointment', *Personnel Management*, vol. 26, no. 5, pp. 63–4.

Rumelt, R. P. (1982), 'Diversification strategy and profitability', *Strategic Management Journal*, vol. 3, pp. 359–69.

Sapolsky, H. (1972), *The Polaris System Development*, Cambridge, Mass: Harvard University Press.

Schein, E. H. (1985), *Organizational Culture and Leadership*. San Francisco: Jossey-Bass.

Stoner, J. A. F. and Freeman, R. E. (1992), *Management*, 5th edition. Englewood Cliffs, NJ: Prentice Hall.

5 Planning: jobs and people

In 1994 Henry Mintzberg asserted that 'the most successful strategies are visions, not plans'. The usefulness of the human resource planning process has always been questioned on the basis of feasibility and implementation problems. In this chapter we will show that human resource planning is a valuable process which, as Walker (1992a) maintains, is necessary to support strategy.

The role of planning

Mintzberg identifies the role of planning in terms of programming the strategic vision, and also in terms of providing information which stimulates the visioning process. It is helpful to look at human resource planning in the same way, which is demonstrated in the simple model shown in Figure 5.1. In more detail, Mintzberg identifies:

- *Planning as strategic programming:* planning can not generate strategies, but it can make them operational by clarifying them; working out the consequences of them; and identifying what must be done to achieve each strategy.

- *Planning as tools to communicate and control:* planning can ensure co-ordination and encourage everyone to pull in the same direction;
    planners can assist in finding successful experimental strategies which may be operating in just a small part of the organisation.

STRATEGIC PLANNING	STRATEGIC VISIONING	STRATEGIC PLANNING
Providing HR data, ideas Asking difficult questions	Defining a vision of the future (organisational and HR)	Programme the vision – HR objectives targets action plans

Figure 5.1 Human resource strategic visioning and strategic planning

- *Planners as analysts:* planners need to analyse hard data – both external and internal – which managers can then make use of in the strategy development process.

- *Planners as catalysts:* raising difficult questions and challenging the conventional wisdom which may stimulate managers into thinking in more creative ways.

Planners, therefore, whether organisational planners or human resource planners, have an essential contribution to make to the strategic visioning carried out by senior managers.

Feasibility and use of human resource planning

Concerns raised about the feasibility of human resource plans focus on the nature of the human resource, the nature of the planning in an uncertain environment and the difficulty of implementing plans.

Hussey (1982) in a book about corporate planning argues that the human resource is far more complex to plan for than the financial resource. He comments on the critical differences between people, the difficulty of moving them around, the costs of overstaffing, and on the importance of treating people as people and not an inanimate resource. In addition individuals have their personal set of values and motivations, and these need to be accounted for in the potential achievement of identified plans.

The balance between visioning and planning will be different depending on the environment. In a highly uncertain environment the emphasis needs to be more on the visioning process. Where things are slightly less chaotic planning has a greater contribution to make. Even so, plans need to be viewed as flexible and reviewed regularly, rather than seeing them as an end point in the process. Planning should not be seen as an isolated event, but rather something that has to be continuously monitored, refined and updated. Bell (1989) argues that while there may be an annual cycle of planning, this should represent a review activity that continues throughout the year; and that each cycle should feed into the next. In spite of the difficulties with planning, Manzini (1984) comments that 'a plan, imperfect though it may be, will generally get us closer to the target than if we had not planned'.

Implementation issues are tied up with the weight that line managers attach to human resource plans. They are more likely to be supportive if they have been involved in the human resource planning process, and if the analyses used are simple rather than complex. Walker (1992b) comments that human resource plans are becoming more flexible and shorter-term, with a clearer focus on human resource issues, simpler data analysis and an emphasis on action planning and implementation. All these suggest that the output of the planning process needs to be user-friendly, and owned by line management rather than the personnel function (see for example Greer, Jackson and Fiorito 1989). Ulrich (1989) points to the need for human resource plans to be seen as the means to an end (achieving the vision), rather than an end in themselves.

> Tony, the Personnel Manager shouted at Ian the Chief Executive: 'What do you mean, it wasn't agreed!'
> 'I mean its the first I've heard that you need £22k for a new apprentice scheme.'
> 'Well, it was in the plan.'
> 'What plan?'
> 'The manpower plan, what other f******g plan would I mean!'
> 'You didn't ask me for the money.'
> 'I asked you in the plan, and you didn't come back and say we couldn't have it.'
> 'I didn't come back and say you could – now let's start at the beginning – tell me why we need to spend it and what will happen if we don't.'
>
> The conversation continued and finally Tony and Ian began to talk about the real issues. Ian never told Tony that he had filed the manpower plan unread, but he did tell him that he wanted next year's plan to be five pages of interpretation and recommendations and not eighty-five pages of figures.

A model of human resource planning

Increasingly there is a need for organisations to integrate the process of planning for numbers and skills of employees; employee behaviour and organisational culture; organisation design and the makeup of individual jobs; and formal and informal systems. These aspects are all critical in terms of programming and achieving the vision. Each of these aspects interrelates with the others. However in the area of human resource planning reality has always been recognised as a long way from identified best practice (see, for example, Ulrich 1989).

Undoubtedly different organisations will place different emphases on each of these factors, and may well plan each separately or plan some and not others. The model we will use for the remainder of this chapter attempts to bring all aspects together, incorporating the more traditional model of 'manpower planning'. Our model identifies 'where we want to be' translated from response to the strategic vision; 'where we are now'; and 'what we need to do to make the transition' – all operating within the organisation's environment. The model is shown in diagramatic form in Figure 5.2.

We will now look in more depth at each of these four areas. It is important to remember that although the steps may logically follow on in the way that they are presented, in reality they may be carried out in parallel and/or in an informal fashion, and each area may well be revisited a number of times.

Analysing the environment

In this chapter we refer to the environment broadly as the context of the organisation, and this is clearly critical in the impact that it has on both organisational and

Figure 5.2   Integrated human resource planning model

human resource strategy. Much strategy is based on a response to the environment – for example, what our customers now want or what competitors are now offering – or a proactive éffort to guess what customers will want or to persuade them what they will need. In human resource terms we need to identify, for example, how difficult or easy it will be to find employees with scarce skills and what these employees will expect of an employer so that we can attract them. (See Appendix, note 1.) We will be concerned with legislation which will limit or widen the conditions of employment that we offer, with what competitors are offering, and what training schemes are available locally or nationally.

Data on relevant trends can be collected from current literature, company annual reports, conferences/courses and from contacts and networking. Table 5.1 gives examples of the many possible sources against each major area. Having acquired and constantly updated data on the environment, one of the most common ways of analysing this is to produce a map of the environment, represented as a wheel. The map represents a time in the future, for instance three years away. In the centre of the wheel can be written the core purpose of the organisation as it relates to people, or potential future strategies or goals. Each spoke of the wheel can then be filled in to represent a factor of the external environment, for example potential employees, a specific local competitor, competitors generally, regulatory bodies, customers, government. From all the spokes the six or seven elements regarded as most important need to be selected.

These can then be worked further by asking what demands each will make of the organisation, and how the organisation will need to respond in order to achieve its goals. From these responses can be derived the implications for human resource activities. For example, the demands of potential employees may be predicted as:

Table 5.1 *Sources of information on environment trends*

Trend area	Possible sources
Social	Census information IPM journals News media *Social Trends* *General Household Survey* *Employment Gazette* Local papers
Demographics	*Labour Market Quarterly* Census information *Employment Gazette* Local Council, TEC
Political and legislative	News media Proceedings of European Parliament Proceedings of British Parliament *Hansard* *Industrial Relations Review and Report* *Industrial Law Journal* IDS Brief
Industrial and technological	*Employment Digest* Journals specifically for the industry *Financial Times* Employers' association Trade association
Competitors	Annual reports Talk to them!

- We need a career not just a job.
- We need flexibility to help with childrearing.
- We want to be treated as people and not machines.
- We need a picture of what the organisation has in store for us.
- We want to be better trained.

And so on.

Managers then consider what the organisation would need to offer to meet these needs in order to meet a declared organisational goal or strategy. It is a good way of identifying human resource issues which need to be addressed. The analysis can also be fed back into identifying and clarifying the future vision or goals in human resource terms. Figure 5.3 gives an outline for the whole process; for a worked example see Appendix, note 2.

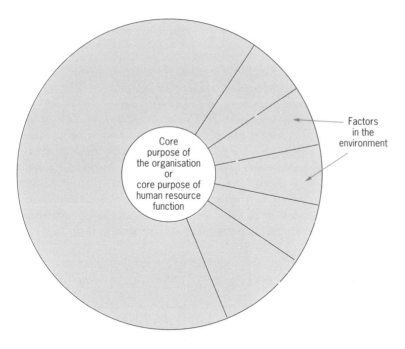

Individual factor in the environment	
Demands from the factor	Demands from the organisation

Figure 5.3 Mapping the environment

REVIEW TOPIC 5.1

Draw a map of the external environment for your organisation for three to five years hence. Individually or as a group, brainstorm all the spokes in the wheel and select the six most important ones. Draw up a demands and responses list for each. Write on a single side of A4 paper a summary of what you think your organisation's priorities should be in the people area over the next three to five years.

Defining the future in human resource terms

Organisation, behaviour and culture

There is little specific literature on the methods used to translate the strategic objectives of the organisation and environmental influences into qualitative or soft human resource goals. In general terms, they can be summed up as the use of managerial judgement. If the activity is seen as vital to the organisation, then senior managers will be involved in the processes and it will be more likely to be identified as part of the strategic visioning rather than a planning activity. Brainstorming, combined with the use of structured checklists or matrices, can encourage a more thorough analysis. Organisational change literature and corporate planning literature are helpful as a source of ideas in this area. Three simple techniques are a human resource implications checklist (see Figure 5.4), a strategic brainstorming exercise (Figure 5.5) and a behavioural expectation chart (Appendix, note 3).

Corporate goal	Human resource implications in respect of:	Methods of achieving this
	New tasks? For whom? What competencies needed? Relative importance of team/individual behaviour? Deleted tasks? How will managers need to manage?	

Figure 5.4   The beginnings of a human resource implications checklist

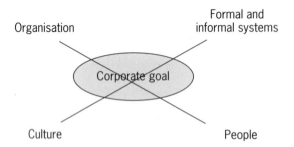

Managers write a corporate goal in the centre and brainstorm changes that need to take place in each of the four areas, one area at a time

Figure 5.5   Strategic brainstorming exercise

Employee numbers and skills (demand forecasting)

There is far more literature in the more traditional area of forecasting employee number demand based on the organisation's strategic objectives. Both objective and subjective approaches can be employed.

Objective methods I: statistical methods

Some statistical methods depend on the assumption that the future situation will display some continuity from the past. Past trends are projected into the future to simulate or 'model' what would happen if they continued – for example, historical trends of employee numbers could be projected into the future. These methods are rarely used in the present climate as they are inappropriate in a context of rapid and often discontinuous change.

Other statistical models relate employee number demand to more specific organisational and environmental circumstances. These models are used to calculate people demand as a result of, usually, organisational activities. Models can take account of determining factors such as production, sales, passenger miles and level of service. These factors can be used separately or in combination with other determining factors. A simple model might relate people demand to production, using a constant relationship, without making any assumptions about economies of scale. In this model if output is to be doubled, then employees would also need to be doubled. (See Appendix, note 4.)

More complicated equations can be formulated which describe the way that a combination of independent factors have affected the dependent employee demand. By inserting new values of the independent factors, such as new projected sales figures, then the demand for employees can be worked out from the equation. The equations can also be represented as graphs making the relationships clear to see. These models can be adapted to take account of projected changes in utilization, due to factors such as the introduction of new technology, or alternative organisational forms, such as high performance teams.

Objective methods II: work study

This method is based on time study and a thorough analysis of the work done to arrive at the person-hours needed per unit of output. Standards are developed for the numbers and levels of employees that are needed to do the work tasks. These standards may be developed within the organisation or elsewhere and are most useful when studying production work. It is important that the standards are checked regularly to ensure they are still appropriate. Work study is usually classified as an objective measure, but Verhoeven (1982) argues that since the development of standards and the grouping of tasks is partly dependent on human judgement, it should be considered as a subjective method.

Subjective methods I: managerial judgement

Sometimes called executive judgement, managerial opinion or inductive method, it can also include the judgements of other operational and technical staff, as well as all levels of managers. This method is based on managers' estimates of manpower demand based on past experience and on corporate plans. Managerial judgements can be collected from the 'bottom up' with lower-level managers providing estimates to be passed upwards in the hierarchy for discussion and redrafting. Alternatively, a 'top-down' approach can be used with estimates made by the highest level of management to pass down the hierarchy for discussion and redrafting. Using this method it is difficult to cope with changes that are very different from past experiences. It is also less precise than statistical methods, but it is more comprehensive. Managerial judgement is a simple method which can be applied fairly quickly and is not restricted by lack of data, particularly historical data, as are statistical techniques. Stainer makes the point that managerial judgement is important even when statistical techniques are used, when he says:

> The aim in employing statistical techniques is to simplify the problem to the extent that the human mind can cope with it efficiently, rather than to eliminate subjective judgement altogether. (Stainer 1971)

(See Appendix, note 5.)

Subjective methods II: Delphi technique
This is a specialised procedure for the collection of managerial opinions based on the idea of the oracle at Delphi. A group of managers anonymously and independently answer questions about anticipated manpower demand. A compilation of the answers is fed back to each individual, and the process is repeated until all the answers converge. Empirical data suggest that this technique is little used at present, although it is often referred to as a common method.

Taking account of changing employee utilisation
The emphasis on employee utilisation varies considerably between different authors – some see it as the most critical issue, whereas others give it only passing attention. There is a vast range of ways to change the way that employees are used.

1.   Introducing new materials or equipment, particularly new technology.

2.   Introducing changes in work organisation, such as:
      (a)   quality circles;
      (b)   job rotation;
      (c)   job enlargement;
      (d)   job enrichment;
      (e)   autonomous work-groups;
      (f)   high performance teams; and
      (g)   participation.

3.   Organisation development.

4.   Introducing changes in organisation structure, such as:
      (a)   centralisation/decentralisation;
      (b)   new departmental boundaries;

(c) relocation of parts of the organisation; and

(d) flexible project structures.

5. Introducing productivity schemes, bonus schemes or other incentive schemes.
6. Encouraging greater staff flexibility and work interchangeability.
7. Altering times and periods of work.
8. Training and appraisal of staff.
9. Developing managers and use of performance management.

Some of these methods are interrelated or overlap and would therefore be used in combination. (See Appendix, note 6.)

Analysing the current situation

Organisation, behaviour and culture

It is in this area that more choice of techniques is available, and the possibilities include use of questionnaires to staff (Appendix, note 7), interviews with staff and managerial judgement. Focus groups are an increasingly popular technique where, preferably, the Chief Executive meets with, for instance, twenty representative staff from each department to discuss their views of the strengths and weaknesses of the organisation, and what can be done to improve them. These approaches can be used to provide information on, for example:

- motivation of employees;
- job satisfaction;
- organizational culture;
- the way that people are managed;
- attitude to minority groups and equality of opportunity;
- commitment to the organisation and reasons for this;
- clarity of business objectives;
- goal-focused and other behaviour;
- organisational issues and problems;
- what can be done to improve; and
- organisational strengths to build on.

Turnover figures, performance data, recruitment and promotion trends and characteristics of employees may also shed some light on these issues.

Data relating to current formal and informal systems, together with data on the structure of the organisation, also need to be collected and the effectiveness, efficiency and other implications of these need to be carefully considered. Most data will be collected from within the organisation, but data may also be collected from significant others, such as customers, who may be part of the environment.

Jennifer Hadley is the Chief Executive of Dynamo Castings, a long established organisation which had experienced rapid growth and healthy profits until the last three years. Around 800 staff were employed, mostly in production, but significant numbers were also employed in marketing/sales and research/development. Poor performance over the last three years was largely the result of the competition who were able to deliver a quality product at a competitive price more quickly. Dynamo retained the edge in developing new designs, but this consumed a high level of resources and was a lengthy process from research to eventual production. Most employees had been with the company for a large part of their working lives and the culture was still appropriate to the times of high profit where life had been fairly easy and laid-back. Messages about difficult times, belt tightening and higher productivity with less people had been filtered down to employees, who did not change their behaviour but did feel threatened.

It was with some trepidation that Jennifer decided to meet personally with a cross-section of each department to talk through company and departmental issues. The first was with research/development. As expected the meeting began with a flood of concerns about job security. No promises could be given. However, the mid-point of the meeting was quite fruitful, and the following, among other, points became clear:

- that development time could be reduced to one year from two if some production staff were involved in the development process from the very beginning;
- that many development staff felt their career prospects were very limited and a number expressed the wish to be able to move into marketing – they felt this would also have an advantage when it came to marketing new products;
- that staff felt fairly paid and would be prepared to forgo salary rises for a year or two if this would mean job security; they liked working for Dynamo and didn't want to move;
- that staff were aware of the difficult position the company was in but they really didn't know what to do to make it any better;
- development staff wanted to know why Dynamo didn't collaborate with Castem Ltd on areas of mutual interest (Jennifer didn't know the answer to this one).

The meeting not only gave Jennifer a better understanding of what employees felt, but also some good ideas to explore. Departmental staff knew their problems had not been wiped away, but did feel that Jennifer had at least taken the trouble to listen to them.

Current and projected employee numbers and skills (employee supply)

Current employee supply can be analysed in both individual and overall statistical terms.

Analysis may be made for any of the following factors, either singly or in combination; number of employees classified by function, department, occupation job title, skills, qualifications, training, age, length of service, performance appraisal results. (See Appendix, note 8.)

Forecasting of employee supply is concerned with predicting how the current supply of manpower will change over time, primarily in respect of how many will leave, but also how many will be internally promoted or transferred. These changes are forecast by analysing what has happened in the past, in terms of staff retention and/or movement, and projecting this into the future to see what would happen if the same trends continued. Bell (1974) provides an extremely thorough coverage of possible analyses, on which this section is based. However, although statistical analyses are most well developed for the forecasting of employee supply, behavioural aspects, which we referred to earlier in this chapter, are also important (see Timperley 1980). These include investigating the reasons why staff leave and criteria that affect promotions and transfers. Changes in working conditions and in personnel policy would be relevant here. Statistical techniques fall broadly into two categories: analyses of staff leaving the organisation, and analyses of internal movements.

Analyses of staff leaving the organisation

Annual labour turnover index   This is sometimes called the percentage wastage rate, or the conventional turnover index. This is the simplest formula for wastage and looks at the number of staff leaving during the year as a percentage of the total number employed who could have left.

$$\frac{\text{Leavers in year}}{\text{Average number of staff in post during year}} \times 100 = \text{per cent wastage rate}$$

(see Appendix, note 9.)

This measure has been criticised because it only gives a limited amount of information. If, for example, there were twenty-five leavers over the year, it would not be possible to determine whether twenty-five different jobs had been left by twenty-five different people, or whether twenty-five different people had tried and left the same job. Length of service is not taken into account with this measure, yet length of service has been shown to have a considerable influence on leaving patterns – such as the high number of leavers at the time of induction.

Stability index   This index is based on the number of staff who could have stayed throughout the period. Usually, staff with a full year's service are expressed as a percentage of staff in post one year ago.

$$\frac{\text{Number of staff with one year's service at date}}{\text{Number of staff employed exactly one year before}} \times 100 = \text{per cent stability}$$

(See Appendix, note 9.)

This index, however, ignores joiners throughout the year and takes little account of length of service. (See Appendix, note 10.)

Bowey's Stability Index Bowey's Index (Bowey 1974) attempts to take account of the length of service of employees.

Cohort analysis   A cohort is defined as a homogeneous group of people. Cohort analysis involves the tracking of what happens, in terms of leavers, to a group of people with very similar characteristics who join the organisation at the same time. Graduates are an appropriate group for this type of analysis. A graph can be produced to show what happens to the group. The graph can be in the form of a survival curve or a log normal wastage curve, which can be plotted as a straight line and can be used to make predictions. The disadvantage of this method of analysis is that it cannot be used for groups other than the specific type of group for which it was originally prepared. The information has also to be collected over a long time-period, which gives rise to problems of availability of data and their validity.

Half-life   This is a figure which expresses the time taken for half the cohort to leave the organisation. The figure does not give as much information as a survival curve, but it is useful as a summary and as a method of comparing different groups.

Census method   The census method is an analysis of leavers over a reasonably short period of time – often over a year. The length of completed service of leavers is summarised by using a histogram, as shown in Figure 5.6. (See Appendix, note 11.)

Retention profile   Staff retained, that is those who remain with the organisation, are allocated groups depending on the year they joined. The number in each year group is translated into a percentage of the total number of individuals who joined during that year.

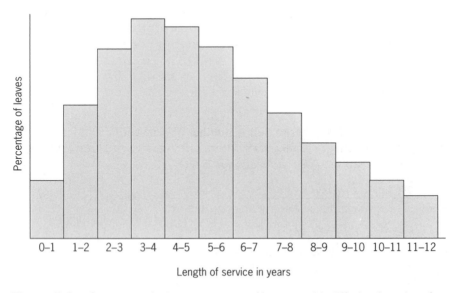

Figure 5.6   Census analysis: percentage of leavers with differing lengths of service.

Analyses of internal movements

These techniques tend to be more sophisticated than those dealing with the analysis of wastage. Age and length of service distributions can be helpful analyses indicating problems that may arise in the future, such as promotion blocks. They need to be used in conjunction with an analysis of previous promotion patterns in the organisation. (See Appendix, note 12.) More sophisticated tools such as the Markov chain and renewal models are rarely used.

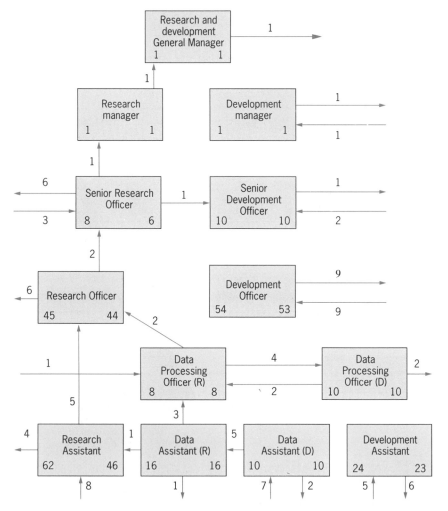

Figure 5.7 Stocks and flows: current establishment and staff in post with movements over the last year. Left side: number inside box = number of posts. Right side: number in box = actual number in post. Arrow into box = recruitment or promotion or sideways move. Arrow from box = leavers or movers. No line between boxes = no movement between those positions in last year

A simpler and more popular technique is a stocks and flows analysis of the whole organisation or a part of it, such as a department. The model is constructed to show the hierarchy of positions and the numbers employed in each. Numbers moving between positions and in and out of the organisation over any time period can be displayed. An example of a stocks and flows analysis is given in Figure 5.7. The model is a visual way of displaying promotion and lateral move channels in operation, and shows what happens in reality to compare with the espoused approach.

Individual analysis   Similar information to the above can be collected on an individual basis to facilitate succession, career, redundancy and relocation planning. Replacement and succession planning are increasingly used and often represented in the form of charts as shown in Figure 5.8. Succession planning is only usually carried out for a select group in the organisation – those who are identified as having high potential – and generally centres around the most senior jobs. The emphasis is on organisational needs – identifying who will be equipped to fill the most senior positions and over what timescale. It is usually

Post	Current post holder	Ready now	Ready soon	Ready future
Marketing Manager	D. Peters	F. Davis	F. Heald	B. Baker
Development Manager	R. Trice	D. Peters	M. Marks	B. Baker L. Brice
Research Manager	J. Moore		J. Old	C. Chane F. Davis
Data Manager	T. Totter	D. Peters	K. James J. Old	C. Churcher

Candidate	Present	Probable	Possible	Future	Development/ Experience needed for each role
D. Peters	Marketing manager	Development manager	Data manager	Marketing director	
F. Davis	Unit leader	Marketing manager		Research manager	
M. Marks	Development team leader		Development manager		

Figure 5.8   Two formats for succession planning

a closed process, so that an individual is not likely to know whether they are on a succession list or chart. In these ways succession is very different from career planning, which we look at in detail in Chapter 25. Walker (1992a) examines the difference between succession planning and replacement planning. He identifies the characteristics of replacement planning as:

- an informal approach, often based on personal knowledge of possible candidates;
- often lacking in a thorough analysis of the challenges within the jobs;
- usually short term; and
- concentrates on vertical moves with little consideration of lateral or diagonal moves.

Walker describes succession planning as overcoming these weaknesses, being more systematic and longer term with a thorough analysis of the demands of future jobs and of the strengths, weaknesses and experiences of key employees. The emphasis is on developing individuals for the potential challenges ahead of them.

REVIEW TOPIC 5.2

1. For what reasons do employees leave organisations?
2. What are the determinants of promotion in your organisation? Are they made explicit? Do staff understand what the determinants are?
3. What would be your criteria for promotion in your organisation?

Reconciliation, decisions and plans

We have already said that, in reality, there is a process of continuous feedback between the different stages of human resource planning activities as they are all interdependent. On the soft side (organisation, behaviour and culture) there is a dynamic relationship between future vision, environmental trends and the current position. Key factors to take into account during reconciliation and deciding on action plans are the acceptability of the plans to both senior managers and other employees, the priority of each plan, key players who will need to be influenced and the factors that will encourage or be a barrier to successful implementation. Piercy (1989), in relation to strategic planning generally, offers a series of tools to help managers work through these issues.

On the hard side feasibility may centre on the situation where the supply forecast is less than the demand forecast. Here, the possibilities are to:

1. Alter the demand forecast by considering the effect of changes in the utilisation of employees, such as training and productivity deals, or high performance teams.

2. Alter the demand forecast by considering using different types of employees to meet the corporate objectives, such as employing a smaller number of staff with higher level skills, or employing staff with insufficient skills and training them immediately.

3. Change the company objectives, as lack of human resources will prevent them from being achieved in any case. Realistic objectives may need to be based on the manpower that is, and is forecast to be, available.

When the demand forecast is less than the internal supply forecast in some areas, the possibilities are to:

1. Consider and calculate the costs of overemployment over various timespans.
2. Consider the methods and cost of losing staff.
3. Consider changes in utilisation: work out the feasibility and costs of retraining, redeployment, and so on.
4. Consider whether it is possible for the company objectives to be changed. Could the company diversify, move into new markets, etc.?

We have also noted the interrelationship between the soft and the hard aspects of planning. For example, the creation of high performance teams may have implications for different staffing numbers, a different distribution of skills, alternative approaches to reward and a different management style. The relocation of supplier's staff on customer premises, in order to get really close to the customer, could have implications for relocation, recruitment, skills required and culture encouraged. The development of a learning organisation may have implications for turnover and absence levels, training and development provision, culture encouraged and approach to reward.

Once all alternatives have been considered and feasible solutions decided upon, specific action plans can be designed covering all appropriate areas of human resource management activity. For example:

1. *Human resource supply plans:* plans may need to be made concerning the timing and approach to recruitment or down-sizing. For example, it may have been decided that, in order to recruit sufficient staff, a public relations campaign is needed to promote a particular company image. Promotion, transfer and redeployment and redundancy plans would also be relevant here.

2. *Organisation and structure plans:* these plans may concern departmental existence, remit and structure and the relationships between departments. They may also be concerned with the layers of hierarchy within departments and the level at which tasks are done, and the organisational groups within which they are done. Changes to organisation and structure will usually result in changes in employee utilisation.

3. *Employee utilisation plans:* any changes in utilisation that affect human resources demand will need to be planned. Some changes will result in a sudden difference in the tasks that employees do and the numbers needed; others will result in a gradual movement over time. Managers need to work out new tasks to be done, old ones to be dropped and the timescale by which they need the right number of peo-

ple fully operational. Other plans may involve the distribution of hours worked, for example the use of annual hours contracts; or the use of functional flexibility where employees develop and use a wider range of skills. There are implications for communications plans as the employees involved will need to be consulted about the changes and be prepared and trained for what will happen. There will be interconnections with supply plans here; for example, if fewer employees will be needed, what criteria will be used to determine who should be made redundant and who should be redeployed and retrained, and in which areas?

4. *Training and management development plans:* there will be training implications from both the manpower supply and manpower utilisation plans. The timing of the training can be a critical aspect. For example, training for specific new technology skills loses most of its impact if it is done six months before the equipment arrives. If the organisation wishes to increase recruitment by promoting the excellent development and training that it provides for employees, then clear programmes of what will be offered need to be finalised and resourced so that these can then be used to entice candidates into the organisation. If the organisation is stressing customer service or total quality, then appropriate training will need to be developed to enable employees to achieve this.

5. *Performance plans:* performance plans directly address performance issues for example the introduction of an objective-setting and performance management system; setting performance and quality standards; or culture change programmes aimed at encouraging specified behaviour and performance.

6. *Appraisal plans:* the organisation needs to make sure that it is assessing the things that are important to do. If customer service is paramount then employees need to be assessed on aspects of customer service relevant to their job, in addition to other factors. This serves the purpose of reinforcing the importance of customer service, and also provides a mechanism for improving performance in this area, and rewarding this where appraisal is to be linked to pay.

7. *Reward plans:* it is often said that what gets rewarded gets done, and it is crucial that rewards reflect what the organisation sees as important. For example, if quantity of output is most important with respect to production workers, bonuses may relate to number of items produced. If quality is most important, then bonuses may reflect reject rate, or customer complaint rate. If managers are only rewarded for meeting their individual objectives there may be problems if the organisation is heavily dependent on team work.

8. *Employee relations plans:* these plans may involve unions, employee representatives or all employees. They would include any matters which need to be negotiated or areas where there is the opportunity for employee involvement and participation.

9. *Communications plans:* the way that planned changes are communicated to employees is critical. Plans need to include methods for not only informing

employees what managers expect of them, but also methods to enable employees to express their concerns and needs for successful implementation. Communications plans will also be important if, for example, managers wish to generate greater employee commitment by keeping employees better informed about the progress of the organisation.

Once the plans have been made and put into action, the planning process still continues. It is important that the plans be monitored to see if they are being achieved and if they are producing the expected results. Plans will also need to be reconsidered on a continuing basis in order to cope with changing circumstances.

☐ SUMMARY PROPOSITIONS

5.1 Human resource planning activities are all interdependent.

5.2 Human resource planning methods range from sophisticated statistical techniques to simple diagnostic tools to analyse judgemental data.

5.3 As human resource planning deals with people, planners need to plan for what is acceptable as well as what is feasible.

5.4 Human resource planning is a continuous process rather than a one-off activity.

5.5 Human resource plans cover areas such as people supply, utilisation, communications, training/development, performance, appraisal, organisation, reward and employee relations.

References

Bell, D. J. (1974), *Planning Corporate Manpower*, London: Longman.

Bell, D. (1989), 'Why manpower planning is back in vogue', *Personnel Management*, July.

Bowey, A. (1974), *A Guide to Manpower Planning*, London: Macmillan.

Greer, C. R., Jackson, D. L. and Fiorito, J. (1989), 'Adapting human resources planning in a changing business environment', *Human Resource Management*, Spring, vol. 28, no. 1.

Hussey, D. (1982), *Corporate Planning: Theory and Practice*, (2nd edn), Oxford: Pergamon Press.

Manzini, A. O. (1984), 'Human resource planning: observations on the state of the art and the state of practice', *Human Resource Planning*, vol. 7, Pt 2, pp. 105–10.

Mintzberg, H. (1994), 'The fall and rise of strategic planning', *Harvard Business Review*, January/February.

Piercy, N. (1989), 'Diagnosing and solving implementation problems in strategic planning', *Journal of General Management*, vol. 15, no. 1, pp. 19–38.

Schuler, R. S. and Walker, J. W. (1990), 'Human resources strategy: focusing on issues and actions', *Organisational Dynamics*, Summer.

Smith, A. R. (ed.) (1980), 'Corporate manpower planning: a personnel review', *Review Monograph*, Aldershot: Gower.

Stainer, G. (1971), *Manpower Planning*, London: Heinemann.

Timperley, S. R. (1980), 'Towards a behavioural review of manpower planning'. In A. R. Smith (ed.), *Corporate Manpower Planning*, Aldershot: Gower.

Ulrich, D. (1989), 'Strategic human resource planning: why and how?' *Human Resource Planning*, vol. 10, no. 1.

Verhoeven, C. T. (1982), *Techniques in Corporate Manpower Planning*, Boston/The Hague/London: Kluwer/Nijhoff.

Walker, J. W. (1992a), *Human Resource Strategy*, New York: McGraw Hill.

Walker, J. W. (1992b), 'Human resource planning, 1990s style', *Human Resource Planning*, vol. 13, no. 4.

Appendix

The City Hotel is located in the middle of a medium-sized city. It caters mainly for business trade during the week and for holiday trade during the weekends and in the summer. In the summer and at weekends there is, therefore, a greater demand for catering and waiting staff as there is a greater demand for lunches. During the same periods there is a lesser demand for housekeeping staff as the guests are mostly longer-stay. The hotel has been gradually improved and refurbished over the past five years and trade, although reasonably good to begin with, has also gradually improved over the period. There are plans to open an extension with a further twenty bedrooms next year.

Note 1

There has been a particular problem in recruiting kitchen assistants, waiting and bar staff. This is partly due to local competition, but also to the fact that late starting and early finishing times make travel very difficult. Often there are no buses at these times and taxis are the only available transport. One or two hotels in the area have begun a hotel transport system, and the City Hotel management have decided to investigate this idea in order to attract a higher number of better quality applicants. A second problem has been identified as the lack of availability of chefs and receptionists of the required level of skill. It is felt that the local colleges are not producing potential staff with sufficient skills, and therefore the management of the City Hotel have decided to consider the following.

1. A training scheme, either run internally or in conjunction with other hotels.
2. Better wages to attract the better trained staff from other employers.
3. Investigation of other localities and the possibility of providing more staff.

Note 2

Having mapped the environment, the hotel management looked at the demands and responses for each priority area. For 'customers' the beginnings of the list are shown in Table A5.1.

Table A5.1 *Demands and responses for the 'customer' factor*

Customer demands	Responses
Polite staff	Our staff pride themselves on being courteous
Staff understand that we are busy people	We will make procedures quick and simple, staff will respond to needs immediately
Sometimes we need facilities we have not arranged in advance	We will be flexible and enthusiastic in our response
And so on	

Note 3

The management of the City Hotel decided that one of their key objectives over the next three years was to become known for excellence of customer service. This was seen as a key tool to compete with adjacent hotels. Managers used brainstorming to identify the staff behaviours that they wanted to see in place, and summarised their ideas in the format in Table A5.2.

In addition to this a suggestion scheme was instigated to collect ideas for improvement in customer service, with a payment of £50 to be made for each successful suggestion.

Table A5.2 *Behavioural expectations chart: organisational goal = excellence in customer service*

Behaviours needed	How to create or reinforce
Address customers by name	A customer service training course to be developed
Smile at customer	A group incentive bonus to be paid on basis of customer feedback. Customer service meetings to be held in company time once per week
Respond to requests, e.g. room change, in positive manner	
Ask customers if everything is to their satisfaction	
Answer calls from rooms within four rings	
And so on	

Note 4

The City Hotel management has plans to open a further twenty bedrooms in a new extension during the coming year. On the basis of this simple model the additional staff required could be worked out as follows:

- fifty-five bedrooms require 60 staff;
- the ratio of staff to bedrooms is therefore 1.09 staff per bedroom;
- if the same relationship were maintained (i.e. without any economies of scale) the additional number of staff needed would be: 20 bedrooms × 1.09 staff = 21.8 extra staff needed. Thus total staff needed would = 81.2 full-time equivalent staff.

Note 5

The managerial staff at the City Hotel exercised judgements on the following human resource planning matters:

1. Management considered the probable reasons for the relationship between people demand and time. It was felt that this was most probably due to the gradual improvement in the hotel over the last five years. Since this improvement had virtually reached its potential it was felt that the relationship between employee demand and time would change.
2. Judgements had to be made on whether the occupancy of the new wing would immediately justify all the additional staff to be appointed.
3. The management considered that since the weather had been very poor during the preceding summer, the bookings for the following summer period might be slightly down on the previous year and this shortfall might not be made up by increasing business trade.
4. Judgements were made as to whether staff could be better utilised, with the effect that the additional numbers of staff projected might not be so great.

Note 6

The managers of the City Hotel decided to encourage greater staff flexibility and interchangeability. This interchangeability would be particularly useful between waiting duties and chamber duties. At the present time waiting duties are greatest at the weekend and least during weekdays, whereas chamber duties are the other way around. The effect of this is that waiting staff and chamber staff both have a number of hours of enforced idle time, and the feeling was that there was some over-staffing. By securing flexibility from staff (by paying a flexibility bonus) it was felt that the smooth running and efficiency of the hotel would be considerably increased. It was calculated that the nine chamber posts and eight waiting posts could be covered by sixteen combined posts (all full-time employees).

Note 7

Managers of the City Hotel assessed the levels of customer service at present by collecting questionnaire data from both staff and customers and conducting a series of interviews with staff. They also asked in what areas service could be improved and asked staff how this might be achieved. As well as specific targets for improvement, they found many examples of systems and organisation that did not help staff give the best customer service. Staff understood that getting the paperwork right was more important than service to the customer in checking out and in. The paperwork systems were over-complex and could be simplified. Also, shift-change times were found to correspond with busy checkout times. Plans were developed to improve systems, organisation and communication.

Note 8

The statistical analysis of staff (Table A5.3) was aimed at occupation, age and full-time equivalent posts. This analysis was used primarily for three main purposes:

1. Full-time equivalents needed to be worked out so that this figure could be used in other human resource planning calculations.
2. To consider the occupational balance of staff and to give information which would be useful from the point of view of staff interchangeability.
3. To plan for future retirements and, in consequence, look at recruitment plans and promotion plans.

Table 5.3   *Staff by occupation, number and age*

Broad occupational group	FTE	Actual number of staff	Ages
General managers and department heads	4 + 5	4 + 5	(45, 43, 30, 21) (51, 47, 45, 35, 32)
Reception/accounts/clerical	7	8	(55, 24, 24, 23, 21, 21, 21, 18)
Chamber staff	9	12	(52, 51, 35, 35, 34, 33, 31, 31, 30, 29, 20, 19)
Porters	3	3	(64, 51, 20)
Chefs	8	8	(49, 47, 41, 40, 39, 24, 23, 21)
Other kitchen staff	12	16	(59, 59, 57, 52, 51, 31, 29, 28, 27, 27, 24, 24, 24, 23, 19, 18)
Bar/waiting staff	10	14	(51, 45, 35, 35, 33, 32, 30, 29, 26, 26, 25, 25, 20, 21)
Handyperson/gardener	2	2	(64, 63)
Total	60	72	

Note 9

At the City Hotel eighteen staff had left during the preceding year. The annual labour turnover index was therefore worked out to be:

$$\frac{18}{70^*} \times 100 = 25.7 \text{ per cent}$$

(*The average number of staff employed over the year is different from the maximum number of staff that have been employed and were desired to be employed.)

Note 10

At the City Hotel, of the eighteen staff that had been recruited over the year, three of these had been replacements for the same kitchen assistant's job, and two had been replacements for another kitchen assistant's job. The stability index was therefore worked out as:

$$\frac{54}{69^*} \times 100 = 78.26 \text{ per cent stability}$$

(At exactly one year before there were only 69 of the desired 72 staff in post.)

Note 11

A histogram (Figure A5.1) was plotted of leavers over the past year from the City Hotel. It shows how the majority of leavers had shorter lengths of service, with periods of employment of less than six months being most common.

Note 12

Analysis of the age distribution (Table A5.3) indicates that there may be some difficulties with promotions. In particular, a problem was identified for management promotions. There are four general managers, the youngest being twenty-one. In the past such a junior manager would have been promoted after two years' service, which they had just completed. The ages of the other managers indicate that there will be no retirements in the immediate future and management staff turnover has, in the past few years, been low. In view of this it was thought likely that the junior manager would leave shortly. This was not desired since they were particularly able, so ways of dealing with this promotion block were considered, such as creating of a new post, which might retain the junior manager's services until a promotion became available.

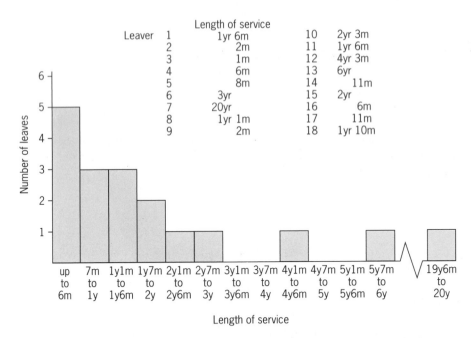

Figure A5.1 A histogram of the lengths of service of the eighteen employees leaving the City Hotel in the previous year

6 Structure and culture

Organisations have a structure and a culture. The structure is a framework that can be described and altered at will. The culture is much more difficult to grasp and understand. It is also much more difficult to change. There are theories of organisational design that are directed towards the structure; no one has yet claimed to design a culture. Yet structure and culture are as interdependent as lungs and oxygen in providing the business with life and purpose.

Gradually, attitudes towards structure are altering. Few people now see the design of an organisation as a single act of creation, deploying power and wisdom to put people into a constructive working relationship with each other: the moment comes and the organisation is created in an instantaneous big bang.

Sometimes organisations are brought into being in almost that way. Richard Branson apparently worked out a complete organisation structure for his Virgin Atlantic airline as a preliminary to setting up the company and then recruiting the 102 people needed to fit into all the positions of the organisation chart.

> Jethro said to Moses, '... select capable men from all the people – men who fear God, trustworthy men who hate dishonest gain – and appoint them as officials over thousands, hundreds, fifties and tens. Have them serve as judges for the people at all times, but have them bring every difficult case to you; the simple cases they can decide themselves. That will make your load lighter, because they will share it with you... you will be able to stand the strain and all these people will go home satisfied.' (Authorised Version of the Bible, Exodus 18:21–23.)

However attractive this idea may be, it is the minority of managers who find themselves in that situation. For most people the organisation is in a steady state of being not right: a pattern of working relationships bedevilled by inefficiency, frustration and obsolescence. For them organisation design is a process of tinkering, pushing and shoving, achieving piecemeal improvements where possible and occasionally coping with a cataclysm – such as a need to shed half the workforce – that seems to leave the worst possible combination of human resources in its wake.

This is especially likely to be the experience of personnel officers. In the 1980s our research showed personnel specialists to be involved usually only at the margin of significant changes in work organisation. That has now begun to change, but too often involvement is in sorting out a mess rather than in finding ways of avoiding the mess. Evans and Cowling found that personnel directors rarely had the responsibility for initiating organisational change.

> Most personnel executives in British organisations may be described as having a 'team' role rather than a 'leadership' role in the field of organisational restructuring... they are not in most cases initiators of major organisational change nor do they generally have a major role in advising on the forms that new structures might take. (Evans and Cowling 1985)

Whether one is creating the single grand design, coping with the steady state or trying to change the structure, it is necessary first to understand the process of organising and the alternative main forms of organisation, before proceeding to consider methods of intervention and the significance of culture.

The fundamentals of the organising process

Organising requires both *differentiation* and *integration*. The process of differentiation is concerned with setting up the arrangements for an individual job or task to be undertaken effectively, while integration is co-ordinating the output of the individual tasks so that the whole task is completed satisfactorily. There is no one best way of doing either. The organising of the individual job will vary according to the degree of predictability in what has to be done, so that the organising of manufacturing jobs tends to emphasise obedience to authority, clearly defined tasks and much specialisation. Jobs which have constantly fresh problems and unpredictable requirements, such as marketing and social work, produce frequent redefinition of job boundaries, a tendency to flexible networks of working relationships rather than a clear hierarchy and a greater degree of individual autonomy. Explanations of this process can be found in Burns and Stalker (1961), and Van de Ven, Delbecq and Koenig (1974).

The integrating process will be influenced by the degree of differentiation. The greater the differentiation, the harder the task of co-ordination. Also Lawrence and Lorsch (1967), in arguably the most influential work on organisation ever written, demonstrated that the nature of the integration problem varies with the rate at which new products are introduced. Galbraith (1977) further showed the importance of the capacity of the organisation to process information about events that cannot be predicted in advance. As the level of uncertainty increases more information has to be processed, with organisation being needed to provide the processing capacity.

We can now see how differentiation and integration are put into action in face of uncertainty to produce a working organisation. There are three fundamentals: task identity and job definition, structure and decision-making complexes.

Task identity and job definition

A job holder has a label or title which provides the basic identity of tasks the job holder performs, the job content and boundaries. Some of the titles are explicit and understood well enough to meet most organisational requirements. Hearing that someone's job is Marketing Director, Office Cleaner, Commissionaire, Plumber, Photographic Model or Train Driver provides you with a good initial understanding of that person's role in the business. Other titles are imprecise or confusing. A single issue of a national newspaper includes the following among the advertised vacancies: Clerical Assistant, Jazz Assistant Administrator, Plastic Executive, Administrator, Information Specialist, Third Party Products Manager, Sub Titler and Editorial Services Controller. Some of these are general titles that are widely used to cover jobs without highly specific content, others probably are precisely understood by those with experience in a particular industry or business, even though they puzzle those of us without that insider knowledge.

There are still many questions to be answered so that other members of the organisation, and those outside, can understand the job holder's status, power, expertise, scope of responsibility and reliability. These questions are especially important where jobs adjoin each other. Where does A's responsibility finish and B's begin? Do areas of responsibility overlap? Are there matters for which no one appears to be responsible?

REVIEW TOPIC 6.1

Write down job titles in your organisation that you do not understand, or which you regard as confusing. How would you change them so that they become more effective labels? How many job titles include words such as 'senior', 'principal' or 'manager' which have no significance other than to confer status on the job holder?

The standard device for clarifying task identity and job definition is the job description, but this is frequently seen as the epitome of stifling, irrelevant bureaucracy, as well as being lost in a filing cabinet. It is an invaluable device for allocating people to jobs and tasks to people in a way that can be understood and to avoid gaps and duplication, but there is always the risk that it becomes a straitjacket rather than a framework. In stable organisations the job description is probably an acceptable mechanism for clarifying the boundaries and content of jobs. In organisations where uncertainty is the only thing that is certain, the job description will be less acceptable and appropriate, but identifying the task and defining the job remain fundamental to the organising process.

Structure

People work together, even though the extent to which jobs interlock will vary, so the organisation designer has to decide how identified tasks should be grouped together. There are four common bases for such groupings. First is grouping according to *function*, so that the sales personnel are put together in one group, public relations in another group, research in another, and so on. The logic here is that the group members share expertise and can therefore understand each other, offering valid criticism, leadership and mutual support.

A second grouping principle is to put people together on the basis of *territory*, with employees of different and complementary skills being co-ordinated in a particular locality. This is usually where there is a satellite separated geographically from the main body of the organisation, such as the Glasgow office of a nationwide business having a handful of people based in Glasgow covering duties such as sales, service and maintenance, warehousing, invoicing and stock control. The best-known example is the department store or the high street branch of a national bank.

A third alternative is to group on the basis of *product*, so that varied skills and expertise are again brought together with a common objective; not this time a group of customers in a particular territory, but a product that depends on the interplay of skill variety. Child (1984) gives the example of the hospital, where personnel with medical, nursing, clerical and technical skills are deployed in groups specialising in such 'products' or activities as maternity, paediatrics and accidents. He then explains the difference between the functional and product logics:

> The product-based logic of tasks recognizes how the contributions of different specialists need to be integrated within one complete cycle of work... The product logic is primarily technological, envisaging a flow of work laterally across functional areas. The functional logic is primarily hierarchical, drawing attention to the vertical grouping of people in depth within the boundaries of separate, specialized sections of the company. (Child 1984, p. 87)

The location of kettles

In a school the number and location of kettles is a main determinant of the informal structure. Usually there is at least a kettle – and sometimes more elaborate water-boiling equipment – in the staffroom. There is also a kettle in the general office which supplies the Head-teacher and some or all of the Deputies and senior teachers. This is a valuable clue to status in the informal structure: who within the senior staff is part of the inner coffee cabinet? Some staff have kettles in their classroom or office and *may* invite a colleague or two to join them in the early morning or at break times. These are usually Heads of Department or Heads of Year marking out a clear status division. Departmental offices and prep. rooms often have kettles used to make coffee during non-contact periods for members of staff in that particular grouping.

The fourth alternative grouping logic is by *time period*, a form which is dictated by operating circumstances. Where a limited number of people work together at unusual times, such as a night shift, then that time period will be the group boundary for organisational purposes and group members would probably identify first with the group and may feel estranged from the rest of the organisation.

Decision-making complexes

Organisational affairs are pushed along by decisions being made, some by individuals and some made collectively. The scope of decisions to be made by individuals is usually determined by their labelling or by their position in the hierarchy. Some matters, however, are reserved for collective decision. The strategies that emerge from the boardroom have to have majority support among those taking part in the discussion, even if one person may dominate due to ownership influence or personal status. Decisions about the corporate plan, overall marketing strategy and policy on acquisitions are other decisions that are usually made collectively. The organisation designer is interested in determining the nature of the groups that make these decisions and in resolving which matters should be decided in this way.

We use the term decision-making *complexes* rather than decision-making groups, as the decision is made on the basis of more consultation than simply the face-to-face discussion in the meeting which produces the decision. In large undertakings a decision-making group is surrounded by working parties, aides, personal assistants, special advisers and secretaries who provide position papers, draft reports, mediate between factions and prepare the ground. All these preliminaries partly shape the decision that is eventually made.

Alternative forms of organisation structure

Charles Handy (1993) drew on earlier work by Roger Harrison (1972) to produce a four-fold classification of organisations, which has caught the imagination of most managers who have read it. Here we present a slightly different explanation, but acknowledge the source of the main ideas. There is no single ideal organisational form:

> organizations are as different and varied as the nations and societies of the world. They have differing cultures – sets of values and norms and beliefs – reflected in different structures and systems. And the cultures are affected by the events of the past and by the climate of the present, by the technology of the type of work, by their aims and the kind of people that work in them. (Handy 1993, p. 180)

Despite this variety, three broad types of structure are found most often and a fourth type is becoming more common.

Figure 6.1   Entrepreneurial organisation structure

The entrepreneurial form

The entrepreneurial form emphasises central power. It is like the spider's web, with one person or group so dominant that all power stems from the centre, all decisions are made and all behaviour reflects expectations of the centre (Figure 6.1). There are few collective decisions, much reliance on individuals, and with actions stemming from obtaining the approval of key figures. It is frequently found in businesses where decisions must be made quickly and with flair and judgement rather than careful deliberation. Newspaper editing has an entrepreneurial form of organisation and most of the performing arts have strong centralised direction.

This is the form of most small and growing organisations as they owe their existence to the expertise or initiative of one or two people, and it is only by reflecting accurately that originality that the business can survive. As the business expands this type of structure can become unwieldy because too many peripheral decisions can not be made without approval from the centre, which then becomes overloaded. It is also difficult to maintain if the spider leaves the centre. A successor may not have the same degree of dominance. In some instances the problem of increasing size has been dealt with by maintaining entrepreneurial structure at the core of the enterprise and giving considerable independence to satellite organisations, provided that overall performance targets are met.

The bureaucratic form

The bureaucratic form emphasises the distribution rather than centralisation of power and responsibility. It has been the conventional means of enabling an

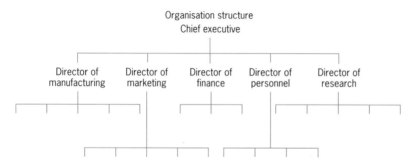

Figure 6.2 Typical bureaucratic organisation structure

organisation to grow beyond the entrepreneurial form to establish an existence that is not dependent on a single person or group of founders (Figure 6.2). Through emphasising role rather than flair, operational processes become more predictable and consistent, with procedure and committee replacing individual judgement. Responsibility is devolved through the structure and it is a method of organisation well suited to stable situations, making possible economies of scale and the benefits of specialisation. There is seldom the flexibility to deal with a volatile environment and a tendency to be self-sufficient:

> The bureaucratic approach is intended to provide organizational control through ensuring a high degree of predictability in people's behaviour. It is also a means of trying to ensure that different clients or employees are treated fairly through the application of general rules and procedures. The problem is that rules are inflexible instruments of administration which enshrine experience of past rather than present conditions, which cannot be readily adapted to suit individual needs, and which can become barriers behind which it is tempting for the administrator to hide. (Child 1984, p. 8)

Bureaucracy has been the standard form of structure for large organisations for thousands of years and remains the dominant form today. It has, however, come under criticism recently because of its inappropriateness in times of change and a tendency to frustrate personal initiative. 'Bureaucracy' is definitely a dirty word, so companies work hard at overcoming its drawbacks.

The matrix form

The matrix form emphasises the co-ordination of expertise into project-orientated groups of people with individual responsibility. It has been developed to counter some of the difficulties of the entrepreneurial and bureaucratic forms (Figure 6.3). It was first developed in the United States during the 1960s as a means of satisfying the government on the progress of orders placed with contractors for the supply of defence material. Checking on progress proved very difficult with a bureaucracy, so it was made a condition of contracts that the contractor should appoint a project

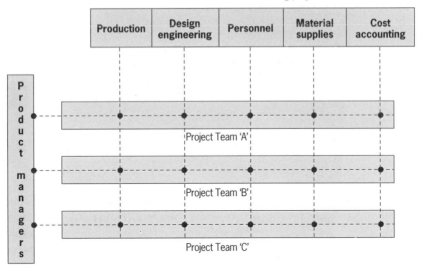

Figure 6.3   Typical matrix organisation structure

manager with responsibility for meeting the delivery commitments and keeping the project within budget. In this way the government was able to deal with a single representative rather than with a number of people with only partial responsibility. The contractors then had to realign their organisation so that the project manager could actually exercise the degree of control necessary to make the responsibility effective. This is done either by appointing a product manager with considerable status and power, or by creating product teams with specialists seconded from each functional area. The first method leaves the weight of authority with the functional hierarchy, while the product managers have a mainly co-ordinating, progress chasing role as lone specialists. The second method shifts power towards the product managers, who then have their own teams of experts, with the functional areas being seen as a resource rather than the centre of action and decision. A third, but less common, situation is a permanent overlay of one set of hierarchical connections laid horizontally over a pre-existing conventional, vertical hierarchy. This brings the relative power distribution into approximate balance, but can also make decision making very slow as a result of that equilibrium.

Matrix is the form that appeals to many managers because it is theoretically based on expertise and provides scope for people at relatively humble levels of the organisation to deploy their skills and carry responsibility. It has, however, recently lost favour because it can generate expensive support systems for product managers needing additional secretaries, assistants and all the panoply of office, as well as the unwieldy administration referred to above.

One way in which matrix has found a new lease of life is in the increasing internationalisation of business, where the impracticability of bureaucracy is most obvious. International business tends to run on matrix lines with complex patterns of working relationship and a greater emphasis on developing agreement than on telling people what to do.

The independence form

The independence form emphasises the individual and is almost a form of non-organisation. The other three are all methods of putting together the contribution of a number of people so that the sum is greater than the parts, results being achieved by the co-ordination of effort. The independence form is a method of providing a support system so that individuals can perform, with the co-ordination of individual effort being either subsidiary or absent (Figure 6.4).

Barristers' chambers and doctors' clinics work in this way and it is a form of organisation attractive to those of independent mind who are confident of their ability to be individually successful. Some firms of consultants and craft workshops operate similarly, with a background organisation to enable the specialists to operate independently. It has been regarded as unsuitable for most types of undertaking because of the lack of co-ordination and control, but there is growing interest in it with increasing emphases on individual responsibility and professional skill in business. The vague shape can be discerned in many businesses for the reasons outlined in Chapter 1: the decline of organisation as entity.

Figure 6.4   The independence form of organisation

Differentiated structures

This four-fold classification is a means of analysis rather than a description of four distinct types of organisation with any undertaking being clearly one of the four (Table 6.1). Bureaucracies will typically have matrix features at some points and few entrepreneurial structures are quite as 'pure' as described here. Probably any organisation you could name could be classified as having one of these four features dominant and in some there is one form dominant in one section of the business and another form dominant elsewhere. Large banks, for example, are bureaucratic in their retailing operations, as consistency is of paramount importance and any changes need to be put into operation simultaneously by a large number of people while being comprehensible to a large number of customers. The same banks will, however, tend to an entrepreneurial emphasis in their merchant banking activities and to independence in currency dealings.

New forms of structure ?

There is much discussion about new forms of organisation that will be needed in the future, based on an assessment of current and evolving activities that could make a new form of organisation viable. The following are some of the reasons for this view.

- *Big is no longer always beautiful:*   most organisational structures evolved on an implicit assumption that the business would expand, but this is no longer seen as the sole form of growth: diversification and change are equally interesting, and sometimes wiser, alternatives.

- *Business is not necessarily directed towards permanence:*   until quite recently enterprises were established with the objective of continuing indefinitely, often with a semi-dynastic objective – 'all this will be yours one day, my lad'. There

Table 6.1 *Conditions favouring different organizational forms*

Form	Conditions
Entrepreneurial	Dominance of single person or group at centre, due to ownership, expertise or the need of the operation for a strong controlling figure Modest size, simple technology and single, dominant technical expertise Uncertain or rapidly changing environment
Bureaucratic	Complex organisation with devolved power and expertise Large size, complex technology and varied technical expertise Stable environment
Matrix	Complex organisation with bureaucratic features and need to devolve responsibility and enhance responsiveness to clients
Independence	Simple organisation form to support independent activities of specialists, with little co-ordination Professional, rather than management, orientation among specialists

is now greater emphasis on terms such as project and venture, setting up an enterprise that will run for a time and then be closed or sold on.

- *The customer is king:* there is an increased emphasis on the importance of the customer and meeting the customer's needs, so that gradually preoccupation with internal affairs and organisational politics declines and the people of the organisation become less inward-looking, with issues of hierarchical status having less importance.

- *The proliferation of expertise:* running a business requires an increasing variety of skills and diverse expertise, so that management relies on people knowing what to do and being required to get on with it. Seldom is a single business big enough to employ all the experts it requires, so many skills have to be bought in on a temporary basis from consultants or contractors.

- *Information technology:* gradually computerised management information systems are able to produce the quality of control data that can depersonalise the management process to a greater extent. Objectives for individuals and sections have a greater degree of quantification and performance is measurable.

    Running alongside this is the practice of teleworking, whereby the people of the business work either from or at home, maintaining contact with the centre and with other colleagues by electronic mail, fax, computer networking and computer conferencing. Working completely *at* home is not widely popular as most people feel a need for the direct contact, socialisation, understanding and stimulus which can only come from meeting people face to face and participating in the multitude of interpersonal interactions that a business needs to drive itself forwards. Working *from* home is more attractive to many, and an interim position is what is sometimes called tele-cottaging, where you spend part of your time in the office at 'work' and part of your time in your office at home. Human resource management as a development of personnel management is partly a response to these factors and ever-growing interest in performance appraisal and performance management is another manifestation.

- *The boundaryless organisation:* in our discussion above about job descriptions, one of the reasons for them was to define the boundaries between jobs. The idea that a job has boundaries is very unpopular with some managers, as they believe it limits and constrains, but some commentators describe the boundaryless organisation (for example, Devanna and Tichy 1990). This is taking the concept of the core and periphery workforce rather further, particularly in reference to the supply chain, and loosens many familiar constraints:

  > A boundaryless organization eliminates barriers that separate functions (e.g., marketing versus manufacturing), domestic and foreign operations, different levels of work (managerial versus hourly), and between the organization and its customers and suppliers. Boundaryless organizations ensure that the specifications and requirements of the suppliers, producers, and consumers are all well integrated to achieve objectives. (Milkovich and Boudreau 1994, p. 123)

- *Delayering:* a popular managerial pastime has become the process of taking out layers of management in the hierarchy in order to speed response times and make the operation more efficient. Drucker (1988) suggests the need for a considerable reduction in the number of layers in the management hierarchy, with the idea that the organisation of the future will be like a symphony orchestra, with a range of highly skilled experts who know exactly what to do, provided that a conductor provides co-ordination and brio. That superb metaphor is slightly weakened, as he concedes, by the fact that a business does not have the main co-ordinating mechanism of the symphony orchestra: the score to read from.

We believe that the key to finding a new organisational form lies in reviewing the notion of hierarchy. The analyses of some economists (notably Marglin 1974; Williamson 1975) give us a different angle on working relationships within organisations, as they look for a rational basis. The entrepreneurial, bureaucratic and matrix forms all take hierarchy as a given and the guiding principle is 'to whom are you accountable', just as the law sees employees as servants of a master – the employer – and the legal basis on which most of us work is a contract of *employment*. If you start without the hierarchical assumption, it is just as feasible to construe working relationships as transactions. This produces a choice, as the working relationship can either be set in a market where one buys services from another, or it can be set in a hierarchy where one obtains work from another.

Tentatively we describe the new approach to organisation structure as *professional*. It has many features of the independence form and some of matrix.

Fundamental to its operation is the core/periphery type of split in the workforce. The core contains all those activities which will be carried out by employees, while the periphery contains activities that will be put out to tender by contractors or moved elsewhere in the supply chain. The crucial decisions relate to which activities should be in which area. The core should contain those skills which are specialised to the business, rare or secret. Logically all the other activities are put to the periphery, but suppose there is an unexpected shortage of people to provide peripheral skills? In approaching privatisation several British water authorities reduced their employment of civil engineers because they were expensive and the work could be done on an occasional basis by consultants. Gradually, however, there developed a shortage of civil engineers in the consultancy firms, so that the simple rules of the market place ceased to operate. The consultants were normally too small to carry trainees in the same way that the water authorities had done. Should water authorities now employ more core civil engineers?

REVIEW TOPIC 6.3

If you were running an airport, which of the following activities would you locate in the core and which on the periphery of your business:

1. Baggage handling
2. The fire service
3. Catering
4. Newsagency

5. Airport information
6. Car park attendance
7. Maintenance of premises and services
8. Cleaning

The approach to the core employees is to give them a strong sense of identification with the business and its success, usually through developing a corporate culture, with shared values and reinforced, consistent behaviours. Those on the periphery have a close specification of what is required from them and their continued engagement depends on meeting the terms of the contract.

The obvious way in which this form of organisation is unattractive to most people is the lack of secure employment. Kanter (1989, p. 358) believes there is no escape from this and that security in the future will come from *continued employability* rather than continuity of employment. There will be no safe havens for those who can no longer keep up. This seemingly harsh message may nevertheless be the way of overcoming the greatest weaknesses of bureaucracy, as the safe havens are usually in senior posts!

The lessons of the last twenty years for the organisation designer are that tinkering with structure will be fruitless without thinking through the purpose of the organisation, the nature of the demands being placed on it from outside, the types of operation which are to be organised and the people available. Efficient bureaucrats may not make good entrepreneurs, independence is clearly inappropriate if the operation is one with closely interlocking tasks, and moving to a matrix may not be the best way of dealing with a dramatic change in the product market.

Organisational culture

Organisational culture is the characteristic spirit and belief of an organisation demonstrated, for example, in the norms and values that are generally held about how people should behave and treat each other, the nature of working relationships that should be developed and attitudes to change. These norms are deep, taken-for-granted assumptions that are not always expressed, and are often known without being understood.

Through the 1980s in particular, there was great interest in organisational culture as the key to improved organisational effectiveness (for example, Deal and Kennedy 1982; Handy 1985) and has been to complement the earlier preoccupation with organisational structure. Organisation charts may be useful in clarifying reporting relations and subtleties of seniority, but the culture or ethos of the business is believed to be an equally important determinant of effectiveness. Just as most of the developments described earlier in this chapter have been attempts to reduce the rigidity of structure – particularly in bureaucracies – the interest in culture is an attempt to achieve the same objective, but by redefining the problem.

The history and traditions of an organisation reveal something of its culture because the cultural norms develop over a relatively long period, with multiple layers of practice both modifying and consolidating the norms and providing the framework of ritual and convention in which people feel secure, once they have internalised its elements.

Although it sounds strange to attribute human qualities to organisations, they do have distinctive identities. Olins (1989) cites the example of the world's great chemical companies, which superficially seem similar and produce virtually identical products selling at the same price. Yet they each have strong identities and in culture are as different as individual human beings.

Corporate culture

Corporate culture is a more self-conscious expression of specific types of objective in relation to behaviour and values. This entices customers to buy, it entices prospective employees to seek jobs and causes them to feel commitment to the organisation:

> ... research demonstrates that a good organisation which is well known is admired more and liked better than an equally good company which is not so well known. It will attract more and better people to work for it, can more readily make acquisitions and more effectively launch new products: it will perform better. (Olins 1989, p. 53)

This identity can be expressed and reinforced in various ways, such as a formal statement from the Chief Executive or in such comments as 'we don't do things that way here'. There is the logo, the stationery, the uniform. In one way or another it is an attempt to ensure commitment. Through all employing organisations there is inevitably some withholding of co-operation by staff, even where they accept the authority of managers and their right to manage (Anthony 1986, p. 41). This is, in part, because managers have an unrealistic expectation about co-operation and in part because of the limited extent to which the authority of position can be exercised. Corporate culture can get around this problem.

It is important that those employed in an organisation should try to understand the culture they share. Managers in general, and personnel managers in particular, have to understand the extent to which culture can be changed and how the changes can be made, even if the changes may be much harder and slower to make than most managers believe and most circumstances allow.

As we have already said, culture is often not expressed and may be known without being understood. It is none the less real and powerful, so that the enthusiasts who unwittingly work counter-culturally will find that there is a metaphorical but solid brick wall against which they are beating their heads. Enthusiasts who pause to work out the nature of the culture in which they are operating can at least begin the process of change and influence the direction of the cultural evolution, because culture can never be like a brick wall. It is living and growing, able to strengthen and support the efforts of those who use it, as surely as it will frustrate the efforts of those who ignore it.

A further important aspect of organisational cultures is the extent to which they are typically dominated by traditional male values of rationality, logic, competition and independence, rather than the traditional female values of emotional expression, intuition, caring and interdependence (Marshall 1985). Is it necessary that organisational cultures should be so biased? Is that the only way to prosper? Perhaps not, but it seems that an organisation has to be set up from scratch by women if it is to develop a different culture:

> Women … may not be properly represented at important levels of big corporations, but they are now doing remarkably well in the firms they have set up themselves. Here, they don't have to play the male game according to male rules. They are free to make up their own rules, make relationships rather than play games, run their businesses more on a basis of trust than of fear, co-operation rather than rivalry … (Moir and Jessell 1989, p. 167)

Goffee and Scase (1985) studied women executives and found abundant evidence of women being very successful when able to operate outside a male-dominated culture. Indeed, the cause of equality for women at work may well be jeopardised rather than helped by the argument that the only non-genital differences between men and women are socially determined (Tiger 1970).

REVIEW TOPIC 6.4

Is your organisation dominated by male characteristics? Where are there signs of female values? How could the female values spread further in the organisation? What would be the effect on the success of the organisation?

Culture in national context

No organisation is an island, so attempts to foster or alter corporate culture must take account not only of the intentions of those in charge and the expectations of those employed, but also of developments in the surrounding society, both nationally and internationally.

In Britain the idea of an enterprise culture in the 1980s was more than the platform of a political party; it was the articulation of an idea whose time had come. There was a sudden upsurge of new businesses, mostly small and specialised, but there was also an associated change in values and expectations among many working people, especially the young, which was to increase interest in careers, mentoring, customised pay arrangements, networking and others. Whatever business you were in, you had to take on board this change of cultural emphasis. Throughout the 1980s the enterprise emphasis lost some of its momentum, although people remain more willing to take risks in order to achieve what they want from life.

Concern for the environment has developed rapidly in the 1990s so that the expression of environmental responsibility is becoming necessary in the product market, but it is also necessary as a feature of the corporate culture to which employees will respond. It is becoming more difficult to get people to commit themselves to projects that they regard as unworthy. They may do it for the money, but will not offer commitment. Increasingly people look to their workplace for personal opportunities to do what is worthwhile. The extraordinary success of such television spectaculars as 'Bandaid' and 'Children in Need' have been built mainly on money raised by groups of people operating in, or from, their place of work. Marketing specialist Elizabeth Nelson reports the result of consumer surveys:

> Throughout the political spectrum there is a growing awareness that the State should be made more efficient, via competition. Individual responsibility plus collective efficiency is a model for the next twenty years. Our surveys show that there is a strong majority even among the very rich prepared to pay more in tax to alleviate poverty. (Nelson 1989, p. 296)

Concern for the environment is growing apace at the national political level. At local level there is not only concern about the ozone layer and the greenhouse effect, but noise, dirt, smells and inconvenience to fellow citizens. Corporate culture has to assimilate these concerns.

REVIEW TOPIC 6.5

How could your organisation be more protective of the environment?
What would be the costs of the changes you describe?
What would be the benefits of the changes you describe?

Culture in international context

As business becomes increasingly international, personnel managers must also become international, although not at quite the same speed as their marketing colleagues. International cultural issues are a puzzle. The Frenchman Philippe Poirson explains the differences of cultural emphasis in management between the Americans, Japanese and French by pointing to the continuing dominance of the Protestant work ethic:

> ... belief in the redemptive virtue of work has built a system of values for many founders and directors of American business organizations ... profit is legitimate, success in business evaluable, 'work ethics' highly developed. (Poirson 1989, p. 6)

In contrast, the Japanese are oriented to human efficiency rather than human functioning because of their quite different heritage. The idea of individual autonomy is a relatively recent development of European/American influences. To a great extent the Japanese continue to espouse the values of an agricultural, feudal nation, living in an introverted manner by developing specific sociability:

> ... the group's superiority over the individual remains a fundamental particularity of Japanese sociability. However, the new role of firms seems slowly to replace the one traditionally held by the house and the village. (Poirson 1989, p. 7)

He suggests that the French have a social pact which differs from the American in the approach to the 'book of rules'. For the Americans this is sacrosanct and liberty is the ability to spread one's own sovereignty – even if it impedes others – provided that it is done within the rules. In France, however, there is:

> ... a duty of moderation in acts susceptible to hinder the situation of others. This attitude of moderation is not explicitly codified, neither is it codifiable, but it indicates a certain tendency in French culture. (Poirson 1989, p. 7)

The history of the European Economic Community in attempting to establish a supranational institution is one of constant, but reluctant, recognition of the stubbornness of national differences and the accentuation of regional differences among, for instance, the Basques and the Flemish. Nationality is important to personnel management because of its effect on human behaviour and the consequent constraints on management action.

Identity

Nationality is a root source of our individual identity, with all its affiliations and allegiances. Arabs have a tradition of hospitality to guests that can cause them to be deeply offended when invitations are declined, the Japanese have great difficulty about losing face and the Germans have made efficiency and attention to detail a national characteristic. There is also the difficulty that we tend to associate certain characteristics unthinkingly with certain nationalities, yet not all Spaniards are hot-tempered and not all Scots are mean.

> The French respond positively to drama and crisis. This is neatly exemplified by the cover of a French book on management, *Gerer et Dynamiser Ses Collaborateurs* (Bournois and Poirson 1989). The use of the word 'dynamiser', meaning to energise, is rather more vigorous than the English equivalent of 'motivate' and more dramatic than 'empowerment', but most interesting is the cover picture of a man. Not a man in thick-rimmed glasses sitting at a desk, nor in earnest conversation with colleagues while studying a set of accounts. Instead, he has both arms upraised in triumph and both feet off the ground in a leap of exultation. His jacket is undone and his hair is tousled.

Conditioning

Family conventions, religious traditions and forms of education differ markedly between countries and every adult is partly a product of these features of conditioning, with the attendant values, imperatives and beliefs that shape behaviour and expectation. American children are taught very early the values of individuality and doing their own thing; Japanese children are taught to conform, to work within a group and to develop team spirit. Barratt is an American management development specialist who has extensive dealings with the Arab world and comments:

> The Arab executive is likely to try to avoid conflict...on an issue favoured by subordinates but opposed by the executive, he is likely to let the matter drop without taking action ... He values loyalty over efficiency. Many executives tend to look on their employees as family and will allow them to by-pass the hierarchy in order to meet them. (Barratt 1989, p. 29)

Political and legal system

Different nations are distinct political units, so that the political institutions and the ways in which they are used are different. Not only just formal, but also informal, political realities are resistant to change. The laws and the systems of law differ, so that some countries, such as Australia and the United States, have legally binding arbitration as a way of resolving industrial disputes. Not only is this a practice that we do not have in Britain, it also means that the status of the contract of employment is different.

Hofstede (1980) analysed no fewer than 116,000 questionnaires administered to employees in forty different countries and concluded that national cultures could be explained by four key factors.

Individualism

This is the extent to which people expect to look after themselves and their family only. The opposite is collectivism, which has a tight social framework and in which people expect to have a wider social responsibility to discharge because others in the group will support them. Those of a collectivist persuasion believe they owe absolute loyalty to their group.

Power distance

This factor measures the extent to which the less powerful members of the society accept the unequal distribution of power. In organisations this is the degree of centralisation of authority and the exercise of autocratic leadership.

Uncertainty avoidance

The future is always unknown, but some societies socialise their members to accept this and take risks, while members of other societies have been socialised to be made anxious about this and seek the security of law, religion or technology.

Masculinity

The division of roles between the sexes varies from one society to another. Where men are assertive and have dominant roles these values permeate the whole of society and the organisations that make them up, so there is an emphasis on showing off, performing, making money and achieving something visible. Where there is a larger role for women who are more service oriented with caring roles, the values move towards concern for the environment and the quality of life, putting the quality of relationships before the making of money and not showing off.

Hofstede found some clear national cultural differences between nationalities. The findings were then compared with the large-scale British study of organisations carried out in the 1970s (Pugh and Hickson 1976) and an unpublished analysis of MBA students' work at INSEAD, which suggested that there were clusters of national cultures that coincided with different organisational principles. Hofstede argues (1991, pp. 140–6) that countries emphasising large power distance and strong uncertainty avoidance tended to have forms of organisation that relied heavily on hierarchy and clear orders from superiors: a *pyramid of people*.

In countries with small power distance and strong uncertainty avoidance the implicit form of organisation relies on rules, procedures and clear structure: a *well-oiled machine*.

The implicit model of organisation in countries with small power distance and weak uncertainty avoidance was a reliance on *ad hoc* solutions to problems as they arose, as many of the problems could be boiled down to human relations difficulties: a *village market*.

The picture is completed by the fourth group of countries where there is large power distance and weak uncertainty avoidance. Here problems are resolved by constantly referring to the boss who is like a father to an extended family, so there is concentration of authority without structuring of activities: the *family*. Table 6.2 shows which countries are in the different segments.

This classification of cultural diversity helps us to make sense of how people in different countries operate. The implicit form of organisation for Britain is a village market, for France it is a pyramid of people, for Germany it is a well-oiled machine and for Hong Kong it is a family. If we can understand the organisational realities and detail in those four countries, we then have clues about how to cope in Denmark, Ecuador, Austria or Indonesia because they each share the implicit organisational form of one of the original four.

Table 6.2   *Types of organisation implicit in various countries*

Pyramid of people	Well-oiled machine	Village market	Family
Arab-speaking	Austria	Australia	East Africa
Argentina	Costa Rica	Britain	Hong Kong
Belgium	Finland	Canada	India
Brazil	Germany	Denmark	Indonesia
Chile	Israel	Ireland	Jamaica
Colombia	Switzerland	Netherlands	Malaysia
Ecuador		New Zealand	Philippines
France		Norway	Singapore
Greece		South Africa	West Africa
Guatemela		Sweden	
Iran		United States	
Italy			
Japan			
Korea			
Mexico			
Pakistan			
Panama			
Peru			
Portugal			
Salvador			
Spain			
Taiwan			
Thailand			
Turkey			
Uruguay			
Venezuela			
Yugoslavia			

In Hofstede's second book he produces a refinement of the uncertainty avoidance dimension: 'Confucian dynamism', or long-term versus short-term orientation. Management researchers are typically from Western Europe or the United States, with that type of cultural bias. Working with the Canadian Michael Bond, Hofstede used a Chinese value survey technique in a fresh study and uncovered a cultural variable – long-term orientation – that none of the original, western questions had reached. The highest scoring countries on this dimension were China, Hong Kong, Taiwan, Japan and South Korea. Singapore was placed ninth. Leaving out the

---

In this chapter there is not space to consider some of the problems in the worldwide use of English as the language of business, and therefore the language of luxury hotels. Here are two examples.

From the Petaling Jaya Hilton in Malaysia: 'Do not use the lift in case of fire'.

From the Chicago Grosvenor in the United States: 'Walk up one floor and down two floors for improved elevator service'.

special case of China, we see that the other five countries are those known as the 'Five Dragons' because of their dramatic rate of economic growth. As Hofstede says:

> The correlation between certain Confucian values and economic growth is a surprising, even a sensational, finding. (Hofstede 1991, p. 167)

The 'Confucian' values attached to this long-term orientation included perseverance, clearly maintained status differentials, thrift and having a sense of shame. In many ways these values are valuable for business growth, as they put social value on entrepreneurial initiative, support the entrepreneur by the willing compliance of others seeking a place in the system, encourage saving and investment and put pressure on those who do not meet objectives.

Developing organisational culture

The most penetrating analysis of organisational culture is by Schein (1985), who distinguishes between the ways in which an organisation needs to develop a culture which enables it to adapt to its changing environment (pp. 52–65) and, at the same time, build and maintain itself through processes of internal integration (pp. 65–83).

How do cultures change? How do they become consolidated? The general comment of Schein is that there are primary and secondary mechanisms, the primary mechanisms being:

(a) what leaders pay most attention to;
(b) how leaders react to crises and critical incidents;
(c) role modelling, teaching and coaching by leaders;
(d) criteria for allocating rewards and determining status; and
(e) criteria for selection, promotion and termination. (pp. 224–37)

This places great emphasis on example-setting by those in leadership roles. If the manager walks around a construction site without a hard hat, then it is unlikely that other people will regard such headgear as important. The comment about how leaders react to crises and critical incidents is interesting. At one level this is to do with reactions such as calmness or urgency, but it is also a question of what is identified by leaders as crises and critical incidents. If there is great attention paid by managers to punctuality and less to quality, then punctuality receives greater emphasis in the eyes of everyone.

The comment about coaching and teaching by leaders indicates the degree of social integration necessary between the opinion formers and those holding the opinions and producing the behaviour that those opinions shape. Research on how people learn demonstrates quite clearly that attitude formation is developed effectively by social interaction and scarcely at all by other methods. Exhortation and written instructions or assurances are likely to do little to change the culture of an organisation: working closely with people can.

The most significant reinforcement of attitudes and beliefs comes from that which is tangible and visible. What do people need to do to get a pay rise? What do you have to do to get promoted? What can lead to people being fired? Those working in and around organisations usually want the first two and try to avoid the third. If loyalty is rewarded you will get loyalty, but may not get performance. If performance is rewarded, people will at least try to deliver performance.

This line of argument by Schein presents two difficulties. First, such emphasis on 'leadership' can imply dependence on one Great Leader to whom everyone else responds. Secondly, it is too easy to confuse cultural leadership with position leadership; those who are most effective in setting the tone may not be those in the most senior posts even though they are well placed for this.

Focusing on the Great Leader also emphasises hierarchical principles of organisation, with all the drawbacks we have already seen. Organisational culture is the concern of all members and change in a culture is effective and swift only when there is wide agreement, and ownership concerning the change to be sought. Wide agreement about important aspects of culture seems to be best obtained, paradoxically, through a recognition and toleration of a legitimate plurality of views and styles on less central matters. Differences will not be resolved by the Great Leader exercising 'the right to manage', but through discussion among all parties concerned.

REVIEW TOPIC 6.6

Think of an organisation of which you are or have been a member that had a strong leader. This may not necessarily have been an employing organisation, but a school, youth club, operatic society, political association, etc.

Did the leader shape the culture?
Did the culture resist the leader?
How did the shaping or resistance manifest itself?

Elevated position in a hierarchy, though possibly helpful, is not a guarantee of effectiveness in the pursuit of, or opposition to, cultural change.

A third difficulty is an assumption, in much of the theory, that the stamp of its culture leaves an identical mark across all of an organisation. We referred above to a 'legitimate plurality of views and styles' as a counterweight to the Great Leader. In fact, we have to go further because all organisations, especially professional organisations, contain groupings each with a distinctive culture, depending on its members' views, the nature of its expertise or tasks, its history and so on. A visitor walking round the premises of any organisation notices different cultures in different areas; when this variety is respected, the culture of the organisation as a whole will be quite different from that in an organisation where such variety is suppressed.

Schein's secondary mechanisms for the articulation and reinforcement of culture are:

(a) the organisational structure;
(b) systems and procedures;
(c) space, buildings and facades;
(d) stories and legends about important events and people; and
(e) formal statements of philosophy and policy. (pp. 237–42)

This introduces a wider range of possible actions, but notice what comes last! So often we find in practice that attempts to develop aspects of culture actually begin with formal statements of policy, or that cultural inertia is attributed to the lack of such statements. The connection with structure can not be emphasised enough as a bureaucratic structure will, for instance, be the biggest single impediment to introducing a corporate culture emphasising risk-taking and personal initiative. The use of space, facades and stories appeals to the romance that is in all of us. The company logo now assumes extraordinary significance in providing a symbol of corporate identity which everyone can see, understand and share. The stories that circulate on the grapevine may be those of management incompetence or greed. On the other hand, they may be stories of initiative or dedication to duty. There may be stories only about managers in key positions, or about how X saved the day by extraordinary initiative and Y got a letter from the overseas visitor who had appreciated a small act of kindness. These are the things which shape culture and managers can influence all of them, for it is the cultural leaders who will make all of these things happen.

Without a central sense of unity, organisations are no more than a collection of people who would rather be somewhere else because they lack effectiveness and conviction in what they are doing. The effective organisation has a few central ideals about which there is a high degree of consensus and those ideals are supported and put into operation by simple rules and clear procedures. The organisation that depends principally on rules for its cohesion is in the process of decay.

Kanter (1989, pp. 361–5) believes that the demands of the future will require seven particular qualities from managers. First, the ability *to operate without relying on the might of hierarchy* behind them. Managers will have to rely on their personal capacities to achieve results rather than depending on the authority of their position.

Second will be a need *to compete in a way that enhances rather than undercuts co-operation*. This is a tall order, but the argument is that the nature of competitive striving must be to stimulate those with whom one has a working relationship, instead of trying to win the fight.

Her third quality is *a high standard of ethics*. Her reasoning follows closely from the previous point and is very similar to the old-fashioned British idea of 'a gentleman's word is his bond'. Collaborations, joint ventures and similar alliances make it necessary for people to be candid and to reveal information, but also being able to rely on partners not to violate that trust. This sounds optimistic, but the logic is clear enough.

The fourth requirement is *humility, as there will always be new things to learn.*

Fifth is *the need to develop a process focus.* How things are done will be just as important as what is to be done. There may be problems to solve that present intriguing intellectual challenges, but success lies not in being able to decide what should be done, but in being able to implement the decision: to make it happen.

The sixth suggestion is the need to be *multifaceted and ambidextrous*:

> able to work across functions and business units to find synergies that multiply value, able to form alliances when opportune but to cut ties when necessary, able to swim effectively in the mainstream and in newstreams. (Kanter 1989, p. 364)

Her final suggestion is that it is necessary to *gain satisfaction from results*: a shift of emphasis from status to contribution and from attainment of position to attainment of results.

REVIEW TOPIC 6.7

How many of Kanter's seven qualities do you have?

How appropriate are these qualities for where you are in your organisation now?

How necessary do you think each of these qualities will be in your
future career?

☐ SUMMARY PROPOSITIONS

6.1 Organisation design is occasionally a process of creating an entire organisation from scratch, but for most people it is modifying parts of an existing organisation.

6.2 Personnel officers rarely play a significant role in organisation design.

6.3 The fundamentals of organisation design are task identity and job definition, structure and decision-making complexes.

6.4 Alternative forms of structure are entrepreneurial, bureaucratic, matrix and independence. A new form of professional organisation can also be seen.

6.5 The culture of an organisation is the characteristic spirit and belief of its members, demonstrated by the behavioural norms and values held by them in common.

6.6 Corporate culture is a culture that those directing the organisation seek to create and foster in the interests of the organisation achieving its objectives.

6.7 No organisation is an island, so attempts to foster or alter corporate culture must take account not only of the intentions and expectations of those within the organisation, but also of developments in the surrounding society, both nationally and internationally.

6.8 The most significant differences in work values and attitudes between cultures can be measured on the four criteria of power distance, uncertainty avoidance, individualism and masculinity.

References

Barratt A. (1989), 'Doing business in a different culture', *Journal of European Industrial Training*, vol. 13, no. 4, pp. 28–31.

Burns, T. and Stalker, G. M. (1961), *The Management of Innovation*, London: Tavistock.

Child, J. (1984), *Organization: a guide to problems and practice*, 2nd edition. London: Harper & Row.

Deal, T. E. and Kennedy, A. A. (1982), *Corporate Cultures: the Rites and Rituals of Corporate Life*, Reading, Mass: Addison-Wesley.

Devanna, M. A. and Tichy, N. (1990), 'Creating the Competitive Organization of the 21st Century: The Boundaryless Corporation', *Human Resource Management*, vol. 29, no. 4, Winter, pp. 455–71.

Drucker, P. F. (1988), 'The Coming of the New Organization', *Harvard Business Review*, vol. 66, no. 1, January–February.

Evans, A. and Cowling, A. (1985), 'Personnel's part in organisation restructuring', *Personnel Management*, January.

Galbraith, J. R. (1977), *Organizing Design*, Wokingham: Addison Wesley.

Goffee, R. and Scase, R. (1985), *Women in Charge*, London: Allen & Unwin.

Handy, C. B. (1985, 1993), *Understanding Organizations*, 3rd and 4th editions, Harmondsworth: Penguin.

Harrison, R. (1972), 'How to describe your organization', *Harvard Business Review*, September/October.

Hofstede, G. (1980), *Culture's Consequences*, Beverly Hills, California: Sage.

Hofstede, G. (1991), *Cultures and Organizations: Software of the Mind*, London: McGraw Hill.

Kanter, R. M. (1989), *When Giants Learn to Dance*, New York: Simon & Schuster.

Lawrence, P. R. and Lorsch, J. W. (1967), *Organization and Environment*, Cambridge, Mass.: Harvard University Press.

Marglin, S. (1974), 'What Do Bosses Do?' In A. Gorz (ed.) *Division of Labour*, Hemel Hempstead: Harvester Press.

Marshall, J. (1985), 'Paths of personal and professional development for women managers', *Management Education and Developement*, vol. 16, pp. 169–79.

Milkovich, G. T. and Boudreau, J. W. (1994), *Human Resource Management*, 7th edition, Burr Ridge, Illinois: Richard D. Irwin Inc.

Moir, A. and Jessel, D. (1989) *Brain Sex*, London: Michael Joseph.

Nelson, E. (1989), 'Marketing in 1992 and Beyond', *Royal Society of Arts Journal*, vol. cxxxvi, no. 5393, April, pp. 292–304.

Olins, W. (1989), *Corporate Identity*, London: Thames & Hudson.

Poirson, P. (1989), *Personnel Policies and the Management of Men* (translated by Thierry Devisse) France: Ecole Supérieure de Commerce de Lyon.

Pugh, D. S. and Hickson, D. J. (1976), *Organisational Structure in its Context*, Farnborough: Saxon House.

Schein, E. H. (1985), *Organizational Culture and Leadership*, San Francisco: Jossey-Bass.

Tiger, L. (1970), 'The biological origins of sexual discrimination', *The Impact of Science on Society*, vol. 20, no. 1.

Van de Ven, A. H., Delbecq, A. L. and Koenig, R. (1976), 'Determinants of coordination modes within organizations', *American Sociological Review*, April.

Williamson, O. E. (1975), *Markets and Hierarchies: Analysis and Antitrust Implications*, New York: Free Press.

7 Organisational communication and systems

Without communication a business would not exist, let alone survive. Communication is the essence of organisation both as entity and as process that we have considered in earlier chapters. The mission statement, strategies, policies, procedures and drills, the organisation chart, the balance sheet, the budget, the training manual, job descriptions, appraisal forms, plans, forecasts, memoranda, briefings, contracts, statements of objectives, electronic mail, computer conferencing, presentations, conversations, meetings and interviews are all different manifestations of this one activity that holds everything together and makes things happen. In this chapter we look first at the scope of communicating in organisations, then consider in more detail the processes and the barriers to their effectiveness, before reviewing different techniques and systems.

Meaning and scope of communication

Communication involves both the giving out of messages from one person and the receiving and understanding of those messages by another or others. If a message has been given out by one person but not received or understood by another, then communication has not taken place. The methods of communicating in organisations include speech, non-verbal communication, writing, audiovisual and electronic means. These methods are considered in greater detail later in the chapter. The method used will depend on the precise message that needs to be passed on. In general, messages may contain factual information, opinion and emotion.

In organisations a wide variety of messages will need to be communicated. Some messages are individually specific – for example, a supervisor giving feedback on a completed task or expressing concern at continued lateness; or an individual explaining their future career plans. Others are team or group oriented – for example, current group objectives; a change in team structure or office accommodation; or sharing action plans for the week. A third group of messages are concerned with all employees – for example, quarterly business results, new company image, revised payment system; or expressions of employee confusion over a new organisational programme or change being introduced. In this chapter we will concentrate on communication relevant to all or groups of employees. Individually specific communication is dealt with elsewhere in this book, for example in the chapters on performance management, appraisal, discipline and grievance.

From the above examples it is clear that organisational communication is not only top-down, but also from the bottom-up and lateral. All aspects are important and all are included in this chapter. The key to success of many organisational communications systems is the extent to which they provide for two-way, or three-way, communication rather than simply one-way traffic.

Within any organisation there are both formal and informal channels of communication. The formal channels are those that are officially acknowledged and approved, such as circulars, meetings, posters, and so on. Informal channels of communication can either facilitate or inhibit communication through official channels (Glen 1975). Foy (1983) argues that in order to improve corporate communication the grapevine should not be eliminated, but an effort should be made to ensure that official communication channels match the informal ones. The informal channels of communication are not officially acknowledged but are, however, often privately acknowledged and approved and sometimes deliberately used: government 'leaks' are a good example. In other organisations the same type of leak may be used from time to time to see what the reaction would be to a proposed management initiative, so that the initiative can be modified before being made official. It is a form of consultation that can save face by avoiding a formal espousal of a strategy that is shown to be unsatisfactory.

Within organisations the existence of such informal channels of communication often encourages managers to communicate officially, as the information will in any case be passed on. On these grounds it may be assumed that an increase in official communication would result in a decrease in the unofficial informal communication. Interestingly, this has been shown not to be the case and that increasing official communication results in increasing informal communication. Effectiveness in communication usually requires a careful blend of both formal and informal channels, with formal statements of fact and reasons, supported by informal explanations and interpretations.

In this chapter we will concentrate on information which was deliberately intended to be communicated, and which is backed up by an explicit system of communication.

Purposes of communication in organisation

Greenbaum (1974) described four major purposes of organisation communication. He identified *regulation* purposes where communication is intended to ensure that employee behaviour is consistent and congruent with the goals of the organisation. Secondly, *innovation* purposes whereby the organisation seeks to change the way that things are done. Thirdly, *integration* purposes where the aim is to encourage employees to identify with the organisation and raise morale. And, lastly, *information* purposes which involve the passing on of factual information which employees will need in order to do their jobs. Clutterbuck and Dearlove (1993) offer a slightly different classification. They identify *task* communication which is specific information needed to do the job; *educational* or *context* communication, which is the background information, and *motivational* communications. In order to achieve some of these purposes communications may well be designed to be persuasive, for example safety campaigns. There is, however, an increasing emphasis on upwards communications and in particular a focus on involving employees as in, for example, suggestion schemes, focus groups and quality circles (although revitalised circles as part of a total quality management (TQM) approach may have a different emphasis). We look in more detail at focus groups towards the end of this chapter and return to the other approaches in Part 6 on Involvement.

Upwards communication is important for the following reasons

1. It helps managers to understand employees' concerns.
2. It helps managers to keep more in touch with employees' attitudes and values.
3. It can alert managers to potential problems.
4. It can provide managers with workable solutions to problems.
5. It can provide managers with the information that they need for decision making.
6. It helps employees to feel that they are participating and contributing and can encourage motivation, and commitment to future courses of action.
7. It provides some feedback on the effectiveness of downwards communication, and ideas on how it may be improved.

McClelland (1988) suggests that the following factors, among others, are important for successful upwards communication: access to senior managers, sufficient business understanding, an atmosphere of trust with no fear of reprisals and sufficient feedback.

Lateral communication is important, among other reasons, for ensuring coordination of activities and goals.

REVIEW TOPIC 7.1

In your organisation:

1. What formal channels of lateral communication are there?
2. How effective are these? Why?
3. Suggest ways in which lateral communication could be improved.

Organisational communication is also directed at the outside world as well as employees. Company newspapers, for example, are often partly aimed at informing employees of what's going on in the company, but also seen as a way to project an image to the outside world. Carlisle (1982) notes this function as a key part of organisational communication.

The process of communicating: the telecommunications analogy

A convenient and well-established method of approaching and understanding communication is to draw the analogy with telecommunications. Here one examines the human process by comparing it with the electronic process. Figure 7.1 shows how the communication process begins with some abstract idea or thought in the mind of the person seeking to convey information. The first step in the communication process is for the central nervous system of that person to translate the abstractions through the vocal organs into speech patterns or into some form of written or other visual message. If the channel of communication is speech, then the patterns of speech travel through the air as sound waves to be received by the ears and conveyed as nervous impulses to the brain. If the channel of communication is visual, as in written communications, the message is either manually, mechanically or electronically transferred and is received by the eyes and conveyed again by nervous impulses to the brain.

The message is unscrambled in the central nervous system of the receiver, which then instructs the listener to understand; the final stage comes when there is registration and the receiver understands.

Through these various stages of translation from the mind of one to the mind of the other there is a number of points at which error is possible, and even likely. It is almost impossible to know whether the abstract idea in the mind of one person has transferred itself accurately to the mind of the other. One essential element in the whole process is feedback. This completes the circuit so that there is some indication from the listener that the message has been received and understood. It is probable that the feedback response will give some indication to the transmitter of the quality of the message that has been received. If the transmitter expects a reaction of pleasure and the feedback received is a frown, then it is immediately known that there is an inaccuracy in the picture that has been planted in the mind of the receiver, and the opportunity arises to identify the inaccuracy and correct it.

A further element in the communication process is that of 'noise'. This is used as a generic term to describe anything that interferes in the transmission process: inaudibility, inattention, physical noise and so forth. The degree to which some noise element is present will impair the quality of both transmission and feedback.

More recent analysis of the communication process has led to a greater understanding of the setting in which communication takes place, so that now perhaps we focus more on understanding the process and the activity of receiving and interpreting information than we do on the activities involved in transmitting information. Shoveller (1987) lists no fewer than twenty-four reasons why communications in organisations may fail. These range from people failing to accept the responsibility to communicate to lack of interest on behalf of the recipient.

Drucker (1970) has described the four fundamentals of communication as: (1) perception; (2) expectation; (3) involvement; and (4) not information. Here Drucker is emphasising that it is the recipient who communicates. The traditional

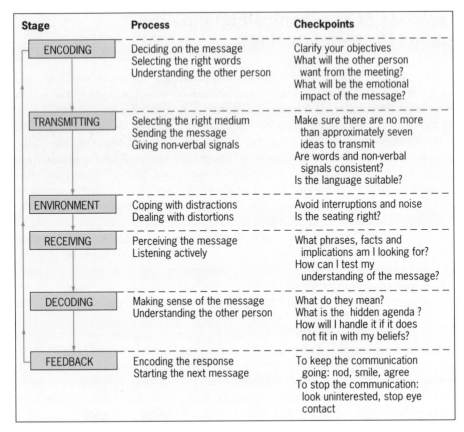

Stage	Process	Checkpoints

ENCODING	Deciding on the message
	Selecting the right words
	Understanding the other person
		Clarify your objectives
		What will the other person
		  want from the meeting?
		What will be the emotional
		  impact of the message?

TRANSMITTING	Selecting the right medium
	Sending the message
	Giving non-verbal signals
		Make sure there are no more
		  than approximately seven
		  ideas to transmit
		Are words and non-verbal
		  signals consistent?
		Is the language suitable?

ENVIRONMENT	Coping with distractions Dealing with distortions	Avoid interruptions and noise Is the seating right?

RECEIVING	Perceiving the message
	Listening actively
		What phrases, facts and
		  implications am I looking for?
		How can I test my
		  understanding of the message?

DECODING	Making sense of the message Understanding the other person	What do they mean? What is the hidden agenda ? How will I handle it if it does not fit in with my beliefs?

FEEDBACK	Encoding the response
	Starting the next message
		To keep the communication
		  going: nod, smile, agree
		To stop the communication:
		  look uninterested, stop eye
		  contact

Figure 7.1   The process of communication (Torrington *et al.* 1985: used with the permission of the Institue of Personnel Management)

communicator only 'utters'. Unless someone hears, there is no communication, only noise. The utterer does not communicate, but only makes it possible or difficult for the recipient to perceive.

Barriers to communication

It is the listener or reader who will determine the extent to which the message is understood. What we hear, see or understand is shaped very largely by our own experience and background so, for example, instead of hearing what people tell us, we hear what our minds tell us they have said – and the two may be different. There are various ways in which expectation determines communication content and a number of these ways of determination can impair the accuracy of message trans-mission. They act as 'noise', interfering both with transmission and feedback. We will look at some of the principal difficulties.

The frame of reference

Few of us change our opinions alone. We are likely to be influenced by the opinions developed within the group with which we identify ourselves: the reference group. If a particular group of people hold certain values in common, individual members of that group will not easily modify their values unless and until there is a value shift through the group as a whole. This is perhaps most apparent in the relative intractability of opinions relating to political party allegiance. There are certain clearly identifiable social class groupings who tend to affiliate to particular political parties; and a change in that affiliation by an individual is rare and difficult. Managers frequently direct to an individual a message, request, instruction or rebuke which would find a more likely response if it were mediated through a representative of the group of employees rather than being directed at an individual. An interesting example of this is the way in which safety campaigns (Strauss and Sayles 1972) are mounted, where the attempt is usually by the use of slogans and posters in order to persuade individual employees about the importance of safe working practices and similar aspects of behaviour rather than negotiating a change of behaviour through group representatives.

Whenever a matter is being discussed, the people among whom it is being considered will view it from their particular personal frame of reference. Where the frames of reference of transmitter and receiver differ widely, there may be substantial difficulties in accurate transmission of messages and even greater difficulties in ensuring that the response of the receiver is that which the transmitter intended.

The stereotype

An extreme form of letting expectation determine communication content is stereotyping, where we expect a particular type of statement or particular type of attitude from a stereotype of a person. It is, for instance, quite common for the English to expect certain types of behaviour and intention from the Irish ('never stop talking and always ready for a fight'). Equally, there is a stereotype expectation about the Scots, that they will be mean or at least extremely careful with their money. People also have stereotypes of certain office holders. There is a widespread stereotype of shop stewards which shows them as being militant, politically extreme in one, and only one, direction, unreasonable, unintelligent and obstructive. Equally, there are widespread stereotypes of different types of manager and for some people there is a stereotype of managers as a whole. One of the greatest difficulties in achieving equal opportunities at work is the challenging of deeply held stereotypes about men and women. Stereotypes about women include the view that they are unwilling to be away from home due to family commitments, that they do not want to rise too high in the hierarchy and that they will invariably leave to have children. Men, on the other hand, are often seen as career-driven and intent on promotion. There are also stereotypes relating to age, such as an older person being seen as unable to stand the pace, no longer able to think quickly and unwilling to change.

The effect of these stereotypes in communication matters is that the person who encounters someone for whom they have a stereotype will begin hearing what the person says in the light of the stereotype held.

Cognitive dissonance

Another area of difficulty, which has been explored extensively by Festinger (1957) and others, is the extent to which people will cope successfully with information inputs that they find irreconcilable in some particular way. If someone receives information that is consistent with what they already believe they are likely to understand it, believe it, remember it and take action upon it. If, however, they receive information that is inconsistent with their established beliefs, then they will have genuine difficulty in understanding, remembering and taking action. This is because one of the ways of dealing with the discomfort of dissonance is to distort the message so that what they hear is what they want to hear, what they expect to hear and can easily understand rather than the difficult, challenging information that is being put to them.

The halo or horns effect

A slightly different aspect of expectation determining communication content is the halo or horns effect, which causes the reaction of receivers of information to move to extremes of either acceptance or rejection. When we are listening to someone in whom we have confidence and who has earned our trust we may be predisposed to agree with what they say because we have placed an imaginary halo around their head. Because of our experience of their trustworthiness and reliability we have an expectation that what they say will be trustworthy and reliable. On the other hand, if we have learned to distrust someone, then what we hear them say will be either ignored or treated with considerable caution. Perhaps the most common example of this is the reaction that people have to the leaders of political parties when they appear on television.

Semantics and jargon

One difficulty about transferring ideas from one person to another is that ideas cannot be transferred because meaning cannot be transferred – all the communicators can use as their vehicle is words or symbols, but unfortunately the same symbols may suggest different meanings to different people. The meanings are in the hearers rather than the speakers and certainly not in the words themselves. A simple example of this is 'quite ill' which could have a variety of weightings according to how it was heard and the circumstances in which the comment was made.

The problem of jargon is where a word or a phrase has a specialised meaning that is immediately understandable by the cognoscenti, but meaningless or misleading to those who do not share the specialised knowledge. The Maslovian hierarchy of human needs is by now quite well known in management circles. On one occasion a lecturer was describing the ideas that were implicit in this notion and was rather surprised some months later in an examination paper to see that one of the students had heard not 'hierarchy' but 'high Iraqui'. The unfamiliarity of the word 'hierarchy' had been completely misinterpreted by that particular receiver, who had imposed her own meaning on what she heard because of the need to make sense of what it was that she received.

Another interesting example was in a school of motoring, where for many years trainee drivers were given the instruction 'clutch out' or 'clutch in', which nearly always confused the trainee. Later the standard instruction was altered to 'clutch down' or 'clutch up'.

	Sender	Recipient	Social/environmental
Barriers in sending a message	Unaware message needed Inadequate information in message Pre-judgements about message Pre-judgements about recipient		
Barriers to reception		Needs and anxieties Beliefs and values Attitudes and opinions Expectations Pre-judgements Attention to stimuli	Effects of other environmental stimuli
Barriers to understanding	Semantics and jargon Communication skills Length of communication Communication channel	Semantic problems Concentration Listening abilities Knowledge Pre-judgements Receptivity to new ideas	
Barriers to acceptance	Personal characteristics Dissonant behaviour Attitudes and opinions Beliefs and values	Attitudes, opinions and prejudices Beliefs and values Receptivity to new ideas Frame of reference Personal characteristics	Interpersonal conflict Emotional clashes Status differences Group frame of reference Previous experience of similar interactions
Barriers to action	Memory and retention Level of acceptance	Memory and attention Level of acceptance Flexibility for change of attitudes, behaviour, etc. Personal characteristics	Conflicting messages Actions of others Support/resources

Figure 7.2 The main barriers to effective communication

Not paying attention and forgetting

The final combination of problems to consider here is first the extent to which people do not pay attention to what is being said or to what they see. There is a human predilection to be selective in attention. There are many examples of this, perhaps the most common being the way in which a listener can focus attention on a comment being made by one person in a general babble of sound by a group of people. This is complicated by the problem of noise, which we have already considered, but it has the effect of the listener trying very hard to suppress all signals other than the particular one that they are trying to pick up.

The rate at which we forget what we hear is considerable. We have probably forgotten half the substance of what we hear within a few hours of hearing it, and no more than 10 per cent will remain after two or three days. Figure 7.2 provides a summary of the main phases in communication and the barriers to effectiveness.

> ### REVIEW TOPIC 7.2
>
> When a computer system is designed in-house, analysts from the computer services department will liaise with members of the user department. Why is the computer system that results from this rarely what the user department wanted?

Ways of communicating in organisations

As discussed at the beginning of this chapter, there is a number of communication media: speech, non-verbal communication, writing, audiovisual and electronic means. Using each medium there is a variety of methods of communication which can be employed in organisations. A summary of communication media and the main methods of organisational communication are found in Table 7.1. Some methods are appropriate only for downwards communication, such as films and posters, other methods are suitable only for upwards communication, such as suggestion schemes. Many methods, however, are suitable for both downwards and upwards communication as well as for lateral communication. The choice of communication method will depend not only on the direction of the communication but also on the specific nature of the message to be communicated. Notifying employees about a reorganisation which directly affects them would not be best communicated solely via an official memo. Many messages, however, are best transmitted by the use of more than one communication medium. Company rules, for example, might most effectively be communicated verbally; communication on an induction course supported by a written summary for employees to take away as a reminder. Company performance may well be written about in the company newspaper, but may also be displayed diagrammatically via a poster or on the notice board. As a general rule, messages are more successfully communicated if more than one communication medium is used.

If more than one medium is used it is imperative that each message reinforces the other, and that conflicting messages are avoided. Variety is another important factor when choosing a communication method. If any particular channel of communication is overloaded, this may result in escape, queueing, loss of quality, delegation or prioritising. If, for example, a company tries to communicate too many messages by means of posters, then employees may escape by ceasing to read any posters, or not read them properly, and so on. If a communication channel is overused it becomes less effective, and some authors have noted the danger of a general communications overload. For a full description of all the different methods of communication, see Bland (1980). We do not have the space here to review all the different methods of communication within the work organisation, but we will discuss team briefing in some depth and then briefly cover objective setting cascades, focus groups, staff surveys and customer surveys.

Team briefing

Team briefing is a method of face-to-face communication in groups of about 10–20 employees. The leader of the group provides up to date organisational information, with explanation and rationale, and group members are given an opportunity to ask

Table 7.1   *Different methods of communicating within organisations*

Used mainly for communication	Downwards	Upwards	Laterally
Medium			
Written	×	×	×
Official paperwork	×		×
Info. bulletins	×		
Newsletters/house journals	×		×
Company newspapers	×		×
Company reports	×		
Objective setting cascade	×		
Employee reports	×		
Notice boards	×		
Manuals	×		×
Training handouts	×		×
Suggestion scheme		×	
Attitude survey		×	
Customer surveys			×
Speech			
Mass meetings	×		
Meetings of reps.	×		×
Departmental meetings	×	×	×
Inerdepartmental meetings	×		×
Briefing groups	×	×	
Focus groups		×	
Formal presentations	×		
Conferences/seminars	×		×
'Open door' policy		×	
Audiovisual			
Slides	×		
Tape-slides	×		
Film strips	×		
Film	×		
Television/video	×		
Audio tape	×		
Company radio	×		×
Posters/flip chart/blackboard	×		
Video conferencing	×		×
Electronic			
Electronic mail	×	×	×
CBT	×		
Non-verbal			
Present during any communication via speech and some audiovisual communications			

questions. Townley (1989) suggests that team briefing is probably the most systematic method of providing top-down information to employees. It is a method of communication pioneered by the Industrial Society, particularly John Garnett, and has been encouraged in some form since the mid-1960s.

In 1975 a British Institute of Management (BIM) survey established that 51 per cent of firms regularly used team briefing; by 1986 Millward and Stevens reported that 62 per cent of organisations contacted in the Second Workplace Industrial Relations Survey used team briefing. Marchington, Wilkinson and Ackers (1993) in smaller scale research reported team briefing in 19 of 25 organisations that were contacted. Team briefing is adopted to improve communications with the workforce and to gain the advantages of upwards and downwards communication (p. 135). The Industrial Relations Review and Report comments that organisations introduce team briefing: 'as a means of communicating with their employees, improving employee attitudes and increasing their involvement at work' (Industrial Relations Review and Report, 4 February 1986, p. 2).

Team briefing is often seen as a way of encouraging employee commitment to the organisation, particularly to major organisational change, by providing the reasons behind intended changes and an opportunity for employees to ask questions. Marchington (1987) also suggests other reasons behind the growth of team briefing: employers' desire to avoid industrial action by trade unions by channelling conflict; increasing expectations of employees to have more influence over their lives at work; and legislation requiring employers to develop employee involvement, such as the 1982 Employment Act, are all mentioned. Team briefing also provides other potential advantages, which include the strengthening of the supervisor's role and the discouragement of reliance on shop stewards and informal networks. This is because in the team briefing system the shopfloor workers will be briefed as a group by their supervisor. In particular, Marchington suggests, it enhances the supervisors' reputation as the providers of information and reinforces their role as being accountable for team performance.

The type of information that is transmitted in briefing groups includes management information, sales figures, progress made, policies and the implications of all these for the workers involved. It is critical that the information passed on is made relevant to those who will hear it.

The team briefing system works from the top downwards in gradual stages: it is suggested that these stages do not exceed four. The system starts with a board meeting, or meeting of executives, and this is followed by briefing groups being held at the next level down, using as their base briefing notes issued by the first meeting, but adding any other information that may be relevant at this level. The last level of briefing group is the level of the supervisor or first-line manager briefing the shopfloor workers. Briefing notes from the next level of briefing group are used here, together with local information. It is usually suggested that those who are 'briefers' and lead the briefing group should, between meetings, make notes of any items of importance that should be included in the next meeting. Meetings are held at intervals varying from fortnightly to quarterly, depending on the circumstances, but it is important that meetings are arranged well in advance so that they are clearly seen as part of the structure. Many organisations have a regular interval between meetings.

Training is important for all those who take part in briefing groups, and particularly for those who will act as briefers, as they may be unused to dealing with groups as opposed to individuals. The success of team briefing is heavily dependent on the skills of the briefer.

Briefing groups are not intended to replace other channels of communication but to supplement them, and urgent matters should of course be dealt with immediately and not saved for the next team briefing session (Industrial Relations Review and Report 1986). However, the potential importance of briefing groups in the whole communications structure is exemplified by a comment from Mike Judge of Talbot Motors (in Romano 1984): 'Team briefing is the cornerstone of our communications policy'. Some guidelines on team briefing are found in Figure 7.3.

There can be difficulties, however, in establishing a team briefing system. Marchington (1987) notes that team briefing is 'managerial in tone' and is concerned with reinforcing 'managerial prerogative', and can therefore be seen by the trade unions as a way of weakening their power. He goes on to comment that team briefing stands most chance of success either where there is little or no union organi-

---

Team briefing should be:

Held at regular intervals and not just at times of crisis

Brief, ideally lasting no longer than 30 minutes

Led by the immediate foreman or supervisor of the workgroup

Face-to-face and not reduced to a series of circulars and memos

Structured to cover – progress: how are we doing
                    people: who is coming and going
                    policy: any changes affecting the team
                    points: for further action

Monitored to assess their success or failure

- -

How team briefing works:

1. The briefer collects information relating to progress, people, policy and points for action in preparation for the meeting

2. A few days before the meeting he prepares a local brief which is checked by his manager

3. Following a board meeting, for example, three or four relevant items are typed and sent to briefers at the next level

4. Directors meet with their teams and any questions which can not be answered immediately are noted and answered within 48 hours. In addition to local information, the brief will have explained the items passed down from the board

5. This process continues down the line, ensuring there is a local brief and that management points have been included

6. The majority of people should be briefed at the same time and the number of levels through which information passes should be no more than four

7. After meetings, briefers should find and feedback answers to unanswered questions. Absentees should be briefed on their return

Figure 7.3   Guidelines for team briefing (Romano 1984, p. 40). Reproduced with permission of Findlay Publications Ltd.

sation, or where the union is well established and supported by the company with good channels of communication. The prognosis is not good where there has been previous union conflict or mistrust. In 1993 he found that customised systems were more effective than those bought 'off the peg', and that briefing was more effective where it was consistent with other management practices. He also reported that less than 20 per cent of employees said that it improved their commitment to the organisation, 66 per cent felt that it had not changed their understanding of management decisions and 40 per cent said that it did not lead to an increase in information received.

Beaumont (1993) reports on a team briefing pilot study in the public sector and discovered that there was little employee participation at the sessions. On surveying employees he found that they felt there was overlap between team briefing and the in-house newspaper, that they felt the decisions had already been made and that some items were held back rather than being disclosed.

Objective-setting cascades

Objective-setting cascades are frequently used to communicate the mission and strategic objectives of the organisation to the whole organisation. The purpose is to ensure that all employees can then pull in the same direction, and have something to guide their priorities. To make the organisational mission and strategic objectives more useable they are normally translated into strategic objectives for each level in the organisation, as shown in Figure 7.4. The organisation's strategic objectives determine objectives at the functional level, which in turn determine objectives at the department level, which in turn determine objectives at the group level, which in turn determine objectives at the team level. In theory, if all parts of the organisation achieve their strategic objectives then the strategic objectives at the organisational level will have been achieved.

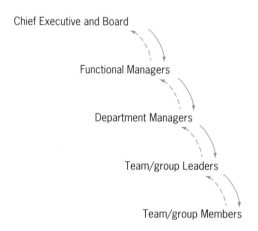

Figure 7.4 Example of an objective setting cascade

The effectiveness of the cascade is partly determined by the way in which the objectives are communicated. If this is done in a one-way top-down manner, with objective being imposed, the results may well be different from using a two-way approach where each level 'offers up' its own objectives in response to higher level objectives.

A further option is for the team leader, for example, to set objectives jointly with their team rather than carrying out this task independently. This allows the opportunity to gain commitment to the objectives via employee involvement.

Focus groups

Focus groups are an increasingly popular way for Chief Executives and the senior team to gather grounded information from all levels in the organisation, rather than from the senior managers with whom they normally communicate. They are usually organised on a departmental basis with the Chief Executive meeting with around twenty employees representing all levels in the department. The focus is on how this group see the organisation; what from their perspective are the strengths and weaknesses; what are the difficulties and opportunities and how can the difficulties be overcome and the opportunities be seized.

Customer feedback systems

Customer feedback systems are a particularly good way of encouraging lateral communication within the organisation. They apply especially to departments who service a wide range of other departments – for example, computer services, site services, personnel – although all departments can identify some internal customers. The focus is on what do we do well, what could be improved and how we could improve. Most feedback systems are paper-based, although some will be face to face.

Staff surveys

Staff surveys are mainly carried out anonymously via questionnaires, although sometimes interviews are held between staff members and an external agency so anonymity can still be maintained. They are a systematic means of collecting the views of employees and Farnham (1993) suggests that they can be used to diagnose organisational problems; assess the effects of change; compare attitudes pre- and post-changes; gather feedback on management action, plans and policies; and identify collective concerns.

What do you think would be the most effective way(s) of communicating the following in a non-unionised organisation with 3000 employees:

1. Instructions from the computer services department on how to use the new computer system.
2. Sales targets for the forthcoming year.
3. Plans to relocate to a new plant five miles away.
4. New absence and holiday reporting procedures.

SUMMARY PROPOSITIONS

7.1 Communication is the flow of information through the organisation structure that can produce understanding and action, but may produce mistrust and inefficiency.

7.2 Formal communication is supported by informal communication, and managerial use of both systems has to be kept in balance.

7.3 Effective communication is multilateral and 'bottom-up', not simply 'top-down'.

7.4 Barriers to communication include the frame of reference, stereotyping, cognitive dissonance, the halo or horns effect, semantics, jargon and not paying attention or forgetting.

References

Beaumont, P. B. (1993), *Human Resource Management: Key Concepts and Skills*, London: Sage.

Bland, M. (1980), *Employee Communication in the 1980s: A personnel manager's guide*, London: Kogan Page.

Carlisle, H. M. (1982), *Management: Concepts, Methods and Applications,* (2nd edn), Chicago: Science Research Associates Ltd.

Clutterbuck, D. and Dearlove, D. (1993), *Raising the Profile: Marketing the HR Function*, London: Institute of Personnel Management.

Drucker, P. (1970), 'What communication means', *Management Today*, March.

Farnham, D. (1993), *Employee Relations*, London: Institute of Personnel Management.

Festinger, L. (1957), *A Theory of Cognitive Dissonance*, Stanford, California: Stanford University Press.

Foy, N. (1983), 'Networkers of the world unite', *Personnel Management*, March.

Glen, F. (1975), *The Social Psychology of Organizations*, Essential Psychology Series, London: Methuen.

Greenbaum, H. W. (1974), 'The audit of organisational communications', *Academy of Management Journal*, pp. 739–54.

Industrial Relations Review and Report (1986), *Team Briefing: Practical steps in employee communications*, IRRR, 4 February.

Marchington, M. (1987), 'Employee participation'. In B. Towers (ed.) *A Handbook of Industrial Relations Practice*, London: Kogan Page.

Marchington, M., Wilkinson, A. and Ackers, P. (1993), 'Waving or drowning in participation', *Personnel Management*, March.

McClelland, V. A. (1988), 'Communication: Upward communication: Is anyone listening?' *Personnel Journal*, June.

Millward, N. and Stevens, M. (1986), *The Second Workplace Industrial Relations Survey, 1980–1984*, Aldershot: Gower.

Romano, S. (1984), 'Shopfloor briefing: Talbot proves its value', *Works Management*, April.

Shoveller, S. E. (1987), 'A problem of communications', *Work Study*, June.

Strauss, G. and Sayles, L. R. (1972), *Personnel: The Human Problems of Management*, Englewood Cliffs, NJ: Prentice Hall.

Torrington, D. P., Weightman, J. D. and Johns, K. (1985), *Management Methods*, London: Institute of Personnel Management.

Townley, B. (1989), 'Employee communication programmes'. In K. Sisson (ed.) *Personnel Management in Britain*, Oxford: Basil Blackwell.

Withers, M. and Hurley, B. (1990), 'Grants grows its own grapevine', *Personnel Management*, November.

8 Information

'I was making decisions by the seat of my pants on the basis of information on one side of A4', a personnel manager told one of the authors, about how his life was before installing a personnel computer system. In this chapter we will look briefly at just how the computer has changed the nature of personnel information.

The opposite problem is the personnel manager who is suffocating under a surfeit of information which has been collected with no real purpose in mind. This means that we need to concentrate on the reasons for collecting information and how it can be used to improve the organisation, as well as what to collect and how to collect it. Four main types of personnel information are explored – individual operating information; strategic aggregate information; and information on the effectiveness and efficiency of personnel systems and of the personnel function. We conclude by reviewing the implications of the Data Protection Act.

A computer revolution?

From the early 1980s there has been a gradual increase in the number of personnel departments using a computer system, and early expectations centred not only on increased efficiency, but also a change in personnel processes and the personnel role in the organisation (see, for example, Kinnie and Arthurs 1993). Such changes have only been evident in a very small number of organisations who use the computer in a sophisticated way (Hall and Torrington 1989). There is much evidence to show that personnel functions do not develop the potential of the computer (Kinnie and Arthurs 1993).

Barriers to extensive computer use may be:

- the use of a centrally imposed system which does not meet local needs;
- problems of inadequate access;
- a system which does not operate in real time;
- a system which does not provide for on-line enquiries;
- a system which does not provide for flexible enquiries;
- lack of integration between systems holding different pieces of personnel information; and

- lack of training, although this did not appear to be the case in the Kinnie and Arthurs survey.

Acquiring a system which meets the department's needs and to which staff are committed is clearly a critical first step. Robertson (1992) describes a helpful approach to designing and installing a new computer system which was used in the Prudential Insurance Company.

REVIEW TOPIC 8.1

- If you do not use a computer in the personnel department, how could a computer be used to meet the department's needs? What specific objectives would you set for a computer system?
- If you do use a computer in the personnel department, how is the computer used to meet the department's needs? What needs are not being met? Why not? What specific objectives would you set for a new or improved system?

In spite of these barriers, personnel people are certainly becoming more familiar with the computer's contribution to personnel information and in writing the bulk of this chapter we have assumed such facilities as:

- producing employee listings according to specified criteria;
- producing a wide range of aggregate statistics in a variety of forms, including matrices, graphs and charts; and
- administrative/operational systems which produce required letters and provide residue data of transactions and timings.

It is the ability to produce such information within minutes or hours rather than days or months that has been the real benefit of the computer so far. We do not discuss the use of different types of systems. For further information on employee database systems – the foundation of most personnel information – see Gallagher (1986) or Norman and Edwards (1984). For further details on administrative systems see, for example, Ive (1982), and for the use of expert systems, for example, Glover (1988). The conference papers resulting from the annual Computers in Personnel Conferences are an excellent source of information and ideas.

Personnel information: a model

The framework in Figure 8.1 shows different types of personnel information that are helpful to the organisation. *Individual information* is an employee's individual record which would include personal information and job and employment history.

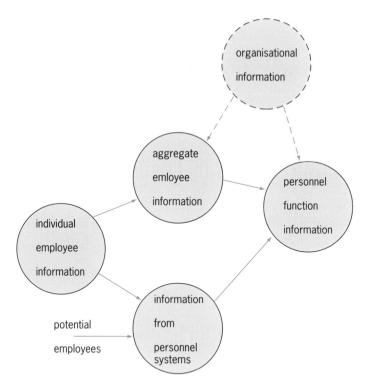

Figure 8.1 A framework for personnel information

This information is helpful as a factual record of past events which can assist operational decisions in respect of the employee, such as a promotion decision based on employee performance and potential ratings, job experiences, qualifications, skills and abilities.

Individual information about each employee is the foundation of *aggregate employee information* and this provides a basis for strategy and policy decisions which would apply across departments, functions or the whole organisation. Aggregate information can also be analysed against organisational information to identify the effectiveness of the workforce as a whole.

Information from *personnel systems and activities* can also provide aggregate information about employees or potential employees; for example, an ethnic breakdown of all applicants to the organisation. It can also provide information about the workload which has been undertaken and the speed and timing of different activities. An example would be volume and pace of recruitment activity over a specified period. This information is helpful for staffing levels, and personnel standards and service agreements with different departments or the whole organisation. It can be helpful in identifying targets or benchmarks towards which the function can strive.

The *information on personnel function* is derived from data about personnel systems, aggregate employee data and other organisational data. Together this will provide information about the function's efficiency, particularly in financial terms. An example here would be personnel staffing ratios and cost benefit analyses of training activity.

In addition there exists *external information* which can be used for comparative purposes.

We will now take each one of these information areas and explore them in more detail

Individual employee information

Individual employee data chiefly comprises information gleaned from the application form together with employment history that has built up since the employee joined. Areas covered usually include the following.

- Basic personal and contract details.
- Training/development/education details.
- Appraisal details/career progression.
- Payment and pension details.
- Fringe benefits.
- Discipline/grievance details.
- Health/safety/welfare details.
- Absence details.
- Termination details, e.g. reason for leaving.

Information relating to these areas may be stored in varying amounts of depth depending on the needs of the particular department, as illustrated in Table 8.1.

Table 8.1 *Individual information stored in a computerised personnel information system: an example showing various levels of information that may be stored*

Increasing depth of information				
Definition of level of depth	**Level 1**	**Level 2**	**Level 3**	**Level 4**
Example of how definition relates to an area of personnel information; educational qualifications	Highest educational qualification	Highest educational qualification, date and subject	All educational qualifications since leaving school with dates and subjects	All educational qualifications, with dates and subject for those after leaving school
Individual example	HND	HND Business Studies 1974	ONC Business Studies 1972 HND Business Studies 1974	5 'O' Levels 1 'A' Level ONC Business Studies 1972 HND Business Studies 1974

In a multinational business unit of around 3500 employees the personnel function used a computer system which had been specified and designed for the Organisational Head Office Personnel Function. The system was helpful but not user-friendly and information was input by personnel staff daily and updated into the records on screen on a monthly basis. There was a large volume to input and only critical areas were updated, for example absence data at the expense of training details. Many departments found that they were unable to get complete and accurate information from the system that could help them in managing their staff. One department dealt with this by buying their own PC and inputting and updating all the personnel data that they required.

One of the chief users of this type of information is the individual's line manager; for example, to check previous training courses attended before agreeing to a training course request, or checking absence history where an employee has had a recent spate of absences. In many cases the line manager does not have easy access to this information either because it is stored in a folder in the personnel department, or it is on a computer system to which the line manager does not have access.

In terms of collecting information to update the file or folder it is the line manager who has current information on absence, training courses attended, appraisal results and so on, yet it is usually the personnel department who input the new data into the system.

REVIEW TOPIC 8.2

What are the respective roles of the personnel function and line managers in your organisation in relation to individual employee data?
What are the reasons for this?
What are the advantages and disadvantages of the way that the roles are divided?
How would you recommend that this situation be changed, and why?

The organisation as a whole also has an interest in individual employee data, which can be used to select individuals for promotion or lateral moves, for relocation or a secondment. If the data is on a computer system it is relatively easy to produce a list of employees who have, for example, electronic engineering skills, French as a second language, a specified performance rating and have worked for the organisation for two years or more. Individual data of a similar nature can also be transferred into a succession planning system (described in more detail in Chapter 5). Lastly individual information can be used in redundancy situations to identify a list of individuals who meet the agreed redundancy criteria.

Aggregate employee information

Aggregated employee information describes the characteristics of the current workforce. It is used at a strategic level in the planning process as described in Chapter 5, and it is also used to inform policy and design changes to improve the current position. Typical areas of information that are analysed include the following.

Skills profile.
Length of service profile.
Absence levels and costing.
Turnover levels and costing.
Age profile.
Gender profile.
Ethnic profile.
Disability profile.
Internal organisational movement.
Salary and benefits costs.

In addition aggregate employee information can be used in conjunction with organisational data to gain measures of workforce effectiveness.

We will look in more detail at some of the above analyses.

Absence analysis and costing

Huczynski and Fitzpatrick (1989) suggest three main approaches to analysing absence, which can be applied on an individual or aggregate workforce basis. For aggregate analysis *absence rate* is the number of days absence, that is when attendance would have been expected, of all employees. *Absence percentage rate* is this figure divided by the total number of actual working days for all employees over the year, multiplied by 100. This simple percentage figure is the one most often used and enables the organisation's absence level to be compared with national figures, or other organisations in the same sector.

Absence frequency rate is the number of spells of absence over the period, usually a year. Comparing this and the absence percentage rate gives critical information about the type of absence problem that the organisation is experiencing.

As well as external comparisons, absence data can be analysed by department, work group, occupation, grade and so on. In this way the analysis will highlight problem areas, and additional analysis can be used to try and identify the causes of differing levels of absence in different parts of the organisation. The data may be supplemented by information from questionnaires or interviews with employees or line managers.

The purpose of producing this information is to understand the causes and extent of absence in order to manage it effectively. So, for example, such analysis may result in a new absence policy, employee communications about the impact of absence, appropriate training for line managers, changes to specific groups of jobs and the introduction of a new type of attendance such as flextime. The information provides a base for future monitoring.

Further analysis of the data can also be used to provide guidelines to line managers in managing individual absence issues. Behrend (1978) provides a method of analysing overall absence so that it shows the absence levels of the highest 25 per cent of the workforce, and of the other three quartiles. This gives line managers an indication of how the absence level of a particular employee compares with the rest of the workforce, and can be used to provide realistic guidelines about what action managers should take when an individual's absence has reached a specific level. Figure 8.2 shows the analysis.

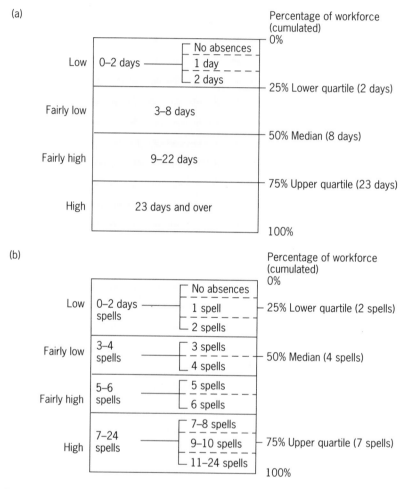

Figure 8.2   An example of the analysis of absence: (a) classification of employees by number of days lost; (b) classification of employees by number of absence spells (Behrend 1978, p. 13). Used with permission of IPD Publications.

The costing of absence needs to have a wider focus than just the pay of the absent individual. Other costs include:

- line manager costs in finding a temporary replacement or rescheduling work;
- the actual costs of the temporary employee;
- costs of showing a temporary employee what to do;
- costs associated with a slower work rate or more errors from a temporary employee; and
- costs of contracts not completed on time.

These costs can be calculated and provide the potential for productivity improvement.

Turnover analysis and costing

In Chapter 5 we looked at the ways of measuring employee turnover, so we move on now to look at its causes and costs. There is little that an organisation can do to manage turnover unless there is an understanding of the reasons for it. Information about these reasons is notoriously difficult to collect. Most commentators recommend exit interviews, but the problem here is whether the individual will feel able to tell the truth and this will depend on the culture of the organisation, the specific reasons for leaving and support that the individual will need from the organisation in the future in the form of references. Despite their disadvantages, exit interviews may be helpful if handled sensitively and confidentially – perhaps by the personnel department rather than the line manager. In addition analyses of differing turnover rates between different departments and different job groups may well shed some light on causes of turnover. Attitude surveys can also provide relevant information.

Once causes have been identified the organisation is in a position to take action. For example, if the reason for staff leaving is that higher wages are offered for similar jobs nearby then the organisation could decide to improve its wage levels. This decision could only be made after consideration of the costs of this compared with the true costs of turnover.

Hugo Fair (1992) argues that there are a wide range of costs to be taken into account when calculating turnover, and Figure 8.3 shows the process of analysis which he suggests. Other reasons for turnover might centre around lack of promotion; difficulties in relating to the line manager; change in the individual's work preferences or needs. Some of these can be improved by actions within the organisation, for example by developing career progression systems and facilitating lateral moves. However, in spite of the high cost of turnover it may not always be desirable to reduce turnover rates to the minimum level possible. Low turnover reduces promotion opportunities, limits the introduction of new blood and new ideas, and encourages the organisation to be static rather than dynamic. Turnover in some organisations can be too low with employees bound by golden handcuffs from finding a better opportunity elsewhere. These employees may stay with the organisation to maintain their living standards, but their enthusiasm and commitment to the job itself may be low.

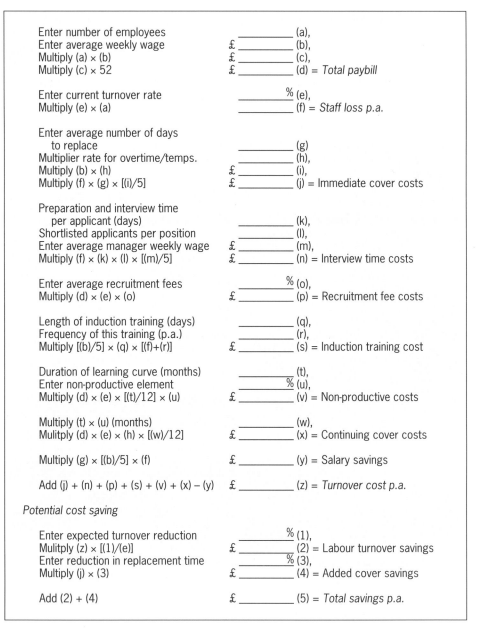

Enter number of employees	_____	(a),
Enter average weekly wage	£ _____	(b),
Multiply (a) × (b)	£ _____	(c),
Multiply (c) × 52	£ _____	(d) = *Total paybill*
Enter current turnover rate	_____ %	(e),
Multiply (e) × (a)	_____	(f) = *Staff loss p.a.*
Enter average number of days to replace	_____	(g)
Multiplier rate for overtime/temps.	_____	(h),
Multiply (b) × (h)	£ _____	(i),
Multiply (f) × (g) × [(i)/5]	£ _____	(j) = Immediate cover costs
Preparation and interview time per applicant (days)	_____	(k),
Shortlisted applicants per position	_____	(l),
Enter average manager weekly wage	£ _____	(m),
Multiply (f) × (k) × (l) × [(m)/5]	£ _____	(n) = Interview time costs
Enter average recruitment fees	_____ %	(o),
Multiply (d) × (e) × (o)	£ _____	(p) = Recruitment fee costs
Length of induction training (days)	_____	(q),
Frequency of this training (p.a.)	_____	(r),
Multiply [(b)/5] × (q) × [(f)+(r)]	£ _____	(s) = Induction training cost
Duration of learning curve (months)	_____	(t),
Enter non-productive element	_____ %	(u),
Multiply (d) × (e) × [(t)/12] × (u)	£ _____	(v) = Non-productive costs
Multiply (t) × (u) (months)	_____	(w),
Mulitply (d) × (e) × (h) × [(w)/12]	£ _____	(x) = Continuing cover costs
Multiply (g) × [(b)/5] × (f)	£ _____	(y) = Salary savings
Add (j) + (n) + (p) + (s) + (v) + (x) – (y)	£ _____	(z) = *Turnover cost p.a.*

Potential cost saving

Enter expected turnover reduction	_____ %	(1),
Mulitply (z) × [(1)/(e)]	£ _____	(2) = Labour turnover savings
Enter reduction in replacement time	_____ %	(3),
Multiply (j) × (3)	£ _____	(4) = Added cover savings
Add (2) + (4)	£ _____	(5) = *Total savings p.a.*

Figure 8.3 A sample form for costing labour turnover (Fair 1992, p. 41). Used with permission of IPD Publications.

On the basis of all the turnover information produced the organisation needs to decide on, and to target, the *optimum* turnover rate for the time being.

Equal opportunities analysis

This analysis aims to provide an organisational profile of ethnic origin, gender, age and disability. The resulting percentages from this can be compared with national and local community figures to give an initial idea of how representative the organisation is. Further analyses break these figures down to compare them by department, job category

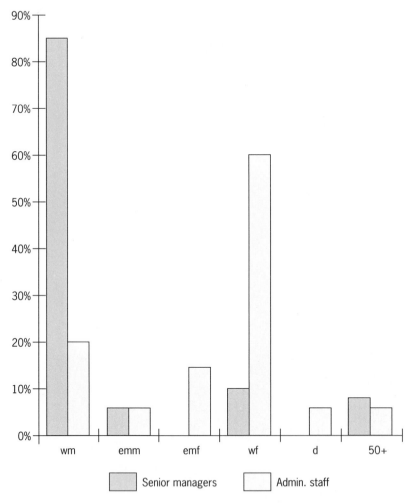

Figure 8.4 Breakdown of senior manager staff group and administrative staff group. wm, white males; emm, ethnic minority males; emf, ethnic minority females; wf, white females; d, disabled; 50+, more than fifty. Percentages of senior manager category and administrative category; each add to over 100% as there is some overlap between the groups into which they are subdivided.

and grade. It is in this type of analysis that startling differences are likely to be found, for example as shown in Figure 8.4. The information gleaned can be used to:

- question the extent and spread of disadvantaged groups in the organisation;
- identify specific barriers to a more representative spread;
- formulate appropriate policy and action plans; and
- set targets to be achieved and monitor year on year compared with these base figures.

Other analyses can be carried out to show promotion, internal moves and secondment figures for disadvantages groups compared with advantaged groups, for example white males. Further mention is made of these and the recruitment system in the following section.

The workforce and organisational performance

There are a range of analyses which can relate the contribution of the workforce to organisational performance. These relationships can be used to control headcount, measure organisational effectiveness and compare this with similar organisations. The information can also be used to communicate to employees what their contribution is to the business.

Profit per employee: one of the ratios used most often is produced by dividing annual profit by the number of employees. This is useful for monitoring improvement, but especially helpful in demonstrating to each employee the importance of cost consciousness. If an employee of an organisation employing 3000 employees realises that profit per employee is only £900 this means far more to that individual than expressing profit as £2.7m. Cost consciousness suddenly becomes important as the fragile and marginal nature of profits is demonstrated.

Turnover per employee: this is a similar ratio but using gross turnover instead of profit, which gives a much clearer idea of the volume of business and the workload of employees. Comparing this ratio to the previous ratio gives pointers to organisational efficiency and again can be used to give employees a better understanding of organisation performance, particularly when turnover is increasing and profit is decreasing. This ratio can also be used to monitor headcount to ensure that it does not rise more rapidly than the workload as expressed by turnover.

People costs: another piece of information relates to the cost of employees in relation to the total costs of production. To work this out turnover less profit (that is the cost of production) is compared with employee costs (salary plus on-costs). The percentage of production costs accounted for by employees will vary markedly according to the nature of the business. For example, in some pharmaceutical businesses people costs will account for 70 per cent of all production costs (due to a heavy emphasis on research and development) whereas in a less people intensive business, as found in other parts of the manufacturing sector, people costs may only account for around 15 per cent. Changes in the percentage of people costs over time would need to be investigated. People costs are a good way of communicating to employees just how important they are to the success of the business.

For a more detailed description of people and organisational costs see Fair (1992).

Information from personnel systems and activities

Information, including costs, can be collected from a range of personnel systems and activities, the most common areas being:

- recruitment systems;
- training activities;
- health and safety systems;
- promotions, relocations and secondments;
- succession planning systems;
- employee support and health programmes;
- assessment centres and other selection procedures; and
- administrative systems.

In this section we will briefly review a sample of systems and activities. Further details will be found in the chapter relevant to the activity itself.

Recruitment systems

Information collected from a computerised, or otherwise well documented, recruitment system may involve the following over a specified period:

- number of vacancies advertised;
- number of vacancies filled;
- number of applications;
- number of candidates selected for first interviews;
- number of candidates attended first interviews;
- number of candidates selected for tests/second interviews;
- number of candidates tested/second interviews; and
- number of offers made.

This analysis will give information on the workload of the recruitment sector. Further analysis by vacancy will give information about hard-to-find skills; accuracy of person specification; appropriateness of advertisement wording and so on. For example, *if* an advertisement for one job:

brought in 400 applications,
15 candidates attended first interview,
3 (of 8) attended tests and second interview,
2 were offered the post and none accepted,

One of the authors of this book marked 150 answers to an examination question on improving equal opportunities. There were many excellent answers describing how organisations carefully monitored all job applications at various stages – particularly in the public sector. The use to which this information was put was less impressive. Most candidates explained that nothing was done with the information. Sometimes monitoring was done using separate sheets sent along with application forms – these sheets were carefully collected, sorted and stored – but not analysed! In other organisations statistical summaries were produced but never discussed, used to inform strategy or policy, or acted upon.

then something in the recruitment process is going wrong!

Further analysis by advertising media can indicate the effectiveness of media and the cost of recruitment as shown in Chapter 12.

Organisations seriously interested in equal opportunities can develop the analysis by breaking down the numbers at each stage by ethnic origin, gender, age and disability. This form of monitoring can identify stages in the procedure where discrimination is most likely to be taking place. The information gleaned can be useful in indicating the use of different advertising media, different selection methods and training for recruiting managers. Continued monitoring and target setting can be used to improve the situation.

Recruitment data can also be broken down by speed and timings of stages which can be helpful in quantifying workload and its peaks and troughs. It can also be used to monitor service contracts with departments where time-based recruitment targets have been agreed.

Training activities

Training course information can cover:

- demand for courses;
- applications for courses;
- places booked;
- cancellations;
- actual attendance; and
- effectiveness/benefit from courses.

Effectiveness and benefit from courses is clearly the most difficult of these to define, and end of course 'happy sheets' can provide some information about specific sessions and how they might be improved, but they say little about the eventual effectiveness of the training once the participants are back on the job.

In manual jobs it may be possible to measure resulting performance by speed or error rate. In other jobs, for example management roles, resulting performance may best be measured by structured interviews with the participant and their immediate manager or through questionnaires. It is important that pre-course performance is compared with post-course performance – however, any changes will not only be due to the course itself as there may be many other intervening factors. Cost of training can be compared against performance improvement to give a cost benefit analysis. Costs amount to far more than the money equivalent of the participant's time off the job.

REVIEW TOPIC 8.3

Identifying a training course at work which runs over around one week. List and quantify all the costs involved and work out the cost per participant.

Employee health programmes

Often referred to as wellness programmes in the United States, these programmes include such activities as healthy eating and drinking promotions, no smoking campaigns, health screening, stress counselling and physical fitness facilities. The rationale behind some programmes is that the cost of the programmes is less than the cost of ill and absent employees, employee rehabilitation, employee turnover and employee replacement. Some organisations will also have more altruistic motives.

The cost of these programmes includes cost of materials, facilities, support staff and employee time off the job where appropriate. These programmes are mostly provided free of charge although there may be some small charges in relation to the use of fitness centres.

Cascio (1991) lists a range of potential outcomes of the use of such programmes which may be costed, which include absence costs, accident costs, turnover costs, productive costs, and costs of hospital visits. These outcomes look attractive to the organisation, but clearly identifying the impact of wellness programmes on these, as opposed to other factors, is no easy matter.

Information on the personnel function

A range of figures is often calculated in relation to the size and effectiveness of the personnel function. Probably the most common is the ratio between headcount in the personnel function and total organisational headcount. One use of this is to control the number of personnel staff to the size of the organisation, once a workable ratio has been identified. Typical ratios lie between 1:50 and 1:100.

Table 8.2 *Some key statistics (with their averages) for Berkshire County Council, (Burn and Thompson 1993, p. 29). Reproduced with permission of the authors.*

Personnel staff to full-time employees	1:95
Managerial/professional personnel staff to full-time employees	1:166
Salary and bonus costs of personnel department staff per organisation employee	£208
Personnel salary and bonus costs as a percentage of the total	1.5%
Overall cost of the personnel function as a percentage of overall organisation costs	1.7%
Recruitment costs per new recruit	£650
Training costs per employee year (internal and external) – private sector	£172pa

Other figures concentrate on the expenditure for which the personnel function is responsible so, for example, the operating budget of the personnel function is added to personnel staff salaries and on-costs. This figure will be monitored annually. Further analyses take this cost and divide it by the number of employees in the organisation, which will give personnel costs per employee.

Another way of reviewing personnel costs is to compare them with all other costs of the organisation. This ratio can then be monitored for changes, and as a way of assessing the productivity of the function.

Berkshire County Council have taken a serious approach to auditing the personnel function, and their approach has three stages (see Burn and Thompson 1993). The first stage is collecting data about the operation of the department compared, corporate statistics and cost effectiveness. This information is then used to identify benchmarks for the future. Some of their key statistics with averages are shown in Table 8.2. The second stage of the process assesses the satisfaction of the customers with the personnel function, using such criteria as professionalism, delivery and commitment. The third step is a check that the department operates good practice in relation to legal and professional codes of practice.

REVIEW TOPIC 8.4

Design a questionnaire to assess customer satisfaction with the personnel function in your organisation.
Who are the customers you will approach?

Confidentiality, privacy and security

Concerns about confidentiality, privacy and security of personal information have always been present but have been highlighted by the growing use of computers.

Confidentiality

Confidentiality relates to information sought, obtained or held by an organisation, the disclosure of which might be detrimental to that organisation or to the third party that supplied it.

> The guarantee given to the reference writer that everything they say will be treated in the strictest confidence is to protect the reference writer, the third party, rather than the person about whom the reference is written.

Privacy

This relates to information sought, obtained or held by an organisation about a past, present or prospective employee, the use of which might be detrimental to that employee. A Home Office document on computers and privacy suggests that there are three areas of potential danger to privacy, as follows.

1. Inaccurate, incomplete or irrelevant information.
2. The possibility of access to information by people who should not need to have it.
3. The use of information in a context or for a purpose other than that for which it was obtained.

The Data Protection Act 1984

The Data Protection Act attempts to regulate the above dangers.

When does the Data Protection Act apply?

The Act applies to organisations holding personal data. Personal data has been defined as:

> data which relates to a living individual who can be identified from the information including an expression of opinion about an individual but not any indication of the intentions of the data user in respect of that individual. (Data Protection Act, sect. 1(3))

All organisations using a computerised personnel information system have to be registered giving the sources and purposes of the information that is held.

Each purpose must be registered. Information that is held manually is not covered by the Act, only data that can be processed by automatic equipment. Users of personal data have an obligation to follow the data protection principles outlined in the Act.

Eight data protection principles
These are:

1. Personal data shall be obtained and processed fairly and lawfully.
2. Personal data shall be held only for specified purposes.
3. Personal data shall not be used or disclosed in a manner incompatible with the specified purposes.
4. Personal data shall be adequate, relevant and not excessive in relation to purpose.
5. Personal data shall be accurate and where relevant kept up to date.
6. Personal data shall not be kept for longer than necessary.
7. An individual is entitled to be informed where data are held about him or her and is entitled to access to the data and where appropriate to have the data corrected or erased.
8. Appropriate security measures should be taken against unauthorised access, alteration, disclosure or destruction, and against accidental loss or destruction.

Implications for personnel managers
In our research in 1986 we found one organisation that had used a Computerised Personnel Information System (CPIS), but had ceased to do so, partly due to worries about the Data Protection Act. Most organisations, however, felt that the Data Protection Act was going to have little effect on the way that they handled personal data. Bell comments that:

> The most significant part of the legislation for personnel managers concerns the seventh principle – the right of access to personal data by the 'data subject', in this case the employee or the applicant for a job, if details are kept on a computer or word processor. (Bell 1984)

It is in this area that personnel managers expressed most concern. Most, though, were happy for individuals to see data about themselves, and in many cases these data had been directly supplied by the individual. There was, however, a distinct tendency not to keep sensitive information on the computer. A few employers expressed concern about occupational health data as there were occasions, for example, where an employee had a terminal illness but for good reasons was not told of their condition. If such data were kept on computer, there would be no way to shield the employee from this information. A number commented that appraisal data were deliberately not kept on the system, partly due to the Data Protection Act, but also because it was already their policy to send an individual's computerised details to them each year for checking. Personnel managers often pointed to a locked drawer in their desk as the place where assessment of performance and potential data and succession planning data were kept. The Data Protection Act gives individuals the right to see any expression of opinion about themselves, but not any indication of the intentions of the data user regarding themselves. Although in many organisations appraisal records are 'open', employers are usually less keen to reveal succession planning and employee potential information. There is concern that some information regarding employee potential may be classified as an expression of opinion and, therefore, if kept on the computer, may be viewed by the individual employee. Top executives were omitted from the system in most cases.

Security

Appropriate security is necessary in order to protect both the individual, as outlined in the Act, and to protect the employer. The most common methods are the use of passwords to gain access to the data, careful positioning of VDUs and printers, regular back-up copies and the use of audit trails to log the day's transactions.

□ SUMMARY PROPOSITIONS

8.1 Too much information can be as bad as too little – the organisation needs to be clear about the purpose for collecting it.

8.2 Personnel information can be seen in four parts – individual employee information; aggregate employee information; information on personnel systems and activities and information on the contribution of the personnel function.

8.3 Personnel information can be used for operational and strategic purposes.

8.4 It is increasingly important to identify the costs and benefits of personnel activities.

8.5 The Data Protection legislation provides legal enforcement for good personnel practice in the areas of confidentiality, privacy and security.

References

Behrend, H. (1978), *How to monitor absence from work: from headcount to computer*, London: IPM.

Bell, D. (1984), 'Practical implications of the Data Protection Act', *Personnel Management*, June.

Burn, D. and Thompson, L. (1993), 'When Personnel calls in the Auditors', *Personnel Management*, January.

Cascio, W. F. (1991), *Costing Human Resources*, Boston: PWS Kent.

Callagher, M. (1986), *Computers and Personnel Management*, London: Heinemann.

Fair, H. (1992), *Personnel and Profit*, London: Institute of Personnel Management.

Glover, D. (1988), 'Expert systems'. In T. Page (ed.) *Computers in Personnel: A Generation On. The CIP 88 Conference Book*, London: Institute of Personnel Management and Institute of Management Studies.

Hall, L. A. and Torrington, D. P. (1986), 'Why not use the computer? The use and lack of computers in personnel', *Personnel Review*, vol. 15, no. 8.

Hall, L. A. and Torrington, D. P. (1989), 'How personnel managers come to terms with the computer', *Personnel Review*, vol. 18, no. 6.

Huczynski, A. A. and Fitzpatrick, M. J. (1989), *Managing Employee Absence for a Competitive Edge*, London: Pitman.

Ive, T. (1982), 'Ready made package or sharing the mainframe?' *Personnel Management*, July.

Kinnie, N. and Arthurs, A. (1993), 'Will personnel people ever learn to love the computer?' *Personnel Management*, June.

Norman, M. and Edwards, T. (1984), *Microcomputers in Personnel*, London: Institute of Personnel Management.

Page, T. (ed.) (1988), *Computers in Personnel: A generation on. The CIP 88 Conference Book*, London: Institute of Personnel Management and Institute of Management Studies.

Robertson, D. (1992), 'A Prudent review of data systems', *Personnel Management*, June.

9 Interactive skill: presentation

Every manager makes presentations. It has become an integral part of organisational life, as it may be that some people read the executive summary sheets at the beginning of reports, and some may even read the report itself, but the main mechanism for conveying ideas is the oral presentation. There are two main reasons for this.

First is the change of emphasis in organisation, that we have already considered at some length: the decline of organisation as entity with the associated rise of organisation as process, and the move away from structure towards culture. Socialisation is valued as a means of creating commitment and the oral presentation to stimulate discussion is the central method of explanation in order to get everyone on the same wavelength.

Second is the decision-making process. Some managers used to cherish the notion that there was always some correct decision lying hidden somewhere like buried treasure that could be reached either by rigorous analysis or by individual wisdom. Although the elaborate decision-making complexes described in Chapter 6 may eventually come up with the best decision they can, and although individual flair can occasionally reach a decision that is breathtaking in its originality, the critical feature of any decision is not only whether it is 'right', but how effectively it can be implemented. Effective implementation means getting people involved, so that they shape the decision and then own it and will make it happen. Presentation is a part of the process of setting a framework within which people can gradually work out the details and commit themselves to action.

Furthermore, having to make a presentation means that at least one person at a meeting is well prepared. Also all of us in contemporary television-dominated society are conditioned to respond to the impact of sound bite and its accompanying projected image. Personnel managers make presentations in all sorts of situations: induction courses, trade union negotiations, employee consultation, training programmes, explanations of company policy, representation at industrial tribunal and so forth. We have placed this chapter at this point in the book in order to emphasise the value to the personnel specialist of presentation on aspects of organisation, strategy and planning. Whatever plans you have someone has to accept and endorse them, and the personnel dimension to anything can be the hardest on which to win support through the difficulty of backing up a case with hard evidence.

'I wish we could get more impact from our personnel people when it comes to meetings of the Board. It is crucial that we get that type of input to the total decision-making process, but time after time they cock it up. The marketing people come in all flash and well-polished. They give you clear and simple messages with state-of-the-art visual aids and lots of impact. The finance people come in and are as miserable as sin, but they explain it with numbers that you can't get away from. The personnel people are woolly, wordy and don't know what they want. What's more, they bang on as if they, and they alone, have some direct line to the Almighty on what is right and wrong, implying that we're just a collection of money-grubbing bastards.'

Director of Manufacturing

Excellence in presentation is rare, even with the most elaborate of technical and professional assistance. It comes from qualities that by now you either have or have not, like mastery of language, fluency, disciplined thinking and social poise. Everyone, however, can become effective in presentation, through appreciating some of the basics, through practice and through feedback.

There is little scope for oratory in organisational life, though there are frequent attempts by individual managers to incorporate aspects of propaganda into addresses they make to groups of employees in an attempt to change their attitudes and behaviour.

More common are addresses intended to increase the knowledge and understanding of audience members, such as on a training course or at a sales presentation. This is where few are effective and many are frightened. It is the widespread fear of speaking in public that gives such power to those who seem to have conquered the fear. Considerable self-confidence comes to those who can cope with something that daunts most people they know. Too many managers regard speaking in public as something beyond them:

> Many managers, both male and female, suffer from the delusion that speaking in public is the same as a theatrical performance, or something suitable only for extroverts. This delusion often serves as a defence. The plain truth is that they fear exposure of their limitations as speakers... If a man has something worth saying, he should not only say it but also learn to say it with full effect. (Bell 1989, p. 46)

There is an old saying that beauty lies in the eye of the beholder: beauty only exists when it is seen and appreciated, so that creating a thing of beauty is creating something that will be seen as beautiful. Everything depends on the reaction of the beholder. Presentation is somewhat similar. Success lies not just in saying the right thing, but in saying it right: what matters is the reaction.

Reverting to the telecommunications analogy in Chapter 7, there may be many different receivers, all of whom have to be kept switched on and tuned in by the speaker. In selection, counselling, appraisal and discipline there is only one receiver; in training there will seldom be more than five or six and negotiations involve only small groups. Presentation will often involve dozens or hundreds of receivers.

Another important difference between this interaction and others is the length of transmission. There is less scope for two-way traffic than there is in the other situations, yet the multitude of receivers will all be operating at varying levels of efficiency. Some will be working efficiently while others are switched off. Some will be producing a decoding of the transmitted message that is quite different from what is intended. It would be unduly optimistic to say that the speaker should get all the receivers working on the same wavelength in the same way, but that should always be the objective.

This can be illustrated by examples from entertainment. As the performance at a pop concert becomes more frenzied and libidinous nearly all members of the audience will combine in a united response, with postural echoes, hands high above heads, glazed expressions and general ecstasy. Some, however, will react quite differently, sitting silent or inattentive. Even the comedian, getting a steadily rising level of laughter from the audience with every succeeding joke, will never make all the audience laugh.

The speaker in the lecture room, at the shareholders' meeting or at the sales conference will never get everyone's attention, but still needs to win over as many members of the audience as possible. As with other performances there is scope for preparation, rehearsal and careful manipulation of the physical environment to achieve the maximum effect. This is why we place great emphasis on preparation.

Preparing the presentation

Objectives

As with almost every aspect of management, the starting point is the objective. What are you aiming to achieve? What do you want the listeners to do, to think, or to feel? Note that the question is not 'What do you want to say?'; the objective is in the response of the listeners. That starting point begins the whole process with a focus on results and payoff, turning attention away from ego. It also determines tone. If your objective is to inform, you will emphasise facts. If you aim to persuade, you will try to appeal to emotion as well as to reason.

The status of the speaker

Are you the right person to deliver this message to this audience? The audience will turn up their receivers if the speaker has authority that fits the message; if not, they will turn off or not even tune in. The main determinant of appropriateness to deliver

At a British Gypsum factory in North West England the general manager called all the shop stewards together simply to announce that the toilet doors were to be painted white. The reason for this was to cope with a long-running problem with graffiti, but the members of the audience dispersed asking each other what he really meant, as it seemed inconceivable that a person in that position should call them together solely for that reason. A few days later a lowly placed chargehand announced that the factory was to be closed; the audience would not believe him and demanded corroboration.

a message is the credence the audience gives to the speaker's standing and expertise. If they see the speaker as a person with information that will be of use to them, then they will accord the necessary status and listen. If the ensuing presentation disappoints them they will not only become inattentive, they are likely to signal their disillusion with demoralising clarity. Audiences show little compunction about humiliating speakers, who assume authority with all its ritual trappings, such as standing while the audience sits, occupying special, distant space and anticipating their attention.

Another aspect of status is hierarchical. Senior members of organisations are expected to speak on important matters ('we want it from the horse's mouth'). When the level of the message does not match the level of the speaker then there will be mistrust.

Who you are and the position you occupy influences what your audience hear you say. The small exception to this is the way in which those with power can invest it in their close aides, such as the Buckingham Palace spokesman. In informal situations, at least, private secretaries and personal assistants to managing directors speak with considerable authority.

The room

The arrangements of the room affect the quality of the presentation. Eye contact with the audience is essential as a means of control and is made difficult if anyone is too close. The seating is best arranged so that there are approximately the right number of seats. Too many will tend to scatter the members of the audience, making it harder for the speaker to encourage them to behave like an audience rather than a collection of individuals. Too few seats can have slight advantages, if the presentation is to be quite brief, if the entrance is at the back of the room and there will be few latecomers. To have all seats full and a small number of standees can create a lively atmosphere. However, the drawbacks of having too few seats will usually outweigh the advantages. If the audience is quiet a single latecomer entering on tip-toe with bated breath will attract the attention of everyone, and half of them will exchange knowing smiles with their neighbours. But latecomers seldom enter on tip-toe with bated breath. They usually say 'Sorry I'm late' with a sheepish grin and then mutter something inaudible about the traffic before tripping over someone's briefcase, while all members of the audience look round to assure themselves that there really isn't any room and commenting on how hot it is.

The position from which to speak is dictated by the arrangements for the audience, but problems that typically curse unprepared speakers are a lack of anywhere to put notes, a distracting background behind the speaker, problems with microphones or some problem with visual aids. Visual aids are referred to shortly, but the problem of the distracting background is not always appreciated. The audience need to look at the speaker so as to concentrate on what they are hearing. Visual aids should embellish the presentation; other visual images will be a distraction. Examples are murals, stained glass windows, blackboards that are not being used or charts on the wall. Speakers who scorn the blackboard because they have a sheaf of acetate sheets to show on the overhead projector often overlook the fact that members of the audience will tend to read what is on the blackboard, even though it was written by someone else the day before.

> One large company has a lecture room in its training centre that is used for management training sessions. On the wall to one side of the speaker's position is a wallchart of the periodic table of chemical elements. During any session all members of an audience spend some time examining the chart, whether they be chemists making sure they can remember the sequence or non-chemists trying to understand it.

Often there is someone introducing the speaker, and this can be the biggest distraction of all if the person deliberately or accidentally impersonates Eric Morecambe listening to Ernie Wise. If you are in the position of introducing someone else, remember not to yawn, pick your nose or register amused disbelief.

REVIEW TOPIC 9.1

The next time you attend a presentation or listen to a speech given by someone else, study the arrangement of the room and note the changes that you would (and could) make if you were the speaker.

The material

What is to be said or, more accurately, what should members of the audience go away having understood and remembered?

Organize your material with an introduction that previews, a body that develops, and a conclusion that reviews. When you organize the body of your presentation, start by sorting out the theme. The theme is a planning device that holds together the various ideas you want to discuss. If the theme of your presentation is informative, then the body should provide facts. If the theme is persuasive, the body should develop persuasive arguments. (Fandt 1994, p. 159)

In the introduction the speaker sets up rapport with the audience. Apart from their attention the speaker will include here an answer to the unspoken question – is it going to be worth our listening? A useful introduction is to explain what the members of the audience will know or be able to do at the end. It is also helpful to sketch out the framework of what is to come, so that people can follow it more readily, but stick to what you promise. If you say there are going to be five points, the audience will listen for five to make sure that they have not missed one. In the main body is the message that is to be conveyed, the development of the argument and the build-up of what it is that the audience should go away having understood and remembered. The conclusion is where the main points are reiterated and confirmed in a brief, integrated summary.

The main body will need to be effectively organised. This will not only help members of the audience to maintain attention, it will also discipline the speaker to avoid rambling, distracting irrelevance or forgetting. The most common methods are as follows.

- Chronological sequence, dealing with issues by taking the audience through a series of events. A presentation to an industrial tribunal often follows this pattern.

- Known to unknown or simple to complex. You start either with a brief review of what the audience already knows or can easily understand and then develop to what they do not yet know or can not yet understand. The logic of this method is to ground the audience in something they can handle so that they can make sense of the unfamiliar. This is the standard method of organising teaching sessions.

- Problem to solution is almost the exact opposite of simple to complex. A problem is presented and a solution follows. The understanding of the audience is again grounded, but this time grounded in anxiety that the speaker is about to relieve.

- Comparison is a method of organisation which compares one account with another. Selling usually follows this path, as the new is compared with the old.

Whatever the method of organisation for the material, the main body will always contain a number of key thoughts or ideas. This is what the speaker is trying to plant in the minds of the audience: not just facts, which are inert, but the ideas which facts may well illustrate and clarify. The idea that inflation is dangerously high is only illustrated by the fact that it is at a particular figure in a particular month.

The ideas in a presentation can be helpfully linked together by a device that will help audience members to remember them and to grasp their interdependence. One method is to enshrine the ideas in a story. If the story is recalled the thoughts are recalled with it, as they are integral to the structure. Classic examples of this are the New Testament parables, but every play, novel or film uses the same method.

Another method is to use key words to identify the points that are being made, especially if they have an alliterative or mnemonic feature, such as 'People, Products, Prosperity'. In a lecture it is common to provide a framework for ideas by using a drawing or system model to show the interconnection of points.

Facts, by giving impact, keep together the framework of ideas that the speaker has assembled. They clarify and give dimension to what is being said. The danger is to use too many, so that the audience are overwhelmed by facts and figures which begin to bemuse them. If the presentation is to be accompanied by a handout, facts may be usefully contained in that, so that they can be referred to later, without the audience having to remember them.

Humour is the most dangerous of all aids to the speaker. If the audience laughs at a funny story, the speaker will be encouraged and may feel under less tension, but how tempting to try again and end up 'playing for laughs'. Laughter is a most seductive human reaction, but too many laughs are even more dangerous than too many facts. What will the audience remember – the joke, or what the joke was to illustrate? Attempted humour is also dangerous for the ineffective comedian. If you tell what you think is a funny story and no one laughs, you have made a fool of yourself (at least in your own eyes) and risk floundering.

REVIEW TOPIC 9.2

Obtain from your library a book or audio cassette of speeches made by an effective orator – such as Winston Churchill, Billy Graham, John Kennedy, Martin Luther King or Nelson Mandela – and make notes of the plan of their material.

Very few people speak effectively without notes, despite the tendency to marvel at those who can. Relying solely on memory risks missing something out, getting a fact wrong or drying up completely. Notes follow the pattern of organisation you have established, providing discipline and limiting the tendency to ramble. It is both irritating and unhelpful for members of an audience to cope with a speaker who wanders off down a blind alley, yet this is very common. When an amusing anecdote pops up in your brain, it can be almost irresistible to share it.

There are two basic kinds of notes: headlines or a script. Headlines are probably the most common, with main points underlined and facts listed beneath. Sometimes there will also be a marginal note about an anecdote or other type of illustration. The alternative of the script enables the speaker to try out the exact wording, phrases and pauses to achieve the greatest effect. The script will benefit from some marking or arrangement that will help you to find your place again as your eyes constantly flick from the page to the audience and back again. This can be underlining or using a highlighter. There are many variations of these basic methods, so that one approach is to use varying line length, while another is to use rows of dots to indicate pause or emphasis.

Some alternative forms of notes

(a) 'People have never fully realised just how destructive a thing worry is.
It truly plays havoc with one's life.
It ruins digestion.
It causes stomach ulcers.
It interferes with sound sleep and forces us to face another day unrested and irritable.
It shortens our tempers and makes us snap at the members of our family.'
(from *Mr Jones, Meet the Master* by Peter Marshall 1964, London: Fontana Books).

(b) The idea that Britain and America are *two nations* divided by a *common language* ... is nowhere more obvious than in management. Differences in connotation and usage of certain terms are most marked ... the most obvious being the word 'manager' itself. This is one of the most *potent symbols* of the American way of life ... representing free enterprise ... and the heroic materialism ... that made the country great.

(c) 1. Goals of the appraisal system.
2. Performance criteria in an environment of quality improvement.
3. Improving the appraisal rating scale.
4. Communicating appraisal results.
5. Making the appraisal system work.

Some people like to have their notes on small cards, so that they are unobtrusive, but this is difficult if the notes are more than headlines. Standard A4 paper should present no problem, provided that the notes are not stapled, well laid out and can be handled discreetly. Never, ever forget to number the pages or cards, as the next time you speak they are going to slip off your lap moments before you are due to begin.

The speaker

The final aspect of preparation is to prepare the speaker, who has to bring the notes to life. Rehearsal can help eliminate potential difficulties, but you need to have someone else in to listen and to comment: the mirror is a poor substitute. Only in this way will there be guidance on what is heard and understood, as well as on what is being said. So the first rehearsal check is on the clarify of expression, does it hang together and make sense? The second rehearsal check is on audibility. Occasional speakers often find it difficult to speak loud enough to be heard at the same time as speaking naturally. Also there is a strange tendency to drop the voice at the end of sentences, losing the last few words. Can you be heard, and can you be heard all the time, or are the last few words in sentences delivered with declining volume?

When John Major became Prime Minister it was the culmination of a career that had not been characterised by strong public speaking. Suddenly every public utterance was of great significance and was listened to by millions. He clearly lacked the degree of vigour and colour in presenting ideas that makes for effective speaking to an audience, but a special problem was virtual inaudibility at the close of sentences. Despite careful coaching it remained a problem that could only be overcome by careful manipulation of the electronic public address system.

Few people avoid stage fright. This is useful up to a point as it keys up the speaker to produce as vivid a performance as possible. Too much stage fright, however, can destroy it. Confidence is essential in getting the audience to listen. Diffidence and nervousness may be engaging qualities in athletes who have just broken a world record or in bridegrooms at wedding receptions, but not for business speakers. It can be reduced by deliberate relaxation, moving consciously a little more slowly than usual and concentrating on the deliberate relaxation of different muscles. There are various ways of relaxing, but some of them require a degree of privacy that may not be feasible. Here are some suggestions, ranging from the simple and discreet to the more elaborate.

- Take several long, deep breaths, filling the base of the lungs from the bottom up.
- Breathe in to a steady count of three and out to an equally steady count of nine; in to four and out to twelve; in to five and out to fifteen and so on.
- Smile as much as possible before starting, as this will remove traces of an anxious frown and relax facial muscles before confronting the audience. It takes sixty-four muscles to frown and only fourteen to smile.

Making the presentation

Now begins the experience that some people find more frightening than any other: facing the audience. Sometimes the result can be exhilarating; all too frequently it is humiliating. The ritual is of one person asserting authority over others and the speaker cannot avoid that role. Disclaimers, apologies and appeals to the better nature of the audience are of no use as the only reason for the event is that the speaker has some authority that members of the audience respect, and that is the expectation to which you have to rise. The audience that is satisfied will 'applaud' and flatter you in a dozen ways: the dissatisfied audience is merciless.

Rapport

Rapport is an unfamiliar French word (although familiar to most personnel specialists) for which there is no English equivalent, meaning to set up some sort of bond or mutual sympathy between people. In presentation it involves presenting yourself before the audience in a way that encourages them to perk up and take notice, wanting to hear what you have to say. It does not just simply happen; you have to *make* it happen.

Appearance is particularly important, not in the sense of best suits or polished shoes, but what the appearance of the speaker says to the audience. The way we present ourselves to others says something of our attitude towards them – we have taken trouble to get ready, or we have not. This may be regarded as the trivia of manners, but virtually everyone works on their appearance in order to feel confident and to create an effect. An audience will scrutinise your appearance closely as they are trapped, with very little else to look at. Do you look prepared and organised? Do you look as if you care what they think? Appearance can also distract. I wonder where she got those earrings? I'm sure he's got odd socks on. That bracelet must have cost a fortune. Is that lapel badge for Round Table or blood donors?

Stance is an expression of authority: you stand, they have to sit. It is not always essential to stand as the organisation of the room will probably give you enough special space to maintain your authority while sitting, but you deny yourself the chance for building up initial confidence slightly if you do not take this opportunity. The speaker's confident manner can make the audience believe that it is all going to be worthwhile. It is not enough, but it helps.

The speaker will also demonstrate and foster contact with the audience and involvement with them. One way is to explain the structure of the presentation, the reasons for it, why the exponent is the person doing it and what the outcome could be for the audience. You need to avoid the risk of creating false hopes, as it is pointless to generate a positive response at the beginning which is let down by what follows, so that the audience leaves disgruntled.

The best method of contact is to look at the audience. This is difficult for inexperienced speakers, who regard the audience as a Hydra-headed monster and dare not look it in the eye, preferring to gaze intently either at their notes, a spot on the floor six inches in front of their feet or the top right hand corner of the ceiling. Such faint hearts should remember a figure from Greek mythology – the Gorgon, one glance from whom turned the observer to stone. The roles of speaker and listener are so clearly dominant and submissive that people in the audience who see the speaker looking at them will appear interested, stop yawning, sit up straight, stop talking, defer the crossword till later or whatever other behaviour is consistent with being observed by an authority figure.

The American Evelyn Mayerson, writing at a time when the male gender was still used almost universally in management texts, suggests that there are three significant non-verbal cues that the speaker gives to affect audience response. The first is energy level:

If he looks as if he needs a lectern to prop him up, he conveys a low energy level. If he seems bursting with vigor, he conveys a high energy level. The freedom with which he turns his head, smiles and moves his hands, the control of the breath as he sends forth his words, his speech volume, his articulation, and his spacing and pausing all contribute to an image of energy level. (Mayerson 1979, p. 183)

Second is flexibility of movement and, thirdly, comes the speaker's warmth and enthusiasm:

Enthusiasm is contagious. If a speaker wants to convince, he has to believe in the issue himself. His belief helps to get the message across. There is a difference between 'We have to do something about wasted materials' said as the speaker picks lint off his trousers, scans the horizon, stifles a yawn, or scratches his head, and 'We have to do something about wasted materials' said with inflection, pausing, direct eye contact and an erect posture. (Mayerson 1979, p. 184)

Do not start by telling a joke unless you are absolutely sure you can get the audience to laugh and that the joke will contribute to, rather than distract from, your message. If you are planning to start by saying, 'My wife (husband, brother, mother, sister) said I should stop boring if I did not strike oil in the first fifteen minutes', think again.

Preview

After you have won over the audience, so that they are eating out of the palm of your hand, you give them a preview. Think of this as an agenda, or as the trailer of a film. You are summarising what is to come, so that the listeners have a framework into which they can fit what they are about to hear.

Development

The form of development is predetermined by the preparation that has been made: the number of ideas, the relevant facts, the illustrations and so on. It is now that the value of that preparation is felt. Do not, however, fall into the trap of thinking that your opening funny story, with eye contact and a list of points to be covered, is all the 'performance' that is required. Audience attention and involvement has to be sustained through the manner of the exposition:

... interest and motivation should be sustained throughout by the use of material or examples which are intrinsically interesting to the audience, dramatic, or simply funny. Concrete examples and stories make the material easier to assimilate, and should be subordinated to the main argument. (Argyle 1972, p. 209)

It is important not to attempt too much, as listeners can not process as much information as readers can. Reverting to the comments at the opening of this chapter, the predisposition towards listening to a presentation instead of reading a report appears to show a preference for the quick and easy rather than for the thorough.

> Most people can not easily comprehend more than three to five main points in a speech. This doesn't mean that you say three things and sit down. It means that you should group your complex ideas into three to five major areas and select supporting visuals that will reinforce your main points. (Fandt 1994, p. 164)

Voice

The voice is the means by which the material is transmitted and the quality of the voice usage will govern what is heard and understood. Try to speak with expression and enthusiasm, remembering inflection and pace.

Inflection refers to the variations in volume and in pitch that give your words expressiveness. Volume is easy to understand, but pitch is less obvious. It describes the range between a squeak and a growl. A low-pitched voice can well express solemnity, while a high-pitched voice is more expressive of excitement.

Pace describes the speed at which you speak. Most inexperienced presenters speak too fast, mainly because of nervousness, so that what they say comes out as a gabble. Those who speak too slowly are likely to bore their audience, who feel that they could cope with things coming at them rather more briskly. Also the speaking goes on for a much longer period without interruption than in normal conversation, so that the speaker needs a slower pace to permit breathing and thinking. There is still the need to vary pace to provide selective emphasis. As ever, the key is to find the right pace, and to vary that pace. A good example is to listen to a commentary on a race, where both pace and pitch rise as the race proceeds. Among the ways of getting pace right are:

- Immediately before starting take a few deep breaths.
- Don't start too quickly, and look across the audience for a moment or two first.
- Use pauses and sometimes additional emphasis to mark a change in direction, to separate stages in the presentation and when using key terms. Pauses help by enabling breathing and emphasis and aiding audience comprehension. They also help to eliminate the nonsense words or 'verbal pauses' that frequently occur as someone is speaking: 'you know', 'as it were', 'at the end of the day', 'um', 'by and large', 'right' and 'OK' being some of the most common. The reason for this type of distracting interjection is that the flow of ideas and the operation of the tongue are not correctly synchronised, so that meaningless words and sounds are produced occasionally to fill the void that the brain has momentarily left. Practice can replace nonsense words with pauses, which are better for the audience and for the speaker.

At all times keep the presentation slow enough to be understood, but fast enough to keep the audience on their toes.

All speakers seem to have a natural tendency for volume to drop at the end of sentences, partly because they are running out of breath. In trying to overcome this difficulty there is the risk of becoming monotonous, as everything is on the same level, without any appropriate reference to the meaning of the words being spoken.

REVIEW TOPIC 9.3

Prepare a five-minute speech on one of these topics:

(i)   walking;
(ii)   gardening;
(iii)   your favourite sport;
(iv)   your hobby; or
(v)   your first boy friend/girl friend.

After careful preparation, deliver the speech in an empty room (the garage would do) and record it. Play it back several times, making critical notes of energy level, voice, pace, pauses, etc., then deliver the speech again while making a recording.

In what ways is it better? In what ways is it not as good? What have you learned about the way you speak? What can you still improve?

Visual aids

We remember what we see for longer than we remember what we are told, and we can sometimes understand what we see better than we can understand what we hear. This is the rationale for the use of blackboards, whiteboards, flip charts, overhead projectors, films, television, working models and experiments. They are, however, aids to, and not substitutes for, the presentation. Too much displayed material can obscure rather than illuminate what is being said. Television news provides a good example of how much can be used. The dominant theme is always the talking head with frequently intercut pieces of film. Very seldom do words appear on the screen and then usually as extracts from a speech or report, where a short sentence or passage is regarded as being especially meaningful. The other way in which words and numbers appear is when facts are needed to illustrate an idea, so that ideas such as football scores or like a change in the value of the pound sterling almost always have the figures shown on the screen to clarify and illustrate. Seldom, however, will more than two or three numbers be displayed at the same time.

Speakers need to remember the size of what they are displaying as well as its complexity. Material has to be big enough for people to read and simple enough for them to follow. Material also has to be timed to coincide with what is being said. Where a speaker is using a display with a good deal of information, it may be sensible to mask it and reveal one section at a time as the exposition proceeds, so that some members of the audience do not move on to a part of the diagram or table that has not yet been explained and which they do not yet understand. Equally, do not leave on an overhead projector an illustration of something from which you have moved on. The audience will be drawn to the powerful, projected image rather than to what you are saying.

Make sure you are familiar with the equipment before you start. If using a flip chart of whiteboard, ensure that there are pens of the right sort that have not dried up. If there is a blackboard, clean it. If there is an overhead projector make sure it is plugged in, that you know how to switch it on and that the bulb has not blown. Then check that the glass is clean (toilet paper is good for this) so that the image is sharp and that the size and focus of the display is correct.

Handouts

It is a common, helpful practice to prepare a handout to accompany the presentation. A typed synopsis of what has been said, or a copy of a diagram that has been displayed, can be helpful in reinforcement but may reduce the level of concentration during the presentation itself. The handout should not duplicate the presentation nor make it irrelevant. Issued beforehand, like a long report, it can form the basis of a presentation that is pointing up or adding to the main points. Issued afterwards, it can reiterate factual details and summarise the main points of the presentation.

Language

Language needs to be what the audience will understand. The larger and more heterogeneous the audience, the more difficult for the speaker to cover that wide range of capacities. Marks (1980, pp. 54–60) has some helpful advice on this and points out how easy it is for professionals to slip into jargon that can puzzle many people, such as the marketing manager to whom everything is a mix and the personnel manager to whom everything is a package. Few things can antagonise an audience more than the feeling that the speaker is trying to impress them with cleverness rather than putting the message over.

Closing

At the end the speaker summarises the points that have been made, reinforces them and leads the audience to some sort of follow-up action. That action may often be no more than to remember something of what has been heard, or to feel reassured, but it is the closing that will lead to the action. The speaker has to avoid an anticlimax which can be caused by signalling the end too clearly: 'Let me sum up what I have been trying to say...'. That both indicates that there is nothing new and confirms the view of the audience that it has not been well done. Instead the exponent aims for a climax – a positive close. Among the ways to do this are telling a story, which brings together and illustrates the points that have been made; raising rhetorical questions to which members of the audience can now see answers where they could not at the beginning; and a straightforward statement which shows the interrelationship of points made earlier.

Pitfalls

The inexperienced speaker should guard against some of the more common pitfalls, one of which is apology. If members of the audience are disciplining themselves to sit still and listen it will not make them more responsive if you start by telling them of your incompetence. Your best hope is to try and conceal it, rather than emphasising it. Shortly after a serious airport disaster, a fire officer addressed a press conference with the opening, 'I cannot promise you that I have expert knowledge on this subject, so perhaps I may share with you some of my own confusion'.

All of us can recall situations in which a speaker's mannerisms distracted us from what was being said. They are a form of displacement activity and should not be restrained to the point of making the presentation wooden or stilted, but can be modified to avoid too much distraction. A common mannerism is walking about. In moderation this provides a mild variation in scene, but some of the more distracting variations are the walks that follow a precise, oft-repeated path, to and fro, or those which include little flourishes like a slow motion, modified goose step. Standing still can be little better if it is accompanied by the act of balancing on the outside edges of one's shoes or using a toe to sketch, with great care and precision, a cross or triangle in the imaginary dust on the floor.

Some people reserve for their public speeches a minute examination of their fingernails or a series of isometric exercises to relieve muscular aches in their shoulders. Rings and bracelets are frequently played with incessantly, but the greatest distractor of all is probably the pair of spectacles that goes on, comes off, gets folded and put away, only to be taken out, unfolded, put on...

Some speakers lose their audience by not stopping when they have finished, rambling from one anticlimactic afterthought to another as the audience chafes because the coffee will be getting cold. When you have said, 'And finally...' you have no more than two minutes left. If you follow this with 'To conclude...' and later, 'As a last word...' and later still, 'And this really is my last word...' you may excite sufficient wrath in the audience for them to start throwing things.

References

Argyle, M. (1972), *The Psychology of Interpersonal Behaviour*, London: Pelican.
Bell, G. (1989), *Speaking and Business Presentations*, London: Heinemann.

Fandt, P. M. (1994), *Management Skills: Practice and Experience*, St Paul, Minnesota: West Publishing.

Marks, W. (1980), *How to Give a Speech*, London: Institute of Personnel Management.

Mayerson, E. W. (1979), *Shoptalk*, Philadelphia: Saunders.

PART III

Resourcing

10 Strategic aspects of resourcing

'Angela's leaving – quick, we must make sure to get the ad in this month's journal.' 'It's hopeless – they all leave just as soon as we've trained them – what's the point?' 'It's not my fault – we just can't get the staff – no wonder quality is so poor.' 'That's it. The results are so bad we'll have to let some of them go – Tony, draw up a short-list of possibles and we'll try and get it sorted this week.'

All too often employee resourcing is a reactive activity, with the absence of any link to organisational strategy and a lack of internal coherence. In order to bridge this gap we suggest the consideration of a range of aspects which together can form the framework for a resourcing strategy that can facilitate the future direction of the organisation. Each of these aspects offers choices for the organisation. We first consider the organisation's response to the resourcing environment, and then look at some different approaches to flexible resourcing. We review the choice to recruit experienced staff or home-grow them, the choice to target specific skills or groups, and the choice of appropriate levels of turnover for the organisation. Finally we take a strategic view of resourcing roles in the organisation.

Responding to external labour markets and demographics

There are four major issues facing employers in the 1990s in relation to the external labour market.

Labour shortages

In 1971 there were around 900,000 live births in the United Kingdom. By 1977, it was less than 700,000 and has since failed to reach 800,000 per annum. Thus, although the workforce is still growing, the extra numbers are in the middle and older age groups rather than among the young. The late 1990s are likely to be characterised by labour shortages, an underlying problem which has been masked so far by the recession. The joker in the pack on this question may well be the effect of the single European market. If some forecasts are proved correct (for example, Rajan 1990), the United Kingdom could suffer substantial job losses in the early years of the single market.

Age composition

By the year 2000 there will be approximately 2.3 million more people aged between 25 and 64 years in the labour force than there are now, and approximately 1.3 million fewer aged under 25 years. The result is a growing workforce of which a higher proportion is older than at present. Employers who rely on young people in certain jobs, or as trainees for specific career plans, will experience particular problems. However, it is likely that the majority of employers will be forced to review policy as regards the preferred age of new recruits.

Sex composition

Due to the decline in population growth, employers will have to rely more on increasing the readiness of individuals to work. Current civilian activity rates (the proportion of the population in or seeking work) are expected to continue their trend of recent years, which means that while male activity rates decline, female rates will continue to increase. So marked are these effects that almost all (90 per cent) of the expected increase in labour supply to 2000 is among women. By 2000, women will comprise 44 per cent of the labour force. The ability of employers to attract female recruits may well depend on provision of facilities such as creches, training for returners and career breaks.

Skill shortage

Demand for labour in manual and unskilled jobs is expected to continue to contract during the 1990s. The growth in demand for labour will therefore be concentrated among the higher skilled occupations, and in particular among professional, scientific and technical occupations (Figure 10.1). University graduates are the main source of supply for these higher skilled occupations, but higher education is also influenced by demographic factors and the need to compete with employers anxious to recruit 'A' level school-leavers. While demand for graduates generally is up, there is a particular need for two specific types: the technologist, required by the electronic, electrical engineering and computing sectors, and the high flyer, increasingly sought to meet the long-term needs of senior management. Many employers are attempting to solve their problems by broadening the entry requirements, so that now nearly half the vacancies currently advertised are open to all graduates.

Change in Employment by Occupation 1991–2000

Figure 10.1   Predictions of labour market demands (Institute for Employment Research 1993). Used with permission of the Institute for Employment Research.

There is some evidence to suggest that so far as these highly qualified staff and new graduates are concerned, eventually the implementation of the single European market will produce a net worsening of supply in the United Kingdom as more potential recruits seek employment overseas (Pearson and Pike 1989). This anticipated trend has so far been held back by practical difficulties in arranging European employment, such as the differences in required vocational qualifications, difficulties in transfer of pension rights and more general factors such as housing and children's education issues. This potential worsening of our supply of well qualified staff may not be offset by predicted UK job losses, as jobs lost are more likely to be those at a lower level in the organisation.

A planned response to demographic change

Overall, these demographic and labour supply factors are certain to cause a tightening of labour markets in all parts of the country. However, what may well exacerbate the situation is the failure of employers to devise and implement suitable responses. Atkinson has suggested a sequential response by firms to the predicted demographic downtown (Figure 10.2) and notes that:

> This shows the most likely types of response and the sequence in which they will be introduced. It suggests that we will see a progression from the tactical towards more strategic responses, and towards an external labour market (supply side) perspective, back to an internal one (demand side). It suggests that firms will progress from doing little or nothing, through competing for available labour, to identifying substitutes for it, ending with the improved deployment and performance of the existing workforce. (Atkinson 1989, p. 22)

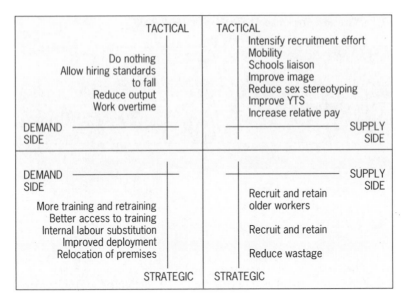

Figure 10.2 Employer's response to shortages (Atkinson 1989, p. 23). Used with permission of the author.

Awareness of labour market changes, although masked at present, can have an impact on current as well as future resourcing strategies. For example, when Ilford were seeking to reduce the size of their current workforce they considered lowering the company retirement age. Although this option had many immediate benefits it was dismissed as it would cause severe problems in the longer term.

Flexible resourcing choices

In Chapter 3 we noted that flexibility was identified as one of the main planks of human resource strategy (see, for example, Guest 1989). We now consider how this may influence resourcing strategy. Organisations have choices in achieving numerical flexibility, temporal flexibility and in how they balance these two aspects. (Other aspects of flexibility – functional and pay – are discussed in Chapters 4 and 32, respectively.)

Numerical flexibility

Numerical flexibility allows the organisation to respond quickly to the environment in terms of the numbers of people employed. This is achieved by using alternatives to traditional full-time permanent employees. The use, for example, of short-term contract staff, staff with rolling contracts, staff on short-term government-supported

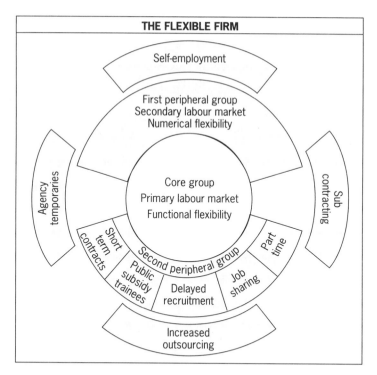

THE FLEXIBLE FIRM

Self-employment

First peripheral group
Secondary labour market
Numerical flexibility

Agency temporaries

Sub contracting

Core group
Primary labour market
Functional flexibility

Short term contracts

Public subsidy trainees

Second peripheral group

Delayed recruitment

Job sharing

Part time

Increased outsourcing

Figure 10.3   Atkinson's model of the flexible firm (from Atkinson 1984). Used with permission of the authors.

training schemes, outworkers and so on, enable the organisation to reduce or expand the workforce quickly and cheaply.

Atkinson (1984) is one of a number of commentators who have described the way in which firms are developing flexibility in their approach to employment, as shown in Figure 10.3. The flexibile firm in this analysis has a variety of ways of meeting the need for human resources. First are core employees who form the primary labour market. They are highly regarded by the employer, well paid and involved in those activities that are unique to the firm or give it a distinctive character. These employees have improved career prospects and offer the type of flexibility to the employer that is so prized in the skilled craftsworker, who does not adhere rigidly to customary protective working practices.

There are then two peripheral groups – first, those who have skills that are needed but not specific to the particular firm, such as typing and word processing. The strategy for these posts is to rely on the external labour market to a much greater extent, to specify a narrow range of tasks without career prospects, so that the employee has a job but not a career. This is a further development of the labour process described by Braverman (1974). Some employees may be able to transfer to core posts, but generally limited scope is likely to maintain a fairly high turnover, so that adjustments to the vagaries of the product market are eased.

The second peripheral group is made up of those enjoying even less security, as they have contracts of employment that are limited, either to a short-term or to a part-time attachment. There may also be a few job sharers and many participants on government training schemes find themselves in this category. An alternative or additional means towards this flexibility is to contract out the work that has to be done, either by employing temporary personnel from agencies or by the entire operation, as sub-contracting.

As we saw in the chapter on organisation structure, a slightly different version of the peripheral workforce is the way in which the organisation boundary may be adjusted by redefining what is to be done in-house and what is to be contracted out to various suppliers.

Temporal flexibility

This type of flexibility concerns varying the pattern of hours worked in order to respond to business demands and employee needs. Moves away from 9–5, 38-hour week include the use of annual hours contracts, increased use of part-time work, job-sharing and flexible working hours. For example, an organisation subject to peaks and troughs of demand (such as an ice-cream manufacturer) could use annual hours contracts so that more employee hours are available to peak periods and less are used when business is slow. Flextime systems can benefit the employer by providing employee cover outside the 9–5 day and over lunchtimes, and can also provide employee benefits by allowing personal demands to be more easily fitted around work demands. Blyton and Morris (1992) also note the opportunity that temporal flexibility offers to improve the utilisation of staff. Evidence suggests that the use of annual hours contracts is increasing, and an Institute of Personnel Management (IPM) survey in 1993 found that 60 per cent of employers using this type of contract had introduced the scheme since 1989 (Hutchinson 1993b).

Welsh Water have introduced a pilot scheme for annual hours contracts in 1991 (Hutchinson 1993a) and found they produced a range of benefits which included a firmer control over overtime, less need for temporary contract labour, increased output, improved management control, reduced absence and a more flexible, co-operative and committed workforce. Since the pilot scheme was introduced they have found that other employees are pressing to be included in the system.

The balance between employee numbers and hours worked

Organisations have a wide range of options in finding a balance that meets their needs. In November 1993 Volkswagen in Germany announced that in their current poor financial situation they were employing too many people. In order to avoid redundancies they agreed with the workforce that hours would be reduced by 20 per cent so that they worked a four-day week, and that wages would be reduced by 10 per cent. There is a good deal of emphasis in Europe on reducing the working week to help reduce redundancies, unemployment and absence levels, and to improve family life.

REVIEW TOPIC 10.1

What evidence can you find in your organisation to support a more flexible approach to resourcing?
What were the driving forces behind these changes?
How have employees responded and why?

Ready-made or home-grown?

Organisations have a choice whether to depend extensively on the talent available in the external labour market or to invest heavily in training and development and career systems to exploit the potential in the internal labour market. Some organisations thrive on high levels of turnover, while others thrive on the development of employees which remain with the organisation in the long term. The emphasis on either approach, or the balance between the two, can be chosen to support organisational strategy.

Sonnenfield *et al.* (1992) propose a model which relates entry and exit of staff with promotion and development of staff in the organisation. One axis of the model is supply flow. They argue that strategically organisations which focus on internal supply tend to see people as assets with a long-term development value rather than costs in terms of annual expenditure. The other axis is labelled the assignment flow, which describes the basis on which individuals are assigned new tasks in the organisation. The criteria for allocation may be in terms of individual contribution to organisation performance, or on group contribution which Sonnenfield *et al.* identify as factors such as loyalty, length of service and support of others. They argue that strategically organisations which emphasise individual contribution expect individuals to provide value on a continuous basis, whereas those which emphasise group contribution see employees as having intrinsic value.

The model proposed describes the combination of these two aspects of resourcing and results in four typical 'career systems', as shown in Figure 10.4. In each box alongside the career system label (academy, club, baseball team and fortress) Sonnenfield *et al.* identify the strategic organisation model and the competitive strategy which are most likely to drive each career system. They also identify the likely orientation of the personnel function.

In this chapter we are concerned with the characteristics of the career systems which are as follows.

● *Academies:* in academies there is a heavy emphasis on individual contribution, in terms of reward and promotion. They are characterised by stability

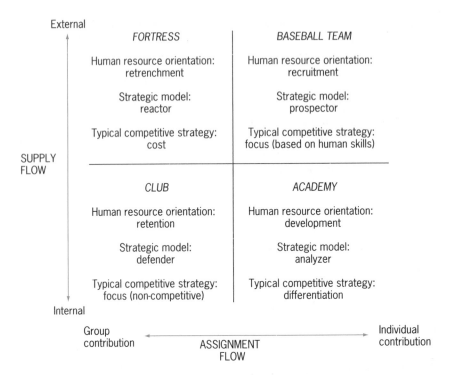

External

FORTRESS

Human resource orientation:
retrenchment

Strategic model:
reactor

Typical competitive strategy:
cost

BASEBALL TEAM

Human resource orientation:
recruitment

Strategic model:
prospector

Typical competitive strategy:
focus (based on human skills)

SUPPLY
FLOW

CLUB

Human resource orientation:
retention

Strategic model:
defender

Typical competitive strategy:
focus (non-competitive)

ACADEMY

Human resource orientation:
development

Strategic model:
analyzer

Typical competitive strategy:
differentiation

Internal

Group
contribution

ASSIGNMENT
FLOW

Individual
contribution

Figure 10.4   A typology of career systems (Sonnenfield *et al.* 1992) in 'Strategic determinants of managerial labour markets' in *Human Resource Management* 27 (4). Copyright © 1992 John Wiley and Sons Inc. Used with permission of John Wiley and Sons Inc.

and low turnover of staff with many employees remaining until retirement. There is an emphasis on development and often competitions for promotion and barriers to leaving the organisation. Examples of typical industries where academies operate are pharmaceuticals and automobiles.

- *Clubs:* again there is a heavy emphasis on the internal labour market, but promotion is more likely to be based on loyalty, length of service, seniority and equality rather than individual contribution. There is an emphasis on staff retention. Sectors where this is likely to operate include public bodies, although the introduction of competitive forces will mean that a different career system may be appropriate.

- *Baseball teams:* these organisations use external labour sources at all levels to seek the highest contributors. There is an emphasis on recruitment to maintain staffing levels. Employees will tend to identify with their profession rather than the organisation, and examples given are advertising, accountancy and legal firms.

- *Fortresses:* these organisations are concerned with survival and can not afford to be concerned with individuals either in terms of reward or promotion. They are more likely to depend on external recruitment, often for generalists who meet the needs of a retrenchment or turnaround situation. Examples given are publishing, retailing and the hotel sector.

REVIEW TOPIC 10.2

Which of the four career systems in the Sonnenfield *et al.* model typifies your organisation?
What characteristics lead you to this conclusion?
How does this career systems strategy fit with your organisational strategy and organisational mission (either explicitly stated or implicit)?

From this discussion it is clear that the balance between retention and turnover is not simply a cost factor but also a critical factor in relating human resource strategy to organisational strategy. Some writers, for example Cann (1993), argue that high turnover levels need not be associated with low training and development levels, and that reasonable levels of turnover are helpful for some industries in terms of distributing skills. We will return to the career system model in Chapter 22 on strategic aspects of development.

Targeting specific competencies

The use of tight job descriptions prepared for recruitment purposes has been questioned in a climate of rapid and constant change (see, for example, Evenden, 1993). Although job descriptions remain of value the way that they are defined is changing to allow more flexibility within a given job and to describe outputs rather than inputs. The emphasis is moving to the person specification, not necessarily restricted to the initial job, but with a focus on qualities and attributes that fit with the strategic direction and culture of the organisation.

A large and previously successful manufacturing organisation needed to change from its bureaucratic approach in order to remain competitive in a tougher market place. The organisation decided that it wanted employees to have a 'can do' attitude; be prepared to try something new and difficult; focus on ends, not means; have a flexible approach to their job; admit their mistakes and learn from them.

This vision of the future clearly had implications for the culture of the organisation and also the characteristics that would be sought in individuals who were recruited and promoted.

Purcell (1992) suggests how employee characteristics and resourcing emphasis can be matched to the strategic position of the organisation in terms of the Boston matrix. For *wildcat* organisations he suggests that employees need to be willing and able to work in a variety of areas with broad skills. For *star* organisations he suggests that a high degree of individualism is required with careful recruitment and selection to employ the best. *Cash cow* organisations, he suggests, need order and stability, and this may result in overmanning in a comfortable organisation. In this type of organisation there may be more encouragement to recruit employees who will not 'rock the boat'. Finally in *dog* organisations he suggests the emphasis will be on reducing surplus labour rather than recruitment in order to enable cost reductions.

Writing from the perspective of differentiated reward structures for chief executives, Miller and Norburn (1981) identify the characteristics of a Chief Executive

Table 10.1 *Matching managers to strategy (Norburn and Miller 1981, p. 24). Used with permission of Braybrooke Press Ltd.*

The objective of the business		The main business activities		The chief executive should be
Growth	1.	Pursuit of increased *market share*	A.	*Young*, ambitious, aggressive
	2.	Earnings generation *subordinate* to building dominant position	B.	Strong development and growth potential
	3.	Focus on *longer term* results	C.	High tolerance for *risk taking*
	4.	Emphasis on *technical innovation* and market development	D.	Highly *competitive* by nature
Earnings	1.	Pursuit of *maximum earnings*	A.	*Tolerates* risk, but doesn't seek it
	2.	Balanced focus on *short range/long range*	B.	Comfortable with variety and flexibility
	3.	Emphasis on complex analysis and clearly articulated *plans*	C.	*Careful* but not conservative
	4.	Emphasis on increased *productivity*, cost improvements, strategic pricing	D.	*Trade-off* artist; short/long, risk/reward
Cash Flow	1.	Pursuit of maximum positive *cash flow*	A.	*Seasoned* and experienced
	2.	Sell off market share to *maximise* profitability	B.	Places high premium on *efficiency*
	3.	Intensive *pruning* of less profitable product/market segments	C.	High tolerance for stability, no charge for sake of it
	4.	Intensive *short range* emphasis/minimise 'futures' activities	D.	*Not* a dreamer, turned on by results *now*

which would match the prevailing business strategy, as shown in Table 10.1. This gives a clear indication of the competencies required for the external recruitment of promotion to the position of Chief Executive in each strategic situation.

Strategic resourcing roles

Increasingly a strategic view is being taken of how resourcing roles are allocated. The traditional view of a heavy involvement of the personnel function in order to provide consistency and expertise is being challenged. There is a shift to greater line manager involvement in resourcing activities with personnel role being devolved. However, this is not necessarily happening in an uncontrolled way. Personnel Officers at Heinz, for example, have produced training for line managers and support material to enable line managers to carry out recruitment activities without direct personnel support.

☐ SUMMARY PROPOSITIONS

10.1 A strategic approach to resourcing requires that account is taken of the changes taking place in the labour market.
10.2 There is an increase in resourcing activities which encourage temporal and numerical flexibility.
10.3 Organisations have strategic choices concerning the use they make of their internal and the external labour market.
10.4 The characteristics sought in recruiting and promoting individuals can be matched to the organisation's strategic direction.
10.5 Organisations have strategic choices about which members of the organisation carry out resourcing activities.

References

Atkinson, J. (1984), 'Manpower strategies for flexible organisations', *Personnel Management*, August.
Atkinson, J. (1989), 'Four stages of adjustment to the democratic downturn', *Personnel Management*, August.
Blyton, P. and Morris, J. (1992), 'HRM and the limits of flexibility', in P. Blyton and P. Turnbull (eds) *Reassessing Human Resource Management*. London: Sage.
Blyton, P. and Turnbull, P. (1992), *Reassessing Human Resource Management*, London: Sage.
Braverman, H. (1974), *Labour and Monopoly Capital*, New York: Monthly Review Press.
Cann, T. (1993), 'Why poaching is good practice', *Personnel Management*, October.
Evenden, R. (1993), 'The strategic management of recruitment and selection', in R. Harrison (ed.), *Human Resource Management – Issues and Strategies*, Wokingham, England: Addison–Wesley.

Guest, D. (1989), 'Personnel and HRM: can you tell the difference?', *Personnel Management*, January, pp. 48–51.

Harrison, R. (ed.) (1993), *Human Resource Management – Issues and Strategies*, Wokingham, England: Addison-Wesley.

Hutchinson, S. (1993a), 'The changing face of annual labour', *Personnel Management*, April.

Hutchinson, S. (1993b), *Issues in People Management No 5. Annual Hours Working in the UK*, London: Institute of Personnel Management.

Institute for Employment Research, (1993), 'Change in employment by occupation 1991–2000', in *Review of Economy and Employment*, Institute for Employment Research.

Norburn, D. and Miller, P. (1981), 'Strategy and executive reward: the mismatch in the strategic process', *Journal of General Management*, vol. 6, no., 4 pp. 17–27.

Pearson, R. and Pike, G. (1989), *The Graduate Labour Market in the 1990s*, Falmer, Sussex: Institute of Manpower Studies.

Purcell, J. (1992), 'The impact of corporate strategies on human resource management'. In G. Salaman *et al.* (eds) *Human Resource Strategies*. London: Sage.

Rajan, A. (1990), *1992: A zero sum game*, Birmingham: The Industrial Society.

Salaman, G. *et al.* (eds) (1992), *Human Resource Strategies*, London: Sage.

Sonnenfield, J. A., *et al.* (1992), 'Strategic determinants of managerial labour markets'. In G. Salaman *et al.* (eds) *Human Resource Strategies*. London: Sage.

11 Contracts of employment, contractors and consultants

It has been conventional to think of employment as full-time employment, but gradually a range of alternative forms is emerging. Full-time employment has been in steady decline for some time and the fall in the numbers of people registered as unemployed has been attributable mainly to the increasing number of part-time jobs available. Employers increasingly use a number of different forms of contract: not only different contracts of employment, but also contracts for the provision of services from sub-contractors and consultants.

The proportion of the labour force that works part-time varies across the European Union. Table 11.1 shows the figures for 1991. Since the development of the factory system employees have always been required to attend work at rigidly predetermined blocks of time, with some variation available through the use of overtime. The logic of this was not seriously questioned until 1968 when the concept of flexible working hours developed in West Germany. Although the majority of people still work some version of '9–5', there is a growing range of different practices, which have been evolving since the idea of flexible working hours broke the mould.

By the 1980s there was considerable interest in finding variations so as to introduce greater flexibility in the staffing of business and to provide individual

Table 11.1   *Proportion of the labour force working part-time in the European Union in 1991*

Spain	3%
Greece	4%
Italy	5.5%
Luxembourg	7%
Portugal	7%
Ireland	8%
Belgium	12%
France	12%
Germany	15%
United Kingdom	22%
Denmark	23%
Netherlands	33%

Source: *Labour Force Survey* 1993, p. 119.

employees with the scope to match working requirements with personal and domestic preferences. This interest was reflected in a number of reports and publications, such as BIM (1985) and Clutterbuck (1985).

The development of working patterns

By 1859 the *normal working week* in Britain had been established as 60 hours spread over 6 days of 10 hours each. Bienefeld (1972) has analysed how normal weekly hours fell at four distinct periods, as shown in Table 11.2. Since then there has been a further drop to approximately 38 hours a week, although the pattern of a normal week is now harder to distinguish. Furthermore, there is a wide variation according to type of employment.

Bienefeld argues that these reductions in working hours all came at a time when economic conditions were favourable, unemployment was low and union bargaining power high, and that the reason for unions seeking the reductions was in anticipation of future employment when the trade cycle moved from relative prosperity to relative recession:

> The four periods during which there were reductions in hours were marked by a configuration of economic factors that distinguished rises in money wages; they were periods of great prosperity, hence low unemployment, and hence great union bargaining power; finally, they were periods when unemployment was not felt to be a serious threat. (Bienefeld 1972, p. 224)

While that analysis may be an accurate explanation of the decline in working hours in the past it must be a poor predictor for the future, as it is difficult to envisage all the factors ever again being present at the same time. There has always been an obvious tension between unions seeking a reduction in the working week without a loss of earnings while employers have needed to be convinced that reductions in hours will not reduce productivity. When hours were very long there was a

Table 11.2 *Percentage reduction in British working hours between 1850 and early 1960s*

Period	Weekly hours' reduction	Percentage fall
1850–75	60–50	10%
1896–1920	54–48	11%
Late 1940s	48–44	8%
Early 1960s	44–40	9%

Table 11.3 *Average weekly hours worked in different parts of the British economy in 1992*

Agriculture	51.3
Industry	42.3
Services	36.4
Total	38.6

Source: *Labour Force Survey* 1993, p. 147.

convincing argument based on fatigue. More recently, moves have been based on a bargain: a reduction in hours in exchange for some major union concession, such as a change in working practices, that gives the management greater control of operations. The whole concept of a normal working week has been eroded as work becomes less rigidly constrained into predetermined blocks of time.

It is interesting that during industrial action by electricity power workers in the early 1970s, the government introduced a three-day week to save fuel. In most instances production remained as high, or nearly as high, as it had been during the previous five-day week.

Shift working can be traced back to the dawn of human history, with many examples for soldiers and sailors, for instance. In industry split shifts were operated as early as 1694 in glass-making, and there was a 1785 experiment in the largest ironworks in South Wales of three eight-hour shifts as an alternative to the norm of two twelve-hour shifts. Recently, there has been an extension of shift-working patterns and an increase in the number of people working shifts. Atkinson (1982, p. 2) calculated that by 1980 one manual worker in four worked on shifts in the manufacturing sector and that 22 per cent of all industrial workers were employed in this way. By 1993 the number of people working shifts and other forms of unsocial hours in the United Kingdom had risen further.

It would be misleading to add all the percentages and conclude that two-thirds of the working population work 'unsocial' hours, as some work on more than one of the periods shown in Table 11.4. It is still striking that a quarter of all those in employment worked on Saturdays, although many of these will be part-timers.

The need to stagger working hours grows greater rather than less. The bank that is open only from 10.00 a.m. to 3.00 p.m. is now a rarity; the airport channelling people onto aircraft will be operating from very early morning to late evening; public houses remain open all day and a high street store will typically be open for at least 70 hours a week. Initially most attempts to stagger working hours were in order to ease public transport problems: now they are to find ways of staffing the business. At one time *part-time working* was relatively unusual and was scarcely economic for the employer, as the national insurance costs of the part-time employee were disproportionate to those of the full-timer. The part-time contract was regarded as an indulgence for the employee and only a second-best alternative to the employment of someone full-time. This view was endorsed by lower rates of

Table 11.4   *People usually engaged in weekend working, shift work and night work, Spring 1993*

	Total number	% age of all in employment
Saturdays only	6,054,000	23.9
Both Saturdays and Sundays	2,543,000	10.0
Sundays only	2,990,000	11.8
Shifts, including both weekend and night shifts	3,954,000	15.6
Nights	1,544,000	6.1

Source: *Social Trends* 1994, p. 60.

pay, little or no security of employment and exclusion from such benefits as sick pay, holiday pay and pension entitlement. How things have changed!

In the last twenty-five years the proportion of the workforce on part-time contracts has increased so dramatically that it reached 22 per cent of total employees by 1991, as already shown. This rise is interrelated with the increased proportion of women in the workforce: 90 per cent of the recent rise in part-time working has been female. This has coincided with campaigns to enhance the employment opportunities of women, with the Equal Opportunities Commission advocating the development of job sharing, a specialised form of part-time working where two people split a full-time job between them so that the employer has a full-time service and the employees have only a half-time commitment. Although increasing, and probably continuing to do so, part-time still lacks the status of full-time employment and it is now more often described as a problem to be overcome rather than an opportunity for flexibility. A leavening of part-time posts provides flexibility to the management in staffing the operation and employment opportunity for those who do not seek full-time work. Too many part-time posts destabilise the staffing of the operation through increasing the training costs, requiring close supervision and costly administration while deploying people who have little understanding of the business. At the same time people who are seeking full-time work are denied the opportunity.

Flexible working hours were initially seen as a way of overcoming travel-to-work problems and as an inducement to prospective employees to join a company that offered this type of flexibility. By the 1980s there was a lessening of interest in this type of scheme but it remains in wide use, both to provide flexibility and as a means of achieving better management control of employee working hours (IDS 1983). Union resistance has reduced, but there is still fear that overtime opportunities may be reduced and attention distracted from the need to reduce working hours (Lee 1983).

Compressed hours is a method of reducing the working week by extending the working day, so that people work the same number of hours but on fewer days. An alternative method is to make the working day more concentrated by reducing the length of the midday meal-break. The now commonplace four-night week on the night shift in engineering was introduced in Coventry as a result of absenteeism on the fifth night being so high that it was uneconomic to operate.

Other more unusual variations include the idea of **annual hours contracts**, whereby the employee contracts to provide the employer with a specified number of hours' work per year and then enjoys considerable latitude in deciding when to work those hours, subject to employer needs and priorities. A **zero hours contract** is

---

The Times reports (14 June 1994, p. 29) that Marks & Spencer is the blue-chip operator of part-time working, with forty years experience, and is frequently sought out by other businesses to find out how it is done. They now feel that some stores are using too many part-timers and are aiming to reduce its part-time workforce from 80 per cent to 70 per cent.

the least attractive form of part-time working as the employee is not guaranteed any hours of work at all, but may be called in if there is a need.

There are already considerable changes in working patterns and further extensions of variations seem likely. The advantage to the employer is flexibility, not only to cope with the commercial ebb and flow but also to maintain a level of manning for a period of organisation operation that is now almost always longer than a standard working week for an individual employee. The appeal to the employee is more diverse. For some there is the attraction of working only part-time, for others there is a more comfortable interface between work and non-work, and for yet others there is the opportunity of combining more than one form of employment.

Flexibility is, however, not valued in organisations if it leads to instability and it is not welcome to those doing the work of the organisation if it denies them the satisfaction of their reasonable, work-related personal needs.

REVIEW TOPIC 11.1

What types of job would you regard as most appropriate for the following variations of the conventional nine-to-five working pattern?

1. Shift working.
2. Part-time working.
3. Job sharing.
4. Flexible hours.
5. Compressed hours.
6. Annual hours.

What types of job would not be suitable for each of these?

Shift working

There are situations where there is no alternative to working shifts or at least abnormal hours. In the continuous process industries such as steel-making and glass manufacture, the need for employees to be in attendance at all hours is dictated by the impracticality of interrupting the manufacturing cycle. In other circumstances there is the overwhelming imperative of customer demand, so that commuter trains are used more out of normal working hours than within them, and morning newspapers have to be prepared in the middle of the night.

The operation of shifts carries an implicit assumption that it is unattractive to the individual employee: it carries a premium payment all of its own and the drafters of incomes policies in the 1970s brought a new phrase into common usage by introducing the notion of special treatment for those who work 'unsocial hours'. Such a generalisation may make sound industrial relations sense, but is no more accurate a statement about individuals than the statement that gentlemen prefer blondes. Wedderburn (1975) gives examples of the range of reactions he discovered in interviewing 50 shiftworkers:

> One young couple work the same shift so that they can use their spare time together working on their old house; another couple work opposing shifts, so that they can manage a handicapped child between them. One young father loves shiftwork because he sees more of his infant children; another feels he is losing contact with his time-locked school children. One can fish all day in uncrowded waters; another gave up fishing because weekend shiftwork meant that he missed crucial competitions. One foreman enjoys the total responsibility that shiftwork gives him; another fears that he has missed his chances of promotion, isolated on shiftwork. (Wedderburn 1975)

For most people the prospect of working shifts may well be appalling, but for a substantial minority it provides a welcome element of flexibility in the employment contract at a time in their lives when it is perhaps very convenient for them to spend a period working unusual hours – for a higher rate of pay.

There are various patterns of working shifts, each of which brings with it a slightly different set of problems and opportunities.

The part-timer shift

Here a group of people are employed for a few hours daily at the beginning or end of normal working hours. The most common group are office cleaners, who may work from 6 a.m. to 9 a.m. or for a similar period in the evening. Also there are some shifts for four or five hours in the evening. Common here are supermarket shelvers, who stock shelves in readiness for the store opening the following morning.

The advantage to employers is in using relatively small units of time that would be insufficient for a full-time employee, and it is a very convenient working arrangement for a fairly large number of people. Where the employer is seeking a short spell of additional work from people who require little training (either because the work is straightforward or because the skills are generally available) the part-time shift may be an ideal arrangement. It may be less satisfactory as a permanent type of employment.

The permanent night shift

The permanent night shift is another arrangement which creates a special category of employee who is set apart (or cut off) from everyone else. They are working full-time, but have no contact with the rest of the organisation's members, who leave before they arrive and return after they have left. Apart from specialised applications such as national newspapers, this form is usually used either to undertake cleaning and maintenance of plant while it is idle or to increase output on a rather more permanent basis than can be achieved through part-time shifts.

The attraction of this arrangement is that it makes use of plant at times when it would otherwise be idle and, if it is used for maintenance, it avoids maintenance interrupting production. It also avoids the upheaval of the existing workforce that would be involved by introducing double-day shifts.

The drawbacks can be considerable. Employees are operating permanently outside normal working hours, and as they are full-time employees that may be even more critical than it is with part-timers. There is an inevitable 'apartheid' for the regular night worker, who is out of touch with the mainstream of union and company activities. A further problem is the provision of services, such as catering, medical and routine personnel services. For the evening worker these are either unnecessary or can be provided relatively cheaply by a few daily employees working occasional overtime. For night workers the services are both more difficult to provide and more costly. Night working is the form that is likely to be most difficult for employees to sustain, as most human beings are diurnal rather than nocturnal creatures. A small minority seem to genuinely prefer working regular nights and maintain this rhythm for their working lives over many years, but for most it will be undertaken either reluctantly or for relatively short periods.

Alternating day and night shifts

If night working is being used to increase output rather than for cleaning and maintenance, then alternation is a possibility. It mitigates many of the difficulties of regular night working, but does present employees with the problem of regular, drastic changes in their daily rhythms

Double-day shifts

The double-day shift variation is suprisingly unpopular. Instead of working a normal day shift, employees work either from 6 till 2 or 2 till 10. This means that plant is in use for sixteen hours, all employees are present for a large part of the 'normal' day, there is no night working and the rotation between the early and late shift enables a variety of leisure activities to be followed.

One problem is the fact that it may be the first experience of shifts for the bulk of employees, if it is introduced in place of a system of regular days or regular days and nights. There may be difficulties about transport in the early morning and there is the inconvenience of eating at unfamiliar times.

Three-shift working

Three-shift working represents a further development and the most widespread pattern: from 6 till 2, 2 till 10 and 10 till 6. The 24-hour cycle is covered so that there is continuous operation. There is a further subdivision: *discontinuous* three-shift working is where the plant is running but stops for the weekend, and *continuous* shift-working is an extension into the weekend whereby the plant never stops. Here we have the inescapable night shift and, with continuous working, the final loss of the sacrosanct weekend. If shifts are run on the traditional pattern of changing every week the shift workers have the unattractive feature of the 'dead fortnight' of two weeks when normal evening social activities are not possible because of late return home after a 2 till 10 shift or early departure for a 10 till 6 shift. The most common solution to this is to accelerate the rotation with a 'continental' shift pattern, whereby a shift team spend no more than three consecutive days on the same shift.

Reductions in the number of hours in the basic working week have induced a range of variations in shiftworking pattern that were not necessary until the 40-hour barrier was broken. Useful examples of such variations have been described by IDS (1985).

Part-time working

Although there has been some increase in part-time working for men, it has grown rapidly among women, because so many women either wish to work only part-time or because their share of domestic responsibilities only allows them to work in this way. Many of them will be working short shifts and sometimes two will share a full working day between them. Others will be in positions for which only a few hours within the normal day are required or a few hours at particular times of the week. As described, retailing is an occupation that has considerable scope for the part-timer, as there is obviously a greater need for counter personnel on Saturday mornings than on Monday mornings. Also, many shops are now open for longer periods than would be normal hours for a full-time employee, so that the part-timer helps to fill the gaps and provide the extra manning at peak periods. Catering is another example, as are market research interviewing, office cleaning, typing and some posts in education. Another aspect of the increasing number of women returning to part-time employment is the provision of funded creche facilities for children (Falconer 1990). As labour shortages become more acute, this issue is likely to become of greater importance to both employers and potential employees.

A specialised form of part-time work is that which is a kind of overtime, in which a person works extra time for a second employer in order to increase earnings. Known as *moonlighting*, this includes such jobs as taxi-driving and bartending as well as the more specialised tasks such as dealing with other people's income tax claims. The second employer gains considerable benefit, obtaining the services of perhaps a skilled and experienced employee without having to invest in that person's training or future career.

Flexible working hours

A typical arrangement for flexible working hours is where the organisation abandons a fixed starting and finishing time for the working day. Instead employees start work at a predetermined time in the period between 8.00 a.m. and 10.00 a.m. and finish between 4.00 p.m. and 6.00 p.m. They are obliged to be present during the core time of 10 till 4, but can use the flexible time at the beginning and end of the working day to produce a pattern of working hours that fits in with their personal needs and preferences. The main advantage of this scheme is that it enables people to avoid peak travel times and the awkward rigidity of the inflexible starting time. From the organisation's point of view it can eliminate the tendency towards a frozen period at the beginning and end of the day when nothing happens – for the first twenty minutes everyone is looking at the paper or making coffee, and for the last twenty minutes everyone is preparing to go home. If the process of individual start-up and slow-down is spread over a longer period the organisation is operational for longer.

The scheme described above assumes that the necessary number of hours will be worked each day. The variations on the theme increase flexibility by allowing a longer settlement period, so that employees can work varying lengths of time on different days, provided that they complete the quota appropriate for the week or month or whatever other settlement period is agreed. This means that someone can take a half-day off for shopping or a full day off for a long weekend, as long as the quota is made up within a prescribed period.

As most organisations depend on a high degree of interaction between staff members for their operations to be viable, all are required to be in attendance for the core time period of the day, although this is waived in schemes where people are allowed to take half or whole days off. A further control is on the bandwidth, which is the time between the earliest feasible starting time and the latest possible finishing time. If this becomes too great the working day attenuates in a rather costly way.

One feature of flexible hours which is often resented by employees is the way in which their attendance is registered, as there has been a tendency to reintroduce time clocks or the more sophisticated elapsed time recorders as a way of controlling the attendance of the individual person. While it is conventional for employees to 'fight' mechanical time recording because of its rigidity, there is also the feeling that it is at least fair. There can be no suspicion that some people are not putting in their full complement of hours, nor that some have bluer eyes than others. On the other hand it is less likely to generate an atmosphere where people develop the type of open-ended approach to working hours that some managers regard as commitment.

In many areas of white-collar employment time-keeping is a matter of mutual trust rather than control. In this type of situation there might be strong resistance to mechanical time recording, largely because the motives for its introduction would be suspect. Management will also have reservations about installing expensive time-recording equipment that has not previously been necessary.

Annual hours

New working patterns offer the opportunity to reduce costs and improve performance. Organisations need a better match between employee working hours and the operating profile of the business in order to improve customer response time and increase productivity.

The 'annual hours' approach has proved to be an effective method of tackling the problem. Central to each annual hours agreement is that the period of time wihin which full-time employees must work their contractual hours is defined over a whole year. All normal working hours contracts can be converted to annual hours; for example, an average 38-hour week becomes 1732 annual hours, assuming five weeks' holiday entitlement. The principal advantage of annual hours in manufacturing sectors which need to maximise the utilisation of expensive assets comes from the ability to separate employee working time from the operating hours of the plant and equipment. Thus we have seen the growth of five-crew systems, in particular in the continuous process industries. Such systems are capable of delivering 168 hours of production a week by rotating five crews. In 365 days there are 8760 hours to be covered, requiring 1752 annual hours from each shift crew, averaging just over 38 hours for 46 weeks. All holidays can be rostered into 'off' weeks, and fifty or more weeks of production can be planned in any one year without resorting to overtime. Further variations can be incorporated to deal with fluctuating levels of seasonal demand.

Of course, there are many sectors of industry which do not have an operational need to work 168 hours a week and yet they wish to improve productivity. Lynch provides an example:

> a company that is operating a three shift system on a 37½ hour week (Monday to Friday) may currently use weekend hours at premium rates to meet extra production, this being the only flexible option available. A move to six-day working (i.e. from 112 operating hours to 144) would increase production by 28%. A move to seven-day working would increase production by 50%. (Lynch 1988, p. 37)

The move to annual hours is an important step for a company to take and should not be undertaken without careful consideration and planning. Managers need to be sure of all the consequences. Tangible savings include all those things that are not only measurable but are capable of being measured before the scheme is put in. Some savings such as reduced absenteeism are measurable only after the scheme has been running and therefore cannot be counted as part of the cost justification.

Distance working and sub-contracting

In the quest for greater flexibility many employers are beginning to explore new ways of getting work done which do not involve individuals working full-time on their premises.

Working overseas, selling in the field and home-working are the most obvious types of distance working. Other types of distance employment include teleworking, working on far-flung sites, or off-site as sub-contractors and consultants. Contractually 'distant' or 'peripheral' working can include anything that is different from the traditional full-time contract even though employees may be geographically present for part or all of the time; for example, part-time and job sharing, temporary and short-term working, on-site sub-contracting and consultancy.

Between 1986 and 1993 the number of self-employed people in Britain increased from 2,566,000 to 2,902,000 moving from 11 per cent to just over 12 per cent of the working population, although the population was slightly higher in 1991 (*Social Trends* 1994, p. 58). Rothwell (1987) has identified several issues relating to the employment of distance workers. These are considered next.

Finding the right people

One source may be existing staff who would prefer more flexible working arrangements, or those who have left employment for family reasons, travel, redundancy or early retirement. Sub-contractors whose businesses have been set up as a result of company hive-offs or buy-outs are another potential source. Information regarding the relevant public and private agencies, sub-contractors and consultants may well be something which more managers need to acquire. More effective relationships can be established by taking time to classify needs and developing longer-term arrangements with public/private agencies and with sub-contractors.

Job specification and selection

Job specification is important in all selection processes but is critical in most forms of geographically and contractually distant working, particularly in sub-contracted work. It is important to set out clearly defined parameters of action, criteria for decision and issues which need reference back. Person specifications are also crucial, since in much distance working there is less scope for employees to be trained or socialised on-the-job. In addition, 'small business' skills are likely to be needed by teleworkers, networkers, consultants and sub-contractors.

Communication and control

Attention needs to be given to the initial stages of settling in these distance workers. Those off-site need to know the pattern of regular links and contacts to be followed. Those newly recruited to the company need the same induction information as regular employees. In fact, those working independently with less supervision may need additional material, particularly on health and safety. Heightened team building skills will also be needed to encompass staff who are working on a variety of different contracts and at different locations.

Pay and performance

A key aspect of the employment of distance workers is the close link between pay and performance. Managers must be able to specify job targets and requirements accurately and to clarify and agree these with the employees or contractors concerned. Where a fee rather than a salary is paid, the onus is on the manager to ensure that the work has been completed satisfactorily. Others (consultants, teleworkers, networkers) may be paid on the basis of time, and it is for the supervisor to ensure the right level and quality of output for that payment.

It is doubtful whether pay levels of peripheral staff can be related to existing job-evaluated systems or salary structures. Indeed, one great advantage of extending the variety of peripheral workers is the ability to move outside those constraints, which may no longer be appropriate. Concepts of the total compensation package may need to be examined more closely in deciding how much less relevant to distance workers will financial services (e.g. low interest loans) become, while the provision of home computers becomes more important.

REVIEW TOPIC 11.2

Consider either the organisation where you work or an organisation where you have a fair idea of what is involved in a number of different jobs, such as a hospital or a television company. Which jobs would it be most suitable, from a management point of view, to staff on the following bases?

Compressed hours
Annual hours
Short-term contracts
Consultancy

The contract of employment

The contract of employment governs the relationship between an employer and an employee. Other types of contract will be made between an employing organisation and those who do the work of the business without being its employees. The contract will be one of the following:

- *Permanent:* This is open-ended and without a date of expiry.

- *Fixed-term:* This has a fixed starting and finishing date, though it may have provision for notice before the agreed finishing date.
- *Temporary:* Temporary contracts are for people employed explicitly for a limited period, but with the expiry date not precisely specified. A specialised form of temporary contract is where someone is employed to carry out a specified task, so that expiry date is when the task is complete.

Employees who work sixteen hours a week or more have the same legal rights as full-timers, but those who work between eight and sixteen hours only acquire these rights when they have been in continuous service with the employer for five years. Employers are not legally obliged to pay the same rates to those working part-time as to those working full-time, but they are bound by the Equal Pay Act, so that part-timers could have a claim for equal pay if they can identifiy a full-time worker of the opposite sex carrying out similar work.

Expiry or performance of contract may be the most normal form of termination for most contracts, consultants or short-term workers. Termination of part-timers will be likely to follow the same legal and contractual procedures as for other staff, depending on their length of service, notice of period of terms and conditions agreed with unions and incorporated into their contracts. Where dismissal is for reasons of redundancy, selection only of part-timers or of other peripheral groups could constitute unlawful 'indirect' discrimination if these were mainly of one sex; proportionate percentage selection of part-time and full-time employees might be more appropriate unless the work was only performed by one group and no suitable alternative offers at all could be made.

Termination of peripheral workers' contracts or disciplinary dismissal may call for legal advice, given the complexity of the position of many categories of flexi-workers.

Table 11.5 *Checklist for preparing a contract of employment*

1. Name of employer; name of employee
2. Date on which employment began
3. Job title
4. Rate of pay, period and method of payment
5. Normal hours of work and related conditions, such as meal-breaks
6. Arrangements for holidays and holiday pay, including means whereby both can be calculated precisely
7. Terms and conditions relating to sickness, injury and sick pay
8. Terms and conditions of pension arrangements, including a note about whether or not the employment is contracted out under the provisions of the Social Security Pensions Act 1975
9. Length of notice due to and from employee
10. Disciplinary rules and procedure
11. Arrangements for handling employee grievances
12. (Where applicable) Conditions of employment relating to trade union membership

The Preying Mantis

'Of all the businesses, by far,
Consultancy's the most bizarre.
For, to the penetrating eye,
There's no apparent reason why,
With no more assets than a pen,
This group of personable men
Can sell to clients more than twice
The same ridiculous advice,
Or find, in such a rich profusion,
Problems to fit their own solution.

The strategy that they pursue –
To give advice instead of do –
Keeps their fingers on the pulses
Without recourse to stomach ulcers,
And brings them monetary gains,
Without a modicum of pain.
The wretched object of their quest,
Reduced to cardiac arrest,
Is left alone to implement
The asinine report they've sent.
Meanwhile the analysts have gone
Back to client number one,
Who desperately needs their aid
To tidy up the mess they made.
And on and on – ad infinitum –
The masochistic clients invite 'em.
Until the merciful reliever.
Invokes the company receiver.

No one really seems to know
The rate at which consultants grow,
By some amoeba-like division?
Or chemobioligic fission?
They clone themselves without an end
Along their exponential trend.
The paradox is each adviser,
If he makes his client wiser,
Inadvertently destroys
The basis of his future joys.
So does anybody know
Where latter-day consultants go?

Ralph Windle, 1985

The *Bertie Ramsbottom Ballad* within the box incorporates nearly all the nightmares about consultants. Although the ballad is directed at external consultants whose services are bought in, many of the reservations also apply to much personnel work, which is advisory and seeking to bring about change in the attitudes and practices of managerial colleagues.

Some personnel activities are undoubtedly best undertaken by consultants. An example is the use of personnel tests in selection. These have been available for many years as a means of making selection more systematic and objective, yet their use remains limited and is sometimes misguided. Few employing organisations are big enough to have a scale of recruitment *for similar posts* that produces a large enough set of results for analysis and comparison to be fruitful. The Royal Air Force selects trainee pilots using a battery of tests developed over many years. There is also a wealth of evidence from tests and subsequent performance, for the ability to fly an aircraft to be predicted with reasonable accuracy from test results alone.

Few other employers can accumulate enough evidence to make comparable predictions, but specialist firms of consultants can, at least theoretically, produce occupational norms to provide useful performance indicators from test results. Duncan Wood (1985) asked senior representatives of fourteen well-established consultancies to rank seven reasons for their use in personnel work. The result was:

First: to provide specialist expertise and wider knowledge not available within the client organisation.
Second: to provide an independent view.
Third: to act as a catalyst.
Fourth: to provide extra resources to meet temporary requirements.
Fifth: to help develop a consensus when there are divided views about proposed changes.
Sixth: to demonstrate to employees the impartiality/objectivity of personnel changes or decisions.
Seventh: to justify potentially unpleasant decisions. (Wood 1985, p. 41)

In earlier research it was found that confident and competent personnel managers can call on the services of outside experts without fear of jeopardising their own position and being able to specify closely what they require (Torrington and Mackay 1986).

REVIEW TOPIC 11.3

What personnel problems currently facing your organisation do you think might best be approached by using outside consultants? Why? How would you specify the requirements?

What personnel problems currently facing your organisation would you not remit to outside consultants? Why not?

Where the personnel function is under-resourced, or where the personnel manager lacks professional expertise, then consultants will be used reluctantly, with a poor specification of requirements and the likelihood of an unsatisfactory outcome for both client and consultant.

In deciding whether or not outside consultants should be used for a specific assignment we suggest the following approach.

Describe the problem

What is the matter about which you might seek external advice? This may not be obvious, as worrying away at an issue can show that the real matter needing to be addressed is not what is immediately apparent. If, for example, the marketing manager leaves abruptly – as they often seem to do – the immediate problem will present itself as 'We must find a replacement'. So you begin to think of ringing up the executive search consultant you used when you needed someone for the Middle East in a hurry. Working at finding a correct description of the problem could suggest that the presenting cause is easy to deal with because young X has been waiting for just such an opportunity for months and all the signals suggest that X would be ideal. The 'real' problem may turn out to be what caused the marketing manager to leave, or whether there is a string of other 'young X's waiting in the wings. It could require attention to succession planning, remuneration strategy, management development, organisation structure or many more alternative possibilities.

Formulate an approach

The next step is to rough out an approach to the problem, with the emphasis here on 'rough'. If you knew the answer you would not need any further advice; if you have no idea of the answer you cannot brief a consultant (but you might give him a blank cheque!). What is needed is a clear but not inflexible strategy so that you can go through the remaining stages of making up your mind without putting the consultant, and yourself, in the wrong framework. If you decide that the problem behind the departure of the marketing manager is a combination of succession planning and remuneration policy, the approach you would then formulate would be based on ideas about how those two issues could be tackled, without an absolute commitment to a single method or technique.

Work out how you could do it in-house

The '5 W-H method', could be used at this stage, as you decide how it could be tackled by using your own existing resources, how much it would cost, how long it would take and what the repercussions would be, such as stopping work on something else.

Whether one is specifying a brief for an outside consultant or coming to terms oneself with a problem that has been presented, there is a need for some device to describe the problem as a preliminary to formulating an approach to solving it. Priestley and his colleagues (1978, p. 28) suggest a simple '5 W-H' method which is What? Who? Where? When? Why? and How? A typical problem could be approached thus:

What is the problem?	Communications in the office are poor.
Who is involved?	Everyone, but most problems are at the level of first-line supervision.
Where is it worst?	In Accounts and in the Print Room.
When is it worst?	At the end of the week and at the end of the month.
Why does it happen?	Because of an erratic flow of work between the two departments, which is worst at those times.
How could it be tackled?	By getting the first-line supervisors to tackle it, smooth out the flow of work, helping them to appreciate the effect of their work flows on the other departments, etc.

This is a very simple problem with a minimal number of questions serving to do no more than illustrate the method. Each question would probably have dozens of supplementaries in order to fill out the details of a complex problem.

The main value of the consultant at this stage is the ability to raise questions that those close to the matter have not thought about. This is not because consultants are cleverer, but because they have a different pattern of experience and take for granted different things from those who are looking at the presenting problem every day.

Find out how it could be done by consultants

Provided you have done the first two steps satisfactorily, it should be possible to brief one or more potential outside suppliers of expertise, so that they can bid for the business. If the problem is not correctly described there may be bids for the wrong things, and if the approach is not accurately formulated the consultant will be obliged to carry out a preliminary study, at your expense, to formulate an approach for you. When this happens you are beginning to lose control of the operation. Even if consultants are not as rapacious and asinine as Bertie Ramsbottom suggests, they too have a business to run and will not welcome failure through an assignment being misconceived, so they will guard against the risk. The main questions to ask of the consultants are, again, how it would be done, how much it would cost and how long it would take.

Decide between the alternatives

A set of alternatives from which to choose gives you the opportunity to compare relative costs, times and likely outputs, as well as implications. In making the final

Table 11.6 *Categorisation of views from sixty-two respondents about outside consultants*

A.		Favourable views
	1	The personnel manager knows what to do, but proposals are more likely to be implemented if endorsed by outside experts
	2	The outsider can often clarify the personnel manager's understanding of an issue
	3	Specialist expertise is sometimes needed
	4	The personnel manager has insufficient time to deal with a particular matter on which a consultant could work full-time
	5	The consultant is independent
	6	Using consultants can be cheaper than employing your own full-time, permanent specialists
B		Less favourable views
	1	The personnel function should contain all the necessary expertise
	2	In-house personnel specialists know what is best for the company.
	3	Other members of the organisation are prejudiced against the use of outside advisers
	4	Using consultants can jeopardise the position of the personnel specialists and reduce their influence.

decision the comments in Table 11.6 are helpful, but the most important point to remember is that the responsibility is inescapably yours. If the consultant can produce the 'best' outcome, have you the resources to implement it? Can you wait? If you can save £10,000 by relying on your own staff and time, will you produce an outcome that adequately meets the needs of your rough-cut approach? The eventual outcome is all that matters.

☐   SUMMARY PROPOSITIONS

11.1 Patterns of employment are changing in order to give the employer greater flexibility in staffing the organisation and to give the employee greater autonomy.

11.2 Significant reductions in working hours have usually come in times of relative prosperity.

11.3 The use of shift working is increasing.

11.4 The use of part-time working (particularly by women) has increased considerably in recent years.

11.5 The use of flexible working hours is now well established. The logical development of this principle – annual hours – is gaining increased application.

11.6 Distance working is developing slowly and presents particular problems in selection, job specification, communication and control, pay and performance.

11.7 Contracts of employment exist only for employees and can be permanent, temporary or fixed-term.

11.8 The use of outside consultants for personnel activities is rising.

11.9 In deciding between outside and in-house resources, the stages are to describe the problem, formulate an approach, work out how to do it in-house, find out how it could be done by consultants, and then decide between alternatives.

References

Atkinson, J. (1982), *Shiftworking*, IMS Report no. 45, London: Institute of Manpower Studies.

Bienefeld, M. A. (1972), *Working Hours in British Industry: An Economic History*, London: Weidenfeld & Nicolson.

British Institute of Management (BIM) (1985), *Managing New Patterns of Work*, London: British Institute of Management Foundation.

Central Statistical Office (1994), *Social Trends 24*, London: HMSO.

Clutterbuck, D. (1985), *New Patterns of Work*, Aldershot: Gower.

Falconer, H. (1990), 'Children at work', *Personnel Today*, April, p. 14.

Incomes Data Services (IDS) (1983), *Flexible Working Hours*, IDS Study 301. London: Incomes Data Services Ltd.

Incomes Data Services (1985), *Improving Productivity*, IDS Study 331. London: Incomes Data Services Ltd.

Lee, R. A. (1983), 'Hours of work – who controls and how?' *Industrial Relations Journal*, vol. 14, no. 4.

Lynch, P. (1988), 'Matching worked hours to business needs', *Personnel Management*, June, pp. 36–9.

Office des Publications Officielles des Communautés Européennes (1993), *Labour Force Survey*, Luxembourg.

Rothwell, S. (1987), 'How to manage from a distance', *Personnel Management*, September, pp. 22–6.

Torrington, D. P. and Mackay, L. E. (1986), 'Will consultants take over the personnel function?' *Personnel Management*, February, pp. 34–7.

Wedderburn, A. (1975), 'Waking up to shiftwork', *Personnel Management*, vol. 7, no. 2.

Windle, R. (1985), *The Bottom Line*, London: Century-Hutchinson.

Wood, D. (1985) 'The uses and abuses of personnel consultants', *Personnel Management*, October, pp. 40–7.

12 Recruitment

In the last edition of this book our chapter on recruitment opened with the following quotation:

> Recruitment is the biggest single challenge facing personnel managers in the 1990s. Current skill shortages and forecasts of a huge drop in the number of young people available for work in the coming decade point to rapidly deteriorating recruitment prospects ... the situation looks bleak for those employers who fail to change their ways and are slow to look to non-traditional methods of recruitment, as well as more innovative forms of employment. (Curnow 1989)

That conclusion was reached following a survey of more than 1000 personnel professional carried out by *Personnel Management* (November 1989) with the assistance of MSL International. It is now clear that the prediction was incorrect and very few employers, apart from those in specialised areas, report significant recruitment problems. The general level of unemployment is, however, falling steadily and recruitment will always be a major feature of the personnel function. There is always a need for replacement employees and those with unfamiliar skills that business growth makes necessary. Recruitment is also an area in which there are important social and legal implications, but perhaps most important is the significant part played in the lives of individual men and women by their personal experience of

On graduating from university, Howard was employed as a management trainee by a large bank and was soon assigned to taking part in 'milk round' interviews of prospective graduate recruits, which he found interesting and a boost to his ego. After two years in the bank a programme of reorganisation led to Howard being out of a job. It was seven months before he was employed again and he had undergone many disappointments and frustrations. His new post was again in recruitment and he wrote himself a short homily on a postcard which he kept propped up on his desk. It said: when you turn someone down, remember:

First, what the experience of rejection can do to a person.
Second, that the rejected person may be a customer.
Third, you may want to recruit that person later.

recruitment and the failure to be recruited. Everyone reading these pages will know how significant those experiences have been in their own lives.

In this chapter we shall consider various aspects of an employer's recruitment strategy; determining the vacancy, the range of recruitment methods available, recruitment advertising and several features of recruitment method, including employee documentation and shortlisting.

Determining the vacancy

Is there a vacancy? Is it to be filled by a newly recruited employee? These are the first questions to be answered in recruitment. Potential vacancies occur either through someone leaving or as a result of expansion. When a person leaves, there is no more than a prima facie case for filling the vacancy thus caused; there may be other ways of filling the gap. Vacancies caused by expansion may be real or imagined. The desperately pressing need of an executive for an assistant may be a plea more for recognition than for assistance. The creation of a new post to deal with a specialist activity may be more appropriately handled by contracting that activity out to a supplier. Recruiting a new employee may be the most obvious tactic when a vacancy occurs, but it is not necessarily the most appropriate. Listed below are some of the options.

- *Reorganise the work:* jobs may be rearranged so that the total amount of work in a section is done by the remaining employees without replacement of the leaver. One clue to the likelihood of this being the right move lies in the reasons for leaving. If the person has left because there was not enough to do, or because the other employees formed a tight-knit group that was difficult to break into, then there may be grounds for considering this strategy. It can also work between departments, with people redundant in one are being redeployed elsewhere.

- *Use overtime:* extra output can be achieved by using overtime, although there is always the possibility that the work to be done is simply expanded to fill the greater amount of time available for its completion. Few personnel managers like the extensive use of overtime and it lacks logic at a time of high unemployment, but it may be the best way of dealing with a short-term problem where, for instance, one employee leaves a month before another is due back from maternity leave.

- *Mechanise the work:* there are all sorts of ways in which the work of a departing member of staff can be mechanised, though it is seldom feasible to mechanise, automate or robotise on the basis of a single, casual vacancy. However, the non-replacement of a departing member of staff is often used to justify the expense of introducing new equipment.

- *Stagger the hours:* as we saw in Chapter 11, there can be staffing economies in introducing shifts, staggering hours or trying flexible working hours. It is again rarely practicable to take these steps when there is a single vacancy, although sometimes a staggering of hours can work in that sort of situation.

- *Make the job part-time:* replacing full-time jobs with part-time jobs has become a widespread practice and has the attraction of making marginal reductions more possible at the same time as providing the possibility of marginally increasing the amount of staff time available in the future by redefining the job as full-time. It also provides potential flexibility by making it possible to turn one full-time job into two part-time posts located in two separate places.

- *Sub-contract the work:* by this means the employer avoids ongoing costs and obligations of employing people by transferring those obligations to another employer. It is simpler to do this when the work can be easily moved elsewhere, such as some features of computer programming, than when the work has to be done on your own premises, with the comparisons of terms and conditions that inevitably take place. Also the advantages of avoiding employment costs and obligations have to be offset against the disadvantages of less direct control and probably higher overall costs in the medium term.

- *Use an agency:* a similar strategy is to use an agency to provide temporary personnel, who again do not come onto the company payroll.

REVIEW TOPIC 12.1

Can you think of further ways of avoiding filling a vacancy by recruiting a new employee? What are the advantages and disadvantages of the methods you have thought of? For what types of job with which you are familiar would each of your methods, and those listed above, be most appropriate?

If your decision is that you are going to recruit, there are then four questions to determine the vacancy:

1. What does the job consist of?

2. In what way is it to be different from the job done by the previous incumbent?

3. What are the aspects of the job that specify the type of candidate?

4. What are the key aspects of the job that the ideal candidate wants to know before deciding to apply?

The conventional personnel approach to these questions is to produce job descriptions and personnel specifications; methods of doing this are well established (see Table 12.1). Good accounts are to be found in Ungerson (1983) and Pearn and Kandola (1988). We have found, however, that less than half of personnel departments use job analysis and its products for recruitment and selection, usually

Table 12.1 *Job description for senior sales assistant*

Job title:
    Senior Sales Assistant

Context:
    The job is in one of the thirteen high technology shops owned by 'Computext'
    Location – Leeds
    Supervised by, and reports directly to the Shop Manager
    Responsible for one direct subordinate – Sales Assistant

Job summary:
    To assist and advise customers in the selection of computer hardware and software,
        and to arrange delivery and finance where appropriate
    Objective is to sell as much as possible, and for customer and potential customers to
        see 'Computext' staff as helpful and efficient

Job content: *Most frequent duties in order of importance*

1. Advise customers about hardware and software
2. Demonstrate the equipment and software
3. Organise delivery of equipment by liaising with distribution department
4. Answer all after-sales queries from customers
5. Contact each customer two weeks after delivery to see if they need help
6. Advise customers about the variety of payment methods
7. Develop and keep up to date a computerised stock control system

    Occasional duties in order of importance
1. Arrange for faulty equipment to be replaced
2. Monitor performance of junior sales assistant as defined in job description
3. Advise and guide, train and assess junior sales assistant where necessary

Working conditions:
    Pleasant 'business-like' environment in new purpose-built shop premises in the city
    centre. There are two other members of staff and regular contact is also required
    with the Delivery Department and Head Office. Salary is £12,000 p.a. plus a twice
    yearly bonus depending on sales. Five weeks' holiday per year plus statutory
    holidays. A six-day week is worked

Other information:
    There is the eventual possibility of promotion to shop manager in another location
    depending on performance and opportunities

Performance standards:
    There are two critically important areas
1. Sales volume. Minimum sales to the value of £400,000 over each six-month
    accounting period
2. Relations with customers:
    *   customers' queries answered immediately
    *   customers always given a demonstration when they request this
    *   delivery times arranged to meet both customer and delivery department's
        needs
    *   complaints investigated immediately
    *   customers assured that problem resolved as soon as possible
    *   customers never blamed
    *   problems that cannot be dealt with referred immediately to
        Manager

because they wish to avoid the close definition and inflexibility that careful specification often implies. Our set of four questions is offered as an alternative.

Methods of recruitment

Once an employer has decided that external recruitment is necessary, a cost effective and appropriate method of recruitment must be selected (see Table 12.2). The survey mentioned at the opening of this chapter investigated the methods used by the 1000+ personnel professionals questioned (Curnow 1989).

The recruitment methods compared

The various methods of recruitment all have benefits and drawbacks, and the choice of a method has to be made in relation to the particular vacancy and the type of labour market in which the job falls. A general review of advantages and drawbacks is given in Table 12.3.

REVIEW TOPIC 12.2

We have seen the significance of informal methods of recruitment whereby new employees come as a result of hearing about a vacancy from friends, or putting their names down for consideration when a vacancy occurs. Employees starting employment in this way present the employer with certain advantages as they come knowing that they were not wooed by the employer: the initiative was theirs. Also they will probably have some contacts in the company already that will help them to settle and cope with the induction crisis. What are the drawbacks of this type of arrangement?

Table 12.2   *Usage of various methods of recruitment by 1000+ personnel professionals questioned by Curnow (1989)*

Advertisements in regional press	87%
Advertisements in specialist press	80%
Advertisements in national press	78%
Job centres	71%
Employment agencies	62%
Recruitment consultants	61%
Executive search consultants	36%
Career conventions	35%
Open days	32%
Recruitment fairs	32%
University milk rounds	21%
Radio/advertising	17%
Other forms of recruitment	6%

Table 12.3 *Advantages and drawbacks of different methods of recruitment*

Job Centres

Advantages	(a)	Applicants can be selected from nationwide sources with convenient, local availability of computer-based data
	(b)	Socially responsible and secure
	(c)	Can produce applicants very quickly
Drawbacks	(a)	Registers are mainly of the unemployed rather than of the employed seeking a change

Commercial employment agencies

Advantages	(a)	Established as the normal method for filling certain vacancies, e.g. secretaries in London
	(b)	Little administrative chore for the employer
Drawbacks	(a)	Can produce staff who are likely to stay only a short time
	(b)	Widely distrusted by employers (Knollys 1983, p. 234)

Management Selection Consultants

Advantages	(a)	Opportunity to elicit applicants anonymously
	(b)	Opportunity to use expertise of consultant in an area where employer will not be regularly in the market
Drawbacks	(a)	Internal applicants may feel, or be, excluded
	(b)	Cost

Executive Search Consultants ('headhunters')

Advantages	(a)	Known individuals can be approached directly
	(b)	Useful if employer has no previous experience in specialist field
	(c)	Recruiting from, or for, an overseas location
Drawbacks	(a)	Cost
	(b)	Potential candidates outside the headhunter's network are excluded
	(c)	The recruit may remain on the consultant's list and be hunted again

Visiting universities ('the milk round')

Advantages	(a)	The main source of new graduates from universities
	(b)	Inexpensive and administratively convenient through using the free services of the University Appointments Service
Drawbacks	(a)	Interviewees are often enquirers rather than applicants
	(b)	Interviewing schedules can be fatiguing

Schools and the Careers Service

Advantages	(a)	Can produce a regular annual flow of interested enquirers
	(b)	Very appropriate for the recruitment of school-leavers, who seldom look further than the immediate locality for their first employment
Drawbacks	(a)	Schools and the advisers are more interested in occupations than organisations

Recruitment advertising

Apart from using recruitment consultants, most employers will deal with an advertising agency to help with drafting the advertisements and placing them in suitable media. The basic service such an agency will provide is considerable:

only one copy of the text need be supplied no matter how many publications are to be used; the agency will book space; prepare the layout and typography; read and correct proofs; verify that the right advertisement has appeared in the right publications at the right time; and only one cheque has to be raised to settle the agency's monthly account. (Plumbley 1985, p. 55)

These basic technical services are of great value to the personnel manager and are 'free' in that the agency derives its income from the commission paid by the journals on the value of the advertising space sold. The personnel manager placing, for instance, £50,000 of business annually with an agency will appreciate that the agency's income from that will be between £5000 and £7500, and will expect a good standard of service. The important questions relate to the experience of the agency in dealing with recruitment, as compared with other types of advertising, the quality of the advice they can offer about media choice, and the quality of response that their advertisements produce.

Well-known agencies can provide another benefit to the employer wishing to advertise anonymously, as the advertisement can appear under the agency's masthead. This can be more productive than using a box number in those few situations where it is prudent to conceal the company's identity in the early stages. Advantages and drawbacks of various methods of job advertising are shown in Table 12.4.

Advertising media

Choosing the appropriate medium for your advertisement will be a subject for advice from your advertising agency, but remembering the basis of their income you may want to take an independent view as well. The best source of information on what to choose will be previous experience. If three column centimetres of classified advertising in your local weekly free-sheet have always produced an adequate number of prospective sales representatives before, why change? Many posts, however, do not recur often enough to provide that background data. Also, the labour market is changing constantly and last year's experience may be this year's irrelevance.

The key pieces of information are circulation and readership, as these tell you both how wide the readership is and how much of that will be wasted. Table 12.5 shows the circulation and percentage share of the main daily and Sunday newspapers over two decades, indicating a decline in the sale of quality dailies over that period. To this must be added the information about who constitutes the readership. The National Readership Survey, which is commissioned annually by the media owners, gives figures based on occupations showing, for instance, that 61,000 accountants read the *Daily Telegraph* and 73,000 graduate engineers read the *Daily Express*, suggesting that you advertise for accountants in one paper and for engineers in the other.

The 'Recruitment Report' section of *Personnel Management* (see Table 12.6) reports monthly on the distribution of recruitment advertising in quality newspapers, but the main source of detailed information about the readership of news-

Table 12.4 *Advantages and drawbacks of various methods of job advertising*

Internal advertisement

Advantages	(a)	Maximum information to all employees, who might then act as recruiters
	(b)	Opportunity for all internal pretenders to apply
	(c)	If an internal candidate is appointed there is a shorter induction period
	(d)	Speed
	(e)	Cost
Drawbacks	(a)	Limit to number of applicants
	(b)	Internal candidates not matched against those from outside
	(c)	May be unlawful if indirect discrimination. See Chapter 21

Vacancy lists outside premises

Advantages	(a)	Economical way of advertising, particularly if premises are near a busy thoroughfare
Drawbacks	(a)	Vacancy list likely to be seen by few people
	(b)	Usually possible to put only barest information, such as the job title, or even just 'Vacancies'

Advertising in the national press

Advantages	(a)	Advertisement reaches large numbers
	(b)	Some national newspapers are the accepted medium for search by those seeking particular posts
Drawbacks	(a)	Cost
	(b)	Much of the cost 'wasted' in reaching inappropriate people

Advertising in the local press

Advantages	(a)	Recruitment advertisements more likely to be read by those seeking local employment
	(b)	Little 'wasted' circulation
Drawbacks	(a)	Local newspapers appear not to be used by professional and technical people seeking vacancies

Advertising in the technical press

Advantages	(a)	Reaches a specific population with minimum waste
	(b)	A minimum standard of applicant can be guaranteed
Drawbacks	(a)	Relatively infrequent publication may require advertising copy six weeks before appearance of advertisement
	(b)	Inappropriate when a non-specialist is needed, or where the specialism has a choice of professional publications

papers and journals is British Rate and Data (BRAD), which includes advertising rates, dates by which advertisements have to be received and occasional additional information by the publisher, for example:

> Accountancy Age, Britain's only weekly newspaper for accountants, is received by over 72,000 qualified accountants in industry, commerce, public practice, the City and both national and local government. It has the highest circulation and the highest readership among qualified accountants of any publicaion in the UK. (BRAD 1984, p. 237)

Table 12.5   *Circulation of market shares of national newspapers*

| | Readership (millions) | | |
	1971	1988	1992
Popular dailies	38.8	33.3	29.7
Sun	8.5	11.3	9.7
Daily Mirror	13.8	8.7	9.7
Daily Express	9.7	4.3	3.8
Daily Mail	4.8	4.3	4.5
Daily Star		3.3	2.4
Today		1.5	1.5
Quality dailies	6.5	7.0	6.5
Daily Telegraph	3.6	2.7	2.5
Guardian	1.1	1.3	1.3
The Times	1.1	1.1	1.0
Independent		1.1	1.1
Financial Times	0.7	0.8	0.6
Popular Sundays	53.1	40.9	39.4
News of the World	15.8	13.2	12.5
Sunday Mirror	13.5	8.9	8.8
Sunday People	13.4	7.8	6.1
Sunday Express	10.4	5.7	4.9
Sunday Sport			1.3
Mail on Sunday		5.3	5.8
Quality Sundays	8.2	8.2	8.3
Sunday Times	3.7	3.8	3.5
Observer	2.4	2.1	1.7
Sunday Telegraph	2.1	2.3	1.8
Independent on Sunday			1.3

Source: Based on *Social Trends 20* 1990, p. 157 and *Social Trends 24* 1994, p. 133.

Table 12.6   *Percentage share of recruitment advertising in quality newspapers, April 1994*

Newspaper	Percentage share
Guardian	42.8
Daily Telegraph	12.4
Times	10.8
Financial Times	9.6
Independent	7.0
Sunday Times	12.7
Independent on Sunday	2.9
Observer	1.7

Source: *Personnel Management* 1994, p. 79.

Drafting the advertisement

The decision on what to include in a recruitment advertisement is important because of the high cost of space and the need to attract attention; both factors will encourage the use of the fewest number of words. The agency placing it will be able to advise on this, as they will on the way the advertisment should be worded, but the following is a short checklist of items that must be included.

Name and brief details of employing organisation

The recruiter seeking anonymity will usually eschew press advertising in favour of some other medium. The advertisement that conceals the identity of the advertiser will be suspected by readers, not least for fear that they might be applying to their present organisation. If the advertisement conceals the name but gives clues to the identity of the organisation ('our expanding high-precision engineering company in the pleasant suburbs of...') then there is the danger that the reader will guess... wrongly. Brief details will fill in some of the uncertainty about what exactly the organisation is and does. The better known the employer, the less important the details.

Job and duties

The potential applicant will want to know what the job is. The title will give some idea, including a subjective assessment of its status, but rarely will this be sufficient. Particularly for knowledge workers, some detail of duties will be sought. Potential candidates are increasingly interested in the training and development that will be available. If space permits, this should also be included.

Key points of the personnel specification

If you really believe that the only candidates who will be considered are those with a specific qualification, then this may be included in the advertisement. Not only do you preclude other applicants who would be wasting your time and theirs, you also bring the vacancy into sharper focus for those you are seeking. But do you want to limit your search to that extent? If, for instance, you ask for 'full, clean driving licence', do you really wish to exclude all those who have ever had any sort of endorsement, or only those who have current endorsements? Do you really mean a *clean* driving licence or a valid licence? Other typical key points are further qualifications and experience, as long as these can be expressed clearly. 'Highly qualified' and 'considerable experience' are valueless in an advertisement.

Salary

Many employers are coy about declaring the salary that will accompany the advertised post. Sometimes this is reasonable as the salary scales are well known and inflexible, as in much public sector employment. Elsewhere the coyness is due either to the fact that the employer has a general secrecy policy about salaries and does not want to publicise the salary of a position to be filled for fear of dissatisfying holders of other posts, or does not know what to offer and is waiting to see 'what the mail brings'. Figure 12.6 lists the phrases about salary used in a single issue on one quality paper. This includes some of the common jargon terms. 'c.' is an abbreviation of the Latin *circa*, meaning about, 'k' means 1,000, as in kilometre, 'neg' is short for negotiable, and 'OTE' stands for on-target-earnings.

The other common feature of phrases about salary is to include words which are meaningless. Table 12.7 includes 'attractive', 'competitive', 'excellent', 'exceptional', 'significant' and 'substantial' as explanations of the income level. It is very difficult indeed to argue that these terms mean anything that would cause an applicant to apply for one job rather than another.

REVIEW TOPIC 12.3

Table 12.7 contains phrases about the value in pay terms of eighteen different jobs. Try putting them in rank order of actual cash value to the recipient. Then ask a friend to do the same thing and compare your lists.

What to do

Finally, the advertisement tells potential applicants what to do. This will vary according to the nature of the post. It is conventional for manual employees to call at the personnel department, while managerial employees will be more disposed to write. Applicants who obey the instruction 'write with full details to...' will be understandably discouraged if the response to their letter is an application form to be completed, giving roughly the same information in a different way. Application forms are now generally accepted, but applicants not only feel it is unnecessary to be asked for the same information twice, they also develop reservations about the administrative efficiency of the organisation that they had been thinking of joining.

Table 12.7 *Phrases used about salary in job advertising*

1.	*c.* £60,000 + bonus + car + benefits
2.	from *c.* £35–
3.	£30,000–£40,000 + substantial bonus + car
4.	You will already be on a basic annual salary of not less than £40,000
5.	Six figure remuneration + profit share + benefits
6.	*c.* £60,000 package
7.	Attractive package
8.	Substantial package
9.	£50,000 OTE plus car and substantial benefits
10.	*c.* £45k + bonus + benefits
11.	*c.* £60,000 + excellent package
12.	£ excellent + benefits
13.	To £35,000 + car + benefits
14.	*c.* £35,000 + car + benefits + exceptional OTE opportunities
15.	*c.* £60k package + banking benefits
16.	Competitive salary + benefits
17.	Significant salary and associated benefits
18.	£ Neg.

Source: *The Sunday Times*, 26 June 1994.

Advertising control

The personnel manager needs to monitor the effectiveness of advertising and all other methods of recruitment, first to ensure value for money and secondly to ensure that the pool of applicants produced by the various methods is suitable. Jenkins (1983, p. 259) provides a useful example of monitoring the effectiveness of advertising for management trainees in retailing.

Table 12.8 shows a number of interesting points, the first being that employment decisions are mainly taken by applicants rather than by employers. Of the 370 originally expressing interest, over half eliminated themselves by not returning the application form. Of the twenty-three to whom jobs were offered more than a third did not take up the offer. An important part of the whole employment process is making sure that inappropriate people eliminate themselves from consideration, and they can only do this when given sufficient information to make that decision. The table also provides the information on approximately what number of initial applications are needed to produce a specific number of accepting candidates and what it costs to fill the vacancies by this means. We would suggest this type of simple, clear recording of developments is the most useful way of building up a stock of control data on which to develop a recruitment advertising strategy.

Table 12.8   *Monitoring the effectiveness of advertising for management trainees in retailing*

Medium	National press
Size of advertisement	60 column cm
Initial response	370
Booklets and application forms sent out	321
Applications returned	127
Selection board attended	95
Jobs offered	23
Jobs accepted	19
Employment actually started	15
Total cost	£1,440
Cost per starter	£96

Source: Jenkins 1983, p. 259

Employment documentation

Table 12.8 shows the importance of one type of documentation – the booklet sent out to applicants – as a means of focusing the minds of recruits on whether the job will suit them or not. We must also remember the significance of informal recruitment and the need to have information available to the casual enquirer, as well as documents for reference, such as the works rules or details of the pension scheme. We shall review some of the key documents.

The job description

As we saw in the last chapter, the job description is a basic element in providing information to applicants so that they can confirm or withdraw their application.

The advertisement

A copy of the advertisement will not only be needed for internal purposes and for the advertising agent; it can also form the basic information to the job centre and to casual inquirers.

The 'glossy'

Larger organisations tend to produce recruitment literature for general use or to target specific potential employees such as graduates. These publications are usually described as 'glossies', indicating some suspicion about their contents.

A study by Cooksey examining student attitudes towards recruitment brochures found that 'the company brochure was the single most important influence on students' decisions to apply to a particular company' (Cooksey 1988, p. 75). However, the influence factors lie not in the glossy presentation but in the *content* of the brochure – information about the company, training, promotion prospects, etc.

REVIEW TOPIC 12.4

Recruiters are interested in the job to be done, so that they concentrate on how the vacancy fits into the overall structure of the organisation and on the type of person to be sought. Applicants are interested in the work to be done, as they want to know what they will be doing and what the work will offer to them. Think of your own job and list both types of feature.

The job to be done	The work that is offered
1..	....
2..	....
3..	....
4..	....
5..	....

How does your listing of features on the right-hand side alter the wording of advertisements and other employment documentation?

Correspondence

It is essential to have some method of tracking recruitment, either manually or by computer, so that an immediate and helpful response can be given to applicants enquiring about the stage their applications have reached.

It is also necessary to ensure that all applicants are informed about the outcome of their application. This will first of all reduce the number of enquiries that have to be handled, but it is also an important aspect of public relations, as the organisation dealing with job applicants may also be dealing with prospective customers. Many people have the experience of applying for a post and then not hearing anything at all. Particularly when the application is unsolicited, personnel managers may feel that there is no obligation to reply, but this could be bad business as well as disconcerting for the applicant. Standard letters ('I regret to inform you that there were many applications and yours was not successful...') are better than nothing, but letters containing actual information ('out of the seventy-two applications, we included yours in our first shortlist of fifteen, but not in our final shortlist of eight') are better. Best of all are the letters that make practical suggestions, such as applying again in six months' time, asking if the applicant would like to be considered for another post elsewhere in the organisation, or pointing out the difficulty of applying for a post that calls for greater experience or qualifications than the applicant at that stage is able to present.

Miscellaneous information

Among the items of peripheral value in the employment process are works rules, general terms and conditions of employment, publicity material about products, the annual report, house magazines, etc.

Recruitment monitoring and evaluation

How effective is the recruiting you undertake? It is an expensive, time-consuming process with legal pitfalls, so you need some process to monitor the effectiveness of the process. One method is that illustrated in Table 12.4. Wright and Storey (1994, p. 209) suggest four numbers to collect:

- Number of initial enquiries received which resulted in completed application forms.
- Number of candidates at various stages in the recruitment and selection process, especially those shortlisted.
- Number of candidates recruited.
- Number of candidates retained in organisation after six months.

There needs, however, to be more than this in order to get to the more intangible questions, such as 'did the best candidate not even apply?'

The most important source of information about the quality of the recruitment process is the people involved in it. Do telephonists and receptionists know how to handle the tentative employment enquiry? What did they hear from applicants in the original enquiries that showed the nature of their reaction to the advertisement? Is it made simple for enquirers to check key points by telephone or personal visit? Is there an unnecessary emphasis on written applications before anything at all can be done? Useful information can also be obtained from both successful and unsuccessful applicants. Those who have been successful will obviously believe that recruitment was well done, while the unsuccessful may have good reason to believe that it was flawed. However, those who are unsuccessful sometimes ask for feedback on the reasons. If a recruiter is able to do that, it is also a simple development to ask the applicant for comment on the recruitment process.

Shortlisting

Shortlisting of candidates can be problematic in some instances because of small numbers of applicants and in other instances because of extremely large numbers of applicants. This can occasionally be attributed to inadequate specification of the criteria. For example:

> One advertisement that was placed in 1983, seeking management trainees and offering a salary in excess of £20,000, asked only for applicants to be of graduate level with some managerial or consulting experience. It appeared in the national press and gave very little additional information. Needless to say, it produced a huge response, as a large number of people, attracted by the salary, would meet the rather vague criteria. (Lewis 1985, p. 123)

There are, however, many instances when a job is attractive and widely understood as being similar to many others (like headteacher, sales representative or management trainee) where an inconspicuous advertisement can produce large numbers of applicants. The conventional method of handling these is to compare key points on the application form with the personnel specification, but large numbers sometimes induce a further stage of arbitrary preselection on the basis of some additional, whimsical criterion. Methods we have heard about include ruling out:

applicants over 45;
married women;
unmarried women;
unmarried men;
handwritten applications;
typewritten applications;
applicants who have been unemployed; and
applicants with poor hand-writing.

No doubt there are other arbitrary criteria being adopted by managers appalled at making sense of 100 or so application forms and assorted curricula vitae. Apart from those that are unlawful, these criteria are grossly unfair to applicants if not mentioned in the advertisement, and are a thoroughly unsatisfactory way of recruiting the most appropriate person. In addition, an increasing number of employers who fail to apply fair and objective selection and promotion procedures can expect to be given a tough time in the courts (Aikin 1988).

Care with shortlisting improves the prospects of being fair to all candidates and lessens the likelihood of calling inappropriate people for interview. Where selection is to be made by a panel, it also provides panel members with practice at working together and can clarify differences in attitude and expectation between them. The following outline procedure has been developed for use in that most difficult of situations: selection by a heterogeneous panel with a long list of applicants:

Stage 1: Panel members agree essential criteria for those to be placed on the shortlist.

Stage 2: Using those criteria, selectors individually produce personal lists of, for instance, ten candidates. An operating principle throughout is to concentrate on who can be included rather than who can be excluded, so that the process is positive, looking for strengths rather than shortcomings.

Stage 3: Selectors reveal their lists and find their consensus. If stages 1 and 2 have been done properly the degree of consensus should be quite high and probably sufficient to constitute a shortlist for interview. If it is still not clear, they continue to:

Stage 4: Discuss those candidates preferred by some but not all in order to clarify and reduce the areas of disagreement. A possible tactic is to classify candidates as 'strong', 'possible' or 'maverick'.

Stage 5: Selectors produce a final shortlist by discussion, guarding against including compromise candidates: not strong, but offensive to no one.

☐ SUMMARY PROPOSITIONS

12.1 Alternatives to filling a vacancy include reorganising the work; using overtime; mechanising the work; staggering the hours; making the job part-time; sub-contracting the work; using an employment agency.

12.2 Recent trends indicate a greater use by employers of recruitment agencies and executive consultants, open days, recruitment fairs, etc. Relocation constraints have also prompted a move towards the use of regional as opposed to national recruitment advertising.

12.3 Advertising agencies and specialist publications provide a wealth of information to ensure that advertisements reach the appropriate readership.

12.4 Recruiters need to think not only of the job that has to be done, but also of the work that is offered.

12.5 Increasing the amount of information provided to potential applicants reduces the number of inappropriate applications.

12.6 The most important feature of candidate decision-making in recruitment is finding an answer to the question, 'how much will I get paid?' Advertisements are frequently misleading on this.

12.7 Care with shortlisting increases the chances of being fair to all applicants and lessens the likelihood of calling inappropriate people for interview.

References

Aikin, O. (1988), 'Subjective criteria in selection', *Personnel Management*, September, p. 59.

British Rate and Data (BRAD) (1984), vol. 31, no. 12., London: BRAD.

Cooksey, L. (1988), 'Recruitment brochures – are students getting the message?' *Personnel Management*, p. 75.

Curnow, B. (1989), 'Recruit, retrain, retain; personnel management and the three R's', *Personnel Management*, November, pp. 40–7.

Jenkins, J. F. (1983), 'Management trainees in retailing.' In B. Ungerson (ed.) *Recruitment Handbook*, 3rd edition, Aldershot: Gower.

Knollys, J. G. (1983), 'Sales staff', Ungerson, B. (ed.), *Recruitment Handbook*, (3rd edn), Aldershot: Gower.

Lewis, C. (1985), *Employee Selection*, London: Hutchinson.

Pearn, M. and Kandola, R. (1988), *Job Analysis: A Practical Guide for Managers*. London: Institute of Personnel Management.

Plumbley, P. R. (1985), *Recruitment and Selection*, 4th edition. London: Institute of Personnel Management.

Ungerson, B. (1983), *How to Write a Job Description*. London: Institute of Personnel Management.

Wright, M. and Storey, J. (1994), 'Recruitment'. In I. Beardwell, and L. Holden (eds), *Human Resource Management*. London: Pitman.

13 Selection: methods and decisions

While the search for the perfect method of selection continues, in its absence personnel and line managers continue to use a variety of imperfect methods to aid the task of predicting which applicant will be most successful in meeting the demands of the job. Selection is increasingly important as more attention is paid to the costs of poor selection, and as reduced job mobility means that selection errors are likely to stay with the organisation for longer.

Legislation promoting equality of opportunity has underlined the importance of using well-validated selection procedures and there is increasing emphasis on ensuring that the selection process discriminates fairly, and not unfairly, between applicants.

In this chapter we first consider the role of personnel management in selection, and selection as a two-way process. next we look at selection criteria and choosing appropriate selection methods. Various selection methods are then considered, including application forms, testing, interviews, group selection and assessment centres, references, use of consultants and some less traditional methods, such as graphology. We conclude by looking at selection decision-making, the validation of selection procedures and selection and the law.

The role of personnel management in selection

Personnel managers still have a key role in the selection process although in many organisations this is increasingly less direct, as indicated in Chapter 10. From an emphasis on direct involvement in shortlisting, interviewing and control and administrative procedures, the nature of involvement is shifting towards provision of specialist advice, guidance and training and evaluation of selection effectiveness.

Personnel managers are able to draw on their expertise to recommend the most effective selection methods for each particular job or group of jobs. They are also in a position to encourage the development and use of personnel specifications as an aid to selection. A member of the personnel department will normally be the organisation's expert on test use and have the British Psychological Society (BPS) certificate of competence. In an organisation where tests are particularly appropriate selection methods they will advise managers on the most suitable test to use, although test administration may be devolved to department level. In a more general sense personnel managers can act as an advice centre on selection methods for line managers, and they are usually involved in the formal and informal training in selection skills, particularly interviewing skills. Increasingly 'how to do it' packs are produced by the personnel department so that line managers have specialist information about selection activities at their fingertips. Personnel departments still play a co-ordinating role in selection activities in many organisations.

Selection as a two-way process

The various stages of the selection process provide information for decisions by both the employer and potential employee. This is not, however, a traditional view as employment decisions have long been regarded as a management prerogative and are still widely regarded in this way. This view is likely to persist for various reasons, as follows.

1. It is attractive to managers because it underlines their authority, and they frequently feel that the ability to choose their subordinates is a key to their own effectiveness.
2. It is supported by much academic research. Psychologists have studied individual differences, intelligence and motivation extensively and have produced a number of prescriptions for those managing selection procedures on how to make sound judgements about candidates.
3. Candidates are convinced of their helplessness in selection, which they see as being absolutely controlled by the recruiting organisation.

Despite these features of the situation, we continue to advocate a more reciprocal approach to employment decision-making which is increasingly being accepted (Lewis 1985), in the belief that managers will be more effective in staffing their organisations if they can bring about some shift of stance in that direction. We must be concerned not only with the job to be done, but also with the work that is offered.

Throughout the selection process applicants choose between organisations by evaluating the developing relationship between themselves and the prospect. This takes place in the correspondence from potential employers; in their experience of the selection methods used by the employer; and in the information they gain on interview. Applicants will decide not to pursue some applications. Either they will have accepted another offer, or they will find something in their correspondence with the organisation that discourages them and they withdraw. Jenkins (1983) gives a specific example of how applicants drop out, to which we referred in more detail in Chapter 12. After newspaper advertising 321 booklets and application forms were sent out to 321 applicants: 127 were returned, so 60 per cent withdrew at that point. Dropping out late was only slightly less in percentage terms. Posts were offered to twenty-three candidates and accepted by nineteen, of whom only fifteen started. Thirty-five per cent dropped out.

This type of example illustrates that the managers in the organisation do not have total control over who is employed and that there are two parties to the bargain. Figures of the type that Jenkins provides can be viewed with pride or alarm. It might be that 194 applicants received the information booklet and were immediately able to make a wise decision that they were not suited to the organisation and that time would be wasted by continuing. On the other hand, it might be that potentially admirable recruits were lost because of the way in which information was presented, lack of information, or the interpretation that was put on the 'flavour' of the correspondence.

Herriot (1985) gives a good example of the criteria that graduates use to select potential employers. The frame of reference for the applicant is so different from that of the manager in the organisation that the difference is frequently forgotten. It would not be unrealistic to suggest that the majority of applicants have a mental picture of their letter of application being received through the letterbox of the company and immediately being closely scrutinised and discussed by powerful figures. The fact that the application is one element in a varied routine for the recipient is incomprehensible to some and unacceptable to many. The thought that one person's dream is another's routine is something the applicant cannot cope with.

If they have posted an application with high enthusiasm about the fresh prospects that the new job would bring, they are in no mood for delay and they may quickly start convincing themselves that they are not interested, because their initial euphoria has not been sustained. They are also likely to react unfavourably to the mechanical response that appears to have been produced on a photocopier that was due for the scrapheap. Again there is a marked dissonance between the paramount importance of the application to the applicant and its apparent unimportance to the organisation. Some of the points that seem to be useful about correspondence are:

1. Reply, meaningfully, fast. The printed postcard of acknowledgement is not a reply, neither is the personal letter which says nothing more than that the application has been received.
2. Conduct correspondence in terms of what the applicants want to know. How long will they have to wait for an answer? If you ask them in for interview, how long will it take, what will it involve, do you defray expenses, can they park their car, how do they find you, etc.?

Selection criteria and the person specification

Unless the criteria against which applicants will be measured are made explicit, it will be impossible to make credible selection decisions. It will be difficult to select the most appropriate selection procedure and approach, and it will be difficult to

Table 13.1 *Two well-used human attribute classification systems: Rodger's seven-point plan and Fraser's five-fold grading*

Rodger's seven-point plan	Fraser's five-fold grading
Physical make-up	Impact on others
Attainments	Qualifications or acquired knowledge
General intelligence	Innate abilities
Special aptitudes	Motivation
Interests	Adjustment or emotional balance
Disposition	
Circumstances	

validate the selection process. Selection criteria are normally presented in the form of a person specification representing the ideal candidate. There are a wide range of formats for this purpose – the two most widely known are Alec Rodger's seven-point plan and John Munro Fraser's five-fold framework. Both are shown in Table 13.1.

Lewis (1985) suggests that selection criteria can be understood in terms of three aspects: organisational criteria, departmental or functional criteria and individual job criteria.

Organisational criteria

Organisational criteria are those attributes that an organisation considers valuable in its employees and that affect judgements about a candidate's potential to be successful within an organisation. For example, the organisation may be expanding and innovating and require employees who are particularly flexible and adaptable. These organisational criteria are rarely made explicit and they are often used at an intuitive level. They are made less subjective if a group of selectors join together to share their ideas of what characteristics are required if an individual is to be successful in the organisation.

Functional/department criteria

Between the generality of organisational criteria and the preciseness of job criteria there are departmental criteria, such as the definition of appropriate interpersonal skills for all members of the personnel department.

Individual job criteria

Individual job criteria contained in job descriptions and person specifications are derived from the process of job analysis. It is these criteria derived from the tasks to be completed that are most often used in the selection process. A sample person specification drawn up on this basis can be found in Table 13.2.

Table 13.2 *Person specification for the job of Senior Sales Assistant using Rodger's seven-point plan*

Physical make-up	
Essential:	Tidy and dressed in business-like manner
Attainment	
Preferred:	GCSE Maths grade A; Essential: grade D–E
Preferred:	Attendance at a programming course, in or out of school; or demonstrate some self-taught knowledge of programming
Essential:	Keyboard skills – 40 wpm minimum
General intelligence	
Essential:	Above-average and quick to grasp the meaning of problems.
Special aptitudes	
Essential:	Ability to relate to people – to be outgoing and form relationships quickly.
Interests	
Essential:	Interested in both computer hardware and software.
Disposition	
Essential:	Patience
Circumstances	
Essential:	Circumstances that enable attendance at work every Saturday.

Although it is reasonably easy to specify the factors that should influence the personnel specification, the process by which the specification is formed is more difficult to describe. Smith and Robertson (1993) identify a lack of research in this area. Van Zwanenberg and Wilkinson (1993) offer a dual perspective. They describe 'job first – person later' and 'person first – job later' approaches. The first starts with analysing the task to be done, presenting this in the form of a job description and from this deriving the personal qualities and attributes, or competencies, that are necessary to do the task. The difficulty here is in the translation process and the constant change of job demands and tasks.

The alternative approach suggested by van Zwanenberg and Wilkinson starts with identifying which individuals are successful in a certain job and then describing their characteristics. The authors note that the difficulty here is in choosing which attributes are key and need to be specified.

Wilkinson and van Zwanenberg (1994) also report on the development of a computer-based expert system which can be used to guide line managers through the development of a person specification for managerial jobs.

Choosing selection methods

It is unusual for one selection method to be used alone. A combination of two or more methods is generally used, and the choice of these is dependent upon a number of factors:

1. *Selection criteria for the post to be filled:* for example, group selection methods and assessment centre activities would only be useful for certain types of job, such as managerial and supervisory.

2. *Acceptability and appropriateness of the methods:* for the candidates involved, or likely to be involved, in the selection. The use, for example, of intelligence tests may be seen as insulting to applicants already occupying senior posts.

3. *Abilities of the staff involved in the selection process:* this applies particularly in the use of tests and assessment centres. Only those staff who are appropriately qualified by academic qualification and/or attendance on a recognised course may administer psychological tests.

4. *Administrative ease:* for administrative purposes it may be much simpler to, for instance, arrange one or two individual interviews for a prospective candidate rather than organise a panel consisting of four members, each needing to make themselves available at the same time.

5. *Time factors:* sometimes a position needs to be filled very quickly, and time may be saved by organising individual interviews rather than group selection methods which would mean waiting for a day when all candidates are available.

6. *Accuracy:* accuracy in selection generally increases in relation to the number of appropriate selection methods used.

7. *Cost:* the use of tests may cost a great deal to set up but once the initial outlay has been made they are reasonably cheap to administer. Assessment centres would involve an even greater outlay and continue to be fairly expensive to administer. Interviews, on the other hand, cost only a moderate amount to set up in terms of interviewer training and are fairly cheap to administer. For the costlier methods great care needs to be taken in deciding whether the improvement in selection decision-making would justify such costs.

Selection methods

Application forms

Growing use is being made of the application form as a basis for employment decisions. For a long time it was not really that at all, but a personal details form, which was intended to act as the nucleus of the personnel record for the individual when they began work. It asked for some information that was difficult to supply, such as national insurance number, and some that seemed irrelevant, such as the identity of the family doctor and next-of-kin. It was largely disregarded in the employment process, which was based on an informal and unstructured 'chat'. As reservations grew about the validity of interviews for employment purposes, the more productive use of the application form was one of the avenues explored for improving the quality of decisions.

Forms were considered to act as a useful preliminary to employment interviews and decisions, either to present more information that was relevant to such deliberations or to arrange such information in a standard way rather than the inevitably idiosyncratic display found in letters of application. This made sorting of applications and shortlisting easier and enabled interviewers to use the form as the basis for the interview itself, with each piece of information on the form being taken and developed in the interview.

More recently the application form has been extended by some organisations to play a more significant part in the employment process. One form of extension is to ask for very much more, and more detailed, information from the candidate.

Another extension of application form usage has been in weighting, or biodata. Biodata has been defined by Anderson and Shackleton (1990) as 'historical and verifiable pieces of information about an individual in a selection context usually reported on application forms'. This method is an attempt to relate the characteristics of applicants to characteristics of successful job holders. The method is to take a large population of job holders and categorise them as good, average or poor performers, usually on the evaluation of a supervisor. Common characteristics are sought out among the good and poor performers. The degree of correlation is then translated into a weighting for evaluating that characteristic when it appears on the application form, or the additional biodata form. The obvious drawbacks of this procedure are first, the time that is involved and the size of sample needed, so that it is only feasible where there are many job holders in a particular type of position. Secondly, it smacks of witchcraft to the applicants who might find it difficult to believe that success in a position correlates with being, *inter alia*, the first-born in one's family. However, Robertson and Makin (1986) report that biodata was used by 8 per cent of major British companies at the time of their survey.

Generally, application forms are used as a straightforward way of giving a standardised synopsis of the applicant's history. This helps applicants present their case by providing them with a predetermined structure, it speeds the sorting and shortlisting of applications and it guides the interviewers as well as providing the starting-point for personnel records. In application form design the following points are worth checking.

> Marks & Spencer is one of the largest recruiters of graduates in the country and receives, each year, huge numbers of applications. Working with biodata analysis, the application forms are first screened in a purely mechanical way, with points being scored for certain criteria, before initial shortlists are drawn up. In this way the company avoids the need to spend expensive executive time in scrutinising all the application forms. This is a very workable strategy when you have a very large number of applicants.

```
BETA BROTHERS: JOB APPLICATION

JOB APPLIED FOR _____
PERSONAL DETAILS
Surname _____ Forenames _____
Address _____
              _____ Tel no._____
Date of birth _____
_____

JOB DETAILS
Present/last job _____
Employer _____
Date started _____ Date finished _____
Immediately previous job _____
Employer _____
Date started _____ Date finished _____
Immediately previous job _____
Employer _____
Date started _____ Date finished _____
_____

EDUCATION AND TRAINING
Highest educational qualification _____
Training/apprenticeship _____
_____
_____
_____

IS THERE ANYTHING YOU'D LIKE TO ADD? Please write overleaf
_____

WHERE DID YOU HEAR OF THIS JOB?    _____
_____

SIGNED _____ Date _____
_____

When you have completed this form, please return it to:
Mrs J. Rank, Personnel Officer, Beta Brothers, Toolmakers, 71 Western Estate,
Greater Manchester.

We will let you know of the progress of your application within the next 14 days. If you do
not hear from us please telephone 432–1256
```

Figure 13.1   A sample application form for skilled, semi-skilled and unskilled jobs

1. Handwriting is usually larger than typescript. Do the boxes on the form provide enough room for the applicant to complete their information?
2. Forms that take too long to complete run the risk of being completed perfunctorily or not being completed at all. Is the time the form takes to complete

appropriate for the information needs of the employment decision?

3. Some questions are illegal, some are offensive, others are unnecessary. Does the form call only for information that is appropriate to employment decision-making?

4. Allan (1990) also suggests that in the age of word processors there is no excuse for failing to produce separate application forms for each vacancy advertised, or for not personlising forms and making them more user-friendly. One way of increasing user-friendliness is to use introductory paragraphs explaining why the information in each section is being sought.

An example of an application form that could be used for unskilled and semi-skilled jobs is found in Figure 13.1.

REVIEW TOPIC 13.1

Design an application form for senior management posts maximising critical information, but asking only for information that is strictly relevant.

Self-assessment

There is increasing interest in providing more information to applicants concerning the job. This may involve a video, an informal discussion with job holders, or further information sent with the application form. This is often termed as giving the prospective candidate a 'realistic job preview', enabling them to assess their own suitability to a much greater extent. Another way of achieving this is by asking the candidates to do some form of pre-work. This may involve asking them questions regarding their previous work experiences which would relate to the job for which they are applying. For further information see Wanous (1992).

Telephone screening

Telephone screening can be used instead of an application form if speed is particularly important, as interviews with appropriate candidates can be arranged immediately. This method works best where a checklist of critical questions has been prepared so that each candidate is being asked for standardised information. There are, however, problems with this method. Because the organisational response to prospective employee is immediate the decision can be haphazard unless preset standards are agreed in advance. The difficulty with setting standards in advance is that these may turn out to be inappropriate in either selecting too many or too few candidates to interview. The standards can, of course, be changed as enquiries are coming in but the best candidate, who may have called early, might not be invited to interview if the standards were intially too high. Also, since organisational response

One large employer requests CVs from applicants and, on the basis of these, invites a selected number to take part in a telephone interview. A date and time are given and an idea of the questions that will be asked so that the candidate can prepare. The interview takes about 15 to 20 minutes, and time is allowed for the candidate to ask questions of the interviewer as well. Candidates are also told in advance of the telephone interview that if they are successful at this stage they will be invited to a one-day assessment centre on a specified date. After the telephone interview candidates are notified in writing whether or not they will move on to the assessment centre stage of the selection procedure.

has to be immediate there is no time for reflection and little opportunity to be flexible.

Other, more recent approaches to telephone interviews often form part of a structured selection procedure.

REVIEW TOPIC 13.2

What are the advantages of using telephone interviews of the type described in the box?

For what types of job would you use this approach to selection?

Testing

The use of tests in employment procedures is surrounded by strong feelings for and against, and a lively debate on the value of personality tests is found in Fletcher *et al.* (1990). Those in favour of testing in general point to the unreliability of the interview as a predictor of performance and the greater potential accuracy and objectivity of test data. Tests can be seen as giving a credibility to selection decisions. Those against either dislike the objectivity that testing implies or have difficulty in incorporating test evidence into the rest of the evidence that is collected. Questions have been raised as to the relevance of the tests to the job applied for and the possibility of unfair discrimination and bias. Also, some candidates feel that they can improve their prospects by a good interview performance and that the degree to which they are in control of their own destiny is being reduced by a dispassionate routine.

The use of tests for employment selection is, however, increasing (see for example Fletcher, 1993). Shackleton and Newell (1991) report results from their survey. They found that the use of personality tests had increased to 37 per cent compared with 12 per cent in a similar Robertson and Makin study five years previously. Similarly, the use of cognitive tests had increased from 9.3 per cent to 41.1

Table 13.3 *The use of psychological tests for selection purposes by job grade (Newell and Shackleton 1994, p. 18). Used with permission of the* Human Resource Management Journal.

Job grade	Recruitment and Selection	
	n	%
Administrative	12	40
Secretarial	11	37
Manual	6	20
Graduates	27	90
Junior management	21	70
Middle management	24	80
Senior management	21	70

per cent. Newell and Shackleton (1994) report that testing is more likely to be used for management and graduate jobs than for administrative, secretarial or manual jobs, as shown in Table 13.3. Tests are chosen on the basis that test scores relate, or correlate, with subsequent job performance, so that a high test score would predict high job performance and a low test score would predict low job performance.

Critical features of test use

A number of different types of validity can be applied to psychological tests. Personnel managers are most concerned with predictive validity, which is the extent to which the test can predict subsequent job performance. Predictive validity is measured by relating the test scores to measures of future performance, such as error rate, production rate, appraisal scores, absence rate, or whatever criteria are important to the organisation. If test scores relate highly with future performance then the test is a good predictor.

Reliability

The reliability of a test is the degree to which the test measures consistently whatever it is intended to measure. If a test is highly reliable then it is possible to put greater weight on the scores that individuals receive on the test. However, a highly reliable test is of no value in the employment situation unless it also has a high validity.

Use and interpretation

Tests need to be used and interpreted by trained or qualified testers. Test results require a very careful interpretation, especially personality tests, as some aspects of personality will be measured that are irrelevant to the job. Wills (1990) reports concerns that tests are carried out by unqualified testers. The British Psychological Society has now introduced a certificate of competence for occupational testing at level A and is developing a level B certificate. For a helpful explanation of competence certificates see Barton (1991). Both the BPS and the Institute of Personnel and Development have produced codes of practice for occupational test use. It is recommended that tests are not used in a judgemental, final way, but to stimulate discussion with the candidate based on the test results. Research by Newell and Shackleton (1994) suggests, unfortunately, that tests are not used as the basis for discussion. Feedback to testees is also identified as a key issue, yet again Newell and Shackleton found that this does not always take place.

Context of tests

Test scores need to be evaluated in the context of other information about individuals. Selection decisions need to be made up of a number of different pieces of information. Test results cannot be seen as having a simple relationship with job performance as, for example, there are many relevant aspects of an individual which a test cannot measure.

Problems with using tests

1. In the last section we commented that a test score that was highly related to performance criteria has good validity. The relationship between test scores and performance criteria is usually expressed as a correlation coefficient (r). If $r = 1$ then test scores and performance would be perfectly related; if $r = 0$ there is no relationship whatsoever. Correlation coefficients of $r = 0.4$ are comparitively good in the testing world and this level of relationship between test scores and performance is generally seen as acceptable. Tests are, therefore, not outstanding predictors of future performance. Robertson and Smith (1989) carried out a meta-analysis of research on the validity of test results. They found that correlations for cognitive tests were between 0.25 and 0.45, and that those of personality tests were between 0.15 and 0.10.

2. Validation procedures are very time-consuming, but are essential to the effective use of tests.

3. The criteria that are used to define good job performance in developing the test are often inadequate. They are subjective and may account to some extent for the mediocre correlations of test results and job performance.

4. Tests are job-specific. If the job for which the test is used changes, then the test can no longer be assumed to relate to job performance in the same way. Also, personality tests only measure how individuals see themselves at a certain point in time and cannot therefore be reliably re-used at a later time point.

5. Test may not be fair as there may be a social, sexual or racial bias in the questions and scoring system. People from some cultures may, for example, be unused to 'working against the clock'. Wood and Barron (1992) provide some further examples of how tests may discriminate in an unlawful or unhelpful way.

Wood and Baron (1992) describe how in 1991 some guards at Paddington Station took British Rail to an industrial tribunal. These guards maintained that the selection processes that British Rail used for train drivers discriminated unfairly against ethnic minorities. As part of the settlement British Rail promised to improve the situation. One action was to run workshops on test taking. They found that the ethnic minority guards were not used to a test taking culture and so they produced an open learning pack which gave them helpful hints on taking tests and gave them material to practice with. As a result five of the seven guards passed the selection test which enabled them to train as train drivers.

Used with permission of the authors.

REVIEW TOPIC 13.3

In what ways could you measure job performance for:

- A mobile telephone engineer?
- A clerk?
- A supervisor?

Types of test for occupational use

People differ in their performance of tasks, and tests of aptitude measure an individual's potential to develop in either specific or general terms. This is in contrast to attainment tests, which measure the skills an individual has already occupied. The words aptitude and ability are often used interchangeably as, for example, by Ghiselli (1966). However, some authors see them as slightly different things. Lewis (1985) defines ability as being a combination of aptitude and attainment. For the purposes of this chapter we shall use aptitude and ability interchangeably, and as something quite separate from attainment. When considering the results from aptitude tests it is important to remember that there is not a simple relationship between a high level of aptitude and a high level of job performance as other factors, such as motivation, also contribute to job performance. Aptitude tests can be grouped into two categories: those measuring general mental ability or general intelligence, and those measuring specific abilities or aptitudes.

General intelligence tests

Intelligence tests, sometimes called mental ability tests, are designed to give an indication of overall mental capacity. A variety of questions are included in such tests, including vocabulary, analogies, similarities, opposites, arithmetic, number extension and general information. As Plumbley (1985) indicates, it has been shown that a person's ability to score highly on such tests correlates with the capacity to retain new knowledge, to pass examination and to succeed at work. However, the intelligence test used would still need to be carefully validated in terms of the job for which the candidate was applying. Examples of general intelligence tests are the AH4 (Heim, in Sweetland, Keyser and O'Connor 1983), and the Wechsler Adult Intelligence Scale Revised (Wechsler, in Sweetland, *et al.* 1983).

Special aptitude test

These are tests that measure specific abilities or aptitudes, such as spatial abilities, perceptual abilities, verbal ability, numerical ability, motor ability (manual dexterity) and so on. There is some debate over the way that general intelligence and special abilities are related. In the United Kingdom the design of ability or aptitude tests has been much influenced by Vernon's (1961) model of the structure of abilities. Vernon suggested a hierarchical model of abilities with general intelligence at the top and abilities becoming more specific and finely divided lower down in the hierarchy. Here an individual's potential ability to perform a task is the result of a combination of the specific appropriate ability and general intelligence. In the United States abilities are generally seen as more distinct (Thurstone 1938), and less emphasis is put on general intelligence as a contributing factor. The development of tests of specific aptitudes obviously influenced by the model of intelligence and ability that is used. Tests of special abilities are those such as the Bennett Mechanical Comprehension Test (Bennett, in Sweetland, *et al.* 1983).

Trainability tests

These are used to measure a potential employee's ability to be trained, usually for craft-type work. The test consists of the applicants doing a practical task that they have not done before, after having been shown or 'trained' how to do it. The test measures how well they respond to the 'training' and how their performance on the task improves. Because it is performance at a task that is being measured these tests are sometimes confused with attainment tests; however, they are more concerned with potential ability to do the task and reponse to training.

Attainment tests

Whereas aptitude tests measure an individual's potential, attainment or achievement tests measure skills that have already been acquired. There is much less resistance to such tests of skills. Few candidates for a typing post would refuse to take a typing test before interview. The candidates are sufficiently confident of their skills to welcome the opportunity to display them and be approved. Furthermore, they know what they are doing and will know whether they have done well or badly. They are in control, while they feel that the tester is in control of intelligence and personality tests, as the candidates do not understand the evaluation rationale. These tests are often devised by the employer.

Personality tests

Swinburne (1985) commented that there are very many articles on training and management development which continue to emphasise the importance of personality for competence in management jobs (Harrison 1979; Hollis 1984; Willis 1984) and yet there is a dearth of papers on the use of personality questionnaires for selection, guidance or development. Swinburne argues that the lack of papers may well reflect the state of the art, in that although the need for personality assessment is high, few questionnaires lend themselves easily to occupational use. An additional reason is that there is even more resistance to tests of personality than to tests of aptitude, partly because of the reluctance to see personality as in any way measurable. In spite of this there has been a marked increase in personality test use over the last ten years and Fletcher (1993) reports that the largest increase in new tests being produced is in the area of personality.

Theories of human personality vary as much as theories of human intelligence. The psychiatrist Karl Jung was content to divide personalities into extroverts and introverts; more recently Eysenck (1963) regarded the factors of neuroticism and extroversion as being sufficient. The most extensive work has been done by Cattell (1965) who identified sixteen factors. Among them were: reserved/outgoing; affected by feelings/emotionally stable; submissive/dominant; tough-minded/sensitive; group dependent/self-sufficient and trusting/suspicious.

It is dangerous to assume that there is a standard profile of 'the ideal employee'. Miller (1975) quotes the example of two establishments in the same organisation using the Cattell inventory to produce a profile of systems analysts. Though the work of each group was similar, the factors most associated with success in the two locations were different.

Another problem with the use of personality tests is that they rely on an individual's willingness to be honest, as the socially acceptable answer or the one best in terms of the job are often easy to pick out (Lewis 1985). There is a further problem that some traits measured by the test will not be relevant in terms of performance on the job.

Some examples of personality tests in common use are Cattell's 16PF (Cattell, Eber and Tatsuoka 1962) and the OPQ (Saville and Holdsworth Ltd 1984). For further information on the new fourth version of the 16PF see Lord (1994).

Interest tests

Interest tests suffer from the same problems as personality tests, without the literature to support their theoretical usefulness. They may perhaps be useful when selecting school-leavers for a range of possible jobs, but otherwise their occupational use is not usually recommended.

Interviewing

Interviewing is the most common method of selection, and both one-to-one and panel interviews are explored in Chapter 15.

Group selection methods and assessment centres

Group methods

The use of group tasks to select candidates is not new, dating back to the Second World War, but such measures have gained greater attention through their use in assessment centres. Plumbley (1985) describes the purpose of group selection methods as being to provide evidence about the candidate's abilities with respect to the following.

1. To get on with others.
2. To influence others and the way they do this.
3. To express themselves verbally.
4. To think clearly and logically.
5. To argue from past experience and apply themselves to a new problem.
6. The type of role they play in group situations.

These features are difficult, on the whole, to identify using other selection methods and one of the particular advantages of group selection methods is that they provide the selector with examples of behaviour on which to select. When future job performance is being considered it is behaviour in the job that is critical, and so selection using group methods can provide direct information on which to select rather than indirect verbal information or test results.

Plumbley (1985) identifies three main types of group task that can be used, each of which would be observed by the selectors.

1. *Leaderless groups:* a group of about six to eight individuals are given a topic of general interest to discuss.
2. *Command or executive exercises:* the members of the group are allocated roles in an extensive brief based on a real-life situation. Each member outlines his/her solution on the basis of their role and defends it to the rest of the group.
3. *Group problem solving:* the group is leaderless and has to organise itself in order to solve, within time-limits, a problem which is relevant to the job to be filled.

Business games and case studies may also be used. There are further details about these techniques as they are used in the training situation in Chapter 24. Participants are observed during the group activities, and the observers note the quality and quantity of social and intellectual skills of each individual.

Group selection methods are most suitable for management and sometimes supervisory posts. One of the difficulties with group selection methods is that it can be difficult to assess an individual's contribution, and some individuals may be unwilling to take part.

REVIEW TOPIC 13.4

To what extent does an individual's behaviour on these group selection tasks accurately reflect behaviour on the job? Why?

Assessment centres

Assessment centres could be described as multiple method group selection (Lewis 1985). The group selection techniques outlined above form a major element of assessment centre selection, and are used in conjunction with other work simulation exercises, such as in-basket tasks (described in more detail in Chapter 35), psychological tests and a variety of interviews. Assessment centres are used to assess, in depth, a group of broadly similar applicants. At the end of the procedure the judges have to come to agreement on a cumulative rating for each individual, related to job requirements, taking into account all the selection activities. The procedure as a whole is then validated against job performance rather than each separate activity. The predictive validities from such procedures are not very consistent, but there is a high 'face validity' – there is a feeling that this is a fairer way of selecting people. The chief disadvantages of these selection methods are that it is a costly and time-consuming procedure, the time commitment being extended by the need to give some feedback to candidates who have been through such a long procedure which involves psychological assessment. Fletcher (1986) gives some guidelines on how this feedback can be organised. Time commitment is also high in the development of such activities. Smith and Tarpey (1987) describe how inter-rater reliability can vary in the assessment of in-tray exercises. Reliability was much improved by the quality of assessor training, greater clarity in marking instructions, more time allowed for marking and a structure approach to marking. All these activities are time-consuming. Survey evidence suggests that the use of assessment centres is increasing (Iles 1992), and Mabey (1989) reported that 37 per cent of the UK organisations he surveyed used group exercises, in-basket exercises and role-play exercises.

Work sampling

Work sampling of potential candidates for permanent jobs can take place by assessing candidates' work in temporary posts or on government training schemes in the same organisations. For some jobs, such as photographers and artists, a sample of work in the form of a portfolio is expected to be presented at the time of interview.

References

One way of informing the judgement of managers who have to make employment offers to selected individuals is the use of references. Previous employers or others with appropriate credentials are cited by candidates and then requested by prospective employers to provide information. There are two types: the factual check and the character reference.

The factual check

This is fairly straightforward as it is no more than a confirmation of facts that the candidate has presented. It will normally follow the employment interview and decision to offer a post. It does no more than confirm that the facts are accurate. The knowledge that such a check will be made – or may be made – will help focus the mind of candidates so that they resist the temptation to embroider their story.

The character reference

This is a very different matter. Here the prospective employer asks for an opinion about the candidate before the interview so that the information gained can be used in the decision-making phases. The logic of this strategy is impeccable: who knows the working performance of the candidate better than the previous employer? The wisdom of the strategy is less sound, as it depends on the writers of references being excellent judges of working performance, faultless communicators and – most difficult of all – disinterested. The potential inaccuracies of decisions influenced by character references begin when the candidate decides who to cite. They will have some freedom of choice and will clearly choose someone from whom they expect favourable comment, perhaps massaging the critical faculties with such comments as: 'I think references are going to be very important for this job.' 'You will do your best for me, won't you?'

Cowan and Cowan (1989) ask whether references are worth the paper they are written on and conclude that they are mostly misused, and that two key questions should be: 'Would you re-employ this person?' and 'Do you know of any reason that we should not employ them?'

Other methods

A number of other less conventional methods such as physiognomy, phrenology, body language, palmistry, graphology and astrology have been suggested as possible selection methods. While these are fascinating to read about there is little evidence to suggest that they could be used effectively. Fowler (1990), however, comments on their greater use in the EU and pressures, therefore, for greater use in the United Kingdom. Further research (Fowler 1991) suggests that the extent of use of graphology is much higher in the United Kingdom than reported figures indicate. There is some reluctance on the part of organisations to admit that they are using graphology for selection purposes. For more information on graphology, see Lynch and Wilson (1985), and for graphology and other methods see Mackenzie Davey (1982) and Mackenzie Davey and Harris (1982).

Using consultants

Consultants are increasingly involved in the recruitment and selection process and will in some cases directly apply a variety of the selection methods outlined above, although it is very rare that they would make the final selection decision.

The problem with using consultants is that organisations may have difficulty in communicating their exact requirements to the consultants and that some criteria, for example, ability to fit into the organisation and be successful within it, are best judged directly by a member of the organisation rather than by an intermediary.

Selection criteria	Candidate 1	Candidate 2	Candidate 3	Candidate 4
Criterion a				
Criterion b				
Criterion c				
Criterion d				
Criterion e				
General comments				

Figure 13.2 A selection decision-making matrix

Final selection decision-making

The selection decision involves measuring each candidate against the selection criteria defined in the person specification, not against each other. A useful tool to achieve this is the matrix in Figure 13.2.

This is a good method of ensuring that every candidate is assessed against each selection and in each box in the matrix the key details can be completed. The box can be used whether a single selection method or multiple methods were used. If multiple methods were used and contradictory information is found against any criterion this can be noted in the decision-making process.

When more than one selector is involved there is some debate about how to gather and use the information and judgement of each selector. One way is for each selector to assess the information collected separately, and then meet to discuss assessments. When this approach is used be prepared for very different assessments – especially if the interview was the only selection method used. Much heated and time-consuming debate can be generated – but the most useful aspect of this process is sharing the information in everyone's matrix to understand how judgements have been formed. This approach is also helpful in training interviewers.

An alternative approach is to fill in only one matrix with all selectors contributing. This may be quicker, but the downside is that the quietest member may be the one who has all the critical pieces of information. There is a risk that all the information may not be contributed to the debate in progress. Iles (1992), referring to assessment centre decisions, suggests that the debate itself may not add to the quality of the decision, and that taking the results from each selector and combining them is just as effective.

Validation of selection procedures

We have already mentioned how test scores may be validated against eventual job performance for each individual in order to discover whether the test score is a good predictor of success in the job. In this way we can decide whether the test should be used as part of the selection procedure. The same idea can be applied to the use of other individual or combined selection methods.

The critical information that is important for determining validity is the selection criteria used, the selection processes used, an evaluation of the individual at the time of selection and current performance of the individual.

Unfortunately, we are never in a position to witness the performance of rejected candidates and compare this with those we have employed. However, if a group of individuals are selected at the same time, for example graduate trainees, it will be unlikely that they were all rated equally highly in spite of the fact that they were all considered employable. It is useful for validation purposes if a record is made of the scores that each achieved in each part of the selection process. Test results are easy to quantify, and for interview results a simple grading system can be devised.

Current performance includes measures derived from the job description, together with additional perfomance measures:

1. *Measures from the job description:* quantitative measures such as volume of sales, accuracy, number of complaints, and so on may be used, or qualitative measures like relations with customers and quality of reports produced.
2. *Other measures:* these may include appraisal results, problems identified, absence data and, of course, termination.

Current performance is often assessed in an intuitive, subjective way, and while this may sometimes be useful it is no substitute for objective assessment.

Selection ratings for each individual can be compared with eventual performance over a variety of time-periods. Large discrepancies between selection and performance ratings point to further investigation of the selection criteria and methods used. The comparison of selection rating and performance rating can also be used to compare the appropriateness of different selection criteria, and the usefulness of different selection methods.

Selection, the law and equality of opportunity

The law puts pressure on employers to select employeees in a non-discriminating way in terms of sex and race. There is also some less effective pressure on employers not to discriminate in terms of age and disability (except for positive discrimination). These issues are dealt with in more detail in Chapter 20.

13.1 Selection is a two-way process. The potential employer and the potential employee both make selection decisions.

13.2 A combination of selection methods is usually chosen, based upon the job, appropriateness, acceptability, time, administrative ease, cost, accuracy and the abilities of the selection staff.

13.3 The application form as a selection method is frequently under-used or misused.

13.4 Testing gives the appearance of accuracy but correlations with job performance are not particularly high and they are therefore not necessarily effective predictors. Test use is, however, increasing.

13.5 Assessment centres have the advantage of providing a full range of selection methods and are increasingly used. They have been found to be more valid than other approaches to selection.

13.6 Selection methods should be validated. A simple system is better than no system at all.

References

Allan, J. (1990), 'How to recruit the best people', *Management Accounting*, February.

Anderson, N. and Shackleton, V. (1990), 'Staff selection decision making into the 1990s', *Management Decision*, vol. 28, no. 1.

Bartram, D. (1991), 'Addressing the abuse of psychological tests', *Personnel Management*, April.

Cattell, R. B. (1965), *The Scientific Analysis of Personality*, Harmondsworth: Penguin.

Cattell, R. B., Eber, H. W. and Tatsuoka, M. M. (1962), *Handbook for the Sixteen Personality Factor Questionnaire (16PF)*, London: NEFR Publishing.

Cowan, N. and Cowan, R. (1989), 'Are references worth the paper they're written on?', *Personnel Management*, December.

Eysenck, H. J. and S. B. G. (1963), *The Eysenck Personality Inventory*, London: University of London Press.

Fletcher, C. (1986), 'Should the test score be kept a secret?' *Personnel Management*, April.

Fletcher, C. (1993), 'Testing times for the world of psychometrics', *Personnel Management*, December, pp. 46–93.

Fletcher, C. *et al.* (1990), 'Personality tests: the great debate', *Personnel Management*, September.

Fowler, A. (1990), 'The writing on the wall', *Local Government Chronicle*, 26 January, pp. 20–8.

Fowler, A. (1991), 'An even handed approach to graphology', *Personnel Management*, March.

Ghiselli, E. E. (1966), *The Validity of Occupational Aptitude Tests*, Chichester: John Wiley

Harrison, R. G. (1979), 'New personnel practice: life goals planning and interpersonal skills development: a programme for middle managers in the British Civil Service', *Personnel Review*, vol. 8, no. 1.

Herriot, P. (1985), 'Give and take in graduate selection', *Personnel Management*, May.

Hollis, W. P. (1984), 'Developing managers for social change', *Journal of Management Development*, vol. 3, no. 1.

Iles, P. (1992), 'Centres of Excellence? Assessment and development centres, managerial competence and human resource strategies', *British Journal of Management*, vol. 3, pp. 79–90.

Jenkins, J. F. (1983), 'Management trainees in retailing'. In B. Ungerson (ed.) *Recruitment Handbook*, 3rd edition. Aldershot: Gower.

Lewis, C. (1985), *Employee Selection*, London: Hutchinson.

Lord, W. (1994), 'The evolution of a revolution', *Personnel Management*, February, pp. 65–6.

Lynch, B. and Wilson, R. (1985), 'Graphology – towards a hand-picked workforce', *Personnel Management*, March.

Mabey, B. (1989), 'The majority of large companies use occupational tests', *Guidance and Assessment Review*, vol. 5, no. 3, pp. 1–4.

Mackenzie Davey, D. (1982), 'Arts and crafts of the selection process', *Personnel Management*, August.

Mackenzie Davey, D. and Harris, M. (1982), *Judging People*, Maidenhead: McGraw Hill.

Miller, K. M. (1975), 'Personality assessment'. In B. Ungerson (ed.) *Recruitment Handbook*, 2nd edition. Aldershot: Gower.

Newell, S. and Shackleton, V. (1994), 'The use (and abuse) of psychometric tests in British industry and commerce', *Human Resource Management Journal*, vol. 4, no. 1.

Plumbley, P. R. (1985), *Recruitment and Selection*, 4th edition. London: Institute of Personnel Management.

Robertson, I. T. and Makin, P. J. (1986), 'Management Selection in Britain; a Survey and Critique', *Journal of Occupational Psychology*, vol. 59, pp. 45–57.

Robertson, I. and Smith, M. (eds) (1989), *Personnel selection methods: Advances in selection and assessment*. Chichester, UK: Wiley.

Saville and Holdsworth Ltd (1984), *Manual of the Occupational Personality Questionnaire*, London: Saville and Holdsworth Ltd.

Shackleton, V. and Newell, S. (1991), 'Management selection: a comparative survey of methods used in top British and French companies', *Journal of Occupational Psychology*, vol. 64, pp. 23–36.

Smith, M. and Robertson, I. T. (1993), *The Theory and Practice of Systematic Staff Selection*, (2nd edn). Basingstoke: Macmillan.

Smith, D. and Tarpey, T. (1987), 'In-tray exercises and assessment centres; the issue of reliability', *Personnel Review*, vol. 16, no. 3, pp. 24–8.

Sweetland, R. C., Keyser, D. J. and O'Connor, W. A. (1983), *Tests*, Kansas City: Test Corporation of America.

Swinburne, P. (1985), 'A comparison of the OPQ and 16PF in relation to their occupational application', *Personnel Review*, vol. 14, no. 4.

Thurstone, L. L. (1938), 'Primary mental abilities', *Psychometric Monographs*, no. 1. Chicago: University of Chicago Press.

van Zwanenberg, N. and Wilkinson, L. J. (1993), 'The person specification – a problem masquerading as a solution?', *Personnel Review*, vol. 22, no. 7, pp. 54–65.

Vernon, P. (1961), *The Structure of Human Abilities*, 2nd edition. London: Methuen.

Wanous, J. P. (1992), *Organisational Entry – Recruitment, selection, orientation and socialisation of newcomers*, Reading, Mass.: Addison-Wesley.

Willis, Q. (1984), 'Managerial research and management development', *Journal of Management Development*, vol. 3, no. 1.

Wills, J. (1990), 'Cracking the nut', *Local Government Chronicle*, 26 January, pp. 22–3.

Wilkinson, L. J. and van Zwanenberg, N. (1994), 'Development of a person specification system for managerial jobs', *Personnel Review*, vol. 23, no. 1, pp. 25–36.

Wood, R. and Barron, H. (1992), 'Psychological Testing free from prejudice', *Personnel Management*, December.

14 Ending the employment contract

Having set up the contract of employment in the first place, the personnel manager monitors the performance of that contract to ensure that both parties are satisfied. Eventually the contract has to be terminated, either because the mutual satisfaction no longer holds or because the contract has come to its natural conclusion: retirement, the end of a fixed-term contract or a range of other reasons such as emigration, career change or following a spouse to a different part of the country. In this chapter we look mainly at dismissal, with some comments on resignation, retirement and notice.

Dismissal

Although there has been a long-standing employee right to claim wrongful dismissal by an employer, the legal framework of current practice stems mainly from the 1971 Industrial Relations Act, which first established the right of employees to claim unfair dismissal, with recourse to industrial tribunals, via ACAS conciliation, in search of a remedy.

Before the 1971 Act there were approximately three million dismissals, according to a Ministry of Labour calculation in 1967 (Ministry of Labour 1976 p. 57). That estimate included dismissals of all types and stated that one-third were due to sickness and slightly fewer were due to redundancy. Of less significance were dismissals for unsuitability and misconduct. This was in a situation of untrammelled freedom of action by employers, as well as full employment. No similar authoritative estimate has been made since, but we do have figures for unfair dismissal cases. Since 1979 the number of applications to industrial tribunals has been between 25,000 and 75,000 each year. That is a small proportion of the previously estimated three million, but it is only cases that employees report because they believe they have a chance of compensation. Table 14.1 is based on figures published by ACAS and demonstrates how the number of tribunal applications has varied in recent years.

These figures clearly show the substantial rise in tribunal cases over the past few years. There are always more applications during economic recessions in the

Table 14.1 *Unfair dismissal claims over a ten-year period*

	1983	1989	1993
Cases received for conciliation	37,123	48,817	75,181
Settled by ACAS	15,591	27,749	21,941
Withdrawn	9,171	8,927	22,466
To tribunal	12,575	8,528	21,987

Source: ACAS 1985, p. 84; 1990, p. 59; 1994

wake of company collapses and staff reductions. The rise is thus mostly accounted for by claims relating to redundancy. Not all the increase, however, arises from cases of unfair dismissal. The number of applications to tribunals relating to workplace discrimination has also increased in this period, as have claims brought under the Wages Act. It is interesting to note how the number of cases going to tribunal dropped in the mid-1980s, when the qualifying period in unfair dismissal claims was raised from one to two years.

Despite increased numbers it remains the case that the proportion of actual dismissals which result in a tribunal decision in favour of the ex-employee is very small. A survey for the Department of Employment in 1983–4 showed that only 6 per cent of employers were deterred from taking dismissal action because of fears of an application to tribunal, but 65 per cent reported that they now took greater care in deciding on whether or not to dismiss (Evans, Goodman and Hargreaves 1985, p. 34)

Unfair dismissal

Every employee who has been with an employer for two years has the right not to be unfairly dismissed; the fairness being determined by the provisions of the Employment Protection (Consolidation) Act 1978, though the main structure of unfair dismissal legislation has remained unaltered since it was first introduced in the Industrial Relations Act 1971. In some areas of employment legal provisions have made little difference, as the existing personnel policies of the employer have provided a similar or better degree of protection. The protection of the employee is due to a specific set of rules and precedents that have developed in that particular place of work and which are particularly relevant to it.

Obtaining a legal remedy from the tribunal involves a dependence on interpretation of the law and the situation by outsiders, and this may not necessarily be in the best interests of either participant. The tribunal members are concerned with fairness for employment as a whole; not within one industrial concentration. Furthermore, of course, the tribunal can not intervene to prevent a dismissal from occurring; it can only act after the event. The power to reinstate an employee is rarely used and the compensation ordered by tribunals seldom reaches the maximum figures permitted under the Acts.

This does not mean that the law can safely be ignored by employers, as the level of complaints to tribunals remains low only as long as practice is ahead of legislation. Even a 'cheap' unfair dismissal could be costly in terms of the unfairness stigma which will influence employee relations generally, can have a damaging public relations effect and could jeopardise the career of the manager to blame. Thus the law determines management practice.

REVIEW TOPIC 14.1

Consider the working activities of some of your colleagues (and perhaps your own working activities). What examples are there of behaviour that you feel justify dismissal? Make a list of your ideas and check them when you have finished this chapter and see how many might be classified as unfair dismissals by a tribunal.

Determining fairness

The novel legal concept of fairness relating to dismissal is determined in two stages – potentially fair and actually fair. A dismissal is potentially fair if there is a fair ground for it. Such grounds are as follows.

- *Lack of capability or qualifications:*   if an employee lacks the skill, aptitude or physical health to carry out the job, then there is a potentially fair ground for dismissal.

- *Misconduct:*   this category covers the range of behaviours that we examine in considering the grievance and discipline processes – disobedience, absence, insubordination and criminal acts. It can also include taking industrial action.

- *Redundancy:*   where an employee's job ceases to exist, it is potentially fair to dismiss the employee for redundancy.

- *Statutory bar:*   when employees cannot continue to discharge their duties without breaking the law, they can be fairly dismissed. Most cases of this kind follow disqualification of drivers following convictions for speeding, drunk or dangerous driving. Other common cases involve foreign nationals whose work permits have been terminated.

- *Some other substantial reason:*   this most intangible category is introduced in order to cater for genuinely fair dismissals that were so diverse they could not realistically be listed. Examples have been security of commercial information (where an employee's husband set up a rival company) or employee refusal to accept altered working conditions.

> A charge nurse in a hospital attacked a hospital official, punched him and broke his glasses. He was dismissed for misconduct. Later he was convicted of assault and causing damage. A tribunal found his dismissal to be unfair because he was not given a chance to state his case and because his right of appeal was not pointed out. (*Amar-Ojok* v. *Surrey AHA* (1975))

Having decided whether or not fair grounds existed, the tribunal then proceeds to consider whether the dismissal is fair in the circumstances. Here there are two questions: was the decision a reasonable one in the circumstances? and was the dismissal carried out in line with the procedure'? The second is the easier question to answer as procedural actions are straightforward, and the dismissal should be procedurally fair if the procedure has been carefully followed without any short cuts.

The importance of procedure was reaffirmed by the House of Lords in the case of *Polkey* v. *AE Dayton Services* (1987). This particular case concerned the fairness of redundancy when the employer had failed to consult the employee and had also failed to give proper notice. In giving judgement Lord Mackay ruled that the fact that consultation would have made no difference to the final outcome did not render the dismissal fair.

In determining reasonableness, according to Hepple (1992), there has been a shift in emphasis on the part of the courts since 1971. In his view tribunals have adapted their previous practice of balancing the interests of employer and employee and making judgements based on 'equity and the substantial merits of the case'. Tribunals now judge reasonableness firmly from the perspective of 'progressive management', determining that the employer has acted reasonably if the dismissal is within the range of reasonable responses open to employers in such circumstances.

In this book we have separated the consideration of discipline from the consideration of dismissal in order to concentrate on the practical aspects of discipline (putting things right) rather than the negative aspects (getting rid of the problem). The two cannot, however, be separated in practice and the question of discipline needs to be reviewed in the light of the material in Chapter 30. The question about decisions that are reasonable in the circumstances is a more nebulous one and the most reliable guide is a commonsense approach to deciding what is fair. It would, for instance, be unreasonable to dismiss someone as incapable if the employee had been denied necessary training; just as it would be unreasonable to dismiss a long-service employee for incapacity on the grounds of sickness unless future incapacity had been carefully and thoroughly determined.

Lack of capability or qualifications

The first aspect of capability relates to skill or aptitude. Although employers have the right and opportunity to test an applicant's suitability for a particular post

> An employee of a shop-fitting company tended to irritate the customers, lacking 'the aptitude and mental quality to be co-operative with, and helpful to, important clients'. His employer dismissed him and the tribunal accepted the fairness of the ground but not the procedural fairness of the decision. On appeal the tribunal judgement was overturned as specific warnings of the procedure type would not have altered the employee's performance. He had known for some time that he was at risk because of his difficulty in getting on with the customers and was not able to change his attitude. (*Dunning* v. *Jacomb* 1973)

before that individual is engaged, or before promotion, the law recognises that it is possible that mistakes will be made and that dismissal can be an appropriate remedy for the error, if the unsuitability is gross and beyond redemption. Normally there should be warning and the opportunity to improve before the dismissal is implemented, but there are exceptions if the unsuitability of the employee is based on an attitude that the employee expresses as a considered view and not in the heat of the moment. Another exception is where the employee's conduct is of such a nature that continued employment is not in the interests of the business, no matter what the reasons for it might be.

Where an employee is going through a period of probation at the time of termination, Lewis (1983) suggests that tribunals judge the fairness of a dismissal by soliciting answers to the following questions:

> Has the employer shown that he took reasonable steps to maintain the appraisal of the probationer through the period of probation? Did he give guidance by advice or warning when it would have been useful or fair to do so? Did an appropriate person make an honest effort to determine whether the probationer came up to the required standard, having informed himself of the appraisals made by supervisors and other facts recorded about the probationer? (Lewis 1983, p. 122)

The employer will always need to demonstrate the employee's unsuitability to the satisfaction of the tribunal by producing evidence of that unsuitability. This evidence must not be undermined by, for instance, giving the employee a glowing testimonial at the time of dismissal.

Lack of skill or aptitude is a fair ground when the lack can be demonstrated and where the employer has not contributed to it – by, for instance, ignoring it for a long period – but normally there must be the chance to state a case and/or improve before the dismissal will be procedurally fair. Redeployment to a more suitable job is also an option employers are expected to consider before taking the decision to dismiss.

The second aspect of capability is qualifications; the degree, diploma or other paper qualification needed to qualify the individual to do the work for which employed. The simple cases are those of misrepresentation, where an employee claims qualifications he or she does not have. More difficult are the situations where the employee cannot acquire necessary qualifications.

Dr Al-Tikriti was a senior registrar employed by the South Western Regional Health Authority. The practice of the authority was to allow registrars three attempts at passing the examination of the Royal College of Pathologists. Dr Al-Tikriti failed on the third attempt and was subsequently dismissed. He claimed that the dismissal was unfair on the grounds that he had had insufficient training to pass the exams. The tribunal, having heard evidence from the Royal College, decided that the training had been adequate and found the dismissal to have been fair. (*Al-Tikriti* v. *South Western RHA* 1986)

The third aspect of employee capability is health. It is potentially fair to dismiss someone on the grounds of ill-health which renders the employee incapable of discharging the contract of employment. Even the most distressing dismissal can be legally admissible, provided that it is not too hasty and provided that there is consideration of alternative employment. Employers are expected, however, to take account of any medical advice available to them before dismissing someone on grounds of ill health. Organisations with occupational health services are well placed to obtain detailed medical reports to help in such judgements but the decision to terminate someone's employment is ultimately for the manager to take and, if necessary, to justify at a tribunal. Medical evidence will be sought and has to be carefully considered but dismissal remains an employer's decision, not a medical decision.

Normally, absences through sickness have to be frequent or prolonged, although absence which seriously interferes with the running of a business may be judged fair even if it is neither frequent nor prolonged, but in all cases the employee must be consulted before being dismissed.

Drawing on the judgement of the EAT in the case of *Egg Stores* v. *Leibovici* in 1977, Selwyn lists nine questions that have to be asked to determine the potential fairness of dismissing someone after long-term sickness:

> (a) how long has the employment lasted (b) how long had it been expected the employment would continue (c) what is the nature of the job (d) what was the nature, effect and length of the illness (e) what is the need of the employer for the work to be done, and to engage a replacement to do it (f) if the employer takes no action, will he incur obligations in respect of redundancy payments or compensation for unfair dismissal (g) are wages continuing to be paid (h) why has the employer dismissed (or failed to do so) and (i) in all the circumstances, could a reasonable employer have been expected to wait any longer? (Selwyn 1985, p. 241)

This case was of frustration of contract, and there is always an emphasis in all tribunal hearings that the decision should be based on the facts of the particular situation of the dismissal that is being considered, rather than on specific precedents. For this reason the nine questions are no more than useful guidelines for personnel managers to consider: they do not constitute 'the law' on the matter.

A different situation is where an employee is frequently absent for short spells, as here the employee can be warned about the likely outcome of the absences being repeated:

> The employee...can be confronted with his record, told that it must improve, and be given a period of time in which its improvement can be monitored. Indeed, the employer should not overlook the powerful medicinal effect of a final warning, and a failure to give one may mean that the employee is unaware that the situation is causing the employer great concern. The effect of such a warning might be to stimulate the employee into seeking proper medical advice in case there is an underlying cause of the continuous minor ailments, it may deter the employee from taking time off when not truly warranted, and it may even lead the employee to look for other work where such absences could be tolerated. (Selwyn 1985, p. 244)

In the intriguing case of *International Sports Ltd* v. *Thomson* (1980), the employer dismissed an employee who had been frequently absent with a series of minor ailments ranging from althrugia of one knee, anxiety and nerves to bronchitis, cystitis, dizzy spells, dyspepsia and flatulence. All of these were covered by medical notes. (While pondering the medical note for flatulence, you will be interested to know that althrugia is water on the knee.)

The employer issued a series of warnings and the company dismissed the employee after consulting its medical adviser, who saw no reason to examine the employee as the illnesses had no connecting medical theme and were not chronic. The EAT held that this dismissal was fair.

Misconduct

The range of behaviours that can be described as 'misconduct' is so great that we need to consider different broad categories, the first being disobedience. It is implicit in the contract of employment that the employee will obey lawful instructions; but this does not mean blind, unquestioning obedience in all circumstances: the instruction has to be 'reasonable' and the employee's disobedience 'unreasonable' before

> Two long-service ambulance men were rostered for duty between 9.00 and 5.00 in May 1991. They were, however, kept unusually busy in the morning and by 2.00 had not been able to take their usual lunch-break. At 2.10 they were called out again but chose not to respond on the grounds that they were excessively tired and strained because they had worked for over five hours without a break. They returned to the ambulance station and signed off sick. They were then suspended from duty and subsequently dismissed. The tribunal rejected the ambulance men's argument that they had a legitimate need for food and drink after a long spell on duty and found in favour of the employer. (*Wallburton and Stokes* v. *Somerset Health Authority* 1991)

the dismissal can be fair. The tribunal would seek to establish exactly what the employee was engaged to do and whether the instruction was consistent with the terms of employment.

In the case of *Payne* v. *Spook Erection* (1984) an employee was asked to rank subordinates each week on a merit table, even though he had very little contact with some of the men whose merit he was assessing. The scheme was used as a basis both for promotion and for possible dismissal. Mr Payne refused to operate this system as he averred that his assessments could often amount to no more than guesswork. Because of his disobedience he was dismissed, but this dismissal was found unfair by the EAT.

> In our judgement, a scheme bearing these characteristics can only be described as obviously and intolerably unfair... To hold that an employer has the right to require the implementation of a scheme such as this would be to strike at the principles of the Employment Protection legislation and the codes of practice of recent years. (*Payne* v. *Spook Erection* (1984))

Although it is generally fair to dismiss the employee for absence, including lateness, the degree of the absence will be an issue. Lateness will seldom be seen to justify dismissal, unless it is persistent and after warning. Absence may be appropriate for dismissal if the nature of the work makes absence unsupportable by the employer. It will normally be expected that the employer will take account of an employee's previous record before taking extreme action.

The third area of misconduct is insubordination or rudeness:

> words or conduct showing contempt for one's employers – deserved or otherwise, and as distinct from disagreement or criticism – may make it impossible for the employer to exercise the authority which the law regards as his or to assume that the job in hand will be properly done. (Whincup 1976, p. 85)

It is important that the insubordination should be calculated, rather than a single moment of hysteria. The willingness of the employee to apologise can also be important.

Rudeness to customers is more likely to result in dismissal that a tribunal will find fair.

The employer retains the right to dismiss summarily, without notice, if the employee's conduct merits summary termination. Difficulties occur with the interpretation of certain phrases:

> A woman employee with five years of satisfactory service called her manager a 'stupid punk' in a heated moment and in front of other employees. Later she refused to apologise. The tribunal held that the dismissal was unfair as it was based on a single episode in a substantial period of service. The compensation for the employee was, however, reduced to £20 because she would not apologise. (*Rosenthal* v. *Butler* (1972))

There have been half a dozen cases on the precise meaning of 'fuck off' – apparently a common industrial salutation. In *Flutty* v. *Brekkes*, (1974), a foreman in the course of a discussion with a fish filleter on Hull docks said to him, 'If you don't like the job you can fuck off'. He made no bones about it! The filleter took him at his word and then claimed damages for unfair dismissal. The tribunal held that what the foreman actually means was, 'if you are complaining about the fish you are working on, or the quality of it, or if you do not like what in fact you are doing then you can leave your work, clock off, and you will be paid up to the time when you do so. Then you can come back when you are disposed to start work again the next day.' His remark was therefore no more than 'a general exhortation' whose precise effect the filleter had failed to appreciate. (Whincup 1976, p. 72)

In another case a supervisor was held to have been constructively dismissed when his employer told him to 'fuck off and get some overalls on'. This remark was to be construed as a demotion, repudiating the contract! (*Walker* v. *Humberside Erection Company* (1976)).

Another area of misconduct is criminal action. Tribunals are not courts for criminal proceedings, so that they will not try a case of theft or dishonesty; they will merely decide whether or not dismissal was a reasonable action by the employer in the circumstances. If a man is found guilty by court proceedings this does not justify automatically fair dismissal: it must still be procedurally fair and reasonable, so that theft off-duty is not necessarily grounds for dismissal. On the other hand, strong evidence that would not be sufficient to bring a prosecution may be sufficient to sustain a fair dismissal. Clocking-in offences will normally merit dismissal. Convictions for other offences such as drug handling or indecency will only justify dismissal if the nature of the offence will have some bearing on the work done by the employee. For someone such as an apprentice instructor it might justify summary dismissal, but in other types of employment it would be unfair, just as it would be unfair to dismiss an employee for a driving offence when there was no need for driving in the course of normal duties and there were other means of transport for getting to work.

Examples are, first, of the college lecturer who was convicted of gross indecency in a public lavatory with another man. His subsequent dismissal by the college was held to be fair as he was responsible for a foundation course for students in their mid-teens (*Gardiner* v. *Newport CBC* (1977)). In the case of *Moore* v. *C&A Modes* (1981) there was another criminal offence. This time it was a store supervisor with more than twenty years' service, who was found shoplifting in another store. Although this was a criminal act away from the place of work, the tribunal held that her subsequent dismissal by C&A Modes was fair because the criminal act was directly relevant to her employment, even though the action had taken place elsewhere:

> The employer must satisfy the three-fold test laid down in *British Home Stores* v. *Burchell*. First, the employer must show that he genuinely believes the employee to be guilty of the misconduct in question; second, he must have reasonable grounds upon which to establish that belief; third, he must have carried out such investigation into the matter as was reasonable in all the circumstances. (Selwyn 1985, p. 187)

Redundancy

Dismissal for redundancy is protected by compensation for unfair redundancy, compensation for genuine redundancy and the right to consultation before the redundancy takes place:

> An employee who is dismissed shall be taken to be dismissed by reason of redundancy if the dismissal is attributable wholly or mainly to:
>
> (a) the fact that his employer has ceased, or intends to cease, to carry on the business for the purposes of which the employee was employed by him, or has ceased, or intends to cease, to carry on that business in the place where the employee was so employed, or
>
> (b) the fact that the requirements of that business for employees to carry out work of a particular kind, or for employees to carry out work of a particular kind in the place where he was so employed, have ceased or are expected to cease or diminish. (Employment Protection (Consolidation) Act 1978, Sect. 81)

Apart from certain specialised groups of employee, anyone who has been continuously employed for two years or more is guaranteed a compensation payment from an employer, if dismissed for redundancy. The compensation is assessed on a sliding scale relating to length of service, age and rate of pay per week. If the employer wishes to escape the obligation to compensate, then it is necessary to show that the reason for dismissal was something other than redundancy.

The employer has to consult with the individual employee before dismissal takes place, but there is also a separate legal obligation to consult with recognised trade unions and the Department of Employment. If ten or more employees are to be made redundant, and if those employees are in unions that are recognised by the employer, then the employer must give written notice of intention to the unions concerned and the Department of Employment at least thirty days before the first dismissal. If it is proposed to make more than 100 employees redundant within a three-month period, then ninety days' advance notice must be given. Having done this, the employer has a legal duty to consult with the union representing the employees on the redundancies: he is not obliged to negotiate with them, merely to explain, listen to comments and reply with reasons. Employees also have the right to reasonable time off with pay during their redundancy notice so that they can seek other work.

One of the most difficult aspects of redundancy for the employer is the selection of who should go. The convention is that people should leave on the basis of a long-standing convention known as last-in first-out, or LIFO, as this provides a rough and ready justice with which it is difficult to argue. Our researches show, however, that an increasing number of employers are using other criteria, including skill, competence and attendance record. Less than two-thirds of employers have agreements on redundancy, yet these are the most satisfactory means of smoothing the problems that enforced redundancy causes.

Increasingly, employers are trying to avoid enforced redundancy by a range of strategies, such as not replacing people who leave, early retirement and voluntary redundancy. Part-time employees can be vulnerable as they can be made redundant if their jobs are made full-time, but they are not able to comply with the revised terms.

The large scale of redundancies in recent years has produced a variety of managerial initiatives to mitigate the effects. One of the most constructive has been a redundancy counselling service. Sometimes this is administered by the personnel department through its welfare officers, but many organisations use external services. Burrows (1985) lists fifteen different firms providing redundancy advisory services, and there have been a number of 'outplacement' courses arranged for redundant executives to enable them to set up in business on their own account. Burrows cities evidence from a study by Gibbs and Cross (1985) to say:

> a fraction of one per cent of the total market is reached by the nine prominent redundancy counselling organizations that were surveyed. Information gained from 21 large companies which attempted some form of resettlement assistance indicates that only 51 managers out of 7,604 made redundant were sponsored at redundancy counselling organizations. (Burrows 1985, p. 320)

Some other substantial reason

As the law of unfair dismissal has evolved since 1978 the most controversial area has been the category of potentially fair dismissals known as 'some other substantial reason'. Many commentators see this as a catch-all or dustbin category which enables employers to dismiss virtually anyone, provided a satisfactory business case can be made. All manner of cases have been successfully defended under this heading including the following; dismissals resulting from personality clashes, pressure to dismiss from subordinates or customers, disclosure of damaging information, the dismissal of a man whose wife worked for a rival firm and the dismissal of a landlord's wife following her husband's dismissal on grounds of capability. The majority of cases brought under this heading, however, result from business reorganisations where there is no redundancy. These often occur when the employer seeks to alter terms and conditions of employment and can not secure the employee's agreement. Such circumstances can result in the dismissal of the employee together with an offer of re-employment on new contractual terms. Such dismissals are judged fair provided a sound business reason exists to justify the changes envisaged. It will usually be necessary to consult prior to the reorganisation but the tribunal will not base its judgement on whether the employee acted reasonably in refusing new terms and conditions. The test laid down in *Hollister* v. *The National Farmer's Union* (1979) [ICR 542] by the Court of Appeal merely requires the employer to demonstrate that the change would bring clear organisational advantage. According to the barrister John Bowers:

> A review of the re-organisation case law shows that the EAT and Court of Appeal appear to accept as wholly valid employers' claims that to compete effectively in a free

market they must be allowed latitude to trim and make efficient their workforce and work methods without being hampered by laws protecting their workers. (Bowers 1990)

Automatic decisions

There are some circumstances in which the tribunal is not required to undergo the process of first establishing a fair reason for the dismissal before going on to assess the employer's reasonableness. In these cases the tribunal is required to find the dismissal fair or unfair without regard to the reasonableness of the employer's actions.

Automatically unfair dismissals

1. Dismissals on grounds of pregnancy.
2. Dismissals on grounds of trade union membership or potential membership.
3. Dismissals on grounds of actual or proposed trade union activity undertaken at 'an appropriate time'.
4. Dismissals resulting from an individual's refusal to join a trade union.
5. Dismissals resulting directly from a transfer in the organisation's ownership.
6. When no reason for the dismissal is given.
7. Where the employee has been unfairly selected for redundancy.
8. Dismissal as a result of a past criminal conviction which is spent under the terms of the Rehabilitation of Offenders Act.

The legislation on dismissal for trade union reasons was substantially revised in the Employment Act 1988 and the Trade Union and Labour Relations (Consolidation) Act 1992. Prior to 1988 it was sometimes deemed fair to dismiss an employee who did not wish to join a trade union where a 'closed shop' arrangement was in operation. Parliament has also waived the two-year qualifying period in cases of this kind so any employee can now bring a case of unfair dismissal if they believe their contract to have been terminated as as result of trade union membership or lack of trade union membership. Trade union activity is judged 'appropriate' if it occurs outside normal working hours or during working hours with the employer's consent.

There is now a similar waiving of the qualifying period in cases of dismissal on grounds of pregnancy. New regulations concerning maternity rights came into force in October 1994, tightening up the law in this area which applies to all female employees whatever their length of service, part-time or full-time. Before October 1994 employers could fairly dismiss a pregnant employee if she was incapable of performing her duties on account of the pregnancy or if continued employment would result in a contravention of health and safety law. Women now have the right to medical suspension on full pay in these circumstances and will be automatically successful at a tribunal if dismissed.

Since the introduction in 1981 of Transfer of Undertakings regulations it has also been automatically unfair to dismiss an employee when a business changes hands or when a public corporation is privatised unless it can be shown that the dismissal was for economic, technical or organisation reasons. It is thus not lawful for a new owner of a business to dismiss the existing manager simply to bring someone else in with whom the new owner is familiar. The same rules apply to hospitals becoming NHS Trusts and to local authority services which are transferred following competitive tendering.

There are also a few situations in which a dismissal will be found automatically to be fair. These fall into two categories:

1. Dismissal of employees who are on strike or taking part in some other industrial action.
2. Dismissals for the purpose of safeguarding national security.

Dismissals resulting from industrial action can only be fair if all employees are treated equally. It is not fair only to dismiss some of the strikers.

Constructive dismissal

When the behaviour of the management causes the employee to resign, the ex-employee may still be able to claim dismissal on the grounds that the behaviour of the employer constituted a repudiation of the contract, leaving the employee with no alternative but to resign; the employee may then be able to claim that the dismissal was unfair. It is not sufficient for the employer simply to be awkward or whimsical; the employer's conduct must amount to a significant breach, going to the root of the contract, such as physical assault, demotion, reduction in pay, change in location of work or significant change in duties. The breach must, however, be significant, so that a slight lateness in paying wages would not necessarily involve a breach, nor would a temporary change in place of work: 'If an employer, under the stresses of the requirements of his business, directs an employee to transfer to other suitable work on a purely temporary basis and at no diminution in wages, that may, in the ordinary case, not constitute a breach of contract' (*Millbrook Furnishing Ltd* v. *McIntosh* (1981)).

Some of the more interesting constructive dismissal cases concern claims that implied terms of contract have been breached.

In 1990, a hotel employee resigned after she had been severely reprimanded by a manager in front of other employees. She claimed that she had had no option to resign because she had been made to feel humiliated and degraded. A tribunal and the EAT accepted the woman's claim of constructive dismissal on the grounds that the manager's actions had breached the implied contractual term of 'trust and confidence'. (*Hilton International Hotels* v. *Protopapa* 1990)

There is no scope for an employer to assume an employee has resigned because of having apparently repudiated the employment contract by not turning up. The breach does not exist until the repudiation is accepted by the employer in dismissing the employee. Unless dismissed, the employee still has a binding contract of employment: 'If a worker walks out of his job or commits any other breach of contract, repudiatory or otherwise, but at any time claims that he is entitled to resume work, then his contract of employment is only determined if the employer expressly or impliedly asserts and accepts the repudiation on the part of the worker' *London Transport Executive* v. *Clarke* (1981)).

In all matters of dismissal the personnel manager should follow scrupulously the suggestions regarding disciplinary and grievance handling set out in Chapter 30. Procedural fairness is a significant test in deciding whether a dismissal was actually fair and not just potentially fair; and the consistent, thorough use of procedure and interviewing can frequently make a dismissal unnecessary as all the other possibilities of restoring satisfaction between the parties are explored first.

Wrongful dismissal

In addition to the body of legislation defining unfair dismissal there is a long-standing common law right to damages for an employee who has been dismissed wrongfully. Cases of wrongful dismissal are taken to the county court, rather than to industrial tribunals, and are concerned solely with alleged breaches of contract. Employees can thus only bring cases of wrongful dismissal against his or her employer when they believe their dismissal to have been unlawful according to the terms of their contract of employment. Wrongful dismissal can, therefore, be used when the employer has not given proper notice or if the dismissal is in breach of any clause or agreement incorporated into the contract. This remains a form of remedy that is used by very few people, but it could be useful to employees who have not sufficient length of service to claim unfair dismissal, so the employer who has learned that it is possible to dismiss people unfairly if they do not have two years' service needs to remember that this does not permit wrongful dismissal. There may also be cases where a very highly paid employee might get higher damages in an ordinary court than the maximum that the tribunal can award.

Compensation for dismissal

Having considered the various ways in which the employee might have some legal redress against an employer when the employment contract is terminated, we now consider the remedies. If an employee believes the dismissal to be unfair, the employee should complain to an industrial tribunal. The office of the tribunal will refer the matter first to ACAS in the hope that an amicable solution between the parties can be reached. As was indicated at the beginning of this chapter, a number of issues are settled in this way. Either the discontented employee realises that there is no case, or the employer makes an arrangement in view of the likely tribunal finding. If an agreement is not reached, the case will be heard by an industrial tribunal and, if either party is not satisfied with the finding, they can appeal to the Employment Appeal Tribunal.

The tribunal can make two types of award: either they can order that the ex-employee be re-employed or they can award some financial compensation from the ex-employer for the loss that the employee has suffered. The Employment Protection (Consolidation) Act makes re-employment the main remedy, although this was not previously available under earlier legislation. They will not order re-employment unless the dismissed employee wants it and they can choose between reinstatement or re-engagement. In reinstatement the old job is given back to the employee under the same terms and conditions, plus any increments, etc., to which the individual would have become entitled had the dismissal not occurred, plus any arrears of payment that would have been received. The situation is just as it would have been, including all rights deriving from length of service, if the dismissal had not taken place. The alternative to re-engagement will be that the employee is employed afresh in a job comparable to the last one, but without continuity of employment. The decision as to which of the two to order will depend on assessment of the practicability of the alternatives, the wishes of the unfairly dismissed employee and the natural justice of the award, taking account of the ex-employee's behaviour.

In practice, however, reinstatement and re-engagement occur in less than 5 per cent of successful unfair dismissal cases. The vast majority of applicants come to tribunal seeking financial compensation. Many applicants want their jobs back at the time they make their claim but want cash compensation instead by the time the hearing takes place. Research by Evans, Goodman and Hargreaves (1985, p. 47) showed that 78 per cent of the respondent firms which they investigated would never re-employ a dismissed employee, and only 1 per cent actually had re-employed a dismissed employee.

Tribunals calculate the level of award under a series of headings. First is the basic award, which is based on the employee's age and length of service. It is calculated in the same way as statutory redundancy payments:

- half a week's pay for every year of service below the age of 22 years;
- one week's pay for every year of service between the ages 22 and 41 years; and
- one-and-a-half week's pay for every year of service over the age of 41 years.

The basic award is limited, however, because tribunals can only take into account a maximum of twenty years' service when calculating the figure to be awarded. A maximum weekly salary figure is also imposed by the Treasury, which in 1994 was £205. The maximum basic award that can be ordered is therefore £6150. In many cases, of course, where the employee has only a few years' service the figure will be far lower.

In addition a tribunal can also order compensation under the following headings.

Compensatory awards

These take account of loss of earnings, pension rights, future earnings loss, etc. The maximum level in 1994 was £11,000.

Additional awards

These are used in cases of sex and race discrimination and also when an employer fails to comply with order of reinstatement or re-engagement. In the former case the maximum award is 52 weeks' pay, in the latter 26 weeks' pay.

Special awards

These are made when unfair dismissal relates to trade union activity or membership. They can also be used when the dismissal was for health and safety reasons.

A tribunal can reduce the total level of compensation if it judges the individual concerned to have contributed to their own dismissal. For example, a dismissal on grounds of poor work performance may be found unfair because no procedure was followed and consequently no warnings given. This does not automatically entitle the ex-employee concerned to compensation based on the above formulae. If the tribunal judges them to have been 60 per cent responsible for their own dismissal the compensation will be reduced by 60 per cent. Reductions are also made if an ex-employee is judged not to have taken reasonable steps to mitigate his or her loss.

REVIEW TOPIC 14.2

In what circumstances do you think a dismissed employee might welcome reinstatement or re-engagement, and in what circumstances might the employer welcome it?

Written statement of reasons

The Employment Protection (Consolidation) Act gives employees the right to obtain from their employer a written statement of the reasons for their dismissal, if they are dismissed after at least twenty-six weeks' service. If asked, the employer must provide the statement within fourteen days. If it is not provided, the employee can complain to an Industrial Tribunal that the statement has been refused and the tribunal will award the employee two weeks' pay if they find the complaint justified. The employee can also complain, and receive the same award, if the employer's reasons are untrue or inadequate – provided, again, that the tribunal agrees.

Such an award is in addition to anything the tribunal may decide about the unfairness of the dismissal, if the employee complains about that. The main purpose of this provision is to enable the employee to test whether there is reasonable case for an unfair dismissal complaint or not. Although the statement is admissible as evidence in tribunal proceedings, the tribunal will not necessarily limit their considerations to what the statement contains. If the tribunal members were to decide that the reasons for dismissal were other than stated, then the management's case would be jeopardised.

Resignation

In any organisation there will be a stream of people leaving to move on to other things, even though tightness of the labour market has recently reduced many streams to a trickle. Even the most serious of these losses actually provides an opportunity, as a new person will come in or there will be some reshuffling among the existing stock of employees, so that individuals will find fresh scope, and new ideas and energies will be deployed. What is important to the personnel manager is to find out and analyse reasons for leaving, as this will provide information that can be used to iron out problems.

Most people simply move on, but some move on because the 'push' factors are stronger than the 'pulls'. By interviewing everyone who leaves, the personnel manager can collect the range of reasons for people resigning in order to see what the pattern is in the decisions. The difficulty is that at that time the employee has not only decided to go, but also has another job to go to, so that the reasons that first caused the employee to look around may have been forgotten in the enthusiasm about the attractions of the new job. Also, the new job must be presented as better, otherwise the leaver looks foolish. With these reservations, the personnel manager can see what features of organisational practice are unsettling people.

An important legal point about resignation is that an employer cannot avoid the possibility of an unfair dismissal by offering the employee the choice between resigning or being dismissed. Resignation under duress is likely to be construed as dismissal. This is not the same as giving an employee the choice between performing the contract and resigning. The employee who resigns in that situation is making a personal choice to resign rather than discharge those duties the employer is legally entitled to expect.

Retirement

The final mode of contract termination is retirement, and this has the advantage for the employer that there is usually plenty of notice, so that succession arrangements can be planned smoothly. It is now rare for people to retire abruptly after working at high pressure to the very end. Some sort of phased withdrawal is much preferred, so that the retiree adjusts gradually to the new state of being out of regular employment and with a lower level of income, while the employing organisation is able to prepare a successor to take office.

Another advantage to this arrangement is that there may be 'a life after death' with the retiree continuing to work part-time after retirement, or coming back to help out at peak periods or at holiday times. Many organisations go to great lengths to keep in touch with their retired personnel, often arranging Christmas parties, excursions and other events with people returning year after year.

Early retirement has become a widespread method of slimming payrolls and making opportunities both for some people to retire early and for others to take their place. The nature of the pension arrangements are critical to early retirement strategies, as early retirees are ideally voluntary and the majority of people will accept, or volunteer for, early retirement if the financial terms are acceptable. It is not, of course, possible to draw state retirement pension until the official retirement ages of 60 or 65 years, but many people will accept an occupational pension and a lump sum in their fifties if they see the possibility of a new lease of life to pursue other interests or to start their own business.

Notice

An employee qualifies for notice of dismissal on completion of four weeks of employment with an employer. At that time the employee is entitled to receive one week's notice. This remains constant until the employee has completed two years' service, after which it increases to two week's notice, thereafter increasing on the basis of one week's notice per additional year of service up to a maximum of twelve weeks for twelve years' unbroken service. These are minimum statutory periods. If the employer includes longer periods of notice in the contract, which is quite common with senior employees, then they are bound by the longer period.

The employee is required to give one week's notice after completing four weeks' service and this period does not increase as a statutory obligation. If an employee accepts a contract in which the period of notice to be given is longer then that is binding, but the employer may have problems of enforcement if an employee is not willing to continue in employment for the longer period.

Neither party can withdraw notice unilaterally. The withdrawal will only be effective if the other party agrees. Therefore, if an employer gives notice to an employee and wishes later to withdraw it, this can only be done if the employee agrees to the contract of employment remaining in existence. Equally, the employee cannot change his mind about resigning unless the employer agrees.

Notice only exists when a date has been specified. The statement 'We're going to wind up the business, so you will have to find another job' is not notice: it is a warning of intention.

Personnel managers and the law

Personnel managers should not be overconcerned with the legalism of the tribunal system, as this is a danger that the legal system itself is regularly trying to avoid. The following is an extract from a recent EAT judgement:

Industrial tribunals are not required, and should not be invited, to subject the authorities to the same analysis as a court of law searching in a plethora of precedent for binding or persuasive authority. The objective of Parliament when it first framed the right not to be unfairly dismissed and set up a system of industrial tribunals (with a majority of lay members) to administer it, was to banish legalism and in particular to ensure that, wherever possible, parties conducting their own case would be able to face the tribunal with the same ease and confidence as those professionally represented. A preoccupation with guideline authority puts that objective in jeopardy. (IRLR (1984), p. 131)

The existence of an expanding body of labour legislation greatly enhances the role and authority of personnel managers within organisations. The law relating to employment is steadily becoming more complex and is thus inevitably outside the competence of most line managers. Legal developments can thus only increase the need for personnel managers trained to pilot organisations through these ever more hazardous waters.

☐ SUMMARY PROPOSITIONS

14.1 Of the many dismissals that take place in a year, a minority are reported to tribunal and a small minority are found in favour of the ex-employee.

14.2 The grounds on which an employee can be dismissed without the likelihood of an unfair dismissal claim are lack of capability, misconduct, redundancy, statutory bar, or some other substantial reason.

14.3 If an employee is dismissed on one of the above grounds, the dismissal must still be procedurally fair: following the agreed procedure and being fair in the circumstances.

14.4 An employee who resigns as a result of unreasonable behaviour by the employer could still be able to claim unfair dismissal: constructive dismissal.

14.5 Personnel managers will not wish to discourage employees from resigning, but they will need to monitor reasons for leaving.

14.6 When employees retire from an organisation, a phased withdrawal rather than abrupt termination is likely to be a better arrangement for both employer and employee.

14.7 When contemplating the potential fairness of a dismissal, personnel managers should concentrate on the statute and the facts of the situation rather than examining tribunal precedent.

References

ACAS (1985), *Annual Report 1984*, London: Advisory, Conciliation and Arbitration Service.
ACAS (1990), *Annual Report 1989*, London: Advisory, Conciliation and Arbitration Service.

ACAS (1994), *Annual Report 1993*, London: Advisory, Conciliation and Arbitration Service.

Amar-Ojok v. Surrey AHA [1975] IRLR 252.

Bowers, J. (1990), *Bowers on Employment Law*, London: Blackstone.

Burrows, G. (1985), *Redundancy Counselling for Managers*, London: Institute of Personnel Management.

Dunning & Sons Ltd v. Jacomb [1973] ICR 448, [1973] IRLR 206, 15 KIR 9.

Evans, S., Goodman, J. and Hargreaves, L. (1985), *Unfair Dismissal Law and Employment Practice in the 1980s, DoE Research Paper no. 53*, London: Department of Employment.

Flutty v. D. & D. Brekkes Ltd [1974] IRLR 130.

Gardiner v. Newport County Borough Council [1974] IRLR 262.

George v. Beecham Group Ltd [1977] IRLR 43.

Gibbs, A. and Cross, M. (1985), *A Study of Managerial Resettlement*, London: Manpower Services Commission.

Hepple, B. A. (1992), 'The fall and rise of unfair dismissal'. In W. Mcarthy (ed.) *Legal Interventions in Industrial Relations (1992)*, Oxford: Blackwell.

Hilton International Hotels Ltd v. Prototapa [1991] IRLR 316.

International Sports Co. Ltd v. Thomson [1980] IRLR 340.

Lewis, D. (1983), *Essentials of Employment Law*, London: Institute of Personnel Management.

Lewis, P. (1981), 'Why legislation failed to provide employment protection for unfairly dismissed employees', *British Journal of Industrial Relations*, November, pp. 316–26.

Lewis, P. (1992), 'Unfair dismissal and tribunals'. In B. Towers (ed.) *A Handbook of Industrial Relations Practice*, London: Kogan Page.

London Transport Executive v. Clarke [1981] ICR 355, [1981] IRLR 166.

Ministry of Labour (1976), *Dismissal Procedures*, London: HMSO.

Moore v. C&A Modes [1981] IRLR 71.

Payne v. Spook Erection Ltd [1984] IRLR 221.

Rosenthal v. Louis Butler Ltd [1972] IRLR 39.

Selwyn, N. (1985), *Law of Employment*, 5th edition. London: Butterworth.

Walker v. Humberside Erection Company [1976] IRLR 105.

Whincup, M. (1976), *Modern Employment Law*, London: Heinemann.

15 Interactive skill: selection interviewing

We now discuss one of the most familiar and forbidding encounters of organisational life – the selection interview. Most people have had at least one experience of being interviewed as a preliminary to employment and few reflect with pleasure on the experience. Personnel specialists have a critical role in selection interviewing, carrying out many of the interviews and encouraging good interviewing practice in others by example, support and training.

In this chapter we review the varieties of selection interview and the criticism that has been made of it, in spite of its importance as a selection tool. Interview strategy and the number of interviews and interviewers are then considered, followed by sections on preparation and conduct of the interview. The chapter concludes with a section on making selection decisions.

Varieties of interview

There is a wide variety of practice in selection interviewing. At one extreme we read of men seeking work in the docks of Victorian London and generally being treated as if they were in a cattle market. In sharp contrast is the attitude of Sherlock Holmes to a prospective employer:

> I can only say, madam, that I shall be happy to devote the same care to your case as I did to that of your friend. As to reward, my profession is its reward; but you are at liberty to defray whatever expenses I may be put to, at the time which suits you best. (Conan Doyle 1881)

There is a neat spectrum of employee participation in the employment process which correlates with social class and type of work. While the London docks situation of the 1890s is not found today, there are working situations where the degree of discussion between the parties is limited to perfunctory exchanges about trade union membership, hours of work and rates of pay: labourers on building sites and extras on film sets being two examples. As interviews move up the organisational hierarchy there is growing equilibrium with the interviewer becoming more courteous and responsive to questions from the applicant, who will probably be described as a 'candidate' or someone who 'might be interested in the position'. For the most senior positions it is unlikely that people will be invited to respond to vacancies advertised in the press. Individuals will be approached, either directly or through consultants, and there will be an elaborate pavane in which each party seeks to persuade the other to declare an interest first.

Another indication of the variety of employment practice is in the titles used. The humblest of applicants seek 'jobs' or 'vacancies', while the more ambitious are looking for 'places', 'posts', 'positions', 'openings' or 'opportunities'. The really high-flyers seem to need somewhere to sit down, as they are offered 'seats on the board', 'professorial chairs' or 'places on the front bench'.

The purpose of the selection interview

An interview is a controlled conversation with a purpose. There are more exchanges in a shorter period related to a specific purpose than in an ordinary conversation. In the selection interview the purposes are:

1. To collect information in order to predict how well the applicants would perform in the job for which they have applied, by measuring them against pre-determined criteria.
2. To provide the candidate with full details of the job and organisation to facilitate their decision-making.
3. To conduct the interview in such a manner that candidates feel that they have been given a fair hearing.

Criticism of the selection interview

The selection interview has been extensively criticised as being unreliable, invalid and subjective, although this is directed towards the decisions made and ignores the importance of the interview as a ritual in the employment process.

> The bald conclusion from all the empirical evidence is that the interview as typically used is not much good as a selection device. Indeed, one might wonder, rationally, why the interview was not long ago 'retired' from selection procedures. (Morgan 1973, p. 5)

The most perceptive criticism is by Webster (1964), summarising extensive research. The main conclusions were:

1. Interviewers decided to accept or reject a candidate within the first three or four minutes of the interview and then spent the remainder of the interview time seeking evidence to confirm that their first impression was right.

2. Interviews seldom altered the tentative opinion formed by the interviewer seeing the application form and the appearance of the candidate.
3. Interviewers place more weight on evidence that is unfavourable than on evidence that is favourable.
4. When interviewers have made up their minds very early in the interview, their behaviour betrays their decision to the candidate.

However much this criticism is justified it does not solve the problem, it merely identifies it. Lopez points to the fact that all the complaints and denunciations boil down to the argument that it is the interviewer and not the interview that is the heart of the problem (Lopez 1975, p. 5).

A key skill for personnel and other managers is how to handle this most crucial of encounters. It will not disappear from employment, as we shall see in the next section of this chapter, and the interview provides a number of important advantages which cannot be provided by any other means.

The importance of the selection interview

The selection interview cannot be bettered as a means of exchanging information and meeting the human and ritual aspects of the employment process.

Exchanging information

The interview is a flexible and speedy means of exchanging information over a broad range of topics. The employer has the opportunity to sell the company and explain job details in depth. Applicants have the chance to ask questions about the job and the company in order to collect the information they require for their own selection decision. The interview is also the logical culmination of the employment process, as information from a variety of sources – such as application forms, tests and references – can be discussed together.

Human and ritual aspects

In an interview some assessment can be made of matters that cannot be approached any other way, such as the potential compatibility of two people who will have to work together. Both parties need to meet each other before the contract begins to 'tune in' to each other and begin the process of induction. The interview is valuable in that way to both potential employee and potential employer. As Lopez suggests, it gives interviewees the feeling that they matter as another person is devoting time to them and they are not being considered by a computer. Also, giving applicants a chance to ask questions underlines their decision-making role, making them feel less helpless in the hands of the all-powerful interviewer. Selection interviewing has powerful ritual elements, as the applicant is seeking either to enter, or to rise within, a social system. This requires the display of deferential behaviours:

> ...upward mobility involves the presentation of proper performances and...efforts to move upward...are expressed in terms of sacrifices made for the maintenance of front. (Goffman 1972, p. 45)

At the same time those who are already inside and above display their superiority and security, even unconsciously, in contrast with the behaviour of someone so obviously anxious to share the same privileged position.

Reason tells us that this is inappropriate at the end of the twentieth century as it produces an unreasonable degree of dependency in the applicant; and the books are full of advice to interviewers not to brandish their social superiority, but to put applicants at their ease and to reduce the status differentials. This, however, acknowledges their superiority as they are the ones who take the initiative; applicants are not expected to help the interviewer relax and feel less apprehensive. Also the reality of the situation is usually that of applicant anxious to get in and selector choosing among several. Status differentials can not simply be set aside. The selection interview is at least partly an initiation rite, not as elaborate as entry to commissioned rank in the armed forces, nor as whimsical as finding one's way into the Brownie ring, but still a process of going through hoops and being found worthy in a process where other people make all the rules.

REVIEW TOPIC 15.1

For a selection interview in which you recently participated, either as selector or as applicant, consider the following:

(a)   What were the ritual features?

(b)   Were any useful ritual features missing?

(c)   Could ritual have been, in any way, *helpfully* reduced?

No matter what other means of making employment decisions there may be, the interview is crucial and when worries are expressed about its reliability, this is not a reason for doing away with it: it is a reason for conducting it properly.

Interview strategy

The approach to selection interviewing varies considerably from the amiable chat in a bar to the highly organised, multiperson panel.

Frank and friendly strategy

By far the most common is the approach which Hackett (1978) described as frank and friendly. Here the interviewer is concerned to establish and maintain the rapport. This is done partly in the belief that if interviewees do not feel threatened, and are relaxed, they will be more forthcoming in the information that they offer. It is the most straightforward strategy for both interviewer and interviewee and has the potential advantage that the interviewees will leave with a favourable impression of the company.

Problem-solving strategy

A variation of the frank and friendly strategy is the problem-solving approach. It is the method of presenting the candidate with a hypothetical problem and evaluating his or her answer, like the king in the fairy tale who offered the hand of the princess in marriage to the first suitor who could answer three riddles.

These are sometimes called situational interviews. The questions asked are derived from the job description and candidates are required to imagine themselves as the job holder and describe what they would do in a variety of hypothetical situations. This method is most applicable to testing elementary knowledge, such as the colour coding of wires in electric cables or maximum dosages of specified drugs. It is less effective to test understanding and ability.

There is no guarantee that the candidate would actually behave in the way suggested. The quick thinker will score at the expense of the person who can take action more effectively than they can answer riddles.

Behavioural event strategy

Similar to problem-solving is the behavioural event method. The focus is on the candidate's past behaviour and performance, which is a more reliable way of

> The following intriguing poser was put to a candidate for the position of security officer at a large department store:
>
> > If you were alone in the building and decided to inspect the roof, what would you do if the only door out on to the roof banged itself shut behind you and the building caught fire?
>
> The retired police superintendent to whom that question was posed asked, very earnestly and politely, for six pieces of additional information, such as the location of telephones, time of day, height of building, fire escapes. The replies become progressively more uncertain and the interviewer hastily shifted the ground of the interview to something else.

predicting future performance than asking interviewees what they would do in a certain situation. Examples of questions used in this type of interview are given by Jenks and Zevnik (1989). Candidates are requested to describe the background to a situation and explain what they did and why; what their options were; how they decided what to do; and the anticipated and real results of their action. The success of this method is critically dependent on in-depth job analysis, and preferably competency analysis, in order to frame the best questions.

Stress strategy

In the stress approach the interviewer becomes aggressive, disparages the candidates, puts them on the defensive or disconcerts them by strange behaviour. The Office of Strategic Services in the United States used this method in the Second World War to select men for espionage work, and subsequently the idea was used by some business organisations on the premise that executive life was stressful, so a simulation of the stress would determine whether or not the candidate could cope.

The advantage of the method is that it may demonstrate a necessary strength or a disqualifying weakness that would not be apparent through other methods. The disadvantages are that evaluating the behaviour under stress is problematical, and those who are not selected will think badly of the employer.

The likely value of stress interviewing is so limited that it is hardly worth mentioning except that it has such spurious appeal to many managers, who are attracted by the idea of injecting at least some stress into the interview 'to see what they are made of', 'to put them on their mettle' or some similar jingoism. Most candidates feel that the procedures are stressful enough, without adding to them. In addition, Sidney and Brown comment:

> There is seldom any reason for assuming that the stress of dealing with a hostile...potential...employer...resembles the kind of stress the applicant would be asked to face if he were appointed. The [stress] interview yields possible evidence on only one aspect of personality...and perforce omits much else that should be relevant. (Sidney and Brown 1961, pp. 164–5)

Number of interviews and interviewers

There are two broad traditions governing the number of interviewers. One tradition says that effective, frank discussion can only take place on a one-to-one basis so candidates meet one interviewer, or several interviewers, one at a time. The other tradition is that fair play must be demonstrated and nepotism prevented so the interview must be carried out, and the decision made, by a panel of interviewers. Within this dichotomy there are various options.

The individual interview

This method gives the greatest chance of establishing rapport, developing mutual trust and the most efficient deployment of time in the face-to-face encounter, as each participant has to compete with only one other speaker. It is usually also the most satisfactory method for the candidate, who has to tune in only to one other person instead of needing constantly to adjust their antennae to different interlocutors. They can more readily ask questions, as it is difficult to ask a panel of six people to explain the workings of the pension scheme, and it is the least formal.

The disadvantages lie in the dependence the organisation places on the judgement of one of its representatives – although this can be mitigated by a series of individual interviews – and the ritual element is largely missing. Candidates may not feel they have been 'done' properly. Our recent research indicates that a sole interview with the line manager is very popular in the selection of blue-collar staff, being used in more than one-third of cases. It is much less popular for white-collar and management staff.

Sequential interviews

This is a series of individual interviews. The series most often consists of just two interviews for blue- and white-collar staff, but more than two for managerial staff. The most frequent combination is an interview with the line manager and an interview with a representative of the personnel department. For managerial posts this will be extended to interviews with other departmental managers, top managers and significant prospective colleagues. Sequential interviews are useful as they can give the employer a broader picture of the candidate and they also allow the applicant to have contact with a greater number of potential colleagues. However, the advantages of sequential interviews need to be based on effective organisation and interviews all on the same day. Lopez (1975) argues that it is important that all interviewers meet beforehand to agree on the requirements of the post and to decide how each will contribute to the overall theme. Immediately following the interviews a further meeting needs to take place so that the candidates can be jointly evaluated. One disadvantage of the method is the organisation and time that it takes from both the employer's and the candidate's point of view. It requires considerable commitment from the candidate who may have to keep repeating similar information and whose performance may deteriorate throughout the interviews due to fatigue.

Panel interviews

This method has the specious appeal of sharing judgement and may appear to be a way of saving time in interviewing as all panel members are operating at once. It is also possible to legitimise a quick decision – always popular with candidates – and there can be no doubt about the ritual requirements being satisfied. Muir (1988) also argues that panel interviews are less influenced by personal bias, ensure the candidate is more acceptable to the whole organisation, and allow the candidate to get a better feel for the whole organisation.

The drawbacks can lie in the tribunal nature of the panel. They are not having a conversation with the candidates; they are sitting in judgement upon them and assessing the evidence they are able to present in response to their requests. There is little prospect of building rapport and developing discussion, and there is likely to be as much interplay between members of the panel as there is between the panel and the candidate. Alec Rodger makes the observation:

> The usefulness of the board interview may depend a good deal on the competence of the chairman, and on the good sense of board members.
>
> A promising board interview can easily be ruined by a member who does not appreciate the line of questioning being pursued by one of his fellow-members and who interrupts with irrelevancies. (Rodger 1975)

Panel interviews tend to over-rigidity and give ironic point to the phrase 'it is only a formality'. Ritualistically they are superb, but as a useful preliminary to employment they are questionable.

However, benefits of the panel interview can be gained, and disadvantages minimised, if the interviewers are well trained and the interview well organised, thoroughly planned and is part of a structured interviewing process as, for example, described by Campion, Pursell and Brown (1988).

REVIEW TOPIC 15.2

In your organisation how many interviews and interviewers are used? How effective is this approach and why? In what ways could the approach be improved?

The selection interview sequence

Preparation

We assume that the preliminaries of job analysis, recruitment and shortlisting are complete and the interview is now to take place. The first step in preparation is for the interviewers to brief themselves. They will collect and study a job description or similar details of the post to be filled, a personnel specification or statement of required competencies and the application forms or curricula vitae of the candidates.

Barbara Trevithick applied for a post as personnel officer at a hospital and was invited for interview at 2.00 p.m. On arrival she was ushered into a small windowless room where four other people were waiting. At 2.20 a secretary came in and asked Mr Brown to come with her. At 3.00 Mr Jones was called for. At 3.45 the remaining three candidates went out in search of the secretary to ask what the remaining timetable for the day was to be. The secretary replied that she did not know but the panel members had just gone to the canteen for a cup of coffee. By now Barbara had figured out that her surname was the last in an alphabetical order. Miss Mellhuish was called for interview at 4.10 and Miss Roberts left because her last train home to Scotland was due in twenty minutes. Barbara Trevithick went in for interview at 4.45 to find that two members of the panel 'had had to leave', so she was interviewed by the two surviving members: a personnel officer and a nursing officer. At the close of the interview she asked when the decision would be made and was told that the two interviewers would have to consult with their two absent colleagues in the morning. Three weeks later Barbara rang to ask the outcome, as she had not received a letter, to be told that Mr Brown had been appointed and 'I'm surprised they didn't tell you, as it was offered to him that afternoon, after the coffee break'.

If there are several people to be interviewed the interview *timetable* needs greater planning than it usually receives. The time required for each interview can be determined beforehand only approximately. A rigid timetable will weigh heavily on both parties, who will feel frustrated if the interview is closed arbitrarily at a predetermined time and uncomfortable if an interview that has 'finished' is drawn out to complete its allotted span. However, the disadvantages of keeping people waiting are considerable and under-rated.

The experience of Barbara Trevithick reflects the thinking of some selectors that candidates are supplicants, waiting on interviewers' pleasure, they have no competing calls on their time and a short period of waiting demonstrates who is in charge. There are flaws in this reasoning. At least some candidates will have competing calls on their time, as they will have taken time off without pay to attend. Some may have other interviews to go to. An open-ended waiting period can be worrying, enervating and a poor preliminary to an interview. If the dentist keeps you waiting you may get distressed, but when the waiting is over you are simply a passive participant and the dentist does not have the success of the operation jeopardised. The interview candidate has, in a real sense, to perform when the period of waiting is over and the success of the interaction could well be jeopardised.

The most satisfactory timetable is the one that guarantees a break after all but the most voluble candidates. If candidates are asked to attend at hourly intervals, for example, this would be consistent with interviews lasting between 40 and 60 minutes. This would mean that each interview began at the scheduled time and that the interviewers had the opportunity to review and update their notes in the intervals.

Reception

Candidates arrive on the premises of their prospective employer on the lookout for every scrap of evidence they can obtain about the organisation – what it looks like, what the people look like and what people say. Candidates will make judgements as quickly as interviewers, and we have already seen that at least one study (Webster 1964) found interviewers making their decisions within a few minutes and then using the rest of the time to confirm it. A candidate is likely to meet at least one and possibly two people before meeting the interviewer. First will be the commissionaire or receptionist. There is frequently also an emissary from the personnel department to shepherd them from the gate to the waiting-room. Both are valuable sources of information, and interviewers may wish to prime such people so that they can see their role in the employment process and can be cheerful, informative and helpful.

The candidate will most want to meet the interviewer, the unknown but powerful figure on whom so much depends. Interviewers easily forget that they know much more about the candidates than the candidates know about them, because the candidates have provided a personal profile in the application form.

Interviewers do not reciprocate. To bridge this gap it can be very useful for interviewers to introduce themselves to the candidate in the waiting-room, so that contact is made quickly, unexpectedly and on neutral territory. This makes the opening of the interview itself rather easier.

Candidates *wait* to be interviewed. Although there are snags about extended open-ended waiting periods, some time is inevitable and necessary to enable candidates to compose themselves. It is a useful time to deal with travelling expenses and provide some relevant background reading about the employing organisation.

The appropriate *setting* for an interview has to be right for the ritual and right from the point of view of enabling a full and frank exchange of information. It is difficult to combine the two. Many of the interview horror stories relate to the setting in which it took place. A candidate for a post as Deputy Clerk of Works was interviewed on a stage while the panel of seventeen sat in the front row of the stalls, and a candidate for a headteacher post came in to meet the interview panel and actually moved the chair on which he was to sit. He only moved it two or three inches because the sun was in his eyes, but there was an audible frisson and sharp intake of breath from the members of the panel.

Remaining with our model of the individual interviewer, here are some simple suggestions about the setting.

1. The room should be suitable for a private conversation.
2. If the interview takes place across a desk, as is common, the interviewer may wish to reduce the extent to which the desk acts as a barrier, emphasising the distance between the parties and therefore inhibiting free flow of communication.
3. Visitors and telephone calls should be absolutely avoided, as they do not simply interrupt: they intrude and impede the likelihood of frankness.
4. It should be clear to the candidates where they are to sit.

Interview structure

There are a number of important reasons why the employment interview should be structured:

1. The candidate expects the proceedings to be decided and controlled by the interviewer and will anticipate a structure within which to operate.
2. It helps the interviewer to make sure that they cover all relevant areas and avoid irrelevant ones.
3. It looks professional. Structure can be used to guide the interview and make it make sense.
4. It assists the interviewer in using the time available in the most effective way.
5. It can be used as a memory aid when making notes directly after the interview.
6. It can make it easier to compare candidates.

The selection interview

There are a number of different ways to structure the interview. We recommend the form set out in Table 15.1. This divides activities and objectives into three interview stages: opening, middle and closing. While there are few, if any, alternative satisfactory ways for conducting the beginning and the end of the interview the middle can be approached from a number of different angles, depending on the circumstances.

The interviewer needs to work systematically through the structure that has been planned, but the structure does not have to be adhered to rigidly. As Sidney and Brown (1961) suggest, interviewers should abandon their own route wherever the candidate chooses one that seems more promising.

Table 15.1 *Interview structure: a recommended pattern*

Stage	Objectives	Activities
Opening	To put the candidate at ease, develop rapport and set the scene	Greet candidate by name Introduce yourself Explain interview purpose Outline how purpose will be achieved Obtain candidate assent to outline
Middle	To collect and provide information	Asking questions within a structure that makes sense to the candidate, such as biographical, areas of the application form, or competencies identified for the job Listening Answering questions
Closing	To close the interview and confirm future action	Summarise interview Check candidate has no more questions Indicate what happens next and when

The *opening* of the interview is the time for mutual preliminary assessment and tuning in to each other. A useful feature of this phase is for the interviewer to sketch out the plan or procedure for the interview and how it fits in with the total employment decision process. It is also likely that the application form will provide an easy, non-controversial topic for these opening behaviours.

One objective is for the two parties to exchange words so that they can adjust their receiving mechanism in order to be mutually intelligible. It also provides an opportunity for both to feel comfortable in the presence of the other. Interviewers able to achieve these two objectives may then succeed in developing a relationship in which candidates trust the interviewer's ability and motives so that they will speak openly and fully.

The interviewer's effectiveness will depend greatly on being skilled with rapport. Bayne regards a prerequisite as being a 'calm–alert' state of consciousness that can be sustained throughout the interview:

> At times the good interviewer is sharp and in focus, specific and rational; at other times intuitive, picking up nuances and rationalizations; at others stepping back to see the whole interaction, fitting things together and taking note of the amount of time left and the areas to cover…the interviewer's calmness helps the candidate to relax and his or her clear perception allows productive silences and the easy asking of questions. The state also counteracts habituation to interviews, when the interviewer is calm but bored. And it allows intuitive processes as well as the usual thinking, evaluating ones. (Bayne 1977).

For the middle of the interview the biographical approach is the most straightforward. It works on the basis that candidates at the time of the interview are the product of everything in their lives that has gone before. To understand the candidate the interviewer must understand the past and will talk to the candidate about the episodes of his or her earlier life – education, previous employment, etc.

The advantage of this is that the objectives are clear to both interviewer and interviewee; there is no deviousness nor 'magic'. Furthermore, the development can be logical and so aid the candidate's recall of events. Candidates who reply to inquiries about their choice of 'A' level subjects will be subconsciously triggering their recollection of contemporaneous events, such as the university course they took, which are likely to come next in the interview. The biographical approach is the simplest for the inexperienced interviewer to use as discussion can develop from the information provided by the candidate on the application form.

One American author has produced an interview structure which suggests that the interviewer begins with questions about the employment history of the candidate and then goes through their educational record, early home background and present social adjustment (Fear 1958). This has the advantage that it begins with what the candidate is best able to handle and later moves to those areas that are not so easy to recall.

Some authorities counsel a more detailed approach by prescribing a checklist of questions to be asked. A form designed by Dodd (1970) includes a series of boxes at every stage in which the interviewer is asked to check 'acceptable or unacceptable'. This highly structured method does, of course, turn the interview into an interrogation rather than a conversation, making it very difficult to unearth opinions and attitudes, as well as closing certain avenues of enquiry that might appear as the interview proceeds. Furthermore, it inhibits the candidate from initiating their own topics for discussion.

Some version of sequential categories such as employment, education and training, seems the most generally useful, but it will need the addition of at least two other categories: the work offered and the organisational context in which it is to be done. The middle of the interview can be structured by systematically working through items of the job description as Green (1983) describes, or the person specification. Increasingly, where competencies have been identified for the job, these are used as the basis of the structure.

In the preparatory stage of briefing the interviewer will also prepare notes on two elements to incorporate in their plan: key issues and check-points.

Key issues will be the main two or three issues that stand out from the application form for clarification or elaboration. This might be the nature of the responsibilities carried in a particular earlier post, the content of a training course, the reaction to a period of employment in a significant industry, or whatever else strikes the interviewer as being productive of useful additional evidence.

Check-points are matters of detail that require further information: grades in an examination, dates of an appointment, rates of pay, and so forth.

In *closing* the interview the explanation of the next step needs especial attention. The result of the interview is of great importance to the candidates and they will await the outcome with anxiety. Even if they do not want the position they will probably hope to have it offered. This may strengthen their hand in dealings with another prospective employer – or their present employer – and will certainly be a boost to their morale. The great merit of convention in the public sector is that the chosen candidate is told before the contenders disperse: the great demerit is that they are asked to accept or decline the offer at once.

In the private sector it is unusual for an employment offer to be made at the time of the interview, so there is a delay during which the candidates will chafe. Their frustration will be greater if the delay is longer than expected and they may begin to tell themselves that they are not going to receive an offer, in which case they will also start convincing themselves that they did not want the job, either! It is important for the interviewer to say as precisely as possible when the offer will be made, but ensuring that the candidates hear earlier rather than later than they expect, if there is to be any deviation.

The interviewer will need to call into play at least five key aspects of *method*.

1. Some data can be collected by simple observation of the candidate. Notes can be made about dress, appearance, voice, height and weight, if these are going to be relevant, and the interviewer can also gauge the candidate's mood and the appropriate response to it by the non-verbal cues that are provided.

2. The remainder of the evidence will come from listening to what is said, so the interviewer has to be very attentive throughout; not only listening to the

anwers to questions, but also listening for changes in inflection and pace, nuances and overtones that provide clues on what to pursue further. The amount of time that the two spend talking is important as an imbalance in one direction or the other will mean that either the candidate or the interviewer is not having enough opportunity to hear information. Inclining the body towards the other person is a signal of attentiveness, so we need to remember our *posture*, which should be inclined forward and facing the other squarely with an open posture: folded arms can be inhibiting.

Eye contact is crucial to good listening, but is a subtle art:

> Effective eye contact expresses interest and a desire to listen. It involves focusing one's eyes softly on the speaker and occasionally shifting the gaze...to a gesturing hand, for example, and then back to the face and then to eye contact once again. (Bolton 1987, p. 36)

The distinction between 'focusing one's eyes softly' and staring is vital, though difficult to describe, and competence in eye contact is never easy to establish. It is one of the most intimate ways of relating to a person and many managers fear that the relationship may become too close. Even if you are happy with it, you may find that the other person is uncomfortable with you looking through the 'window' of their eyes.

We have to avoid distracting the other person by physical behaviour that is unrelated to what is being said: fiddling with a pen, playing with car keys, scrutinising your fingernails, wringing your hands, brushing specks of dust off your sleeves are a few typical behaviours that indicate inattention. Skilled listeners not only suppress these, they also develop minor gestures and posture variants that are directly responsive to what the other person is saying.

Being silent, and deliberately leaving verbal lulls in face-to-face situations, provides the opportunity for the other person to say more – perhaps more than was initially intended. Silence still has to be attentive and the longer the silence, the harder it is to be attentive.

3.   In order to have something to hear the interviewer will have to direct the candidate. This, of course, is done by questioning, encouraging and enabling the candidate to talk, so that the interviewer can learn. The art of doing this depends on the personality and style of the interviewer who will develop a personal technique through a sensitive awareness of what is taking place in the interviews. Anstey has described this as the highest stage of interviewing skill:

> Once rapport has been established, the actual questions matter less and less. The candidate senses what one is getting at, without worrying about the form of words, becomes increasingly at ease and responds more spontaneously. This is the ideal... (Anstey 1977)

It is helpful to distinguish between different types of question in selection interviewing. *Closed questions* are used when we want precise, factual infor-

Reflection

The effectiveness of listening can be aided by reflection: the listener picks up and restates the content of what has just been said. It indicates that you are attending to what the other person is saying, have understood it and you are providing the opportunity for any misunderstanding to be pointed out. The standard method is *paraphrasing*, by which the listener states the essence of what has been said. This is done concisely and gives the speaker a chance to review what has been said.

An example of how this would be done is in the following exchange:

Respondent: 'Seniority does not count for as much as it should in my present company'.

Reflection: 'You feel there is not enough acknowledgement of loyalty and long service?'

Alternative reactions would have a different effect, for example:

'You sound like someone who has been passed over for promotion', or

'Oh, I don't know about that'.

Both push the respondent on to the defensive, expecting a justification of what has been said. Another alternative:

'Well, I think seniority is sometimes overemphasised.'

stifles the opinion before it has been fully expressed. The diffident candidate will not develop the feeling further, so the matter cannot be resolved. There is also the danger that any one of these evaluative reactions could evoke a comeback from the respondent which complies with the view suggested by the interviewer. This is the same problem as that of the leading question.

mation. We close the question to control the answer ('Is it Clarke with an e, or without?'). These are useful at the point in the interview where you want clear, straightforward data.

Open-ended questions are quite different as they avoid terse replies, inviting candidates to express their opinions and to explain things in their own words and emphasis. The question does little more than introduce a topic to talk about ('What does your present job entail?'). The main purpose is to obtain the type of deeper information that the closed question misses, as the shape of the answer is not predetermined by the questioner. You are informed not simply by the content of the answers, but by what is selected and emphasised.

Probes are forms of questioning to obtain information that the respondent is trying to conceal. When this happens the questioner has to make an important, and perhaps difficult decision: do you respect the candidate's unwillingness and let the matter rest, or do you persist with the enquiry? Reluctance is quite common in selection interviews where there may be an aspect of the recent employment history that the candidate wishes to gloss over. The most common sequence for the probe takes the following form. (a) Direct questions, replacing the more comfortable open-ended approach ('What were you doing in the first six months of 1988?'). Careful phrasing may avoid a defensive reply, but those skilled at avoiding unwelcome enquiry may still deflect the question, leading to (b) Supplementaries, which reiterate the first question with different phrasing ('Yes, I understand about that period, it's the first part of 1988 that I'm trying to get clear: after you came back from Belgium and before you started with Amalgamated Widgets'.). Eventually this should produce the information. (c) Closing. If the information has been wrenched out like a bad tooth and the interviewer looks horrified or sits in stunned silence, then the candidate will feel put down beyond redemption. The interviewer needs to make the divulged secret less awful than the candidate had feared, so that the interview can proceed with reasonable confidence ('Yes, well you must be glad to have that behind you.').

Some common lines of questioning should be avoided because they can produce an effect that is different from what is intended. *Leading questions* ('Would you agree with me that...?') will not necessarily produce an answer which is informative, but an answer in line with the lead that has been given. *Multiple questions* give the candidate too many inputs at one time ('Could you tell me something of what you did at University – not just the degree, but the social and sporting side as well – and why you chose to backpack your way round the world? You didn't travel on your own, did you?'). This is sometimes found in interviewers who are trying very hard to efface themselves and let the respondent get on with the talking. However helpful the interviewer intends to be, the effect is that the candidate will usually forget the later parts of the question, feel disconcerted and ask, 'What was the last part of the question?' By this time the interviewer has also forgotten, so they are both embarrassed.

Taboo questions are those that infringe the reasonable personal privacy of the candidate. There is a proper place for the probe, but some questions have to be avoided in selection interviews, as they could be interpreted as discriminatory. It is at least potentially discriminatory, for instance, to ask women how many children they have and what their husbands do for a living. Questions about religion or place of birth are also to be avoided. Also some questions may do no more than satisfy the idle curiosity of the questioner. If there is no point in asking them, they should not be put.

4. The best place to make notes is on the application form. In this way they can be joined to information that the candidate has already provided and the peculiar shorthand that people use when making notes during conversations can be deciphered by reference to the form and the data that the note is embellishing. It also means that the review of evidence after the interview has as much information as possible available on one piece of paper. An alternative is to record notes on the interview plan where the structure is based on job specification, person specification or competencies. Interviewers are

strangely inhibited about note-taking, feeling that it in some way impairs the smoothness of the interaction. This apprehension seems ill-founded as candidates are looking for a serious, businesslike discussion, no matter how informal, and note-taking offers no barrier providing that it is done carefully in the form of jottings during the discussion, rather than pointedly writing down particular comments by the candidate which make the interviewer seem like a police officer taking a statement.

5. Data exchange marks a change of gear in the interview. Rapport is necessarily rather rambling and aimless, but data exchange is purposeful and the interviewer needs to control both the direction and the pace of the exchanges. The candidate will be responsive throughout to the interviewer's control, and the better the rapport the more responsive they will be. Skilled interviewers close out areas of discussion and open fresh ones. They head off irrelevant reminiscences and probe where matters have been glossed over. They can never abandon control. Even when the time has come for the candidates to raise all their queries they will do this at the behest of the interviewer and will look to him or her constantly for a renewal of the mandate to enquire by using conversational prefixes such as 'Can I ask you another question?'; 'If it's not taking up your time, perhaps I could ask...?'; 'I seem to be asking a lot of questions, but there was just one thing'.

6. Closing the interview can be as skillful as opening it. Most of the suggestions so far have been to encourage a response, but it is easy to nod and smile your way into a situation of such cosy relaxation that the respondent talks on and on...and on. A surprising number of interviewers have great difficulty closing. *Braking* slows the rate of talking by the candidate. You will seldom need to go beyond the first two or three, but five are described in case of your having to deal with a really tough case. (a) One or two closed questions to clarify specific points may stem the tide. (b) The facial expression changes with the brow furrowed to indicate mild disagreement, lack of understanding or professional anxiety. The reassuring nods stop and the generally encouraging, supportive behaviours of reward are withdrawn. (c) Abstraction is when the eyes glaze over, showing that they belong to a person whose attention has now shifted away from the respondent and towards lunch. (d) To look at one's watch during a conversation is a very strong signal indeed, as it clearly indicates that time is running out. Other, milder ways of looking away are: looking for your glasses, looking at your notes or looking at the aircraft making a noise outside the window. A rather brutal variant is to allow your attention to be caught by something the respondent is wearing – a lapel badge, a tie, a ring or piece of jewellery, perhaps. Putting on your glasses to see it more clearly is really rather going too far! (e) If all else fails, you simply have to interrupt.

    Closing requires the interview to end smoothly. Future action is either clarified or confirmed. Also, candidates take a collection of attitudes away with them, and these can be influenced by the way the interview is closed. There is a simple procedure. (a) First signal, verbal plus papers. The interviewer uses a phrase to indicate that the interview is nearing its end ('Well now, I think we have covered the ground, don't you? There isn't anything more I want to ask you. Is there anything further you want from me?'). In this way you signal the impending close at the same time as obtaining the candidate's confirmation. There is additional emphasis provided by some paper play. A small collection of notes can be gathered together and stacked neatly, or a notebook can be closed. (b) Second signal, the interviewer confirms what will happen next ('There are still one or two people to see, but we will write to you no later than the end of the week'.) (c) The final signal is to stand up: the decisive act to make the close. By standing up the interviewer forces the candidate to stand as well and there remain only the odds and ends of hand-shakes and parting smiles.

References

Anstey, E. (1977), quoted in R. Bayne, 'Can selection interviewing be improved?' *The British Psychology Society Annual Occupational Psychology Conference, Sheffield.*

Bayne, R. (1977), 'Can selection interviewing be improved?' *Paper presented to The British Psychological Society Annual Occupational Psychology Conference, Sheffield.*

Bolton, R. (1987), *People Skills*, Brookvale, New South Wales: Simon and Schuster.

Campion, M. A., Pursell, E. D. and Brown, B. K. (1988), 'Structured interviewing: raising the psychometric properties of the employment interview', *Personnel Psychology*, vol. 41, pp. 25–43.

Conan Doyle, A. (1881), *The Adventures of Sherlock Holmes*, London: John Murray.

Dodd, J. H. B. (1970), 'Personnel selection – interviewing', *Applied Ergonomics*, September.

Fear, R. A. (1958), *The Evaluation Interview*, Maidenhead: McGraw Hill.

Goffman, E. (1972), *The Presentation of Self in Everyday Life*, Harmondsworth: Pelican.

Green, J. (1983), 'Structured sequence interviewing', *Personnel Executive*, April.

Hackett, P. (1978), *Interview Skills Training: Role Play Exercises*, London: Institute of Personnel Management.

Jenks, J. M. and Zevnik, L. P. (1989), 'ABCs of job interviewing', *Harvard Business Review*, July–August.

Lopez, F. M. (1975), *Personnel Interviewing*, 2nd edition, Maidenhead: McGraw-Hill.

Morgan, T. (1973), 'Recent insights into the selection interview', *Personnel Review*, Winter.

Muir, J. (1988), 'Recruitment and selection', *Management Services*, November.

Rodger, A. (1975), 'Interviewing techniques'. In B. Ungerson (ed.) *Recruitment Handbook*, 2nd edition. Aldershot: Gower.

Sidney, E. and Brown, M. (1961), *The Skills of Interviewing*, London: Tavistock.

Webster, E. C. (1964), *Decision Making in the Employment Interview*, McGill University, Canada: Industrial Relations Centre.

PART IV

Performance

16 Strategic aspects of performance

> Two themes have dominated debates among personnel professionals in the last few years; what contribution can personnel make to productivity and performance, and how can the change be managed effectively? (Mueller and Purcell 1992)

Performance is certainly a central topic although there is less written about what we mean by performance. It has been used to describe such aspects as:

- bottom-line profit;
- other financial indicators such as share price;
- doing better than competitors – i.e. moving up the league table;
- maximum organisational effectiveness, given the resources deployed; and
- achieving specified organisational objectives.

Perhaps the most important factor underlying all of these is the idea of performance improvement – whatever criteria are being used to define performance. Increasingly performance is viewed on three different levels – organisational, individual and team.

Another important issue is understanding what factors affect the performance we observe or measure. Only by identifying these factors and working with them are we in a position to influence the resultant performance.

In this chapter we review some major influences on our current thinking about performance. From this we explore in more detail some commonly acknowledged performance variables and then briefly review a range of current strategic performance initiatives. The following three chapters look in more detail at organisational, individual and team performance.

Influences on our understanding of performance

The Japanese influence

The success of Japanese companies and the decline of Western organisations has encouraged an exploration and adoption of Japanese management ideas and practices in order to improve performance. Thurley (1982) described the objectives of personnel policies in Japan as performance, motivation, flexibility and mobility. Delbridge and Turnbull (1992) described type 'J' organisations (based on Japanese thinking) as characterised by commitment, effort and company loyalty. A key theme in Japanese thinking appears to be people development and continuous improvement, or *kaizen*.

Much of this thinking and the specific management techniques used in Japan, such as JIT (just in time), have been adopted into UK organisations, often in an uncritical way and without due regard for the cultural differences between the two nations.

The American excellence literature

Peters and Waterman (1982) identified eight characteristics which they found to be associated with excellent companies – all American. These companies were chosen as excellent on the basis of their innovativeness and on a set of financial indicators, compared on an industry-wide basis. The characteristics they identified were:

- A bias for action – rather than an emphasis on bureaucracy or analysis.
- Close to the customer – concern for customer wishes.
- Autonomy and entrepreneurship – the company is split into small operational units where innovation and initiative are encouraged.
- Productivity through people – employees are seen as the key resource, and the value of the employees' contribution is reinforced.
- Hands-on, value-driven – strong corporate culture promoted from the top.
- Stick to the knitting – pursuing the core business rather than becoming conglomerates.
- Simple form, lean staff – simple organisation structure and small HQ staffing.
- Simultaneous loose–tight properties – company values strongly emphasised, but within these considerable freedom and errors tolerated.

Peters and Waterman identify a shift from the importance of strategy and structural factors to style, systems, staff and skills (from the hard 's' to the soft 's').

In a subsequent book Peters and Austin (1985) identified four key factors related to excellence as concern for customers, innovation, attention to people and leadership.

Guest (1992) analysed why this excellence literature has had such an impact. He goes on to identify a range of methodological and analytical problems associated with the research, which question its validity. For example, he points out that no comparison was made with companies not considered to be excellent. We do not, therefore, know whether these principles were applied to a greater extent in excellent organisations. Hitt and Ireland (1987) go so far as to say that 'the data call into question whether these excellent principles are related to performance'. In addition a number of the companies quoted have experienced severe problems since the research was carried out, and there remains the problem of the extent to which we can apply the results to UK organisations.

HRM and HRM strategy literature

The human resource management (HRM) strategy literature gives an indication of the personnel function's contribution to organisational performance. As we noted in Chapter 3, Guest identified strategic integration, flexibility, commitment and quality as key factors influencing performance outcomes. Sparrow and Pettigrew (1988) have identified HR policies which influence employee values and attitudes. Legge (1989), though, has pointed to some of the inherent contradictions in HRM, for example between commitment and flexibility; between individualism and teamwork and between a strong culture and adaptability. These contradictions can also be seen in some of the performance variables and strategic performance initiatives discussed below.

Some commonly identified performance variables

From the preceding influences it can be seen that a range of variables are emerging which are recognised as having a positive impact on performance. We will explore some well-documented examples in more detail.

Commitment

Commitment has been identified by some writers as resulting in higher performance. Commitment has been described as:

- *Attitudinal commitment:* that is loyalty and support for the organisation, strength of identification with the organisation (Porter 1985), a belief in its values and goals, and a readiness to put in effort for the organisation.
- *Behavioural commitment:* actually remaining with the organisation.

Walton (1985) notes that commitment is *thought* to result in better quality, lower turnover, a greater capacity for innovation and more flexible employees. In turn these are seen to enhance the ability of the organisation to achieve competitive advantage. Iles, Mabey and Robertson (1990) note that some of the outcomes of commitment have been identified as the IR climate, absence levels, turnover levels and individual performance.

Morris, Lydka and O'Creery (1992/3) note that there is very little *evidence* to link high commitment and high levels of organisational performance. Some authors have argued that high commitment could indeed reduce organisational performance. Cooper and Hartley (1990) suggest the commitment might decrease flexibility and inhibit creative problem solving. If commitment reduces staff turnover this may result in fewer new ideas coming into the organisation. Staff who would like to leave the organisation but who are committed to it in other ways, for example through high pay and benefits, may stay but may not produce high levels of performance.

As well as the debate on the value of commitment to organisational performance, there is also the debate on the extent to which commitment can be managed, and how it can be managed. Guest (1992) suggests that commitment is affected by:

> personal characteristics;
> experiences in job role;
> work experiences;
> structural factors; and
> personnel policies.

Morris, Lydka and O'Creery also identify that personnel policies have an effect on commitment. In particular they found career prospects as the most important factor in their research on graduates.

Empowerment

Keenoy (1990) argues that HRM releases untapped reserves of labour resourcefulness by facilitating employee responsibility, commitment and involvement. It is viewed that the organisation will benefit from unleashing these reserves. Alongside this notion of 'exploiting' employee resourcefulness is the idea that this will be used in line with the needs and objectives of the organisation. It is therefore based on trust and an assumption that employees' values will be in line with those of the organisation.

The way that empowerment is facilitated is seen as realising both these expectations. Not only is it essential for appropriate training and resources to be provided for employees, but responsibility for decision-making is pushed down the hierarchy so that those who do the task make the decisions about the task. In this way employees will have a high level of ownership of what they do and bureaucratic control is not necessary as employees will manage themselves. Connock (1992) identifies empowerment as involving greater individual accountability for results with enhanced authority for work teams. He sees strategy as key and within this, confined only by broad job accountabilities, managers and individuals have freedom to act. Connock also identifies the encouragement of innovation and continuous self-improvement as critical.

More critically Sewell and Wilkinson (1992) in their study of total quality management (TQM) (which they identify as very similar to the tenets of HRM) found that empowerment and trust may be the rhetoric, but that management power and control were the reality.

Leadership

Leadership, rather than management, has been identified as one of the keys to a high performance organisation. 'Charismatic leadership' and 'transformational leadership' give some indication of the virtues that great leadership is seen to offer. Leadership is seen as the power to inspire and motivate, the ability to imbue employees with the desire to change the organisation and to be the best. Leaders create the vision and the strategy and present it and themselves in such a way that employees feel enthusiastic and excited by it.

Atwater, Penn and Rucker (1991) carried out some research to try to define which particular traits were present in charismatic leaders. By comparing uncharismatic and charismatic leaders they found that charismatic leaders were different in terms of being dynamic, inspiring, outgoing, sociable, insightful and enterprising.

There is a good deal of research demonstrating the value of leadership in terms of organisational performance. Leaders clearly act as role models within the organisation. Some of the strategy literature, however, does suggest that different types of leaders fit with different types of situation, as we discussed in Chapter 10 on Resourcing Strategy.

There is also a debate over whether leadership can be learned or whether it is innate – Peters and Waterman see it as something that can be learned. Leaders may easily become sidetracked into operational matters (see for example, Garratt 1990 and Argyris 1992), thus compromising their role.

Culture

Meek (1992) suggests that there is a link between culture and organisational effectiveness – and that there is an assumption that the culture will unite all employees behind the stated goals of the organisation. Some organisations have used this link to try and change the organisational culture in an effort to improve organisational performance – we hear of organisations encouraging a 'performance culture' or a 'learning culture'. This, however, is making one very great assumption – that culture can be managed. Kilmann *et al.* (1985) support this view of culture as a variable that can be controlled. Peters and Waterman write of strong organisational cultures as being associated with excellence, and again suggest that it is possible to make a culture strong.

However, there is a strong lobby arguing that culture is an independent variable which can not be manipulated (see for example Meek 1992). He notes that the culture of an organisation is not in the hands of management and therefore it is not a matter of handing down a culture to passive employees. He also suggests, however, that culture is not necessarily static and that management, as opposed to other groups, do have control over some things that will affect the culture, for example logos and mission statements. This argument can be extended to include systems and processes in the organisation – hence those organisations which attempt to induce culture change through the introduction of a system; for example a performance management system, or through quality leadership at Ford (McKinlay, A. and Starkey, K. 1988). The impact of such systems on the culture is neither straightforward nor immediate. Another issue to contend with is the fact that in any organisation there are multiple cultures.

Schein (1992) also makes the point that strong cultures are not necessarily associated with a more effective organisation, and indicates that the relationship is far more complex. He draws out some contradictions – for example, that a strong culture may stand against flexibility and adaptability. He maintains that culture-awareness is important in facilitating strategic decisions.

Flexibility

We have discussed flexibility in some length in Chapter 3 and Chapter 10. It remains here to highlight the link between flexibility and performance. Functional flexibility is particularly important where employees with a wide job remit and a wide range of skills can reduce waiting time (e.g. for maintenance activities on breakdown) and give employees a greater sense of doing a whole job and greater responsibility. All these factors have potential to improve performance.

Learning

We have already noted Garratt's view that for an organisation to survive the extent of learning had to be greater than or equal to the extent of change which it faces. De Gaus (1988) comments that learning is 'an almost priceless competitive advantage'. There is little doubt that organisational and individual learning are associated with organisational performance. However, achieving this learning in practice is, as Whipp (1992) comments, 'problematical in the extreme'.

Some attention has always been given to individual learning – even if only in the form of rhetoric. Increasingly attention is being paid to enabling the whole organisation to learn on a continuous basis and therefore become more effective.

Major performance initiatives

The variables we have reviewed above form the basis for many of the popular performance initiatives which organisations have adopted. There are many small initiatives

Table 16.1 *Some major peformance initiatives*

Organisational focus	Learning organisation Investors in people Total Quality Management (TQM) Performance culture Lean production Just in time (JIT) Standards – BS5750 – ISO9000 Customer care/orientation
Individual focus	Performance management Performance related pay Self-development
Team focus	High performance teams Cross-functional teams Self-regulating teams

in organisation every day which help to improve performance, but we are concentrating here on major strategic initiatives – 'big ideas', as described by Connock (1992).

Mueller and Purcell (1992) make a useful point when they say 'It is the integration of change initiatives with other aspects of organisational life which is the key to success. It is very rare for a single initiative, however well designed to generate significant or lasting benefit'.

This brings us to the concern that many initiatives in the same organisation will give conflicting messages to employees – particularly when they are introduced by different parts of the organisation. For example there may be contradictions between TQM and learning organisations – which we will explore further in Chapter 17.

In Table 16.1 we have listed some of the major performance initiatives. The initiatives are divided according to their primary focus – organisational, individual or team. Some of the initiatives partly cover the same ground, and it would be unlikely to find them in the same organisation.

REVIEW TOPIC 16.1

(a) Identify the main performance initiatives in your organisation
(b) What/who is the source of each initiative?
(c) In what ways do they mutual support each other, and in what ways do they conflict?

☐ SUMMARY PROPOSITIONS

16.1 Performance has become a central topic of debate in organisations.
16.2 In the United Kingdom our views of performance improvement have been

influenced by American excellence literature, the Japanese experience and HRM strategy literature.

16.3 Some commonly identified performance variables have been identified as commitment, empowerment, leadership, culture, flexibility and learning.

16.4 There is an argument that by changing these variables (usually increasing them) changes can be brought about in the organisation's performance.

16.5 Many performance initiatives have these variables at their core.

16.6 There is a counter argument to this based on more complex and sometimes negative relationships.

References

Argyris, C. (1992), 'A leadership dilemma: skilled incompetence'. In G. Salaman *et al.* (eds) *Human Resource Strategies*, London: Sage.

Atwater, L., Penn, R. and Rucker, (1991), 'Personel qualities of charismatic leaders', *Leadership and Organisation Development Journal*, vol. 12, no. 2, pp. 7–10.

Blyton, P. and Turnbull, P. (eds), (1992), *Reassessing Human Resource Management*. London: Sage.

Connock, S. (1992), 'The importance of big ideas to HR managers', *Personnel Managers*, June.

Cooper, J. and Hartley, J. (1991), 'Reconsidering the case for organisational commitment', *Human Resource Management Journal*, vol. 1, no. 3, pp. 18–31.

de Gaus, A. (1988), 'Planning as learning', *Harvard Business Review*, March–April, pp. 70–4.

Delbridge, R. and Turnbull, P. (1992), 'Human resource maximisation: the management of labour under just-in-time manufacturing systems', in P. Blyton and P. Turnbull (eds) *Reassessing Human Resource Management*, London: Sage.

Garratt, B. (1990), *The hearing organisation*, Director Books.

Guest, D. (1992), 'Right enough to be dangerously wrong; an analysis of the "In search of excellence" phenomenon'. In G. Salaman *et al.* (eds) *Human Resource Strategies*. London: Sage.

Hitt, M. and Ireland, D. (1987), 'Peters and Waterman revisited; the unending quest for excellence', *Academy of Management Executive*, vol. 1, no. 2, pp. 91–8.

Iles, P., Mabey, C. and Robertson, I. (1990), 'Human resource management practices and employee commitment. Possibilities, pitfalls and paradoxes', *British Journal of Management*, vol. 1, pp. 147–57.

Keenoy, T. (1990), 'HRM: a case of the wolf in sheep's clothing', *Personnel Review*, vol. 19, no. 2, pp. 3–9.

Kilmann, R. H. *et al.* (1985), *Gaining Control of the Corporate Culture*, San Francisco: Jossey-Bass.

Legge, K. (1989), 'Human resource management: a critical analysis', in Storey, J. (ed.) *New Perspectives on Human Resource Management*, London: Routledge.

McKinley, A. and Starkey, K. (1988), 'Competitive strategies and organisational change', *Organisation Studies*, vol. 9, no. 4, pp. 555–71.

Meek, L. (1992), 'Organisational culture: origins and weaknesses'. In G. Salaman *et al.* (eds) *Human Resource Strategies*, London: Sage.

Morris, T., Lydka, H. and O'Creery, M. F. (1992/3), 'A longitudinal analysis of employee commitment and human resource policies', *Human Resource Management Journal*, vol. 3, pp. 21–38.

Mueller, F. and Purcell, J. (1992), 'The drive for higher productivity', *Personnel Management*, vol. 24, no. 5, pp. 28–33.

Peters, T. and Austin, N. (1985), *A Passion for Excellence*, New York: Random House.

Peters, T. and Waterman, R. (1982), *In Search of Excellence*, New York: Harper & Row.

Porter, M. (1985), *Competitive Advantage*, New York: Free Press.

Salaman, G. *et al.* (eds) (1992), *Human Resource Strategies*, London: Sage.

Sewell, G. and Wilkinson, B. (1992), 'Empowerment or emasculation? Shopfloor surveillance in a total quality organisation'. In P. Blyton and P. Turnbull (eds) *Reassessing Human Resource Management*, London: Sage.

Schein, E. H. (1992), 'Coming to a new awareness of organisational culture'. In G. Salaman *et al.* (eds) *Human Resource Strategies*, London: Sage.

Sparrow, P. and Pettigrew, A. (1988), 'Contrasting HRM responses in the changing world of computing', *Personnel Management*, vol. 20.

Thurley, K. (1982), 'The Japanese model; practical reservations and surprising opportunities', *Personnel Management*, February.

Walton, R. E. (1985), 'From control to commitment in the workplace', *Harvard Business Review*, March–April, pp. 77-84.

Whipp, R. (1992), 'Human resource management, competition and strategy: some productive tension'. In P. Blyton and P. Turnbull (eds) *Reassessing Human Resource Management*, London: Sage.

Organisational performance

There was a time when performance was seen primarily in terms of individual motivation and individual performance. Increasingly the focus has shifted to emphasise performance of the organisation as a whole. This change of emphasis is drawn starkly by Deming (1986) when he asserts that performance variations are the result not of individual differences, but of the systems that are implemented and controlled by managers – factors which are outside the control of the individual. While we do not fully agree with Deming's views on individual performance we recognise that he highlights a critical perspective on the importance of the systems, processes and culture for ultimate organisational performance.

The focus of this chapter is on the whole organisation and its performance although it is inevitable that within this, individual performance and team performance issues will play a part. We will review total quality management (TQM) and learning organisations as major recent initiatives seen to affect organisational performance directly. The word 'initiative' may appear to some protagonists as inappropriate, as both these approaches may be seen as long-term and permanent changes in the philosophy of the organisation and the way that it is managed. It is unfortunate that the way these approaches have been applied does not always (often) live up to such ideals.

The third approach we will briefly review is that of organisation development – a perspective which has enjoyed a checkered past in terms of its perceived value. In spite of this it has not gone away and remains a valuable method and toolkit available to those organisations that are prepared to spend time to understand and apply it. Unlike TQM and learning organisations it lacks instant impact and management appeal, and has yet to be packaged in a user-friendly way.

Total quality management

There have been a variety of quality initiatives in one form or another in recent years – perhaps the most common has been quality circles. Total quality management differs from past approaches in that these without exception were partial,

Table 17.1 *The difference between Quality Circles and TQM (Wilkinson et al. 1992)*

Ideal Types	Quality Circles	TQM
Choice	Voluntary	Compulsory
Structure	Bolt-on	Integrated quality system
Direction	Bottom-up	Top-down
Scope	Within departments/units	Company-wide
Aims	Employee relations improvements	Quality improvements

Reproduced with permission of Human Resource Management Journal.

piecemeal initiatives, inevitably bolted on to existing structures and systems. TQM, on the other hand, is a holistic approach affecting every aspect of the organisation with a view to building quality into everything that is done – it is the philosophy of the way the organisation is managed. Dale and Cooper (1992) noted, for example, that:

> TQM is a much broader concept than the initiatives which have gone before, encompassing not only product, service and process quality improvements but those relating to costs and productivity, and people involvement and development. (p. 11)

Wilkinson *et al.* (1992) provide a helpful comparison of quality circles with TQM, as shown in Table 17.1.

TQM is seen by most commentators to apply to all in the organisation, not just to a selected few who work in production, and concentrates on how different parts of the organisation interact. The emphasis is on problem and defect *prevention*, rather than on fault *detection* as with quality control, with quality no longer belonging to the Quality Department, but to everyone. Quality becomes an integral part of management at all levels. TQM requires that measures of quality have been established and that when new ideas for quality improvement have been found that this best practice is then shared across the organisation to become the new expected minimum standard.

The central focus of TQM is on identifying and meeting customer needs. Customers are identified both externally, as in the eventual purchaser or user of the product or service, and internally, as in organisational departments and members who are supplied with product/media/information/services and so on provided by other members or departments. Total quality is not something that can be 'achieved' but is a focus for continual improvement, as in the Japanese term *kaizen*, which is well described in an article by Walker (1993). Honeycutt (1993) highlights the importance of organisational culture and environment when he says:

> The theory of continuous process improvement refers to substantive, systemic change. The challenge is to create an environment for substantive, systemic change.

Dale and Cooper state that many organisations claim TQM is their primary business strategy in influencing competitive performance, and the number of organisations claiming to have adopted TQM processes is increasing (Pike and Barnes 1994). A US study found that those organisations adopting TQM experienced overall better performance in terms of employee relations, productivity, customer satisfaction, market share and improved production. They also found that none had experienced these benefits immediately (Mendelowitz 1991). TQM is a long-term strategy for improvement, not a short-term fix.

So, TQM is popular in the extreme, but what changes exactly are being implemented? Does TQM mean the same thing in one organisation as another? It would not be surprising that organisations approached TQM in slightly different ways according to their needs. Harari (1993) notes an Ernst and Young study which revealed that no fewer than 945 different tools were used for quality management in different organisations. Honeycutt views TQM as an umbrella for several business concepts, but more fundamentally there are two quite different perspectives on TQM.

1. The 'hard' statistical approaches, which emphasise measurements of production, proportion of products that do not conform to specification, reasons for this, and resultant changes that are required to prevent future similar problems. This perspective depends heavily on two techniques. The first is SQC – statistical quality control – which is used to tally product defects, trace the source, make corrections and make a record of what happens next. The second is SPC – statistical process control – which is used to analyse deviations in the production process during manufacturing.

2. The 'soft' people-based approaches, which emphasise worker empowerment, teamwork, devolved responsibility, open communications, involvement, participation, skill development and generating commitment to the quality objectives of the organisation.

Clearly, these are pure forms and most organisations will implement some combination of these approaches. Historically the statistical approach came first and there is a large degree of movement towards the people-based approaches. Lee and Lazarus (1993) identify a change in TQM from a technical and product focus to an 'analysis of all the processes which relate a company to its customers, suppliers and employees'. They argue that what is new about TQM is the emphasis on customers, the training and empowerment of employees, top management support and commitment.

Many of the reported problems with TQM have been identified as people problems and indicate a neglect of the people issues. An Institute of Personnel Management (IPM) survey in the United Kingdom (reported in Marchington, Dale and Wilkinson 1993) identified that the public sector placed more emphasis on people aspects in their implementation of quality improvement.

The criteria for the 1994 Baldridge National Quality Awards in the United States include both aspects of TQM, with such aspects as quality leadership, quality information and analysis, strategic quality planning, human resource development and management, management of process quality, quality and operational results and customer focus and satisfaction.

What's involved in total quality management?

Dale and Cooper identify seven key elements of total quality management and we use their framework for this section.

Commitment and leadership of the Chief Executive

There is general agreement that commitment from the top of the organisation is essential. Senior managers need to define the quality objectives of the organisation to provide direction and clarity, and to communicate these continually within the organisation. The Chief Executive and top team also act as role models by talking about, asking about and reinforcing quality standards.

Culture change

A culture of not passing on faults to either internal or external customers is clearly important, together with a belief that all tasks can be continually improved. Critically, a culture of viewing mistakes as learning opportunities needs to be developed, and this is often where messages can become confused. Some of the quality literature refers to 'right first time' and 'zero defects' (see Crosby 1979) and this is sometimes passed on or perceived as mistakes not being allowable. If mistakes are not allowable, they are not owned up to (unless this is unavoidable), and if they are not owned up to, others cannot learn from them and the source of problems cannot be tackled.

Planning and organisation

This involves designing quality into the product and identifying fault proof features (to prevent faults in assembly); planning and communicating systems and procedures to be followed to ensure quality; designing work structures to support quality improvement (for example task teams or cross-departmental teams) ensuring the necessary resources are made available for quality improvements; identifying how quality will be measured and monitored.

Education and training

This will be important in the areas of understanding a new approach to the management and philosophy of the organisation; operating within new structures; new criteria and performance standards; learning new skills in a team environment; learning new priorities and new tasks. In team structures team leaders will need particular help in running quality meetings and problem-solving, and in adopting a different management style. Management development generally is a key area, but often overlooked. Jeffery (1992) describes how a TQM environment changes managers' tasks from control to setting direction, and from decision-making to giving guidance, information and support.

Involvement

Involving employees in the process of quality improvement is crucial, whether this be through suggestion schemes, team-based quality meetings or involvement in cross-function project teams looking at quality issues.

Recognition

Senior management need to recognise, celebrate and reward quality improvements. This may be in the form of publicity in company newsletters or local press, company awards and prizes, or simple praise for a job well done. It is also important that other personnel systems, for example the appraisal system, support quality achievements.

Measurement

Level of quality according to agreed measures, costs of quality and quality improvement targets are all important here. One of the tools used is benchmarking, where an organisation or a department within it compares itself on a range of indicators to direct competitors or other organisations in the same sector. On a department basis benchmarking may use comparisons with the 'best' organisations irrespective of sector. Information on these indicators is then used as benchmarks or improvement targets for the organisation so that they can match or exceed the performance of other organisations. Simple indicators for the personnel function might include costs per new recruit or days training per head per year.

REVIEW TOPIC 17.1

In comparing your personnel department against others:

(a) which other personnel departments would you choose to compare yourselves with and why?

(b) what quality measures or indicators would you use for the comparison and why?

What happens in practice?

In an ideal world organisations implementing TQM would follow the above steps on a continuous basis and quality improvements would ensue. This may have been the experience of some excellent organisations, but research increasingly suggests that it is not as simple as this for most. The IPM survey referred to above identifies four of five organisations experiencing people problems in implementing quality initiatives. These problems centred around commitment to the aims of quality initiatives. Dale and Cooper identified middle managers as a block to implementation. This is sometimes because these managers see TQM as representing a greater workload for them without any immediate payoff, or alternatively due to fear of delegating responsibility and being left with neither job nor power. Wilkinson *et al.* (1992) found that rather than TQM uniting middle managers behind a common cause, it actually became a source of competition. Schein (1991) also identified the most commonly cited failure of TQM as the failure of upper and middle management to commit themselves to it. Managers often lack the passion and enthusiasm that TQM requires, and top management all too often delegate their involvement. Miller and Cangeri (1993) remind us that quality needs to be an obsession with everyone in the organisation. A further difficulty for managers is in wrestling with the concepts of TQM – if true TQM requires an environment where mistakes are seen as learning opportunities, how do managers reconcile this with 'zero defect' and 'right first time' and avoid using mistakes as punishment opportunities?

Wilkinson *et al.* (1992) identified some further issues from their research related to difficulties in sustaining TQM:

- that TQM has been adopted as a bolt-on extra rather than a fundamental change in management approach and has not been fully integrated into the organisation;
- where devolution had only superficially taken place within a centralised framework then employees felt their hands were tied in terms of implementing changes through TQM;
- the employee relations aspects of TQM are rarely considered – is it possible for staff to feel and display commitment after only a short training course? and
- there are some contradictions in TQM as while involvement and participation are encouraged, management control is often not relinquished, and is often strengthened through the process.

There is now much literature on the failure of TQM in organisations, and the complexity of this approach to improving organisational performance is being exposed. Of the three cases described by Marchington *et al.* (1993) two of the organisations were about to relaunch TQM.

Sewell and Wilkinson (1992) report on a Japanese-owned organisation in the United Kingdom where all employees were seen as having common status in an environment of a flattened hierarchy and responsibility was pushed down to team level. The company sought to encourage an atmosphere of trust with open communications and participation. Electronic components were assembled in teams and standard times had been identified for each activity. The teams had approximately 40–45 employees with a team leader and, within production limits, the leaders had considerable discretion in the way that staff were deployed. Team members were encouraged to develop new skills and were rewarded for this, and they were encouraged to seek innovations to improve quality and productivity. The team as a whole had to cover for the absence of any team member, and electronic recording meant that the quality levels for the whole team and each individual were identified each day. All information regarding team performance in terms of absence, quality performance, conformity to standard times and production targets was displayed so that it was visible to all members. Individuals who had made mistakes were often called to the front of the line to rectify their error. The monitoring system was extended so that error rate information was placed over the head of each team member for all to see. The effect of this was to set one team member against another as the poor performance of one member affected the performance of the team as a whole.

In this example the rhetoric was to delegate day to day responsibility to the team in order to empower them and increase ownership of the task and commitment, but in reality management retained control.

TQM and the personnel function

The central importance of people to TQM is an invitation to the personnel department to be involved. The bad news is that Storey (1992) reports that in some organisations TQM was implemented with very little involvement of the personnel function. In the IPM survey it was reported that around three-quarters of organisations had involved their human resource function in some way, although in many cases this was limited to operational issues such as training. What possible areas of opportunity does TQM provide?

Business strategy

Ideally the personnel function would be involved in the development of the TQM strategy itself. We have already indicated a general lack of involvement. Before attributing this to the lack of credibility of the personnel function it is worth considering the historical development of TQM. Where TQM is seen from a 'hard' perspective the concentration is on technical quality of the product and process. Is it reasonable, then, to expect a high level of personnel involvement in strategy development? This especially applies in those organisations where TQM has just been applied to the technical/manufacturing function. What is more worrying is those organisations with a soft perspective on TQM – it is here that personnel involvement is crucial – however, there is no research which tells us of personnel involvement specifically in relation to the organisation's approach to TQM.

Human resource strategy

A critical area, but not often emphasised, is the matching of human resource strategy to TQM. For TQM to be effective it is essential that personnel strategies reinforce the quality message rather than pulling in another direction. For example, in the appraisal system are the appraisal criteria in line with quality criteria; in terms of reward does the organisation reward quality or something else and does the process of reward (individual or group-based/skill or job-based) line up with the demands and expectations of TQM?

TQM implementation

We noted previously how the personnel function was involved more heavily in this area. Training course design and delivery, coaching managers, facilitating quality meetings are all key factors here; so are communications about quality and quality improvements.

TQM within the pesonnel function

Applying quality criteria within the personnel function is not only an essential part of TQM, but also enables the function to act as a role model for the rest of the organisation and understand first-hand problems and issues. It gives the function the credibility to carry out implementation activities described above.

REVIEW TOPIC 17.2

How would you define the internal customers of the personnel function? What would be the most appropriate way to explore customer needs and expectations for each group?

Review

The personnel function is well placed to identify some of the effects and issues of the implementation of TQM. Attitude and opinion surveys are clearly one popular way. Working closely with departments as a consultant is another, and in this way richer information can be gathered giving a more in-depth understanding of issues and problems.

Learning organisations

Pedler, Boydell and Burgoyne (1989) have identified current interest in the idea of the learning organisation as a response to poor organisational performance. They describe the history of training and development in organisations in terms of critical problems and solutions. From the problem of skills shortage, leading to systematic skills training, to the problem of poor application of training, leading to an emphasis on self-development, to the problem of poor organisational performance, leading to learning organisations. They define the characteristics of poor organisational performance as:

> sluggishness, an excess of bureaucracy and over-control, of organisations as straitjackets frustrating the self-development efforts of individual members and failing to capitalise upon their potential. (Pedler *et al.* 1989)

Becoming a learning organisation is seen by some as a way of keeping ahead of the competitors and gaining competitive advantage. We have already noted the idea that in times of constant change, learning needs to be greater than, or at least equal to the rate of change in order for the organisation to survive (see p. 59, Chapter 3).

In 1987 Pedler, Boydell and Burgoyne carried out a project entitled 'Developing the Learning Company' and interviewed staff in organisations which were pursuing learning company strategies. They asked why these strategies had been adopted, and found such reasons as the need to improve quality; the wish to become more people oriented in relation to both staff and customers; the need to encourage 'active experimentation' and generally to cope with competitive pressures in order to survive and grow. Other reasons focused on the need to change and cope with change. In Chapter 3 we also noted Pedler *et al.*'s (1989) definition of a learning organisation:

an organisation which facilitates the learning of all its members and continually transforms itself.

The question is – what does this mean in practice? Beard (1993) notes that there is some confusion over this. The confusion, however, lies more in the practices adopted by organisations under the banner of a learning organisation rather than in fundamental ideas. Academics and theorists may place different emphasis on different aspects of a learning organisation, but these are mutually supportive rather than conflicting. There is the common thread of a holistic approach and that organisational learning is greater than the sum of individual learning in the organisation. Different organisations appear to have been inspired by some aspects of this approach, have adopted these and therefore see themselves as learning organisations. In essence they have taken some steps towards their goal, and have certainly improved the level of learning occurring in the organisation, but have taken a partial rather than a holistic approach. In the next section we will consider a wide range of characteristics of learning organisations.

What are the characteristics of learning organisations?

Pedler, Burgoyne and Boydell (1991) identify eleven characteristics of a learning organisation which over time they have grouped into five overall themes. Figure 17.1 shows both the characteristics and themes. We summarise briefly and discuss each of these dimensions below.

- *A learning approach to strategy:* strategy formation, implementation, evaluation and improvement are deliberately structured as learning experiences. Explicit feedback loops are built into the process so that there can be continuous improvement in the light of experience. This approach is very close to Mintzberg's ideas of strategy formation (see, for example, Mintzberg 1987).

- *Participative policy-making:* policy-making is shared with all in the organisation and even further, so that suppliers, customers and the total community have some involvement. The aim of the policy is to 'delight customers', and the differences of opinion and values which are revealed in the participative process are seen as productive tensions. A closeness to the principles of total quality management can be seen here and Nonka and Johansson (1985) note how extensive internal consultations are carried out in Japanese organisations before taking major decisions.

- *Informating:* technology is used to empower and inform employees, and is made widely available. They note that such information should be used to understand what is going on in the company and so stimulate learning, rather than be used to reward, punish or control. There are some clear differences here with the practical example we described earlier in this chapter of information use in a total quality environment. Easterby-Smith (1990) makes the point that good news is often reported, such as sales achieved, rather than the information which would be of more value – that is why some orders were

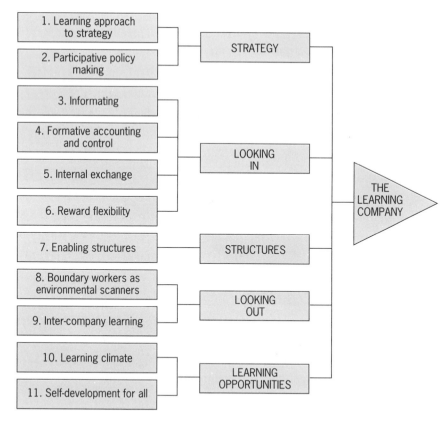

Figure 17.1 Blueprint of a learning company from Pedler *et al.* (1991). Used with permission of McGraw-Hill Book Company.

lost. He also notes the importance of systems that are future orientated rather than past orientated.

- *Formative accounting and control:* Pedler *et al.* (1991) see this as a particular application of informating where accounting, budgeting and reporting systems are designed to assist learning. They also identify a purpose here of delighting the internal customer.

- *Internal exchange:* this involves the general idea of all internal units seeing themselves as customers and suppliers of each other, but causing them to operate in a collaborative way rather than a competitive way. This is, of course, also a key theme in TQM.

- *Reward flexibility:* while noting that money is not seen as the sole reward, Pedler *et al.* (1991) believe that the question of why some receive more money than others is a debate to be brought out into the open. They recommend that alternatives are discussed and tried out, but recognise that this is the most difficult of the eleven characteristics to put into practice.

- *Enabling structures:* this means that roles should be loosely structured in line with the needs of internal customers and suppliers, and in a way that allows for personal growth and experimentation. Internal boundaries can be flexible. Easterby-Smith reports on some research with managers from different organisations. They were asked whether they had learned and developed through their past work experiences, and the results indicated that managers in different organisations would differ greatly in the extent to which they had done this. One of the key characteristics which distinguished organisations where individuals had learned and those where they had not was the use of project groups and transient structures, and individual encouragement to try new ways of working. These structures help to break down barriers between units, provide mechanisms for spreading new ideas and encourage the idea of change.

- *Boundary workers as environmental scanners:* this relates to the need to collect data from outside the organisation, and it is seen as part of the role of all workers who have contact with suppliers, customers and neighbours of the organisation.

- *Inter-company learning:* this entails joining with customers and suppliers in training experiences, research and development and job exchanges. Pedler *et al.* (1991) also note the possibility of learning with competitors. They suggest that benchmarking can be used to learn from other companies.

- *Learning climate:* here the primary task is the encouragement of experimentation and learning from experience. To achieve this current ideas, attitudes and actions need to be questioned and new ideas tried out. Mistakes are allowed because not all new ideas will work. The importance of continuous improvement of customers, suppliers and neighbours in experimentation is suggested. A learning climate suggests that feedback from others is continually requested, is made available and is acted upon.

- *Self-development opportunities for all:* that means that resources and facilities for self-development are available to employees at all levels in the organisation and that coaching, mentoring, peer support, counselling, feedback and so on are available to support individuals in their learning.

One of the authors invited a business speaker to address a course group on the subject of management development. The speaker duly arrived and delivered a summary of his organisation's management development strategy, including its efforts to become a learning organisation. Over coffee, following the lecture the speaker requested feedback from the whole class group so that he could use this to improve his performance on the next occasion. He explained that in everything that the personnel function did they would ask for feedback and incorporate this into future activities. Asking for feedback had become a habit and was not only expected internally, but from external customers too.

> REVIEW TOPIC 17.3
>
> Which of the eleven dimensions identified by Pedler *et al.* (1991) are currently being pursued in your organisation? How is this being done? Which of the eleven would be the most difficult for your organisation to pursue? What are the barriers and how might they be overcome?

Easterby-Smith makes some key points about encouraging experimentation in organisations in relation to flexible structures, information, people and reward. We have discussed flexibility and information in some detail. In respect of people he argues that organisations will seek to select those who are similar to current organisation members. The problem here is that in reinforcing homogeneity and reducing diversity, the production of innovative and creative ideas is restrained. He sees diversity as a positive stimulant (which we discuss further in Chapter 20) and that organisation should therefore select some employees who would not normally fit their criteria, especially those who would be likely to experiment and be able to tolerate ambiguity. In relation to the reward system he notes the need to reinforce rather than punish risk-taking and innovation.

Garratt (1990) concentrates on the role that the directors of an organisation have in encouraging a learning organisation and in overcoming learning blocks. He suggests:

- that the top team concentrate on strategy and policy and hold back from day to day operational issues;
- thinking time is necessary for the top team to relate changes in the external environment to the internal working of the organisation;
- the creation of a top team involving the development and deployment of the strengths of each member;
- the delegation of problem-solving to staff close to the operation; and
- acceptance that learning occurs at all levels of the organisation, and that directors need to create a climate where this learning flows freely.

Clearly, a learning organisation is not something which can be developed overnight and has to be viewed as a long-term strategy.

A word of caution

Hawkins (1994) notes the evangelistic fervour with which Learning Organisations and Total Quality Management are recommended to the uninitiated. His concern with the commercialisation of these ideas is that they become superficial. He argues that an assumption may be made that all learning is good, whatever is being learnt, whereas the value of learning is where it is taking us. Learning, then, is a means rather than an end in itself. Learning to be more efficient at what is being done does

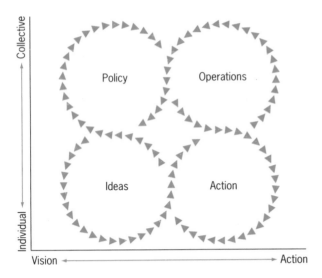

Figure 17.2   The energy flow model from Pedler *et al.* (1991). Used with permission of McGraw-Hill Book Company Europe.

not necessarily make one more effective – it depends on the appropriateness of the activity itself.

The full complexity of the ideas implicit in the words 'learning organisation' require more explanation; for example, the question of how individual learning feeds into organisational learning and transformation, and how this is greater than the sum of individual learning are only beginning to be addressed. Viewing the organisation as a process rather than an entity may offer some help here; another perspective is that of viewing the organisation as a living organism. Pedler *et al.* (1991) make a useful start with their company energy flow model, shown in Figure 17.2.

Organisational development

It is difficult to justify writing a chapter about organisational performance without mentioning organisational development (OD), which has been and remains a key approach to developing performance in some organisations. OD has been described by French and Bell (1984) as an approach to organisational improvement using behavioural science techniques. Hawkins (1994) sees the learning organisation as an umbrella for OD activities while recognising there is value in the slightly different perspectives of each. Other writers have argued that the learning organisation is enabling individuals to do collectively what OD set out to do, but that they are doing it by themselves without external help.

Typically, OD has involved an internal or external consultant/facilitator using behavioural science principles in working on organisational problem-solving.

Currently OD practitioners may be particularly involved in the introduction of change, whether it be technical, cultural or organisational. OD's method of operation centres on not only objectives and aims, but on interpersonal behaviour, attitudes and values within the organisation. There is usually an emphasis on openness between colleagues, improved conflict resolution methods, more effective team management and the collaborative diagnosis and solution of problems. OD does not necessarily include formalised training and development, although it is most likely that this will be incorporated.

Any training strategy typically centres on groups of managers, or directly on organisational processes with the assistance of the change agent or consultant, who helps the participants to perceive, face up to and resolve the behavioural problems experienced. OD is a 'macro' approach to development, in contrast with individual training and development, which is primarily a 'micro' approach.

Specific issues that OD practitioners may be involved with include the following.

- Developing processes for bringing about and implementing change.
- Assessing organisational effectiveness and developing improvement plans.
- Organisation structure and design.
- Bringing about cultural change.
- Designing effective communication processes.
- Building effective work-groups and multidisciplinary teams.
- Managing the implementation and organisational implications of new technology.
- Effective work practices, such as clarification of roles and responsibilities in complex situations, work-group objective-setting.
- Stimulating innovation and creativity.
- Problem-solving and effective decision-making processes.
- Managing interpersonal and inter-group conflict.

Source: Adapted from Purves (1989), Organisation and process consultancy (unpublished).

Van Eynde and Bledsoe (1990) found in their research that OD practitioners were now more likely to be working with client managers on more task-focused issues directly related to organisational effectiveness, and less on improvement of interpersonal relationships, than they were fifteen years ago. Team dynamics, for example, would now be dealt with within the framework of helping a team to resolve a critical issue. Increasingly, OD consultants are involved in helping organisations to envisage the future. The researchers also found that there are increasing opportunities for OD practitioners to work with the highest levels in the organisation, on changes that impact on the whole organisation.

It is through these types of intervention, and from their experiences of the processes used, that managers develop further and are more able to work through similar issues successfully in the future.

17.1 There is an increasing emphasis on organisational performance and the factors which affect it.

17.2 Systems, structures, processes, resources and culture will all have an impact on organisational performance, as well as individual motivation and ability.

17.3 Total Quality Management and Learning Organisations are two important philosophies for improving organisational performance.

17.4 Both of these approaches require a long-term perspective and are more complex than the ways in which they are often presented.

17.5 Total Quality Management has a statistical, 'hard' strand and a people-centred 'soft' strand. Difficulties experienced in adopting TQM have mainly focused on people issues.

References

Beard, D. (1993), 'Learning to change organisations', *Personnel Management*, January.

Blyton, P. and Turnbull, P. (1992), *Reassessing Human Resource Management*, London: Sage.

Crosby, P. B. (1979), *Quality if Free*, New York: McGraw Hill.

Dale, B. and Cooper, C. (1992), *Total Quality and Human Resources: An executive Guide*. Oxford: Blackwell.

Deming, W. E. (1986), *Out of the Crisis*, Cambridge, Mass.: MIT Institute for Advanced Engineering Study.

Easterby-Smith, M. (1990), 'Creating a learning organisation', *Personnel Review*, vol. 19, no. 5, pp. 24–8.

Garratt, B. (1990), *Creating a Learning Organisation*, Cambridge: Director Books.

Harari, O. (1993), 'Ten reasons why TQM doesn't work', *Management Review*, vol. 82, no. 1, January.

Hawkins, P. (1994) 'Organisational learning; taking stock and facing the challenge', *Management Learning*, vol. 25, no. 1.

Honeycutt, A. (1993), 'Total quality management at RTW', *Journal of Management Development*, vol. 12, no. 5.

Jeffery, J. R. (1992), 'Making quality managers: redefining management's role', *Quality*, vol. 31, no. 5, May.

Marchington, M., Dale, B. and Wilkinson, A. (1993), 'Who is really taking the lead on quality?', *Personnel Management*, April.

Mendelowitz, A. I. (1991), *Management Practices – US companies Improve Performance through Quality Efforts*, United States General Account Office (GAO/NSIAD-91-190).

Miller, R. L. and Cangeri, J. P. (1993), 'Why total quality management fails: perspective of top management', *Journal of Management Development*, vol. 12, no. 7.

Mintzberg, H. (1987), 'Crafting strategy', *Harvard Business Review*, July/August, pp. 66–75.

Nonaka, I. and Johansson, J. (1985), 'Japanese management: what about the "hard skills"?', *Academy of Management Review*, vol. 10, no. 2, pp. 181–91.

Pedler, M., Boydell, T. and Burgoyne, J. (1989), 'Towards the learning company', *Management Education and Development*, vol. 20, Pt 1.

Pedler, M., Burgoyne, J. and Boydell, T. (1991), *The Learning Company*, Maidenhead: McGraw Hill.

Pike, J. and Barnes, R. (1994), *TQM in Action*, Chapman and Hall.

Schien, L. (1991), 'Communicating quality in the service sector'. In B. H. Peters and J. L. Peters (eds) *Maintaining Total Quality Advantage*, pp. 40–2. New York: The Conference Board.

Sewell, G. and Wilkinson, B. (1992), 'Empowerment or emasculation? Shopfloor surveillance in a total quality organisation'. In P. Blyton and P. Turnbull (eds) *Reassessing Human Resource Management*, London: Sage.

Storey, J. (1992), *Developments in the management of human resources*, Blackwell.

Van Eynde, D. F. and Bledsoe, J. A. (1990), 'The changing practice of organisation development', *Leadership and Organisation Development Journal*, vol. 11, no. 2, pp. 25–30.

Walker, V. (1993), 'Kaizen – the art of the continual improvement', *Personnel Management*. August.

Wilkinson, A., Marchington, M., Goodman, J. and Ackers, P. (1992), 'Total Quality Management and employee involvement', *Human Resource Management Journal*, vol. 2, no. 4, pp. 1–20.

18 Performance management and individual performance

The treatment of individual performance in organisations has traditionally centred around the assessment of performance and the allocation of reward. Walker (1992) notes that this is partly due to these processes being institutionalised through the use of specific systems and procedures. Performance was typically seen as the result of the interaction between individual ability and motivation.

Increasingly organisations are recognising that planning and enabling performance have a critical effect on individual performance. So, for example, clarity of performance goals and standards, appropriate resources, guidance and support from the individual's manager all become central.

In this chapter we start with the fundamental steps for managing the individual performance, review approaches to the assessment of performance, and then explore how Performance Management Systems attempt to integrate both enabling and assessing individual performance.

The performance cycle

The performance cycle identifies three key aspects of effective performance, as shown in Figure 18.1. These aspects can be used as stepping stones in managing employee performance.

Planning performance

This step recognises the importance of a shared view of expected performance between manager and employee. The shared view can be expressed in a variety of ways, such as a traditional job description, key accountabilities, performance standards, specific objectives or targets and essential competencies.

In most cases a combination of approaches is necessary. There is a very clear trend to use specific objectives with a timescale for completion in addition to the generic tasks, with no beginning and no end, that tend to appear on traditional job

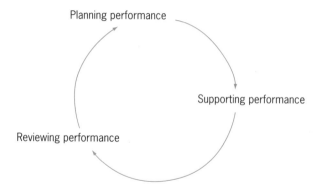

Planning performance

Supporting performance

Reviewing performance

Figure 18.1 Three key aspects of effective performance

descriptions. Such objectives give individuals a much clearer idea of performance expectations and enable them to focus on the priorities when they have to make choices about what they do. A long history of research demonstrates how clarity of goals improves employee performance.

The critical point about a *shared* view of performance suggests that handing out a job description or list of objectives to the employee is not adequate. Performance expectations need to be understood and where possible involve a contribution from the employee. For example, although key accountabilities may be fixed by the manager, they will need to be discussed. Specific objectives allow for, and benefit from, a greater degree of employee input as they will have a valid view of barriers to overcome, effort involved and feasibility. Expressing objectives as a 'what' statement rather than a 'how' statement gives the employee the power to decide the appropriate approach once they begin to work on the issue. Incorporating employee input and using 'what' statements are likely to generate a higher degree of employee ownership and commitment.

Planning the training, development and resources necessary for employees to achieve their objectives is imperative. Without this support it is unlikely that even the most determined employees will achieve the performance required.

Supporting performance

While the employee is working to achieve the performance agreed, the manager retains a key enabling role. Organising the resources and off-job training identified is clearly a must. So too is being accessible. There may well be unforeseen barriers to the agreed performance which it falls within the manager's remit to address, and sometimes the situation will demand that the expected performance needs to be revised. The employee may want to test out possible courses of action on the manager before proceeding, or may require further information. Sharing 'inside' information which will affect the employee's performance is often a key need, although it is also something which managers find difficult, especially with sensitive information. Managers can identify information sources and other people who may be helpful.

Ongoing coaching around the task is especially important. Managers can guide employees through discussion and by giving constructive feedback. They are in a position to provide practical job experiences to develop the critical skills and competencies which the employee needs, and can provide job-related opportunities for practice. Managers can identify potential role models to employees, and help to explain how the high achievers perform so well.

Although it is the employee's responsibility to achieve the performance agreed, the manager has an ongoing role in providing support and guidance and in oiling the organisational wheels.

REVIEW TOPIC 18.1

Do managers actively support employee performance in your organisation?
If they do: By what means do they do this and how effective is it?
If they do not: why not, and what is the impact of this?

Ongoing review

Ongoing review is an important activity for employees to carry out in order to plan their work and priorities and also to highlight to the manager well in advance if the agreed performance will not be delivered by the agreed dates. Joint employee/manager review is also essential so that information is shared. For example, a manager needs to be kept up to date on employee progress while the employee needs to be kept up to date on organisational changes which have an impact on their agreed objectives. Both need to share perceptions of how the other is doing in their role, and what they could do that would be more helpful.

These reviews are normally informal in nature, although a few notes may be taken of progress made and actions agreed. They need not be part of any formal system and therefore can take place where and when the job or the individuals involved demand, and not according to some preset schedule. The purpose of the review is to facilitate future employee performance and provide an opportunity for the manager to confirm that the employee is 'on the right track', or redirect them if necessary. They thus provide a forum for employee reward in terms of recognition of progress. A 'well done' or an objective signed off as completed can enhance the motivation to perform well in the future.

Using the performance cycle

The performance cycle describes effective day to day management of performance.

As such it was often used as the reason why no formal appraisal system was in place – 'because performance is appraised informally on a continuous basis'. In reality performance was usually managed on a *dis*continuous basis, with very little action unless there was a performance problem which needed solving! Even then the problem was often avoided until it had become so severe that someone would begin to talk of disciplinary procedures.

The performance cycle as we have described above is intended to be viewed as a positive management tool to enhance employee performance and to support whatever formal appraisal or Performance Management System is in place.

Appraisal systems

Appraisal systems formalise the review part of the performance cycle. They are typically designed on a central basis, usually by the personnel function, and require that each line manager appraise the performance of their staff on an annual, six-monthly or even quarterly basis. Elaborate forms are often designed to be completed as a formal record of the process.

Appraisal has traditionally been seen as most applicable to those in management and supervisory positions, but increasingly clerical and secretarial staff are being included in the process. Manual staff, particularly those who are skilled or have technical duties, are also subject to appraisal, although to a lesser extent than the other groups. Long (1986) notes that over the past decade there has been a substantial increase in performance reviews for non-managerial staff. Some organisations have a flexible approach whereby individuals in certain grades, for example secretarial and clerical, can elect whether or not to be included in the appraisal system. Other organisations allow those over a certain age to opt out of the system if they so wish.

Why have an appraisal system?

The different purposes of appraisal systems frequently conflict. Appraisal can be used to improve current performance, provide feedback, increase motivation, identify training needs, identify potential, let individuals know what is expected of them, focus on career development, award salary increases and solve job problems. It can be used to set out job objectives, provide information for human resource planning and career succession, assess the effectiveness of the selection process and as a reward or punishment in itself. Fletcher and Williams (1985) have suggested two conflicting roles of judge and helper which the appraiser may be called upon to play, depending on the purposes of the appraisal process. If a single appraisal system was intended both to improve current performance and to act as the basis for salary awards, the appraiser would be called upon to play both judge and helper at the same time. This makes it difficult for the appraiser to be impartial. It is also difficult for the appraisee, who may wish to discuss job-related problems but is very cautious about what they say because of not wanting to jeopardise a possible pay rise. Randell, Packard and Slater, (1984) suggest that the uses of appraisal can be divided into three broad categories, and that an appraisal system should attempt to satisfy only one of these. The categories they suggest are reward reviews, potential reviews and performance reviews. This implies that personnel managers need to think more carefully about the primary purpose of their appraisal system and make sure that procedures, training and individual expectations of the system are not in conflict.

Given that there is a choice about the way the appraisal system will be used, Randell *et al.* (1984) believe that the greatest advantages will be gained by the use of performance reviews. Such reviews include appraisal of past performance, meeting of objectives, identification of training needs, problems preventing better performance, and so on. This poses a great problem, particularly for the private sector but increasingly in the public sector, where there is a predilection to link pay directly to performance. Do these organisations settle just for reward reviews and forgo the advantages of performance reviews? Do they have two different appraisal systems, one for reward and one for performance at two distinctly different times of the year? Do they forget about linking performance and pay? These are key questions in relation to performance management systems, and are discussed later in this chapter.

REVIEW TOPIC 18.2

What are the key purposes of performance appraisal in your organisation?
What conflicts does this create?
How might these conflicts be resolved?

Torrington and Weightman (1989) suggest that from the individual's point of view appraisal may be seen as a time when they can gain feedback on their performance, reassurance, praise, encouragement, help in performing better and some guidance on future career possibilities. For many, however, the process is still seen as irrelevant to their needs and unhelpful – although this is often a reflection on the way that the process operates. Long (1986) found that there was a decreased emphasis on potential assessment and related career planning activity.

Who contributes to the appraisal process?

Individuals are appraised by a variety of people, including their immediate supervisor, their superior's superior, a member of the personnel department, themselves, their peers or their subordinates. Sometimes, assessment centres are used to carry out the appraisal.

Immediate manager
Most appraisals are carried out by the employee's immediate manager. The advantage of this is that the immediate supervisor usually has the most intimate knowl-

edge of the tasks that an individual has been carrying out and how well they have been done. The annual appraisal is also the logical conclusion of ongoing management of performance that should have been taking place throughout the year between the supervisor and the appraisee. Appraisal by the immediate manager is sometimes called appraisal by 'father'. Even when appraisal information is collected from a range of other sources, it is the immediate manager who collates and uses this information with the individual.

Manager's manager

The level of authority above the immediate manager can be involved in the appraisal process in one of two different ways. First, they may be called upon to countersign the manager's appraisal of the employee in order to give a seal of approval to indicate that the process has been fairly and properly carried out. Secondly, the manager's manager may directly carry out the appraisal. This is known as the 'grandfather' approach to appraisal. This is more likely to happen when the appraisal process is particularly concerned with making comparisons between individuals and identifying potential for promotion. It helps to overcome the problem that managers will all appraise by different standards, and minimises the possibility that appraisees will be penalised due to the fact that their manager has very high standards and is a 'hard marker'. Grandfather appraisal is often used to demonstrate fair play.

Member of the personnel department

Much less frequently an employee will be appraised by a member of the personnel department. This happens when there is no logical ongoing immediate manager, for example, in a matrix organisation. Stewart and Stewart (1977) show how this can work in practice by the example of an accountancy and consultancy partnership where work teams are organised according to the particular project in hand. At the end of each project the team manager completes a summary of the performance of each member of the team. This is then forwarded to the 'development manager' in the personnel department. At the end of the appraisal year the development manager collates all the reports on a given employee and produces a composite performance appraisal which is then discussed with the individual. This type of appraisal can be tricky to organise and much depends on the skills of the co-ordinator in the personnel department.

Self-appraisal

Fletcher (1993a) argues that there is little doubt that people are capable of rating themselves, but the question is whether they are willing to do this, and will individuals rate themselves fairly? Is it realistic to expect an individual to rate themselves as middle of the range if their salary depends on the appraisal result? Meyer (1980) reports that when employees were asked to compare themselves with others they tended to overrate themselves; however, when individuals prepared self-appraisals for appraisal interviews they were more modest. Fletcher notes that one of the most fruitful ways for individuals to rate themselves is by rating different aspects of their performance relative to other aspects rather than relative to the performances of other people. He comments that by approaching self-appraisal in this way individuals are more discriminating.

Self-appraisal is relatively new and not heavily used at present. However, individuals do carry out an element of self-appraisal in some of the more traditional appraisal schemes. Some organisations encourage individuals to prepare for the appraisal interview by filling out some form of appraisal on themselves. The differences between the individual's own appraisal and the manager's appraisal can then be a useful starting point for the appraisal interview. The difference between this and self-appraisal is that it is still the superior's appraisal that officially counts, although in the light of the subordinate's comments they might amend some of the ratings that they have given. In many schemes appraisees are asked to sign the completed appraisal form to show that they agree with its conclusions. In the event of disagreement a space is provided for details of controversial items. At the other end of the scale there are 'closed' schemes which not only eschew any form of contribution from the appraisees, but also prevent the appraisees from knowing the ratings that they have been given by their appraiser.

Taylor, Lehman and Forde (1989) recommend a particularly constructive form of self-appraisal, where individuals do this as a mid-point evaluation and concentrate on development, improvement and enrichment strategies. Managers support this process and aid development by coaching. The formal appraisal by the manager does not take place until six months later.

Appraisal by peers

Latham and Wexley (1981) suggest that peer ratings are both acceptably reliable and valid and have the advantage that peers have a more comprehensive view of the appraisee's job performance. They note the problem, though, that peers may be unwilling to appraise each other, as this can be seen as 'grassing' on each other. It is perhaps for this reason that peer appraisal is not often used, despite its claimed advantages. When peer rating is used an individual is rated by a group of peers and the results are averaged. In a time of increasing emphasis on teamwork there is a danger that peer assessment can be dysfunctional and disrupt team harmony (see Williams 1989).

Appraisal by subordinates

Appraisal information from subordinates is another less usual approach, although it is certainly on the increase. Latham and Wexley (1981) identify circumstances where it can be valuable and give an example of an organisation where individuals were rated by both superiors and subordinates, and where any large discrepancies in ratings were seen as areas for follow-up investigation. It is more limited in its value than peer appraisal as subordinates are only acquainted with certain aspects of their manager's work. However, it can be especially useful in providing information on management style and people management skills, which are increasingly seen as critical. Redman and Snape (1992) argue that asking for this type of information from subordinates facilitates empowerment. Recent examples of this include the Post Office (Cockburn 1993) and W H Smith & Son (Fletcher 1993b).

Customer appraisal

An increasingly useful source of appraisal information is from internal and external customers. This information can be collected directly by the direct manager from internal customers – for example, the training manager may collect information from a department on the support given to them by their specified training officer. Collecting information from external customers is a bit more tricky but can be done in a positive manner, framed in terms of improving customer services, and designed to be not too time-consuming.

REVIEW TOPIC 18.3

Almost all organisation members will have contact with a variety of internal customers. Identify your internal customers, or those of another member of staff, and design a short questionnaire to collect feedback that would be important in an appraisal situation.

What difficulties might you encounter in collecting and using this information?

Assessment centres

Assessment centres can be used in the appraisal of potential supervisors and managers. The advantage of assessment centres for this purpose is that ratings of potential can be assessed on the basis of factors other than current performance. It is well accepted that high performance in a current job does not mean that an individual will be a high performer if promoted to a higher level. It is also increasingly recognised that a moderate performer at one level may perform much better at a higher level. Assessment centres use tests, group exercises and interviews to appraise potential.

What is appraised?

Appraisal systems can measure a variety of things. They are sometimes designed to measure personality, sometimes behaviour or performance, and sometimes achievement of goals. These areas may be measured either quantitively or qualitatively. Qualitative appraisal often involves the writing of an unstructured narrative on the general performance of the appraisee. Alternatively, some guidance may be given as to the areas on which the appraiser should comment. The problem with qualitative appraisals is that they may leave important areas unappraised, and that they are not suitable for comparison purposes. Coates (1994) argues that what is actually measured in performance appraisal is the extent to which the individual conforms to the organisation.

When they are measured quantitively some form of scale is used, often comprising five categories of measurement from 'excellent', or 'always exceeds requirements' at one end to 'inadequate' at the other, with the mid-point being seen as acceptable. Scales are, however, not always constructed according to this plan. Sometimes on a five-point scale there will be four degrees of acceptable behaviour and only one that is unacceptable. Sometimes an even-numbered (usually six-point) scale is used to prevent the central tendency. There is a tendency for raters to settle on the mid-point of the scale, either through lack of knowledge of the appraisee, lack of ability to discriminate, lack of confidence or desire not to be too hard on appraisees. Rating other people is not an easy task, but it can be structured so that it is made as objective as possible. If performance appraisal is related to pay then some form of final scale is normally used. A typical approach is for there to be forced distributions on this scale – so for example only a specified proportion of staff fall into the highest, middle and lowest categories.

Avoidance of personality measures

Much traditional appraisal was based on measures of personality traits that were felt to be important to the job. These included traits such as resourcefulness, enthusiasm, drive, application and other traits such as intelligence. One difficulty with these is that everyone defines them differently, and the traits that are used are not always mutually exclusive. Raters, therefore, are often unsure of what they are rating. Ill-defined scales like these are more susceptible to bias and prejudice. Another problem is that since the same scales are often used for many different jobs, traits that are irrelevant to an appraisee's job may still be measured. One helpful approach is to concentrate on the job rather than the person. In an attempt to do this some organisations call their annual appraisal activity the 'job appraisal review'. The requirements of the job and the way that it is performed are considered, and the interview concentrates on problems in job performance which are recognised as not always being the 'fault' of the person performing the job. Difficulties in performance may be due to departmental structure or the equipment being used, rather than the ability or motivation of the employee. Other approaches concentrate on linking ratings to behaviour and performance on the job.

Behaviourally Anchored Rating Scales

One way of linking ratings with behaviour at work is to use Behaviourally Anchored Rating Scales (BARS). These can be produced in a large organisation by asking a sample group of raters to suggest independently examples of behaviour for each point on the scale in order to collect a wide variety of behavioural examples. These examples are then collated and returned to the sample raters without any indication of the scale point for which they were suggested. Sample raters allocate a scale point to each example and those examples, which are consistently located at the same point on the scale, are selected to be used as behavioural examples for that point on the scale. Future raters then have some guidance as to the type of behaviour that would be expected at each point. BARS can be used in conjunction with personality scales, but are most helpful when using scales that relate more clearly to work behaviour. Table 18.1 shows an example of a BARS in relation to 'relations with clients' – for the sake of clarity just one behavioural example is given at each

Table 18.1 *An example of a behaviourally anchored rating scale: relations with clients*

Behavioural example	Points of the rating scale
Often makes telephone calls on behalf of the client to find the correct office for him/her to go to even though this is not part of the job	A
Will often spend an hour with a client in order to get to the root of a very complex problem	B
Usually remains calm when dealing with an irate client	C
If the answer to the client's problem is not immediately to hand s/he often tells them s/he has not got the information	D
Sometimes ignores clients waiting at the reception desk for up to ten minutes even when s/he is not busy with other work	E
Regularly keeps clients waiting for ten minutes or more and responds to their questions with comments such as 'I can't be expected to know that' and 'You're not in the right place for that'	F

point on the scale, whereas in a fully developed scale there may be several at each point. Another advantage of the development of BARS is that appraisers have been involved in the process and this can increase their commitment to the outcome.

Behavioural Observation Scales

Behavioural Observation Scales (BOS) provide an alternative way of linking behaviour and ratings. Fletcher and Williams (1985) comment that these scales are developed by lengthy procedures, and are similar in some ways to BARS. They indicate a number of dimensions of performance with behavioural statements for each. Individuals are appraised as to the ecxtent to which they display each of the characteristics. Figure 18.2 gives an example.

Meeting objectives

Another method of making appraisal more objective is to use the process to set job objectives over the coming year and, a year later, to measure the extent to which these objectives have been met. The extent to which the appraisee is involved in setting these objectives varies considerably. If, as Stewart and Stewart (1977) suggest, these objectives are part of an organisational management by objectives scheme then the individual may be given them, with limited negotiation available. Alternatively, if they are not part of a larger scheme there is a great deal of scope for the individual to participate in the setting of such objectives. One of the biggest problems with appraisal on the basis of meeting objectives is that factors beyond the employee's control may make the objectives more difficult than anticipated, or even impossible. Another problem is that objectives will change over a period and

Leadership/staff supervision

1 Provides help, training and guidance so that employees can improve their performance

Almost never 5 4 3 2 1 Almost always

2 Explains to staff exactly what is expected of them – staff know their job responsibilities

Almost never 5 4 3 2 1 Almost always

3 Gets involved in subordinates' work only to check it

Almost never 5 4 3 2 1 Almost always

4 Consults staff for their ideas on ways of making their jobs better

Almost never 5 4 3 2 1 Almost always

5 Praises staff for things they do well

Almost never 5 4 3 2 1 Almost always

6 Passes important information to subordinates

Almost never 5 4 3 2 1 Almost always

The number of behavioural statements to be rated for any one dimension will be determined through the job analysis used to identify the key dimensions of performance and behavioural statements.

Figure 18.2 An example of a behavioural observation scale (Fletcher and Williams 1985, p. 45; used with the permission of Stanley Thornes Publishers).

so the original list is not so relevant a year later. Kane and Freeman (1986, p. 7) also highlight such difficulties as pressures to set 'easy' objectives, lack of comparability between the objectives of different individuals, unclear specification of measures and an emphasis on short-term, at the expense of long-term, accomplishments. They also discuss the 'fudge factor', where middle managers are pressured from the top to set challenging and stretching objectives for their people, and are pressured from below to set objectives that are not difficult to achieve. In order to please all, the middle manager fudges the issue rather than working it through. If suitable provision can be made for these contingencies and difficulties, appraisal by objectives can be effective and motivating.

Performance against job description

Some systems require the manager to appraise performance against each task specified in the job description or against each key accountability. The appraisal in this case may be in the form of narrative statements and/or a performance rating.

Performance against job competencies

When a competency profile has been identified for a particular job it is then possible to use this in the appraisal of performance. Many appraisal systems combine competency assessment with assessment against objectives or job accountabilities.

Development of appraisal criteria

Stewart and Stewart (1977) suggest a variety of methods by which appraisal criteria can be identified. These include the use of the critical incident technique to identify particularly difficult problems at work, content analysis of working documents and performance questionnaires whereby managers and potential appraisees identify (anonymously) what characterises the most effective job holder and the least effective job holder (see Stewart and Stewart 1977, pp. 37–59). We made the point previously that one of the advantages of BARS was that appraisers are involved in formulating the way that appraisal scales are used. There are, similarly, advantages in involving appraisers in the identification of appraisal criteria, as well as the advantages from an information point of view. There can also be advantages in involving potential appraisees in criteria identification (Silverman and Wexley 1984).

The key question is whether the appraisal criteria are appropriate for the job in question – there are all too many examples of appraisal criteria being chosen and used based on flimsy evidence of appropriateness to the job. Appraising criteria that have little relevance to the job being done is clearly of no value whatsoever.

Effectiveness of appraisal systems

The effectiveness of appraisal systems hinges on the extent to which performance criteria are appropriate for the jobs for which they are used, and that the system itself is appropriate to the needs and culture of the organisation (see for example George 1986). Ownership of the system is also important – if it was designed and imposed by the personnel function there may be little ownership of the system by line managers. Similarly if paperwork has to be returned to the personnel function the system may well be seen as a form-filling exercise for someone else's benefit and with no practical value in performing within the job. Fletcher (1993a) makes the interesting comment that all systems have a shelf-life – perhaps changes are required to the system to renew interest and energy. In any case, as Fletcher also notes, organisations have changed so much, and continue to do so, that it is inevitable that the nature of the appraisal process will change too (see Fletcher 1993b).

Performance Management Systems

Performance Management Systems are increasingly seen as the way to manage employee performance rather than relying on appraisal alone. Bevan and Thompson (1992), for example, found that 20 per cent of the organisations they surveyed had introduced a Performance Management System. Such systems offer the advantage of being closely tied into the objectives of the organisation, and therefore the resulting performance is more likely to meet organisational needs. The systems also represent a more holistic view of performance. Performance appraisal is almost always a key part of the system, but is integrated with ensuring that employee effort is directed towards organisational priorities, that appropriate training and development is carried out to enable employee effort to be successful, and that successful performance is rewarded and reinforced. Given that there is such an emphasis on a link into the organisation's objectives it is somewhat disappointing that Bevan and Thompson found no correlation between the existence of a Performance Management system and organisational performance in the private sector.

As with appraisal systems, some Performance Management Systems will be development-driven and some will be reward-driven. For a good example of a development-driven system, which does include an element of reward, see Sheard (1992) reporting on Performance Management at Zeneca Pharmaceuticals.

There are many different definitions of Performance Management and some have identified it as 'management by objectives' under another name. There are, however, some key differences here. Management by objectives was primarily an off-the-peg system which organisations bought in, and generally involved objectives being imposed on managers from above. Performance Management tends to be tailor-made and produced in-house (that's why there are so many different versions), and there is an emphasis on mutual objective-setting and on ongoing performance support and review.

Figure 18.3 shows a typical system, including both development and reward aspects, the main stages of which are as follows.

1. Written and agreed job description, reviewed regularly. Objectives for the work-group which have been cascaded down from the organisation's strategic objectives. Bevan and Thompson found that Performance Management organisations were more likely to have an organisational mission statement and to communicate this to employees.

2. Individual objectives derived from the above, which are jointly devised by appraiser and appraisee. These objectives are results – rather than task-orientated, are tightly defined and include measures to be assessed. The objectives are designed to stretch the individual and offer potential development, as well as meeting business needs. Many organisations use the 'SMART' acronym for describing individual objectives or targets:

   Specific
   Measurable
   Appropriate
   Relevant
   Timed

This is clearly easier for some parts of the organisation than others. There is often a tendency for those in technical jobs, for example computer systems development, to identify purely technical targets – reflecting heavy task emphasis they see in their jobs. Moving staff to a different view of how their

Figure 18.3 Four stages of a typical performance management system

personal objectives contribute to team and organisational objectives is an important part of the Performance Management process. An objective for a Team Leader in systems development could be:

> To complete development interviews with all team members by end July 1996 (written March 1996).

Clearly, the timescale for each objective will need to reflect the content of the objective and not timescales set into the Performance Management System. As objectives are met managers and their staff need to have a brief review meeting to look at progress in all objectives and decide what other objectives should be added. Five or six ongoing objectives is generally sufficient for one individual to work on at any time.

3. Development plan devised by manager and individual detailing development goals and activities designed to enable the individual to meet the objectives. The emphasis here is on managerial support and coaching, very much as described in the performance support phase of managing individual performance (see earlier in this chapter). Those organisations with a development-driven Performance Management System may well have development objectives alongside performance objectives to ensure that this part of the system is given proper attention.

4. Assessment of objectives. Ongoing formal reviews on a regular basis designed to motivate the appraisee and concentrate on developmental issues. Also, an annual assessment which affects pay received depending on performance in achievement of objectives. Most systems include this link with pay, but Fletcher and Williams (1993a) point to some difficulties experienced. Some organisations (both public and private) found that the merit element of pay was too small to motivate staff, and indeed was sometimes found to be insulting. Although Performance Management organisations were more likely to

have merit, or performance-related pay (Bevan and Thompson 1992), some organisations have regretted its inclusion.

Implementation of Performance Management

Performance Management needs to be line-driven rather than personnel-driven (see for example, Fletcher 1993b), and therefore mechanisms need to be found to make this happen. The incorporation of line managers alongside personnel managers in a working party to develop the system is clearly important. This not only ensures that the needs of the line are taken into account in the system design, but also demonstrates that the system is line led. Training in the introduction and use of the system is also ideally line led, and Fletcher and Williams (1992b) give us an excellent example of an organisation where line managers were trained as 'performance management coaches' who were involved in departmental training and support for the new system.

Bevan and Thompson found incomplete takeup of Performance Management, with some aspects being adopted and not others. They noted that there was a general lack of integration of activities. This is rather unfortunate, as one of the key advantages of Performance Management is the capacity for integration of activities concerned with the management of individual performance.

A large insurance company introduced a Performance Management System, but two years later the system had to be relaunched. The main problem was that the middle managers felt less than keen to agree objectives with their staff because their managers had not done so with them. They had received only very brief training in Performance Management and although the system was designed to be reward-driven the organisation had experienced difficult times during the recession and there had been no additional money available to reward achievement of objectives.

The scheme was introduced by training a series of nominated line manager coaches from each department. They had then to take the message back to their colleagues and train them, tailoring the material to their department (Personnel Training providing the back-up documentation). These were serving line managers who had to give up their time to do the job. Many of them were high-flyers, and they have been important opinion leaders and influencers – though they themselves had to be convinced first. Their bosses could refuse to nominate high quality staff for this role if they wished, but they would subsequently be answerable to the Chief Executive. This approach was taken because it fits with the philosophy of performance management (i.e. high line management participation), and because it was probably the only way to train all the departmental managers in the timescale envisaged.
(Fletcher and Williams 1992b, p. 133)

☐ Summary Propositions

18.1 Effective management of individual performance rests on managing the performance cycle – ongoing performance planning, support and review.

18.2 Appraisal is most often carried out by the immediate manager, but is enhanced by information from other parties.

18.3 There is a conflict in many appraisal systems in the role of the manager – as judge and as helper.

18.4 Performance Management Systems incorporate appraisal activity, but include other aspects such as a link to organisational objectives and a more holistic view of performance.

18.5 So far Performance Management has generally been adopted in a bitty way with a lack of integration between performance activities – there are, however, some good examples of carefully thought through and implemented systems.

References

Bevan, S. and Thompson, M. (1992), 'An overview of policy and practice'. In Institute of Personnel Management, (1992) *Personnel Management in the UK: An analysis of the issues*. London: Institute of Personnel Management.

Coates, G. (1994), 'Performance appraisal as icon; Oscar winning performance or dressing to impress?' *International Journal of Human Resource Management*, no. 1, February.

Cockburn, B. (1993), 'How I see the personnel function', *Personnel Management*, November.

Fletcher, C. (1993a), *Appraisal: Routes to Improved Performance*, London: Institute of Personnel Management.

Fletcher, C. (1993b), 'Appraisal; an idea whose time has gone?', *Personnel Management*, September.

Fletcher, C. and Williams, R. (1992a), 'The route to performance management', *Personnel Management*, October.

Fletcher, C. and Williams, R. (1992b), 'Organisational experience', in Institute of Personnel Management, (1992), *Performance Management in the UK: An analysis of the issues*, London: Institute of Personnel Management.

George, J. (1986), 'Appraisal in the public sector: dispensing with the big stick', *Personnel Management*, May.

Herriot, P. (ed.), (1989), *Assessment and Selection in Organisations*, Chichester: Wiley.

Institute of Personnel Management (1992), *Performance Management in the UK: An analysis of the issues*, London: Institute of Personnel Management.

Kane, J. S. and Freeman, K. A. (1986), 'MBO and performance appraisal; A mixture that's not a solution, Part 1', *Personnel*, December, pp. 26, 28, 30–6.

Latham, G. P. and Wexley, K. N. (1981), *Increasing Productivity Through Performance Appraisal*, Wokingham: Addison-Wesley.

Long, P. (1986), *Performance Appraisal Revisited*, London: Institute of Personnel Management.

Maier, N. R. F. (1958), *The Appraisal Interview: Objectives, Methods and Skills*, New York: Wiley.

Meyer, H. H. (1980), 'Self-appraisal of job performance', *Personnel Psychology*, vol. 33, pp. 291–5.

Randell, G., Packard, P. and Slater, I. (1984), *Staff Appraisal*, London: Institute of Personnel Management.

Redman, T. and Snape, E. (1992), 'Upward and onward: can staff appraise their managers?', *Personnel Review*, vol., 21, pp. 32–46.

Sheard, A. (1992), 'Learning to improve performance', *Personnel Management*, September.

Silverman, S. B. and Wexley, K. N. (1984), 'Reaction of employees to performance appraisal interviews as a function of their participation in rating scale development', *Personnel Psychology*, vol. 37.

Stewart, V. and Stewart, A. (1977), *Practical Performance Appraisal*, Aldershot: Gower.

Taylor, G. S., Lehman, C. M. and Forde, C. M. (1989), 'How employee self-appraisals can help', *Supervisory Management*, August, pp. 33–41.

Torrington, D. P. and Weightman, I. (1989), *The Appraisal Interview*, Manchester: UMIST.

Walker, J. W. (1992), *Human Resource Strategy*, New York: McGraw-Hill.

Williams, R. (1989), 'Alternative raters and methods', In P. Herriot (ed.) *Assessment and Selection in Organisations*. Chichester: Wiley.

19 Team performance

The appointments pages of *Personnel Management* in 1994 were littered with advertisements looking for 'an effective team player' to 'join an established HR team', where one of the 'key organisational issues is team working' so that they can 'add value to the European HR team', 'enhance the skills of the management team', and 'facilitate effective team development'.

Few would disagree that the 1990s is the age of the team and teamwork. Teamwork is used as a way of empowering employees and facilitating the flowering of their full potential in order to enhance organisational performance. A heavy emphasis on teamwork usually corresponds with flatter organisations that have diminished status differentials. Teamwork, of course, is not a new idea, and the autonomous working groups of the 1960s and 1970s are clear forerunners. The similarities are increasing responsibility, authority and a sense of achievement among group members. The protagonists of autonomous working groups were also intent on improving the quality of working life of employees by providing a wider range of tasks to work on and a social environment in which to carry them out. The emphasis in the 1990s is quite different – performance is the unvarying aim. Higher performance is expected due to increased flexibility and communication within teams, increased ownership of the task and commitment to team goals. Some of the most famous autonomous working groups at Volvo in Sweden have now been disbanded because their production levels were too low compared with other forms of production. The teams of the 1990s are designed to outperform other production methods.

So, what is a team? How does it differ from all other groups in organisations? A team can be described as more than the sum of the individual members. In other words, a team demands collaborative, not competitive, effort where each member takes responsibility for the performance of the team rather than just their own individual performance. The team comes first, the individual comes second, and everything the individual member does is geared to the fulfilment of the team's goals rather than their individual agenda. If you think of a football team, a surgical team or an orchestra it is easier to see how each member is assigned a specific role depending on their skills and how individuals use their skills for the benefit of the team performance rather than selectively using them for personal achievement. In a football game, for example, a player making a run towards the goal would pass to another player in a better position to score rather than risking trying to score themselves for the sake of personal glory. We argue that such teamwork is critical to the success of delayered organisations, and we have discussed this issue in Chapter 6 in the context of Drucker's (1988) metaphor of the symphony orchestra.

Moxon (1993) defines a team as having a common purpose; agreed norms and values which regulate behaviour; members with interdependent functions and a recognition of team identity. Kazenback and Smith (1993) have also described the differences that they identify between teams and work groups, and identify teams as having shared leadership roles, mutual accountability and a specific team purpose, amongst other attributes. In organisations this dedication only happens when individuals are fully committed to the team's goals, and derives from an involvement in defining how the goals will be met and having the power to make decisions within teams rather than being dependent on the agreement of external management. These are particularly characteristics of self-managing teams – perhaps the most topical of teams at present. Organisational teams differ, though, in terms of their temporary or permanent nature, the intechangeability of individual members and tasks and the breadth of tasks or functions held within the team.

Time span

Some teams are set up to solve a specific problem, and when this has been solved the team disbands. Other teams may be longer-term project-based, and may disband when the project is complete. Some teams will be relatively permanent fixtures, such as production teams, where the task is ongoing.

Interchangeability

Teams differ in the range of specific skills that are required and the expectation of all members learning all skills. In some production teams interchangeability of skills is crucial and all members will have the potential, and will be expected to learn all skills eventually. In other types of teams, for example cross-functional teams (surgical teams, product development teams) each member is expected to bring their specialist skills to use for the benefit of the team, and they are not expected to be able to learn all the skills of each other member.

Task and functional range

Many production teams will often be designed to cover a whole task and within this there will be a wide range of activities. This clearly differs from the traditional line form of production where the tasks are broken down and segmented. Other teams

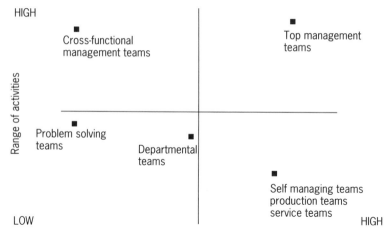

HIGH

Cross-functional
management teams

Top management
teams

Range of activities

Problem solving
teams

Departmental
teams

Self managing teams
production teams
service teams

LOW

HIGH

Interchangeability of team members

Figure 19.1   Different types of teams. High range of activities indicates activities over a broad range of functions; low range of activities indicates activities within a function and within a single task.

will span a range of functions – for example, cross-functional teams involving research, development, marketing and production staff. Figure 19.1 shows how different types of teams can be represented on a framework representing interchangeability and task/functional spread.

REVIEW TOPIC 19.1

Think of the different types of teams in your organisation and plot them on the framework above. What does this tell you about:

(a)   your organisation's approach to teamwork; and

(b)   the different purposes of the different types of teams.

In this chapter we will go on to look at the characteristics of four broad types of teams – production/service teams; cross-functional management teams; problem-solving teams and departmental teams. We will then examine which factors affect how teams perform and what can be done to improve team effectiveness.

Broad team types

Production and service teams

It is these teams which are often referred to as *self-managing teams*, *self-managing work teams* or *self-directed teams*. They are typically given the authority to submit a team budget, order resources as necessary within budget, organise training required, select new team members, plan production to meet predefined goals, schedule holidays and absence cover and deploy staff within the team. There is a clear emphasis on taking on managerial tasks that would previously have been done by a member of the managerial hierarchy. These managerial tasks are delegated to the lowest level possible organisational level in the belief that they will be carried out in a responsible manner for the benefit of the team and the organisation. The payoff from this self-management has been shown in some research as a 30 per cent increase in productivity (Hoerr 1989). These teams are growing in popularity in such areas as car production and the production of electrical and electronic equipment. Teams will be based around a complete task so that they perform a whole chunk of the production process and in this way have something clear to manage. For example, the team will normally include people with maintenance skills, specific technical skills and different types of assembly skills, so that they are self-sufficient and not dependent on waiting for support from other parts of the organisation. The ultimate aim is usually for all members to have all skills needed within the team. Self-managing teams may also be found in the service arena as well as the manufacturing one.

In some teams a leader is appointed from the outset, but in others a leader is left to emerge. Whatever process is used, the leader is the same level of employee as other members and is as fully involved in the task of the team. They are therefore not part of the traditional managerial hierarchy, and yet they will need to take on managerial tasks such as planning, organising, supporting individuals, presenting information and representing the team to the rest of the organisation. The way that the leader carries out these activities and involves others in them will clearly have an impact on the effectiveness of the team. In some teams the leadership may vary

---

The British company Whitbread have established a small, up-market chain of restaurants called 'Thank God it's Friday', which is abbreviated to 'Friday's' or TGIF. The marketing is directed towards the relatively young and affluent and a part of this strategy has been to avoid the traditional hierarchy of the good-food restaurant – Maitre d'Hotel, Chef de Rang, Commis Waiter and so forth – by empowering the person with whom the customer deals directly: the Waiter. This person can take decisions on such things as complimentary drinks without reference to anyone else. There is no manager, but each restaurant has a team leader known as the Coach.

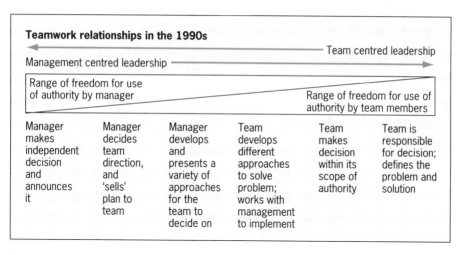

Figure 19.2 Teamwork relationships in the 1990s (Oliva 1992, p. 76). Reproduced with permission of Idea Group Publishing.

according to the nature of task, resting with whoever has the most appropriate skills to offer.

The nature of self-management also has an impact on the role of managers outside the team. Traditionally these managers would carry out the tasks described above and would monitor and control the performance of the team. If these tasks are no longer appropriate then what is the role of the manager – is there a role at all? It will come as no surprise that the formation of self-managed teams are seen as a threat to some managers. However, Casey (1993) comments that 'self-managed teams do not deny the role of manager, they redefine it'. He also notes that the management of the team is a balance between responsibility within the team and management without rather than an-all-or-nothing situation. He suggests a move towards 90 per cent within the team in a self-management situation rather than nearer 30 per cent in a traditional management situation.

Where there are self-managed teams the role of the traditional manager outside the team changes to adviser and coach, as they have now delegated most of their responsibilities for directly managing the team. These managers become a resource to be called on when needed in order to enable the team to solve their own problems. Salem, Lazarus and Cullen (1992) comment that:

> The SMT approach requires a conscious effort on the part of the management to encourage and reinforce both the individual members and the team as a whole. Management's tools are stimulating questions designed to motivate the individual to examine himself or herself in relation to the attainment of the group's objectives. (Salem *et al.* 1992)

Oliva (1992) draws a helpful framework for understanding the respective managerial roles of traditional managers and teams in a team environment, shown in Figure 19.2.

We referred to the High Performance Teams at Digital in Chapter 3 (Buchanan 1992) and you may wish to return to this example on page 60. Another example is Milliken, which won the Baldridge US National Quality Award in 1989. In this organisation employees are called 'associates' and the teams schedule their own work, create team objectives, enrol themselves for training and are empowered to stop production for quality or safety reasons (Oliva 1992).

The self-managing team concept has much to offer in terms of increasing employee ownership and control and thereby releasing their commitment, creativity and potential. There are, of course, potential problems with this approach too. Salem *et al.* (1992) identify the difficulty of returning to traditional systems once employees have experienced greater autonomy; resistance from other parts of the organisation; and peer pressure and its consequences. We would also add resistance from team members. Let us look at some of these in some more detail.

Resistance from other parts of the organisation

As self-managing teams have clear knock-on effects for other parts of the organisation these other parts will react. If traditional managers do not give direction and control to the team an immediate conflict is set up as to who makes the decisions; if they fail to support and coach the team may feel abandoned and insecure. In general the climate of the organisation needs to be supportive in terms of the value placed on individual autonomy and learning. There are also situations where the rhetoric of the organisation is about delegating responsibility to the team but where management fail to relinquish ownership of the task (see the example adapted from Sewell and Wilkinson on page 305 of Chapter 17).

Resistance within the team

Individuals who have spent many years being told what to do may need some time to take this responsibility for themselves. It is clear that operating self-managed teams will be easier on a greenfield site. However, for locations which want to make the transition, the importance of team selection of newcomers and of selecting skills relevant to a team environment as well as essential technical skills will be crucial. Salem *et al.* (1992) note that the most often-cited individual characteristics for a team environment are 'interpersonal skills, self-motivation, ability to cope with peer pressure, level of technical/administrative experience, communication skills and the ability to cope with stress'. Other characteristics which have been noted elsewhere include the ability to deal with ambiguous situations and cope with conflict in a constructive way.

Peer pressure

The by-products of peer pressure have been identified as lower absence levels, due to an awareness that colleagues have to cover for them; and a higher production rate so as not to let colleagues down. However, intense peer pressure can lead to

Meyer (1994) reports that at one Ford manufacturing plant multifunctional teams were used to improve product quality. Team members were trained to collect and analyse data so that they could solve their own quality problems.

Quality engineers had also been appointed in order to assist the teams. The divisional management then asked the engineers for a Divisional Quality report, and in order to complete this the engineers asked the teams for the data that they had collected, and they summarised this.

As time went on the teams began to wait for the engineers to collect and analyse their raw data before they made any decisions regarding quality. They even began to wait for directions from the engineers before taking action. Problems that the teams had previously solved were now being solved with the help of the engineers, who began to ask for more engineers to support this process.

The intention had been to empower the teams, but the teams did not act as though they were empowered as management had still remained in control by asking for quality reports from the engineers.

stress and destroy many of the perceived benefits of team involvement from the employees' perspective. Some of the destructive aspects of peer pressure can also be seen in the Sewell and Wilkinson example in Chapter 17. Banner, Kulisch and Peery (1992) also note issues about the limits of peer involvement when they ask whether team members should exercise discipline over one another and whether they should be responsible for the performance appraisal process.

Cross-functional management teams

Cross-functional management teams are very different from the teams described above, and members are more likely to retain other roles in the organisation. Typically they will see themselves as members of their function, whether it be marketing, research, sales, development and members of a specific project team. Very often the project team will surround the development of a particular product from creation to sales – for example, a new computer package, a drug, a piece of electrical equipment. Members may be allocated to the team by their home function for all or part of their time.

The thinking behind a cross-functional team is that each member brings with them the expertise in their own function and the dedication to the team task around a certain product or project. By bringing individuals together as a team the project gains through the commitment of team members to a task which they feel that they own. Bringing these individuals together enables the development of a common language and the overcoming of departmental boundaries. For a further discussion of the matrix form of organisation in which cross-functional teams are a key feature, see Chapter 6.

Meyer (1994) expresses the importance of measures of performance for cross-functional teams, and sees process measures as key rather than just measures of achievement. His argument is that process measures help the team to gauge their progress and identify and rectify problems. It follows from this that the performance measures used need to be designed by the team and not imposed on them from senior management, as the team will know best what measures will help them to do their job. Inevitably these measures will need to be designed against a strategic context set by higher management. Meyer describes a good example of the problems that can result if managers try and control the performance measurement process rather than empowering team members.

The process of agreeing their own performance measures will also enable the team to identify different assumptions and perceptions that each team member holds, and generate discussion on the exact goals of the team. All this is helpful in bringing the team together, generating a common language and ensuring that everyone is pulling in the same direction.

One special form of cross-functional management team is the top management team of the organisation – the Directors. Clearly this team is different in that it is permanent and not project-based, but the need to work as a team rather than a collection of individuals is a key factor. Kazenback and Smith (1992) note that it is more difficult to get this group to work together as a team as they are more likely to be individualists. Directors often still see themselves as representatives of their function rather than members of a team, and thus will be more likely to defend positions and attempt to influence each other rather than pulling together. Garratt (1990) asks three key questions to top teams to assess whether they are truly direction-giving teams. He asks about regular processes, outside formal meetings, to discuss what's going on in the organisation and what possibilities exist; to what extent the team involve themselves in unstructured visioning before grappling with the down-to-earth business of plans and budgets; and to what extent they assess individual contributions and the skills and resources owned within the team. Garratt explains that he usually gets little evidence of any of these activities taking place.

REVIEW TOPIC 19.2

Think of some functional teams that you either belong to, have belonged to, or have had some contact with.
To what extent, and why, is each truly a team, or just a group of individuals with the title 'team'?

Functional teams

Functional teams, as the name implies, are made up of individuals within a function. For example, the training section of the personnel department may well be referred to as the training team, different groups of nurses on a specific ward are sometimes divided into the 'red' team and the 'blue' team. Sales staff for a particular product or region may refer to themselves as the 'games software sales team' or the 'north west sales team'. Some of the rationale behind this is to give the customer, internal or external, an identified set of individuals to liaise with. Given that these will be a smaller set than those in the whole department it will enable a much closer knowledge of the particular customer in question and a better understanding of customer needs. The extent to which these are really teams as opposed to groups of individuals will vary enormously.

Problem-solving teams

These teams may be within-function or cross-functional. Within-function teams may typically be in the form of quality circles where employees come together voluntarily to tackle production and quality issues affecting their work. Unfortunately, many of these teams have had little clout and recommended changes and improvements have not been possible to implement, due to the retention of management control. Other within-function teams may consist of specially selected individuals who will be involved in the implementation of a major development within the function or department. For example, the implementation of performance management may be supported by specific coaches in each department who carry out related training, offer counselling and advice and who tailor organisation policy so that it meets department needs. These coaches may become the departmental performance management team.

REVIEW TOPIC 19.3

If you have belonged to, or observed, a problem-solving team:

(a) what were the barriers to team formation?
(b) in what ways did team members support the team?
(c) in what ways did team members concentrate on themselves as individuals?

Cross-functional teams may be brought together to solve an identified and specific organisationational problem, and will remain together for a short period until that problem has been solved. They differ from cross-functional management teams as their role is not to manage anything, but rather to collect and analyse data and perspectives and develop an understanding of the nature of the problem. From this they will make recommendations on how to solve the problem which are then passed on to higher management. Usually their remit ends here and there is little or no involvement in implementation. Normally team members will retain their normal work role at the same time as being a team member.

Team effectiveness

For a team to be effective they need a clear and agreed vision, objectives and set of rules by which they will work together. They will need to feel able to be open and honest with each other and be prepared to confront difficulties and differences. It is also important for members to be able to tolerate conflict and be able to use this in a collaborative way in the achievement of the team's objectives. Some researchers have commented upon the size of the team and suggest it should be small enough, say twenty or less, for communications to be feasible. Others have suggested that proximity is important in maintaining communications and team spirit. Below we explore the key issues of selection, training/development, assessment and reward in relation to team effectiveness.

Selecting team members

The effectiveness of any team depends to a large extent on the appropriateness of the team members. For self-managing teams there is a strong lobby for newcomers to be appointed by the team themselves, and indeed some would argue that unless this happens the team is not truly self-managing (see, for example, Banner *et al.* 1992). Other case studies suggest that team members, whether selected by the team or by others, are chosen very carefully in the likeness of the team and with the 'right attitudes'. For all teamwork Kazenbach and Smith identify three critical selection criteria – technical or functional expertise, problem-solving and decision-making skills and interpersonal skills.

Another approach to selection of team members is by understanding the team roles that they are best able to play, so that the team is endowed with a full range of the roles that it will need to be effective. Belbin (1993), through extensive research and the evolution of his original ideas, has identified nine team roles which are important to a team and which individuals may have as strengths or weaknesses. The absence of some or many of these roles can cause problems in team effectiveness. Too many individuals playing the same type of role can cause undue friction in the team and again damage effectiveness. The key lies in achieving a balance. These team roles are as follows.

- *Co-ordinator:* this person will have a clear view of the team objectives and will be skilled at inviting the contribution of team members in achieving these, rather than just pushing his or her own view. The Chairperson is self-disciplined and applies this discipline to the team. They are confident and mature and will summarise the view of the group and will be prepared to take a decision on the basis of this.

- *Shaper:* the shaper is full of drive to make things happen and to get things going. In doing this they are quite happy to push their own views forward, don't mind being challenged and are always ready to challenge others. The shaper looks for the pattern in discussions and tries to pull things together into something feasible which the team can then get to work on.

- *Plant:* this member is the one who is most likely to come out with original ideas and challenge the traditional way of thinking about things. Sometimes they become so imaginative and creative that the team can not see the relevance of what they are saying; however, without the plant to scatter the seeds of new ideas the team will often find it difficult to make headway. The plant's strength is in major new insights and changes in direction and not in contributing to the detail of what needs to be done.

- *Resource investigator:* the resource investigator is the group member with the strongest contacts and networks, and is excellent at bringing in information and support from the outside. This member can be very enthusiastic in pursuit of the team's goals, but can not always sustain this enthusiasm.

- *Implementer:* the individual who is a company worker is well organised and effective at turning big ideas into manageable tasks and plans that can be achieved. They are both logical and disciplined in their approach. They are hardworking and methodical but may have some difficulty in being flexible.

- *Team worker:* the team worker is the one who is most aware of the others in the team, their needs and their concerns. They are sensitive and supportive of other people's efforts, and try to promote harmony and reduce conflict. Team workers are particularly important when the team is experiencing a stressful or difficult period.

- *Completer:* as the title suggests the completer is the one who drives the deadlines and makes sure they are achieved. The completer usually communicates a sense of urgency which galvanises other team members into action. They are conscientious and effective at checking the details, which is a vital contribution, but sometimes get 'bogged down' in them.

- *Monitor evaluator:* the monitor evaluator is good at seeing all the options. They have a strategic perspective and can judge situations accurately. The monitor evaluator can be overcritical and is not usually good at inspiring and encouraging others.

- *Specialist:* this person provides specialist skills and knowledge and has a dedicated and single-minded approach. They can adopt a very narrow perspective and sometimes fail to see the whole picture.

REVIEW TOPIC 19.4

Think of a team situation in which you have been involved, either in a work or social/family setting.

Which roles were present and which were absent?
What was the effect of this balance?

An individual's potential team roles can be interpreted from some of the psychometric tests used in the normal selection procedure. They can also be assessed in a different way. A specific questionnaire has been designed to identify the individual's perceived current team role strengths (that is the roles they have developed and are actually playing). This is particularly helpful for development within the current team, but may be less useful for selection purposes. Although helpful, current team role strengths may not be automatically transferred into another team situation.

Team leader and manager training

Both team leaders and senior managers begin to play new roles in team situations. Team leaders suddenly find themselves with a host of new responsibilities for the support of team members and the planning and organising of team activities – responsibilities for which they have little experience and often no training. Similarly, managers will need some training support in moving from a directive, controlling role to a coaching and counselling role. Training needs to encompass not only new skills but an opportunity to discuss the changing philosophy of the organisation and encourage attitude change.

Team member training

Whether or not the team has an appointed leader all team members will need some training support in working in a different environment with different rules about what they should and should not be doing. Being more involved and taking on more responsibility and sometimes leading activities will require some initial training support. Further training in new technical skills can often be handled within the team once at least one member has the knowledge required and has gained some training skills themselves.

Team development

Teams can be developed in many different ways, and perhaps one of the most critical early on is development through the task itself. For example, teams can develop by jointly describing the core purpose of the team, visualising the future position that they are aiming to achieve, developing the rules and procedures they will use, performance measures and so on. If the team are given some support to do this, perhaps a facilitator from the personnel function or externally, they can not only develop vital guidelines but also understand a way of working things out together, a process which they can use by themselves in the future.

Teams can also develop by looking at the way they have been working together since they came together. One way of doing this is by completing a team roles questionnaire to identify the strengths and weaknesses of each member. This will help to promote a better understanding of why things happen as they do, and also pave the way for some changes. On this basis some individuals can develop their potential in team roles which they are not presently using, but for which they have some preference, and in this way a better balance may be struck making the team more effective. Another process is to review what the team are good and bad at, what different inviduals can do to enable others to carry out their tasks more effectively, and what improvements can be made in the way that the team organises itself. Simple suggestions can be surprisingly effective, such as: 'It would really help me if you gave me a list of telephone numbers where I can leave a message for you when I need to get hold of you urgently' (cross-functional team) and 'I don't understand why we need to lay the figures out in this way and it really gets my back up – will someone take some time out to explain it to me?' Irwin, Plovnick and Fry (1974) identified four major problem areas in relation to group effectiveness – goals, roles, processes and relationships – and these four can be used to provide a framework for team development activities.

Other less direct methods of development involve working through simulated exercises as a team – for example, building a tower out of pieces of paper – and learning from this how the team operate and what they could do to operate better. Outdoor training is also used to good effect in team situations, where the team tackle new, and perhaps dangerous, activities in the outdoors. Typically some activities involve learning to trust and to depend on each other in a real and risky situation and the learning from this, and the trust developed, can then be transferred back into the work situation.

The approach taken to team building needs to be appropriate to the stage of development of the team. Tuckman (1965) identified four stages of team development – forming, storming, norming and performing. Forming centres on team members working out what they are supposed to be doing, and trying to feel part of it. At this stage they are quite likely to be wary of each other and hide their feelings. Storming is the stage where members are prepared to express strongly held views, where there is conflict and competition, and where some push for power while others withdraw. The norming stage is characterised by a desire to begin to organise themselves. Members actually begin to listen to each other, become more open and see problems as belonging to the whole group. Performing is where a sense of group loyalty has developed and where all contribute in an atmosphere of openness and trust. Two very useful and practical texts for managers and facilitators on team building are Woodcock (1979) and Moxon (1993).

Recognition and reward

Like individuals, teams need some form of recognition and reward for their efforts. Recognition may be in the form of articles in company newsletters or local papers about team successes, inscribing the team name on the product or monetary rewards. A sense of team identity is often encouraged by the use of team T-shirts, coffee mugs and other useable items. It is most important that other reward systems in the organisation, for instance based on individual contribution, do not cut across the reinforcement for team performance. In addition, for those teams where the longer-term objective is for all members to acquire the whole range of skills then a payment system which pays for skills gained rather than job done will be important.

Implications for the personnel function

Team-based working gives rise to a number of implications for the personnel function:

- there will need to be increasing emphasis on training the trainers so that teams can do as much of their own training as possible;
- training in selection techniques will need to be made available if teams are to select members without ongoing assistance from the personnel function;
- the personnel function will probably find it useful to produce guidance manuals for teams which give a framework for those personnel activities which will be carried out within the team, and which back-up any training given;
- there will be an increased demand, especially early on, for facilitation skills – a member of the personnel function will need to work with teams in reviewing their effectiveness and working out ways to improve;
- there will also probably be an increased demand for personnel consultancy skills and on-line advice;
- members of the personnel function may well find they spend more time coaching senior managers in changing their role from directing to coaching; and
- the personnel function may well become involved in efforts to change the culture of the organisation so that it is supportive of teamwork. The personnel function may be involved in supporting the changes in senior managers' roles and in helping them view problems as learning opportunities.

Team-based work seems set to increase on the premise that it will improve organisational performance. The two gritty issues which will need to be tackled are that not all employees will feel comfortable or perform their best in a team-based situation, and that not all teams are effective teams.

☐ SUMMARY PROPOSITIONS

19.1 Team-based working has been increasing due to a belief that this empowers employees, encourages them to use their full potential and results in better performance.

19.2 Three key variables in different types of teams are timespan of the team, interchangeability of team members and range of activities and functions involved.

19.3 There are four broad team types – production/service teams; cross-functional management teams; departmental teams and problem-solving teams.

19.4 Team effectiveness is dependent on the team having agreed goals and methods of working, and a climate where team members can be open and honest and use conflict in a constructive way.

19.5 Selection of team members is key and it is important to have a well balanced team in terms of the team roles described by Belbin (1993).

19.5 Increasing team-based work has an impact on the personnel role – including increased consultancy and facilitation, coaching of managers, training team trainers and producing team guides.

References

Banner, D. K. Kulisch, W. A. and Peery, N. S. (1992), 'Self-managing work teams (SMWT) and the Human Resource Function', *Management Decision*, vol. 30, no. 3, pp. 40–5.

Belbin, M. (1993), *Team Roles at Work*, London: Butterworth Heinemann.

Buchanan, D. (1992), 'High performance: new boundaries of acceptability in worker control'. In G. Salaman *et al.* (eds) *Human Resource Strategies*, London: Sage.

Casey, D. (1993), *Managing Learning in Organisations*, p. 60. Milton Keynes: Open University Press.

Garratt, B. (1990), *Creating a Learning Organisation*, Cambridge: Director Books.

Hoerr, J. (1989), 'The pay-off from teamwork', *Business Week*, July, pp. 56–62.

Kazenbach, J. R. and Smith, D. K. (1993), 'The discipline of teams', *Harvard Business Review*, March/April.

Meyer, C. (1994), 'How the right measures help teams excell', *Harvard Business Review*, May/June, pp. 95–103.

Moxon, P. (1993), *Building a Better Team*, Aldershot: Gower in association with ITD.

Oliva, L. M. (1992), *Partners not competitors – the age of teamwork and technology*, London: Idea Group Publishing.

Salaman, G. *et al.* (eds) (1992), *Human Resource strategies*. London: Sage.

Salem, M., Lazarus, H. and Cullen, J. (1992), 'Developing self-managing teams: structures and performance', *Journal of Management Development*, vol. 11, no. 3, pp. 24–32.

Tuckman, B. W. (1965), Development sequences in small groups', *Psychological Bulletin*, vol. 63, pp. 384–99.

Woodcock, M. (1979), *Team Development Manual*, Aldershot: Gower.

20 Managing diversity

We discriminate between people in many aspects of our life and work. The selection process in particular directly discriminates between people in order to offer the reward of a job to one but not the others. Certain forms of discrimination are acceptable but others are not, and have been made unlawful. Facts rather than prejudice, and relevant facts rather then irrelevant facts are important criteria in determining what type of discrimination is acceptable; but the law expects more from employers than this. It forces employers to exercise some form of social responsibility in the decisions they take in respect of potential and present employees. Discrimination in employment is inextricably linked with discrimination in the rest of society.

Disadvantaged groups and the argument for equal treatment

There are always certain groups in any society that are discriminated against unfavourably due to the prejudices and preconceptions of the people with whom they have to deal. The preconceptions are sometimes verbalised but often not, and the people holding these preconceptions may well be unaware of the way that they see and judge things and people. However, verbalised or not, these preconceived ideas influence the actions of the people who hold them and the way they deal with others. The effects of this can be seen in the employment arena. Disadvantaged groups who have already been identified are:

- women;
- people from other racial backgrounds;
- disabled people; and
- older people.

By far the most attention, in terms of public interest and legislation, has been paid to the first two groups. There is, however, some legislation relating to disabled people, and there have been some unsuccessful attempts by private members to establish legislation to protect older workers (see for example EOR No 48 1993c). In the

United States and some other countries legislation affecting the employment of people aged over 40 has already been adopted. The types of preconception that still affect the employment of these four groups are, for example, that women do not want too much responsibility at work because of their home commitments; that women are less reliable workers because of their home commitments; that employees would not want to work for a black supervisor; that the ability to fill out an application form in good English is an indication of an individual's potential to do a manual job; that someone who has suffered from mental illness will automatically crack up under the slightest pressure; that older people are less adaptable; and that they have become less interested in their careers.

These and many other unproven, and often more subtle, preconceptions can affect the access that these groups have to employment, their level of employment and their occupation, the treatment that they receive at work and their terms and conditions of employment.

There are two main schools of thought concerning the action that should be taken to alleviate the disadvantages that these groups suffer. One school supports legislative action, while the other argues that this will not be effective and that the only way is to change fundamentally the attitudes and preconceptions that are held about these groups. So far there has been an emphasis on legislative action in the hope that this will eventually affect attitudes.

Legislation, however, appears to have a poor track-record where social change is involved, and the evidence to date suggests that legislation to equalise employment opportunity has had a minimal impact. There have also been some attempts to change attitudes directly, for example, the International Year for the Disabled in 1981 and Opportunity 2000, which has encouraged employers to publicly commit themselves to the goals of increasing the quantity and quality of women's participation in the workforce, and set relevant organisational goals together with an improvement programme (see for example EOR, No 41 1992a).

A third, more extreme, and often less supported approach comes from those who advocate legislation to promote positive or reverse discrimination in order to compensate for a history of discrimination against specified groups and as a way of redressing the balance more immediately. The arguments for and against such an approach are fully discussed by Singer (1993).

The most pervasive argument against discrimination in employment or anywhere else is the argument based on an appreciation of human rights, and an ethical approach to the treatment of others. Work is a particularly important area as employment experiences have consequences for all aspects of people's lives.

There are also practical arguments supporting the equalisation of employment opportunity. A company that discriminates directly or indirectly against older or disabled people, women or ethnic minorities will be curtailing the potential of available talent, and employers are not well known for their complaints about the surplus of talent. Mahon (1989) demonstrates how an equal opportunities policy at Wellcome has shifted from good employment practice to sound business sense, and from personnel policies to business issues.

In this chapter we will first consider the issues and legislation relating to each disadvantaged group, together with the implications and impact of this; we will then review some of the strategies and actions which are recommended for the successful management of diversity in organisations.

Promoting gender equality

Using the conventional economic activity figures women form a large, and increasing, proportion of the working population. In 1971 women formed around 38 per cent of the workforce; in 1987 this had risen to around 42 per cent, and to 44 per cent by 1991. Comparisons with other countries indicate that there is a high participation rate in the United Kingdom (Women of Europe Supplements 1989), although it is recognised that many work part-time.

The idea of women working to support the family is not new. Prior to the industrial revolution, women took on a heavy productive burden, albeit doing their work from home. After the advent of the factory system women also worked long hours away from the home in factories, and played a much-acclaimed role in outside employment during the two World Wars.

Hakim (1993) puts forward the strong argument, based on alternative analysis, census and employment data, that the increasing participation of women in employment between the 1950s and the late 1980s is a myth, although a real increase does appear to have taken place since the late 1980s. Her analysis shows that:

> the much trumpeted rise in women's employment in Britain consisted entirely of the substitution of part-time for full-time jobs from 1851 to the late 1980s. (Hakim 1993, p. 12)

Hakim concludes from the research that only an increase in full-time employment is likely to have a wider impact on women's opportunities at work and elsewhere. For example, one perspective on the gaining of equality was that as participation rates increased, occupational segregation by sex would decrease as would the pay gap between male and female earnings. The few changes that we have seen in these areas then are most likely to be a direct result of the legislation itself, rather than the impact of increasing participation.

The chief legislation relating to the promotion of gender quality in employment are:

- The Equal Pay Act 1970.
- The Sex Discrimination Act 1975.
- The Employment Protection (Consolidation) Act 1978.
- The Social Security Act 1989.
- The Trade Union and Employment Rights Act 1993.

The Equal Pay Act 1970

This was the first of the legislation promoting equality at work between men and women. The Act was passed in 1970, came into full force on 29 December 1975, and was amended by the 1983 Equal Pay (Amendment) Regulations Statutory Instrument 1983, No. 1794 and the 1983 Industrial Tribunals (Rules and Procedures) (Equal Value Amendment) Regulations, which came into effect from January 1984. A very good guide, particularly to the amendments is to be found in Gill and Ungerson (1984).

The Act specifices circumstances where a woman's pay should be equal to that of a man. These are as follows.

1.   Where the woman can show that she is doing like work to a man – for example, a woman assembly worker sitting next to a male assembly worker, assembling similar items would clearly be entitled to equal pay. An example of this is *Capper Pass* v. *Lawton* where:

> A woman worked as a cook in a company directors' dining-room, providing lunches for between 10 and 20 persons. She sought equal pay with two assistant chefs who worked in the factory canteen and who prepared 350 meals each day. Other differences were that she worked 40 hours per week, and had no one supervising her, whereas the men worked 45 hours per week and were under the supervision of the head chef. The EAT upheld a decision of the Industrial Tribunal that she was entitled to equal pay. The work did not have to be the same; it was sufficient if it was broadly similar and the differences were not of practical importance. (Selwyn 1978, p. 80)

2.   Where a woman can show that she is carrying out work rated as equivalent to that of a man, for example, under a job evaluation scheme. In this case the woman may be in a clerical post, but if the organisation has an overall job evaluation scheme and her job is given the same points as a different job done by a man, then she can claim pay equal to the man.

3.   Since 1984, where a woman can show that her work is of equal value to that of a man's. Equal value is defined in terms of the demands made by the job and include skill, effort and decision-making. To claim under this rule there need be no job evaluation scheme, as demonstrated in the case when a cook at Cammell Laird claimed that her work was of equal value to painters and joiners (see Wainwright 1985). The cook was awarded equal pay.

Selection of a comparator

There is a number of limitations on the job holder which the woman may select as a comparator. The comparator needs to be of a different sex, but employed by the same employer and at an establishment covered by the same terms and conditions.

Enforcement of the Act

A woman may claim on an individual basis to a tribunal. Appeal is possible to an Employment Appeal Tribunal, then the Court of Appeal, and finally the House of Lords. Should the job be declared equal the individual applicant may then receive equal pay, which can be backdated to a maximum of two years before the date at which she applied to the tribunal.

Genuine material factors

An employer, however, may admit that a woman's job is equal to a man's in one of the three ways defined above, but that the pay is different and should remain different 'genuinely due to a material factor which is not the difference of sex' ((S1 (3) Amended Equal Pay Act). A genuinely material factor (GMF) applies in a slightly different way to like work and work rated as equivalent under a job evaluation scheme, from work of equal value cases. In the first the employer may cite a difference of personal factors such as length of service, superior skill or qualifications, higher productivity or red circling (that is protection of a previous higher salary). In relation to equal value cases skill shortages and market forces would come into play.

Ten years on from the amendment regulations there is widespread concern about their ineffectiveness due to complexity of both the substantive and procedural law (Gregory 1992). The Equal Opportunities Review (no. 52 1993) notes that there are fourteen stages to the equal value procedure and that it has been widely criticised by the judiciary for its complexity and obscurity, with severe delays and average claims taking more than two-and-a-half years. Pay differentials between men and women have changed very little except for a hike of women's pay upwards when the 1970 law came into force. Jarman (1994) identifies four current proposals that would improve the chances of equal value claims being made and achieved:

- collective remedies rather than solely successful do not trigger adjustments for other women who are in the same position;
- the provision of legal aid for equal value cases. The EOC claim that the cost of pursuing an equal value case is approximately £6500 and in cases where there is an appeal, costs frequently exceed £50,000 (EOR, no. 52, 1993). Clearly most individuals will have difficulty in funding a claim, and can not proceed unless their case is financed by the EOC;
- independent experts involved in these cases should be full time, be recruited in a different manner and be given adequate training. This redresses the concern that evaluation procedures are less than scientific and many systems have a built-in gender bias; and
- eliminating the material factors clause (with some exceptions), as this clause provides entry for the 'market forces' rationale.

The Sex Discrimination Act 1975

This Act came into force at the same time as the Equal Pay Act: December 1975. The Sex Discrimination Act promotes the equal treatment of women and men in employment and other areas. Equal treatment in employment centres on such activities as selection, the availability of opportunities for training and progression, the provision of benefits and facilities and dismissal. The Equal Opportunities Commission was established by the Sex Discrimination Act, and its duties are primarily to:

1.   Eliminate discrimination on the grounds of sex or married status.
2.   Generally promote equal opportunities between men and women.
3.   Monitor the implementation of the Sex Discrimination Act and the Equal Pay Act.

The Sex Discrimination Act makes discrimination against women or men, or discrimination on the grounds of marital status, unlawful in the employment sphere. The meaning of both direct and indirect discrimination is clarified in the Act.

Ways of discriminating

1.   Direct sex discrimination occurs when a person is treated less favourably due to their sex than a person of the opposite sex would be in similar circumstances. For example, advertising for a man to do a job which could equally well be done by a woman.

2.   Direct marriage discrimination occurs when a married person is treated less favourably, due to their married status, than a single person of the same sex would be treated in similar circumstances. This would apply if a married woman was denied promotion because she was married, and it was considered that she might leave to follow her husband's job or start a family. The Act makes no mention of discrimination against employees on the basis of their unmarried status, and this is not unlawful.

3.   Indirect sex discrimination occurs when a requirement or condition is applied equally to men and women. However, the condition has the effect that in practice it disadvantages a significantly larger proportion of one sex than the other, because they find it harder to fulfil, and it cannot be justified on any grounds other than sex. Indirect sex discrimination has been demonstrated by the age limit of twenty-eight years, maximum, for entry into the executive officer grade of the civil service. In the case of *Price* v. *The Civil Service Commission* it was successfully argued that this was considerably disadvantageous to women as they were often raising a family at this time, and that therefore the age limit constituted indirect discrimination (IPM 1978; EOC 1985b, Sex Discrimination Decisions no. 9).

4.   Indirect marriage discrimination occurs when an employer places a requirement or condition on both married and unmarried people, but the practical effect of this is that a significantly smaller proportion of married people can comply compared with single people of the same sex, and there is no other justification for the condition than their marital status. An employer who offered promotion on the basis that the employee was prepared to be away from home for considerable spells of time, when in reality this was never or rarely required would be indirectly discriminating on the grounds of married status. If the spells away from home were needed in practice then the employer would not be acting unlawfully.

5.   Victimisation occurs when an employer treats an employee of either sex less favourably than other employees would be treated on the grounds that they

have been involved in, or intend to be involved in (or is suspected of either of these), proceedings against the employer under the Sex Discrimination Act or the Equal Pay Act.

Unlawful discrimination

In the employment sphere it is unlawful to discriminate on the basis of sex or married status in relation to potential and present employees.

1. *Potential employees;* it is unlawful to discriminate in recruitment arrangements, for example in advertising and interviewing; and in the terms and conditions of a job offer, for example, in whether a permanent or temporary position is offered. It is also unlawful to discriminate in the adoption of selection criteria, in selection methods and in other selection matters, for example in refusing or deliberately omitting to offer employment because of a person's sex.

   In *Batisha* v. *Say*, a woman was turned down for a job as a cave guide because 'it is a man's job', and in *Munroe* v. *Allied Supplies* a man was not taken on as a cook because women employees would not work with him. In both cases it was held that an act of discrimination had occurred. (Selwyn (1978, p. 70)

2. *Present employees:* it is unlawful to discriminate in the provision of opportunities for promotion, transfer or training; in the provision of facilities or services such as study leave or company cars; and in unfavourable treatment, such as dismissal.

   In *Gubala* v. *Crompton Parkinson*, the choice of a dismissal in a redundancy situation lay between a man and a woman. The woman had longer overall service, but the employers took into account that the man was 58 years old and had a family to support and a mortgage to keep up. The woman was young and married with a husband who was working, and she was dismissed. It was held that this amounted to unlawful discrimination; the tribunal refused to accept the 'breadwinner' criteria as a basis for redundancy selection. (Selwyn 1978, p. 72)

Exceptions to the Sex Discrimination Act

There are some exemptions from the Act; for example, employers are allowed to discriminate due to a genuine occupational qualification (GOQ) for the job – for example in modelling, acting, or jobs such as toilet attendant.

The Act does does not allow positive discrimination, but does allow positive action. For example, if a job has been done solely or mainly by members of one sex over the past year, then employers can provide special training purely for members of the other sex. They are also allowed to specifically encourage applications from this group, but not to favour them in any way in the selection procedure.

Enforcement of the Sex Discrimination Act

There are two aspects to enforcement.

1. The EOC is the only body that can take action about instructions or pressure to discriminate, about discriminatory practices or advertisements, or persistent discrimination.

2.   In all other cases any individual who feel they have suffered as a result of discrimination may make a claim to a Tribunal as described under the Equal Pay Act.

Further details about enforcement may be found in Guidelines for Equal Opportunities Employers (EOC 1986).

The Employment Protection (Consolidation) Act 1978

The 1980 Employment Act provided the right to paid time off during working hours for antenatal care. In effect this was done by adding a new section to the Employment Protection Act 1975 include the right not to be unfairly dismissed due to pregnancy or a reason connected with pregnancy; the right to six weeks' maternity pay; and the right to return to work after the birth of a child. These rights have since been extended.

The Social Security Act 1989

From 1 January 1993 it was unlawful for occupational benefit schemes (including health insurance and pensions) to discriminate directly or indirectly on grounds of sex. Areas such as survivors' benefits, optional pensions and pensionable age are, however, not covered by the Act. Other provisions related to pregnancy and maternity. In-depth explanations of the provisions may be found in Industrial Relations Review and Report (Anon. 1989, no. 384).

Trade Union and Employment Rights Act 1993

This act makes further improvements to women's employment rights, especially in relation to maternity. The main provisions which affect equal opportunities are to:

- make dismissal for any reason connected with pregnancy unlawful;
- remove the service qualification for bringing an unfair dismissal claim on the grounds of pregnancy;
- allow new provision for suspension from work on pregnancy grounds due to health and safety reasons; and
- regardless of service provides for a minimum of fourteen weeks' maternity leave, and specifies that during this period all other terms and conditions except for actual remuneration must be maintained.

In addition the Act allows measures restricting the publicity of sexual harassment cases, new rules for settling sex and race discrimination cases out of court and new rights to challenge collective agreements on the grounds that they are discriminatory. The pregnancy and maternity sections of the act substitute new sections for many provisions in the Employment Protection (Consolidation) Act.

Table 20.1 *Summary of the EOG's model Equal Opportunity Policy*

1.	*Introduction:* desirability of the policy and that it is required to be strictly adhered to
2.	*Definitions:* direct and indirect discrimination defined
3.	*General statement of policy:* a commitment to equal treatment and the belief that this is also in the interests of the organisation. Staff in the organisation should be made aware of the policy and key personnel trained in the policy
4.	*Possible preconceptions:* examples of preconceptions that may be erroneously held about individuals due to their sex or marital status
5.	*Recruitment and promotion:* care to be taken that recruitment information has an equal chance of reaching both sexes and does not indicate a preference for one group of applicants. Care that job requirements are justifiable and that interviews conducted on an objective basis. An intention not to discriminate in promotion
6.	*Training:* an intention not to discriminate with some further details
7.	*Terms and conditions of service and facilities:* an intention not to discriminate
8.	*Monitoring:* nomination of a person responsible for monitoring the effectiveness of the policy and with overall responsibility for implementation. An intention to review the policy and procedures. Intention to rectify any areas where employees/applicants are found not to be receiving equal treatment
9.	*Grievances and victimisation:* an intention to deal effectively with grievances and a note of the victimisation clauses in the Act

Source: Summarised from EOC 1985

Equal opportunity policies

Equal opportunities policies are not required by law but are recommended, and the Equal Opportunities Commission produces a model policy for these employers who wish to adapt this for use in their own organisation. A summary of the EOC's model policy is found in Table 20.1, and the IPD strongly recommend the use of such policies.

Practical implications of the legislation to promote gender equality

The legislation has several implications for personnel management.

Advertisements, notes and circulars

Advertisements must not discriminate on the basis of sex or marital status. This means that job titles should either be sexless, as in 'cashier', 'machinist' or 'salesperson', or indicate an acceptability of either sex, as in 'waiter/waitress' or 'manager/manageress'. If a job title is used indicating one sex, such as 'chairman', this must be accompanied by a statement that both men and women are invited to apply. To save any misunderstandings, it may be wise to use this statement in all advertisements. Illustrations used in advertisements and in recruitment literature should depict both men and women.

Other recruitment procedures

Personnel managers also need to consider the implications of other recruitment procedures. For example, in admitting schoolchildren into the organisation for a careers visit, care should be taken that the boys are not shown only round the parts of the factory where the traditional male jobs are to be found, while the girls are only shown around the canteen and the offices. Similarly, if local schools are visited, then both boys' and girls' schools should be included.

Selection procedures

Equal opportunities legislation reinforces the need for job analysis and the production of job descriptions and person specifications. In particular, the person specification should be carefully considered to ensure that the person requirements are not unnecessarily restrictive and indirectly discriminate between men and women, making it easier for one group to comply. Care should also be taken that any selection tests have been well validated in that they have been demonstrated to predict performance in the job, and that they have been developed using data from both sexes.

The interview

Although interviewers may not be able to banish their personal prejudices and stereotypes, an awareness of these may at least allow some compensation. Other methods, such as interviewing in a structured and consistent way, can also be used to help limit the effects of preconceptions. Care should also be taken to avoid questions that may indicate an intention to discriminate, even where discrimination is not intended; for example, questioning a woman about her husband and domestic arrangements (although these questions would not in themselves constitute discrimination if they were also put to male interviewees and the information collected used in exactly the same way). Similarly, questions about dependants are fair if are asked of both sexes. In fact, discriminating against someone on the grounds of their dependants is not unfair *so long as men and women are treated equally in this respect*. It would, however, be reasonable to assume that an individual applying for a job will have made or will make suitable arrangements for the care of dependants. We recommend that questions about domestic situations and responsibilities should not be asked. Finally, it is always wise to keep notes of an interview and the reasons for rejection in the event of a claim for unfair discrimination.

REVIEW TOPIC 20.1

We have suggested five implications for personnel managers of the legislation relating to women.
What other major implications are the in your organisation?
What is the role of the personnel function in monitoring the effects of the legislation?

Job evaluation

If a scheme is already in existence it should be reviewed periodically to ensure that it does not discriminate between men and women.

Effects of the legislation to promote equal opportunity on the basis of sex

There is some evidence to suggest that women are beginning to enter some previously male-dominated occupations; for example, women priests in the Church of England have now been ordained, but not without deep and continuing debate. Similarly, men are beginning to enter some previously female-only occupations, such as midwifery. There are, however, still few women in higher levels of management and not many male secretaries. An NEDCO report states that only 4 per cent of senior and middle management, 1–2 per cent of senior executives, 1.8 per cent of executive directors and 5.1 per cent of non-executive directors are women (EOR, 1993a, no. 47). Snell, Glucklich and Povall (1981) report that widespread job segregation has continued. Most women remain in clerical and related, catering and cleaning and selling occupations, often characterised by part-time work, and in a mainly narrow range of industrial sectors. Dickens and Colling (1990) explain how continued job segregation in respect of both role and hours/arrangements is one of the influence factors which results in discriminatory agreements between employers and unions. They also highlight the problem of job evaluation schemes which perpetuate old values and hence encourage rather than discourage equality of pay. Some progress has been made towards equal pay but these factors still remain as barriers to be overcome. Women's pay as a percentage of men's pay was 77 per cent in 1990, increased from 63 per cent prior to the Equal Pay Act. However, if overtime earning is taken into account the percentage reduces to 68 per cent (Gregory 1992). The abolition of the Wages Councils will not help in this respect.

Although women have equal access to pension schemes under the Sex Discrimination Act, and many other inequalities in schemes are now illegal under the Social Security Act 1989, McGoldrick's (1984) comments are still appropriate. She notes that pensions schemes still work to women's disadvantage as they are normally organised and administered on the basis of traditional male employment patterns – such as rewarding long, continuous service and based on full-time rather than part-time employment.

There has been a clear removal of overt discrimination, particularly in recruitment advertising, following on quickly from the Acts, but there is much less evidence of changes in training and promotion practices, and no use of the provision enabling positive action in training (Snell, Glucklich and Povall 1981). For a discussion of career development and discrimination see Chapter 25.

In spite of the EOC's model Equal Opportunity Policy and the IPD's support for such policies, our recent research in 1984 indicates that such policies are only produced by 60 per cent of organisations, and that on the whole they are not seen as very useful. Indeed, a large number of organisations saw their policy as irrelevant.

The effects of the legislation have been limited. To some extent this was recognised at the outset:

> Nobody believes that legislation by itself can eradicate overnight a whole range of attitudes which are rooted in custom, and are, for that very reason, often unchallenged because unrecognised. But if the law cannot change attitudes overnight, it can, and does effect change slowly. (Select Committee on the Anti-discrimination Bill (House of Lords) 1972/3, p. 22)

As this comment recognises, the roots of discrimination go very deep. Simmons (1989) talks about challenging a system of institutional discrimination and anti-female conditioning in the prevailing culture. Recognising that men and women present different cultures at work, and that this diversity needs to be managed, is key to promoting a positive environment of equal opportunity, which goes beyond merely fulfilling the demands of the statutory codes. Masreliez-Steen (1989) explains how men and women have different perceptions, interpretations of reality, languages and ways of solving problems which, if properly used, can be a benefit to the whole organisation as they are complementary. She described women as having a collectivist culture where they form groups, avoid the spotlight, see rank as unimportant and have few but close contacts. Alternatively, men are described as having an individualistic culture, where they form teams, 'develop a profile', enjoy competition and have many superficial contacts. The result of this is that men and women behave in different ways, often fail to understand each other and experience 'culture clash'. However, the difference is about how things are done and not what is achieved.

The fact that women have a different culture with different strengths and weaknesses means that women need managing and developing in a different way. They need different forms of support and coaching. For example, women more often need help to understand the need for making wider contacts and how to make them. In order to manage such diversity, key management competencies for the future would be: concern with image, process awareness, interpersonal awareness/sensitivity, developing subordinates and gaining commitment.

Another aspect of the management of diversity is that women need different forms of organisational support, particularly in terms of flexibility, to enable them to combine successfully a career with parenthood. Such forms of support include career breaks, flexible working hours, annual hours, job sharing and part-time work, childcare facilities and support. Liff (1989) also suggests that non-linear career paths and the restructuring of jobs are important. Progress in these areas is patchy. Field and Paddison (1989) comment that women in the United Kingdom spend less time out of paid employment than women in any other EC country, and that 90 per cent of women are returning to work after having children. However, there is less nursery provision for the under-fives in the United Kingdom than the rest of Europe (Anon., Industrial Relations Review and Report 1988). Anecdotal evidence suggests that childcare provision is a difficult need to meet as needs vary so considerably, that it is almost impossible for the employer to win. Some companies have surveyed present and/or potential women employees to help identify some of their support needs, as did Mothercare (Arkin 1990).

Promoting racial equality

Between the 1950s and early 1970s there was immigration largely of black workers from the New Commonwealth countries, and it was an awareness that this group of people was disadvantaged in employment and other areas that prompted anti-discrimination legislation. The legislation, however, is designed to apply to any racial minority group.

Black workers are particularly at risk because not only are their customs and practices often different from those of our indigenous population, although this decreases over time, but their colour clearly identifies them as being different.

Immigrant labour in the United Kingdom was identified as being heavily concentrated in less desirable, non-skilled, manual jobs, causing Smith (1974) to remark that the composition of the minority workforce was 'markedly different, by type of job, from the total workforce' (in Braham *et al.* 1981). Smith also comments that on the basis of the preliminary results of the 1971 Census, minority groups are almost twice as likely as white people to be unemployed. There has been legislation since 1968 making it unlawful for employers to discriminate directly on the grounds of race, colour, nationality or ethnic origin. The Race Relations Act 1976 replaces the 1968 Act and extends it by, for example, making indirect discrimination illegal, using a similar approach to the Sex Discrimination Act. The 1976 Act also set up the Commission for Racial Equality with similar powers to the Equal Opportunities Commission.

The Race Relations Act 1976

The Act identifies ways in which racial minority groups may be discriminated against, and makes these illegal.

1. Direct discrimination occurs if an employer treats an employee, or prospective employee, less favourably than they treat, or would treat other employees, on the grounds of their race. Racial grounds have been defined as colour, race or nationality or ethnic or national origin. Less favourable treatment may occur, for example in selection for recruitment, promotion, shiftwork, overtime and so on. Discrimination may also occur in the work environment, for example in the use of separate canteens.

2. Indirect discrimination is defined in the same way as for the Sex Discrimination Act. An example here would be requiring a good standard of written English for a manual labourer's job:

    > To insist that applicants for a specified job should be of a certain minimum height may well be discriminatory against Indians unless it can be shown that the requirement is justifed. But to insist that workers on a building site should wear steel helmets would not be discriminatory against Sikhs, the condition is capable of being justified irrespective of the race of the person concerned (see *Singh* v. *Lyons Maid* in Selwyn 1978, p. 87)

3. Victimisation provisions give individuals the right of complaint to an industrial tribunal, as with the Sex Discrimination Act, if they feel they have been victimised in their employment because they have been connected with bringing proceedings under the Act.

Some exceptions to the Race Relations Act are specified, and in these areas discrimination in recruitment, training, promotion or transfers on the grounds of 'genuine occupational qualification' is acceptable. These are as follows.

1. *Entertainment:* if it is necessary to have a person of a particular racial group to achieve an authentic presentation.
2. *Artistic or photographic modelling:* if it is necessary to use a person from a particular racial group to provide authenticity for a work of art, visual image or sequence.
3. *Specialised restaurants:* if it is necessary to have a person from a particular racial group to sustain the special setting of an establishment where food or drink is served to the public, such as a Chinese restaurant.
4. *Community social workers:* if a person provides personal services to members of a particular racial group and the services can best be provided by someone of the same racial group.

However, these do not permit discriminatory treatment in the terms and conditions of employment.

Enforcement of the Race Relations Act

The pattern of enforcement is similar to that for the Sex Discrimination Act. Individuals who feel they have been discriminated against can complain to a tribunal, and the Commission for Racial Equality can also bring complaints to a tribunal where there may be direct discriminatory practices, but no particular casualty, or in cases of discriminatory advertisements.

Practical implications of legislation promoting racial equality

The implications for the personnel manager run along the same lines as for the Sex Discrimination Act, in particular the following.

Advertisements
Advertisements should be carefully worded so that there is no indication that people of some racial backgrounds are preferred to others. A statement to this effect, as with the Sex Discrimination Act, may well be the best policy. Illustrations should show a mix of different races. Personnel managers also need to be careful where

they place advertisements. An internally-placed advertisement in an organisation employing only white people may constitute indirect discrimination against those racial groups who will have less chance to hear about the job from their friends.

Selection procedures

The use of a job description and specification are again very helpful here, and care should be taken not to draw up a specification that is unjustifiably demanding. When considering individuals from different racial groups against this specification it is important to distinguish between attainment and potential. People from disadvantaged groups often have a poor record of attainment by employers' standards, but their potential to do the job may at the same time be very good. Also, as a general rule, application forms require a level of English in excess of job requirements and so selection on that basis may constitute unfair discrimination against those whose mother tongue is not English and yet may be suitable employees (Runnymede Trust and BPS 1980).

Selection tests

The use of selection test should be carefully monitored. Many tests discriminate against people from minority backgrounds due to assumptions made when the tests were designed and due to the fact they may have ben standardised on, for example, all-white groups of individuals. Also, people from different racial backgrounds may be at a disadvantage because the ethos of testing is more alien to their culture (IPM 1978).

Personnel managers will overcome these difficulties if they scrutinise very carefully, for example, a test that rejects 70 per cent of black applicants but only 30 per cent of white applicants. They must be able to show that this cut-off point is justifiable and that the test is valid in terms of job performance. It is also worthwhile considering whether there are equally valid selection criteria that can be used which have a less adverse impact on disadvantaged groups. If tests are used, personnel managers should try to ensure that these are 'culture-fair' (although it has been argued that this is impossible (Runnymede Trust 1980, p. 23)); that adequate pretest orientation is given, for example, about the purpose of testing; that pretest practice is given; and perhaps produce a self-help pamphlet.

Interviewing

One of the common problems with interviewing is the tendency of interviewers to select in their own image (Runnymede Trust 1980). This works against minority groups and also reinforces the current structure of the workforce. Interviewers need to be aware of this problem as well as the others mentioned under the Sex Discrimination Act. Interviewers also need consciously to remember that the way individuals present themselves is partly dependent on their culture and background. Things that are acceptable, or even expected, in one culture may not be acceptable in another.

Effects of the legislation to promote equal opportunity on the grounds of race

In spite of the legislation evidence of discrimination continues to exist. The Equal Opportunities Review in 1994 reports that:

> unemployment rates for ethnic minority groups were about double those of the white population, even when age, sex and level of qualification were taken into account (EOC 1994, C p. 25)

The same article demonstrates continued segration in the labour market with about 29 per cent of ethnic minority male employees being employed in the hotel, catering and repairs and distribution sectors, compared with 17 per cent for men who are white. Similar percentages were found for manufacturing industry, but for construction the reverse is true with 11 per cent of white men, but only 4 per cent of racial minorities being employed here.

Evidence of discrimination in the recruitment process is also well documented. Noon's (1993) research involved sending speculative letters to 100 employers randomly selected from the top 1000 employers. Two letters, identical in their request for information on the company's graduate training scheme and the qualifications of the sender, were sent to each company. The only difference was the name – John Evans and Sanjay Patel, identifying them as belonging to different ethnic groups. Although there was no statistical difference in reply rate to each individual, there was a statistical difference in the quality of reply as measured by the helpfulness in terms of information and encouragement given. Evans received the more helpful replies. Those organisations with an Equal Opportunities policy were less likely to discriminate in the type of replies sent to each person, but where different treatment was given this was always in favour of Evans. Brown and Gay (1986) using actors found in their research in Manchester, London and Birmingham that discrimination against ethnic minority candidates took place in one-third of organisations that had advertised vacancies in the press.

In 1984 a code of practice was issued by the Commission for Racial Equality; however, research in 1991 (CRE 1992) showed an almost 'universal disregard' for the code in the hotel sector, a sector of heavy employment for minority racial groups.

The number of successful cases brought before tribunals each year is significant compared with the scale of racial discrimination, which research studies have revealed (Runnymede Trust 1979). There were only forty-seven successful racial discrimination cases at industrial tribunals in 1990–1 (CRE 1992). Jenkins (1986) notes some severe problems with the way that indirect discrimination is framed by the law – that it was ambiguous and placed a burden of proof to show that the discrimination was not justifiable. It is still possible to use selection criteria which demand specific individual job experiences, and also to select on the basis of 'who will fit in' due to business necessity. There are many other concerns about current UK legislation and the authors of *Measure for Measure* note:

The majority (of employers) make no specific efforts to advance equal opportunities practice. A significant minority have issued an equal opportunities policy statement, and pro-active organisations have developed codes of practice, monitoring and positive action programmes. All these practical means of combatting racial discrimination in the workplace are optional rather than required (*Measure for Measure*, DoE 1992)

In addition there is little help from Europe. Contrary to the position of employment concerning fair treatment for women, the United Kingdom generally has better legal protection for racial minority groups, and the EU has been remarkably reticent about agreeing and issuing directives to improve this position. Harmonisation in this case would mean a drop in minimum protection rather than an improvement!

In response to the current position the CRE have made some far-reaching recommendations in their second review (1991, reported in 1992) of the Race Relations Act. These recommendations include:

- a new definition of indirect discrimination;
- ethnic monitoring should be legally binding as in the Fair Employment Act 1989 which required religious monitoring in Northern Ireland;
- employers should have a legal requirement to identify equality targets (not quotas);
- the Act should apply in more areas of employment than it presently does;
- the CRE should be enabled to take on an inspectoral role, to make spot checks on employers' practices, rather than just an investigatory role to research a problem area already identified;
- legal aid for all racial discrimination cases;
- a special tribunal division should be set up to deal with discrimination cases in order to build up expertise;
- tribunal remedies, for example compensation, can apply to more than the individual bringing the case if appropriate others register their involvement;
- tribunals should be able to impose non-discrimination notices, where appropriate, to apply to a situation from which an individual has successfully proved discrimination; and
- the tribunal should have power to impose special training on an organisation

Mars Ltd

Tony Harbour (1980) reports that managers at Mars have been consciously concerned with being an equal opportunities employer for some time, and decided to use ethnic monitoring, partly to see if their ethnic minorities policy was working, and to identify any problems in recruitment, promotion, transfer, merit and disciplinary practices. Ethnic data were asked for on application forms and were also put onto both personnel and payroll records all of which were accessible for the individual concerned. Equality in recruitment was measured by comparing the racial structure of the workforce at Mars with that in the local area, and the racial groups used were: Caucasian, Latin, Negro, Asian, Arabic and Oriental. Comparisons of the racial structure of different work groups, departments and grades were also made.

London Borough of Hackney

John Carr, Equal Opportunities Officer (1980) argues that there is a wide range of employment activities that need to be monitored and suggests a list of the areas that the London Borough of Hackney intend to cover:

(a) Wording, presentation and media used for advertising.
(b) Responses to advertising.
(c) Shortlisting from returned application forms.
(d) Interviewing.
(e) Offers of employment.
(f) Acceptance of offers of employment.
(g) Reviews of probationary periods.
(h) Job specifications and criteria for employment (related to (a)–(f)).
(i) Terms and conditions.
(j) Promotions.
(k) Regrading.
(l) Transfers.
(m) Disciplinary procedures.
(n) Grievance procedure.
(o) Dismissals.
(p) Leavers in employment with the borough.
(q) Reasons for leaving.
(r) Access to and take up of training opportunities.
(s) Existing staff.

(Carr 1980, pp. 20–1)

These monitoring exercises will be used to provide statistical tables reflecting the position of ethnic minorities. Carr suggests that the comparison of statistics over a period of time is the most vital factor and that the frequency of monitoring needs to be carefully considered. He points to the importance of qualitative as well as quantitative information.

where discrimination has been proved, and/or to impose actions to encourage specific racial groups (these are permitted, but voluntary, at present).

The experiences of two organisations voluntarily adopting ethnic monitoring are shown in the boxes.

REVIEW TOPIC 20.2

Prepare an equal opportunity policy for racial equality for the organisation in which you work.

Promoting equality for disabled people

There are 420,000 people who registered as disabled in 1984. The true figure of disabled people in the workforce must be more than this. Walker (1986) notes that disabled people have always experienced higher levels of unemployment than the workforce as a whole and once unemployed, have greater difficulty in returning to work and therefore often remain unemployed for longer periods. The Labour Force Survey in 1992 found that 25 per cent of registered disabled men and 18 per cent of registered disabled women were unemployed compared with 12 per cent and 8 per cent respectively, of their able-bodied counterparts. Their choice of job is often restricted and where they do find work it is likely to be in low-paid, less attractive jobs. The HMSO (1989) reported that disabled employees earned, on average, 20 per cent less than non-disabled employees. Prescott-Clarke (1990) notes that disabled people are underpresented in professional and managerial jobs. Periods of high general unemployment exacerbate these problems. Employers have a wide range of concerns regarding the employment of disabled people. These include worries about general standards of attendance and health, safety at work, eligibility for pension schemes and possible requirements for alterations to premises and equipment.

The legal framework, local Placement, Assessment and Counselling Teams and the Major Organisations Development Unit

Walker (1986) comments that political and moral pressure to make provision for the war disabled, together with a practical need to reduce labour shortages, resulted in the setting up of the Tomlinson Committee on the rehabilitation and resettlement of disabled persons. The recommendations of this committee resulted in the 1944 Disabled Persons (Employment) Act which, together with the 1958 Act of the same name, is the main legislation in operation, with some additional regulations coming into force in 1980. The legislation provides for:

1. Assessment of disabled people.
2. Rehabilitation of disabled people.
3. Retraining of disabled people.
4. A register of people with disabilities.
5. A quota scheme in respect of registered disabled people.
6. Reserved employment for disabled people, see below.
7. Sheltered employment, for example Remploy.

The Manpower Services Commission Employment Division (1984) produced a Code of Good Practice on the Employment of Disabled People (1984), which was updated in 1993 by Employment Services. At Job Centres there are specialist Disablement Employment Advisors who specifically assist disabled people in their search for employment and training. They also liaise with employers regarding the employment of disabled people. These employment advisors are part of the new local Placement,

Assessment and Counselling Teams (PACTs) which replace the old Disablement Resettlement Officers, the Employment Rehabilitation Service and the Disablement Advisory Service. There are 70 PACTs throughout the country. In 1987 the Major Organisations Development Unit (MODU) was set up as part of the disablement branch of Employment Services. Members of MODU provide a consultancy service to large national companies to help them recruit, develop and retain disabled employees.

The quota scheme

It is in the areas of the quota scheme and reserved occupations that the 1944 Act has most implications for employers. The quota scheme is a method of positive discrimination where every employer of more than twenty people has to employ sufficient disabled people to make up 3 per cent of their total workforce. If firms are under their quota they should not employ another non-disabled person until they are up to quota unless they have obtained a special permit.

Government statistics for 1993 (EOR, 1994a, no. 56) show that only 18.9 per cent of employers fulfil their quota obligations. There has been much discussion over the future of the quota scheme, but it has been decided to retain it for the time being in spite of its reducing effectiveness. The Equal Opportunities Review (1994a, no. 56) reports that since the scheme began, only ten firms have been prosecuted. Disablement Employment Advisers have attempted to persuade employers to take on disabled people rather than invoking the law. An MSC working group considering ways of improving the quota scheme has made a number of recommendations including changes in the issue of permits and methods of increasing employers' awareness of the quota scheme (MSC 1985). Walker, however, comments: 'These reforms are no substitute for the establishment of clear rights to employment protection along the lines of other European countries such as West Germany' (Walker 1986, p. 45).

Reserved occupations

In addition, certain jobs are reserved or designated to be filled only be registered disabled people. To date, these jobs are car park and lift attendant.

Policy on the employment of disabled people

All employers with 250 or more staff, on average, are obliged to include in the Directors' Report a statement of their policy on the employment of disabled people. The Code of Good Practice recommends that this policy should include items about: communication and consultation in the drawing up of the policy; objectives of the policy; the role of managers, employees and their representatives; the advice and help that are planned to be used; good practices and the areas where these are particularly important; and how it is planned to monitor and assess the policy.

The disability symbol

This was introduced in 1990 and relaunched in June 1993. The scheme permits an employer to use the disability tick symbol in advertisements if they demonstrate their pursuit of five minimum commitments to disabled people. These commitments are:

- guaranteed job interviews for all disabled applicants who meet the minimum criteria for the job;
- consultation with current disabled employees;
- retention of disabled workers;
- efforts to raise disability awareness; and
- production of an annual review of the commitments and the achievements that have been made.

Examples of employers who have achieved this standard are found in The Equal Opportunities Review no. 43 (1992b) and 56 (1994a).

Access to work scheme

This scheme provides help, which may be worth thousands of pounds, to provide essential equipment and facilities to enable a disabled worker to be appointed to a job.

Promoting equal treatment for older workers

Older workers are the least protected of all the groups we have looked at in this chapter, and in this country there is no specific legisaltion relating to them. The main protection for the older employee is against redundancy, for which they will be financially compensated, but there is no protection for them in seeking fresh employment, training or promotion. The problems of unemployment in the 1980s and 90s have tended to miltate against the employment prospects of those who are older, because the worker population appears to be too large for our total employment requirements. People have been under pressure to retire early in many circumstances and find it very difficult to continue working after normal retirement age.

In the United States and New Zealand legislation has been introduced to prevent discrimination in employment on the grounds of age. There are no signs of this spreading to the United Kingdom, but we need to consider not only whether citizens' rights are being impaired because of the lack of such legislation, but also – as with other types of anti-discrimination legislation – whether the effectiveness of organisations is being impaired by people suggesting to older employees that they are becoming less effective and that they may be standing in the way of the legitimate career aspirations of others.

In a recent survey by the Equal Opportunities Review (no. 48 1993) of 4000 job advertisements, around one-third specified age qualifications, which is slightly more than their survey four years ago. Itzin and Phillipson (1993) in their qualitative and quantitative study of local authorities note some improvements in terms of fewer upper age limits being applied. They did, however find that the wording of some advertisements puts older workers off from applying. Words like 'innovative', 'dynamic' and 'forward thinking' suggest a picture of a young applicant. They also identified discrimination at both the shortlisting and interview stage, with line managers having negative perceptions of older workers – seeing them as less able to cope with change, training or technology and less interested in their careers.

Itzin and Phillipson also found that although three-quarters of the 221 employers who responded to their questionnaire had an Equal Opportunities Policy, only one-third of the 221 included age in this.

Respondents to a survey of IPM members (Warr, reported in EOR 1993c) did identify some ways in which younger employees were preferred, but also a number of ways in which older workers were preferred. Workers over 40 years old were seen to be more loyal and conscientious, to have better interpersonal skills and be more efficient in the job.

The Equal Opportunities Review (1993c) when reviewing the research about older workers concluded that experience in the job counteracts any age related factors lowering productivity; that older workers are generally more satisfied with their jobs and have less accidents and a better absence record; and that in any case there is considerable variation within individuals.

Warr also reports that 86 per cent of personnel managers responding to his survey were keen to see legislation or at least a voluntary code developed by the government to protect older workers from discrimination. There have been a number of failed attempts via Private Members' Bills to institute legislation, and at present legal protection does not seem likely.

Managing diversity

The emphasis so far in this chapter has been on separate groups who are discriminated against in employment, and we have concentrated on the meeting of legal obligations. This is an important starting point, but obviously a limited perspective. The words 'managing diversity' have been used to represent an integrated and more fundamental perspective. Ellis and Sonnenfield (1994) describe managing diversity as:

> ... the challenge of meeting the needs of a culturally diverse workforce and of sensitising workers and managers to differences associated with gender, race, age and nationality in an attempt to maximise the potential productivity of all employees. (p. 82)

We would add employees with disability to this definition.

Jackson *et al.* (1993) propose a series of stages and levels that organisations go through in becoming a multicultural organisation:

- *Level 1, stage 1: the exclusionary organisation.* This organisation maintains the power of dominant groups in the organisation, and excludes others.

- *Level 1, stage 2: the club.* The club still excludes people but in a less explicit way. Some members of minority groups are allowed to join in as long as they conform to predefined norms.

- *Level 2, stage 3: the compliance organisation.* This organisation recognises that there are other perspectives, but don't want to do anything to rock the boat. They may actively recruit minority groups at the bottom of the organisation and make some token appointments.

- *Level 2, stage 4: the affirmative action organisation.* This organisation is committed to eliminating discrimination and encourages employees to examine their attitudes and think differently. There is strong support for the development of new employees from minority groups.

- *Level 3, stage 5: the redefining organisation.* The redefining organisation is not satisfed with being anti-racist and so examines all it does, and its culture, to see the impact of these on its diverse multicultural workforce. It develops and implements policies to distribute power among all diverse groups.

- *Level 3, stage 6: the multicultural organisation.* This organisation reflects the contribution and interests of all its diverse members in everything it does and espouses. All members are full participants of the organisation and there is recognition of a broader social responsibility – to educate others outside the organisation and to have an impact on external oppression.

LaFasto (1993), presents a similar but simpler model and this is shown in Figure 20.1. In a UK situation most organisations remain working towards compliance, but there are a number who are attempting to manage diversity. Ross and Schneider (1992) argue for the business case for diversity to be made, and they identify the difference between seeking equal opportunity and managing diversity. They suggest that diversity approaches are:

- internally driven, not externally imposed;
- focused on individuals rather than groups;
- focused on the total culture of the organisation rather than simply the systems used; and
- the responsibility of all in the organisation and not only the personnel function.

Ross and Schneider (1992) advocate a strategic approach to managing diversity which involves the following.

1. Diagnosis of the current situation in terms of statistics, policy and culture, and looking at both issues and causes.

2. Setting aims which involves the business case for equal opportunities, identifying the critical role of commitment from the top of the organisation, and a vision of what the organisation would look like if it successfully managed diversity.

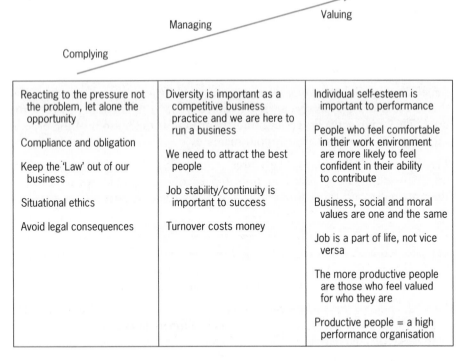

Complying   Managing   Valuing

Reacting to the pressure not the problem, let alone the opportunity	Diversity is important as a competitive business practice and we are here to run a business	Individual self-esteem is important to performance
Compliance and obligation	We need to attract the best people	People who feel comfortable in their work environment are more likely to feel confident in their ability to contribute
Keep the 'Law' out of our business	Job stability/continuity is important to success	Business, social and moral values are one and the same
Situational ethics	Turnover costs money	Job is a part of life, not vice versa
Avoid legal consequences		The more productive people are those who feel valued for who they are
		Productive people = a high performance organisation

Figure 20.1 Conceptual model of diversity (LaFasto 1992). 'Baxter Healthcare Corporation' in Jackson, B.W., Lafasto, F., Schultz, H.G. and Kelly, D. 'Diversity' in *Human Resource Management*, 31 (1 and 2) p. 28. Reprinted by permission of John Wiley and Sons, Inc © 1992 John Wiley and Sons, Inc.

3. Spreading the ownership. This is a critical stage in which awareness needs to be raised, via a process of encouraging people to question their attitudes and preconceptions. Awareness needs to be raised in all employees at all levels, especially managers, and it needs to be clear that diversity is not something owned by the personnel function.

4. Policy development comes after awareness raising as it enables a contribution to be made from all in the organisation – new systems need to be changed via involvement and not through imposition on the unwilling.

5. Managing the transition needs to involve a range of training initiatives. Positive action programmes, specifically designed for minority groups, may be used to help them understand the culture of the organisation and acquire essential skills; policy implementation programmes, particularly focusing on selection, appraisal, development and coaching; further awareness training and training to identify cultural diversity and manage different cultures and across different cultures.

6. Managing the programme to sustain momentum. This involves a champion, not necessarily from the personnel function, but someone who, in addition, continues in their previous organisation role. Also the continued involvement of senior managers is important, together with trade unions. Harnessing initiatives that come up through departments and organising support networks for disadvantaged groups are key at this stage. Ross and Schneider also recommend measuring achievements in terms of business benefit – better relationships with customers, improvements in productivity and profitability, for example – which need to be communicated to all employees.

Ellis and Sonnenfield make the point that training for diversity needs to be far more than a one-day event. They recommend a series of workshops which allow time for individuals to think, check their assumptions and reassess between training sessions. Key issues that need tackling in arranging training are ensuring that the facilitator has the appropriate skills; carefully considering participant mix; deciding whether the training should be voluntary or mandatory; being prepared to cope with any backlash for previously advantaged groups who now feel threatened; and being prepared for the fact that the training may reinforce stereotypes. They argue that training has enormous potential benefits, but that there are risks involved.

Organisations have a long way to go before getting to the stage of really valuing diversity, and in order for them to continue to strive it is important to reinforce the business advantages. Thompson and DiTomaso (reported by Ellis and Sonnenfield) express it very well:

> Multicultural management perspective fosters more innovative and creative decision making, satisfying work environments, and better products because all people who have a contribution to make are encouraged to be involved in a meaningful way... More information, more points of view, more ideas and reservations are better than fewer.

REVIEW TOPIC 20.3

Prepare a strategy for managing diversity which would be appropriate for your organisation, or one with which you are familiar.

SUMMARY PROPOSITIONS

20.1 The essence of much personnel work is to discriminate between individuals. The essence of equal opportunity is to avoid unfair discrimination.

20.2 Equalising employment opportunity is not only meeting legal and social responsibilities, it is also ensuring organisational effectiveness.

20.3 Unfair discrimination often results from people being treated on the basis of limited and prejudiced understanding of the groups to which they belong rather than on the basis of an assessment of them as individuals.

20.4 Legislation can have only a limited effect on reducing the level of unfair discrimination.

20.5 Actual changes in practice relating to equalising opportunity are taking place very slowly.

20.6 Managing and valuing diversity is a positive way forward in this area.

References

Anon. (1988), 'Childcare provision 1 – employers head for the nursery', *Industrial Relations Review and Report*, October, no. 425, pp. 2–7.

Anon. (1989), 'Social Security Act 1989, Guidance note', *Industrial Relations Review and Report, Legal Information Bulletin*, no. 384, pp. 2–8.

Arkin, A. (1990), 'Mothercare makes a play for women returners', *Personnel Management Plus*, July, pp. 20–1.

Braham, P., Rhodes, E. and Pearn, M. (1981), *Discrimination and Disadvantage in Employment*, Milton Keynes: The Open University.

Brown, C. and Gay, P. (1986), *Racial Discrimination 17 Years After the Act*, PSI.

Carr, J. (1980), 'Comments on monitoring'. In *Record Keeping and Monitoring in Education and Employment*. London: Runnymede Trust.

Commission for Racial Equality (1992), *Second Review of the Race Relations Act 1976*, London: CRE.

Dickens, L. and Colling, T. (1990), 'Why equality won't appear on the bargaining agenda', *Personnel Management*, April, pp. 48–53.

DOE, (1992), *Measure for Measure*, Department of Employment.

Ellis, C. and Sonnenfield, J. A. (1993), 'Diverse approaches to managing diversity', *Human Resource Management*, Spring, vol. 33, no. 1, 79–109.

Employment Service (undated), *The Disabled Persons (Employment) Acts 1944 and 1958: Employers' Obligations*. Sheffield: Employment Service.

Equal Opportunities Commission (1985a), *A Model Equal Opportunities Policy*. London: Equal Opportunities Commission.

Equal Opportunities Commission (1985b), *Sex Discrimination Decisions no. 9. Women and Family Responsibilities, Price* v. *Civil Service Commission*, EOC Information Leaflet. London: Equal Opportunities Commission.

Equal Opportunities Commission (1986), *Guidelines for Equal Opportunities Employers*. London: HMSO.

Equal Opportunities Review (1992a), 'Opportunity 2000', *Equal Opportunities Review*, no. 41, pp. 20–6.

Equal Opportunities Review (1992b), 'Positive action on disability', *Equal Opportunities Review*, no. 43, May/June.

Equal Opportunities Review (1993), 'EOC looks to Europe for action over UK equal pay laws', no. 52, November/December.

Equal Opportunities Review (1993a), 'Formulating an equal opportunities policy', *Equal Opportunities Review*, no. 47, January/February.

Equal Opportunities Review (1993b), 'Trade Union and Employment Rights Act and equal opportunities: the EOR guide', *Equal Opportunities Review*, no. 5, July/August.

Equal Opportunities Review (1993c), 'Age discrimination – no change', *Equal Opportunities Review*, no. 48.

Equal Opportunities Review (1993d), 'EOC looks to Europe for action over UK equal pay laws', *Equal Opportunities Review*, November/December, no. 52, pp. 20–4.

Equal Opportunities Review (1994a), 'Positive about disabled people: the disability symbol', *Equal Opportunities Review*, no. 56, July/August.

Equal Opportunities Review (1994b), *Equal Opportunities Review*, no. 54.

Equal Opportunities Review (1994c), 'Statistics: ethnic minorities in the labour market', *Equal Opportunities Review*, no. 56, July/August.

Field, S. and Paddison, L. (1989), 'Designing a career break system', *Industrial and Commercial Training*, January/ February, pp. 22–5.

Gill, D. and Ungerson, B. (1984), *The Challenge of Equal Value*, London: Institute of Personnel Management.

Gregory, J. (1992), 'Equal pay and work of equal value: the strengths and weaknesses of the legislation', *Work Employment and Society*, vol. 6, no. 3, pp. 461–73, September.

Hakim, C. (1993), 'The myth of rising female employment', *Work Employment and Society*, March, vol. 7, no. 1, pp. 121–33.

Harbour, T. (1980), 'Monitoring: the mass experience'. In *Record Keeping and Monitoring in Education and Employment*, Proceedings of a one-day seminar. London: Runnymede Trust.

HMSO (1989), *Disabled adults: services, transport and employment*, London: HMSO.

Home Office (1985), *Sex Discrimination: A Guide to the Sex Discrimination Act 1975*, London: HMSO.

Institute of Personnel Management (1978), *Towards Fairer Selection: A code for non-discrimination*, IPM Joint Standing Committee on Discrimination, London: IPM.

Itzin, C. and Phillipson, C. (1993), *Age Barriers at Work: Maximising the Potential of Mature and Older People*, Solihull: Metropolitan Authorities Recruitment Agency.

Jackson, B. W., LaFasto, F., Schultz, H. G. and Kelly, D. (1993), 'Diversity', *Human Resource Management*, Spring/Summer, vol. 31, nos. 1 and 2, pp. 21–34.

Jarman, J. (1994), 'Which way forward? Assessing the current proposals to amend the British Equal Pay Act', *Work Employment and Society*, June, vol. 8, no. 2, pp. 243–54.

Jenkins, R. (1986), *Racism and Recruitment*, Cambridge: Cambridge University Press.

LaFasto, F. (1993), 'Baxter Healthcare Corporation', in B. W. Jackson, F. LaFasto, H. G. Schultz and D. Kelly, 'Diversity', *Human Resource Management*, Spring/Summer, vol. 31, nos 1. and 2.

Liff, S. (1989), 'Assessing equal opportunities policies', *Personnel Review*, vol. 18, no. 1, pp. 27–34.

Mahon, T. (1989), 'When line managers welcome equal opportunities', *Personnel Management*, October, pp. 76–9.

Manpower Services Commission Employment Division (1984), *The Disabled Persons Register*, Sheffield: Central Office of Information and Manpower Services Commission.

Manpower Services Commission (1985), *Working Group Report on Suggestions for Improving the Quota Scheme's Effectiveness*, Sheffield: Manpower Services Commission.

Martin, J. and Roberts, C. (1980), *Women and Employment: A Lifetime Perspective. Report of the 1980 DE/OPCS Women and Employment Survey*, London: HMSO.

Masreliez-Steen, G. (1989), *Male and Female Management*, Sweden: Kontura Group.

McGoldrick, A. (1984), *Equal Treatment in Occupational Pension Schemes. Research report*. London: Equal Opportunities Commission.

Noon, M. (1993), 'Racial discrimination in speculative application: evidence from the UK's top 100 firms', *Human Resource Management Journal.*

Prescott-Clarke, P. (1990), *Employment and Handicap*, London: Social and Community Planning Research.

Ross, R. and Schneider, R. (1992), *From Equality to Diversity – a business case for equal opportunities*, London: Pitman.

Runnymede Trust (1979), *A Review of the Race Relations Act*. London: Runnymede Trust.

Runnymede Trust and BPS (1980), *Discriminating Fairly: A guide to fair selection. Report by the Runnymede Trust/BPS Joint Working Party on Employment Assessment and Racial Discrimination*. London: Runnymede Trust and BPS.

Select Committee on the Anti-discrimination Bill (House of Lords) (1972–73), *Second Special Report from the Select Committee*, London: HMSO.

Selwyn, N. M. (1978), *Law of Employment*, London: Butterworth.

Simmons, M. (1989), 'Making equal opportunities training effective', *Journal of European Industrial Training*, vol. 13, no. 8, pp. 19–24.

Singer, M. (1993), *Diversity Based Hiring*, United States of America: Avebury.

Smith, D. J. (1974), *Racial Disadvantage in Employment (PEP Study of Racial Disadvantage), vol. XL, Broadsheet 544*. London: The Social Science Institute.

Snell, M. W., Glucklich, P. and Povall, M. (1981), *Equal Pay and Opportunities. A study of the implications and effects of the Equal Pay and Sex Discrimination Acts in 26 organizations, Research Paper no. 2*. London: Department of Employment.

Wainwright, D. (1985), 'Equal value in action', *Personnel Management*, January.

Walker, A. (1986), 'Disabled workers and technology: quota fails to quote', *Manpower Policy and Practice*, Spring.

Women of Europe Supplements (1989), *Women of Europe Supplements*, no. 30.

21 Interactive skill: performance appraisal

W. Edwards Deming has contended that performance appraisal is the number one American management problem. He says it takes the average employee (manager or non-manager) six months to recover from it. I think Dr Deming is about right, though I'd add the setting of objectives and job descriptions to the list of personnel control devices that are downright dangerous – as currently constituted. (Peters 1989, p. 495).

This comment echoes a similar opinion expressed by Douglas McGregor thirty years previously in the classic management text *The Human Side of Enterprise*.

With reactions like this it makes the appraisal interview sound even more suspect than the selection interview, as we saw in Chapter 15. Its use is becoming more widespread, but if it is so difficult to get right, why does it survive? Why persist with something that Tom Peters regards as downright dangerous?

One might just as well ask why marriage survives despite its extensive failure and the innumerable personal tragedies it produces. Why do teachers grade students' work? Why do we all seek advice? Why do audiences applaud? Why do

---

In one recent set of examination scripts for the Institute of Personnel Management the following comments were found:

> Our scheme has been abandoned because of a lot of paperwork to be completed by the manager and the time-consuming nature of the preparation by both appraiser and appraisee. Assessment dragged on from week to week without any tangible outcome, there was no follow-up and few people understood the process. The interview was spent with managers talking generalities and appraisees having nothing to say. (From a large engineering company)

> We have had approximately one new scheme per year over the last six years. These have ranged from a blank piece of paper to multi-form exercises, complete with tick boxes and a sentence of near death if they were not complete by a specified date. (From an international motor manufacturer)

> Our scheme is not objective and has become a meaningless ritual. It is not a system of annual appraisal; it is an annual handicap. (From a public corporation).

wives and husbands seek the views of their spouses on the prospective purchase of a new suit/dress/shirt or hat? The reason is simply that we all seek approval and confirmation that we are doing the right thing, and most of us yearn to advise or direct what other people should do.

At work these basic human drives are classified into activities such as objective-setting, counselling, coaching or feedback on performance. They all have in common the feature of one person meeting face to face with another for a discussion focused on the performance of only one of them.

There are many appraisal schemes being designed and implemented in all areas of employment. Once installed, schemes are frequently being modified or abandoned and there is widespread management frustration about their operation. Despite the problems the potential advantages of appraisal are so great that organisations continue to introduce them and appraisal *can* produce stunning results. Here is another extract from the same set of examination answers referred to above:

> I have had annual appraisal for three years. Each time it has been a searching discussion of my objectives and my results. Each interview has set me new challenges and opened up fresh opportunities. Appraisal has given me a sense of achievement and purpose that I had never experienced in my working life. (From an insurance company)

Contrasted approaches to appraisal

There are two contrasted motivations that drive the appraisal interview: the motivation of management control and the motivation of self-development. These produce appraisal systems that show a mixture of both motivations, with the control approach still being the most common, especially when there is a link with performance-related pay, but the alternative development emphasis is gaining in popularity. Describing them as polar opposites helps to illustrates the key elements.

1. *The management control approach* starts with an expression of opinion by someone 'up there', representing the view of controlling, responsible authority in saying:

    > We must stimulate effective performance and develop potential, set targets to be achieved, reward above-average achievement and ensure that promotion is based on sound criteria.

    Despite the specious appeal of this most reasonable aspiration, that type of initiative is almost always resisted by people acting collectively, either by representation through union machinery or through passive resistance and grudging participation. This is because people whose performance will be appraised construe the message in a way that is not usually intended by the controlling authorities, like this:

    > They will put pressure on poor performers so that they improve or leave. They will also make sure that people do what they're told and we will all be vulnerable

to individual managerial whim and prejudice, losing a bit more control over our individual destinies.

It is the most natural human reaction to be apprehensive about judgements that will be made about you by other people, however good their intentions.
   This approach is likely to engender:

(a) Conflictual behaviour and attitudes within the organisation, including resistance by managers to the amount of administrative work involved in the process.
(b) Negotiated modifications to schemes. These are 'concessions' made to ease the apprehension of people who feel vulnerable. These frequently make the schemes ineffective.
(c) Tight bureaucratic controls to ensure consistency and fairness of reported judgements.
(d) Bland, safe statements in the appraisal process.
(e) Little impact on actual performance, except on that of a minority of self-assured high achievers at one extreme and disenchanted idlers at the other.
(f) Reduced openness, trust and initiative.

This approach works best when there are clear and specific targets for people to reach, within an organisational culture that emphasises competition. There are considerable problems, such as who sets the standards and who makes the judgements? How are the judgements, by different appraisers of different appraisees, made consistent? Despite its drawbacks, this approach is still potentially useful as a system of keeping records and providing a framework for career development that is an improvement on references and panel interviews. It is most appropriate in bureaucratic organisations. The emphasis is on FORM-FILLING.

2. *The development approach* starts with the question in the mind of the individual job holder:

> I am not sure whether I am doing a good job or not. I would like to find ways of doing the job better, if I can, and I would like to clarify and improve my career prospects.

This question is addressed by job holders *to themselves*. Not: 'Am I doing what you want?', but, 'Where can I find someone to talk through with me my progress, my hopes, my fears. Who can help me come to terms with my limitations and understand my mistakes? Where can I find someone with the experience and wisdom to discuss my performance with me so that I can shape it, building on my strengths to improve the fit between what I can contribute and what the organisation needs from me?'

Those in positions of authority tend to put a slightly different construction on this approach, which is something like:

This leads to people doing what they want to do rather than what they should be doing. There is no co-ordination, no comparison and no satisfactory management control.

This approach to appraisal:

(a) develops co-operative behaviour between appraisers and appraisees and encourages people to exercise self-discipline, accepting autonomous responsibility;

(b) confronts issues, seeking to resolve problems;

(c) does not work well with bureaucratic control;

(d) produces searching analysis directly affecting performance; and

(f) requires high trust, engenders loyalty and stimulates initiative.

This approach works best with people who are professionally self-assured, so that they can generate constructive criticism in discussion with a peer; or in protegé/mentor situations, where there is high mutual respect. The emphasis is on INTERVIEWING, rather than on form-filling. Despite the benefits of this approach, there are two problems: first is the lack of the *systematic* reporting that is needed for attempts at management control of, and information about, the process; second is the problem of everyone finding a paragon in whom they can trust.

REVIEW TOPIC 21.1

To what extent can the benefits of both approaches be created in a single scheme?
Who should conduct the appraisal interview?

Despite the problems the potential advantages of performance appraisal are so great that attempts are made to make it work. Appraisal is, however, valueless unless the general experience of it is satisfactory. Appraisees have to find some value in the appraisal process itself and have to see tangible outcomes in follow-up. Appraisers have to find the appraisal process not too arduous and have to see consructive responses from appraisees. When general experience of appraisal is satisfactory, it becomes an integral part of managing the organisation and modifies the management process.

Who does the appraisal?

Individuals are appraised by a variety of people, including their immediate superior, their superior's superior, a member of the personnel department, themselves, their peers or their subordinates. Sometimes, assessment centres are used to carry out the appraisal. You may find it helpful to refer to Chapter 18 to remind yourself in more detail about these options.

There are, however, many problems for those carrying out the appraisal. For example:

- *Prejudice:* the appraiser may actually be prejudiced against the appraisee, or be anxious not to be prejudiced; either could distort the appraiser's judgement.
- *Insufficient knowledge of the appraisee:* appraisers often carry out appraisals because of their position in the hierarchy rather than because they have a good understanding of what the appraisee is doing.
- *The 'halo effect':* the general likeability (or the opposite) of an appraisee can influence the assessment of the work that the appraisee is doing.
- *The problem of context:* difficulty of distinguishing the work of appraisees from the context in which they work, especially when there is an element of comparison with other appraisees.

> ## REVIEW TOPIC 21.2
>
> Think of jobs where it is difficult to disentangle the performance of the individual from the context of the work. How would you focus on the individual's performance in these situations?

Problems for both the appraiser and the appraisee include:

- *The paperwork:* documentation soon becomes very cumbersome in the attempts made by scheme designers to ensure consistent reporting.
- *The formality:* although appraisers are likely to try and avoid stiff formality, both participants in the interview realise that the encounter is relatively formal, with much depending on it.

Among the other common problems that often cause appraisal schemes to fail are:

- *Outcomes are ignored:* follow-up action agreed in the interview for management to make fails to take place.
- *Everyone is 'just above average':* most appraisees are looking for reassurance that all is well, and the easiest way for appraisers to deal with this is by a statement or inference that the appraiser is doing at least as well as most others, and better than a good many. It is much harder to deal with the situation of facing somone with the opinion that they are average – who wants to be average?
- *Appraising the wrong features:* sometimes behaviours other than the real work are evaluated such as time-keeping, looking busy and being pleasant, because they are easier to see.

The appraisal interview

The different styles of appraisal interview were neatly described forty years ago by the American psychologist Norman Maier (1958). His three-fold classification remains the most widely adopted means of identifying the way to tackle the interview. The *problem-solving* style has been summarised as:

> The appraiser starts the interview by encouraging the employee to identify and discuss problem areas and then consider solutions. The employee therefore plays an active part in analysing problems and suggesting solutions, and the evaluation of performance emerges from the discussion at the appraisal interview, instead of being imposed by the appraiser upon the employee. (Anderson 1993, p. 102)

This is certainly the most effective style, consistent with the development approach to appraisal set out at the opening of this chapter, provided that both the appraiser and appraisee have the skill and ability to handle this mode. It is the basis on which this chapter is written, but it is not the only way. Maier's alternatives were first *tell and sell*, where the appraiser acts as judge, using the interview to tell the appraisee the result of the appraisal and how to improve. This 'ski instructor' approach can be appropriate when the appraisees have little experience and have not developed enough self-confidence to analyse their own performance. *Tell and listen* still casts the appraiser in the role of judge, passing on the outcome of an appraisal that has already been completed and listening to reactions. These could sometimes change the assessment, as well as enabling the two people to have a reasonably frank exchange.

A number of recent articles suggest *a contingency approach* to the personal interaction in the appraisal interview. George suggests that effective appraisal depends on the style of appraisal not conflicting with the culture of the organisation. He suggests that the degree of openness that is required is 'unlikely to materialize without an atmosphere of mutual trust and respect – something which is conspicuously lacking in many employing organizations' (George 1986, p. 32).

George also comments on the links between the appraisal system and other personnel and organisational systems:

> An investment in a system must involve statements about certain desired organizational characteristics and about the treatment of people in an organization. It is very mistaken, therefore, to regard appraisal as merely a technique or a discrete process with an easily definable boundary. (George 1986, p. 33)

Appraisal therefore needs to reflect the wider values of the organisation if it is to be properly integrated and survive in an effective form.

Other aspects of the contingency approach to appraisal include the appraiser's style in relation to their normal management style and in relation to the needs and personality of the appraisee. Pryor (1985) argues that appraisers should aim to achieve consistency between their normal day to day management style and the style that they adopt in appraisal interviews. George talks of the few really open relationships that individuals have at work and how in the appraisal situation we may be expecting interactions of a nature and quality which are not evident in most relationships. Pryor offers a reappraisal of Maier's three styles, particularly the usefulness of tell-and-sell and tell-and-listen. He suggests that they can be effectively adapted to the needs of appraisees with little experience who require less participation in the appraisal interview.

It is tempting to identify Maier's problem-solving approach as 'the best', because it appears to be the most civilised and searching, but not all appraisal situations call for this style, not all appraisees are ready for it and not all appraisers normally behave in this way.

The appraisal interview sequence

Certain aspects of the appraisal interview are the same as those of the selection interview discussed in Chapter 15. There is the inescapable fact that the appraiser determines the framework of the encounter, there is need to open in a way that develops mutual confidence as far as possible, and there is the use of closed and open-ended questions, reflection and summarising. It is also a difficult meeting for the two parties to handle.

> The appraisal interview is a major problem for both appraisers and appraisees. The appraiser has to have a degree of confidence and personal authority that few managers have in their relationship with all those who they have to appraise. The most contentious aspect of many appraisal schemes is the lack of choice that appraisees have in deciding who the appraiser should be. Interview respondents regularly cite the interview as something that they dread. (Torrington, 1994, p. 152).

For the appraisee there are concerns about career progress, job security, the ongoing working relationship with the appraiser, and the basic anxieties relating to self-esteem and dealing with criticism.

The fundamental difference between selection and appraisal that every appraiser has to remember is that the objective is to reach an understanding that will have some impact on the future performance of the appraisee: it is not simply to formulate a judgement by collecting information, as in the selection situation. A medical metaphor may help. A surgeon carrying out hip replacements will select people for operation on the basis of enquiring about their symptoms and careful consideration of the decision. A physician examining a patient who is overweight and short of breath may rapidly make the decision that the patient needs to lose weight and take more exercise. It is, however, not the physician but the patient who has to implement that decision. The physician can help with diet sheets, regular check-ups and terrifying advice; the real challenge is how to get the patient to respond.

The easy part of appraisal is sorting out the facts. The tricky part is actually bringing about a change in performance. The interview – like the discussion in the physician's consulting rooms – is crucial in bringing about a change of attitude, fresh understanding and commitment to action.

Preparation

Brief the appraisee on the form of the interview, possibly asking for a self-appraisal form to be completed in readiness. To some extent this is establishing rapport in advance, with the same objectives, and makes the opening of the eventual interview easier.

Asking for the self-appraisal form to be completed will only be appropriate if the scheme requires this. As we have seen, self-appraisal gives the appraisee some intitiative, ensures that the discussion will be about matters which the appraisee can handle and on 'real stuff'.

The appraiser has to review all the available evidence on the appraisee's performance, including reports, records or other material regarding the period under review. Most important will be the previous appraisal and its outcomes.

Most of the points made in Chapter 15 about preparing for the selection interview apply to appraisal as well, especially the setting. Several research studies (e.g. Anderson and Barnett 1987) have shown the extremely positive response of appraisees who felt that the appraiser had taken time and trouble to ensure that the setting and supportive nature of the discussion was considerate of the appraisee's needs.

Interview structure

A recommended structure for a performance appraisal interview is shown in Figure 21.1. Alternative frameworks can be found in Anderson (1993, pp. 112–13) and Dainow (1988).

Rapport is unusual because it is attempting to smooth the interaction between two people who probably have an easy social relationship, but now find themselves ill at ease with each other. This is not the sort of conversation they are used to having together, so they have to find new ground rules. The pre-interview appraisee briefing is an important step towards this, but the opening of the interview itself still needs care. The mood needs to be light, but not trivial, as the appraisee has to be encouraged towards candour rather than gamesmanship.

1.	Purpose and rapport	Agree purpose with appraisee Agree structure for meeting Check that pre-work is done
2.	Factual Review	Review of known facts about performance in previous period. Appraiser reinforcement.
3.	Appraisee views	Appraisee asked to comment on performance over the last year. What has gone well and what has gone less well; what could be improved; what they liked; what they disliked; possible new objectives.
4.	Appraiser views	Appraiser adds own perspective, asks questions and disagrees, as appropriate, with what appraisee has said.
5.	Problem-solving	Discussion of any differences and how they can be resolved.
6.	Objective setting	Agreeing what action should be taken, and by whom.

Figure 21.1 Structure for a performance appraisal interview

Factual interview is reviewing aspects of the previous year's work that are unproblematic. Begin by reviewing the main facts about the performance, without expressing opinions about them but merely summarising them as a mutual reminder. This will include the outcome of the previous appraisal and will help to key in any later discussion by confirming such matters as how long the appraisee has been in the job, any personnel changes in the period, turnover figures, training undertaken and so forth.

The appraiser will still be doing most – but not all – of the talking, and can isolate those aspects of performance that have been disclosed which are clearly satisfactory, mention them and comment favourably. This will develop rapport and provide the basic reassurance that the appraisee needs in order to avoid being defensive. The favourble aspect of performance will to some extent be *discovered* by the factual review process. It is important that 'the facts speak for themselves' rather than appraiser judgement being offered. Not, for instance:

> Well, I think you are getting on very well. I'm very pleased with how things are going generally.

That sort of comment made at this stage would have the appraisee waiting for...'but...', as the defences have not yet been dismantled. A different approach might be:

> Those figures look very good indeed...How do they compare with...? That's X% up on the quarter and Y% on the year... That's one of the best results in the group... You must be pleased with that... How on earth did you do it?

This has the advantage of the evidence being there before the eyes of both parties, with the appraiser pointing out and emphasising, and it is specific rather than general; precise rather than vague. This type of suggested approach invariably raises the question from appraisers about what to do in a situation of poor performance. Appraising stars is easy; what about the duds? The answer is that all appraisees have some aspects of their performance on which favourable comment can be made, and the appraisal process actually identifies strengths that might have been previously obscured by the general impression of someone who is not very good. You may discover something on which to build, having previously thought the case was hopeless. If there is not some feature of the performance that can be isolated in this way, then the appraiser probably has a management or disciplinary problem that should have been tackled earlier.

The appraiser then asks for the *appraisee's views* on things that are not as good as they might be in the performance, areas of possible improvement and how these might be addressed. These will only be offered by the appraisee if there has been effective positive reinforcement in the previous stages of the interview. People can only acknowledge shortcomings about performance when they are reasonably sure of their ground. Now the appraisee is examining areas of dissatisfaction by the process of discussing them with the appraiser, with whom it is worth having the discussion, because of the appraiser's expertise, information and helicopter view. There are three likely results of debating these matters:

- some will be talked out as baseless;
- some will be shown to be less worrying than they seemed when viewed only from the single perspective of the appraiser, and ways of dealing with them become apparent;
- some will be confirmed as matters needing attention.

This stage in the interview is fraught with difficulties for the manager, and is one of the reasons why an alternative style is sometimes preferred:

> ...some employees prefer to be told rather than invited to participate... the manager receives extra pay and status for making decisions, so why should the manager expect them to do his or her job as well? (Wright and Taylor 1984, p. 110)

These, however, are problems to be recognised and overcome: they are not reasons for not bothering to try.

Appraiser views can now be used in adding to the list of areas for improvement. In many instances there will be no additions to make, but usually there are improvement needs that the appraisee can not, or will not, see. If they are put at this point in the interview, there is the best chance that they will be understood, accepted and acted upon. It is not possible to guarantee success. Demoralised collapse or bitter resentment is always a possibility, but this is the time to try, as the appraisee has developed a basis of reassurance and has come to terms with some shortcomings that he or she had already recognised.

The appraiser has to judge whether any further issues can be raised and if so, how many. None of us can cope with confronting all our shortcomings, all at the same time, and the appraiser's underlying management responsibility is that the appraisee is not made less competent by the appraisal interview. There is also a fundamental moral responsibility not to use a position of organisational power to damage the self-esteem and adjustment of another human being.

Problem-solving is the process of talking out the areas for improvement that have been identified, so that the appraisee can cope with them. Underlying causes are uncovered through further discussion. Gradually huge problems come into clearer and less forbidding perspective, perhaps through being analysed and broken up into different components. Possibilities for action, by both appraiser and appraisee, become clear.

These central stages of the interview – factual exchange, appraisee views, appraiser views and problem-solving – need to move in that sequence. Some may be brief, but none should be omitted and the sequence should not alter.

The final stage of the encounter is to agree what is to be done: objective-setting. Actions need to be agreed and nailed down, so that they actually take place. One of the biggest causes of appraisal failure is with action not being taken, so the objectives set must not only be mutually acceptable, they must also be deliverable. It is likely that some action will be needed from the appraiser as well as some from the appraisee.

Making appraisal work

There are many reports of organisations installing an appraisal system only to find that they have to change it or completely abandon it after only a short time. Other organisations battle on with their systems, but recognise that they are ineffective or inadequate or disliked. What can be done to encourage the system to work as effectively as possible?

Effectiveness will be greater if all involved are clear about what the system is for. The personnel manager and senior managers need to work out what they want the appraisal system to achieve and how it fits in with the other personnel activities that feed into it and are fed by it, such as career planning, training and human resource planning. Those who have to operate the system also have to appreciate its objective, otherwise they are simply filling in forms to satisfy the irksome personnel people, as we saw at the opening of this chapter. Finally, those whose performance is to be appraised will answer questions and contribute ideas with much greater constructive candour if they understand and believe in the purposes of the scheme.

It is vital that the system is visibly owned by senior and line management in the organisation, and that it is not something that is done for the personnel department. This may mean, for example, that appraisal forms are kept and used within the department and only selected types of data are fed through to the personnel function or other departments. Ideally, the form itself should be a working document used by appraiser and appraisee throughout the year.

The more 'open' the appraisal system is, that is the more feedback that the appraisee is given about his or her appraisal ratings, the more likely the appraisee is to accept rather than reject the process. Similarly, the greater the extent to which appraisees participate in the system, the greater the chance of gaining their commitment, subject to the reservation already made: not all appraisees are ready and willing to participate, and not all organisational cultures support participative processes.

The involvement of both appraisers and appraisees in the identification of appraisal criteria has already been noted. Stewart and Stewart (1977) suggest that these criteria must be:

1. Genuinely related to success or failure in the job.
2. Amenable to objective, rather than subjective judgement, and helpful if they are:
   (a) Easy for the appraiser to administer.
   (b) Appear fair and relevant to the appraisee.
   (c) Strike a fair balance between catering for the requirements of the present job while at the same time being applicable to the wider organisation.

Appraisers need training in how to appraise and how to conduct appraisal interviews. Appraisees will also need some training if they have any significant involvement in the process. In our recent research we found that just over a third of the organisations that had appraisal systems trained all interviewers in appraisal interviewing. A further 18 per cent said that all interviewers had some training in interpersonal skills and that appraisal was included in this. Almost a quarter provided appraisal interviewing training for those who felt that they needed it. However, over 20 per cent provided no training at all. An excellent performance appraisal system is of no use at all if managers do not know how to use the system to best effect. Sims (1988) quotes an ineffective system which was sophisticated and well designed, but which line managers did not have the skills to use.

The appraisal system needs to be administered so that it causes as few problems as possible for both parties. Form-filling should be kept to a minimum, and the time allocated for this activity should be sufficient for it to be done properly, but not so much that the task is seen as unimportant and low priority.

Appraisal systems need to be supported by follow-up action. Work plans that are agreed by appraiser and appraisee need to be monitored to ensure that they actually take place, or that they are modified in accordance with changed circumstances or priorities. Training needs should be identified and plans made to meet those needs. Other development plans may involve the personnel department in arranging temporary transfers or moves to another department when a vacancy arises. In order to do this, it is vital that appraisal forms are not simply filed and forgotten.

References

Anderson, G. C. (1993), *Managing Performance Appraisal Systems*, Oxford: Blackwell.
Anderson, G. C. and Barnett, J. G. (1987). 'The Characteristics of Effective Appraisal Interviews', *Personnel Review*, vol. 16, no. 4.
Dainow, S. (1988), 'Goal-oriented appraisal', *Training Officer*, January, pp. 6–8.
George, J. (1986), 'Appraisal in the public sector: dispensing with the big stick', *Personnel Management*, May.

Maier, N. R. F. (1958), *The Appraisal Interview: Objectives, Methods and Skills*, New York: Wiley.

McGregor, D. (1960), *The Human Side of Enterprise*, London: McGraw Hill.

Peters T. (1989), *Thriving on Chaos*, London: Pan Books.

Pryor, R. (1985), 'A fresh approach to performance appraisal', *Personnel Management*, June.

Sims, R. R. (1988), 'Training supervisors in employee performance appraisals', *European Journal of Industrial Training*, vol. 2, no. 8, pp. 26–31.

Stewart, V. and Stewart, A. (1977), *Practical Performance Appraisal*, Aldershot: Gower.

Torrington, D. P. (1994), 'Sweets for the sweet: performance-related pay in Britain', *International Journal of Employment Studies*, vol. 1, no. 2, pp. 149–64.

Wright P. L. and Taylor D. S. (1984), *Improving Leadership Peformance*, Hemel Hempstead: Prentice Hall International.

PART V

Development

22 Strategic aspects of development

Extract from the diary of Len Hodge, Personnel Director

First Monday of the month again – Board meeting. This was the opportunity I'd been waiting for – with some trepidation. My function had produced firm proposals on a new training and development strategy which I was to present to the Board. Development for all was the theme, with key competencies being identified at each level of the organisation and everyone being entitled to six days off job training per year, plus coaching on the job to meet individual development goals. A real step in the right direction at last. All I had to do was to get the Board's backing and we'd be off.

I began to present the scheme complete with user friendly overheads, information packs to employees and a manager guidance and support package. My colleagues listened intently, for about 5 minutes, then all hell broke loose.

'So what's going to happen to production when they're all off swanning around training – we're understaffed anyway?' – that was Gary the Production Manager.

Brian from Marketing chipped in next: 'They'll be poached as soon as they're trained if word gets out about this – we'll be doing it for nothing'.

But worst of all was Karen the MD: 'Why are you proposing this anyway. Granted we desperately need some skills training for those new machines and to encourage flexibility – but we didn't ask for all this. How will it improve business performance? What are we going to get out of all the money this is going to cost us?'

I had hoped more of Karen. She was usually very supportive when I came up with training proposals to solve business problems – well crises would be a better word – we did what I suggested and it usually worked.

This time my words fell on stony ground – no one was interested.

Where do we go from here???

Employee development has traditionally been seen as a cost rather than an investment in the United Kingdom, although this is certainly changing in some organisations. Comparatively speaking organisations in the United Kingdom give little support to training and development compared with our European partners (see, for example, Handy 1989 and Constable and McCormick 1987).

REVIEW TOPIC 22.1

Before you read on…

What went wrong in the Board meeting?
Why do you think that the Directors reacted as they did?
What could Len have done differently to improve his chances of success?
Where does Len go from here?

It is widely agreed that it is difficult to provide evidence of a causal link between employee development and organisational performance. Harrison (1993) argues that this is partly because the terms 'employee development' and 'business success' are poorly defined.

Employee development is necessarily an act of faith. It is so difficult to tie performance improvements down to the development itself (aside from other influences) and to understand the nature of the causal link. For example, is performance better because of increased or different employee development, because the reward package has improved, or because we have a clearer set of organisational and individual objectives? If there is a link with employee development initiatives is it that employees have better skills, or are better motivated, or they have been selected from a more able group of candidates attracted to the organisation as it offers a high level of development?

Miller (1991), writing specifically of management development, points to a lack of relationship between business strategy and development activity. Pettigrew, Swallow and Hendry (1988) did find, however, that development issues get a higher priority when they are linked to organisational needs and take a more strategic approach.

Miller makes the point that although at organisational level it is difficult to quantitatively identify the direct impact of strategic investment in development this is well supported by anecdotal evidence and easily demonstrated at macro level.

Harrison notes a number of triggers for employee development activity which include:

organisational strategy;
external labour market shortages;
changes in internal labour market needs;
changes in internal systems and values; and last but not least
government initiatives and external support.

It is in this context that we consider employee development strategy. In the following chapter we look in more detail at government support for National Vocational Qualifications (NVQs) and the competence movement more generally (including the Management Charter Initiative competencies). In this chapter we will concentrate on internal changes, especially organisation strategy, and to a lesser extent external labour market conditions.

Organisational strategy and employee development strategy

McClelland's research published in 1994 is one of the many to show that many organisations do not consider development issues as part of their competitive strategy formulation, although he found that those that do identified it to be of value in gaining as well as maintaining competitive advantage.

Those organisations which do consider employee development at a strategic level usually see employee development as a key to *implementing* business strategy. This necessitates an emphasis on identifying development needs from an organisational perspective rather than, but not at the complete expense of, individually identified development needs.

Miller has demonstrated how management development can be aligned with the strategic positioning of the firm. He has produced a matrix demonstrating how development content and processes can reflect either stable growth; unstable growth; unstable decline and competitive positions, as shown in Table 22.1. He offers the model as suggestive, only, of the 'possibilities in designing strategically-oriented management development programmes'.

Not only is it critical for individuals to be developed to meet currently identified strategic needs, but also for needs in the future. There has been an upsurge of

One large organisation had a well-established training function and on an annual basis they traditionally sat down to plan the year ahead. They would plan how many of what type of courses depending on the demand in the previous year and the availability of appropriate staff. New courses would be introduced where a need had been identified and were piloted. Course evaluation data (collected mainly from participants, but sometimes from their managers) was used to inform course demand and course structure and content.

Individuals were booked on training courses following discussion with their manager regarding their individual needs. There were often problems resulting from long waiting lists and individuals being nominated for courses for which they were not eligible (defined by the nature of their job) – it appeared that individuals sometimes nominated themselves and the manager rubber-stamped this.

Some years later, after efforts on the part of general management and training and development management to employ a more strategic approach to the business, the picture was very different. Performance management had been introduced as the cornerstone of people management resulting from a multifunctional high-level working party. A course was devised and delivered in chunks of one and two days and this was delivered to *all* staff, with slightly differing versions for managers and non-managers. The course was an integrating mechanism for all people management activities and most importantly it promoted a cohesive *style and philosophy* of people management that the organisation felt was critical in the achievement of its business objectives. Not only was senior general management involved in the initial stages of the course, but key line managers were involved in delivering the subsequent modules.

Table 22.1 *Linking management development to strategic situations (Miller 1991, p. 47). Reproduced with permission of the author.*

		Environment condition		
	Stable	**Unstable growth**	**Unstable decline**	**Competitive**
Content	Environment scanning skills	Environment scanning skills	Stakeholder relations	Competitive strategy development
	Understanding sources of stability (e.g. geographically isolated product market, state of technology)	Industry analysis skills	Executive retention skills	Competitor analysis
		Sales, marketing	Understanding competitor environment	Marketing/cost control (dependent on competitive strategy)
		Financial control		
		Creative thinking	Negotiating skills	
	Defence strategies	Team building	Diversification skills (technology, human resources)	Industry analysis (dependent on competitive strategy)
	Industrial relations skills (but depends on source of stability)	Organisation structure skills		
		Forecasting techniques		
Process	Slow pace but 'eventful'	Fast-moving	Medium pace	High-pressure
	Modest emphasis individual development	High-pressure	Co-operative environment	Competitive
		Intense		
	Non-competitive but 'aggressive'	Team-orientated	Reactive	
		Proactive		
	Reactive			

interest in 'anticipatory learning' where future needs are predicted and development takes place in advance. The *Journal of Management Education and Development* devoted an entire issue to anticipatory learning (1994) which included some ideas on how it might be identified and achieved. Buckley and Kemp (1987) suggest that anticipatory learning is most important at corporate level, and that a strategic approach at business unit or functional level may be shorter-term and more immediately relevant.

What can be said with confidence is that the future will be different from the present and that the skills and competencies needed will therefore be different. Of paramount importance therefore is the ability to learn. Watkins (1987) suggests that development for strategic *capability*, rather than simply targeting development on achieving business objectives, needs to reinforce an entrepreneurial and innovative culture in which learning is part of everyday work. He identifies the importance of acting successfully in novel and unpredictable circumstances and that employees acquire a 'habit of learning, the skills of learning and the desire to learn'.

Mabey and Iles (1993) note that a strategic approach to development differs from a tactical one in that a consistent approach to assessment and development is identified with a common skills language and skills criteria attached to overall business objectives. They also note the importance of a decreasing emphasis on subjective assessment. To this end many organisations have introduced a series of development centres, similar to assessment centres (discussed in Chapter 13), but with a clear outcome of individual development plans for each participant related to their current levels of competence and potential career moves, and key competencies required by the organisation. In Table 22.2 we offer a list of questions that are raised if an organisation wishes to adopt a strategic approach to employee development.

Influence of the external labour market

The external availability of individuals with the skills and competencies required by the organisation will also have an impact on employee development strategy. If skills and individuals are plentiful the organisation has the choice of whether, and to what extent it wishes, to develop staff internally. If skills or individuals are in short supply then internal development invariably becomes a priority. Predicting demographic and social changes is critical in identifying the extent of internal development required and also who will be available to be developed. In-depth analysis in these areas may challenge traditionally held assumptions about who will be developed, how they will be developed and to what extent they will be developed. For example, the predicted shortage of younger age groups in the labour market coupled with a shortage of specific skills may result in a strategy to develop older rather than younger recruits. This poses potential problems about the need to develop quickly aligned with developing older workers, some of whom may learn more

Table 22.2

- What are the key competencies that the organisation needs at each level to meet its objectives now and in the future?
- How are we going to assess current levels of these competencies?
- To what extent (as determined by the organisation's strategy and the external labour market) should these be developed internally?
- Which approaches to, and methods of, development will be most effective in helping us to build up the required competencies?
- Who is most appropriately involved in these processes?
- How are we going to ensure that our employee development strategy is reinforced by, and reinforces other HR strategies?

slowly. What is the best form of development programme for employees with a very varied base of skills and experiences? Another critical issue is that of redeployment of potentially redundant staff and their development to provide shortage skills.

Prediction of skills availability is critical, as for some jobs the training required will take years rather than months. Realising in January that the skills required by August by the organisation will not be available in the labour market is too late if the development needed takes three years!

The external labour market clearly has a big impact on employee development strategy, but it is important that in this respect and in relation to organisational strategy that there is a high level of integration between employee development strategy and other aspects of human resource strategy.

Integration with other human resource strategy

Where there is a choice between recruiting required skills or developing them internally, given a strategic approach, the decision will reflect on the positioning of the organisation and its strategy. In Chapter 10 on Strategic Aspects of Resourcing we looked at this balance in some depth and you may find it helpful to re-read pages 187 to 191. A further issue is that of ensuring consistency between the skills criteria used for recruitment and development.

From a slightly different perspective, the organisation's development strategy, either explicit or implicit, is often underestimated in terms of its impact on recruitment and retention. There is increasing evidence to show that employees and potential employees are more interested in development opportunities, especially structured ones, rather than improvements in financial rewards. Development activity can drive motivation and commitment, and can be used in a strategic way to contribute towards these. For these ends, publishing and marketing the strategy is crucial, as well as ensuring that the rhetoric is backed up by action. There is also the tricky question of access to and eligibility for development – if it is only offered very selectively it can have the reverse of the intended impact.

However, not all employees see the need for, or value of, development and this, in particular, means that the organisation's reward systems need to be supportive of the development strategy. If we want employees to learn new skills and become multiskilled, it is skills development we need to reward rather than the job that is currently done. If we wish employees to gain vocational qualifications we need to reflect this in our recruitment criteria and reward systems. Harrison notes that these links are not very strong in most organisations.

Other forms of reward, for example promotions and career moves, also need to reflect the development strategy; for example, in terms of providing appropriate, such as matrix, career pathways if the strategy is to encourage a multifunctional, creative perspective in the development of future general management. Not only do the pathways have to be available, they must also be used, and this means encouraging current managers to use them for their staff. In Chapter 25 we explore such career issues in more depth.

Finally, an organisation needs to reinforce the skills and competencies that it wishes to develop by appraising those skills and competencies rather than something else. Developmentally based appraisal systems can clearly be of particular value here.

Training and development roles

Most organisational examples suggest that the formation of training and development strategy is not something which should be 'owned' by the personnel and training function. The strategy needs to be owned and worked on by the whole organisation, with the personnel/training function acting in the roles of specialist/expert and co-ordinator. The function may also play a key role in translating that strategy into action steps. The actions themselves may be carried out by line management, the personnel/training function or outside consultants.

Involvement from line management in the delivery of the training and development strategy can have a range of advantages. Top management have a key role in introducing strategic developments to staff – for example, the creation of an organisation-wide competency identification programme; the creation of a system of development centres or introduction of a development-based organisational performance management system. Only in this way can employees see and believe that there is a commitment from the top. At other levels line managers can be trained as trainers, assessors and advisers in delivering the strategy. This is not only a mechanism for getting them involved, but also for tailoring the strategy to meet the real and different needs of different functions and departments.

Consultants may, of course, be used at any stage. They may add to the strategy development process, but there is always the worry that their contribution comes down to an offering of their ready-packaged solution, with a little tailoring here and there, rather than something which really meets the needs of the organisation. It is useful to have an outside perspective, but there is an art in defining the role of that outside contribution.

In terms of delivery consultants may make a valuable contribution where a large number of courses have to be run over a short period. The disadvantages are that they can never really understand all the organisational issues, and that they may be seen as someone from outside imposing a new process on the organisation.

Approaches to development

The approaches to and methods of development chosen need to be the most effective in achieving the skills and competencies required by the organisation. They will also need to be appropriate to the culture of the organisation. Schein (1961) produces an argument based on development as a process of influence and attitude change and shows how different approaches to development would meet differing organisation needs. For example, although there is great agreement on the value and importance of on-job coaching, this may not be the most appropriate method of development if the organisation wished to encourage innovation, creativity and a holistic organisation perspective. Coaching would be a mechanism of continuing the traditions of the past; whereas cross-functional moves, job rotations, secondments and periods spent in another organisation would be more likely to produce new insights and an organisational perspective.

Another question is the organisation's approach to national initiatives such as National Vocational Qualifications and competencies identified by the Management Charter Initiative. Both of these reflect the general move from education to job related training and both aim to develop specific competencies to a predefined standard. The work-based nature of these initiatives means that organisations adopting and encouraging them are landed with a heavy time commitment, particularly in the assessment process. A further issue is the extent to which the employer decides to tailor the standards to meet their own specific needs. Similarly, a commitment to 'Investors in People' requires significant time and effort, particularly in relation to the processes involved in development. The initial targets set for the number of employers seeking and achieving the Investors in People recognised status are proving to have been very ambitious.

Raskas and Hambrick (1994) show in the context of multifunctional development how business strategy, culture, skills required and individual characteristics need to be considered when deciding the exact approach to be adopted. A contingency approach to employee development strategy is therefore essential – there are no pre-packaged solutions.

Evaluation of training and development

One of the most nebulous and unsatisfactory aspects of the training job is evaluating its effectiveness, yet it is becoming more necessary to demonstrate value for money. Evaluation is straightforward when the output of the training is clear to see, such as reducing the number of dispatch errors in a warehouse or increasing someone's typing speed. It is more difficult to evaluate the success of a management training course or a programme of social skills development, but the fact that it is difficult is not enough to prevent it being done.

A familiar method of evaluation is the post-course questionnaire, which course members complete on the final day by answering vague questions that amount to little more than 'good, very good or outstanding'. The drawbacks with these are, first, that there is a powerful halo effect as the course will have been, at the very least, a welcome break from routine and there will probably have been some attractive fringe benefits such as staying in a comfortable hotel and enjoying rich food.

Secondly, the questionnaire tends to evaluate the course and not the learning, so that the person attending the course is assessing the quality of the tutors and the visual aids, instead of being directed to examine what has been learnt. Easterby-Smith and Tanton (1985) surveyed evaluation of training in fifteen organisations to conclude:

> All but one of the 15 organizations conducted some form of evaluation on a regular basis, and invariably this consisted of an end-of-course questionnaire... The impression gained from training managers was that this was regarded largely as part of the ritual of course closure; they commented that completed questionnaires were normally filed away – the data thus produced was rarely used in decisions about training... if a negative comment is voiced by one individual, that criticism is often seen to reflect poorly on the individual rather than on the course. (Easterby-Smith and Tanton 1985, p. 25)

The authors then advocate the simple strategy of asking participants and their bosses to complete short questionnaires at the beginning of the course to focus their minds on what they hope to get from it. At the end of the course there is a further questionnaire focusing on learning and what could be applied when back on the job. Later, they complete further questionnaires to review the effects of the course on subsequent working performance. This overcomes the problem of learning remaining a detached experience inducing nostalgic reflection but no action, but it also encourages the course participant to concentrate on what he or she is learning and not on assessing objectively the quality of the service.

Taking the broader issue of evaluating training in general rather than the experience of trainees, researchers at Warwick University concluded:

> Evaluation is notoriously difficult, but our research indicates that those firms which have the most positive attitudes (and carry out the most training) typically employ 'soft' criteria relating to broad human resource goals (recruitment and retention, career management etc.), and tend to be sceptical about 'hard' cost–benefit evaluation, related to bottom-line outcomes. (Pettigrew, Sparrow and Hendry 1988, p. 31)

The amount of money available for training and development and the way in which costs are allocated and analysed within the business will have a significant impact on what development strategies are feasible and supportable.

> The Manpower Services Commission survey calculated that with a total training expenditure of £2 billion per year, this works out at £200 per employee and represents only 0.15% of the average firm's turnover. This lack of investment is not only foolhardy but considerably below that of others: in fact only one seventh of the American figure and one fourteenth of the best in West Germany. (Open University 1986, p. 5)

Two years later the Manpower Services Commission had become the Training Commission and had conducted a further survey reported by Sloman (1989). This reached the conclusion that in 1986/7 British employers spent £14.4 billion on the provision of training for their workforce, which worked out at £800 per employee. Despite the wildly differing conclusions about how much is actually spent, they at least demonstrate that we do not spend as much on training as other countries, but not widespread agreement on who should pay more.

An analysis by the Industrial Society (1985) shows how companies in different areas distribute their training budget and what proportion it is of turnover. In answer to a questionnaire with 134 useable responses, 64.6 per cent of responding organisations said that they spent less than 0.5 per cent of their annual turnover on training their employees, including all twelve of the public service respondents. Only seven respondents spent more than 1.5 per cent. The items comprising the training budget were staff education schemes, equipment costs, training centres and consultants. The survey does not reveal whether salary costs for training staff are included, but 77 per cent of firms include trainees' expenses and only 35 per cent include trainees' salaries.

☐ SUMMARY PROPOSITIONS

22.1 The personnel/training function does not own employee development strategy – it must be owned by the organisation as a whole.

22.2 Employee development strategy needs to focus on the organisation strategy and objectives and involves identifying the skills and competencies required to achieve this now and in the future.

22.3 Employee development strategy will also be influenced by the external labour market, government initiatives and competitor activity.

22.4 It is important that employee development strategy is reinforced by, and reinforces, other HR strategy.

22.5 The methods of employee development chosen need to be aligned not only with the competencies and skills to be developed, but also the strategic position of the organisation, its culture and the individuals involved.

References

Buckley, J. and Kemp, N. (1987), 'The strategic role of management development', *Management Education and Development*, vol. 18, Pt 3, pp. 157–74.

Constable, R. and McCormick, R. J. (1987), *The Making of British Managers*, London: British Institute of Management.

Easterby-Smith, M. and Tanton, M. (1985), 'Turning course evaluation from an ends to a means', *Personnel Management*, April.

Handy, C. (1988), *Making Managers*, London: Pitman.

Harrison, R. (1993), *Human Resource Management: Issues and strategies*, Wokingham: Addison–Wesley.

Industrial Society (1985), *Survey of Training Costs*, London: The Industrial Society.

Journal of Management Education and Development, 'Anticipatory learning: learning for the twenty-first century', vol. 12, no. 6.

Mabey, C. and Iles, P. (1993), 'Development practices: succession planning and new manager development', *Human Resource Management Journal*, vol. 3, no. 4.

McClelland, S. (1994), 'Gaining competitive advantage through strategic management development', *Journal of Management Development*, vol. 13, no. 5, pp. 4–13.

Miller, P. (1991), 'A strategic look at management development', *Personnel Management*, August.

Open University (1986), *Managing People: 2*, Milton Keynes: The Open University.

Pettigrew, A. M., Sparrow, P. and Hendry, C. (1988), 'The forces that trigger training', *Personnel Management*, vol. 20, no. 12, pp. 28–32.

Raskas, D. F. and Hambrick, D. C. (1994), 'Multi-functional management development: A framework for evaluating the options', *Organisational Dynamics*, vol. 21, Autumn, 1992.

Schein, E. (1961), 'Management development as a process of influence', *Sloan Management Review*, vol. 2, no. 2, May.

Sloman, M. (1989), 'On-the-job training: a costly poor relation', *Personnel Management*, vol. 21, no. 2, February.

Watkins, J. (1987), 'Management development policy in a fast changing environment: The case of a public sector service organisation', *Management Education and Development*, vol. 18, Pt 3, pp. 181–93.

23 Competence, competencies and NVQs

There has always been a tension in education and training between what the trainee knows and what they can do after the training is complete. Knowledge has an ancient history of being highly desirable: witness Eve's trouble because of the serpent and the tree of knowledge in the Garden of Eden. Our literature and our folklore is full of the value of knowledge, including its best-known aphorism by Francis Bacon four hundred years ago, that knowledge is itself power.

In every country of the world education has been developed, with all its mystique and influence, to communicate knowledge and to develop understanding. In developing countries it is usually the first priority of economic growth. For all people the search for better understanding is a human quality that is self-perpetuating once the appetite has first been stimulated.

The search for knowledge also develops a prestige for certain types of knowledge and for the institutions that trade in that knowledge. In Britain and France the areas with the greatest prestige have been those which are closest to art and pondering the human condition: English, history, classical civilisation and language, philosophy and theology, followed by those allied to elite professions, such as medicine and the law. Science took longer to achieve similar prestige and it is still physics and chemistry that are valued ahead of engineering. Knowledge rather than practical skills carries status, and the educational institutions with the highest prestige are those universities with the strongest reputation in these areas.

This preference for knowledge has carried through into the labour market. We still pay more to people who manipulate words than to those who manipulate materials. Reading the news on television pays much more than making the world's most advanced aircraft or electronic equipment. Writing computer programmes for arcade games pays much more than making the equipment on which the games run.

> Many people love studying, but in some places it seems to have become a public nuisance. In a shopping mall on Orchard Road in Singapore a cafe proprietor concerned about the popularity of the establishment with students has a large notice:
> 'NO STUDYING IN THE CAFE'.

It has become very difficult to recruit able students to study physics at university, and it is a bitter frustration for their teachers that many of them will move, on graduation, to merchant banking or accountancy.

Elsewhere it is different. The inevitable comparison is with Germany and Japan, countries where the practical skills of engineering, for instance, carry much greater prestige. This comparison has increasingly led policy-makers and those in education to seek ways to shift the emphasis in education away from esoteric knowledge towards practical, vocational skills. This has proved remarkably difficult, as education is a large vested interest in any advanced society and change is resisted, however inevitable it may be. In the last fifty years there have been moves to set up technical schools in the late 1940s, which failed almost completely. We have had technological universities, many of which became universities much like any other. We had degrees in technology that were designated as BSc*, to show that they weren't real degrees at all. We had the industrial training boards in the 1960s, rapidly followed by polytechnics in the 1970s, but the training boards were abolished and the polytechnics developed degrees in social sciences more rapidly than in vocational science and engineering.

By the end of the 1980s government policy achieved an unprecedented degree of centralised control on schooling through the national curriculum and on higher education through controlling student numbers and having differential fee regimes. Central to this control has been a heightened emphasis on practical vocational skills: what the student is able to do that is vocationally useful when the training is complete. The end result should be that the student is competent to do something that is useful. Furthermore, the education and training agenda has been placed under greater employer influence than previously.

REVIEW TOPIC 23.1

Think of your own schooling. Single out three things you learned at school that have subsequently been useful to you in your working life. Then single out the three topics or subjects which you found most interesting to study. What changes would you make if you could have your time over again?

Competencies

The vehicle for this revolution is an array of National Vocational Qualifications (NVQs), which are based on assessed competencies, so let us now see what competencies are. The basic idea of competency-based training is that it should be criterion-related, directed at developing the ability of trainees to perform specific tasks directly related to the job they are in or for which they are preparing, expressed in terms of performance outcomes and specific indicators. It is a reaction against the confetti-scattering approach to training as being a good thing in its own right, concerned with the general education of people dealing with general matters.

The key research work on competencies is by Richard Boyatsis, who carried out a large-scale intensive study of 2000 managers, holding forty-one different jobs in twelve organisations. He defines a competency as: 'an underlying characteristic of a person which results in effective and/or superior performance in a job' (Boyatsis 1982, p. 21).

It may be a *trait*, which is a characteristic or quality that a person has, such as efficacy, which is the trait of believing you are in control of your future and fate. When you encounter a problem, you then take an initiative to resolve the problem, rather than wait for someone else to do it. It may be a *motive*, which is a drive or thought related to a particular goal, such as achievement, which is a need to improve and compete against a standard of excellence. It may be a *skill*, which is the ability to demonstrate a sequence of behaviour that is functionally related to attaining a performance goal. Being able to tune and diagnose faults in a car engine is a skill, because it requires the ability to identify a sequence of actions, which will accomplish a specific objective. It also involves being able to identify potential obstacles and sources of help in overcoming them. The skill can be applied to a range of different situations. The ability to change the sparking plugs is an ability only to perform that action.

It may be a person's *self-image*, which is the understanding we have of our-selves and an assessment of where we stand in the context of values held by others in our environment. For example: 'I am creative and innovative. I am expressive and I care about others'. In a job requiring routine work and self-discipline, that might modify to: 'I am creative and innovative. I am too expressive. I care about others and lack a degree of self-discipline'. It may be a person's *social role*, which is a perception of the social norms and behaviours that are acceptable and the behaviours that the person then adopts in order to fit in. It may be a *body of knowledge*. If these are the elements of competency, some of them can be developed, some can be modified and some can be measured, but not all.

Boyatsis makes a further distinction of the threshold competency, which is: 'A person's generic knowledge, motive, trait, self-image, social role, or skill which is essential to performing a job, but is not causally related to superior job perfor-mance', such as being able to speak the native tongue of one's subordinates. Table 23.1 summarises these.

Competencies are required for superior performance and are grouped in clus-ters, shown in Table 23.2.

- The *goal and action management cluster* relates to the requirement to make things happen towards a goal or consistent with a plan.
- The *leadership cluster* relates to activating people by communicating goals, plans and rationale and stimulating interest and development.
- The *human resource management cluster* relates to managing the co-ordina-tion of groups of people working together towards the organisation's goals.

Table 23.1 *The seven threshold competencies identified by Richard Boyatsis*

	Threshold competencies
Use of unilateral power:	Using forms of influence to obtain compliance
Accurate self-assessment:	Having a realistic or grounded view of oneself, seeing personal strengths and weaknesses and knowing one's limitations
Positive regard:	Having a basic belief in others; that people are good; being optimistic and causing others to feel valued
Spontaneity:	Being able to express oneself freely or easily, sometimes making quick or snap decisions
Logical thought:	Placing events in causal sequence; being orderly and systematic
Specialised knowledge:	Having useable facts, theories, frameworks or models
Developing others:	Helping others to do their jobs, adopting the role of coach and using feedback skills in facilitating self-development of others

- The *focus on others cluster* relates to maturity and taking a balanced view of events and people.
- The *directing subordinates cluster* relates to providing subordinates with information on performance, interpreting what the information means to the subordinates and placing positive or negative values on the interpretation.

The Boyatsis framework is set out at some length because of its influence. It is the basis of the work carried out by many consultants in the training field. It has, however, suffered criticism. Academics were sceptical about the methods of investigation and practitioners found the framework too complex to translate into action. Boyatsis may be slipping into history, but his work remains an invaluable point of reference because of the way it demonstrates the scale and complexity of the management job. Subsequently definitions of competency and lists of competencies have come thick and fast from the training and development specialists. There is no need for us to add to those, but we can offer some clarification. First of all competency is not the same as competence. Competence is the general ability to do something to an acceptable level (a competent witness, a competent answer, a competent driver) and is in contrast to incompetent, which is a pretty drastic condemnation. Competency is not as modern and trendy as many of its advocates believe. It appears in Shakespeare's *Merchant of Venice* and is a word that has long been available as an alternative to competence. What is new is its use in training in a quite specific way to describe a range of things one has to be able to do in order to achieve competence:

> A competency is a set of behaviour patterns that the incumbent needs to bring to a position in order to perform its tasks and functions with competence. (Woodruffe, 1992)

Table 23.2 *The five clusters of management competencies identified by Richard Boyatsis (1982)*

Management competency clusters
The *goal and action management* cluster

Concern with impact: being concerned with symbols of power to have impact on others, concerned about status and reputation

Diagnostic use of concepts: identifying and recognising patterns from an assortment of information, by bringing a concept to the situation and attempting to interpret events through that concept

Efficiency orientation: being concerned to do something better

Proactivity: being a disposition toward taking action to achieve something

The *leadership* cluster

Conceptualisation: developing a concept that describes a pattern or structure perceived in a set of facts: the concept emerges from the information

Self-confidence: having decisiveness or presence; knowing what you are doing and feeling you are doing it well

Use of oral presentations: making effective verbal presentations in situations ranging from one-to-one to several hundred people (plus threshold competency of logical thought)

The *human resource management* cluster

Use of socialised power: using forms of influence to build alliances, networks, coalitions and teams

Managing group process: stimulating others to work effectively in group settings (plus threshold competencies of accurate self-assessment and positive regard)

The *focus on others* cluster

Perceptual objectivity: being able to be relatively objective, avoiding bias or prejudice

Self-control: being able to inhibit personal needs or desires in service of organisational needs

Stamina and adaptability: being able to sustain long hours of work and have the flexibility and orientation to adapt to changes in life and the organisational environment

The *directing subordinates* cluster

(Threshold competencies of developing others, spontaneity and use of unilateral power)

Competencies in the United Kingdom

In the United Kingdom, competencies have been developed in line with other aspects of change in education, such as experiential learning, the national curriculum and GCSE, attempts to develop the ability of learners to do rather than to know, as well as introducing greater flexibility into the learning process, so that career aspirants are not restrained by elitist exclusiveness of either educational institutions or professional associations. This is partly due to a long-standing disappointment about British industrial performance, easily attributable to poor management

(Constable and McCormick, 1987). There is therefore a political momentum behind the competence movement beyond considerations of education and training. It is heavily promoted by the Training and Enterprise Directorate of the Department of Employment.

The principles of competencies are:

1. *Open access.* There should be no artificial barriers to training, such as it being available only to people who are members of a professional body, for example the Institute of Personnel and Development or the Law Society, or those in a particular age group.

2. There is a focus on what people can *do*, rather than on the process of learning. Masters' students in a university typically cannot graduate in less than twelve months. With competency-based qualifications, you graduate when you can demonstrate competence, however long or short a period it takes you to achieve the standard.

3. *National* vocational qualifications, which are the same wherever the training takes place, so that the control is in the hands of the awarding body rather than the training body, and there is only one strand of qualification for each vocational area: no multiplication of rival qualifications. The overall control is with the National Council for Vocational Qualifications (NCVQ).

4. The feature of performance *standards* as the basis of assessment; not essays or written-up case studies, but practical demonstrations in working situations, or replicas, of an ability to do the job at a specified standard. Although training schemes are littered with euphoria about excellence, the competency basis has only one standard. The only degree of differentiation between trainees is the length of time taken to complete the qualification.

5. *Flexibility and modularisation.* People must be able to transfer their learning more or less at will between 'providers', so that they are not tied to a single institution and without needless regulations about attendance. Woolwich Building Society runs a scheme with one of the new London universities whereby employees can obtain a BA in Business Studies without ever visiting the university itself.

6. *Accreditation of prior learning.* You can accredit prior learning, no matter how you acquired it. If you have been able to acquire a competence by straightforward experience or practice at home, and if you can reach the performance standard, you can receive the credit for it.

7. The approach to training is the establishment of a *learning contract* between the provider and the trainee, whereby the initiative lies with the trainee to specify the assistance and facilities that are needed and the provider agrees to provide them. The idea of this is that the learner is active in committing to the learning process.

8. Flexibility in assessment is partly achieved by the *portfolio* principle, as you accumulate evidence of your competence from your regular, day to day working and submit it for assessment as appropriate.

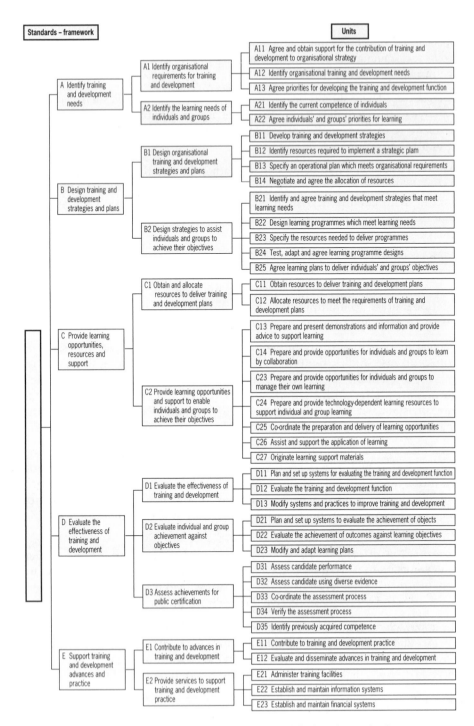

Standards – framework

Units

A Identify training and development needs

- **A1 Identify organisational requirements for training and development**
  - A11 Agree and obtain support for the contribution of training and development to organisational strategy
  - A12 Identify organisational training and development needs
  - A13 Agree priorities for developing the training and development function
- **A2 Identify the learning needs of individuals and groups**
  - A21 Identify the current competence of individuals
  - A22 Agree individuals' and groups' priorities for learning

B Design training and development strategies and plans

- **B1 Design organisational training and development strategies and plans**
  - B11 Develop training and development strategies
  - B12 Identify resources required to implement a strategic plam
  - B13 Specify an operational plan which meets organisational requirements
  - B14 Negotiate and agree the allocation of resources
- **B2 Design strategies to assist individuals and groups to achieve their objectives**
  - B21 Identify and agree training and development strategies that meet learning needs
  - B22 Design learning programmes which meet learning needs
  - B23 Specify the resources needed to deliver programmes
  - B24 Test, adapt and agree learning programme designs
  - B25 Agree learning plans to deliver individuals' and groups' objectives

C Provide learning opportunities, resources and support

- **C1 Obtain and allocate resources to deliver training and development plans**
  - C11 Obtain resources to deliver training and development plans
  - C12 Allocate resources to meet the requirements of training and development plans
- **C2 Provide learning opportunities and support to enable individuals and groups to achieve their objectives**
  - C13 Prepare and present demonstrations and information and provide advice to support learning
  - C14 Prepare and provide opportunities for individuals and groups to learn by collaboration
  - C23 Prepare and provide opportunities for individuals and groups to manage their own learning
  - C24 Prepare and provide technology-dependent learning resources to support individual and group learning
  - C25 Co-ordinate the preparation and delivery of learning opportunities
  - C26 Assist and support the application of learning
  - C27 Originate learning support materials

D Evaluate the effectiveness of training and development

- **D1 Evaluate the effectiveness of training and development**
  - D11 Plan and set up systems for evaluating the training and development function
  - D12 Evaluate the training and development function
  - D13 Modify systems and practices to improve training and development
- **D2 Evaluate individual and group achievement against objectives**
  - D21 Plan and set up systems to evaluate the achievement of objects
  - D22 Evaluate the achievement of outcomes against learning objectives
  - D23 Modify and adapt learning plans
- **D3 Assess achievements for public certification**
  - D31 Assess candidate performance
  - D32 Assess candidate using diverse evidence
  - D33 Co-ordinate the assessment process
  - D34 Verify the assessment process
  - D35 Identify previously acquired competence

E Support training and development advances and practice

- **E1 Contribute to advances in training and development**
  - E11 Contribute to training and development practice
  - E12 Evaluate and disseminate advances in training and development
- **E2 Provide services to support training and development practice**
  - E21 Administer training facilities
  - E22 Establish and maintain information systems
  - E23 Establish and maintain financial systems

Figure 23.1 Management Charter Initiative middle level standards

9. *Continuous development.* Initial qualification is not enough. Updating and competence extension will be needed and failure to do this will lead to loss of qualification.

10. The standards to be achieved are determined by designated *lead bodies*, which are large committees of practitioners, or professional bodies, so that vocational standards are decided by those in charge of the workplace instead of by those in charge of the classroom. One of these is the Management Charter Initiative (MCI), which has set standards for management at the administrative and middle level and has recently published standards for the strategic level. These are intended to equate to Certificate, Diploma and MBA. Figure 23.1 lists the middle level standards.

11. *Assessment.* Written examinations are not regarded as being always the most appropriate means of assessing competence. Assessment of whether or not the learner has attained the appropriate standard must be by a *qualified assessor*, who becomes qualified by demonstrating competence according to two units of the scheme produced by the Training and Development Lead Body. Assessment may be partly by portfolio (see 8 above), but has to be *work-based*. Originally it was to be in the workplace, but that proved impracticable to implement.

12. *General National Vocational Qualifications* are school- or college-based and take the place of BTec and similar qualifications. The general intention is that NVQs should run alongside traditional academic qualifications at under-graduate level.

NVQs have had a rough side since the concept was first introduced, coming under some heavy criticism and not being extensively taken up. The most common reservations about NVQs are as follows.

1. *Assessment.* The emphasis has been shifted away from learning towards assessment. The assessment process is itself somewhat laborious. Research by the Institute of Manpower Studies (1994) found that the most common problem about introducing NVQs was finding the time to organise the assessments. The study found that 5 per cent of employers were using NVQs and half of them reported this difficulty.

2. *Bureaucracy.* NVQs have developed an entire vocabulary to bring the concept into action, and this causes difficulties. One of the key terms is 'range indicators' and at a recent meeting of fifty personnel practitioners, no one could produce a definition that the rest of the group could accept. Also the assessment process specifies a number of different standards of performance that have to be demonstrated and assessed. Each of these has to be described succinctly and the performance measured.

3. *The generality of the standards.* Those employers who take up NVQs are likely to modify them for their own use. In research at UMIST over three years more

than twenty employer schemes for MCI have been examined, and each one is tailored to the needs of the particular business. This is due to two reasons. First, the national standards are seen as being too general and secondly, because employers are concerned to train for their own needs rather than for national needs of skilled human resources. This begins to undermine the concept of a *national* qualification.

4. *The quality of the standards.* It is very difficult to ensure a satisfactory quality of assessment, where so much depends on a large number of individual assessors. The initial emphatic opposition to written examination has modified, especially as NVQs are contemplated for some of the well-established professions, such as medicine and the law.

5. *The training agenda.* Within a large vested interest such as British higher education, there is obviously some resistance to the idea that educators are not competent to set the training agenda.

> There seems to be a drift towards a training agenda in management education, such that students are technically equipped to take up a task but intellectually incapable of addressing the ideas that have shaped the creation of that task. (Berry 1990)

Those who have championed the concept of employers setting the agenda are equally concerned that employers risk losing the control they have achieved.

> ... if we do not move towards a market system, and the Government continues to fund and intervene heavily in the development and design process, NVQs could soon be a dead duck and vocational qualifications would, once again, be knowledge-based and controlled mainly by educationalists. The opportunity for a system which matches employers' needs and individuals' aspirations to the greater benefit of UK plc would have been lost. (Marshall, 1994)

A useful review of NVQ problems and the NCVQ approach to their resolution is provided by McKiddie (1994). An excellent practical guide to the approach can be found in Fletcher (1991). Opposition from the academic world continues (for example, Smithers 1994), although some universities now provide programmes leading to NVQs.

Other competence-based approaches

Although there has been much controversy about NVQs, they are not the only form of competence-based training that is being provided. Boam and Sparrow (1992) describe a number of different schemes. Although competence-based training has become the received wisdom on approaches to management training, all the lists we have seen have been difficult to use in practice, mainly due to an understandable attempt to be precise or over-inclusive.

Torrington, Waite and Weightman (1992) developed a composite model to describe the work of personnel specialists working in the health service. We are therefore presenting a crude model here as a framework which could be applied to other groups of jobs. It is crude because the boundaries must be blurred: ambiguity is essential if we are to make sense.

Our analysis starts from this point, by considering not whether a person is able to do a job, but what skills are required in order to be able to do a job: not 'this is how you do recruitment', but 'these are the skills you need in order to do recruitment excellently'. This is the approach of competence analysis, distinguishing between the competent performance of a job and the competencies required in order to perform a job excellently.

The basis of this model is an analysis of the jobs that need doing by personnel managers. The following list we feel encompasses the main areas of expertise that a large NHS personnel department could need to have. The composite is based on eight facets of the personnel operational role:

1.   The personnel manager as *selector*.
2.   The personnel manager as *paymaster*.
3.   The personnel manager as *negotiator*.
4.   The personnel manager as *performance monitor*.
5.   The personnel manager as *welfare worker*.
6.   The personnel manager as *human resource planner*.
7.   The personnel manager as *trainer*.
8.   The personnel manager as *communicator*.

Every mainstream personnel management job consists of one or more of these roles. Selector and Trainer are those most commonly found to comprise a complete job. Some combination of two or three is usual. All the roles are highly interdependent.

Figure 23.2 summarises the main areas of expertise or *professional competence* that are comprehended by each professional role. There is also a list of generic competencies which are more general competencies used in at least two, and sometimes more, of the professional roles.

The idea of the Job Composite Model, therefore, is that each individual's job will be a composite of activities drawn from the professional list and from the shorter list of *generic competencies*. Job-specific individual training needs can then be derived by using our self-assessment questionnaire, which is a more detailed version of Figure 23.2 developed from these two lists of competencies.

There have been many criticisms of the type of analysis we are putting forward here, not least of which is the belief that a competence-based approach cannot take into account individual differences.

> Users of competency-based assessment should be aware that it provides one relatively partial view of performance. Its strong emphasis on the need for scientific rigour tends to lead to a rather narrow perspective which, on its own, is barely capable of reflecting the rich and often paradoxical nature of human behaviour. (Jacobs 1989)

Name. . . . . Date . . . .

Current post . . . .

Using the job composite model of personnel competencies, complete the following checklist by assessing your present expertise in each of the identified competencies as either A,B,C,D or E, indicating:

A   Little or no expertise;
B   Some expertise, but a need for further development or updating now;
C   Expert;
D   Considerable expertise, but some further development or updating necessary soon;
E   Not relevant to the present post.

Professional competencies
1. *The PM as selector*
....   Vacancy identifications
....   Job analysis
....   Recruitment advertising
....   Selection process
....   Psychometric testing
....   Selection decision-making
....   Letters of offer
....   Contracts of employment
....   Employee records
....   Induction/socialisation

2. *The PM as paymaster*
....   Job evaluation
....   Pay determination
....   Employee benefits
....   Performance-related pay
....   Salary administration
....   Salary structures
....   Pensions and sick pay
....   Taxation and National Insurance

3. *The PM as negotiator*
....   Consultation
....   Employee involvement
....   Negotiating bodies
....   Trade union recognition
....   Agreements and procedures
....   Grievance and discipline
....   Redundancy and dismissal
....   Industrial tribunals

4. *The PM as performance monitor*
....   Appraisal/assessment
....   Attendance management
....   Management of poor performance

5. *The PM as welfare officer*
....   Health and safety
....   Counselling services
....   Occupational health
....   Health and safety legislation

6. *The PM as human resource planner*
....   Supply and demand forecasting
....   Modelling and extrapolation
....   Manpower utilisation
....   Planning
....   Statistical method
....   Computer analysis

7. *The PM as trainer*
....   Identification of training needs
....   Design of training
....   Delivery of training
....   Evaluation of training

8. *The PM as communicator*
....   Bulletins
....   Community relations
....   Team briefing
....   In-house magazine

Generic competencies
9. *Managing oneself*
....   Personal organisation
....   Time management
....   Interpersonal communication
....   Assertiveness
....   Problem-solving and decision making
....   Report writing
....   Reading
....   Presentations
....   Managing stress

10. *Working in the organisation*
....   Networking
....   Working in groups
....   Power and authority
....   Influencing
....   Negotiating

11. *Getting things dones*
....   Setting objectives
....   Goal planning and target setting
....   Managing external consultants
....   Using statistics
....   Information technology literacy
....   Keyboard skills
....   Minute-taking
....   Record-keeping
....   Setting up systems and procedures

12. *Working with people*
....   Interviewing
....   Listening
....   Counselling
....   Conducting and participating in meetings
....   Team-building

Figure 23.2   Personnel competencies

One way around this problem is to construct competence analysis in terms of self-assessment, enabling staff at all levels and varying from tyro to past master to assess their own training needs.

Our research has demonstrated the need for this approach caused by the wide differences in practice between parts of the organisation, which make it quite inappropriate to have an 'ideal' model of, for example, a personnel department. These are some of the main differences we found between Health Service Districts:

- The different levels of funding received.
- The different skills and experience of the people.
- The differing hierarchical position of personnel, including the relationship to the general manager.
- The differing relationships with Region.
- Differing perceptions of the personnel role held by personnel directors, their staff and their colleagues.
- The differing nature of the districts themselves: size, labour markets, medical specialisms, and so forth.

Below we give some hypothetical examples of the sort of competencies, both professional and generic, that particular job holders might conclude were necessary for them to do their work. These lists might be arrived at by the job-holder alone or in consultation with their boss and/or colleagues.

A pay strategy post

Appropriate professional competencies:

1. Job analysis
1. Job evaluation
2. Pay determination
2. Employee benefits
2. Performance-related pay
2. Salary administration
2. Salary structures
2. Pensions/sick pay
2. Taxation and National Insurance
3. Consultation
3. Employee involvement
3. Negotiating bodies
3. Agreement and procedures
6. Planning
6. Computer analysis

Appropriate generic competencies:

9. Personal organisation
9. Interpersonal communication
9. Problem-solving and decision-making
9. Report-writing
9. Making presentations
10. Networking
10. Influencing
11. Statistics
11. Information technology literacy
11. Setting up systems and procedures
12. Conducting and participating in meetings

Most of the other competencies listed would probably be scored E (no current or foreseeable need for competence in this area). Of the competencies listed which are needed, some no doubt will have been scored A or B, suggesting some difficulty. These then need prioritising.

A recruitment officer post

Appropriate professional competencies:

1. Vacancy identification
1. Job analysis
1. Recruitment advertising
1. Selection process
1. Selection decision-making
1. Letters of offer
1. Contracts of employment
1. Induction socialisation
3. Agreements and procedures
6. Supply and demand forecasting

Appropriate generic competencies:

9. Managing oneself
9. Time management
9. Interpersonal communication
12. Interviewing

REVIEW TOPIC 23.2

How many of the generic competencies listed in Figure 23.2 are common to most jobs?

□ SUMMARY PROPOSITIONS

23.1 The level of training provision in most companies is lower than is needed for international competitiveness, economic performance and the reasonable expectations of employees.

23.2 Effective company training cannot come from the training officer or department alone. It must involve both the workplace and the line manager of the trainee.

23.3 Training is one of the first casualties of financial economies in organisations because of the problem of results, the lack of external controls and lack of advocacy by personnel managers.

23.4 A greater interest in marketing has provided some stimulus to training in more efficient companies.

23.5 Training is not only responding to requirements; it is also seeking out training needs before they become obvious and anticipating ways in which training could make a contribution to business growth.

23.6 Evaluation of training is more effective when directed at trainees' behaviour and how this has changed than when directed at their opinions.

23.7 Training costs constitute a lower proportion of company turnover than in West Germany and the United States.

References

Berry, A. J. (1990), 'Masters or subjects?', *British Academy of Management Newsletter*, no. 5, February.

Boam, R. and Sparrow, P. (1992), *Designing and Achieving Competency*, Maidenhead: McGraw Hill.

Boyatsis, R. E. (1982), *The Competent Manager*, New York: Wiley.

Constable, J. and McCormick, R. (1987), *The Making of British Managers*, Corby: British Institute of Management.

Fletcher, S. (1991), *NVQs, Standards and Competence*, London: Kogan Page.

Jacobs, R. (1989), 'Getting the measure of management competency', *Personnel Management*, vol. 21, no. 6, June, pp. 32–7.

Marshall, V. (1994), 'Employers beware: don't lose control of your NVQs', *Personnel Management*, vol. 26, no. 3, pp. 30–3.

Smithers, A. (1994), 'Whither Competences?', reported in *Times Higher Education Supplement*, 22 April.

Torrington, D. P., Waite, D. and Weightman, J. B. (1992), 'A continuous development approach to training health service professionals', *Journal of European Industrial Training*, vol. 16, no. 3, pp. 3–12.

Woodruffe, C. (1992), 'What is meant by competency?', in R. Boam, and P. Sparrow (eds), *Designing and Achieving Competency*, pp. 16–30, London: McGraw Hill.

Management development

If we want to develop managers so that they are effective contributors to the organisation we need to have a clear view of what an effective contribution would look like. The use of personal competencies, as described in the last chapter, can be helpful in describing the way that an effective manager behaves, but the truth is that there can be no universal prescription of an effective manager. Effectiveness will vary with organisational context, and on whose perspective we are adopting. What makes an effective manager is a complex of personality, innate skills, developed skills, experiences and learning.

In this chapter we do not attempt prescription. We do consider the growth and identity of management development, review some differing perspectives on its nature and goals, and in particular concentrate on the processes that contribute towards management development.

The growth of management development

There is a strong myth-making tradition attached to the development of effective management as those senior in organisations have sought to preserve their elite status. Initially, there was no question of acquiring skill; entry to a management position came as part of the right of ownership, the favour of the owner or the natural entitlement of those in a particular social position. As the size of organisations and the number of managers began to increase, there was a move to professionalisation to justify managerial status, with the development of professional or quasiprofessional bodies, controlling entry by examination and election. This, together with organisational complexity, produced specialisation and the longest-running feature of management development: management training courses. Run by educational establishments, professional bodies, employers or consultants, there is a wide range of courses which seek to communicate some distilled wisdom relating to the management task. Although the training course is well established, it was joined during the 1960s by a fresh idea – that of developing individuals. Instead of managers being fed information on a course, their managerial capacity and potential would be developed by a wide variety of experiences, through which they would acquire greater understanding, awareness, sensitivity, self-confidence and those other aspects of effectiveness that were regarded as most important but which could not be inculcated. This change of emphasis was accompanied by growing use of employee appraisal to determine individual development needs, rather than leaving trainers to produce universal programmes. There was also some move towards putting the control of the development programme in the hands of the individual being developed, instead of the experts. In reporting on one such experiment Graves concludes: 'managers are better able to develop their own skills if given development opportunities rather than training ... training should be based on managerial needs as perceived by the managers rather than development needs perceived by the trainers' (Graves 1976, p. 15). Furthermore, such development may well take place on the job in the everyday ebb and flow of events rather than in the specially contrived circumstances beloved by trainers. In this way the learning is not only relevant to the job being done, it may also alter the manager's approach to their work as they become more questioning of events and more analytical of processes: 'The remarkable and persuasive reason for saying that nonetheless managers can become more effective as learners lies in the dedication to doing things, being active, that is the hallmark of so many of them' (Mumford 1981, p. 380). Mumford continues by suggesting that the art of encouraging learning is: 'to ask them to undertake activities associated with learning which build on existing managerial processes and rewards' (Mumford 1981).

The focus in management development has moved to emphasise activities such as coaching, action learning, natural learning and self development. In line with this increased emphasis on learning in the job, there has also been an upsurge of interest in mentoring, which like many of the best management development ideas describes a process long familiar to experienced managers, but substantially unrecognised and underused (Mumford 1985). This process is largely uncontrolled at present, although there is a clear increase in formal mentoring schemes. An understanding of mentoring and of the contributions of peers gives critical insight into the role of work relationships in the development of managers.

Interest in mentoring has also highlighted a particular problem for the development of women managers, that of finding a role model. It appears that, for the few women who are mentors or protegées, the nature of the relationship is different from that of men. This brings us to the thorny problem of whether the training and development needs of women managers are different from those of men and whether there should be separate development programmes especially for women.

The identity of management development

We can see from the above that management training contributes to management development but is not synonymous with it, as managers also learn and develop in many other ways. Management training and management development can be differentiated in four important ways.

1.   Management development is a broader concept and is more concerned with developing the whole person rather than emphasising the learning of narrowly defined skills.
2.   Management development emphasises the contribution of formal and informal work experiences.
3.   The concept of management development places a greater responsibility on managers to develop themselves than is placed on most employees to train themselves.
4.   Although in training generally there always needs to have a concern with the future, this is especially emphasised in managerial development. Managers are developed as much for jobs that they will be doing as for the jobs that they are doing. Both the organisation and the managers benefit from this approach. Management development is a vital aspect of career management, and from the organisation's point of view both are methods of satisfying human resource needs while allowing individuals to achieve their career goals.

REVIEW TOPIC 24.1

There is a growing emphasis on anticipatory learning which involves learning for the demands of the future rather than the demands of the present.

How can managers identify the demands and needs of the organisation in the future?

What do managers do?

The question 'what do managers do?' has an air of naivete, insolence and even redundancy about it. Yet it is a question which is begged by many management-related issues... The vast and growing industry of management education, training and development presumably rests upon a set of ideas about what managers do and, hence, what managers are being educated, trained and developed for (Hales 1986, p. 88).

There has been much theorising and uncertainty about the nature of managerial work. Managerial work has been studied from a variety of perspectives, including what managers do, how they distribute their time, with whom they interact, informal aspects of their work and themes that pervade management work (Hales 1986).

Among the mass of theorising has been the research of Stewart (1976) in analysing work in terms of the relationships involved, and also some common recurrent management activities which are liaison, maintenance of work processes, innovation and setting the boundaries of the job. Mintzberg (1973) suggests that managerial work comprises various combinations of ten distinct roles in three general categories: decision-making, interpersonal and information-processing. A little earlier Scholefield (1968) had produced the suggestion that managers should do three things: operate the firm, make innovations and stabilise the organisation. Other management researchers (for example, Torrington and Weightman 1982) have concentrated on the nature of the skills involved in management work, and have investigated how managers' time is allocated between the technical, administrative and managerial aspects of their jobs. Leavitt (1978) suggests four key ideas about the nature of the managing process. First, managing always includes some influencing and implementing activities, as managers have to get other people to do things. Secondly, managing also includes a great deal of problem-solving, with managers not only having to work against tight deadlines, but also work on a dozen problems at the same time. Thirdly, managers have to be problem finders, and need to take an active rather than an entirely passive stance.

A final aspect of managing, as suggested by Leavitt (1978), is that it takes place in an organisation and that managers operate in a position that is peculiarly dependent, while seeming to be independent.

One of the central themes of managerial work is that to a large extent managers define the work that they will do. This is undoubtedly one of the factors which makes managerial work so hard to characterise. Hales comments that: 'Managerial jobs seem, in general, to be sufficiently loosely defined to be highly negotiable and susceptible to choice of both style and content' (Hales 1986, p. 101). Fletcher carries this point further: 'Management is neither art nor science nor skill. At base there is nothing to do. A manager is hired for what he knows other firms do, what he can find to do, and what he can be told to do' (Fletcher 1973, p. 136).

Hales (1986) comments that this opportunity for choice and negotiation, together with variation and contingency, pressure and conflict, and lack of opportunity for reflection are central themes in managerial work. In the same vein Mumford (1987) characterises the reality of management as very different from the logical rational and organising processes that it may superficially appear to be about. He suggests that management is an interactive activity with multi-programmed tasks being carried out at a hectic pace and dependent on the use of informal networks. In addition he argues that a manager's work is more often constrained than innovative and unplanned rather than proactive.

All these ideas clearly have a bearing on the objectives of management development. However, a useful counterblast to all this theorising is the iconoclasm of Mant (1977), whose scepticism is so perceptive and persuasive that one is left with the feeling that he might just be right when he argues that we tend to undervalue a large number of jobs that are of true social and economic importance, such as 'salesman' and 'housewife', while ascribing enormous significance to the job of manager, which seems non-existent in some of the world's more successful industrial societies.

The goals of management development

Undoubtedly, those people who design management development programmes and experiences aim to encourage the development of effective managers. One of the greatest difficulties is that although there is much research about what managers do, much less is written about the relationship between this and their effectiveness. Hales (1986) comments that some of the more celebrated writings on effective management are singularly reticent about specifying what effective managers are effective at. We have already noted that the use of competency description can be helpful here, but some of the most helpful comments have been made by Pedler, Burgoyne and Boydell (1991) who identify eleven necessary qualities of effective managers. These include command of basic facts, relevant professional knowledge, continuing sensitivity to events, problem-solving and decision-making skills, social skills, emotional resilience, proactivity, creativity, mental agility, balanced learning habits and skills and self-knowledge. A glance back at Mumford's characterisation of the reality of management will show some immediate contradictions. We can only conclude that there is much uncertainty about what managers do, and it is not surprising therefore that the goals of management development are often uncertain and frequently spurious. The goals of the organisers of development may differ markedly from those undergoing the process. Among the generalisations we can make are that management development has traditionally been an elitist process, although this may be changing with greater development for all; emphasis will be on skills at doing, rather than knowledge about; and dominant will be the capacity of the individual manager to be socially adroit and to evaluate information as a preliminary to making choices between alternatives.

Following on from the last section we would suggest that it would be fruitful, among other things, to develop managers who can structure their own jobs and manage themselves and their careers. Much of the management development that takes place does so without any externally imposed goals – it takes place in the context of the job and is guided to a greater or lesser extent by managers themselves. The capacity of managers to develop others is increasingly seen as fundamental. The process of managerial development at work has been identified as incurring emotional costs (Snell 1988) and this may influence the goals themselves.

We move on to review some aspects of organising development experiences, including informal and formal training input. We discuss the nature of management learning and based on this, how learning techniques and support can be used together with job experiences to contribute to their development as managers.

Approaches to management development

Education and training courses

A training course will usually be a key feature in a formal programme of development, and these may be standard offerings by various specialist bodies or in-house courses developed for their own specialist needs. Increasingly, these options are being combined so that there is the possibility of an externally provided course tailored to suit an organisation's particular needs.

First are the pre-experience courses: full-time education leading to academic qualification with a management sciences or business studies label and undertaken by young people as a preliminary to a career. These have been developed in the United Kingdom since the mid-1960s and have proved very popular with students at universities and polytechnics. They are often described as 'vocational' and intended to be a practical preparation for a management-type occupation on completion. They can never, however, be vocational in the same sense as degrees in areas such as medicine or architecture because there is relatively little practical element in the course. The sandwich courses that incorporate periods of work in the 'real' world may help to bring the feet of students nearer to the ground, but they cannot give any meaningful experience in, and practice at, managerial work. The courses provide an education, normally based on a study of the academic disciplines of economics, mathematics, psychology and sociology and incorporating some work in the more specialised disciplines such as industrial relations and organisational behaviour, as well as an introduction to the practical areas like accounting, marketing, personnel and production. The student should emerge with a balanced understanding of the workings of an industrial society and an industrial economy, and they will have some useful blocks of information which may well be at the frontiers of knowledge in management thought. The student should also have developed the more traditional qualities of maturity and the ability to analyse and debate that university education purports to nurture: they will not be trained to be a manager.

Second are the post-experience courses: full-time education usually leading to a diploma or master's degree with a management or business label and undertaken during a career. Although such courses were being run in this country early in this century, the great boom came after the establishment of the London and Manchester Business Schools and other management centres in the 1960s. The main difference is not only that students are older, but that they study on the basis of experience they have had and with the knowledge of the work to which they will return. Members of a course at a business school may be seconded or supported on a part-time basis by their employer at a time when they have already held a management post. The material of the course may not be very different from that of the pre-experience course, but the student's perception will be very different and their application of any new insights or skills will be more immediate.

Neither pre-experience nor post-experience courses of the type described here will feature strongly the skills element mentioned on pages 421–2.

The third category can be generally described as consultancy courses. Varying from a half-day to several weeks in length, they are run by consultants or professional bodies for all comers. They have the advantage that they bring together people from varying occupational backgrounds and are not, therefore, as introspective as in-house courses and are popular for topical issues. They are, however, often relatively expensive and superficial, despite their value as sources of industrial folklore, by which we mean the swapping of experiences among course members. The most valuable courses of this type are those that concentrate on specific areas or knowledge, such as developing interviewing or disciplinary skills, or being introduced to a new national initiative. This short-course approach is probably the only way for managers to come to terms with some new development, such as a change in legislation, because they need not only to find an interpretation of the development, they also need to share views and reactions with fellow managers to ensure that their own feelings are not idiosyncratic or perverse.

A fourth category is in-house courses which are often similar in nature to the consultancy courses. Such in-house courses are often run with the benefit of some external expertise, but this is not always the case. In-house courses can be particularly useful if the training needs to relate to specific organisational procedures and structures, or if it is geared to encouraging managers to work more effectively together in the organisational environment. The drawbacks of in-house courses are that they suffer from a lack of breadth of both content and input from managers, and there is no possibility of learning from people in other organisations.

Lastly, and on the fringe of education and training courses, are outdoor (sometimes known as outward bound) – type courses. Outdoor courses attempt to develop such skills as leadership, getting results through people, self-confidence in handling people and increasing self-awareness through a variety of experiences including outdoor physical challenges. One course brochure states:

> A range of intellectual, emotional and physical challenges is presented which involves
> working in a variety of environments; in group syndicate rooms, outdoor project areas,
> creative workshops, on rivers and lakes and in the hills and mountains. (Brathay 1986)

The nature of learning

There has been a significant amount of work done which helps us understand how managers, and others, learn from their experiences. Kolb *et al.* (1984) argued that it is useful to combine the characteristics of learning, which is usually regarded as

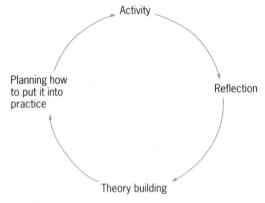

Figure 24.2 The learning cycle (adapted from Kolb (1984) and Honey and Mumford (1989))

Gwen is a management trainer in a large organisation running a number of in-house management courses. She has just moved into this position from her role as section leader in the research department – the move was seen as a career development activity in order to strengthen her managerial skills.

Gwen is working with her manager to learn from her experiences. Here is an extract from her learning diary based on the learning cycle:

Activity – I've had a go at running three sessions on my own now, doing the input and handling the questions.

Reflection – I find the input much easier than handling questions. When I'm asked a question and answer it I have the feeling they're not convinced by my reply and I feel awkward that we seem to finish the session hanging in mid-air. I would like to be able to encourage more open discussion.

Theory building – If I give an answer to a question it closes off debate by the fact that I have 'pronounced' what is 'right'. If I want them to discuss I have to avoid giving my views at first.

Planning practice – When I am asked a question rather than answering it I will say to the group 'What does anyone think about that?' or 'What do you think?' (to the individual who asked) or 'What are the possibilities here?' I will keep encouraging them to respond to each other and reinforce where necessary, or help them change tack by asking another question.

passive, with those of problem-solving, which is usually regarded as active. From this combination Kolb developed a four-stage learning cycle which was further developed by Honey and Mumford (1989). The four stages, based on both influences, are shown in Figure 24.2.

Each of these four stages of the learning cycle is critical to effective learning, but few people are strong at each stage and it is helpful to understand where our strengths and weaknesses lie. Honey and Mumford designed a questionnaire to achieve this and which identified individuals' learning styles as 'activist', 'reflector', 'theorist' and 'pragmatist'. Understanding our strengths and weaknesses enables us to choose learning activities which suit our style, and also gives us the opportunity to decide to strengthen a particularly weak learning stage of our learning cycle.

Activists learn best from 'having a go', and trying something out without necessarily preparing. They would be enthusiastic about role play exercises and keen to take risks in the real environment.

Reflectors are much better at listening and observing. They are effective at reflecting on their own and others' experiences and good at analysing what happened and why.

Theorists' strengths are in building a concept or a theory on the basis of their analysis. They are good at integrating different pieces of information, and building models of the way things operate. They may choose to start their learning by reading around a topic.

Pragmatists are keen to *use* whatever they learn and will always work out how they can apply it in a real situation. They will plan how to put it into practice. They will value information/ideas they are given only if they can see how to relate them to practical tasks they need to do.

An understanding of the way that managers learn from experience is paralleled by a change in emphasis in management development from formal training course offering to learning through the job itself, with appropriate support. The remainder of approaches to management development rely heavily on learning from experience.

REVIEW TOPIC 24.2

Identify a management skills area which you need to develop.

(You may find it particularly helpful to choose an interpersonal area, for example assertiveness, influencing others, presentation, being more sociable, contributing to meetings, helping others.)

Keep a learning diary over the next few weeks logging anything which is relevant to your development area. Use the framework which Gwen used on page 425.

At the end of the period review what you have learned in your development area and also what you have learned about the learning cycle.

Action learning

The iconoclasm of Mant (1977), referred to earlier in this chapter, is mild compared with that of Revans (see, for example, Revans 1972, 1974), one of the great original thinkers to study management. As a professor of management he became more and more disenchanted with the world of management education which he saw developing around him. Among the many aphorisms attributed to him was: 'If I teach my son to read, how do I know he will not read rubbish; if I teach him to write, how do I know that he will not write yet another book on management education?' Despairing of the way in which the London and Manchester Business Schools were established, Revans resigned his chair in Manchester and moved to Belgium to start his first action learning project. This was based on his conviction that managers do not need education but the ability to solve problems. His method has been, basically, to organise exchanges, so that a manager experienced in one organisation is planted in another to solve a particular set of problems that is proving baffling. He or she brings a difference of experience, a freshness of approach, and they are not dependent on their new, temporary organisational peers for their career growth. They work on the problem for a period of months, having many sessions of discussion and debate with a group of other individuals similarly planted in unfamiliar organisations with a knotty problem to solve. The learning stems from the immediate problem that is presented, and from all the others that emerge, one by one, in the steps towards a solution. This presents a need that the student has to satisfy and all the learning is in terms of what they discover they need to know rather than what someone else feels is necessary. It is an idea of startling simplicity. Its relative unpopularity in academic circles is easy to understand, but in management circles there has been some diffidence because the action learning approach nearly always stirs something up, and not all organisations have the nerve to risk the soul-searching and upheaval that is caused.

Coaching

Coaching is an informal approach to management development based on a close relationship between the developing manager and one other person, usually their immediate manager, who is experienced in management. The manager as coach helps trainees to develop by giving them the opportunity to perform an increasing range of management tasks, and by helping them to learn from their experiences. They work to improve the trainee's performance by asking searching questions, discussion, exhortation, encouragement, understanding, counselling and providing information and feedback. It is vital that the coach is someone who has experienced those things which the trainee is now learning, as Henry Boettinger, that most elegant of writers on management, makes the point:

> Only someone who can actually perform in an art is qualified to teach it. There is no question that constructive criticism from an informed bystander is helpful; actors, for instance, can learn a great deal about human motivation from psychiatrists. Nevertheless, this kind of procedure is different from the one an actor goes through to show another how to express human feelings. (Boettinger 1975)

The coach, as the immediate manager of the learner, is also in an excellent position to provide the appropriate learning opportunities in terms of new/challenging tasks, membership of working parties and committees, secondments, deputising and so on. Mumford (1994) has written an excellent guide to the ways that managers can help other managers to learn.

Mentoring

> As a training and development tool, it [mentoring] is not a new concept. For centuries wise men have offered counsel to the young. In ancient Greece, Odysseus entrusted the education of his son Telemachus to a trusted counsellor and friend. This trusted and wise friend, Mentor, reputedly became the counsellor, guide, tutor, coach, sponsor and mentor for his protege, Telemachus. (Hunt and Michael 1983)

Mentoring is seen as offering a wide range of advantages for the development of the protegé, coaching as described above being just one of the benefits of the relationship. The mentor would occasionally be the individual's immediate manager, but

```
Mentoring relationships                  Peer relationships

Career-enchancing functions              Career-enhancing functions
 • sponsorship                            • information sharing
 • coaching                               • career strategising
 • exposure and visibility                • job-related feedback
 • protection
 • challenging work assignments

Psychosocial functions                   Psychosocial functions
 • acceptance and confirmation            • confirmation
 • counselling                            • emotional support
 • role modelling                         • personal feedback
 • friendship                             • friendship

Special attribute                        Special attribute
 • complementarity                        • mutuality
```

Figure 24.3   Development functions – comparison of mentoring and peer
relationships (Kram and Isabella 1985). Reproduced with the
permission of the American Academy of Management.

more often it is a more senior manager in the same or a different function. Kram
(1983) identifies two broad functions of mentoring; first, career functions, which are
those aspects of the relationship that primarily enhance career advancement; secondly,
psychosocial functions, which are those aspects of the relationship that primarily
enhance a sense of competence, clarity of identity and effectiveness in the managerial
role. Figure 24.3 shows these functions in more detail and compares them with the
functions of peer relationships, which we discuss in the following section. There is a
much greater stress in the mentoring relationship than in the coaching relationship, on
career success and individuals selected for mentoring because, among other things,
they are good performers, from the right social background, and know the potential
mentors socially (Kanter 1977). There are advantages in the relationship for mentors
as well as protegés – these include reflected glory from a successful protegé, the development of supporters throughout the organisation and the facilitation of their own
promotion by adequate training of a replacement (Hunt and Michael 1983).

   Managers are also seen as responsible for developing talent, and mentorship
may be encouraged or formalised as, for example, in the Bell Laboratories and some
departments of the US Government (Stumpf and London 1981). The difficulties of
establishing a formal programme include the potential mismatch of individuals,
unreal expectations on both sides, and the time and effort involved. Gibb and
Megginson (1993) surveyed a number of formal mentoring schemes and describe
that such UK schemes offer a slightly different perspective than the US approach.
They argue from the literature and from their research that the mentoring relationship is multifaceted, and that in the United Kingdom in particular there is greater
emphasis than in the United States on learning support, often based around the
restructuring of our qualification system. In these situations the protegés were more
likely to have specific learning goals. An example might be mentoring in support of

achieving MCI competencies or other competency-based qualifications. In the formal schemes surveyed just less than half the protégés were working on a learning contract (see page 433 of this chapter for further details).

Four mentoring roles were identified by Gibb and Megginson from the literature – these were helping to improve performance, helping career development, acting as a counsellor and sharing knowledge. Burke and McKeen (1989) offer a thoughtful discussion of the advantages and disadvantages of formal programmes.

Peer relationships

Although mentor–protégé relationships have been shown to be related to high levels of career success, not all developing managers have access to such a relationship. Supportive peer relationships at work are potentially more available to the individual and offer a number of benefits for the development of both individuals. The benefits that are available depend on the nature of the peer relationship, and Kram and Isabella (1985) have identified three groups of peer relationships which are differentiated by their primary development functions and which can be expressed on a continuum from 'information peer' through 'collegial peer' to 'special peer'. Table 24.1 shows the developmental functions and the characteristics of each type of relationship. Most of us benefit from one or a number of peer relationships at work but often we do not readily appreciate their contribution towards our development. Peer relationships most often develop on an informal basis and provide mutual support. Some organisations, however, formally appoint an existing employee to provide such support to a new member of staff through their first 12–18 months in the organisation. These relationships may, of course, continue beyond the initial period. The name for the appointed employee will vary from organisation to organisation, and sometimes the word 'coach' or 'mentor' is used – which can be confusing! Cromer (1989) discusses the advantages of peer relationships organised on a formal basis and references the skills and qualities sought in peer providers, which include accessibility, empathy, organisational experience and proven task skills.

REVIEW TOPIC 24.3

Consider each significant peer relationship that you have at work. Where does each fit on the continuum of relationships shown in Table 24.1, and what contributions does it make towards your development?

Natural learning

Natural managerial learning is learning that takes place on the job and results from managers' everyday experience of the tasks that they undertake. Natural learning is

Table 24.1   *Peer relationships and the characteristics of each type*

	Information peer	Collegial peer	Special peer
Primary functions	Information-sharing	Career strategising Job-related feedback Friendship	Confirmation Emotional support Personal feedback Friendship
Level of commitment	Demands little, but offers many benefits	Information-sharing joined by increasing levels of self-disclosure and trust	Equivalent of best friend
Intensity of relationship	Social, but limited in sharing of personal experience	Allows for greater self-expression	Strong sense of bonding
Issues worked on	Increases individual's eyes and ears to organisation (work only)	Limited support for exploration of family and work issues	Wide range of support and work issues
Needs satisfied	Source of information regarding career opportunities	Provides direct honest feedback	Offers chance to express one's personal and professional dilemmas, vulnerabilities and individuality

Source: Adapted from Kram and Isabella 1985, pp. 119–20. Reproduced with the permission of the American Academy of Management.

even more difficult to investigate than either coaching, mentoring or peer relationships, and yet the way that managers learn from everyday experiences, and their level of awareness of this, is very important for their development. Burgoyne and Hodgson (1983) collected information from managers by having them 'think aloud' while doing their work. They identified three levels of learning. The first level of learning is when the manager took in some factual information that had an immediate relevance but did not have any long-term effect on his view of the world in general. At the next level the manager learnt something that was transferable from the present situation to another – they had changed their conception about a particular aspect of their view of the world in general, this aspect being situation-specific. For example, managers use incidents to add to their personal stock of 'case law' and from this select models when dealing with future situations. In some cases managers specifically set aside time for reflective learning so that they can derive critical insights and new approaches for use in the future. Some managers also learnt through deliberate problem-solving: Burgoyne and Hodgson describe a manager who was unhappy with the way that he used his time and who tried a new approach, was unsatisfied and so tried another, liked it and kept it. Level three learning was similar to level two, but as not situation-specific. Perhaps one of the most valuable insights from this research is that some learning occurred as a direct result of the research process, due to managers verbalising what was happening or had happened, and thus becoming more conscious of the processes taking place. Mumford comments: 'In my view the focus should be on what managers do and how they can be helped to learn from what they do' (Mumford 1985, p. 30).

Self-development

To some extent self-development may be seen as a conscious effort to gain the most from natural learning in a job. The emphasis in self-development is that each individual is responsible for, and can plan, their own development, although they may need to seek help when working on some issues. Self-development involves individuals in analysing their strengths, weaknesses and the way that they learn, primarily by means of questionnaires and feedback from others. This analysis may initially begin on a self-development course, or with the help of a facilitator, but would then be continued by the individual back on the job. From this analysis individuals, perhaps with some help at first, plan their development goals and the way that they will achieve these, primarily through development opportunities within the job. When individuals consciously work on self-development they use the learning cycle in a more conscious way than described in natural learning above. They are also in a better position to seek appropriate opportunities and help, in their learning, from their manager.

Many of the activities included in self-development would be based on observation, collecting further feedback about the way they operate, experimenting with different approaches, and in particular reviewing what has happened, why and what they have learned. A managers' guide to self-development has been published by Pedler, Burgoyne and Boydell (1986), which provides some structured analyses and activities for managers to work through. Honey and Mumford (1989) have also produced a *Manual of Learning Opportunities* which is helpful in this respect.

A logical extension of self-development within the job is the development of career planning where individuals can work through a guidebook which helps them identify their career goals, the ways they learn, and their development needs, liaising with their supervisor to check assumptions, share information and receive help. This process has been described by Burgoyne and Germain (1984) in relation to research staff at Esso, and we will return to this aspect of development in Chapter 25 on Career Planning.

Self-development groups

Self-development or management learning groups are another way in which managers can support their development. Pedler (1986) describes how self-development groups originated from his work on individual self-development and provides an insight into how groups operate and develop.

Typically, a group of managers are involved in a series of meetings where they would jointly discuss their personal development, organisational issues and/or individual work problems. Groups may begin operating with a leader who is a process expert, not a content expert, and who therefore acts as a facilitator rather than, but not to the complete exclusion of, a source of information. The group itself is the primary source of information and as their process skills develop they may operate without outside help. The content and timings of the meetings can be very flexible, although clearly if they are to operate well they will require a significant level of energy and commitment. Blennerhasset (1988) gives an example of using such groups prior to further development of Information Technology (IT) and demonstrates changes in individual attitudes and behaviour and beneficial effects for the organisation.

Self-development groups can be devised in a variety of contexts. They can be part of a formal educational course, for example the Diploma in Management Studies, where a group of managers from different organisations come together to support their development; they constitute the whole of a self-development 'course'; or they can be an informal group within an organisation. However the group origi-

---

David wanted to improve his influencing skills and has sent the following draft learning contract to his manager for discussion:

Goal
>   To improve my influencing skills with both peers and more senior managers.

Specific objectives
>   To prepare for influencing situations.
>   To try and understand better the perspective of the other.
>   To identify the interpersonal skills required – probably active listening, reflecting, summarising, stating my needs, collaboration (but maybe more)
>   To be able to identify that I have had more influence in decisions made.

Activities
>   Watch a recommended video on influencing skills.
>   Re-read my notes from the interpersonal skills course I attended.
>   Watch how others in my department go about influencing.
>   Ask other people (supportive ones) how they go about it.
>   Identify possible influencing situations in advance, and plan for what I want and what might happen.
>   Reflect back on what happened, and work out how to do better next time.
>   Ask for feedback.

Resources
>   Video
>   Notes
>   The support of others.

Assessment
>   I could ask for feedback from colleagues and my manager.
>   My own assessment may be helpful.
>   Make a log over time of decisions made and my originally preferred outcome.

nates it is important that the group understands what every member hopes to get out of the group, the role of the facilitator (if there is one), the processes and rules that the group will operate by and how they agree to interact. Martin (1988) identifies some of the problems and issues in running self-development groups, particularly the nature of the facilitator role.

Learning contracts

There is increasing use of management learning contracts – sometimes used within more formalised self-development groups; on other management courses; as part of a mentoring or coaching relationship; or in working towards a competency-based qualification. These contracts are a formal commitment by the learner to work towards a specified learning goal, with an identification of how the goal might be achieved. Boak (1991) has produced a very helpful guide to the use of such contracts and suggests that they should include:

- an overall development goal;
- activities to be undertaken;
- resources required; and
- method of assessment of learning.

The value that individual managers gain from learning contracts is dependent on their choice to participate, their identification of the relevant goal and the importance and value they ascribe to achieving it. Only with commitment will a learning contract be effective, because at the end of the day it is up to the individual learner manager to make it happen.

Appraisal, performance management and MbO

Although different in their emphasis these approaches have been grouped together as they provide some similarities in terms of management development. They can all provide some performance targets and feedback on the extent to which they have been achieved. Some developmentally based Performance Management Systems include specific development goals as well as performance goals, aiming for integration between the two, with an emphasis on coaching as the key development mechanism.

We have identified the main approaches to management development and have focused on learning from the work itself – with support. Management development is, however, no solution to incorrect selection. Many organisations have now produced competency profiles of what makes an effective manager in their context, and not all of these are easily developable – for example creativity and being socially at ease. Sisson (1994) suggests that some of the desirable indicators for managers in the future are being an active analyst, willing to take risks, strong personal goals and wide vision. As we noted in Chapter 6 Kanter (1989) believes that the organisation of the future will require seven particular qualities from managers – the ability to operate without relying on hierarchy; competing in a way that enhances rather than undercuts co-operation; a high standard of ethics; humility to learn new things; a process focus; to be multifaceted and ambidextrous and to gain satisfaction from results rather than contribution. Again some of these are not so easy to develop from a very low base level. We suggest that those qualities which are harder to develop should be key criteria in the selection process.

☐ SUMMARY PROPOSITIONS

24.1 The emphasis on formal development programmes is declining in favour of greater interest in approaches to on-the-job development, such as mentoring, peer relationships and self-development.

24.2 Management development is different from management training as it is broader and geared more towards the future. It places a greater responsibility on managers to develop themselves.

24.3 There is great uncertainty about what managers do, and to some extent managers define their own jobs. It would be fruitful to help them to develop the skills to do this.

24.4 It is critical to help managers to learn from their own experiences. It is also critical for managers to develop skills in helping others to develop.

24.5 Management development is no substitute for poor management selection.

References

Blennerhasset, E. (1988), 'Research report: Management learning groups – a lesson in action', *Journal of European Industrial Training*, vol. 12, no. 8, pp. 5–12.

Boak, G. (1991), *Developing Managerial Competencies. The management learning contract approach*, London: Pitman.

Boettinger, H. M. (1975), 'Is management really an art?' *Harvard Business Review*, January–February.

Brathay, (1986), *Brathay Leadership and Development Training*, Ambleside, Cumbria: Brathay.

Burgoyne, J. G. and Germain, C. (1984), 'Self-development and career planning: an exercise in mutual benefit', *Personnel Management*, April.

Burgoyne, J. and Hodgson, V. E. (1983), 'Natural learning and managerial action: a phenomenological study in the field setting', *Journal of Management Studies*, vol. 20, no. 3.

Burke, R. J. and McKeen, C. A. (1989), 'Developing formal mentoring programs in organizations', *Business Quarterly*, vol. 53, Pt. 3, pp. 76–9.

Cromer, D. R. (1989), 'Peers as providers', *Personnel Administrator*, vol. 34, Pt 5, pp. 84–6.

Fletcher, C. (1973), 'The end of management'. In J. Child (ed.), *Man and Organisations*, London: George Allen & Unwin.

Gibb, S. and Megginson, D. (1993), 'Inside corporate mentoring schemes – a new agenda of concerns', *Personnel Review*, vol. 22, no. 1, pp. 40–54.

Graves, D. (1976), 'The managers and management development', *Personnel Review*, Autumn.

Hales, C. P. (1986), 'What do managers do? A critical review of the evidence', *Journal of Management Studies*, vol. 53, no. 1.

Honey, P. and Mumford, A. (1989), *The Manual of Learning Opportunities*, Maidenhead: Peter Honey.

Hunt, D. M. and Michael, C. (1983), 'Mentorship: a career training and development tool', *Academy of Management Review*, vol. 8, no. 3.

Kanter, R. M. (1977), *Men and Women of the Corporation*, New York: Basic Books.

Kolb, D. A., Rubin, I. M. and McIntyre, J. M. (1984), *Organisational Psychology* (4th edition), Englewood Cliffs, NJ: Prentice Hall.

Kram, K. E. (1983), 'Phases of the mentor relationship', *Academy of Management Journal*, vol. 26, no. 4.

Kram, K. E. and Isabella, L. A. (1985), 'Mentoring alternatives: the role of peer relationships in career development', *Academy of Management Journal*, vol. 28, no. 1.

Leavitt, H. J. (1978), *Management Psychology*, 4th edition, Chicago: University of Chicago Press.

Mant, A. (1977), *The Rise and Fall of the British Manager*, Basingstoke: Macmillan.

Martin, P. (1988), 'Self-development groups in the context of a structured management development programme', *Management Education and Development*, vol. 19, Pt 4, pp. 281–97.

Mintzberg, H. (1973), *The Nature of Managerial Work*, London: Harper & Row.

Mumford, A. (1981), 'What did you learn today?' *Personnel Management*, August.

Mumford, A. (1985), 'What's new in management development?' *Personnel Management*, May.

Mumford, A. (1987), 'Using reality in management development', *Management Education and Development*, vol. 18, Pt 3.

Mumford, A. (1994), *How managers develop managers*, Aldershot: Gower.

Pedler, M., Burgoyne, J. and Boydell, T. (1986), *A Manager's Guide to Self-development*, London: McGraw-Hill.

Pedler, M. (1986), 'Developing within the organisation – experiences of management self-development groups', *Management Education and Development*, vol. 17, Pt 1, Spring pp. 5–21.

Revans, R. W. (1972), 'Action learning – a management development programme', *Personnel Review*, Autumn.

Revans, R. W. (1974), 'Action learning projects'. In B. Taylor and G. L. Lippitt (eds) *Management Development and Training Handbook*, Maidenhead: McGraw-Hill.

Scholefield, J. (1968), 'The effectiveness of senior executives', *Journal of Management Studies*, May.

Sisson, K. (1994), *Personnel Management – A comprehensive guide to theory and practice*, 2nd edition, Oxford: Blackwell.

Snell, R. S. (1988), 'The emotional cost of managerial learning at work', *Management Education and Development*, vol. 19, Pt 4, pp. 322–40.

Stewart, R. (1976), *Contrasts in Management*, Maidenhead: McGraw-Hill.

Stumpf, S. A. and London, M. (1981), 'Management promotions; individual and organizational factors influencing the decision process', *Academy of Management Review*.

Torrington, D. and Weightman, I. (1982), 'Technical atrophy in middle management', *Journal of General Management*, vol. 7, no. 4.

25 Career development

June had applied for four promotions over the last two years. She knew she was ready to move on, but had been turned down on each occasion. There was no feedback from her manager about her applications, but she was beginning to think that her career had come to a dead end.

Larry, with a PhD in chemistry, was appointed to a junior research role four years ago, and he was promoted to a senior post two years ago. He saw his role as limited and he felt he was wasting his talents. There was no logical promotion route from where he was, unless he wanted to move into management which he didn't. Larry saw his only option as moving out of the organisation.

Brenda performed really well in a senior production role. She could see only two potential promotions in the function and these were not likely to become available within the next five years. She wanted to move into marketing which would provide a fresh challenge and broaden her perspective. Her manager kept blocking her efforts to move, continued to express her value to the production function, and told her to be patient.

Phil was trapped. He was at the top of the unqualified scientist career ladder and the company had indicated that this was as far as he would go. He didn't think studying for a degree would improve his chances much either. He was well paid and tempted to stay put although he felt bored and frustrated and had ceased to perform to the best of his ability.

Sarah felt as if she didn't count. She loved her job in the sales support team and was good at what she did. She did, however, want more, but not too much more. The next logical move was to apply for a position as a representative and her manager had indicated she stood a fair chance of success. This was no good to her at present as she did not feel able to combine the travelling with her family responsibilities. What she would have liked was some challenging expansion of her current role. Her requests were ignored – her manager had defined her as 'not a career woman'.

Some of the problems outlined in the above examples include lack of feedback on career development possibilities; lack of a technical promotion ladder to run in parallel with a management promotion ladder; avoidance of cross-functional moves; the desire to hold on to good people rather than encouraging their development elsewhere; lack of support for those individuals who are not seen as having the potential to move to a more senior position; lack of development opportunities within current job and the writing off of those people who do not conform to standard career development patterns. These problems typify a lack of attention to career development in the organisation. We suggest that organisations ignore career development at their peril.

In this chapter we will look at the changing context of career development and then offer some definitions, and consider why it is important both to the individual and the organisation. Following this we will review some of the concepts behind career development and then explore what we can do to manage our own careers and what organisations can do to support this process and reap the benefits.

The context of career development

Careers are different than they were. It is now much more likely that individuals will progress in a variety of organisations rather than remaining with one for the whole of their working lives. It is also more likely that they will make one or more career transitions, that is, changing to a different career area in the same or a different organisation, during their working lives. The opportunities for upward promotion in organisations are decreasing as organisations are delayered, and yet this remains as the most desirable career move for many employees. Organisations continue to work on making lateral moves and career development through job expansion a more realistic and attractive alternative. Constant organisation change and reshaping makes career planning over the longer term an exercise in fortune telling, and in any case there is clear evidence that individuals do not plan their careers to any great extent. Individuals expect to have a greater say in their career within an organisation and are generally keener to develop careers which take account of personal and family needs, including childrens' education, partner's career and quality of life. Career development is no longer a stand-alone issue and needs to be viewed in the context of the life and development of the whole person, not just the person as employee.

Definitions and importance of career development

A career can be defined as the pattern or sequence of work roles of an individual. Traditionally the word would be applied only to those occupying managerial and professional roles but increasingly it is seen as appropriate for everyone in relation to their work roles. Also traditionally the word career has been used to imply upward movement and advancement in work roles, whereas we now recognise other moves as legitimate expressions of career development, including development and extension within the job itself.

We view career development as something experienced by the individual, and therefore not necessarily bounded by one organisation. This also means that the responsibility for managing a career is with the individual, although the organisation may play a key role in facilitating and supporting this.

The primary purpose of career development, then, is to meet the needs of the individual at work, although clearly it makes sense to meet organisation needs at the same time where this is possible. Career success is seen through the eyes of the individual, and can be defined as individual satisfaction with career through meeting personal career goals, while at the same time making a contribution to the organisation. In this respect our perspective differs from, for instance, Stamp (1989) who in her article on career development gives the needs of the individual and the organisation equal weight. Although in this chapter we prioritise the needs of the individual, in Chapter 5 we have prioritised the needs of the organisation when we reviewed replacement and succession planning.

In considering the priority we have given to the individual in career development, it is also worth noting the general benefits that this can provide for the organisation as it:

● makes the organisation attractive to potential recruits;
● enhances the image of the organisation, by demonstrating a recognition of employee needs;
● is likely to encourage employee commitment and reduce staff turnover;
● is likely to encourage motivation and job performance as employees can see some possible movement and progress in their work; and perhaps most importantly exploits the full potential of the workforce.

Before we look at how individuals can manage their career development and how organisations can support this, we need to review some of the concepts underlying the notion of career, as an understanding of these is important for both the individual and the organisation in selecting the most appropriate career activities.

Understanding careers

Career development stages

Many authors have attempted to map out the ideal stages of a successful career. These are compatible with the life stages outlined by such writers as Levinson (1978), but more specifically Schein offers nine stages of the career life cycle and these are shown in Table 25.1. Other authors such as Super (1980) and Hall and Nougaim (1968) have suggested five. In this section we use the five stages outlined by Greenhaus and Callanan (1993).

Table 25.1 *Schein's stages of the Career Development Cycle*

0–21	Growth, fantasy, exploration
16–25	Entry into the world of work
16–25	Basic training
17–30	Full membership in early career
25+	Full membership in mid-career
35–45	Mid-career crisis
40+	Late career
40+	Decline and disengagement
	Retirement

Source: Summarised from Schein 1978, pp. 40–6.

Stage 1. Occupational choice: preparation for work

Greenhaus and Callanan suggest that this stage may last until around age 25 years, or may reappear for those who wish to change career later in life, and involves the development of an occupational self-image. The key theme is a matching process between the strengths, weaknesses, values and desired lifestyle of the individual and the requirements and benefits of a range of occupations. One of the difficulties that can arise at this stage is a lack of individual self-awareness. There are countless tests available to help identify individual interests, but these can only complete part of the picture. Perhaps more effective are structured exercises which help people look at themselves from a range of perspectives. Other problems involve individuals limiting their choice due to social, cultural, gender or racial characteristics. We often use role models to identify potential occupations. On some occasions these extend the range of options we consider, but this process may also close them down. Another difficulty at this stage is gaining authentic information about careers which are different from the ones pursued by family and friends.

Stage 2. Organisational entry

There is some overlap between stage one and stage two which occurs, typically between the ages of 18 and 25 years, involves the individual in both finding a job which corresponds with their occupational self-image, and in starting to do that job. Problems here centre around the accuracy of information that the organisation provides, so that when the individual begins work their expectations and reality are very different. Recruiters understandably 'sell' their organisations and the job to potential recruits, emphasising the best parts and neglecting the downside. Applicants often neglect to test out their assumptions by asking for the specific information they really need. In addition schools, colleges and universities have, until recently, only prepared students for the technical demands of work, ignoring other skills that they will need – such as communication skills, influencing skills and dealing with organisational politics. To aid organisational entry Wanous (1992) has suggested the idea of realistic recruitment whereby organisations present a more balanced view of what to expect from the organisation and the job. Candidates are then in a better position to choose for themselves, and if they choose to join they have a more accurate picture of what to expect. There is evidence to suggest that pointing out the negative as well as the positive aspects of a job does not deter applicants from accepting an offer. Once someone has joined the organisation appropriate induction programmes and a mentoring scheme can facilitate an understanding of what the job and organisation is really like.

REVIEW TOPIC 25.1

Think of three different jobs in your organisation which have been/may be recruited externally. If a 'realistic recruitment' approach were adopted:

● what information would you give to the candidates about each job and the organisation so that a balanced picture was presented?

● what methods would you use to communicate this information?

Stage 3. Early career – establishment and achievement

The age band for early career is suggested by Greenhaus and Callanan as between 25 and 40 years.

The Establishment stage involves the process of fitting into the organisation and understanding how things are done. The new recruit not only needs to learn the specific tasks of the job, but also how the organisation works and what things are rewarded and punished. Individuals seek to be recognised as belonging, and need some form of approval from the organisation. Thorough induction programmes are important, but more especially it is important to provide the new recruit with a 'real' job and early challenges rather than a roving commission from department to department with no real purpose (as often found on trainee schemes). Feedback and support from the immediate manager are also key.

The achievement part of this stage is concerned with demonstrating competence and gaining greater responsibility and authority. It is this stage where access to opportunities for career development becomes crucial. Development within the job and opportunities for promotion and broadening moves are all aided if the organisation has a structured approach to career development involving career ladders, pathways or matrices. Feedback remains important, as do opportunities and support for further career exploration and planning.

Stage 4. Mid-career

Greenhaus and Callanan suggest that this stage usually falls between the ages of 40 to 55 years, and may involve further growth and advancement or the maintenance of a steady state. In either case it is generally accompanied by some form of re-evaluation of career and life direction. A few will experience decline at this stage. For those individuals who continue to advance, organisational support as described above remains important. For others a different type of support may be required as some people whose career has reached a plateau will experience feelings of failure. Motivation and job performance may decrease. Greenhaus and Callanan suggest that organisational support in these cases needs to involve the use of lateral career paths, job expansion, developing these individuals as mentors of others, further training to keep up to date and the use of a flexible reward system.

Stage 5. Late career

The organisation's task in this stage, from 50 years onwards, is to encourage people to continue performing well. Despite the stereotypes that abound defining older workers as slower and less able to learn, Mayo (1991) argues that if organisations believe these employees will do well and treat them as such, then they will perform well. Greenhaus and Callanan point out that the availability of flexible work patterns, clear performance standards, continued training and the avoidance of discrimination are helpful at this stage, combined with preparation for retirement.

The profile of a traditional/ideal career and some alternatives are shown in Figure 25.1.

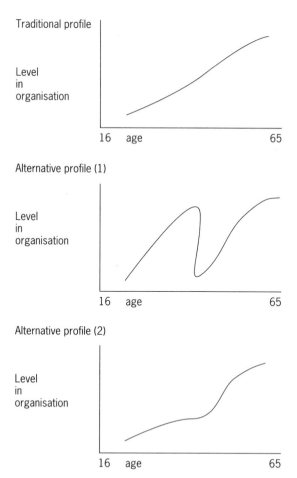

Figure 25.1   Traditional ideal and alternative career profiles

Career anchors

Based on a longitudinal study of forty-four male Sloan graduates completed in 1973, 10–12 after graduation, Schein identified a set of five 'career anchors' and proposed that these explained the pattern of career decisions that each individual had taken. Schein (1978) described career anchors as much broader than motivation, and inclusive of the following:

- self-perceived talents and abilities;
- self-perceived motives and needs; and
- self-perceived attitudes and values.

Our perception of ourselves in these areas comes from direct experiences of work – from successes, from self-diagnosis and feedback. The conclusions reached by the individual through work experiences both drive and constrain future career development. Schein sees career anchors as a holistic representation of the person which takes into account the interaction between the factors identified above. Career anchors can be used to identify a source of stability in the person which has determined past choices and will probably determine future ones.

The most problematic aspect of career anchors is the accuracy of the individual's self-perceptions, and the question of what happens in mid-career to those who feel their attitudes and values are changing. Schein acknowledges that career anchors are learned rather than reflecting latent abilities. The identification and assessment of one's own career anchors can be very helpful to those who do not feel comfortable with the career path they are following.

Career anchors are the sort of things that people are very reluctant to abandon. Not only do we all need to identify and understand what our anchors are in order to make sure we are doing the right thing, we also need to appreciate that there are things that we will continue to need even if we make a career change.

Schein originally identified five career anchors and later supplemented them with another four. Schein suggests that people may have more than one career which is important to them. The original five are:

- *Technical/functional competence:* those who have this as their career anchor are interested in the technical content of their work and their feelings of competence in doing this. They tend not to be interested in management itself, as they prefer to exercise their technical skills. They would, however, be prepared to accept managerial responsibilities in their own functional area.

- *Managerial competence:* for those with this career anchor, the exercising of managerial responsibility is an end in itself, and technical/functional jobs simply a way of getting there. These individuals are most likely to end up in general managerial jobs and possess three key competences. The first is analytical competence to solve problems with incomplete information in areas of uncertainty. The second is the interpersonal competence to influence and control; and the third is emotional resilience, and the ability to be stimulated by crises rather than be paralysed by them.

- *Security and stability:* it is characteristic of those with this career anchor to be prepared to do what the organisation wants of them in order to maintain job security and the present and future benefits which go with this. They will conform to the organisation's requirements and trust that they will be well looked after. Most will therefore remain with one organisation for life, although there are alternative patterns such as remaining in the same geographical area while moving between different employers, and making separate financial provision for the future. Because they have not sought career success in terms of hierarchical promotion those with this career anchor often feel a sense of failure, and find it hard to accept their own criteria for career success. This group are more likely to integrate career with home life.

- *Creativity:* individuals with creativity as a career anchor feel the need to build something new. They are driven by wanting to extend themselves, become involved in new ventures and projects and could be described as entrepreneurial. Should their new ventures turn into thriving businesses they may become bored by the need to manage it and are more likely to hand this aspect over to others.

- *Autonomy and independence:* the desire to be free of organisational constraints in the exercise of their technical/functional competence is what drives those with this career anchor. These people tend to find organisational life restrictive and intrusive into their personal lives and prefer to set their own pace and workstyle. They will usually work alone or in a small firm. Consultants, writers and lecturers are typical of the roles that this group occupy.

The four additional anchors which Schein proposed are:

- *Basic identity:* those with this career anchor are driven by the need to achieve and sustain an occupational identity. Typically these people are in lower level jobs where their role is represented visually perhaps with badges or uniforms. In this way their role is defined externally, and some may seek for example to be associated with a prestigious employer.

- *Service to others:* the driving force here is the need to help others, often through the exercise of interpersonal competence, or other skills. The need is not to exercise such competence as an end in itself, but for the purpose of helping others, and typical examples would be teachers and doctors.

- *Power, influence and control:* this career anchor can be separate from the managerial anchor or may be a pronounced part of it. Those driven by this career anchor may pursue political careers, teaching, medicine, or the church as these areas may give them the opportunity to exercise influence and control over others.

- *Variety:* those who seek variety may do so for different reasons. This career anchor may be relevant for those who have a wide range of talents, who value flexibility or who become very easily bored.

Table 25.2   *Derr's career orientations (1986)*

Getting high	Excited by the actual content of the work done
Getting ahead	Motivated by advancement in their chosen field and will want to climb the organisation's career ladder
Getting secure	Seeking a solid position in the organisation
Getting free	Seeking an autonomous working environment to create and structure one's own work
Getting balanced	Values career but attaches greater importance to family and other non-work interests

Derr (1986) proposed an alternative set of career types with the emphasis on the development of this aspect of self-identity as an ongoing process. Derr's five types are shown in Table 25.2.

Complicating issues and organisational implications

Much of the original work done on describing career stages and career anchors was carried out by analysing the experiences of those who were both male and white, so the analyses are clearly inadequate for our contemporary world of work. The development by Schein of his original set of career anchors is an indication of how understanding is being reshaped, but we still lack satisfactory explanations of career development that can embrace the full variety of ethnic backgrounds, gender and occupational variety.

There is considerable evidence that racial minorities and women limit their career choices, both consciously and unconsciously, for reasons not to do with their basic abilities and career motives. Social class identity may have the same impact. Employees need at least to be aware of such forces and ideally would explore such constraints with their employees to encourage individual potential to be exploited to the full.

The acceptance of such idealised career development stages as described above leaves little room for family and other interference in career development, and until recently there has been no place in career development; or even in the thinking about careers for those who do not conform to the career stages outlined. There are hopeful signs of increasing recognition that career and life choices need to be explored in unison. There has also been little recognition of the commercial environment and the impact that this has on career development stages for many individuals. We look at three major influences below – parenting; partner's career; and recession and redundancy.

Parenting is a powerful influence, particularly, but *not only* on women's careers. This may create the desire to take a few years out from employment; putting a halt on advancement aspirations while children are young; or taking a different career path which combines more effectively with child raising. Gold and Pringle (1989) note that the interruption of a woman's career pathway is often identified as one of the reasons for the lower status and salary they receive in management positions. Such people are often classified as not interested in their career development. The following quote from a female chartered accountant, reported by Lewis and Cooper (1989), is telling:

> If you are trying to get back into the profession at the age of 40, there isn't much chance. This is the problem, the child rearing years are the same years when you have to build your career. For a woman who drops out for a period of, say five to ten years, it would be difficult to get back. You would be out of touch anyway.

A more positive reaction would be to view their career development curve as having a different, but equally legitimate shape (see Figure 25.1).

Partners' careers. Career choices are increasingly likely to be taken in combination with the career choice of a partner rather than in isolation, although the burden of adapting one's own career choices to fit in with those of a partner still falls on women. Traditional patterns of job-seeking activity for dual career couples would be for the man to choose a job first and the woman to follow. Lewis and Cooper (1989) identify a range of alternatives, including direct reversal of the traditional pattern. More egalitarian strategies are that:

- each partner seeks opportunities independently and the best joint option is chosen;
- both partners seek to be employed by the same organisation on a joint basis;
- each partner selects the best opportunity for them and geographical distance is dealt with by one partner living away from home during the working week.

As alternative strategies become more common career decisions become more complex and organisations need to work harder at understanding and working with the influences at play. Geographical mobility generally becomes more difficult and Evans (1986) notes that resistance to this is increasing.

Jennifer is a thoroughly professional lecturer who appears to enjoy her job immensely. When asked about her career ambitions she described her present job as taking time out of her career plan. Prior to lecturing she was committed to her role as Personnel Adviser in a large company and had ambitions to be Personnel Director. On the birth of her children she knew that she could not effectively combine her Personnel Adviser role and childrearing to her satisfaction. Hence her decision to take a different career path for ten years with the objective of returning to industry when her children were older.

Paul was a lecturer in the same department, and was intent upon an academic career. Soon after he joined he agreed with his partner to take sole responsibility for the children. Over the next eleven years Paul did little research and publication but concentrated very effectively on his teaching role. When his children left home he devoted all his energy to his career, taking on much more responsibility and applying for promotion. He had delayed the start of the 'achievement' phase of his career and consequently pursued it more intensely and desired that his employer would support his continued promotion at a later stage in his life.

Job loss and career transitions. There is increasing evidence of mobility between organisations and of career transitions both within organisations and without. Some of this is prompted by redundancies due to recession and redesign of jobs due to new technology. Increasingly men as well as women are experiencing a career break, whether chosen or not. All of these factors divert individual career development from the idealised pattern.

Individual career management

If we identify a career as the property of the individual then clearly the responsibility for managing this rests on the individual, who should identify career goals, adopt strategies to support them and devise plans to achieve the goal.

In reality, however, there is a considerable amount of research indicating that many people fail to plan. Pringle and Gold (1989), for example, found a lack of career planning in their sample of fifty 'achieving' men and women managers. Only around a quarter of people had plans for the future and many identified luck, opportunity or being in the right place at the right time as the reason they had achieved promotions. Harlan and Weis (1982) found both men and women drifting into positions created through coincidences.

Of course, we don't know how well these people would have done had they planned – they may have done even better. Whether this is the case or not we would argue that planning is an essential ingredient of individual career management even if only to provide a framework for decisions about the opportunities that arise through identification of priorities. We would also argue that the more an individual attempts to manage their career the more likely it is that opportunities will arise and the more likely we are to be able to do something constructive with them.

Mayo suggests that in defining a career goal it is too difficult for a person to try and specify the ultimate goal of their career. He suggests that career aiming points are more appropriate if based on a 10–15-year time span, maybe shorter for younger people. This lines up well with Greenhaus and Callanan, who provide a strong case for career goals to be identified in the context of the career stage which the individual is in at the time. They also argue that career management needs to be an ongoing process, and suggest a career management model, appropriate to any stage in the career development cycle, which we show in Figure 25.2. A career goal will be specific to the individual, for example to become an internal senior organisational consultant by the age of 35 years. The range of strategies that an individual may adopt in pursuit of their goal can be described in terms of more general groups. The list below describes the type of strategies, identified from a review of the literature by Gould and Penley (1984).

● *Creating opportunities:* this involves building the appropriate skills and experiences that are needed for a career in the organisation. Developing those skills which are seen as critical to the individual's supervisor and department are most useful, as is exercising leadership in an area where none exists at present.

Figure 25.2   Career management model. Figure adapted from *Career Management* 2nd edition by Jeffrey H. Greenhaus and Gerald Callanan © 1993 by Harcourt Brace and Company. Reproduced by permission of the publishers.

- *Extended work involvement:* this necessitates working long hours, both at the workplace and at home, and may also involve a preoccupation with work issues at all times.
- *Self-nomination/self-presentation:* the individual who pursues this strategy will communicate the desire for increased responsibility to their managers. They will also make known their successes, and build an image of themselves as someone who achieves things.
- *Seeking career guidance:* this involves seeking out a more experienced person either within the organisation or without, and looking for guidance or sponsorship. The use of mentor relationships would come into this category.
- *Networking:* networking involves the development of contact both inside and outside the organisation in order to gain information and support.
- *Interpersonal attraction:* this strategy involves building the relationship with one's immediate manager on the basis that they will have an impact on career progression. One form of this is 'opinion conformity' – that is, sharing the key opinions of the individual's manager, perhaps with minor deviations. Another is expressed as 'other enhancement' which may involve sharing personal information with one's manager and becoming interested in similar pursuits.

Gould and Penley interviewed 414 clerical, professional and managerial employees of a municipal bureaucracy to establish which strategies they used to relate this to salary progression as one indicator of career progression. They found the following:

- managers used these strategies more than non-managers;
- non-'plateaud' managers used them more than 'plateaud' managers;
- salary progression was related to the use of extended work involvement, creating opportunities, and for non-managers only 'other enhancement';
- men were more likely to use extended work involvement than were women; and

- for managers the use of networking and self-nomination/self-presentation were best related to salary progression.

These results obviously need to be interpreted in the context of the employing organisation – different career strategies will be most effective in different contexts. The findings are still illuminating and there are some clear pointers here to the disadvantages that women experience with career progression – for example, the greater limitations on extended work involvement and the difficulty of breaking into male networks:

> women in management often find it difficult to break into the male-dominated 'old boy network' and therefore are denied the contacts, opportunities and policy information it provides. (Davidson and Cooper 1992, p. 129)

The career strategies explored above are clearly most appropriate in the early and mid-career stages, and other strategies will best fit other stages.

REVIEW TOPIC 25.2

What general types of career strategy would be appropriate for:

- organisational entry
- late career

Compare your views with people you know who are in each of these career stages.

Organisational support for career development

Although career management is primarily the individual's responsibility there is a great deal that organisations can do to support this. Organisations can help individuals with:

- career exploration – providing tools and help for self-diagnosis and supplying organisational information;
- career goal setting – providing a clear view of the career opportunities available in the business, making a wider range of opportunities available to meet different career priorities;
- career strategies and action planning – providing information and support; what works in this organisation; what's realistic; and
- career feedback – providing an honest appraisal of current performance and career potential.

The ways that organisations can make this contribution are through the following activities.

Career pathways and grids

A career path is a sequence of job roles or positions, related via work content or abilities required, through which an individual can move. Publicised pathways are helpful to an individual in identifying a realistic career goal within the organisation. Traditional pathways were normally presented as a vertical career ladder. The emphasis was on upward promotion within a function, often formally or informally using age limits and formal qualifications for entry to certain points of the ladder. Joining the pathway at other than the normal entry point was very difficult. These pathways tended to limit career opportunities as much as they provided helpful information. The emphasis on upward movement had the result that career progress for the majority was halted early on in their careers. The specifications of age and qualification meant that the pathways were restricted to those who had an 'ideal' career development profile (for example it excluded those who had taken career breaks, or who had lots of relevant experience but no formal qualifications). Lack of flexibility in these pathways tended to stifle cross-functional moves and emphasised progression via management rather than equally through development of technical expertise. An example of a traditional career pathway is shown in Figure 25.3.

There is now increasing use of alternative approaches which are often designed in the form of a grid with options at each point so that lateral, diagonal and even downwards moves can be made, as well as the traditional upwards ones. In addition these grids may be linked into grids for other parts of the business, and therefore facilitate cross-functional moves. Ideally positions are described in behavioural terms, identifying the skills, knowledge and attitudes required for a position rather than the qualifications needed or age range anticipated. An example of a career grid is shown in Figure 25.4.

Not only do career pathways and grids need to be carefully communicated to employees, they also need to reflect reality, and not simply present an ideal picture of desirable career development. Managers who will be appointing staff need to be

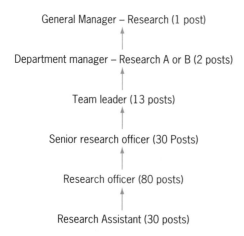

Figure 25.3   Traditional career pathway

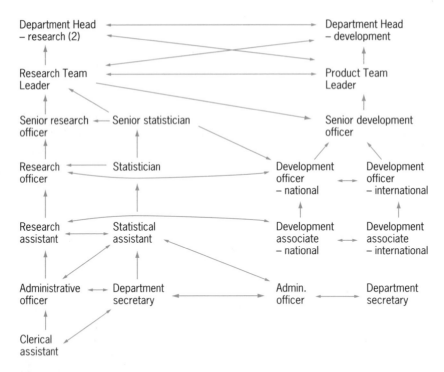

Figure 25.4 Career grid or matrix

fully on board with the philosophy of career development and the type of moves that the organisation wishes to encourage. It is important that the organisation reinforces lateral moves by developing a payment system that rewards the development of skills and not only organisation level.

Managerial support

Managerial support is critical, not only in terms of appointing staff but also in supporting the career development of their current staff. Direct feedback on current performance and career potential is vital especially in the form of strengths and weaknesses, and what improvement would be critical. The immediate manager is in a good position to refer the individual to other managers and introduce them into a network which will support their career moves. In addition the manager is in the ideal position to provide job challenges and experiences within the current job which will equip the incumbent with the skills needed for the desired career move. Walker (1992) notes that:

> The manager can provide valuable input in terms of honest feedback relative to the individual's capabilities, information about the organisation's needs and future direction, and ideas and suggestions for training and use of company resources. (Walker 1992, p. 208)

Unfortunately, as Evans (1986) notes, managers often do not see these responsibilities as part of their job and see them as belonging to the personnel department. Managers often feel constrained by their lack of knowledge about other parts of the organisation, and often withdraw from giving accurate feedback about career potential, particularly when they know that what they have to say is not what the individual wishes to hear. Managers are also sometimes tempted, in their own interests, to hold on to good employees rather than encouraging them to develop elsewhere.

REVIEW TOPIC 25.3

As a member of the personnel function pursuing an organisational philosophy of flexible career moves and continuous career development, how would you:

- encourage managers to adopt this philosophy?
- prepare them for the skills they will need to use?

What other career development support could immediate managers give in addition to the suggestions made above?

Career counselling

Occasionally immediate managers will be involved in career counselling in terms of drawing out the strengths, weaknesses, values and interests of their staff. In many cases, however, those who seek such counselling would prefer to speak in confidence to someone independent of their work situation. In these circumstances a member of the personnel department may act as counsellor. In more complex cases, or those involving senior members of staff, professionals external to the organisation may be sought. This is also more likely to be the case if the career counselling is offered as part of an outplacement programme resulting from a redundancy situation.

Career workshops

These workshops are usually, but not always, conducted off-site, and offered as a confidential programme to help individuals assess their strengths and weaknesses, values and interests, identify career opportunities, set personal career goals, and begin to develop a strategy and action plan. Career goals will not necessarily be restricted to the current employing organisation – and one objective of the workshop is often to broaden career perspectives. Workshops may last two to three days, and normally involve individual paper and pencil exercises, group discussions, one-to-one discussions and private conferences with tutors. For some people these can be quite traumatic events as they involve whole life exploration, and often buried issues are confronted which have been avoided in the hurly-burly of day to day life. The most difficult part for many individuals is keeping the momentum going after the event by continuing the action planning and self-assessment of progress.

Self-help workbooks

As an alternative to a workshop there are a variety of self-help guides and workbooks which can assist you to work through career issues by presenting a structure and framework. Organisations such as 'Lifeskills' provide a range of workbooks appropriate for different stages of career development.

Another excellent example is the work of Burgoyne and Germain (1982) at Esso Chemicals. The two driving forces here were the need to spend more effective career planning time with employees and the anticipated needs of the organisation in the year 2000. A guide was produced that staff could work through at their own speed using friends and colleagues to check their responses and assessments. The guide was designed to help them integrate career planning and self-development, and covered the following areas:

- your skills and job;
- your life and work;
- the world in which you live and work;
- exploring career options;
- what can you learn to help you in the future?
- how do you solve problems?
- what should you be planning to learn?
- how best do you learn?
- how do you keep up to date?
- opportunities and resources for learning; and
- planning your self-development.

It is critical that in completing the guide individuals also had a series of meetings with their immediate manager to test out their assessments and assumptions and share information.

Career centres

Career centres can be used as a focal point for the provision of organisational and external career information. The centre may include a library on career choices and exploration, information on organisational career ladders and grids, current opportunities to apply for, self-help workbooks and computer packages.

Assessment and development centres

Assessment centres for internal staff have traditionally taken the form of pass/fail assessment for a selected group of high potential managers at a specific level. They were focused on organisation rather than individual needs. Recent changes to some of these centres have moved the focus to the individual and there has been less limitation in who is allowed to attend. The emphasis in these centres, usually termed 'development centres', is to assess the individual's strengths and weaknesses and provide feedback and development plans so that each individual can make the most of their own specific potential. The outcome is less pass/fail, than more action plans for personal and career developments.

Whatever career activities are in place in the organisation it is important to ensure that:

- there is a clear and agreed philosophy communicated to all in the organisation;
- managers are supported in their career development responsibilities;
- career opportunities are communicated to staff;
- there is an appropriate balance between open and closed internal recruitment;
- the reasons for the balance are explained;
- knowledge, skills and attitude development are rewarded as well as achievement of a higher organisational level; and
- attention is given to career development within current job.

REVIEW TOPIC 25.4

What are the advantages and disadvantages of open and closed internal recruitment?

In which circumstances might it be appropriate to give a greater emphasis to closed recruitment?

In which circumstances might it be appropriate to give a greater emphasis to open recruitment?

Perhaps the most outstanding challenge is to come in terms with the fact that careers have changed due to a changing organisation structure and competitive demands; individuals in our current labour market have a greater say in their career and how it relates to their whole life; and that alternative career profiles are equally legitimate.

☐ SUMMARY PROPOSITIONS

25.1 Careers are owned by individuals and the primary responsibility for managing them falls to the individual; organisations have a role in supporting and encouraging this.

25.2 It is important for individuals and organisations to understudy the dynamics of careers in order that they may manage or support them more effectively.

25.3 Career development can be described in stages, for example occupational choice, organisational entry, early career, mid-career, late career. These stages may follow a traditional pattern but there are equally legitimate alternative forms.

25.4 Career anchors represent the self-perceived talents, values and needs of individuals. They help to explain past career choice and have a bearing on future choices. Individual people usually have a combination of anchors.

25.5 Individuals can most effectively manage their careers on a continuous basis. Career management involves identifying a career goal, career strategies and a career action plan, together with collecting feedback and monitoring their progress.

25.6 Organisations can support and encourage individual career management by providing flexible and realistic career grids, honest feedback, opportunities for individual career exploration and planning.

References

Burgoyne, J. and Germain, C. (1982), 'Self development and career planning: an exercise in mutual benefit', *Personnel Management*, April, pp. 21–3.

Davidson, M. J. and Cooper, C. L. C. (1992), *Shattering the Glass Ceiling*, London: Paul Chapman Publishing Ltd.

Derr, C. B. (1986), *Managing the New Careerists: The Diverse Career Success Orientations of Today's Workers*, San Francisco: Jossey-Bass.

Evans, P. (1986), 'New directions in career management', *Personnel Management*, December pp. 26–9.

Harlan, A. and Weiss, C. L. (1982), 'Sex differences in factors affecting managerial career advancement'. In P. Wallace (ed.) *Women in the Workforce*, Chapter 4, Boston, Mass: Auburn House.

Greenhaus, J. H. and Callanan, G. A. (1993), *Career Management*, Fort Worth, Texas: Dryden Press.

Gould, S. and Penley, L. (1984), 'Career strategies and salary progression: a study of their relationships in a municipal bureaucracy', *Organisational Behaviour and Human Performance*, vol. 34, pp. 244–65.

Hall, D. T. and Nougaim, K. (1968), 'An examination of Maslow's need hierarchy in an organisational setting', *Organisational Behaviour and Human Performance*, vol. 13, pp. 12–35.

Levinson, D. J., Darrow, C. N., Klein, E. B., Levinson, M. H. and McKee, B. (1978), *The Seasons of a Man's Life*, New York: Knopf Lewis and Cooper 1978.

Lewis, S. and Cooper, C. L. (1989), *Career Couples*, London: Unwin Hyman.

Mayo, A. (1991), *Managing Careers: Strategies for Organisation*, London: Institute of Personnel Management.

Pringle, J. K. and Gold, U. O'C. (1989), 'How useful is career planning for today's managers?', *Journal of Management Development*, vol. 8, no. 3, pp. 21–6.

Schein, E. (1978), *Career Dynamics: matching individual and organisational needs*, Reading, Mass: Addison-Wesley.

Stamp, G. (1989), 'The individual the organisation and the path to mutual appreciation', *Personnel Management*, July, pp. 28–31.

Super, D. E. (1980), 'A life span, life space approach to career development', *Journal of Vocational Behaviour*, vol. 16, pp. 282–98.

Walker, J. W. (1992), *Human Resource Strategy*, New York: McGraw Hill.

Wanous, J. P. (1992), *Recruitment, Selection, Orientation and Socialisation of Newcomers*, Reading, Mass: Addison-Wesley.

26 Interactive skill: teaching

Within the personnel function, and in all other management roles, there is always a need to enable people to learn. There are all manner of ways in which this can be done, especially with the development of technical aids, but this chapter concentrates on the face-to-face learning situation: teaching. We use that simple, traditional term despite its connotations of narrowness. Many people visualise teaching as a process in which someone who knows instructs someone who does not, but enabling people to learn goes beyond simple instruction. Learners frequently have to discover for themselves, as this is the only way in which they will understand, and they frequently can only learn by their interaction with other people in a group, as it is the group process alone that can help them develop their social skills.

Teaching a person to do something is different from teaching someone to understand something and understanding something intellectually is different from understanding and changing how you interact with other people. In this chapter we are going to consider two different approaches to teaching: learning in groups and job instruction, with the most detail about the last, which remains essential despite the increasing emphasis quite rightly placed on other types of learning:

> Notwithstanding the amazing development that have taken place in recent years with alternative modes of delivery, there is still a great demand for classroom-based, tutor delivered training. People do, however, demand and expect training to be lively and stimulating. They will not put up with dull and irrelevant training ... (Truelove 1992, p. 172)

Approaches to learning

Different types of learning require fundamentally different methods and approach by the teacher. One recent, popular classification is to distinguish between memorising, understanding and doing (MUD) that was the result of research by Downs and Perry (1987). Their work was based on identifying blockages to learning especially by adults and was widely promoted in the late 1980s by, among others, the Manpower Services Commission. A more detailed classification was shown in the

CRAMP taxonomy (ITRU 1976), developed after a study of the work of the Belbins (Belbin and Belbin 1972) and following an earlier analysis by Bloom (1956). This system divides all learning into five basic types.

Comprehension

Comprehension is where the learning involves knowing how, why and when certain things happen, so that learning has only taken place when the learner understands: not simply when the learner has memorised. Examples would be having enough understanding of how German grammar works to be able to put the words of a sentence into the right order, or knowing enough of the law of employment to decide whether or not someone has been dismissed unfairly.

Reflex learning

Reflex learning is involved when skilled movements or perceptual capacities have to be acquired, involving practice as well as knowing what to do. Speed is usually important and the trainee needs constant repetition to develop the appropriate synchronisation and co-ordination. Many of the obvious examples lie outside the interests of most personnel managers, such as juggling, gymnastics or icing a cake, but there are many examples in most organisations, such as driving a fork-lift truck, spot welding, fault-finding and typing. One of the most widespread in management circles is the use of a keyboard. It is interesting how the status of the keyboard has altered. On promotion to supervisory, administrative or managerial positions, ex-secretaries have regarded it as essential that they should never use a keyboard again for fear that they would revert to being seen as 'merely a secretary'. Now the use of a keyboard is an essential managerial adjunct to making the most of information technology (Hall and Torrington 1989).

Attitude development

Attitude development is enabling people to develop the capacity to alter their attitudes and social skills. Much of the customer care training currently being conducted has this as its basis. The theory is that dealing with customers requires people to be confident of their own ability to deal with others, shedding some of their feelings of insecurity and discovering how they are able to elicit a positive response. This can only partly be achieved by the process of 'scripting', whereby staff have a set formula to follow. We are all familiar with making a telephone call which brings a response along the lines of, 'Good morning. Bloggs, Blenkinsop, Huggins and Scratchit. Mandy speaking. How may I help you?' Attitude development aims to enable people to develop positive attitudes about themselves and their relationships with others, so that they can cope effectively with other people.

Memory training

Memory training is obviously concerned with trainees remembering how to handle a variety of given situations. Pharmacists learn by rote a series of maximum dosages, for example, and an office messenger will need to remember that all invoices go to Mr Brown and all cheques to Mrs Smith. Police officers remember the registration numbers of cars better than most of us, and we all need to remember telephone numbers and PIN numbers. This is distinguished from comprehension because understanding is not necessary, only recall, and it is worth referring back to the example above of understanding German grammar. Learning grammatical rules by rote does not enable one to use that knowledge, because understanding is also required. Learning your PIN number does not require any understanding at all.

Procedural learning

Procedural learning is similar to memory except that the drill to be followed does not have to be memorised, but located and understood. Examples are the procedure to be followed in shutting down a plant at Christmas, or dealing with a safety drill.

Most forms of training involve more than one type of learning, so that the apprentice vehicle mechanic will need to understand how the car works as well as practising the skill of tuning an engine, and the driver needs to practise the skill of co-ordinating hands, feet and eyes in driving as well as knowing the procedure to follow if the car breaks down. Broadly speaking, however, comprehension-type learning is best approached by a method that teaches the whole subject as an entity rather than splitting it up into pieces and taking one at a time. Here the lecture or training manual are typically used. Attitude change is now often handled by group discussion, but reflex learning is best handled by part methods which break the task down into sections, each of which can be studied and practised separately before putting together a complete performance, just as a tennis player will practise the serve, the smash, the forehand, the backhand and other individual strokes before playing a match in which all are used. Memory and procedural learning may take place either by whole or by part methods, although memorisation is usually best done by parts.

REVIEW TOPIC 26.1

(a) Think of things that you have learned in the recent past and identify whether the learning was comprehension, reflex, attitude development, memorisation or procedural.

(b) How would you classify learning for the following:
Swimming
Calorie-counting in a diet
Parenting
Safe lifting
Selection interviewing
Learning Russian
Running a business
Preparing for retirement

Types of learner

Learners differ according to their prior knowledge, the quality and nature of their previous education and their age. CRAMP (comprehension, reflex, attitude, memory, procedure) was developed on the basis of research among adults; most teaching carried out under the aegis of personnel management is with adults, so we need some understanding of how learners differ. An excellent analysis has been produced by Robert Quinn (1988) based on earlier work by Dreyfus, Dreyfus and Athanasion (1986). It also appears in Quinn's work on management skills (Quinn *et al.* 1990). He believes that mastery of an activity involves a learning process that takes place over an extended period of time and the capacity to learn evolves at the same time. The inference of this is that our approach to organising facilities for others to learn will be influenced by how far their learning capacity has developed. There are five stages.

The novice

The novice learns facts and rules without criticism or discussion, accepting that there are ways of doing things that others have devised, and that's that.

The advanced beginner

The advanced beginner goes a little further by being able to incorporate the lessons of experience, so that understanding begins to expand and embellish the basic facts and rules. As you begin to experience working in an organisation, aspects of cultural norms become apparent that are just as important as the basic rules. You find out the subtleties of the dress code and working relationships and extend competence by trying out very slight departures from the rigidity of the rules.

Competency

Competency represents a further development of confidence and a reduced reliance on absolute rules by recognising a wider variety of cues from the working context. There is a greater degree of learning by trial and error, experimenting with new behaviours. It is not abandoning the rules, but being able to use them more imaginatively and with an interpretation that suits one's own personal strengths and inclinations.

Proficiency

Proficiency is where the learner transcends analysis to being able to use intuition:

> Calculation and rational analysis seem to disappear. The unconscious, fluid, and effortless performance begins to emerge, and no one plan is held sacred. You learn to unconsciously 'read' the evolving situation. You notice cues and respond to new cues as the importance of the old ones recede. (Quinn *et al.* p. 315)

Expert

Expert is the term used to describe those rare people who produce masterly performance simply by doing what comes naturally, because all the learning has fused

David teaches a teacher-training course which has a mixture of students. Most are recent graduates with little working experience but well developed study skills. A minority are a little older, usually mothers with growing children who have experience, but whose study skills are rusty. He finds that the mature students tend to dominate discussion at the beginning of the course, as they constantly relate everything to their own experience and circumstances, while the recent graduates feel at a loss and put down. After a few weeks the younger students become more assertive in discussion as they gain confidence from their developing understanding, and the mature students are less dominant because they are beginning to question some of the taken-for-granted certainty of their earlier opinions. Mutual respect gradually develops and both groups learn from each other. David classifies the recent graduates as novices rapidly becoming advanced beginners and the mature students as competents who have to revert to novices in order to move on to proficiency.

together to develop a capacity based on having in their heads 'multidimensional maps of the territory' that are unknown to other people and they are thus able to meet effortlessly the contradictions of organisational life.

That is a neat and helpful model, although it could also be used as an excuse for sloppy thinking and an inability to see that there has been a sea change that undermines the expert's certainties. Personnel students have ground into them the risks of snap judgements in selection interviewing ('I can tell as soon as they come through the door') and there will always be a temptation for established managers to take short cuts on the basis of their assumed expertise without realising that the rules have been changed, so that they are playing the wrong game.

Leading group discussion

Members of a discussion group both compete and co-operate. They will co-operate in the shared task of seeking understanding and developing answers, but they will also compete in wanting to appear shrewd, fluent and perceptive, especially if there are inequalities of status in the group. They will be even more anxious not to appear foolish. Members of the group will look to the teacher for structure at the beginning: a strong indication of how to get started and assistance in developing the social interaction of the group process. As discussion unfolds the teacher will become less obviously necessary to the group, but will still need to control the exchanges to ensure their effectiveness. This later control is the hardest part, as the voluble need to be reigned in frequently and the diffident encouraged.

Small informal groups are being used more extensively in business life, especially since the introduction of team briefing, quality circles and similar attempts at employee involvement. This is an important aspect to the background of using group methods in teaching. Working in groups becomes more familiar, so learning in groups becomes more the accepted norm. The increasing use of groups generally

The Higher Education Funding Council for England has undertaken the assessment of teaching assessment through the universities it supports. A part of this process is assessing the effectiveness of individual teaching sessions. Here is an extract from one of these assessments:

> The student group was a mixture of those in their late teens who had recently left school and a number of married women 'returners' who were preparing to re-enter the labour market. There was an easy relationship between the teacher and the students, so that discussion of the case study began without delay and everyone took some part. There was, however, increasing diversity and generality in the discussion that often dwelt on personal opinions of the group members on matters that had no relevance to the case study. When the session closed after 50 minutes one was left with the impression that all students had enjoyed a *conversation* but it was difficult to believe that much *learning* had taken place.

is based on the belief that some tasks are better undertaken by groups than by individuals. Blau and Scott (1963) offer three reasons for this view:

(a) The sifting of suggestions in social interaction serves as an error-correction mechanism.

(b) The social support furnished in interaction facilitates thinking.

(c) The competition among members for respect mobilises their energies for contributing to the task.

For the teacher that analysis provides the value of using groups for learning: clarification, thinking and motivation. One must, however, avoid the risk of thinking that group-working is the *only* effective means of teaching, especially when one considers the time that is involved. Not only do groups move at the speed of the slowest learner, there is also the problem that each group member may have a problem that others do not share, so much time may be spent by the group laboriously reaching only a modest level of learning development.

Group leadership and group roles

In all informal groups the position of the leader is crucial, and in teaching situations the leadership role is clearer than in most, as the teacher is the acknowledged expert in the group, although many teachers may feel no more than competent or proficient! The size of the group will influence group effectiveness, according to the task. The larger the group the greater the problems of coordination. Most experienced teachers feel that groups relying mainly on discussion as the means of learning begin to lose their effectiveness if there are more than twelve or fifteen members, and that numbers should be lower when the material is particularly abstruse. It is interesting to compare with other group learning situations. A class in school will seldom be so small, but the student learning depends on a higher level of individual student activity, such as reading a passage in the book, working out an equation, translating a poem or carrying out an experiment. Apprentice classes are able to work with larger numbers, again because so much of the learning is practical work by the individual student. Hare (1962) argues that there should always be an odd number of group members so that a single group member could be in a minority without the same pressure to conform with the majority that would exist in a smaller group, and there are enough people for members to shift roles easily. Where the group task is not wholly one of social interaction, then the size could increase.

Membership of the group will be either more or less homogeneous, or it will be mixed. Most personnel managers organising teaching will be working with homogeneous groups in the sense that they will have a number of points in common, such as membership of the company, or all being recently recruited, or all needing to understand the new computing system. Typically the teacher will probably increase the homogeneity by, for instance, grouping all the supervisors in one group, all the engineers in another and all the marketing staff in a third. Similarity of interests and background aids co-operation and understanding.

Mixed group composition is better when the differences of perspective or interest are the core of the training task, because they are differences that have to be overcome, or where a diversity of opinion and expertise is needed to achieve understanding.

Every group leader needs to be able to assess the members of the group and work out how to mobilise their diverse competences and contributions to best effect. Here is a list of types of people and their distinctive contributions to group discussion. It is modelled on the work of Belbin that was described fully in Chapter 19.

The Shaper influences discussion by developing thoughtful argument and following through particular topics that have been raised, always wanting to make sense of things and get them into shape.

The Ideas Person contributes novel suggestions and is likely to provide possibilities of breaking out of stalemate situations, or distracting everyone with a fresh idea just at the point where most people are about to succeed in mastering something else.

The Radical believes that the group's task cannot be begun until something else has been done first – and the 'something else' is always beyond the group's control. Groups discussing employee relations issues are vulnerable to discussion that rapidly settles down to bemoaning capitalist society, the failure of the labour movement or male repression of women.

The Steady Eddy is always cautious and aware of problems. This anxiety not to rock the boat can help a group to calm down when the Radicals and Ideas People get going, but a group comprised entirely of Steady Eddies would achieve little. They can be useful for knowing what next week's topic is and for explaining that the right books are not in the library.

The Team Worker keeps the group going by joking when discussion gets too tense and always finding points on which to agree with other people. They are more useful than Steady Eddies, but it gets a bit boring when everyone agrees with everything.

The Monitor likes to review progress and summarise what has been said. In most teaching situations this is the main role of the leader, but a leader who is a natural ideas person will value a Monitor to keep track of what is happening.

The Shrinking Violet has difficulty in getting in to the discussion and is intensely concerned not to sound foolish, requiring careful assistance – but not condescension – from the leader. They have to be assisted because they worry everyone else as well as themselves. The silent figure who never speaks can soon become identified as someone who thinks deeply and has probably spotted flaws in the argument that no-one else can see.

The Completer likes to push things along, get things done and formulate conclusions. The trouble is that this may be done too soon and may deflect the group from facing up to tricky issues.

REVIEW TOPIC 26.2

Rewrite the above list in the ranked order that most accurately describes your behaviour in group learning situations. Could you alter that ranking by changing your mode of participation? Do you want to? Why?

At the next meeting you attend, classify each participant in *one only* of the eight categories. Does the meeting need different people?

The group work sequence

Preparation

Do all members of the group know each other? With a close-knit team, like a senior management group, introductions will obviously not be needed, but there may be a new member of the group, there may be members whose presence puzzles others (or themselves), and sometimes the group will be made up of relative strangers. The group leader has four basic strategies available for making sure that people know each other.

1. *Assume introductions are not needed.* The leader does not make any introductions, assuming them to be unnecessary.

2. *Introduce individuals.* Leader makes introductions 'from the chair', of those who are new to those who are established and vice versa, for example:

    > I think we mostly know each other, but Chris is with us for the first time, as last week he was on assignment in Italy. Chris, on your right is Roger, from customer service, Sheila, from Distribution and Jan, who…

3. *Ask people to introduce themselves.* 'Perhaps we could just go round the group, saying who we are and what our role is… I'm Simon Rowntree, from Central Personnel. I've been seconded for three months to act as trainer on all these sessions. On my right is… ?'

4. *Ask people to introduce others.* The leader asks pairs in the group to interview each other for five minutes and then introduce the person they have interviewed to everyone else. This method is particularly useful for a group of strangers, as it initiates discussion and eliminates the self-consciousness felt by many in saying 'I am...'

The leader sets the scene by reminding everyone of why they have assembled and summarising what it is they have to do. At this stage members of the group will welcome clear guidance and a suggested structure for the meeting, but the leader will need their consent by signing off with a comment such as:

'Is that all right?'
'Is there anything I've missed, do you think?'

The leader now opens the discussion by introducing the topic – or the first of several topics – for the group to develop. There are various ways of doing this.

(a) *Setting out background information.* Adding to the initial introductory comments by providing more general information in a way that will focus the thinking of group members.

(b) *Providing factual data.* Giving group members specific details about the initial topic and inviting their analysis.

(c) *Offering an opinion.* Leading the group towards a conclusion by declaring your own beliefs first is a strong but risky opening. If you are articulating a view that most people will support, then the group will make quick progress, but you may prevent people developing true understanding. In your inescapable role as expert, you may not be challenged. If there is likely to be dissent then proceedings will be slowed down, as members of the group have to first grapple with the task of disagreeing with the leader, and then they have to sound out support for their own views.

(d) *Asking a question.* Directing everyone's thinking by posing a question that opens up the topic. It is wise to move from the general to the particular, by setting up the initial discussion around the broader aspects of the question which can later be brought into much sharper focus.

Although the teacher will be less dominant as the discussion gets under way, there is still a need for control and direction, using the following methods.

(a) *Bringing people in.* Without direction some group members will never speak and others will scarcely stop, but productive discussion will result from a blend of contributions from Shapers, Steady Eddies, Completers and so on. The teacher will not only bring people in in a general way ('What do you think, Frank?') but will also shape the discussion by bringing people in for specific comment ('How does John's idea fit in with what you were saying earlier, Helen?').

(b) *Shutting people up.* Curbing the voluble is difficult and can make everyone feel awkward if it is not well done, yet the discussion will not work if it is dominated by one or two people. Equally, the teacher will fail if the voluble person is expressing a point of view for which there is broad support, so that the understanding is not moving on. Techniques for the teacher to use in shutting people up are:

- put one or two closed questions to a person in the middle of a diatribe;
- give them a job to do ('Could you just jot down for us the main points of that, so that we can come back to it later?'); and
- orientate them towards listening ('Can you see any problems with what Sheila has suggested?').

There is little need to sustain discussion on matters where everyone is agreed. Agreeing with each other is useful for social cohesion, but the leader needs regularly to direct discussion back to points of disagreement and misunderstanding. It helps to bring in someone who has previously been neutral or silent on the matter and who may therefore have a different perspective.

Periodically the discussion will need to be summarised and a new direction introduced. Members of the group need to confirm the summary. This is usually a job for the teacher, but there may be a monitor in the group to take it on.

Occasionally someone in the group will make a contribution that others do not understand, so the teacher will seek clarification, ensuring that the responsibility for the confusion is *not* on the person making the statement. 'Could you just go over that again, Fred' is better than 'I think what Fred is trying to say is...'

The session must close and not simply run out of time. It is superficially pleasing when everyone is still keenly discussing when time is up, but it does leave things up in the air. The teacher needs to pick out from the discussion one or two workable hypotheses or points of general consensus and put them to the meeting for acceptance. Group members will look to the teacher for that type of closure so that they have confirmation that their time has been well spent: only the teacher can really see the wood for the trees. The best discussions finish on time!

Job instruction

The first step in learning a skill is for the learner to understand the task and what needs to be done to produce a satisfactory performance. This provides the initial framework for, and explanation of, the actions that are to be developed later, although more information will be added to the framework as the training proceeds. The job of the teacher at this point is to decide how much understanding is needed to set up the training routine, especially if part methods are to be used for the later practice. Trainees are usually keen to get started with 'hands-on' experience, so long and detailed preliminaries are best avoided.

The second step is to practise the performance, so the instructor has to decide how to divide the task up into separate units or sub-routines to aid learning. Typists begin their training by learning sub-routines for each hand before combining them into routines for both hands together, but pianists spend very short periods of practice with one hand only. The reason for this seems to be that typists use their two hands in ways that are relatively independent of each other with the left always typing 'a' and the right always typing 'p', so that co-ordination of the hands is needed only to sequence the actions. In playing the piano there is a more complex integration of the actions performed by the two hands so that separate practice can impair rather than enhance later performance. A further aspect of learning to type is to practise short letter sequences that occur frequently, such as 'and', 'or', 'the', 'ing' and 'ion'. These can then be incorporated into the steadily increasing speed of the typist. A feature of this type of development is the extent to which the actions become automatic and reliable. The amateur typist will often transpose letters or hit the wrong key, writing 'trasnpose' instead of 'transpose' or 'hte' instead of 'the'. The skilled typist will rarely do this because the effect of the repeated drills during training will have made the sub-routines not only automatic but also correct.

The third element is feedback, so that learners can compare their own performance with the required standard and see the progress they are making. The characteristics of good feedback are immediacy and accuracy. If the feedback comes immediately after the action the trainee has the best chance of associating error with the part of the performance that caused it, whereas delayed feedback will demonstrate what was wrong, but the memory of what happened will have faded. If you are being taught to drive a car, one of the early lessons is changing gear. If you think you understand what the instructor tells you, you need to try it out straight away, so that you have first the feedback of your own performance in seeing if you execute the manoeuvre effectively and then the feedback from the instructor, who screams in anguish before telling you what you did wrong. If you are learning photography you do not have that element of immediate feedback, so that you have to recall everything that took place in taking the photograph when you eventually receive the prints.

The second characteristic of feedback is that it should be as accurate as possible in the information it provides on the result and the performance. The driving instructor may say, 'That's fine', or may say, 'That was better than last time because you found the gear you were looking for, but you are still snatching. Try again and remember to ease it in'. The second comment provides a general indication of making progress, it provides an assessment of the performance and specific comment that should improve the next attempt.

The job instruction sequence

Preparation

The instructor will have two sets of *objectives*, organisational and behavioural. Organisational objectives specify the contribution to the organisation that will be made by the learner at the end of training. It will be general but necessary. If a company trains its own word processor operators and secretaries, for instance, it might be that the organisational objectives will be to teach people to word process and to transcribe from handwritten copy or dictating machine, but not to take shorthand. These are different from educational objectives, which focus on the trainee or student rather than on organisational needs, so that tutors in secretarial colleges are more likely to organise training around what will be useful in a number of occupational openings. The instructor will need to work out organisational objectives which may or may not include broader educational features.

Behavioural objectives are specifically what the learner should be able to do when the training, or training phase, is complete. Organisational objectives for trainee word processor operators may be simply to ensure a constant supply of people able to type accurately and at reasonable speed. In behavioural terms that would be made more specific by setting standards for numbers of words to be typed to a predetermined level of accuracy per minute.

REVIEW TOPIC 26.3

Think of a training experience involving learning how to *do* something that you are contemplating for yourself or for someone else in your organisation. Note down organisational objectives and behavioural objectives for the training.

Next the instructor will decide what learning *methods* are to be used. We have already seen that the main elements of job instruction are understanding, practice and feedback, so the instructor decides how much initial explanation is needed, and how many other explanations will be necessary at different stages of the training, together with the form that is appropriate. Words alone may be enough, but audio-visual illustration and demonstration will probably be needed as well. There are rapid developments in computer-based training and interactive video that can provide frequent explanations and feedback on trainee performance (Rushby 1987).

The two questions about practice are to decide on the sub-routines and any necessary simulation, such as the working of a flight simulator in pilot training. Most feedback is by the instructor talking to the learner, but it may be necessary to devise ways of providing greater accuracy or speed to the feedback by methods such as television recording or photography. The most common method of job instruction is the *progressive part* method that had its most comprehensive explanation by Seymour (1966). The task to be undertaken by the learner is broken down into a series of sub-routines. The learner then practises routine 1, routine 2 and then 1 + 2.

The next step is to practise routine 3, 2 + 3 and 1 + 2 + 3, so that competence is built up progressively by practising a sub-routine and then attaching it to the full task, which is constantly being practised with an increasing number of the different components included. The components are only practised separately for short periods before being assimilated, so there is no risk of fragmentary performance.

This only works if the job can be subdivided into components. Where this is not possible, simplification offers an alternative. In this method the task to be performed is kept as a whole, but reduced to its simplest form. Skilled performance is then reached by gradually increasing the complexity of the exercises. In cookery the learner begins with simple recipes and gradually develops a wider repertoire.

There are some specialised methods of memory training which can be listed here, as well as ways of training for perceptual skill. Both types of ability appear to be increasing in importance in organisational life.

The most familiar way of memorising is the mnemonic or jingle, wherein a simple formula provides the clue to a more comprehensive set of data. Laser is much easier to remember than light amplification by stimulated emission of radiation and most people employed in schools will remember how the Great Education Reform Bill of 1988 was reduced to the shorthand of GERBIL in staff room discussions. If the initial letters are not easily memorable, the mnemonic is replaced by the jingle. The denseness of ROYGBIV has led generations of school children to remember that Richard Of York Gave Battle In Vain as a way of recalling the sequence of red, orange, yellow, green, blue, indigo and violet in the spectrum. Arthur Spits in Claude's Milk is a rather less familiar way of remembering that there are five types of arthropod: Arthropods, Spiders, Insects, Crustaceans and Myriapods. One does have to be sure, however, both that the mnemonic or jingle will itself be remembered and that it will subsequently be possible to remember what is to be called.

REVIEW TOPIC 26.4

What do the following sets of letters mean:
DERV, DFE, DSS, RADAR, TINA LEA, UNESCO, UNPROFOR ?

Apart from the obvious, why should anyone remember the phrase, 'Most Engineers Prefer Blondes'?

For some tasks the use of *rules* reduces the volume of material to be memorised. There are many fault-finding rules, for instance, where the repairer is taught to use a systematic series of rules. The stranded motorist who telephones the vehicle rescue service for assistance will probably be asked a first question, 'Have you run out of petrol?' The answer 'Yes' identifies the fault, while 'No' leads to the second question, 'Is there any spark?' so that the mechanic who comes to help already has some areas of fault eliminated.

Deduction is a method that puts information into categories so that if something does not fit into one category the learner then uses deduction to conclude that it must belong in another. At the beginning of this chapter was the example of the office messenger remembering that invoices go to Mr Brown and cheques to Mrs Smith. If there was also a Ms Robinson, who received all sales enquiries, complaints, unsolicited sales promotion material, tax returns, questionnaires, applications for employment and so on, the messenger would not need to remember what did go to Ms Robinson, but what did not: invoices to Mr Brown, cheques to Mrs Smith and everything else to Ms Robinson. Some interesting examples of using deduction in training are to be found in Belbin and Downs (1966).

For memorisation of information the *cumulative part* method is slightly, but significantly, different from the progressive part method already described in that the learner constantly practises the whole task, with each practice session adding an extra component. This is distinct from progressive part in which components are practised separately before being built into the whole. This can be especially useful if the more difficult material is covered first, as it will then get much more rehearsal than that coming later.

A method for the development of perceptual skills is *discrimination*, which requires the learner to distinguish between items that appear similar to the untrained eye or ear. In a rough-and-ready way it is the procedure followed by the birdwatcher or the connoisseur of wine. First the trainee compares two items which are clearly dissimilar and identifies the points of difference. Then other pairs are produced to be compared, with the differences gradually becoming less obvious. Discrimination can be aided by *cueing*, which helps the learner to identify particular features in the early attempts at discrimination by providing arrows or coloured sections. Some people start learning to type with the keys coloured according to whether they should be struck with the left or right hand, or even according to the particular finger which is appropriate. Gradually the cues are phased out as the learner acquires the competence to identify without them.

Magnification is a way of developing the capacity to distinguish small faults in a process or even small components in machinery. Material for examination is magnified at the beginning of training and then reduced back to normal as competence is acquired. Inspectors of tufted carpet start their training by being shown samples of poor tufting that have been produced using much larger material than normal. Later they examine normal material under a magnifying glass and eventually they are able to examine the normal product. A helpful discussion of magnification method can be found in Holding (1965).

The various training methods to be used are put together in a *training programme*. This sets out not only what the instructor is going to do, but also the progress the trainee is expected to make. Of critical importance here is pacing; how much material has to be taken in before practice begins, how long there is to practice before being able to proceed to a new part and how frequently progress is checked by the teacher. Individual trainees will each have their own rate at which they can proceed and will need differing levels of initial explanation and demonstration before practice can start. Training programmes require sufficient flexibility to accommodate the varying capacities that learners bring to their training.

A useful feature of the training programme is providing scope for learners to be involved in determining their own rate of progress and some self-discovery, to avoid spoon-feeding. At the outset trainees are so conscious of their dependency that all measures that build up confidence, independence and autonomy are welcome.

Repetition does not necessarily make material automatic. Acker Bilk played 'Stranger on the Shore' thousands of times, and many excellent teachers reuse exactly the same material repeatedly. The Scottish playwright James Barrie studied medicine in his youth and took with him to university a set of verbatim anatomy notes that had been compiled by his father thirty years earlier. His father said the lectures were so interesting that it would be better if he did not have to make notes. As Barrie attended the lectures, he was astonished to find that little had changed. At one point the lecturer took hold of a gas bracket and related an anecdote. On looking at his father's notes he saw, 'At this point Professor X took hold of a gas bracket and told this story...'

The instruction

When instructor and trainee meet for the first time there is a mutual appraisal. The process is basically 'getting-to-know-you' but the exchanges are important, as the two people have to work together and the learner will be uncertain in an unfamiliar situation, and absolutely dependent upon the instructor. Some instructors and some training programmes appear to emphasise the inferiority of the learner deliberately as a prerequisite of the training process; Hollywood frequently produces films about the training of marines or other members of the American military that show the trainees being systematically humiliated by instructors who could have given lessons to Attila the Hun. Individual instructors in less melodramatic situations sometimes like to assert their superiority, but it is essential that the learners feel confident in the instructor as someone skilled in the task that is to be learned and enthusiastic about teaching it to others. They will also be looking for reassurance about their own chances of success by seeking information about previous trainees.

The explanation of procedure will follow as soon as the meeting phase has lasted long enough. Here is the first feature of pacing that was mentioned as part of preparation. There has to be enough time for meeting to do its work, but long, drawn-out introductions can lead to impatience and wanting to get started.

The procedure is the programme, with the associated details of timing, rate of progress, training methods and the general overview of what is to happen. The most important point to the trainee is obviously the end. When does one 'graduate'? What happens then? Can it be quicker? Do many people fail? What happens to them? The instructor is, of course, more interested in the beginning of the programme rather than the end, but it is only with a clear grasp of the end that the trainee can concentrate on the beginning. Clarifying the goal reinforces the commitment to learning.

With long-running training programmes where an array of skills has to be mastered, the point of graduation may be too distant to provide an effective goal so that the tutor establishes intermediate goals: 'By Friday you will be able to...'. This phase benefits from illustration; a timetable, a chart of the average learning curve, samples of work by previous trainees all make more tangible the prospect of success. The more complete the mental picture of the operating framework that the learner is putting together. It is also helpful to avoid the explanation becoming mechanical, like the tourist guide at a stately home. If the instructor has explained the procedure so often that it has become automatic, it is no longer the vivid stimulus to learning that is so necessary. It is a time for as much interchange as possible, with questions, reiteration, further explanation, clarification and confirmation.

The task that the trainee has to perform first is demonstrated and explained. The purpose is not to display the teacher's advanced skills, but to provide a basis for the learner's first, tentative (and possibly incorrect) attempts. The demonstration is thus done without any flourishes, and as slowly as possible, because the teacher is not only demonstrating skill but also using skill to convince the trainees that they can do the job. Accompanying the demonstration, an explanation gives reasons for the different actions being used and describing what is being done so that the learners can watch analytically. Their attention is drawn to features they might overlook, the sequence of actions is recounted and key points are mentioned.

The task must be presented to the learner in its simplest possible form, with a straightforward, unfussy, accurate demonstration accompanied by an explanation which emphasises correct sequence, reasons why, features that might be overlooked in the demonstration and the key points that lead to success. Where possible, the tutor should not mention what *not* to do. Incorrect aspects of performance can be dealt with later; at this stage the direction should be on what *to* do.

The presentation is followed, and perhaps interrupted, by questions from the learners on what they did not follow or cannot remember. The success of this will depend on the skill of the instructor in going through the opening stages of the encounter. Many trainees are reluctant to question because they feel that the question reveals their ignorance, which will be judged as stupidity. The experienced instructor can stimulate the questioning and confirming by the trainees through putting questions to them. This is effective only when done well, as there is the obvious risk of inhibiting people by

> 'Now, tell me the three main functions of this apparatus'.
> 'Can anyone remember which switch we press first?'

Little better are the vague requests for assent:

> 'Do you understand?'
> 'Am I making myself clear?'
> 'Is that all right, everybody?'

These are leading questions. They will be some use as there will be nods and grunts from the trainees to provide response, but it is most unlikely that people will do more than offer the easy, regular 'yes'. The job of the teacher is to help learners build the picture in their own minds without the feeling that they are being tested. This will only come with good rapport. After the presentation the trainees have their first attempt at the task.

They expect to do badly and need confidence from the tutor, who has to steer a difficult path between too much or too little intervention. Too much and the trainees do not 'feel their feet' and acquire the confidence that comes from sensing the strength and purpose of their own first faltering steps. Too little intervention means that trainees learn about their lack of competence, which is reinforced by a performance which falls short of what presentation had suggested as being possible. This shows again the importance of presentation, which has to be pitched at the level that will make initial performance feasible, without building up expectations that cannot be realised.

Among the considerations for teachers are the varying potential of individual trainees and the ritual elements of training. Some trainees will be able to make initial progress much more rapidly than others, so that pegging all to the same rate of advance will inhibit both. The ritual features depend on the acknowledgement by the trainee of the absolute, albeit temporary, superiority of the tutor. It has already been pointed out that there is a reluctance to question during presentation; there are also intermittent displays of deference to the teacher. This enables learners to perform badly during practice without losing face. However, deference to a superior figure is normally offered on the assumption that the novice is being helped towards the advanced level of skill that the superior possesses. If early practice of a taught skill produces abject performances by the learners, then they either lose confidence or resent the instructor for highlighting their inadequacy.

Learning theory tells us the importance of the law of effect, which practice makes possible, but it also tells us that there is likely to be a point at which the learner makes a sudden leap forward – the point at which the penny drops and there is a shared excitement. In the words of Professor Higgins about Eliza: 'I think she's got it. By Jove, she's got it'. Practice leads up to the point where the learning spurts forward and it then provides the reinforcement of that learning by continued rehearsal and confirmation.

The most effective reinforcement for learners is realising that they can perform, like the child who at last finds it possible to remain upright and mobile on a bicycle. Learners cannot usually rely on their own interpretation of success: they will need constant assessment by the teacher. Many of the textbooks on teaching and learning emphasise the value of praise, a little of which apparently goes a long way, for example:

> When they are learning people need to know where they stand, they need to know how they are progressing. The knowledge of their progress spurs them on to greater achievements. In this respect praise is always far more helpful than criticism. (Winfield 1979)

Effective reinforcement enables trainees to understand both the result and the actions or behaviour which produced the result, so the tutor needs to identify the particular ways in which progress is being made and explain their merit, as well as explaining what caused the progress to happen. When trainees are approaching full competence, with the associated self-confidence, then they are able to cope with more direct criticism.

References

Belbin, E. and Belbin, R. M. (1972), *Problems in Adult Retraining*, London: Heinemann.
Belbin, E. and Downs, S. (1966), 'Teaching and paired associates', *Journal of Occupational Psychology*, vol. 40, pp. 67–74.

Blau, P. M. and Scott, W. R. (1963), 'Processes of Communication in Formal Organisations', in Argyle, M. (ed.), *Social Encounters*, Harmondsworth, Middlesex: Penguin Books.

Bloom, B. S. (1956), *Taxonomy of Educational Objectives: The Cognitive Domain*, London: Longman.

Downs, S. and Perry, P. (1987), *Helping Adults to Become Better Learners*, Sheffield: Manpower Services Commission.

Dreyfus, H. L., Dreyfus, S. E. and Athanasion, T. (1986), *Mind over Machine: The Power of Human Intuition and Expertise in the Era of the Computer*, New York: Free Press.

Hall, L. A. and Torrington, D. P. (1989), 'How personnel managers come to terms with the computer', *Personnel Review*, vol. 18, no. 6.

Hare, A. P. (1962), 'Small Groups' in *American Behavioural Scientist*, May/June.

Harrison, R. (1988), *Training and Development*, London: Institute of Personnel Management.

Holding, D. H. (1965), *Principles of Training: Research in Applied Learning*, Oxford: Pergamon.

Industrial Training Research Unit (ITRU) (1976), *Choose an Effective Style: a Self-Instructional Approach to the Teaching of Skills*, Cambridge: ITRU Publications.

Quinn, R. E. (1988), *Beyond Rational Management: Mastering the Paradoxes and Competing Demands of High Performance*, San Francisco: Jossey-Bass.

Quinn, R. E., Faerman, S. R., Thompson, M. P. and McGrath, M. R. (1990), *Becoming a Master Manager*, New York: Wiley.

Rushby, N. (ed.) (1987), *Technology based Learning: Selected Readings*, London: Kogan Page.

Seymour, W. D. (1966), *Industrial Skills*, London: Pitman.

Truelove, S. (1992), *Handbook of Training and Development*, Oxford: Blackwell.

Winfield, I. (1979), *Learning to Teach Practical Skills*, p. 81. London: Kogan Page.

PART VI

Involvement

When we surveyed the activities and priorities of personnel specialists in the early 1980s, there was no doubt about the pre-eminence of employee relations as being the activity on which they spent most of their time and as being most central to the personnel function (Mackay and Torrington 1986, pp. 149 and 161). Only in recruitment and selection did they feel that they had a slightly greater degree of discretion and scope in decision-making (*ibid*. pp. 146–8). Furthermore it was a time of increasing management assertiveness in this area (*ibid*. p. 79).

Ten years later the emphasis has changed. In the early stages of the work by the Personnel Standards Lead Body in developing the occupational map, one group of consultants decided that employee relations was not a part of personnel work at all! It certainly has lost the pre-eminent position it held through most of the post-war period, with training and development, performance management, team building and other activities taking greater attention. The agenda has also changed. The focus is no longer on collective bargaining and procedural agreements, but on holistic approaches to the relationship with the workforce, such as employee involvement, total quality management and team briefing. No longer is there an attempt to control affairs by getting a firm agreement to a set of arrangements that will not be changed by either side, but rather there is an attempt to reach a much less settled relationship, within which working practices change constantly and the employment relationship is less formalised. To some commentators the agenda is human

Table 27.1 *Replies in interviews on employee relations with senior personnel specialists (Mackay and Torrington 1986, p. 79)*

Percentage of replies to the question, 'Is there a more "bullish" approach being taken to employee relations in this organisation?'		
	%	*n*
Yes, more bullish	61.0	25
No, it was always bullish	10.0	4
No, not more bullish	29.0	12

Using the term 'employee relations' instead of the broader 'industrial relations' was new and was viewed as being more managerialist.

resource management, not as a term to describe the varied activities of personnel specialists, but as a description of the current management approach to industrial relations. The arena has become both bigger and smaller, as the focus has shifted away from national-level determination of terms and conditions towards arrangements determined within the enterprise, at the same time as the European context of labour law and the social contract have expanded the general context.

The two main trends have been more local determination and more emphasis on commitment:

> ... two core themes appear to underscore many of the new developments. One is to internalise the personnel function as far as possible within the enterprise, thereby loosening employee relations from wider labour institutions and influences... The other is to establish *gemeinshaft* arrangements inside the enterprise in an effort to increase corporate identity and loyalty amongst employees. (Teague 1991, p. 4)

By the mid-1990s we find employee relations alive and well as a management activity, although not as salient as industrial relations was in the 1970s, and the overriding characteristic of employee relations is employee involvement.

The development of employee involvement

The whole concept of employee involvement has its roots in broader concepts such as industrial democracy and workers' control, which themselves have an ancient lineage. More than 2000 years ago there was a series of so-called 'Servile Wars' in Rome, where slaves rose up against their overseers. The last of these was led by a Thracian shepherd, Spartacus, who assembled an army of 90,000 rebellious slaves before eventual defeat. His example was remembered in modern times when a movement was started in Berlin at the beginning of the twentieth century called the Spartacists. This was led by Rosa Luxembourg, who has become an icon of the labour movement.

The inspiration for industrial democracy was the Marxist analysis of how the proletariat is exploited by the capitalists and the middle class, with the inevitable result that the proletariat will eventually overthrow the capitalist system and establish a system of workers' control. This idea received considerable impetus from the inequities of the factory system that followed the industrial revolution, alluded to in our opening chapter.

This was the time when 'industry' came to mean the large-scale manufacture of goods as well as meaning habitual diligence. The size of employing organisations began to grow, industrial cities mushroomed, there was large-scale migration from the country to the city, expanding population, division of labour, ghastly working conditions and the emergence of the new social class, the *bourgeoisie*. Perhaps of greatest importance, there was a degree of speed of change in people's lives that was unprecedented.

The degree of exploitation of the urban proletariat was so extreme, in such a novel form, that its members attempted collective organisation to resist it. Early trade unions were ineffective and seldom lasted, but by 1880 the British trade union movement had established itself and taken on a form that has not been much altered since. Not only were the methods of industrial action set, so too were the subtle class distinctions between craft and general unions. It was an essentially British invention and the basic intractability of British trade unions today, as they find it so difficult to adapt policies and practices appropriate to the times, can be seen as a problem of a movement that began when employee representation was being first thought about. At the same time that trade unions were becoming established as part of the social order, the revolutionary philosophy of Karl Marx was being propounded. Asserting that social change results from a class struggle for control of the means of production Marx predicted the eventual, inevitable victory of the proletariat despite the contemporary subjection of the worker whose labour is bought and sold as a commodity under capitalism, with the economic and human interests of employees being sacrificed. He also argued that conflict in the social relations of industry was a result of *inherent* exploitation.

Marxisim has not had the same effect on the British labour movement as has been seen in other countries of Europe, where it is common to have some unions that are communist and some that are Catholic, but it has had an undoubted influence on thinking about industrial relations, mainly because it provides an explanation of the phenomenon and an integrating conceptual framework.

While Marxists argue that change in industrial relations will only be peripheral and unimportant until a complete social revolution has taken place, a more generally accepted view was proposed by Sidney and Beatrice Webb in the late nineteenth century. They concentrated on the industrial order rather than the more general social order and saw trade unions as organisations to further the interests of their members within the system of industrial government, mainly by influencing the wage–work bargain. Any political action is seen as a means towards the end of reforming the way industry is governed rather than transforming the whole society of which industry is a part. This can be described as the mainstream of industrial relations thinking, which reached its apogee in the 1960s in the work of Flanders (1964), Clegg (1960) and the recommendations of the Donovan Commission (1968). Through the first half of the twentieth century trade unions, employers' associations and the various institutions of collective bargaining developed steadily. The General Strike of 1926 was a trauma from which two main lessons were learned. The union movement learned that a general strike would bring no miracles of social change in a British context and those who had so implacably opposed it, particularly in the employer ranks, learned that 'beating' the strike did not cause the trade unions to wither and die, even though they suffered considerable losses in membership, funds and morale.

The next major development came in the mid-1960s, but in 1958 there was a new academic explanation of industrial relations. Dunlop (1958) set out his idea of industrial relations as a system with different types of relations at the varying levels of plant, enterprise, industry or nation in any political or economic setting. He attempted to put forward a comprehensive model that would aid subsequent research. Initially the reaction was mainly of interested disagreement, but recent years have seen more detailed and constructive attempts to move forward from his position.

By the time Dunlop produced his book most British managers were resigned to a rather defeatist attitude towards the organisation of employment where trade unions were recognised. Little by little more was conceded to the unions, who had effected a vice-like grip on production around which nothing could be altered. Restrictive or protective practices were deeply entrenched. This coincided with bad news in the production market. Exports were slipping and the economic growth of other countries was outstripping that of Britain. Productivity bargaining became fashionable as managements sought initiatives with trade unions that had previously seemed impracticable. A Royal Commission on trade unions and employers' associations (1968) was set up in order to make proposals for change. The title of the Commission itself was interesting, as it was set up to look at the collectives rather that the processes in which they were engaged. The report of the Commission reflected a significant change in thinking. The trouble lay not with trade unions, nor with employers, but with the processes for their interactions. Collective bargaining itself needed reform. National agreements were frequently inadequate as a framework for employment relations in a factory as their formality and precision was shadowed by a series of informal, imprecise arrangements that governed what actually happened on the floor of factories.

It was these informal undertakings that needed attention in order to improve the disorder of the workplace. They should be reviewed and a greater degree of formality introduced so that everyone knew more reliably where they stood. No dramatic legislative intervention; no fundamental restructuring in the direction of industrial democracy; and no question of the government taking over. The Royal Commission commented favourably on the productivity agreements that were being concluded, seeing in these deals many of the features which it saw as being necessary at plant level: managers and shop stewards taking responsibility for their own affairs and leaving national agreements as a framework for their affairs, and gradually bringing about the changes in employment and working relationships that were so urgent.

Productivity bargaining received another boost from a new body, the National Board for Prices and Incomes. For the first time there was a statutory prices and incomes policy, which sought to control income growth by statute rather than exhortation and example. One of the agents of this policy was an investigative Prices and Incomes Board. This was soon to become politically unacceptable, but for a few years it produced a series of excellent reports on a variety of investigations into employment matters and advocated the extension of productivity bargaining as a means of achieving economic growth as well as improved industrial relations. Although it was to disappear so soon, it helped to develop the idea of plant-level agreement, which was the productivity bargaining inheritance and brought about that major, and apparently long-term, shift of emphasis towards local agreement on the features of the employment contract.

The proposals of the Royal Commission were not universally accepted. A few weeks before it was published another document, called *Fair Deal at Work*, was produced. This was a statement of policy by the Conservative party, then in opposition. The proposals were radically different in tenor and were not widely discussed or analysed because the Royal Commission report followed so soon afterwards. The importance of *Fair Deal at Work* (1968) was seen in 1970, when a change of government brought in draft legislation based on the earlier policy statement. This became the Industrial Relations Act of 1971, one of the most controversial pieces of legislation of the post-war period. There was a fundamental difference between it and the Royal Commission view. Instead of seeing reform of collective bargaining and more effective management, *Fair Deal at Work* and the Industrial Relations Act set out to contain collective bargaining and to control trade unions. The resistance of unions was fierce and the reaction of managements generally apathetic or hostile. Within four years the Act was repealed. There were other legacies of the Act that it is not appropriate to discuss here, but one rather intangible effect was a further strengthening of the 'establishment' position of unions. The General Strike of 1926 may have demonstrated that unions would not wither on the vine, but the Industrial Relations Act brought a form of official acceptance that had previously been missing. For a Conservative government to introduce legislation conferring the legal right to belong to a union and various other union rights was a significant step, even if the unions did not want most of the rights they were given.

The twentieth century British view of industrial democracy was based on the idea that employers were powerful, the state was powerful and it was therefore important that trade unions should be powerful, so that the three stakeholders in industrial relations should be in some form of power balance. This was articulated by Clegg (1960). During the 1970s there was a lively debate about industrial democracy and various forms of employee participation in the management decision-making processes of business. This was driven by the relatively strong position held by trade union leaders in the various industries and the need of a Labour government to gain their support at a time of a slender majority in the House of Commons. The most thorough-going idea was for the introduction of industrial democracy, which was by then conceived as the participation of employees being developed via representative democracy at the boardroom level to influence, or to make, the major strategic decisions of the organisation.

The main focus of the debate was the Committee of Inquiry on Industrial Democracy. Their majority proposal was that boards of companies should be reconstituted to give equal representation to shareholders and employee representatives, with a smaller number of independents holding the balance.

The proposals were met with varying degrees of horror in management circles and less than rapture among trade unions. The eventual government reaction to the ideas was contained in a White Paper more than twelve months later, which declared that there would not be a standard form of participation, like that proposed by the Committee of Inquiry, imposed by law. Increased participation would result mainly from exhortation, although companies employing 5000 people or more would be legally obliged to discuss with employees all major proposals affecting the workforce and those employing 2000 or more would be required to concede a legal right to employee representation a few years later.

The 1979 change of government led to these proposals being shelved, but interest continued among both managers and trade unionists. Dowling *et al.* surveyed the attitudes of executives in twenty-five large private companies and the regional officers of fourteen trade unions. Both groups were opposed to worker directors and were relieved that the likelihood of such legislation had receded:

> Managers tended to favour forms of 'participation' which emphasized communication and consultation, whereas the trade union officials favoured extensions to the range of issues subject to collective bargaining or joint regulation. (Dowling *et al.* 1981, p. 190).

In 1984 Hanson and Rathkey published the results of a survey of shopfloor opinion carried out in four different companies that would have been affected by the Bullock proposals (1977) to try to establish a shopfloor view of the industrial democracy idea. One of their most conclusive findings was that employees were very little interested in employees making decisions without management involvement. Also, twice as many people wanted involvement only in matters concerning their own work and conditions as those who wanted involvement in both that and issues concerning the management of the company as a whole.

The managerial interest is usually in some form of sharing control in order to regain control and they are clearly committed to the idea that managers are the people to make decisions, although employees may be consulted and have things explained to them in order to obtain their commitment to management objectives. Difficult trading conditions have also increased managerial willingness to disclose information about company affairs. An amendment to the Employment Act 1982, introduced by the House of Lords, is a requirement for companies with more than 250 employees to include in their annual report a statement of action taken to introduce or develop arrangements for employee participation, specifically:

- Systematically providing employees with information on matters which concern them.
- Consulting with employees or their representatives on management decisions likely to affect employees' interests.
- Encouraging employee involvement through means such as shareholding.
- Providing information on financial and economic matters affecting the business.

Management interest was centred on the idea of employee involvement as a way of meeting the demands of the 1982 Act, although ACAS were not initially impressed:

> The pressing need is for employees to be further involved in consultative and decision-making processes in the organizations in which they work, if their talents and energies are to be released and their willing commitment secured to the measures necessary for economic recovery. ACAS officials report that progress in this area has been slow and there remains much to be done. (ACAS 1985, p. 16)

Another view of participation is that it should develop first at the place of work itself, with autonomous working groups taking over their own supervision, and with managers giving much more attention to the design of jobs and finding ways in which individual employees can participate more in the day by day decisions that affect their work. The argument supporting this is that board-level decisions are of little interest or immediacy to employees and that their participation will be apathetic or incompetent, while what they really care about is what they themselves do from day to day, as implied by the Hanson and Rathkey (1984) survey.

Another type of initiative is harmonisation of terms and conditions between different categories of employee. One-third of the respondents in our earlier research had made some moves in this direction (Mackay and Torrington 1986). Changes were mainly in holidays, hours and method of payment. Sound practical guidance on making moves towards harmonisation is to be found in Roberts (1985).

The most popular current methods of involvement appear to be team briefing and total quality management, although the Investors in People initiative is promising. We will consider each of these shortly, but this review of how employee involvement has developed can be wound up by considering the idea that involvement progresses in cycles or waves. This was scouted by Ramsay (1991) and developed in the seminal work of Marchington and his colleagues (1992 and 1993). While Ramsay saw a pattern that amounted to reinventing the wheel, the Marchington analysis sees that each wave of development is different from its predecessors, even though there may be similarities in their stimuli. Like so many aspects of management practice there are fashions, so that joint consultation was in vogue at one time, team briefing became the popular notion of the early 1980s, followed by employee share ownership, total quality management and so forth. This is similar to the analysis put forward in our opening chapter, that personnel management is constantly picking up new ideas and orientations. They rarely disappear, but the emphasis is constantly changing.

Team briefing

> Teamwork has been one of the key ingredients of the new industrial relations and human resource management movements. *Fortune* business magazine in the United States heralded it as 'possibly *the* productivity breakthrough of the 1990s'. (Storey and Sisson 1993, p. 91)

That is a bold claim and it covers aspects of work organisation that are rather broader than team briefing. Teamworking is a direct descendant of the concept of autonomous working groups, that had their highest profile in the Volvo plant at Kalmar, and a rather vague movement of the 1960s, called Quality of Working Life (QWL). At Volvo there were the twin aims of improving the quality of working life and enhancing productivity. QWL was directed mainly at making life more tolerable, as the title implies, and it is difficult to see what impact it had. More recently teamworking has become more comprehensive in its approach and its objectives. It is very fully explained in the work of Buchanan (1993) and Buchanan and McCalman (1989).

The timeliness of this approach was linked to the shop steward tradition, as well as to the production and market imperatives that were its main drives. The shop steward had been the main focus of representation and loyalty in the collective bargaining framework of industrial relations. As the collective bargaining influence waned, a vacuum needed to be filled. Management seized on the opportunity to maintain and develop group cohesion around work activities that were aligned directly with organisational requirements. Teamworking aims to focus work activity among small face-to-face groups of about a dozen members, who are mutually supportive and who operate with minimal supervision. Within the teamworking framework and ethos, team briefing is an initiative that attempts to do a number of different things simultaneously. They provide authoritative information at regular intervals so that people know what is going on, the information is geared to achievement of production targets and other features of organisational objectives, it is delivered face-to-face to provide scope for questions and clarification, and it emphasises the role of supervisors and line managers as the source of information:

> They are often used to cascade information or managerial messages throughout the organisation. The teams are usually based round a common production or service area, rather than an occupation, and usually comprise between four and fifteen people. The leader of the team is usually the manager or supervisor of the section and should be trained in the principles of skills of how to brief. The meetings last for no more than 30 minutes, and time should be left for questions from employees. Meetings should be held at least monthly or on a regular pre-arranged basis. (Holden 1994, p. 567)

With goodwill and managerial discipline team briefing can be a valuable contributor to employee involvement, as it deals in that precious commodity: information. Traditionally there has perhaps been a managerial view that people doing the work are not interested in anything other than the immediate and short-term and that the manager's status partly rests on knowing what others don't know. For this reason all the managers and supervisors in the communications chain have to be committed to making it a success, as well as having the training that Holden refers to above. Team briefing becomes easier once it is established as a regular event. The first briefing will probably go very well and the second will be even better. It is important that management enthusiasm and commitment do not flag just as the employees are getting used to the process.

During the early 1980s there was a boost to the team briefing process because so many managements had so much bad news to convey. When you are losing money and profitability, there is a great incentive to explain to the workforce exactly how grim the situation is, so that they do not look for big pay rises. Team briefing as a means to maintain the team ethos continues, but the main method of teamworking has changed to the quality initiative.

Total Quality Management

Total Quality Management – universally abridged to TQM – can be regarded as one of the biggest developments in management during the latter part of the twentieth century. Although a bold and sweeping statement, it has survived and flourished for a sustained period, it has achieved a British Standard definition and has attained the magical 'senior management support' that all personnel managers seem to regard as essential. What may be even more significant is that it has crossed international boundaries, especially the crucial boundary between East and West, as the basic concept was invented by an American, taken to Japan because of American indifference and re-exported when it was so successful:

> ... many of the products the Japanese now sell successfully were invented in America and manufactured according to standards set by an American. Here, in his own country, he is largely unknown – almost a prophet without honor. Yet in Japan, he is a national celebrity. (Stoner and Freeman 1992, p. 7)

The prophet without honour at home was the late W. Edwards Deming, who went to Japan as a struggling engineer in 1950 to propose a management approach to achieving quality production. Thirty years later it was picked up by the Americans and is now established throughout the world as a fundamental approach to management that can apply in any culture.

Initially TQM was an engineering approach, concerned with measurement and with procedures being managerially imposed in organisations, lacking the voluntary nature of the earlier quality circles (Sewell and Wilkinson 1992). In Britain TQM is gradually being seen as needing an extra dimension, developing from its engineering basis to give more attention to social factors, such as commitment, self control and trust. Guest (1992) is one of several analysts who has identified a logical link between the needs of HRM and the opportunity of TQM.

TQM can only logically appear in a chapter on employee involvement if it goes beyond the type of managerially determined electronic surveillance described by Sewell and Wilkinson above. The recent path-breaking work by Wilkinson and his colleagues suggests that TQM in Britain is taking that course (1991, 1992, 1994).

Investors in people

The government commits a considerable proportion of its annual expenditure to vocational training. Opposition parties, employer bodies and trade unions claim that the commitment should be even greater. All interests share a concern that British training has not succeeded in developing the type of skilled and committed workforce that is needed in the current economic context of intense international competition.

Among a range of national initiatives is 'Investors in People', or IIP, which aims to develop employer commitment to developing their staff in line with business objectives. This is widely regarded as an initiative of considerable potential, as it should achieve the twin objectives of skill and commitment at the same time as improving business effectiveness. Very few companies have achieved the required standard and there was little sign that the national objectives would be reached until the Spring of 1994, when IIP was relaunched. By the Autumn the level of commitment to the IIP concept had increased although only 350 companies had achieved the standard.

It may be that more skilful marketing and clearer explanation is what is required to make IIP successful. We believe that is only a small part of what is needed. What will convince employers and employees is a convincing analysis and explanation of the tangible benefits that IIP is producing in the business where the standard has been achieved. The unanswered questions include:

1. *Process benefits:* how has IIP changed attitudes of training expenditure away from cost and towards investment? How is the return on training measured? Does IIP help to justify training expenditure? Does it provide a focus for existing initiatives?

2. *Business benefits:* what have been the benefits to the business from the IIP award? How have these benefits been measured? How do they split between tangible and the intangible? Are they real or assumed?

3. *Employees:* what have been employee attitudes toward IIP? How has their commitment been won? How has anxiety about employment insecurity been allayed (if it has)? What do employees see as the personal benefits to them?

4. *The personnel function:* how has the personnal function featured in IIP, as instigator and creative leader, as administrative support, as bystander, or as something else? Is the personnel function the key to success in IIP?

IIP offers an excellent prospect of real progress in finding a way to create more effectively competitive business through developing skills and commitment to those who work in the businesses, but it may be just one more wave in employee investment.

Strategy and employee involvement

The position adopted on employee involvement by management is one of the most profound of all strategic issues, with ethical, social and political dimensions, as well as affecting all aspects of human resource management.

Many managers look for what one might call the bottom-line argument. Does employee involvement 'work'? Does it enhance employee commitment and effectiveness? There is a simplistic answer to that sort of question which runs that it must 'work' because it makes sense: people will support that which they have helped to create. Without involvement there will not be commitment and motivation, both of which are much lauded as necessary features of corporate culture. There are, however, limitations to the validity of that argument.

The channel of involvement is through the work that people do, yet the work that some people do lacks sufficient job content for involvement to offer any scope for the degree of personal commitment that involvement requires. There is a

> Mary, a programmer, is married to John, a bricklayer. They take it in turns to work full-time while the other looks after the domestic duties and picks up casual work. They each aim to work full-time for four to five months a year and to spend two to three months travelling round Europe in their motor caravan with their two small children. They both find it reasonably easy to obtain the short spells of working that they need, as they are both highly skilled and efficient. To them employee involvement is an irrelevance and they seek clearly defined tasks with specific objectives.

constant cry that there is a shortage of skilled people, yet many jobs call for little skill. If one is engaged on routine, mind-deadening tasks, offers of involvement are difficult to understand and respond to. In jobs of this nature the best prospect for the people doing the work is to find some degree of mental and emotional detachment from it, rather than involvement.

Some people find the implications of involvement stressful, as they feel under pressure to display acceptable behaviours, like enthusiasm and withholding criticism, which they regard as phoney and unnecessary.

The decline of organisation as entity also reduces the scope for involvement. If the employer distances the employees by some form of casualisation, the message is clear. 'You are not a part of the business. We are keeping you at arm's length. There are insiders and outsiders; you are an outsider, not a stakeholder'.

A different type of justification for employee involvement is that it is a straightforward legal and moral obligation of any employer to treat employees decently and with respect. That includes providing information, explanation of management decisions, training and career opportunities, opportunities to complain and to suggest improvements. If that is the management motivation towards involvement then it is providing opportunity rather than making demands that go beyond the bounds of the employment contract, so there is as much scope to opt out of involvement as there is to opt in.

The management strategy on involvement will therefore stem from the values and personal priorities of the management team as well as the type of business that is being managed. It is difficult to devise involvement strategies that are equally appropriate for all members of the business. The opportunities for involvement of senior managers are infinitely greater than those of security guards, because their jobs are so much more varied and individualised. The need for employee involvement in – for instance – a theatre company is much stronger than in running a pub with part-time bar staff.

☐ SUMMARY PROPOSITIONS

27.1 A collective approach to employee relations and employee involvement does not now have the emphasis it had in the period before 1980.

27.2 Employee involvement practices have evolved from a specifically British view of industrial democracy as a means of balancing the relative power of employers, trade unions and the state that was propounded by Clegg in the 1960s.

27.3 It is possible to identify waves in employee involvement approaches with different ideas being adopted as others recede in popularity.

27.4 The current popular ideas are team briefing, total quality management and investors in people. All these are firmly managerial, with the power balance ideas of industrial democracy largely missing.

27.5 The approach a business adopts to employee involvement will depend on the personal views and priorities of the management team, as well as the nature of the business itself.

References

ACAS (1985), *Annual Report, 1984*, London: HMSO.

Buchanan, D. (1993), 'Principles and practice of work design'. In K. Sisson (ed.) *Personnel Management*, 2nd edition, Oxford: Blackwell.

Buchanan, D. and McCalman, J. (1989), *High Performance Work Systems: The Digital Experience*, London: Routledge.

Lord Bullock (1977), *Report of the Committee of Inquiry on Industrial Democracy*, London: HMSO.

Clegg, H. A. (1960), *A New Approach to Industrial Democracy*, Oxford: Blackwell.

Clegg, H. A. (1972), *The System of Industrial Relations in Great Britain*, Oxford: Blackwell.

Code of Industrial Relations Practice (1972). London: HMSO.

Dowling, M., Goodman, J., Gotting, D. and Hyman, J. (1981), 'Employee participation: survey evidence from the north west', *Employment Gazette*, April.

Dunlop, J. T. (1958), *Industrial Relations Systems*, London: Harper & Row.

Conservative Political Centre (1968), *Fair Deal at Work*.

Flanders, A. (1964), *The Fawley Productivity Agreement*, London: Faber & Faber.

Guest, D. (1992), 'Human resource management in the UK.' In B. Towers (ed.) *The Handbook of Human Resource Management*, Oxford: Blackwell.

Hanson, C. and Rathkey, P. (1984), 'Industrial democracy: a post-Bullock shopfloor view', *British Journal of Industrial Relations*, vol. 22, no. 2, pp. 154–68.

Holden, L. (1994), 'Employee Involvement'. In I. Beardwell and L. Holden (eds) *Human Resource Management*, London: Pitman.

Mackay, L. E. and Torrington, D. P. (1986), *The Changing Nature of the Personnel Function*, London: Institute of Personnel Management.

Marchington, M. P., Goodman, J. F. B., Wilkinson, A. J. and Ackers, P. (1992), *New Development in Employee Involvement*, Employment Department Research Series No. 2, London: HMSO.

Marchington, M. P., Wilkinson, A. J. and Ackers, P. (1993), 'Waving or drowning in participation?', *Personnel Management*, March, pp. 46–50.

Ramsay, H. (1991), 'Re-inventing the wheel? A review of the development and performance of employee involvement', *Human Resource Management Journal*, vol. 1, no. 4, pp. 1–22.

Roberts, C. (ed.) (1985), *Harmonization: Whys and Wherefores*, London: Institute of Personnel Management.

Royal Commission on Trades Unions and Employers' Associations (1968), Cmnd 3623, London: HMSO. (The Donovan Commission).

Royal Commission on Trades Unions and Employers' Associations (1968), *Report*. London: HMSO.

Sewell, G. and Wilkinson, B. (1992) 'Empowerment or emasculation? Shopfloor surveillance in a total quality organisation'. In P. Blyton and P. Turnbull (eds) *Reassessing Human Resource Management*. London: Sage.

Stoner, J. A. F. and Freeman, R. E. (1992), *Management*, 5th edition. Englewood Cliffs, New Jersey: Prentice Hall International.

Storey, J. and Sisson, K. (1993), *Managing Human Resources and Industrial Relations*, Buckingham: Open University Press.

Teague, P. (1991), 'Human resource management, labour market institutions and European integration', *Human Resource Management Journal*, vol. 2, no. 1.

Walker, K. F. (1977), 'Towards useful theorising about industrial relations', *British Journal of Industrial Relations*, November, pp. 307–16.

Wilkinson, A. J., Allen, P. and Snape, E. (1991), 'TQM and the management of labour', *Employee Relations*, vol. 13, no. 1, pp. 24–31.

Wilkinson, A. J., Marchington, M. P., Goodman, J. F. B. and Ackers, P. (1992), 'Total Quality Management and employee involvement', *Human Resource Management Journal*, vol. 2, no. 4, pp. 1–20.

Wilkinson, A. J. (1994), 'Managing human resources for quality'. In B. G. Dale (ed.) *Managing Quality*, 2nd edition. London: Prentice Hall International.

Trade Union recognition and consultation

Trade union recognition is widespread in Britain, although there has been a drop of almost three million union members since the peak figure of thirteen and a half million in 1979. By 1990 the total membership of the Trades Union Congress had declined from 12,128,000 in 1979 to 8,405,000 and the number of unions affiliated to the TUC had moved from 112 in 1979 to 78 in 1990. After dropping sharply in 1980 to 464,000, membership of unions not affiliated to the TUC had reached 1,400,000 by 1990. Furthermore, much of the expansion in the economy had been in companies that are electing not to recognise trade unions. The Workplace Industrial Relations Survey (Millward *et al.* 1992) provides comprehensive information about all aspects of industrial relations and Table 28.1 shows the decline.

Some people see trade unionism in terminal decline as no longer relevant to an advanced society. Others believe that unionism has moved to a marginal position in employee relations, and some sense a resurrection, based on support from the European Commission and a new style of leadership within the TUC itself:

> There are signs the tide is turning in favour of the unions. Mind-blowing militants still wave red flags, but they are nobodies going nowhere. The rise of middle class unemployment, the hopelessness of many young people without jobs, the entrenchment of union reform and the resentment created by boardroom greed all favour the restoration of responsible trade unionism. (Jones 1994)

It remains to be seen whether this resurrection will actually take place, but we can be sure that some personnel managers are in establishments where unions are not

Table 28.1 *Changes in the proportion of establishments recognising trade unions between 1980 and 1990 (Millward et al. 1992)*

Establishments recognising trade unions in 1980 and 1990 (%)						
	Manufacturing		Services		Public sector	
	1980	1990	1980	1990	1980	1990
Manual workers	65	44	33	31	76	78
Non-manual	27	23	28	26	91	84
All workers	65	44	41	36	94	87

recognised and where recognition is unlikely, some are in establishments where they are working towards recognition, but the great majority are in a situation where unions are recognised to some degree for at least part of the workforce. Thus most personnel managers are in a situation where they have to carry on managing recognition rather than initiating or rejecting it.

The issue of trade union recognition is not as burning as it was in the 1970s, but most organisations have recognised unions and ACAS still has some 15 per cent of the collective conciliation workload in this area. Managements may recognise unions, they may involve employees, consult with them, participate with them or harmonise terms and conditions. After detailed examination of employee relations practice in four very different organisations, Marchington and Parker (1990) concluded that unions were becoming less central to employee relations, but not because of deliberate management attempts to 'take them on':

> unions were not on the whole central to workplace employee relations, and in some cases their role was becoming more marginal. This factor did not, however, arise from any concerted management strategy directed specifically at labour relations, but was more appropriately seen as a consequence of other actions taken in pursuit of wider corporate goals – in particular to increase employee commitment to produce quality and customer service. (Marchington and Parker 1990, p. 257)

Management always needs the collective consent of its employees: it also needs a mandate to manage. In most situations this is at least partly delivered by trade union recognition. The recent changes in union membership, employment legislation, high unemployment and economic recession have provided academic analysts with the challenge of describing how employee relations strategies have changed. We still lack a full explanation, but one of the best-known approaches has been the attempt of Purcell and Sisson (1983) to categorise management styles in industrial relations. These are summarised in Table 28.2 and the key distinguishing

Table 28.2   *Categories of management styles in employee relations*

Style	Characteristics
Traditional	Fire-fighting approach. Employee relations not important until there is trouble. Low pay. Hostile to trade unions. Authoritarian. Typical in small, owner-managed business
Paternalist	Unions regarded as unnecessary because of employer's enlightenment. High pay. Concentration on encouraging employee identification with business objectives
Consultative	Union participation encouraged through recognition. Problem-solving, informal approach to employee relations. Emphasis on two-way communications
Constitutional	Similar to *consultative*, but emphasis on formal agreements to regulate relationship between two powerful protagonists
Opportunistic	Large company devolving responsibility for employee relations to subsidiaries, with no common approach but emphasis on unit profitability

Source: Purcell and Sisson 1983, pp. 112–18.

feature is of a collective view of the workforce. From a personnel management perspective this is a useful way of separating out this category of personnel work from the rest and, for instance, having sections in books like this with the title 'Employee Relations'. This is a useful set of categories, although some organisations do not fit easily into any one of them. Most large, long-established companies will be in one of the last three; most public sector organisations will be in category four; and many of the newer business will be in some version of category two.

REVIEW TOPIC 28.1

Which of the five categories in Table 28.2 most closely fits your establishment? Does the category vary for different groups of employees?

Collective consent

Taking a strictly managerial view of trade unions and their recognition, the interest is the degree to which recognition will deliver collective consent to a general framework of rules and guidelines within which management and employees operate.

Collective consent implies the acceptance of a situation, while agreement has the more positive connotation of commitment following some degree of initiative in bringing the situation into existence.

We are not, therefore, necessarily describing active employee participation in managerial decision-making. The range is wider, to include the variety of circumstances in which employees consent collectively to managerial authority, so long as they find it acceptable.

In order to couch the discussion in terms that can embrace a variety of styles we set out seven categories of consent, in which there is a steadily increasing degree of collective employee involvement. We begin with a category in which there is straightforward and unquestioning acceptance of management authority, and then move through various stages of increasing participation in decision-making and the necessary changes in management style as the power balance alters and the significance of bargaining develops and extends to more and more areas of organisational life.

1. *Normative:* we use this term in the sense of Etzioni (1961), who described 'normative' organisations as being those in which the involvement of individuals was attributable to a strong sense of moral obligation. Any challenge to authority would imply a refutation of the shared norms and was therefore unthinkable. Many of the exercises in corporate culture are construed by some as strategies to develop this type of consent, with strong emphasis on commitment and the suppression of views opposed to managerial orthodoxy.

2. *Disorganised:* in organisations that are not normative there may be collective consent simply because there is no collective focus for a challenge, so

disorganised consent is where there may be discontent but consent is maintained through lack of employee organisation. A Victorian sweatshop would come into this category.

3. *Organised:* when employees organise it is nearly always in trade unions and the first collective activities are usually in dealing with general grievances. It is very unlikely that there will be any degree of involvement in the management decision-making processes. Employees simply consent to obey instructions as long as grievances are dealt with.

4. *Consultative:* consultation is as a stage of development beyond initial trade union recognition, even though some organisations consult with employees before – often as a means of deferring – trade union recognition. This is the first incursion into the management process as employees are asked for an opinion about management proposals before decisions are made, even though the right to decide remains with the management.

5. *Negotiated:* negotiation implies that both parties have the power to commit and the power to withhold agreement, so that a decision can only be reached by some form of mutual accommodation. No longer is the management retaining all decision-making to itself; it is seeking some sort of bargain with employee representatives, recognising that only such reciprocity can produce what is needed.

6. *Participative:* when employee representatives reach the stage of participating in the general management of the organisation in which they are employed, there is a fundamental change in the control of that organisation, even though this may initially be theoretical rather than actual. Employee representatives take part in making the decisions on major strategic issues like expenditure on research, the opening of new plants and the introduction of new products. In arrangements for participative consent there is a balance between the decision-makers representing the interests of capital and those representing the interests of labour, though the balance is not necessarily even.

7. *Controlling:* if the employees acquire control of the organisation, as in a workers' co-operative, then the consent is a controlling type. This may sound bizarre, but there will still be a management apparatus within the organisation to which employee collective consent will be given or from which it will be withheld.

All of the above categories require some management initiative to sustain collective consent. In categories (1) and (2) it may be exhortation to ensure that commitment is kept up, or information supplied to defer organisation. In each subsequent category there is an increasing bargaining emphasis that becomes progressively more complex.

The implication of the last few paragraphs is that there is a hierarchy of consent categories, through which organisations steadily progress. Although this has frequently been true in the past, it is by no means necessary. Some may begin at (6) or (7): there is no inflexible law of evolution and change can also move in the opposite direction.

REVIEW TOPIC 28.2

At the end of Chapter 27 three current approaches to employee involvement were set out: team briefing, total quality management and Investors in People. Where would you place each of those in these seven categories of consent?

Trade Union recognition and bargaining units

When a trade union has recruited a number of members in an organisation, it will seek recognition from the employer in order to represent those members. The step of recognition is seldom easy but is very important as it marks an almost irrevocable movement away from unilateral decision-making by the management. We can examine some of the questions to be considered.

Why should a union be recognised at all?

If the employees want that type of representation they will not readily co-operate with the employer who refuses. In extreme cases this can generate sufficient antagonism to cause industrial action in support of recognition. A more positive reason is the benefits that can flow from recognition: there are employee representatives with whom to discuss, consult and negotiate so that communication and working relationships can be improved. The 1980s saw, however, a decline in union membership and effectiveness in resisting management initiatives.

There are now few situations in which an employer is forced to recognise a union or unions for the first time if that is contrary to management policy, so an important consideration is how – if at all – union recognition can be used to support management strategy:

> With private sector employers facing increasingly competitive open markets, and the public sector being privatised or deregulated, there has been a shift towards employment flexibility... These new arrangements are generally not conducive to employment stability and membership retention in the trade unions. (Farnham 1993, p. 281)

Employers are apprehensive about the degree of rigidity in employment practice that union aims for security of employment appear to imply and are therefore considering recognition claims more carefully; collective consent can be achieved by other means in some situations, provided that the management work hard at the job of both securing and maintaining that consent.

When should a union be recognised?

A union should be recognised only when it has sufficient support from the employees, but there is no simple way of determining what is sufficient. The Industrial Relations Act 1971 specified that 51 per cent of the employees must be in membership, but current legislation lays down no percentage. The first thirteen cases brought to ACAS (Advisory, Conciliation and Arbitration Service) after the passing of the Employment Protection Act 1975 produced recommendations for recognition where the level of membership varied from 21 to 100 per cent and in five cases the figure was below 40 per cent. Among the factors that influenced ACAS in whether or not to recommend recognition were the degree of union organisation and efficiency, the number of representatives, the size of constituency and the degree of opposition to recognition from non-union employees. A frequent encouragement for the management of an organisation to recognise a union relatively quickly is where there is the possibility of competing claims, with some employees seeking to establish another union because they do not like the first.

For whom should a union be recognised?

A union should be recognised for that group of employees who have sufficient commonality of interests, terms and conditions for one union to be able to represent them and the management to be able to respond. This group of employees is sometimes described as that making up a bargaining unit; the boundaries of the units need careful consideration by the management to determine what is most appropriate and what consequent response to recognition claims they will make. A number of boundaries are generally acknowledged: manual employees are usually represented by different unions from white-collar employees, and skilled employees are sometimes represented by a different union from the semi-skilled and unskilled as well as from those possessing different skills. Other boundaries are less easy, particularly where a distinction may be drawn on the grounds of hierarchical status, as between those who are paid monthly and those paid weekly. Where status is related to responsibility for subordinates there appears to be another accepted boundary: the supervisor will not be represented by the same union as the supervised, although one or two levels may be included sometimes in the same unit.

These traditional boundaries are gradually becoming blurred, as is described in the opening of Chapter 32 looking at the long-standing difference between wages and salaries. The Trade Union Reform and Employment Rights Act 1993 provides employees with a statutory right to join the union of their choice, regardless of what might be convenient for the local management, so that the famous Bridlington agreement on dealing with disputes between unions about membership is effectively redundant, but a management can still decide which union, if any, to *recognise*.

The most common type of new recognition arrangement is where an employer agrees recognition terms with one union only. These are popularly known as 'single-union' agreements, but they are more far-reaching in their departure from traditional arrangements than simply focusing on a single union. They are typically on green-field sites and in businesses of technological sophistication. Their essential novelty is the closeness and extent of the working relationship between management and union. Union officials find that they have less freedom of action on some matters than their members expect, but also find they are involved in the full range of human resource management questions, not simply the familiar terrain of collective bargaining.

For what should a union be recognised?

The terms and conditions of employment of the employees who are members of the bargaining unit. A union can seek recognition on anything that might be covered in a contract of employment, but the employer may agree to recognition only for a limited range of topics. The irreducible minimum is assistance by a union representative for members with grievances, but the extent to which matters beyond that are recognised as being a subject of bargaining depends on which consent category the organisation is in. It also depends on the possible existence of other agreements that could take some matters out of the scope of local recognition. Again, the new-style agreements frequently cover a wider range of issues.

The legal position on recognition

Trade unions seek recognition from employers by the traditional means of recruiting members and making representations to the management. If they are not successful then they have to take risks by, for instance, calling on their members to take industrial action to persuade the employer into a position where recognition will be granted. Disputes in support of a claim for recognition are very rare.

The Employment Protection Act 1975 provided an alternative method for trade unions to seek recognition via ACAS from an employer who was reluctant to recognise. These provisions were so unpopular that they were repealed by the Employment Act 1980, but it is worth a brief review to consider why the measures were originally introduced and what led to their repeal.

The 1975 legislation was based on the premise that an employer's right to refuse recognition to a trade union should be open to some question other than that of union bargaining power, in order to ensure basic rights of representation to employees and union members employed in situations where trade union organisation was weak. Many unions ignored the 1975 measures entirely and most employers objected to the one-sided nature of legislation, whereby unions could ask for an investigation of an issue but employers could not. ACAS became concerned about the variety of hats they were being asked to wear. Their main duties are to improve industrial relations and to extend collective bargaining, but it was difficult to reconcile that with the compulsory arbitration that the 1975 provisions involved.

Although unions can no longer seek recognition by this method, it is still vital for them to be recognised if they are to enjoy other legal rights. The remaining provisions of the 1975 Act include rights for recognised trade unions only to receive collective bargaining information, time off for industrial relations, trade union and public duties and consultation on proposed redundancies. The 1974 Health and Safety Act provisions for safety representatives only apply to recognised unions, as do the planning information rights under the 1975 Industry Act, and the workplace facilities and secret ballot provisions of the Employment Act 1980.

If an individual employer is a member of an employers' association that recognises a particular union for national and collective bargaining, that does not mean that the individual employer necessarily recognises the same union for any purpose at establishment level.

The correct legal definition of recognition is 'for the purpose of collective bargaining' with collective bargaining defined in Section 29(1) of the Trade Union and Labour Relations Act 1974 as matters relating wholly or mainly to one of the following:

1. Terms and conditions of employment, or the physical conditions in which any workers are required to work.
2. Engagement or non-engagement, or termination or suspension of employment or the duties of employment of one or more workers.
3. Allocation of work or the duties of employment as between workers or groups of workers.
4. Matters of discipline.
5. The membership or non-membership of a trade union on the part of a worker.
6. Facilities for officials of trade unions.
7. The machinery for negotiation or consultation and other procedures, relating to any of the foregoing matters, including the recognition by employers or employers' associates of the right of a trade union to represent workers in any such negotiation or consultation or in the carrying out of such procedures.

The Transfer Regulations of 1981 require that union recognition continues and collective agreements remain in force after the transfer of an undertaking to new ownership provided that the transferred undertaking retains 'an identity distinct from the remainder of the transferee's undertaking'.

Management organisation for recognition

The 'category of consent' for an organisation will influence its style of management and the structure of its management organisation, with the most important change coming when an organisation moves from the second to the third category mentioned earlier in this chapter (see under Collective Consent). That is the point at which there is some guarantee of commitment by management to procedure and the acknowledgement that a limited range of management decisions could be successfully challenged by the employees, causing those decisions to be altered.

As personnel managers have become more dominant in the management handling of employee relations issues, the traditional pattern of personnel and line management has altered. There is still, however, a notional distinction between the personnel and line roles. The Commission on Industrial Relations has made this comment:

1. The line manager is necessarily responsible for industrial relations within his particular area of operations. He needs freedom to manage his plant, department or section effectively within agreed policies and with access to specialist advice.

2. The personnel manager should help by supplying expert knowledge and skill and by monitoring the consistent execution of industrial relations policies and programmes throughout the company. He needs the backing of top management and must establish the authority which comes from giving sound advice. (CIR 1973, p. 26)

The same publication indicates (*ibid*. p. 13) that the simple distinction between advisory and executive roles is more useful as an instrument of analysis than as a means of describing current practice, which varies so much. Some organisations give full executive authority to industrial relations specialists. Parker, Hawes and Lumb illustrate the variation with two quotations from company policy statements:

> Management responsibility for the conduct of industrial relations is...delegated by the accountable line manager to his senior industrial relations executive who will make industrial relations decisions or review such decisions and ensure their consistency with established policy, practices and procedure...

> The management of employees is the responsibility of line management; the role of personnel specialists is to advise and assist line management in the exercise of that responsibility and to provide requisite supporting services. (Parker *et al*. 1971, p. 23)

Although the use of the exclusive male gender is now dated, the fundamental nature of the responsibility split seems to remain. What has changed is the nature of the advice offered. It used to be of the type offered by a well-meaning mother-in-law. It was thoughtful, genuinely intended to be helpful and was sometimes welcome, but its basis was simply general experience and good intentions. The recipient could use or ignore it at will, depending on the commonsense assessment of its value. Legislation has caused the need for advice of the type offered by a professional. This is thoughtful, intended to be helpful, but may not be welcome. It will be based on an informed examination of statute and precedent, and will include a full appreciation of the strategic implications of whatever is being considered. No personnel manager can now regard the general company strategy as something of concern only for other members of the management team. Although this is such an obvious point, it needs reiteration as a number of those applying for courses in personnel management retain a view that personnel is much more even-handed and some commentators castigate personnel managers for adopting a managerial approach. One recent commentary criticised personnel managers for abandoning their social and religious principles, adopting a managerial rather than independent professional stance, ignoring the pluralistic nature of work organisations and consolidating an exploitative relationship between people at work (Hart, 1993). Today's personnel manager is inescapably and necessarily a representative of management interests. In union recognition issues in particular, there is no point in having a personnel manager involved who does *not* adopt that perspective.

The personnel manager therefore carries a quite different type of authority. It may also be that people see the need not only for advice, but also for representation by someone who knows the esoteric rules of procedure and behaviour in a highly stylised form of discussion.

As well as advice, the employer needs to see that all employment matters are administered in a way that is consistent with the legislative framework, and part of that requirement is that managerial actions should be consistent with each other.

In many management decisions with relation to employees correctness lies not only in the intrinsic quality of the decision but also in the consistency of management handling of similar matters previously and in other parts of the organisation. In labour law consistency is an important feature of justice, and it can be achieved in an organisation either by having inflexible rules or by having a single source of control on decisions made.

The need for specialist advice based on a sound knowledge of the law and the need for an associated control over a wide range of management decisions have changed the range of options open to the employer in deploying personnel experts. The personnel officer may be charged with the task of deciding action on all employment matters and then implementing those decisions. Alternatively, the officer may monitor tentative decisions by others, which are agreed or vetoed before they are confirmed and implemented by those who formulated them. There is no place for mothers-in-law.

Organisational strategy for union recognition

There is a sequence of steps in the strategy of an organisation's management for union recognition.

Management attitudes

However dominant personnel specialists may be on employee relations matters, the other members of management do not simply leave them to get on with trade union recognition while they pursue their other and more interesting preoccupations. The step of recognition, or the extension of recognition, and all that follows can affect other policy matters such as the introduction of new products, investment in new plant, the manning of equipment and the opening or closure of establishments.

Equally, policy decisions to do with marketing, manufacturing, financing or new technology are likely to have employment repercussions. Union recognition or extension of recognition represents the introduction of change that can have major implications in all parts of the life of the organisation. Because of this it is important that collective management attitudes towards recognition should have as wide a degree of consensus as possible. Then policy on recognition and its consequences can be fully integrated with other aspects of policy.

The previous three sentences represent a homily that has been repeated for years, and managers are frequently sceptical about such bland exhortations to do something which they know to be extremely difficult. Some of the problems lie in the specialised nature of the issue. The very existence of trade unions is resented by some and the alleged behaviour of trade unionists has been given as the reason for the fall of governments, let alone managerial ineffectiveness. The reasons justifying trade union recognition in general, and on some contentious matters in particular, are not readily appreciated and when understood may still be disputed. Another difficulty is the need for a positive rather than grudging approach to recognition. If the management of an organisation recognises a trade union only because they feel there is no alternative, then they will derive scant benefit from the arrangement. As with other aspects of change in organisations it can be an initiative towards improvement and development or it can be a defensive reaction to something distasteful and unwanted. It is also typical for the new convert to trade union recognition to be disappointed with the outcome. The conventional illustration of this attitude is where management have been persuaded that rank-and-file employees will make a contribution to better management decisions if they are involved through their union being recognised. A few months later there are bitter, disillusioned remarks about the unwillingness of the employees to discuss anything other than trivial matters such as the colour of their overalls.

These and other problems about the integration of policy and a management consensus on recognition can probably only be resolved by full and lengthy discussion by members of management to find and then agree on a collective view.

Preparing to recognise

Does a management respond or initiate on recognition? Does it wait for a claim and then treat it on its merits or does it invite a claim? The answer to this question will come from a consideration of timing. It has already been suggested in this chapter that care has to be taken with a recognition claim that the time is ripe, not too soon or too late. There is always a danger that recognition will be harder if deferred. The Commission on Industrial Relations (CIR) found several situations like this:

> the success of the company's products in the markets of the world meant that management had to concentrate, to the virtual exclusion of all else, on increasing output... The problems arising from the needs and aspirations of a large number of people had been largely shelved under the presence of the more immediate need to meet production targets. (CIR 1973, p. 12)

Another argument in favour of a recognition initiative by the management is that most of the areas of employment where recognition has not yet been granted are white-collar; one of the traditional reasons for white-collar employees not joining unions is their feeling that the management do not approve. They may tend to identify with the management and do not want to do things that are disliked.

Preparing to recognise requires a decision on whether to wait or to initiate. It also requires decisions on strategy about which union would be most 'appropriate', what the boundaries of the bargaining units could be and on what matters recognition would be contemplated.

Organisation, communication and responsibility

How are the management to organise themselves to make recognition work? This process will involve a re-examination of the decision-making processes so that the additional input of employee consent can be incorporated with the other variables to be evaluated. It does not mean that managers have to obtain permission from their employees before they do anything – even though this is how union recognition is often caricatured. The decision-making processes have to be examined and the boundaries of managerial roles redrawn. Any recognition step involves removing one or more items from the list that are customarily a subject for unilateral decision and on to the list of those for joint regulation. When that happens it will involve not only a different approach but also a different process of discussion and validation within the management ranks.

The contract for recognition

Ideally, there will be some written statement to which both parties assent; this will include the basic factual information about which union is a party to the agreement, what the bargaining unit is and what the subjects of recognition are. It may include much more, as it is an opportunity to declare aspects of the policy of the organisation – either the policy of the organisation's management or the policy of management and employee representatives combined. This can pave the way for openness between the parties, awareness of what is happening and consistency in management.

Such a statement will also have the advantage of focusing the attention of policy-makers on the purposes and implications of it. The drafting of the statement could well be the basis of the full and lengthy discussion suggested earlier in this chapter. The CIR give us a useful summary of the benefits of a written statement of policy:

> Firstly, the processes involved in producing the document will themselves have been valuable in focusing minds on the purpose of the policy. They clarify intentions and eliminate uncertainties which may exist when reliance is placed on custom and practice

or when policy is a matter of surmise. Secondly, a written document provides an objective reference point in the communication of policy to managers, employees and their representatives. Thirdly, by making clear the starting point of policy it provides a basis for change. A written policy need not be inflexible but should be reviewed and adapted as circumstances require. By being written it should, in fact, be easier to change than policies which are embedded in custom and practice, tradition and precedent. (CIR 1973, p. 6)

We have already referred to the move by some employers to sign single-union agreements when setting up new plants. These avoid, on one hand, a long-running series of arguments with unions seeking recognition and, on the other hand, the problems of fragmented bargaining arrangements. It also shifts any rivalry between unions to the stage before recognition. Pirelli General approached five different unions in south Wales:

> In each case the company outlined in some detail its proposed personnel philosophy and policies for the new factory, and each union was asked whether it wished to be considered for single recognition on those broad terms. All five unions...responded positively and enthusiastically. The prize ... was the creation of new jobs and new union recruits in an area of very high unemployment. (Yeandle and Clark 1989, p. 37)

☐ SUMMARY PROPOSITIONS

28.1 Employee consent to the exercise of management authority may be strengthened if the management recognises a trade union to provide a focused, collective questioning of that authority and consequent co-operation.

28.2 Management need to decide what bargaining units there should be, which union should be recognised for each unit, when it should be recognised and what the scope of recognition should be.

28.3 Managements at new sites often seek a 'new-style' recognition agreement with a single union and covering a wide range of human resource matters.

28.4 The step of recognition requires re-examination of management decision-making processes and will involve the personnel manager in taking the leading role in employment matters.

28.5 A written statement of policy on recognition can provide the basis for mutually beneficial development of collective consent.

References

Commission on Industrial Relations (CIR) (1973), *The Role of Management in Industrial Relations*, London: HMSO.

Etzioni, A. (1961), *A Comparative Analysis of Complex Organizations*, New York: Free Press.

Farnham, D. (1993), *Employee Relations*, London: Institute of Personnel Management.

Hart, T. (1993), 'Human resource management: time to exorcize the militant tendency', *Employee Relations*, vol. 15, no. 3, pp. 29–36.

Marchington, M. P. and Parker, P. S. (1990), *Changing Patterns of Employee Relations*, Hemel Hempstead: Harvester Wheatsheaf.

Millward, N., Stevens, M., Smart, D. and Hawes, W. (1992), *Workplace Industrial Relations Survey*, Aldershot: Dartmouth.

Parker, P. A. L., Hawes, W. R. and Lumb, A. L. (1971), *The Reform of Collective Bargaining at Plant and Company Level*, London: HMSO.

Purcell, J. and Sisson, K. (1983), 'Strategies and practice in the management of industrial relations'. In G. S. Bain (ed.) *Industrial Relations in Britain*, Oxford: Basil Blackwell.

Yeandle, D. and Clark, I. (1989), 'Growing a compatible IR set up', *Personnel Management*, vol. 21, no. 7, July, pp. 36–9.

29   Health, safety and welfare

There is always a conflict between the needs of the employer to push for increased output and efficiency and the needs of the employee to be protected from the hazards of the workplace. In the mid-nineteenth century these tensions centred almost entirely on the long hours and heavy physical demands of the factory system. In the closing years of the twentieth century the tensions are more varied and more subtle but concern about them remains as great, being expressed by employers, employees, trade unions, government agencies and campaign groups.

Increasingly, aspects of protection are being provided by statute, and James comments that:

> As a result of the directives adopted by the European Community, UK health and safety law is undergoing its most fundamental process of change since the passing of the Health and Safety at Work Act 1974. (James 1992)

In addition some aspects result from the initiatives of managements, employees and their representatives. No matter what the source of the initiative or the nature of the concern, the personnel manager is often the focus of whatever action has to be taken.

In this chapter we first consider definitions of health, safety and welfare and then discuss the development and importance of this area of work and the role of personnel management. Following this we cover legislation relating to health, safety and welfare and then look at the management of health and safety matters. We conclude by discussing some more general aspects of occupational health and welfare.

Definitions of health, safety and welfare

The dictionary defines 'welfare' as 'wellbeing', so health and safety are strictly aspects of employee welfare, which have been separately identified as being significant areas of welfare provision for some time. Other authors (e.g. Beamont 1984), have also noted that welfare can be very broadly defined. Using Fox (1966) as an example, he notes that welfare has been defined to encompass not only the early concern with workers' physical working conditions (sanitation, canteens, hours of work, rest pauses, etc.), but also the 'human relations school of thought', due to the achievement of job satisfaction being seen as a way to achieve higher productivity. He also notes the importance attached to counselling by early welfare workers and the human relations school.

There are two primary areas of benefit to the individual from the provision of welfare facilities – physical benefits and emotional/psychological benefits. Physical benefits would stem primarily from measures to improve health and safety, as well as from the provision of paid holidays, reduced working hours, and so on. Emotional welfare stems chiefly from any provisions made to improve mental health, for example, counselling, improved communications, or anything involving the 'human relations' needs of people at work. These benefits are, however, highly interrelated, and most welfare activities would potentially have both physical and emotional benefits. It can also be argued that employers provide for the material and intellectual welfare of their employees in the material provisions of sick pay and pensions, and in the intellectual benefits that come from the provision of satisfying work and appropriate training and development. However, since these aspects are covered elsewhere in this book, we shall concentrate on physical and emotional welfare in this chapter.

Many provisions are less clearly seen as welfare when, for example, they are long-standing provisions made by many employers, such as canteens and time off for doctor's appointments. Other provisions are less clearly seen as welfare when they are enshrined in the contract of employment and therefore seen as standard. Holiday entitlement would come into this group: however, the amount of holiday is far from standard. In the United Kingdom holiday entitlement generally ranges from three to six weeks a year, which compares very favourably with the two weeks to which many US employees are entitled.

The development and importance of health, safety and welfare provision and the role of personnel management

The development of health, safety and welfare provision is to a large extent interrelated with the development of personnel management itself. As mentioned in Chapter 1, one of the early influences on the development of personnel management was the growth of industrial welfare workers at the turn of the century. Enlightened employers gradually began to improve working conditions for employees and the industrial welfare worker was often concerned in implementing these changes. Much of this work was carried out voluntarily by employers, although not necessarily from altruistic motives alone. Another influence on personnel management was that of the 'human relations school', in particular the work of Elton Mayo at the Hawthorne plant of the Western Electric Company. Here there was an employee counselling programme, which operated from 1936 to 1955. It was found that such a programme was beneficial both for the mental health of the employees and their work. Other aspects of welfare provision, particularly with respect to safety, such as limitations on the hours of work of children, were enshrined in the law from as early as the 1840s and these again have become identified with the personnel function. Our research in 1984 shows that in 53.4 per cent of those firms with a safety officer this person comes within the ambit of the personnel function. In those firms without a health and safety officer the personnel department had a primary responsibility for health and safety. The activities of the personnel department in relation to health and safety are shown in Table 29.1. As health and safety legislation has become more pervasive, in particular with the Health and Safety at Work Act 1974, and the surge of regulations stemming from it (many resulting from the need to harmonise health and safety regulation through the EU), the personnel department has taken the role of advising managers on the consequences of this, as with the constant updating of other employment.

However, personnel managers often find their welfare origin a source of embarrassment, feeling that it has contributed to their 'soft' image, and accordingly were not sorry when the emphasis on welfare decreased between the 1950s and the 1970s. There is considerable support for the view that the personnel function can only achieve authority and status in the organisation when its activities have moved substantially beyond the welfare function (Fox 1966). More recently Mackay comments:

> Today, the personnel function seeks to be, and often is, a full member of the management team, aiming to participate and contribute to the success and survival of the organization ... It is the credibility of personnel management in the eyes of other managers that matters, not their credibility in the eyes of the workforce. (Mackay (1986), The workforce and the personnel function, UMIST, Manchester, p. 3. unpublished paper)

Watson (1977) has also noted the need for personnel to distance itself from its welfare image in order to facilitate full acceptance as part of the management team.

During the 1970s, however, there was some attempt to rediscover welfare (Kenny 1975). In the 1980s this renewed interest was maintained; the personnel function still had a role to play in welfare provision. The issues have changed from the early days. There has been a change in emphasis from purely physical to both physical and emotional welfare. In aspects of occupational health related to stress and personal problems, the involvement of line managers (Slaikeu and Frank 1986) and separate occupational counselling services have been advocated. Whatever role personnel managers may play in health, safety and welfare, our research indicates that they do not rate this area of their work very highly in terms of the time that they devote to it and the importance they accord to it among their other activities. Health, safety and welfare was ranked ninth out of fourteen for time spent, eleventh out of fourteen for importance, and eleventh out of fourteen for degree of increase in importance (Torrington, Mackay and Hall 1985).

The importance of health, safety and welfare from the employees' point of view is clear – their lives and futures are at risk. Health and safety has been given increasing emphasis by the trade unions, especially from the late 1960s. Eva and Oswald (1981), in their book on the trade union approach to health and safety, identify a number of health and safety concerns of the unions in the early 1970s,

Table 29.1 *Activities of the personnel department in relation to health and safety activities*

| Activity | Role of personnel department | | | |
	Undertakes wholly	Undertakes in part	Does not undertake	Total
Formulating policy statement on safety	32	43	25	100
Formulating safety regulations	19	44	37	100
Formulating safe systems of work	9	47	43	99
Formulating accident reporting procedures	41	37	22	100
Recording industrial accidents and notifiable diseases	43	31	26	100
Formulating accident investigation procedures	29	35	34	98
Advising management of health and safety legislation	44	38	18	100
Designing, providing, recording health and safety training	32	44	24	100
Compiling, analysing health and safety statistics	37	23	40	100
Designing safety publicity, leaflets	18	22	60	100
Liaising with occupational health and other bodies	34	33	33	100
Liaising with inspectorate	33	38	29	100
Monitoring health and safety policy, procedures	35	29	26	100
Advising on provision of protective clothing	26	39	35	100

(a) Figures are percentages of 350 potential responses indicating the role of the personnel department in each of the health and safety activity areas.
(b) Figures may not total 100 due to rounding.

which include the rising number of accidents; new technologies creating new hazards and new diseases; and new diseases caused by working conditions being detected. Since that time some improvements have been made:

> For the third successive year the rate of fatal accidents fell in 1992–3 to 1.3 per 100,000 employees, generally less than a quarter of the rate 30 years ago. The rate of major injuries fell to 81 per 100,000 (Anon 1994, reporting on the 1992–3 *Health and Safety Commission Annual Report*)

The Health and Safety Commission acknowledges that as well as representing genuine improvements in safety these reflect the move away from high risk-heavy industry. The annual report also notes that 140,365 injuries caused an absence from work of more than three days, and that an estimated 3000 of the deaths were due to asbestos. With such a rate of injury and death few would fail to acknowledge the continued importance of health and safety issues.

From the point of the view of the employer there is a variety of reasons for supporting health, safety and welfare provision, apart from the ethical perspective and their legal obligations. It would be unfair to say that altruism does not play a part in employers' motives for improving these provisions, but there are other major influencing factors. The number of working days lost due to accidents at work was 10½ million in the year 1981/2 (Health and Safety Executive 1985). If this figure were reduced by only a small percentage, the employer would save a considerable amount of money and trouble. One of the side-effects of employees with personal problems is that the quality of their work is often affected, as indicated by Knox and Fenley: 'One of the earliest signs of problem drinking is a detrimental change in attitude, performance and efficiency at work which can be detected by an alert supervisor many years before other serious consequences of alcoholic dependence' (Knox and Fenley 1985, p. 32). There is also a general feeling that employees whose health, safety and welfare needs are well looked after by the employer will be more productive and loyal employees, and may cause fewer industrial relations problems, as indicated by the following quotes from a personnel director: 'It's very difficult for people who have been treated well to take a militant attitude to one per cent one way or the other on a pay deal' (Mackay 1986, p. 13; unpublished paper); and a personnel manager: 'Let's be honest. From our point of view, I far prefer to have a contented employee, because he's doing a good job and generating income for the company' (*ibid.*).

However, there is a continual conflict between health, safety and welfare considerations and other business priorities, as Beaumont, Leopold and Coyle (1982) comment:

> Many safety officers interviewed suggested that, as a result of the recession, production considerations consistently tended to outweigh health and safety matters as a priority in management calculations. As one health and safety officer put it, trying to bring about improvements in health and safety now was very much an uphill battle. (Beaumont *et al.* 1982, p. 38)

Very recently Leach (1994) reported the following quote from a line manager (who had previously been a safety officer): 'I think in general managers don't see them (health and safety issues) as important as ... other issues that they would deal with disciplinary on [*sic*]. I mean you do take short cuts, I do myself. I mean I am not practising a lot of what I used to preach, there's no doubt about it. Managers know it is a part of their job, but I don't think they personally see it (health and safety offences) as an offence as such'.

Health, safety and welfare legislation

In the area of health and safety legislative intervention has existed continuously for well over 100 years, longer, we consider, than for any other matter. Prior to 1974 the principal statutes were the Factories Act (1961), the Offices, Shops and Railway Premises Act (1963) and the Fire Precautions Act (1971). These three Acts have all been brought up to date by the Health and Safety at Work Act (1974). In addition there are a host of health and safety regulations primarily extending the Health and Safety Act to expand specific areas of the legislation, the most significant of which is the Control of Substances Hazardous to Health Regulations (1988) (COSHH). Increasingly, regulations have been based on EU directives, such as noise control and the manual handling of heavy loads, use of visual display units (VDUs) and use of carcinogens and biological agents. Regulations are also supplemented by an increasing number of Codes of Practice which are not legally enforceable.

Health and Safety legislation is increasing at a high rate and the IPD (1994) note that:

> This is now the most highly regulated area of employment and more proposals are on the table.

European Union directives are implemented via our national law such as implementing further regulations under the Health and Safety at Work Act. The reason that EU directives have increased so rapidly in this area is that the Single European Act (1987) added another article into the Treaty of Rome. This article allowed health and safety directives to be accepted by a qualified *majority* vote as a move towards harmonising EU health and safety legislation.

The Factories Act 1961

This statute applies to all factories where two or more persons are employed in manual labour by way of trade or for the purpose of gain in a range of operations. The Act sets out to ensure that minimum standards are maintained in factories on cleanliness, space for people to work in, temperature and ventilation, lighting, toilet facilities, clothing, accommodation and first-aid facilities. Many of the standards are fairly obvious, such as keeping factories clear of the effluvia from drains, but some of them provide very precise levels that have to be met. Part of the enforcement machinery is the Factory Inspector, whose authority was reinforced under the Health and Safety at Work Act.

The Offices, Shops and Railway Premises Act 1963

The Offices, Shops and Railway Premises Act was introduced to extend to these buildings protection similar to that provided for factories. The legislation covers the type of premises described, and the general provisions are very similar to those of the Factories Act, dealing with cleanliness, lighting, ventilation and so on. There is a difference in terms of the minimum space provision and temperature requirements.

The Fire Precautions Act 1971

The Fire Precautions Act lists designated premises for which a fire certificate is required, and this list includes premises being used as a place of work. When issuing a fire certificate a fire authority can impose requirements on the certificate holder. These may concern such things as:

- The means of escape from the building.
- Instruction and training for employees on what to do in the case of a fire.
- Limits to the number of people on the premises.

The Health and Safety at Work Act 1974

The Health and Safety at Work Act 1974 is an attempt to provide a comprehensive system of law, covering the health and safety of people at work:

> The objectives of the Act, which are very ambitious, include both raising the standards of safety and health for all persons at work, and protection of the public, whose safety and health may be put at risk by the activities of persons at work. Because it is of general application, it brings within statutory protection many classes of persons who were previously unprotected. (Howells and Barrett 1982, p. 1)

The Act is an enabling Act and, as Howells and Barrett (1982) comment, for this reason its provisions are of necessity wide and remain somewhat vague, except where they have been interpreted by the courts or augmented by regulations produced under the Act by the Secretary of State. By September 1985, 147 regulations had been issued under the Act (Health and Safety Executive 1985) although some of these are modifications or repeals of existing health and safety laws. The Act imposes, for the first time, criminal liability to comply with its provisions. The legislation is based largely on the recommendations of the Robens Committee (1970–2) and creates various new bodies and reinforces the authority of others as detailed below.

The Health and Safety Commission

The Health and Safety Commission was formed under the Act and has a chairman and between six and nine other members appointed by the Secretary of State to represent employers, employees and local authorities. The commission is responsible for carrying out the policy of the Act and providing advice to local authorities and others to enable them to discharge the responsibilities imposed upon them by the Act. It issues codes of practice and regulations, as well as having the power to make investigations and inquiries.

The Health and Safety Executive

The Commission, together with the Secretary of State, appoints three people to form the Health and Safety Executive whose duty it is to make adequate provision for the enforcement of the Health and Safety at Work Act, and to undertake the daily administration of affairs. There can also be other enforcement bodies as well as the Executive, for example local authorities.

The Factory Inspectorate

Factory inspectors had been employed for some time prior to the 1974 Act, and we have previously mentioned them regarding the enforcement of the 1961 Factories Act. As the enforcing authority of the Health and Safety at Work Act, the Executive is given the power to appoint inspectors. The role of the Inspectorate was strengthened by the 1974 Act as they were given the power to issue improvement and prohibition notices to appropriate employers. In general, inspectors have the right to enter employers' premises; carry out examinations/investigations; take measurements, photographs and recordings; take equipment and materials; and examine books and documents. Initially, the number of inspectors was increased from 681 in 1973 to 986 in 1980. However, by 1985 the number had fallen to 823. See Davis (1979) for further coverage of this aspect.

The Employment Medical Advisory Service

The Employment Medical Advisory Service was set up in 1972 to provide general advice to the government on industrial medicine matters and a corps of employment medical advisers to carry out medical examinations of employees whose health may have been endangered by their work. Responsibility for this service is now delegated by the Secretary of State to the Health and Safety Commission.

Enforcement of the Health and Safety at Work Act

Employer health and safety policy
Every employer is required to prepare a written statement of their general policy on health and safety, and the organisation and arrangements for carrying out that policy which are in force at the time. All employees must be advised of what the policy is. It is perhaps inevitable that many employers have regarded this as a statutory chore and have gone through the motions of articulating a policy in terms of the bare minimum that is possible, rather than thinking out a policy statement that will have genuine impact on safe working. The report of the inspectorate for 1976 is very critical of companies where this happens, especially where the policy is a hollow

statement without action to implement the declared intentions. Other specific criticisms were the lack of information in policy statements about particular hazards and how they could be dealt with, and a failure to stress management responsibility for safety as strongly as those of safety representatives (Health and Safety Commission 1978).

Booth (1985) makes similar criticisms based on research carried under the auspices of the PPITB (Printing and Publishing Industry Training Board). He comments that of the 121 policy documents investigated, most expressed a clear commitment to health and safety but few contained appropriate details of the necessary arrangements for implementing the policy.

Another requirement of the Act is updating: 'it is the duty of every employer to prepare, and as often as may be appropriate revise, a written statement of general policy with respect to the health and safety at work of his employees' (Health and Safety at Work Act 1974, sect. 2(3)). If a safety policy is produced as something to be filed away and forgotten, there is little chance that arrangements for coping with new hazards or changed working conditions will be made. The need for safety policy statements to be specific to the circumstances makes it difficult to offer models, but a useful starting point is provided by Armstrong:

> The general policy statement should be a declaration of the intention of the employer to safeguard the health and safety of his employees. It should emphasize four fundamental points: first, that the safety of employees and the public is of paramount importance; second, that safety will take precedence over expediency; third, that every effort will be made to involve all managers, supervisors and employees in the development and implementation of health and safety procedures; and fourth, that health and safety legislation will be complied with in the spirit as well as the letter of the law. (Armstrong 1977, p. 337)

REVIEW TOPIC 29.1

Devise a health and safety policy for your organisation. Include information about:

1. General policy on health and safety.
2. Specific hazards and how they are to be dealt with.
3. Management responsibility for safety.
4. How the policy is to be implemented.

Managerial responsibility

The management of the organisation carry the prime responsibility for implementing the policy they have laid down, and they also have a responsibility under the Act for operating the plant and equipment in the premises safely and meeting all the Act's requirements whether these are specified in the policy statement or not. In the case of negligence, proceedings can be taken against an individual, responsible manager as well as against the employing organisation. The appointment of a safety officer can be one way of meeting this obligation. The officer does not become automatically responsible for all managerial failures in the safety field, but does become an in-house factory inspector.

Employee responsibility

For the first time in health and safety legislation a duty is placed on employees while they are at work to take reasonable care for the safety of themselves and others, as well as their health, which appears a more difficult type of responsibility for the individual to exercise. The employee is, therefore, legally bound to comply with the safety rules and instructions that the employer promulgates. Rose (1976) reported that nine employees had been prosecuted under this section of the Act.

Employers are also fully empowered to dismiss employees who refuse to obey safety rules on the grounds of misconduct, especially if the possibility of such a dismissal is explicit in the disciplinary procedure. An employee who refused to wear safety goggles for a particular process was warned of possible dismissal because the safety committee had decreed that goggles or similar protection were necessary. His refusal was based on the fact that he had done the job previously without such protection and did not see that it was now necessary. He was dismissed and the tribunal did not allow his claim of unfair dismissal (*Mortimer* v. *V. L. Churchill* 1979).

Safety representatives

To reinforce the employees' role in the care of their own health and safety, provision has been made for the appointment of safety representatives by trade unions. The Safety Representatives and Safety Committees Regulations 1978 sets out the functions of safety representatives and provides for various types of inspection and investigation which they may carry out. Safety representatives have a legal duty of consultation with employers and are entitled to paid time off for training to enable them to carry out their function. There is also a Code of Practice for Safety Representatives recommending that they keep themselves informed, encourage co-operation with management and bring matters to their employer's attention (Davis 1979). However, in practice, things do not always work out this well, as Codrington and Henley comment:

> The innovations of [HASWA] can only produce significant improvements in the construction industry's appalling safety record if there are improvements in trade union site organization, for without it safety representatives have very little real power or authority... With a declining membership and increasing fragmentation of employment relationships on site, the construction unions will only have limited resources available to encourage the development of safety representatives' activities. (Codrington and Henley 1981, p. 308)

Safety committees

Although the Act does not specifically instruct employers to set up safety committees, it comes very close:

> it shall be the duty of every employer, if requested to do so by the safety representatives ... to establish, in accordance with regulations made by the Secretary of State, a safety committee having the function of keeping under review the measures taken to ensure

the health and safety at work of his employees and such other functions as may be pre-scribed. (Health and Safety at Work Act 1974, sect. 2(7))

Safety representatives also have to be consulted about the membership of the committee, and detailed advice on the function and conduct of safety committees is provided in the guidance note on safety representatives (Health and Safety Commission 1976).

Research by Leopold and Coyle (1981) has shown that there has been a great increase in the number of safety committees in operation since the passing of the Act, especially in companies employing fewer than 200 people and in those indus-tries where there was previously a low level of accidents. They also found the effec-tiveness of such committees to be much dependent on the employment of trained safety officers. This was generally confirmed by the work of Donnelly and Barrett (1981).

Safety training

There is a general requirement in the Act for training to be given, along with infor-mation, instruction and supervision, to ensure 'the health and safety at work of his employees'. There is thus fairly wide scope to determine what is appropriate in the differing circumstances of each organisation. We deal more fully with safety train-ing and other methods of persuasion later in this chapter.

Codes of practice

The Commission is empowered to follow the growing practice of issuing codes of practice for people to follow in various situations. Codes have been issued covering such aspects as:

- The protection of persons against ionising radiation.
- Control of lead pollution at work.
- Time off for the training of safety representatives.
- Control of substances hazardous to health (various).

The codes are not legally enforceable, but the use or not of the codes may be interpreted in a legal case as an indication of the employer's efforts in that area of health and safety.

Improvement notices

Inspectors can serve improvement notices on individuals whom they regard as being in breach of the HASWA provisions, or earlier legislation, such as the Factories Act 1961. This notice specifies the opinion of the inspector and the reasons for it, as well as requiring the individual to remedy the contravention within a stated period. Most frequently, this will be issued to a member of the management of an organis-ation, depending on which individual the inspector regards as being appropriate, but such a notice could also be issued to an employee who was deliberately and knowingly disobeying a safety instruction.

Prohibition notices

An alternative, or subsequent, power of the inspector is to issue a prohibition notice where they believe that there is a risk of serious personal injury. This prohibits an operation or activity being continued until specified remedial action has taken place. In 1983, 3805 prohibition notices were issued compared with 12,268 improvement notices (HSE 1986).

It is possible for employers to appeal against both improvement and prohibition notices. In 1978 an employer appealed successfully against a prohibition notice issued against a hand-operated guillotine that had been used – as had nine similar machines – for eighteen years without accident. Another successful appeal was against an improvement order that was issued requiring safety shoes to be provided free of charge to employees. The tribunal found that the cost of £20,000 in the first year and £10,000 a year thereafter was disproportionate to the risk involved, and that the fact of the shoes being provided free did not make it more likely that they would be worn (LDS 1978).

Control of Substances Hazardous to Health Regulations, 1988

These regulations, which came into force on 1 October 1989, were made under the Health and Safety at Work Act 1974. They comprise nineteen regulations plus four approved codes of practice and were described by Norman Fowler, Secretary of State, in 1988, as the most far-reaching health and safety legislation since the Health and Safety at Work Act (Powley 1989).

The purpose of the legislation is to protect all employees who work with any substances hazardous to their health, by placing a requirement on their employer regarding the way and extent that such substances are handled, used and controlled.

The regulations apply to all workplaces, irrespective of size and nature of work – so, for example, they would apply equally to a hotel as to a chemical plant, and in firms of a handful of employees as well as major p.l.c.s. The regulations not only place a responsibility for good environmental hygiene on the employer, but on employees too. All substances are included, except for asbestos, lead, materials producing ionising radiations and substances underground, all of which have their own legislation, as explained by Riddell (1989).

The regulations require employers to focus on five major aspects of occupation in respect of hazardous substances. These are:

1.   Assessing the risk of substances used, and identifying what precautions are needed. This initial assessment of substances already in use, and those that are intended for use is a major undertaking in terms of both the number of substances used and the competency of the assessor. Cherrie and Faulkner (1989) report that one employer in their survey used more than 25,000 different substances! The assessment needs to be systematic, and key questions to ask are contained in the HSE's guide (1985), *Introduction to COSHH*. Assessors may be internal or external consultants or specialists. Should the internal approach be adopted, the assessors require rigorous training and education as at ICI, described by Mountfield (1989).

2. Introducing appropriate measures to control or prevent the risk. These may include:

    (a) removing the substance, by changing the processes used;
    (b) substituting the substance; and
    (c) controlling the substance where this is practical, for example, by totally or partially enclosing the process, or by increasing ventilation or instituting safer systems of work and handling procedures.

    These measures would be designed to undercut Maximum Exposure Limits (MEL) and meet Occupational Exposure Standards (OES). For a fuller explanation of MEL and OES, see Powley (1989).

3. Ensure that control measures are used – that procedures are observed and that equipment involved is regularly maintained. Where necessary, exposure of the substance to employees should be monitored. This would particularly apply where there could be serious health implications if measures were to fail or be suboptimal. Records of monitoring should be made and retained.

4. Health surveillance: where there is a known adverse effect of a particular substance, regular surveillance of the employees involved can identify problems at an early stage. When this is carried out, records should be kept and these should be accessible to employees.

5. Employees need to be informed and trained regarding the risks arising from their work and the precautions that they need to take.

Although the legislation has been widely publicised and produced in a clear and appropriate format as judged, for example, by Foy (1989), there is early survey evidence of the lack of awareness, understanding and training in smaller firms from Cherrie and Faulkner (1989). The authors recommend three major initiatives to prepare this sector of employers better, which are that:

1. A major publicity campaign should be aimed specifically at small firms.
2. Small organisations need better access to professional health and safety advice.
3. The regulations must be enforced effectively.

Further regulations resulting from EU directives

The following information is based in the IPD Executive brief: *Personnel Management and Europe* (1994).

Management of Health and Safety at Work Regulations, 1992

This implements the Framework and Temporary Workers Directives. The Framework Directive is an umbrella directive, in a similar way as the Health and Safety at Work

Act is an umbrella act. Additional rules known as 'daughter directives' covering specific areas have been issued within the framework of this directive.

Workplace (Health, Safety and Welfare) Regulations, 1992

This implements the first daughter directive, the Workplace Directive, which sets minimum design requirements, including provision of rest and no smoking areas.

Provision and Use of Work Equipment Regulations, 1992

This implements the Work Equipment Directive (the second daughter directive), and sets minimum standards for the safe use of machines and equipment.

Personal Protective Equipment at Work Regulations, 1992

This implements the third daughter directive on Personnel Protective Equipment, and requires employers to provide appropriate protective equipment, and workers to use this correctly.

Manual Handling Operations Regulations, 1992

This implements the fourth daughter directive on Heavy Loads, and requires employers to reduce the risk of injury by providing lifting equipment where appropriate and training in lifting.

Health and Safety (Display Screen Equipment) Regulations, 1992

This implements the Display Screen Equipment (VDU) Directive (fifth daughter directive), and requires employers to provide free eye tests, glasses where appropriate, regular breaks, appropriate training and organisation of equipment to reduce strain.

COSHH (Amendment) Regulation, 1992

This implements the Carcinogens Directive, increasing the safeguards on employees by proving for risk assessments every five years.

The Control of Asbestos at Work (Amendment) Regulations, 1992 and The Asbestos (Prohibitions) Regulations, 1992

This implements the Asbestos Directive (which does not come under the framework directive) and concerns worker protection. Other regulations will be introduced shortly to implement the Biological Agents Directive, the Construction Sites Directive and the Health and Safety Signs Directive. All these are daughter directives.

Further directives awaiting implementation through national legislation relate to the Protection of Pregnant Workers, Drilling Industries, Mines and Quarries and Fishing Vessels. Other directives, not under the framework directive, include directives on Young Workers, Working Time, Explosive Atmospheres and Ships.

The Management of Health, Safety and Welfare

There are a number of ways in which managerial responsibility can be discharged to implement the policy statement and ensure compliance with legal requirements.

Making the work safe

Making the work safe is mainly in the realm of the designer and production engineer. It is also a more general management responsibility to ensure that any older equipment and machinery that is used is appropriately modified to make it safe, or removed. The provision of necessary safety wear is also a managerial responsibility – for example, making sure goggles and ear protectors are available.

Enabling employees to work safely

Whereas making the work safe is completely a management responsibility, the individual employee may contribute his or her own negligence to work unsafely in a safe situation. The task of the management is two-fold; first, the employee must know what to do; secondly, this knowledge must be translated into action: the employee must comply with the safe working procedures that are laid down. To meet the first part of the obligation the management need to be scrupulous in communication of drills and instructions and the analysis of working situations to decide what the drills should be. That is a much bigger and more difficult activity than can be implied in a single sentence, but the second part of getting compliance is more difficult and more important. Employee failure to comply with clear drills does not absolve the employer and the management. When an explosion leaves the factory in ruins it is of little value for the factory manager to shake his head and say: 'I told them not to do it'. We examine the way to obtain compliance shortly, under the discussion about training and other methods of persuasion.

The initiative on safe working will be led by the professionals within the management team. They are the safety officer, the medical officer, the nursing staff and the safety representatives. Although there is no legal obligation to appoint a safety officer, more and more organisations are making such appointments. One reason is to provide emphasis and focus for safety matters. The appointment suggests that the management mean business, but the appointment itself is not enough. It has to be fitted into the management structure with lines of reporting and accountability which will enable the safety officer to be effective and which will prevent other members of management becoming uncertain of their own responsibilities – perhaps to the point of thinking that they no longer exist. Ideally, the safety officer will operate on two fronts: making the work safe and ensuring safe working, although this may require an ability to talk constructively on engineering issues with engineers as well as being able to handle training and some industrial relations-type arguments. Gill and Martin (1976) have demonstrated that there is usually a clear dissonance between what is prescribed and what takes place, because the engineering approach produces complex and detailed manuals based on the belief that safety is a technical rather than human problem, whereas the people who do the work tend to produce different working practices based on experience:

> When we came to study the chemical plants we found an apparent paradox. On the one hand there existed a comprehensive body of written safety practices and procedures to cater for every conceivable contingency, and on the other hand actual working practice often differed considerably from the rules specifying safe working practices. Nevertheless the plants ran well and both the frequency of dangerous incidents and accidents were very low by national standards. (Gill and Martin 1976, p. 37)

The medical officer (if one is appointed) will almost certainly be the only medically qualified person and can therefore introduce to the thinking on health and safety discussions a perspective and a range of knowledge that is both unique and relevant. Secondly, the medical officer will probably carry more social status than the managers dealing with health and safety matters and he or she will be detached from the management in their eyes and his or her own. Doctors have their own ethical code, which is different from that of the managers. They are an authoritative adviser to management on making the work safe and can be an authoritative adviser to employees on working safely. They are an invaluable member of the safety committee and a potentially important feature of training programmes.

Occupational nurses also deal directly with working safely and often play a part in safety training, as well as symbolising care in the face of hazard.

Safety training and other methods of persuasion

Safety training has three major purposes. First, employees should be told about and understand the nature of the hazards at the place of work; secondly, employees need to be made aware of the safety rules and procedures; and thirdly, they need to be persuaded to comply with them. The first of these is the most important, because employees sometimes tend to modify the rules to suit their own convenience. Trainers cannot, of course, condone the short-cut without implying a general flexibility in the rules, but they need to be aware of how employees will probably respond. In some areas the use of short-cuts by skilled employees does not always mean they are working less safely, as Gill and Martin (1976) have demonstrated, but there are many areas where compliance with the rules is critical, for example, the wearing of safety goggles.

Persuading employees to keep to the safety rules is difficult and there often appears to be a general resistance on the part of the employees. A study by Pirani and Reynolds (1976) throws some light on this, as they used the repertory grid technique to obtain from both managers and employees a construct of the safety conscious employee:

> The management sample saw this 'ideal' safety-conscious operative as a half-witted, slow but reliable person who gave little trouble. They saw him as a worker who could be left safely alone but prone to making trivial complaints. He certainly was not depicted as a worker to be respected. The major construct to emerge from the operatives' data alone was that the ideal safety conscious man was rather a 'cissy' and somewhat unsociable. It is important to note, however, that individual operatives did not see him in these terms but felt that this was how the rest of the operatives would view him – a feeling substantiated by a large sample of operatives. (Pirani and Reynolds 1976, p. 26)

Safety training needs to be carried out in three settings: at induction, on the job and in refresher courses. A variety of different training techniques can be employed, including lectures, discussions, films, role-playing and slides. These methods are sometimes supplemented by poster or other safety awareness campaigns and communications, and disciplinary action for breaches in the safety rules. Management example in sticking to the safety rules no matter what the tempo of production needed can also set a good example. A four-stage systematic approach to health and safety training is described by Culliford (1987).

Research by Pirani and Reynolds (1976) indicated that the response to a variety of methods of safety persuasion – poster campaigns, film shows, fear techniques, discussion groups, role-playing and disciplinary action – was very good in the short-term (over two weeks) but after four months the initial improvement had virtually disappeared for all methods except role-playing. From this it can be concluded that: first, a management initiative on safety will produce gratifying results in the obeying of rules, but a fresh initiative will be needed at regular and frequent intervals to keep it effective. Secondly, the technique of role playing appears to produce results that are longer-lasting.

Also important is external training for managers, supervisors and safety representatives. Following the 1974 Act, a substantial provision for health and safety training and education was introduced in colleges of further education, but in recent years there has been a decline in the take-up of places (Booth 1985).

REVIEW TOPIC 29.2

- Why do you think that there has been a decline in the take-up of places on health and safety courses at colleges?
- What are the implications of this decline? Why?

Job descriptions and the role of the supervisor

Attention can be drawn to the safety aspects of work by inserting a reference to safe working practices in job descriptions. In particular, the supervisor's role in ensuring safe working practices should be made as specific as possible in the supervisor's job description.

Risk assessment

Risk assessment is one of the newer approaches to health and safety which concentrates on accident prediction – as opposed to the more traditional prevention of re-occurrence after the event (Booth 1985). This approach reflects current concerns that expenditure on health and safety matters should be cost effective, and the Royal Society (1983) paper on the subject discusses risk decision-making based on cost–benefit models.

Occupational health and welfare

Occupational health and welfare is a broad area, which includes both physical and emotional wellbeing. The medical officer, occupational health nurse and welfare officer all have a contribution to make here. In a broader sense so do the dentist, chiropodist and other professionals when they are employed by the organisation. The provision of these broader welfare facilities is often found in large organisations located away from centres of population, especially in industrial plants, where the necessity of at least an occupational health nurse can be clearly seen.

In terms of physical care the sorts of facility that can be provided are:

1. Emergency treatment, beyond immediate first-aid, of injuries sustained at work.
2. Medical, dental and other facilities, which employees can use and which can be more easily fitted into the working day than making appointments with outside professionals.
3. Immediate advice on medical and related matters, especially those connected with work.
4. Monitoring of accidents and illnesses to identify hazards and danger points, and formulating ideas to combat these in conjunction with the safety officer.
5. On-site medicals for those joining the organisation.
6. Regular medicals for employees.
7. Input into health and safety training courses.
8. Regular screening services. For example, cervical cancer screening at British Shipbuilders, Leyland Vehicles and United Biscuits.
(*Personnel Management* 1986)

In terms of emotional welfare (although this cannot necessarily be clearly separated from physical welfare) Slaikeu and Frank (1986) make a convincing case for provision by the employer:

> Research shows that marital, family, financial or legal crises are workers' most prevalent problems. Poor resolution of such crises can lead to long-term psychiatric damage

resulting in depression, alcoholism, physical illness and even death. Untreated and unresolved crises affect worker productivity and contribute to labour turnover; the annual cost to US business of alcoholism alone is put at five billion. The 'hard' costs of ill and unhappy employees (absence, recruitment, and training expenses) are high enough. Still greater are inefficient and inadequate job performance, discredit to the company and diminished morale engendered among co-workers. The bottom line?

Estimated cost for 'emotional problems' in US business and industry is $17 billion a year. (*Management Today*, 1986 p. 35)

This, however, only deals with the emotional problems that employees bring with them to work and the effects that these have on their work. What about problems that are caused by the work itself, and the interaction between 'home' and 'work' problems? There is not only a financial argument for the provision of health and welfare assistance here, but possibly a moral argument as well. It is very difficult, of course, to ascribe some problems to a definite cause; however, Eva and Oswald (1981) argue that conditions of work, speed of work, how boring or demanding the job is, and how the job affects family and social life are all major elements in the causation of stress.

Stress at work is not a new idea, although it was originally viewed in terms of 'executive stress' (for example, Levinson 1964), and seen only to apply to those in senior management positions. There is a large number of books and articles on the subject of stress at work (for example, Cooper and Marshall 1980; Palmer 1989; Nykodym and George 1989). Stress is now also seen to apply to those in manual work (Cooper and Smith 1985). It is the response of individuals to work pressure, however, that determines whether they display symptoms of stress. Different people react to the same pressures in different ways. It has been shown that the experience of stress is related to 'type A' coronary-prone behaviour. Stress is a threat to both physical and psychological wellbeing. Glowinkowski summarises the effects of stress:

> While stress can be short-lived it can represent a continuous burden leading to short-term outcomes such as tension, increased heart rate, or even increased drinking or smoking. In the long term, stress is said to cause disorders such as depression, coronary heart disease, diabetes melitus and bronchial asthma... Indeed, while stress may be a direct causal factor in heart disease, its effects may be indirect. Stress may increase smoking and cause overeating, which are also high risk factors in coronary artery disease (Glowinkowski 1985, pp. 1–2)

In relation to the variety of psychological and physical problems, there is a number of facilities that the employer can provide to ease the difficulties that employees may be experiencing.

Someone to talk to/someone to advise

This could be the individual's manager, or the personnel manager, but it is often more usefully someone who is distinct from the work itself. An occupational health nurse, welfare officer or specialised counsellor are the sort of people well placed to deal with this area. There are two benefits that come from this, the first being advice and practical assistance. This would be relevant, for example, if the individual had financial problems, and the organisation was prepared to offer some temporary assistance. Alternatively, the individual could be advised of alternative sources of help, or referred, with agreement, to the appropriate agency for treatment.

The second benefit to be gained is that from someone simply listening to the individual's problem without judging it – in other words, counselling. De Board (1983) suggests that the types of work-related problems that employees may need to be counselled on are: technical incompetence, underwork, overwork, uncertainty about the future and relationships at work. Counselling aims to provide a supportive atmosphere to help people to find their own solution to a problem.

Organisation of work

This is a preventive measure involving reorganisation of those aspects of work that are believed to be affecting the mental health of employees and this may include changes that could be grouped as 'organisational development', such as job rotation and autonomous work-groups. Eva and Oswald (1981) suggest greater control over the speed and intensity of work, an increase in the quality of work and a reduction in unsocial hours. Individually based training and development programmes would also be relevant here. Specifically for the executive, there is growing use of the 'managerial sabbatical'. In the United States some companies have begun to give a year off after a certain number of years' service in order to prevent 'executive burnout'. In the United Kingdom, the John Lewis Partnership has a programme allowing six months away from work.

Positive health programmes

Positive health programmes display a variety of different approaches aimed at relieving and preventing stress and associated problems. Some approaches are not new and include the use of yoga and meditation. Others, such as 'autogenic training', are based on these principles but are presented in a new guise. Autogenic training is developed through exercises in body awareness and physical relaxation which lead to passive concentration. It is argued that the ability to do this breaks through the vicious circle of excessive stress, and that as well as the many mental benefits there are benefits to the body including relief of somatic symptoms of anxiety and the reduction of cardiovascular risk factors (Carruthers 1982). A newer approach is 'chemofeedback', which is geared towards the connection between stress and coronary heart disease, high blood pressure and strokes. Chemofeedback (Positive Health Centre 1985) is designed as an early warning system to pick up signs of unfavourable stress. The signs are picked up from the completion of a computerised questionnaire together with a blood test. This approach is being offered as a 'stress-audit' on a company-wide basis. Other issues currently in the health and safety arena are passive smoking, alcohol and drug abuse, the control of HIV and the threat of violence.

> ### REVIEW TOPIC 29.3
>
> 'We are buying their [the employees'] skills and their energy and indus-
> try and commitment. While they are at work we don't feel we've got
> responsibility to manage their social life, marriages, religious faith or
> anything else...' (personnel manager).
>
> How do you think employees see the provision of facilities at work to
> deal with their personal, emotional problems?

☐ SUMMARY PROPOSITIONS

29.1 Occupational welfare is the 'wellbeing' of people at work, encompassing occupational health and safety.

29.2 There are four aspects of welfare at work: physical, emotional, intellectual
and material.

29.3 The history of personnel management is interrelated with the development of
welfare. Many personnel managers find this association a disadvantage when
trying to develop the authority and status of personnel management.

29.4 There was a surge in interest in health, safety and welfare in the late 1960s
and early 1970s and this culminated in the Health and Safety at Work Act
1974, and its associated regulations.

29.5 By the early 1980s the interest in safety had waned but there was increasing
interest in occupational health and welfare, particularly related to stress, alcoholism and counselling.

29.6 The efforts of the EU to ensure harmonisation of health and safety has resulted in a major surge of legislation in the early 1990s.

References

Anon. (1994), 'Record Low for workplace deaths', *Employment Gazette*, January, p. 9.

Armstrong, M. (1977), *Handbook of Personnel Management Practice*, London: Kogan Page.

Beaumont, P. B. (1984), 'Personnel management and the welfare role', *Management
Decision*, vol. 22, no. 3.

Beaumont, P. B., Leopold, J. W. and Coyle, J. R. (1982), 'The safety officer: an emerging
management role?' *Personnel Review*, vol. 11, no. 2.

Booth, R. (1985), 'What's new in health and safety management?' *Personnal Management*, April.

Carruthers, M. (1982), 'Train the mind to calm itself', *General Practitioner*, 16 July.

Cherrie, I. and Faulkner, C. (1989), 'Will the COSHH regulations improve occupational
health?' *Safety Practitioner*, February, pp. 6–7.

Codrington, C. and Henley, J. S. (1981), 'The industrial relations of injury and death', *British
Journal of Industrial Relations*, November.

Cooper, C. L. and Marshall, I. (1980), *White Collar and Professional Stress*. Chichester: Wiley.

Cooper, C. L. and Smith, M. I. (eds) (1985), *Job Stress and Blue Collar Work*, Chichester: Wiley.

Culliford, G. (1987), 'Health and safety training', *Safety Practitioner*, July, pp. 10–14.

Davis, K. P. (1979), *Health and Safety*, Wokingham: Van Nostrand Reinhold.

de Board, R. (1983), *Counselling People at Work: An Introduction for Managers*, Aldershot: Gower.

Donnelly, E. and Barrett, B. (1981), 'Safety training since the Act', *Personnel Management*, June.

Eva, D. and Oswald, R. (1981), *Health and Safety at Work*, London: Pan Books.

Fox, A. (1966), 'From welfare to organization', *Nev Society*, 9 June.

Foy, K. (1989), 'COSHH package appraisal', *Safety Practitioner*, February, pp. 18–19.

Gill, I. and Martin, K. (1976), 'Safety management: reconciling rules with reality', *Personnel Management*, June.

Glowinkowski, S. P. (1985), 'Managerial Stress: a longitudinal study', unpublished PhD thesis, UMIST, Manchester.

Health and Safety Commission (1976), *Safety Representatives and Safety Committees*, London: HMSO.

Health and Safety Commission (1978), *Health and Safety in Manufacturing and Service Industries (1976)*, London: HMSO.

Health and Safety Executive (HSE) (1985), *Statistics for Health and Safety (1981/2)*, London: HMSO.

Health and Safety Executive (HSE) (1986), *Health and Safety Executive Statistics (1983)*, London: HMSO

Health and Safety Executive (HSE) (1988), *Introduction to COSHH*, London: HMSO.

Howells, R. and Barrett, B. (1982), *The Health and Safety at Work Act: A Guide for Managers*, London: Institute of Personnel Management.

Incomes Data Services (1978), *IDS Brief No. 145*, London: Incomes Data Services.

Institute of Personnel and Development (IPD) (1994), *Personnel Management and Europe*, IPD Brief, July.

James, P. (1992), 'The Health and safety agenda', *Personnel Management*, March, p. 23.

Kenny, T. (1975), 'Stating the case for welfare', *Personnal Management*, vol. 7, no. 9.

Knox, I. and Fenley, A. (1985), 'Alcohol problems at work: some medical and legal considerations', *Personnel Review*, vol. 14, no. 1.

Leach, J. (1994), *The devolution of personnel responsibilities*, unpublished paper.

Leopold, I. and Coyle, R. (1981), 'A healthy trend in safety committees', *Personnel Management*, May.

Levinson, H. (1964), *Executive Stress*, New York: Harper & Row.

Mortimer v. V. L. Churchill (1979), News and notes, *Personnal Management*, March, 1986.

Mountfield, B. (1989), 'Preparing for COSHH at ICI', *Occupational Health Review*, June/July, pp. 6–7.

Nykodym, N. and George, K. (1989), 'Stress busting on the job', *Personnel*, July, pp. 56–9.

Palmer, S. (1989), 'Occupational stress', *The Safety and Health Practitioner*, August, pp. 16–18.

Pirani, M. and Reynolds, J. (1976), 'Gearing up for safety', *Personnel Management*, February.

Positive Health Centre (1985), *Chemo Feedback*, London: Positive Health Centre.

Powley, D. (1989), 'Life under the COSHH', *Manufacturing Engineer*, September, pp. 24–31.

Riddell, R. (1989), 'Why COSHH will hit hard on health and safety', *Personnel Management*, September, pp. 46–9.

Rose, P. (1976), 'Surveying the new safety structure', *Personnel Management*, November.

Royal Society (1983), *Risk Assessment: A Study Group Report*, London: The Royal Society.

Slaikeu, K. and Frank, C. (1986), 'Manning the psychological first aid post', *Management Today*, February.

Torrington, D. P., Mackay, L. E. and Hall, L. A. (1985), 'The changing nature of personnel management', *Employee Relations*, November/December.

Watson, T. J. (1977), *The Personnel Managers*, London: Routledge & Kegan Paul.

30 Grievance and discipline

Organisations are systems to distribute power and obedience, and the individuals who become employees of the organisation surrender a segment of their personal autonomy to become relatively weaker, making the organisation inordinately stronger. The benevolence of the organisation cannot be guaranteed, so individual employees seek to limit its power in relation to themselves.

Usually, the authority to be exercised in an organisation is impersonalised by the use of role in order to make it more effective. If a colleague mentions to you that you have overspent your budget, your reaction might be proud bravado unless you knew that the colleague had a role such as company accountant, internal auditor or financial director. Everyone in a business has a role – most people have several – and each role confers some authority. The canteen assistant who tells you that the steak and kidney pudding is off is more believable than the managing director conveying the same message. Quality assurance staff in factories are likely to wear white coats and send unfavourable reports in writing so as to deploy the authority of their role rather than test the authority of their own selves.

Dependence on role is not always welcome to those in managerial positions, who are fond of using phrases such as 'I know how get the best out of people', 'I understand my chaps' and 'I have a loyal staff'. Partly this may be due to their perception of their role as being to persuade the reluctant and command the respect of the unwilling by the use of personal leadership qualities, and it is indisputable that some managers are more effective with groups of staff than others, but there is more to it than personal skill: we are predisposed to obey.

The Milgram experiments with obedience

Obedience is the reaction expected of people by those in authority positions, who prescribe actions which otherwise may not necessarily have been carried out. Milgram (1974) conducted a series of experiments to investigate obedience to authority and highlighted the significance of obedience and the power of authority in our everyday lives. Subjects were led to believe that a study of memory and learning was being carried out which involved giving progressively more severe electric shocks to a learner when incorrect answers were given. If the subject questioned the procedure a standard response was received from the authority figure conducting the experiment, such as:

1. 'Please continue' or 'Please go on'.
2. 'The experiment requires that you continue'.
3. 'It is absolutely essential that you continue'.
4. 'You have no other choice: you must go on'.

These responses were given sequentially: (2) only after (1) had failed, (3) after (2), and so on.

The 'learner' was not actually receiving shocks, but was a member of the experimental team simulating progressively greater distress as the shocks were made stronger. Eighteen different experiments were conducted with more than 1000 subjects, with the circumstances varying between each experiment. No matter how the variables were altered the subjects showed an astonishing compliance with authority even when receiving 'shocks' of 450 volts. Up to 65 per cent of subjects continued to obey through the experiment in the presence of a clear authority figure and as many as 20 per cent continued to obey when the authority figure was absent.

Milgram was widely criticised for this study, largely because of questions about the ethics of requiring subjects to behave in such a distressing way, but we cannot evade the fact that he induced a high level of obedience from a large number of people who otherwise considered their actions to be wrong. Understandably, the reaction of Milgram to his own results was of dismay that:

> With numbing regularity good people were seen to knuckle under to the demands of authority and perform actions that were callous and severe. Men who are in everyday life responsible and decent were seduced by the trappings of authority, by the control of their perceptions, and by the uncritical acceptance of the experimenter's definition of the situation into performing harsh acts. (Milgram 1974, p. 123)

Our interest in Milgram's work is simply to demonstrate that we all have a predilection to obey instructions from authority figures, even if we do not want to. Milgran explains the phenomenon of obedience for us by an argument which he summarised thus:

> (1) organized social life provides survival benefits to the individuals who are part of it, and to the group; (2) whatever behavioural and psychological features have been necessary to produce the capacity for organized social life have been shaped by evolutionary forces; (3) from the standpoint of cybernetics, the most general need in bringing self-regulating automata into a co-ordinated hierarchy is to suppress individual direction and control in favour of control from higher level components; (4) more generally, hierarchies can function only when internal modification occurs in the elements of which they are composed; (5) functional hierarchies in social life are characterised by each of these features, and (6) the individuals who enter into such hierarchies are, of necessity, modified in their functioning. (*ibid.* p. 132)

He then points out that the act of entering a hierarchical system makes people see themselves acting as agents for carrying out the wishes of another person, and this results in these people being in a different state, described as the agentic state. This is the opposite to the state of autonomy when individuals see themselves as acting on their own. Milgram then sets out the factors that lay the groundwork for obedience to authority.

1. *Family:* parental regulation inculcates a respect for adult authority. Parental injunctions form the basis for moral imperatives as commands to children have a dual function. 'Don't tell lies' is a moral injunction carrying a further implicit instruction 'And obey me!'. It is the implicit demand for obedience that remains the only consistent element across a range of explicit instructions.

2. *Institutional setting:* children emerge from the family into an institutional system of authority: the school. Here they learn how to function in an organisation. They are regulated by teachers, but can see that the teachers themselves are regulated by the headteacher, the school governors and central government. Throughout this period they are in a subordinate position. When, as adults, they go to work it may be found that a certain level of dissent is allowable, but the overall situation is one in which they are to do a job prescribed by someone else.

3. *Rewards:* compliance with authority is generally rewarded, while disobedience is frequently punished. Most significantly, promotion within the hierarchy not only rewards the individual but ensures the continuity of the hierarchy.

4. *Perception of authority:* authority is normatively supported: there is a shared expectation among people that certain institutions do, ordinarily, have a socially controlling figure. Also, the authority of the controlling figure is limited to the situation. The usher in a cinema wields authority which vanishes on leaving the premises. As authority is expected it does not have to be asserted, merely presented.

5. *Entry into the authority system:* having perceived an authority figure, this figure must then be defined as relevant to the subject. The individual does not only take the voluntary step of deciding which authority system to join (at least in most of employment), but also defines which authority is relevant to which event. The firefighter may expect instant obedience when calling for everybody to evacuate the building, but not if asking employees to use a different accounting system.

6. *The overarching ideology:* the legitimacy of the social situation relates to a justifying ideology. Science and education formed the background to the experiments Milgram conducted and therefore provided a justification for actions carried out in their name. Most employment is in realms of activity regarded as legitimate, justified by the values and needs of society. This is vital if individuals are to provide willing obedience, as it enables them to see their behaviour as serving a desirable end.

Of all the strange creatures in science fiction, among the most durable are the Daleks of Dr Who. They moved smoothly and rapidly in pursuit of their prey, with turret-like heads that swivelled weird antennae searching for their victims. Although they were remorseless robots they were reassuringly vulnerable, especially to one of Dr Who's friends, the Brigadier. Of particular significance in making them safe for small children to watch were their voices, strident but high-pitched and verging on hysteria. Their opening battle cry was a relentless monotone, 'Exterminate...exterminate...' but when they were baffled or outwitted, the voices rose to a paranoid screech, 'You will obey...you will obey'. Once you heard that you could come out from under the bed-clothes, because you knew they were asserting in vain an authority they could not implement. Dr Who and his companions were not in the Daleks' hierarchical structure and would not see themselves in an agentic state, so the Daleks could not prevail.

Managers are positioned in an organisational hierarchy in such a way that others will be predisposed, as Milgram demonstrates, to follow their instructions. Managers put in place a series of frameworks to explain how they will exact obedience: they use *discipline*. Because individual employees feel their relative weakness, they seek complementary frameworks to challenge the otherwise unfettered use of managerial disciplinary power: they may join trade unions, but they will always need channels to present their *grievances*.

In this chapter we are concerned uniquely with discipline and grievance within organisations, but it is worth pointing out that managers are the focal points for the grievances of people outside the organisation as well, but those grievances are called complaints. You may complain *about* poor service, shoddy workmanship or rudeness from an employee, but you complain *to* a manager.

Personnel managers make one of their most significant contributions to organisational effectiveness by the way they facilitate and administer grievance and disciplinary issues. First, they devise and negotiate the procedural framework of organisational justice on which both discipline and grievance depend. Secondly, they are much involved in the interviews and problem-solving discussions that eventually produce solutions to the difficulties that have been encountered. Thirdly, they maintain the viability of the whole process which forms an integral part of their work: they monitor to make sure that grievances are not overlooked and so that any general trend can be perceived, and they oversee the disciplinary machinery to ensure that it is not being bypassed or unfairly manipulated.

Grievance and discipline handling are one of the personnel roles that few other people want to take over. Ambitious line managers may want to select their own staff without personnel intervention or by using the services of consultants. They may try to brush their personnel colleagues aside and deal directly with trade union officials or organise their own management development, but grievance and discipline is too hot a potato.

Although it may seem like a thankless task that is 'pushed on to' personnel, it is now a major feature of personnel influence and authority within the organisation.

The requirements of the law regarding explanation of grievance handling and the legal framework to avoid unfair dismissal combine to make this an area where personnel people must be both knowledgeable and effective. That combination provides a valuable platform for influencing other aspects of organisational affairs. The personnel manager who is not skilled in grievance and discipline is seldom in a strong organisational position.

What do we mean by discipline?

Discipline is regulation of human activity to produce a controlled performance. It ranges from the guard's control of a rabble to the accomplishment of lone individuals producing spectacular performance through self-discipline in the control of their own talents and resources.

First there is managerial discipline, in which everything depends on the leader from start to finish. There is a group of people who are answerable to someone who directs what they should all do. Only through individual direction can that group of people produce a worthwhile performance, such as the person leading the community singing in the pantomime or the person conducting an orchestra. Everything depends on the leader.

Secondly there is team discipline, whereby the perfection of the performance derives from the mutual dependence of all, and that mutual dependence derives

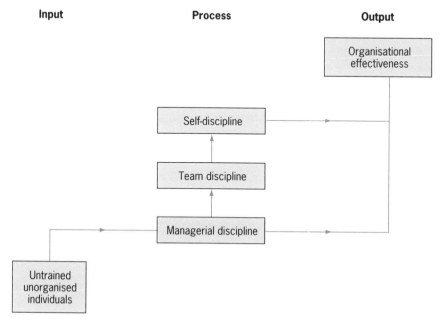

Figure 30.1   Three forms of discipline

from a commitment by each member to the total enterprise: the failure of one would be the downfall of all. This is usually found in relatively small working groups, such as a dance troupe or an autonomous working group in a factory.

Thirdly there is self-discipline, like that of the juggler or the skilled artisan, where a solo performer is absolutely dependent on training, expertise and self-control.

Discipline is, therefore, not only negative, producing punishment or prevention. It can also be a valuable quality for the individual who is subject to it, although the form of discipline depends not only on the individual employee but also on the task and the way it is organised. The development of self-discipline is easier in some jobs than others and many of the job redesign initiatives have been directed at providing scope for job holders to exercise self-discipline and find a degree of autonomy from managerial discipline. Figure 30.1 shows how the three forms are connected in a sequence or hierarchy, with employees finding one of three ways to achieve their contribution to organisational effectiveness. However, even the most accomplished solo performer has been dependent on others for training and advice, and every team has its coach.

REVIEW TOPIC 30.1

Note three examples of managerial discipline, team discipline and self-discipline from your own experience.

Managers are not dealing with discipline only when they are rebuking late-comers or threatening to dismiss saboteurs. As well as dealing with the unruly and reluctant, they are developing the co-ordinated discipline of the working team, engendering that *esprit de corps* which makes the whole greater than the sum of the parts. They are training the new recruit who must not let down the rest of the team, puzzling over the reasons why A is fitting in well while B is still struggling. Managers are also providing people with the equipment to develop the self-discipline that will give them autonomy, responsibility and the capacity to maximise their powers. The independence and autonomy that self-discipline produces also produces the greatest degree of personal satisfaction – and often the largest pay-packet. Furthermore the movement between the three forms represents a declining degree of managerial involvement. If you are a leader of community singing, nothing can happen without you being present and the quality of the singing depends on your performance each time. If you train jugglers, the time and effort you invest pays off a thousand times while you sit back and watch the show.

What do we mean by grievance?

Contemporary British texts virtually ignore grievance handling, but the Americans maintain sound coverage. Mathis and Jackson (1994) have a particularly helpful review. Some years ago Pigors and Myers (1977, p. 229) provided a helpful approach to the topic by drawing a distinction between the terms dissatisfaction, complaint and grievance as follows:

Dissatisfaction: anything that disturbs an employee, whether or not the unrest is expressed in words.

Complaint: a spoken or written dissatisfaction brought to the attention of the supervisor and/or shop steward.

Grievance: a complaint that has been formally presented to a management representative or to a union official.

This provides us with a useful categorisation by separating out grievance as a formal, relatively drastic step, compared with commonplace grumbling. It is much more important for management to know about dissatisfaction. Although nothing is being expressed, the feeling of hurt following failure to get a pay rise or the frustration about shortage of materials can quickly influence performance.

Much dissatisfaction never turns into complaint, as something happens to make it unnecessary. Dissatisfaction evaporates with a night's sleep, after a cup of coffee with a colleague, or when the cause of the dissatisfaction is in some other way removed. The few dissatisfactions that do produce complaint are also most likely to resolve themselves at that stage. The person hearing the complaint explains things in a way that the dissatisfied employee had not previously appreciated, or takes action to get at the root of the problem.

Grievances are rare since few employees will question their superior's judgement and fewer still will risk being stigmatised as a troublemaker. Also, many people do not initiate grievances because they believe that nothing will be done as a result of their attempt.

Personnel managers have to encourage the proper use of procedures to discover sources of dissatisfaction. Managers in the middle may not reveal the complaints they are hearing, for fear of showing themselves in a poor light. Employees who feel insecure, for any reason, are not likely to risk going into procedure, yet the dissatisfaction lying beneath a repressed grievance can produce all manner of unsatisfactory work behaviours, from apathy to arson. Individual dissatisfaction can lead to the loss of a potentially valuable employee; collective dissatisfaction can lead to industrial action.

Roethlisberger and Dickson (1939, pp. 225–69) differentiated three types of complaint, according to content.

The first kind referred to tangible objects in terms that could be defined by any competent worker and could be readily tested:

- the machine is out of order;
- this tool is too dull;
- the stock we're getting now is not up to standard;
- our cement is too thin and won't make the rubber stick.

Second were those complaints based partly on sensory experience, but primarily on the accompanying, subjective reactions:

- the work is messy;
- it's too hot in here;
- the job is too hard.

These statements include terms where the meaning is biologically or socially determined and can therefore not be understood unless the background of the complaint is known; seldom can their accuracy be objectively determined. A temperature of 18 degrees centigrade may be too hot for one person but equable for another.

The third type of complaint they differentiated were those involving the hopes and fears of employees:

- the supervisor plays favourites;
- the pay rates are too low;
- seniority doesn't count as much as it should.

These complaints proved the most revealing to the investigators as they showed the importance of determining not only what employees felt but also why they felt as they did; not only verifying the facts ('the manifest content') but also determining the feelings behind the facts ('the latent content').

Roethlisberger and Dickson concluded, for instance, that one employee who complained of his supervisor being a bully was actually saying something rather different, especially when the reason given was the fact that the supervisor did not say 'good morning'. Later, it was revealed that the root of his dissatisfaction was in his attitude to any authority figure, not simply the supervisor about whom he had complained.

Each of the types of dissatisfaction manifested in this analysis are important for the management to uncover and act upon, if action is possible. Action is likely to be prompt on complaints of the first type, as they are neutral: blame is being placed on an inanimate object and individual culpability is not an issue. Action may be taken on complaints of the second type where the required action is straightforward – such as opening a window if it is too hot – but the problem of accuracy is such that there may be a tendency to smooth over an issue or leave it 'to sort itself out' in time. The third type of complaint is the most difficult, and action is therefore less likely to be taken. Supervisors will often take complaints to be a personal criticism of their own competence, and employees will often translate the complaint into a grievance only by attaching it to a third party such as a shop steward, so that the relationship between employee and supervisor is not jeopardised.

The framework of organisational justice

Now we look at the ways of dealing with the dissatisfaction that causes grievance and discipline.

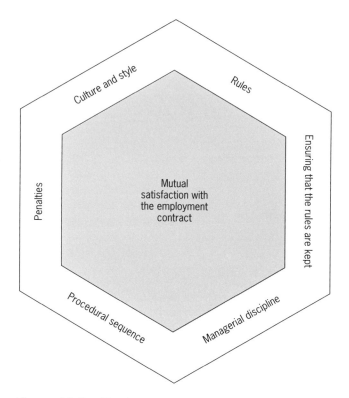

Figure 30.2 The framework of organisational justice.

The organisation requires a framework of justice to surround the everyday employment relationship so that managers and supervisors, as well as other employees, know where they stand when dissatisfaction develops. Figure 30.2 shows a framework of organisational justice.

> REVIEW TOPIC 30.2
>
> Think of an example from your own experience of dissatisfaction caus-
> ing inefficiency that was not remedied because there was no complaint.
> Why was there no complaint?

Awareness of culture and appropriateness of style

The culture of an organisation profoundly affects the behaviour of people within it and develops norms that are hard to alter. It is important to recognise the importance of this influence. If, for instance, everyone is in the habit of arriving ten minutes late, a 'new broom' manager will have a struggle to change the habit. Equally, if everyone is in the habit of arriving punctually, then a new recruit who often arrives late will come under strong social pressure to conform, without need for recourse to management action. Culture also affects the freedom and candour with which people discuss dissatisfactions with their managers without allowing them to fester.

The style adopted by managers in handling grievances and discipline will reflect their beliefs. The manager who sees discipline as being punishment and who regards grievances as examples of subordinates getting above themselves will behave in a relatively autocratic way, being curt in disciplinary situations and dismissive of complaints. The manager who sees disciplinary problems as obstacles to achievement that do not necessarily imply incompetence or ill-will by the employee will seek out the cause of the problem. The problem may then be revealed as one requiring firm, punitive action by the manager, but it may alternatively be revealed as a matter requiring management remedy of a different kind. In either case the manager will be supported by the bulk of the employees. The manager who listens out for complaints and grievances, gets to the bottom of the problems and finds solutions will run little risk of rumbling discontent from people obsessed by trivial problems.

Rules

Every workplace has rules; the difficulty is to have rules that people will honour. Some rules come from statutes, such as the tachograph requirement for HGV drivers, but most are tailored to meet the particular requirements of the organisation in which they apply. For example, rules about personal cleanliness are essential in a food factory but less stringent in a garage.

Rules should be clear and readily understood. The number of rules should be sufficient to cover all obvious and usual disciplinary matters. To ensure general compliance it is helpful if rules are jointly determined, but it is more common for management to formulate the rules and for employee representatives eventually to concur with them. Employees should have ready access to the rules, through the employee handbook and noticeboard, and the personnel manager will always try to ensure that the rules are known as well as published.

The Department of Employment (1973) suggest that rules fall into six categories, relating to different types of employee behaviour, as follows.

1. Negligence is failure to do the job properly and is different from incompetence because of the assumption that the employee can do the job properly, but has not. The incompetent employee, unable to do the job properly, should not be subject to discipline.

2. Unreliability is failure to attend work as required, such as being late or absent.

3. Insubordination is refusal to obey an instruction, or deliberate disrespect to someone in a position of authority. It is not to be confused with the use of bad language. Some of the most entertaining cases in industrial tribunals have involved weighty consideration of whether or not colourful language was intended to be insubordinate.

4. Interfering with the rights of others covers a range of behaviours that are deemed socially unacceptable. Fighting is clearly identifiable, but intimidation may be more difficult to establish. Less clear as a basis for rules that must be obeyed is the prohibition of practical jokes and pernicious gossip.

5. Theft is another clear-cut aspect of behaviour that is unacceptable when it is from another employee. Theft from the organisation should be supported by very explicit rules, as stealing company property is regarded by many offenders as one of the perks of the job. How often have you taken home a box of paper clips or a felt-tip pen without any thought that you were stealing from the employer?

6. Safety offences are those aspects of behaviour that can cause a hazard.

The Institute of Personnel Management conducted a survey (1979) of disciplinary practice in nearly 300 organisations and found that the three main reasons for disciplinary action were: poor timekeeping, unauthorised absence and poor standards of work; so the rules most frequently invoked were those relating to negligence and unreliability. Rules are not, however, only a basis for imposing penalties. Their greatest value is in providing guidelines on what people should do, and the majority will comply. The number of drivers killed on the roads has declined sharply because the great majority of drivers obey the law on wearing seat belts. The date for introducing the legislation was, however, deferred twice to ensure that

---

In a recent discussion with a group of senior managers, the following were identified as legitimately taken at will by employees:

> paper clips, pencils, disposable pens, spiral pads, local telephone calls, plain paper, computer paper and disks, adhesive tape, overalls and simple uniform.

Among the more problematic were:

> redundant or shop-soiled stock. One DIY store insisted that the store manager should personally supervise the scrapping of items that were slightly damaged, to ensure that other items were not slightly damaged on purpose.

> Surplus materials. One electricity supplier had some difficulty in eradicating the practice of surplus cable and pipe being regarded as a legitimate prerequisite of fitters at the end of installation jobs, as they suspected their engineers were using the surplus for private work. Twelve months later the level of material requisition had declined by 14 per cent.

it was introduced at a time when there would be general acceptance rather than widespread defiance of the law.

Ensuring that the rules are kept

Although the majority of car drivers wear seat belts, the majority of dog owners never had dog licences. It is not sufficient just to have rules, they are only effective if they are observed. How do we make sure that employees stick to the rules?

1. Information is needed so that everyone knows what the rules are and why they should be obeyed. Written particulars may suffice in an industrial tribunal hearing, but most people follow the advice and behaviour of their colleagues in determining how they will behave, so informal methods of communication are just as important as formal statements.

2. Induction is a means of making the rules coherent and reinforcing their understanding. The background can be described and the reason for the rule explained, perhaps with examples, so that the new recruit not only knows the rules but understands why they should be obeyed.

3. Placement and relocation can both avoid the risk of rules being broken by placing a new recruit with a working team that has high standards of compliance. If there are the signs of disciplinary problems in the offing, then a quick relocation can put the problem employee in a new situation where offences are less likely.

4. Training increases the new recruit's awareness of the rules, improving self-confidence and self-discipline. For established employees there will be new working procedures or new equipment from time to time and again training will reduce the risk of safety offences, negligence or unreliability.

5. Review of the rules periodically ensures that they are up to date, and also ensures that their observance is a live issue. If, for instance, there is a monthly works council meeting, it could be appropriate to have a rules review every twelve months. The simple fact that the rules are being discussed will keep up the general level of awareness of what they are.

6. Penalties make the framework of organisational justice firmer if there is an understanding of what penalties can be imposed, by whom and for what. It is not feasible or desirable to have a fixed scale, but nor is it wise for penalties to depend on individual managerial whim. This area has been partially codified by the legislation on dismissal, but the following are some typical forms of penalty:

   (a) *Rebuke:* this is probably used too little by managers nowadays. This is the simple 'Don't do that' or 'Smoking is not allowed in here' or 'If you're late again, you will be in trouble'. This is all that is needed in most situations, as someone has forgotten one of the rules, or had not realised it was to be taken seriously, or was perhaps testing the resolution of the management. Too frequently, managers are reluctant to risk defiance and tend to wait until they have a good case for more serious action rather than deploying their own, there-and-then authority.

(b) *Caution:* slightly more serious and formal is the caution, which is then recorded. This is not triggering the procedure for dismissal, it is simply making a note of a rule being broken and an offence being pointed out.

(c) *Warnings:* when the management begin to issue warnings great care is required, as the development of unfair dismissal legislation with its associated code of practice has made the system of warnings an integral part of disciplinary practice which has to be followed if the employer is to succeed in defending a possible claim of unfair dismissal at tribunal. For the employer to show procedural fairness there should normally be a formal oral warning, or a written warning, specifying the nature of the offence and the likely outcome of the offence being repeated. It should also be made clear that this is the first, formal stage in the procedure. Further misconduct could then warrant a final written warning containing a statement that further repetition would lead to a penalty such as suspension or dismissal. All written warnings should be dated, signed and kept on record for a period agreed by rules known by both sides. Details must be given to the employee and to his or her representative, if desired. The means of appeal against the disciplinary action should also be pointed out.

(d) *Disciplinary transfer or demotion:* this is moving the employee to less attractive work, possibly carrying a lower salary. The seriousness of this is that it is public, as the employee's colleagues know the reason. A form of disciplinary transfer is found on assembly lines, where there are some jobs that are more attractive and carry higher status than others. Rule breakers may be 'pushed down the line' until their contempt is purged and they are able to move back up. Demotion is rare and seldom effective because the humiliation is so great. Those demoted usually either leave or carry on (probably because they cannot leave) with considerable resentment and having lost so much confidence that their performance remains inadequate.

(e) *Suspension:* a tactic that has the benefit of being serious and avoids the disadvantage of being long-lasting, similar to demotion. The employer has a contractual obligation to provide pay but not to provide work, so it is easy to suspend someone from duty – with pay – either as a punishment or while an alleged offence is being investigated. If the contract of employment permits, it may also be possible to suspend the employee for a short period without pay.

(f) *Fines:* these are little used, because of contractual problems, but the most common is deduction from pay for lateness.

The important general comment about penalties is that they should be appropriate in the circumstances. Where someone is, for instance, persistently late or absent, suspension would be a strange penalty. Also penalties must be within the law. An employee cannot be demoted or transferred at managerial whim, and fines or unpaid suspension can only be imposed if the contract of employment allows such measures.

7.   Procedural sequence is essential to the framework of organisational justice. It should be the clear, unvarying logic of procedure, and be well-known and trusted. Procedure makes clear, for example, who does and who does not have the power to dismiss. The dissatisfied employee who is wondering whether or not to turn a complaint into a formal grievance knows who will hear the grievance and where an appeal could be lodged. This security of procedure, where step B always follows step A, is needed by managers as well as by employees, as it provides them with their authority as well as limiting the scope of their actions.

8.   Managerial discipline. Finally, managers must preserve general respect for the justice framework by their self-discipline in how they work within it. With very good intentions some senior managers maintain an 'open door' policy with the message: 'My door is always open...call in any time you feel I can help you'. This has many advantages and is often necessary, but it has danger for matters of discipline and grievance because it encourages people to bypass middle managers. They welcome the opportunity to talk to the organ grinder rather than the monkey. There is also the danger that employees come to see the settlement of their grievances as being dependent on the personal goodwill of an individual rather than on their human and employment rights.

Managers must also be consistent in their handling of discipline and grievance issues. Whatever the rules are, they will be generally supported only as long as they deserve such support. If they are enforced inconsistently they will soon lose any moral authority and depend only on the fear of penalties. Equally, the manager who handles grievances quickly and consistently is well on the way to enjoying the support of a committed group of employees.

The other need for managerial discipline is to test the validity of the discipline assumption. Is it a case for disciplinary action or for some other remedy? There is little purpose in suspending someone for negligence when the real problem is lack of training. Many disciplinary problems disappear under analysis, and it is sensible to carry out the analysis before making a possibly unjustified allegation of indiscipline.

Grievance procedure

The formality of the grievance procedure is often resented by managers, who believe that it introduces unnecessary rigidity into the working relationship: 'I see my people all the time. We work side by side and they can raise with me any issue they want, at any time they want. ...' The problem is that many people will not raise issues with the immediate superior that could be regarded as contentious, in just the same way that managers, as was mentioned earlier, frequently shirk the rebuke as a form of disciplinary penalty. Formality in procedure provides a framework within which individuals can reasonably air their grievances and avoids the likelihood of managers dodging the issue when it is difficult. It avoids the risk of inconsistent *ad hoc* decisions and the employee knows at the outset that the matter will be heard and where it will be heard. The key features of grievance procedure are fairness, facilities for representation, procedural steps and promptness.

1. Fairness is needed not only to be just but also to keep the procedure viable. If employees develop the belief that the procedure is only a sham, then its value will be lost and other means will be sought to deal with grievances. Fairness is best supported by the obvious even-handedness of the ways in which grievances are handled, but it will be greatly enhanced if the appeal stage is either to a joint body or to independent arbitration – usually by ACAS – as the management is relinquishing the chance to be judge of its own cause.

2. Representation can be of help to the individual employee who lacks the confidence or experience to take on the management single handedly. A representative, such as a shop steward, has the advantage of having dealt with a range of employee problems and may be able to advise the person with the grievance whether the claim is worth pursuing. There is always the risk that the presence of the representative produces a defensive management attitude affected by a number of other issues on which the manager and shop steward may be at loggerheads, so the managers involved in hearing the grievance have to cast the representative in the correct role for the occasion.

3. Procedural steps should be limited to three. There is no value in having more just because there are more levels in the management hierarchy. This will only lengthen the time taken to deal with matters and will soon bring the procedure into disrepute. The reason for advocating three steps is that three types of management activity are involved in settling grievances.

    The first step is the preliminary, when the grievance is lodged with the immediate superior of the person with the complaint. In the normal working week most managers will have a variety of queries from members of their departments, some of which could become grievances, depending on the manager's reaction. Usually the manager will either satisfy the employee or the employee will decide not to pursue the matter. Sometimes, however, a person will want to take the issue further. This is the preliminary step in procedure, but it is a tangible step as the manager has the opportunity to review any decisions made causing the dissatisfaction, possibly enabling the dissatisfied employee to withdraw the grievance.

    The hearing is when the complainant has the opportunity to state the grievance to a more senior manager, who is able to take a broader view of the

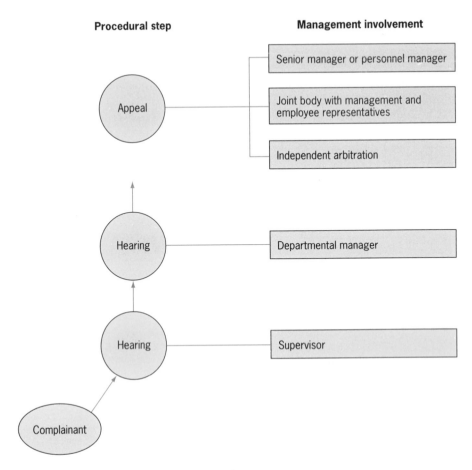

Procedural step   **Management involvement**

Appeal
- Senior manager or personnel manager
- Joint body with management and employee representatives
- Independent arbitration

Hearing — Departmental manager

Hearing — Supervisor

Complainant

Figure 30.3   Outline grievance procedures

matter than the immediate superior and who may be able both to see the issue more dispassionately and to perceive solutions that the more limited perspective of the immediate superior obscured. It is important for the management that the hearing should finalise the matter whenever possible, so that recourse to appeal is not automatic. The hearing should not come to be seen by the employees as no more than an irritating milestone on the way to the real decision-makers. This is why procedural steps should be limited to three.

If there is an appeal, this will usually be to a designated more senior manager, and the outcome will be either a confirmation or modification of the decision at the hearing.

4. Promptness is needed to avoid the bitterness and frustration that can come from delay. When an employee 'goes into procedure', it is like pulling the communication cord in the train. The action is not taken lightly and it is in anticipation of a swift resolution. Furthermore, the manager whose decision is

being questioned will have a difficult time until the matter is resolved. The most familiar device to speed things up is to incorporate time limits between the steps, specifying that the hearing should take place no later than, for instance, four working days after the preliminary notice and that the appeal should be no more than five working days after the hearing. This gives time for reflection and initiative by the manager or the complainant between the stages, but does not leave time for the matter to be forgotten.

Where the organisation has a collective disputes procedure as well as one for individual grievances, there needs to be an explicit link between the two so that individual matters can be pursued with collective support if there is not a satisfactory outcome. An outline grievance procedure is shown in Figure 30.3.

Disciplinary procedure

Procedures for discipline are very similar to those for grievance and depend equally on fairness, promptness and representation. There are some additional features.

Authorisation of penalties

The law requires that managers should not normally have the power to dismiss their immediate subordinates without reference to more senior managers. Whatever tangible penalties are to be imposed, they should only be imposed by people who have that specific authority delegated to them. Usually this means that the more serious penalties can only be imposed by more senior people, but there are many organisations where such decisions are delegated to the personnel department.

Investigation

The procedure should also ensure that disciplinary action is not taken until it has been established that an offence has been committed that justifies the action. The possibility of suspension on full pay is one way of allowing time for the investigation of dubious allegations, but the stigma attached to such suspensions should not be forgotten.

Information and explanation

If there is the possibility of disciplinary action the person to be disciplined should be told of the complaint, so that an explanation can be made, or the matter denied, before any penalties are decided. If an employee is to be penalised, then the reasons for the decision should be explained to make sure that cause and effect are appreciated. The purpose of penalties is to prevent a recurrence. An outline disciplinary procedure is in Figure 30.4.

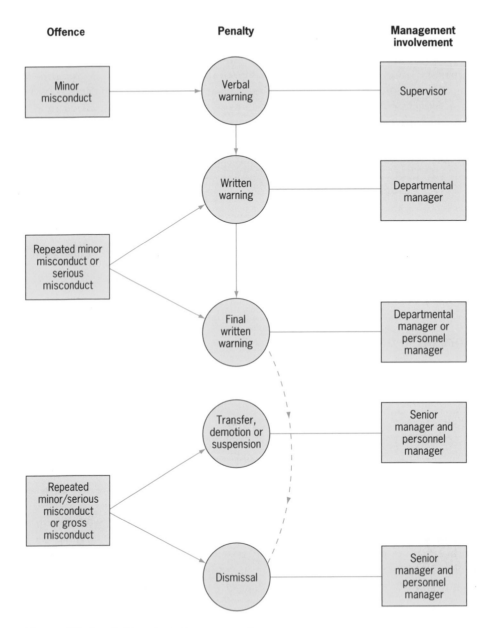

	Offence		Penalty		Management involvement

Offence — Penalty — Management involvement

Minor misconduct → Verbal warning — Supervisor

Written warning — Departmental manager

Repeated minor misconduct or serious misconduct → Final written warning — Departmental manager or personnel manager

Transfer, demotion or suspension — Senior manager and personnel manager

Repeated minor/serious misconduct or gross misconduct → Dismissal — Senior manager and personnel manager

Figure 30.4 Outline disciplinary procedure

Disputes

Procedures for the avoidance of disputes are drawn up mainly in national negotiations between employers' associations and trade unions or between single employers and unions. Disputes can arise for a wide range of reasons, but their essence is that they are collective: employees are acting in concert, and almost always using union machinery, to persuade the management to alter a decision. Sometimes the grievance of an individual can escalate into a collective dispute if employees together feel that a matter of principle is at stake. Disciplinary penalties, especially dismissals, can also become matters for collective employee action, when the dismissal is regarded as unfair or victimisation.

There are usually more steps in a procedure for collective dispute than for individual grievances and provisions to preclude strikes, lock-outs or other forms of industrial action before procedure is exhausted.

Are grievance and discipline processes equitable?

For these processes to work they must command support, and they will only command support if they are seen as equitable, truly just and fair. At first it would seem that it is concern for the individual employee that is paramount, but the individual cannot be isolated from the rest of the workforce. Fairness should therefore be linked to the interests that all workers have in common in the organisation and to the managers, who must also perceive the system as equitable if they are to abide by its outcomes.

Procedures have a potential to be fair in that they are certain. The conduct of employee relations becomes less haphazard and irrational; people 'know where they stand'. The existence of a rule cannot be denied and opportunities for one party to manipulate and change a rule are reduced. Procedures also have the advantage that they can be communicated. The process of formalising a procedure that previously existed only in custom and practice clarifies the ambiguities and inconsistencies within it and compels each party to recognise the role and responsibility of the other. By providing pre-established avenues for responses to various contingencies there is the chance that the response will be less random and so more fair. The impersonal nature of procedures offers the possibility of removing hostility from the workplace, since an artificial social situation is created in which the ritual displays of aggression towards management are not seen as personal attacks on managers.

The achievement of equity may not match the potential. Procedures cannot, for instance, impart equitability to situations that are basically unfair. Thus attempting to cope with an anomalous pay system through grievance procedure may be alleviating symptoms rather than treating causes. It is also impossible to overcome accepted norms of inequity in a plant, such as greater punctuality being required of manual employees than of white-collar employees.

A further feature of procedure equity is its degree of similarity to the judicial process. All adopt certain legalistic mechanisms, such as the right of individuals to be represented and to hear the case against them, but some aspects of legalism, such as burdens of proof and strict adherence to precedent, may cause the application of standard remedies rather than the consideration of individual circumstances.

The 'red-hot stove' rule of discipline offers the touching of a red hot stove as an analogy for effective disciplinary action:

1. The burn is immediate. There is no question of cause and effect.
2. You had warning. If the stove was red-hot, you knew what would happen if you touched it.
3. The discipline is consistent. Everyone who touches the stove is burned.
4. The discipline is impersonal. A person is burned not because of who he is, but because he touched the stove.

REVIEW TOPIC 30.3

Think of an attempt at disciplinary action that went wrong. Which of the features of the red-hot stove rule were missing?

Notions of fairness are not 'givens' of the situation; they are socially constructed and there will never be more than a degree of consensus on what constitutes fairness. Despite this, the procedural approach can exploit standards of certainty and consistency which are widely accepted as elements of justice. The extent to which a procedure can do this will depend on the suitability of its structure to plant circumstances, the commitment of those who operate it and the way that it reconciles legalistic and bargaining elements.

☐ SUMMARY PROPOSITIONS

30.1 The authority of managers to exercise discipline in relation to others in the organisation is underpinned by a general predilection of people to obey commands from those holding higher rank in the hierarchy of which they are members.

30.2 The exercise of that discipline is limited by the procedural structures for grievance and discipline.

30.3 Grievance and discipline handling are two areas of personnel work that few other people want to take over and provide personnel managers with some of their most significant contributions to organisational effectiveness.

30.4 Discipline can be understood as being either managerial, team or self-discipline, and they are connected hierarchically.

30.5 Dissatisfaction, complaint and grievance is another hierarchy. Unresolved employee dissatisfaction can lead to the loss of potentially valuable employees. In extreme cases it can lead to industrial action.

30.6 Grievance and disciplinary processes both require a framework of organisational justice.

30.7 The procedural framework of disciplinary and grievance processes is one of the keys to their being equitable.

References

Department of Employment (1973), *In Working Order*, London: HMSO.

Institute of Personnel Management (1979), *Disciplinary Procedures and Practice*, London: Institute of Personnel Management.

Mathis, R. L. and Jackson, J. H. (1994), *Human Resource Management*, 7th edition, Minneapolis/St Paul: West.

Milgram, S. (1974), *Obedience to Authority*, London: Tavistock.

Pigors, P. and Myers, C. S. (1977), *Personnel Administration*, 8th edition, Maidenhead: McGraw-Hill.

Roethlisberger, F. J. and Dickson, W. J. (1939), *Management and the Worker*, Cambridge, Mass.: Harvard University Press.

31

Interactive skill: grievance and disciplinary interviewing

We now consider the interviews that managers carry out with employees during disciplinary and grievance processes, as it is in these encounters that any managerial or employee initiative succeeds or fails. Procedures can do no more than force meetings to take place: it is the meetings themselves that provide answers.

Many contemporary views of discipline are connected with the idea of punishment, as we saw in the last chapter; a disciplinarian is one seen as an enforcer of rules, a hard taskmaster or martinet. To discipline schoolchildren is usually to punish them by keeping them in after school or chastising them. Disciplinary procedures in employment are usually drawn up to provide a preliminary to dismissal, so that any eventual dismissal will not be viewed as unfair by a tribunal. This background makes a problem-solving approach to discipline difficult for a manager, as there is always the sanction in the background making it unlikely that the employee will see the manager's behaviour as being authentic. There will always be a feeling – somewhere between outright conviction and lingering uncertainty – that a manager in a disciplinary interview is looking for a justification to punish rather than looking for a more constructive solution. The approach of this chapter is based on the more accurate notion of discipline implied in its derivation from the Latin *discere*, to learn and *discipulus*, learner. In disciplinary interviews the manager is attempting to modify the working behaviour of a subordinate, but it does not necessarily involve punishment.

The idea of grievance similarly has problems of definition and ethos. In the last chapter we used the convenient scale of dissatisfaction–complaint–grievance as an explanation, but that is a convenient technical classification. The general sense of the word is closer to the dictionary definitions which use phrases such as '...a real or imaginary wrong causing resentment...' or '... a feeling of injustice having been unfairly treated...'. Notions of resentment and injustice seem too heavy for situations where the basic problem is that the maintenance crew have fallen down on the job or the central heating is not working properly. Where we have unresolved problems about our jobs – even when we are deeply worried by them – we are often reluctant to construe our feelings as 'having a grievance'. We just want to get more information, or an opportunity for training, a chance to talk to someone a little more senior. Very few people indeed want to be seen as grumbling. Customers are generally reluctant to grumble about the service they receive because it is too much trouble, because no one would listen, or just because they do not want to make a fuss; yet they can simply walk away. Compared with customers, employees are much less inclined to complain, or even to point out problems, for fear of being categorised as a nuisance.

Despite the difficulties, the aim of this chapter is to formulate an approach to the interview that achieves an adjustment in attitude, with the changed attitude being confirmed by subsequent experience. Either the manager believes that the employee's subsequent working behaviour will be satisfactory, or the employee believes that his or her subsequent experience in employment will be satisfactory. The interview only succeeds when there is the confirmation.

In his profound and simple book of 1960, Douglas McGregor advocated an approach to management based on the strategy of *integration* and *self-control*. He regarded forms and procedures as having little value and emphasised the importance of social interaction as well as the difficulty of achieving any change in people's interactive behaviour:

> Every adult human being has an elaborate history of past experience in this field and additional learning is profoundly influenced by that history. From infancy on, his ability to achieve his goals and satisfy his needs – his 'social survival' – has been a function of his skills in influencing others. Deep emotional currents – unconscious needs such as those related to dependency and counterdependency – are involved. He has a large 'ego investment' and his knowledge and skill in this area, and the defences he has built to protect that investment are strong and psychologically complex. (McGregor 1960, p. 75)

Managers undoubtedly spend a great deal of their time in interviews of one type or another and grievance and disciplinary interviews are among the least popular parts of their managerial day; nearly as difficult as performance appraisal and potentially even less pleasant. It may be that the ability of managers to handle the grievance/discipline interview will be the most important test of their effectiveness in organising the efforts of their working group.

Just as we set grievance and discipline alongside each other in the last chapter, similarly we examine here the grievance/disciplinary encounter in the same framework, as both are trying to tackle dissatisfaction with the employment situation of a particular person, where resolution of the problem is not straightforward. If Jim sets fire to the Works Director's office and he admits to the police that he did it for a lark because he was bored, then any disciplinary interview ought not be too difficult. If Joe is not working as well as he used to, but nobody quite knows why and he refuses to say anything about it to anyone, then there is the less straightforward situation with which the approach of this chapter might help.

REVIEW TOPIC 31.1

What grievance or disciplinary incidents can you recall where the situation was not clear-cut and where an interview with a manager produced a resolution to the problem that was effective, although quite different from what had been anticipated by the manager at the beginning of the interview?

There is a risk of some managers looking for problems that do not exist anywhere than in the imagination of the manager. George was a supervisor in charge of several cleaning gangs and he prided himself on his avuncular concern for their welfare (some of the more cynical cleaners described him as 'bloody nosey').

One day, Mildred stopped at his office to say that she was going to leave at the end of the month because she had decided to give up work. Mildred had been a cleaner in the company for fifteen years and was highly regarded by George. She was 59 and her husband had recently retired. Her two children were both independent, so she and her husband had decided that she would give up work in April, so that they could both get used to retirement before the summer rather than wait until her 60th birthday in November.

George decided that there was 'more to this than met the eye' and spent half an hour asking Mildred a series of questions about her health, her children, her relationship with her husband and how she spent her spare time. Mildred became more and more exasperated, eventually storming out to see her shop steward.

Sometimes people say what they mean, mean what they say and that's that: problem-solving interviewing is definitely not required.

The nature of grievance and disciplinary interviewing

Many grievance or discipline interviews are simple: giving information, explaining work requirements and delivering rebukes, but from time to time every manager will need to use a problem-solving approach, involving sympathy, perception, empathy and the essential further feature that some managers provide only with reluctance: time. The method will be analytical and constructive; not only for the interviews built in to the grievance and discipline procedure, but also for interviews that avoid recourse to the rigid formality of procedure. We see such interviews as one of the means towards *self-discipline* and *autonomy* of employees, reducing the need for supervision. The sequence we advocate has discipline and grievance intertwined for much of the process but diverging in the interview itself.

As we have shown in the previous chapter, a grievance may be expressed only in manifest form, requiring interviewing to understand its latent content in order that appropriate action is taken to remove the underlying dissatisfaction. Discipline problems will have underlying reasons for the unsatisfactory behaviour and these need to be discovered before solutions to the problems can be attempted.

The discipline and grievance sequence

Figure 31.1 shows a model of the interviews we are going to describe.

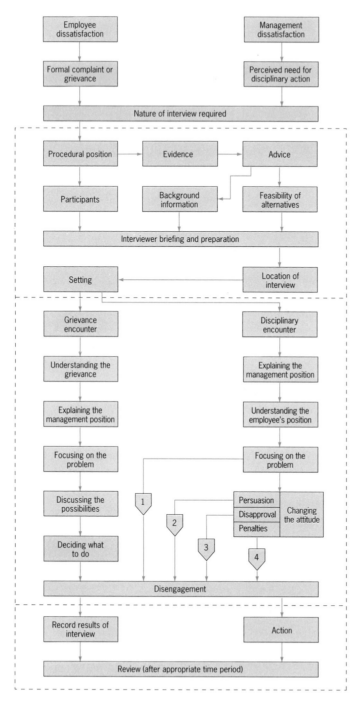

Figure 31.1 The grievance and disciplinary interviews

Preparation

The first requirement is to check the procedural position and to ensure that the impending interview is appropriate. In a grievance situation, for instance, is the employee pre-empting the procedure by taking the matter to the wrong person or to the wrong point in procedure? This is most common when the first-line supervisor is being bypassed, either because the employee or the representative feel that it would be a waste of time, or perhaps because the supervisor is unsure of the appropriate action and is conniving at the procedure being side-stepped. It is also possible that the supervisor knows what to do but is shirking the responsibility or the potential unpopularity of what has to be done. Whatever the reason for such bypassing it is usually to be avoided because of the worrying precedents that it can establish.

In disciplinary matters even more care is needed about the procedural step as the likelihood of penalties may already have been set up by warnings, thus reducing the scope for doing anything else in the impending interview apart from imposing a further penalty. In the majority of cases we believe that interviews will precede procedure, in which case the parties to the interview are less constrained by procedural rules. In these situations the manager will be at pains to establish that the interview is informal and without procedural implications. Alternatively the interview may be in a situation where the likelihood of a move into procedure is so remote that the manager will be at pains to avoid any such reference, for fear of the complainant taking fright.

Who will be there? Here there are similar procedural considerations. *In* procedure there is the likelihood of employee representation, *out of* procedure there is less likelihood of that, even though the employee may feel anxious and threatened without it. If the manager is accompanied in the interview, the employee may feel even more insecure, and it is doubtful how much can be achieved informally unless the employee feels reasonably secure and able to speak frankly.

What are the facts that the interviewer needs to know? In grievance it will be necessary to know the subject of the grievance and how it has arisen. This type of information will have been filtered through the management hierarchy and may well have been modified in the process, so it needs to be considered carefully and any additional background information collected.

Disciplinary interviews always start at the behest of the management so the manager will again need both to collect evidence and to consider how it may have been interpreted by intermediaries. This will include some basic details about the interviewee, but mainly it will be information about the aspects of the working performance that are unsatisfactory and why. Too often this exists only in opinions that have been offered and prejudices that are held. This provides a poor basis for a constructive interview, so you need to ferret out details, with as much factual corroboration as possible, including a shrewd guess about the interviewee's perspective on the situation.

It is almost inevitable that the interviewee will start the interview defensively, expecting to be blamed for something and therefore ready to refute any allegations, probably deflecting blame elsewhere. The manager needs to anticipate the respondent's initial reaction and be prepared to deal with the reaction as well as with facts that have been collected. Unless the interview is at an early, informal stage, the manager also needs to know about earlier warnings, cautions or penalties that have been invoked.

For both types of interview there will be more general information required. Not just the facts of the particular grievance or disciplinary situation, but knowledge to give a general understanding of the working arrangements and relationships, will be required. Other relevant data may be on the employee's length of service, type of training, previous experience and so forth.

Most managers approaching a grievance or disciplinary interview will benefit from advice before starting. It is particularly important for anyone who is in procedure to check the position with someone such as a personnel officer before starting, as the ability to sustain any action by management will largely depend on maintaining consistency with what the management has done with other employees previously. The manager may also have certain ideas of what could be done in terms of retraining, transfer, or assistance with a domestic problem. The feasibility of such actions need to be verified before broaching them with an aggrieved employee or with an employee whose work is not satisfactory.

Where is the interview to take place? However trivial this question may seem it is included for two reasons. First, because we have seen a number of interviews go sadly awry because of the parties arriving at different places; this mistake seems to happen more often with this type of encounter than with others. Secondly, because there may be an advantage in choosing an unusually informal situation – or an unusually formal location, according to the manager's assessment. A discussion over a pie and a pint in the local pub may be a more appropriate setting for some approaches to grievance and disciplinary problems, although they are seldom appropriate if the matter has reached procedure. Also employees frequently mistrust such settings, feeling that they are being manipulated or that the discussion 'does not count' because it is out of hours or off limits. If, however, one is trying to avoid procedural overtones, this can be a way of doing it.

Unusual formality can be appropriate in the later stages of procedure, especially in disciplinary matters, when proceedings take on a strongly judicial air. An employee is not likely to take seriously a final warning prior to probable dismissal if it is delivered over a pint in a pub. The large, impressive offices of senior managers can provide appropriate settings for the final stages of procedure.

REVIEW TOPIC 31.2

What incidents have you experienced or heard about where the location of the interview was clearly unsuitable?

The grievance interview

The first step in the grievance interview is for the manager to be clear about what the grievance is; a simple way of doing this is to state the *subject* of the grievance and get confirmation from the employee that it is correct. The importance of this lies in the probability that the manager will have a different perspective on the affair from the employee, particularly if it has gone beyond the preliminary stage. A supervisor may report to a superior that Mr X has a grievance and '... will not take instructions from me...', but when the interview begins Mr X may state his grievance as being that he is unwilling to work on Saturday mornings. In other situations it might be the other way around, with the supervisor reporting that Mr X will not work on Saturday mornings and Mr X saying in the interview that he finds the style of his supervisor objectionable. Even where there is no such confusion, an opening statement and confirmation of the subject demonstrate that they are talking about the same thing.

Having clarified or confirmed the subject of the grievance, the manager will then invite the employee to state the case. This will enable the employee to explain why she or he is aggrieved, citing examples, providing further information and saying not just 'what' but also 'why'. Seldom will this be done well. The presentation of a case is not a particularly easy task for the inexperienced, and few aggrieved employees are experienced at making a case of this type. Furthermore there is the inhibition of questioning the wisdom of those in power and some apprehension about the outcome. After the declaration of case the manager will need to ask questions in order to fill in the gaps that have been left by the employee and to clarify some points that were obscure in the first telling. As a general rule it seems better to have an episode of questioning after the case has been made, rather than to interrupt on each point that is difficult. Interruptions make a poorly argued case even more difficult to sustain. There may, however, be disguised pleas for assistance that provide good opportunities for questioning to clarify '... I'm not very good with words, but do you see what I'm getting at...?', '...do you see what I mean?', or 'Am I making myself clear?' Among the communication ploys that the manager will need at this stage could be the method of *reflection* that is described by Beveridge:

> ... a selective form of listening in which the listener picks out the emotional overtones of a statement and 'reflects' these back to the respondent without making any attempt to evaluate them. This means that the interviewer expresses neither approval or disapproval, neither sympathy nor condemnation. Because the respondent may be in an emotional state, sympathy is liable to make him feel resentful and angry. Any attempt to get the respondent to look objectively and rationally at his problem at this stage is also likely to fail; he is still too confused and upset to be able to do this and will interpret the very attempt as criticism. (Beveridge 1968, p. 121)

After all the necessary clarification has been obtained the manager will restate the employee grievance, together with an outline of the case that has been presented, and will ask the employee to agree with the summary or to correct it. By this means the manager is confirming and demonstrating an understanding of what the grievance is about and why it has been brought. The manager is not agreeing with it or dismissing it; all that has happened is that the grievance is now understood.

This phase of the interview can be summarised in sequential terms:

Manager	Employee
1. States subject of grievance	
	2. Agrees with statement
	3. States case
4. Questions for clarification	
5. Re-states grievance	
	6. Agrees or corrects

The grievance is now understood

The next phase is to set out the management position on the grievance. This is not the action *to be taken* but the action that *has been taken* with the reasons for it and may include an explanation of company policy, safety rules, previous grievances, supervisory problems, administrative methods and anything else which is needed to make clear why the management position has been what it has been. The manager will then invite the employee to question and comment on the management position to ensure that it is understood and the justifications for it are understood, even if they are not accepted. The objective is to ensure that the parties to the discussion see and understand each other's point of view.

The management position is now understood

Setting out the two opposed positions will have revealed a deal of common ground. The parties will agree on some things, though disagreeing on others. In the third phase of the interview the manager and employee sort through the points they have discussed and identify the points of disagreement. At least at this stage the points on which they concur can be ignored as the need now is to find the outer limits. It is very similar to the differentiation stage in negotiation.

Points of disagreement are now in focus

As a preliminary to taking action in the matter under discussion, the various possibilities can be put up for consideration. It is logical that the employee suggestions are put first. Probably this had already been done either explicitly or implicitly in the development of the case. If, however, specific suggestions are invited at this stage they may be different ones, as the aggrieved employee now understands the management position and is seeing the whole matter clearly due to the focusing that has just taken place. Then the manager will put forward alternatives or modifications, and such alternatives may include – or be limited to – the suggestion that the grievance is mischievous and unfounded so that no action should be taken.

Nevertheless, in most cases there will be some scope for accommodation even if it is quite different from the employee's expectation. Once the alternative suggestions for action are set out, there is time for the advantages and disadvantages of both sets to be discussed.

Alternatives have now been considered

A grievance interview is one that falls short of the mutual dependence that is present in negotiation, so that the decision on action is to be taken by the manager alone; it is not a joint decision even though the manager will presumably be looking for a decision that all parties will find acceptable. In bringing a grievance the employee is challenging a management decision and that decision will now be confirmed or it will be modified, but it remains a management decision.

Before making the decision the manager may deploy a range of behaviours to ensure that the decision is correct. It may be useful to test the employee's reaction by thinking aloud, '… well, I don't know, but it looks to me as if we shall have to disappoint you on this one…' There may be an adjournment for a while to seek further advice or to give the employee time to reflect further, but there will be little opportunity for prevarication before the manager has to decide and then explain the decision to the employee. In this way the manager is not simply deciding and announcing, but supporting the decision with explanation and justification in the same way that the employee developed the case for the grievance at the beginning. There may be employee questions, who may want time to think, but eventually the management decision will have to be accepted, unless there is some further procedural step available.

Management action action is now clear and understood

The disciplinary interview

Discipline arises from management dissatisfaction rather than employee dissatisfaction with the employment contract, so the opening move is for a statement of why such dissatisfaction exists, dealing with the *facts* of the situation rather than managerial feelings of outrage about the facts. The importance of this is that the interview is being approached by the manager as a way of dealing with a problem of the working situation and not – yet – as a way of dealing with a malicious or indolent employee. If an employee has been persistently late for a week, it would be unwise for a manager to open the disciplinary interview by saying '… your lateness this week has been deplorable…' as the reason might turn out to be that the employee has a seriously ill child needing constant attendance through the night. Then the manager would be seriously embarrassed and the potential for a constructive settlement of the matter would be jeopardised. An opening factual statement of the problem, '… you have been at least twenty minutes late each day this week…' does not

In the booklet *I'd Like to Have a Word With You*, Tietjin describes various types of difficult interviewee, one of which is 'the professional weeper':

> This is the person who can turn on tears like turning on a tap. Some people are quite unmoved by tears, but lots of bosses find tears and emotion very hard to cope with. They are either very embarrassed or very apologetic that their words could have had such an effect. (1987, p. 26)

Another difficult interviewee is 'the counter-attacker':

> who operates on the maxim that the best defence is attack. Once you have stated your reasons for the interview, he will leap straight into the discussion, relishing the opportunity to 'have it out'. The obvious danger is that you respond to his aggression, that a battle of words will ensue and that nothing else will happen. (p. 28)

Notice that Ms Tietjin leaves the gender open in the first instance and specific in the second!

prejudge the reasons and is reasonably precise about the scale of the problem. It also circumscribes management dissatisfaction by implying that there is no other cause for dissatisfaction: if there is, it should be mentioned.

Now the manager needs to know the explanation and asks the employee to say what the reasons for the problem are. The manager may also ask for comments on the seriousness of the problem itself, which the employee may regard as trivial, while the manager regards it as serious. If there is such dissonance it needs to be drawn out. Getting the employee reaction is usually straightforward, but the manager needs to be prepared for one of two other types of reaction. Either there may be a need to probe because the employee is reluctant to open up or there may be angry defiance. Disciplinary situations are at least disconcerting for employees and are frequently very worrying and surrounded by feelings of hostility and mistrust, so that it is to be expected that some ill-feeling will be pent up and waiting for the opportunity to be vented.

If the employee sees something of the management view of the problem and if the manager understands the reasons for it, the next requirement is to seek a solution. We have to point out that a disciplinary problem is as likely to be solved by management action as it is to be solved by employee action. If the problem is lateness one solution would be for the employee to catch an earlier bus, but another might be for the management to alter the working shift to which the employee is assigned. If the employee is disobeying orders, one solution would be to start obeying them, but another might be for the employee to be moved to a different job where orders are received from someone else. Some managers regard such thinking as unreasonable, on the grounds that the contract of employment places obligations on individual employees that they should meet despite personal inconvenience. The answer to this type of query seems to lie in the question not of how people *should* behave, but how they *do*. Can the contract of employment be enforced on an unwilling employee? Not if one is seeking such attitudes as enthusiasm and co-operation or behaviour such as diligence and carefulness. The disenchanted employee can always meet the bare letter rather than the spirit of the contract, but there is some evidence of increasing strictness.

> There appears to be growing managerial concern about absence and timekeeping... There has been a move towards closer monitoring of attendance and the enforcement of standards. In one firm subjected to case study analysis, absence control was high on the managerial agenda... workers were more aware of pressures to work harder and tightening discipline. (Edwards 1989, p. 320)

The most realistic view of the matter is that many disciplinary problems require some action from both parties, some require action by the employee only and a small proportion require management action only. The problem-solving session may quickly produce the possibility for further action and open up the possibility of closing the interview.

First possible move to disengagement

The simple, rational approach that we have outlined so far may not be enough, due to the unwillingness of employees to respond to disciplinary expectations. They may not want to be punctual or to do as they are instructed, or whatever the particular problem is. There is now a test of the power behind management authority. Three further steps can be taken, one after the other, although there will be occasions when it is necessary to move directly to the third.

(i)   *Persuasion.* A first strategy is to demonstrate to employees that they will not achieve what they want, if their behaviour does not change:

> You won't keep your earnings up if your output doesn't meet the standard.

> It will be difficult to get your appointment confirmed when the probationary period is over if...

By such means employees may see the advantages of changing their attitude and behaviour. If they are so convinced, then there is a strong incentive for them to alter, because they believe it to be in their own interests.

Second possible move to disengagement

(ii) *Disapproval.* A second strategy is to suggest that the continuance of the behaviour will displease those whose goodwill the employee wishes to keep:

> The Management Development Panel are rather disappointed...

> Some of the other people in the department feel that you are not pulling your weight.

A manager using this method will need to be sure that what is said is both true and relevant. Also the manager may be seen by the employee as shirking the issue, so it may be appropriate to use a version of, 'I think this is deplorable and expect you to do better'.

We asked for a restraint from judgement in the early stages of the interview, until the nature of the problem is clear. The time for judgement has now come, with the proper deployment of the rebuke or the caution.

Third possible move to disengagement

(iii) *Penalties.* When all else fails or is clearly inappropriate – as with serious offences about which there is no doubt – penalties have to be invoked. In rare circumstances there may be the possibility of a fine, but usually the first penalty will be a formal warning as a preliminary to possible dismissal. In situations that are sufficiently grave summary dismissal is both appropriate and possible within the legal framework.

Fourth possible move to disengagement

We have indicated possible moves to disengagement at four different points in the disciplinary interview. Now we come to a stage that is common for both grievance and disciplinary encounters from the point of view of describing the process, although the nature of disengagement will obviously differ. Essentially the manager needs to think of the working situation that will follow. In a grievance situation can the employee now accept the decision made? Are there faces to be saved or reputations to be restored? What administrative action is to be taken? In closing a disciplinary interview, the manager will aim for the flavour of disengagement to be as positive as possible so that all concerned put the disciplinary problem behind them. In those cases where the outcome of the interview is to impose or confirm a dismissal, then the manager will be exclusively concerned with the fairness and accuracy with which it is done, so that the possibility of tribunal hearings is reduced, if not prevented. It can never be appropriate to close an interview of either type leaving the employee humbled and demoralised.

References

Beveridge, W. E. (1968), *Problem-Solving Interviews*, London: Allen & Unwin.
Edwards, P. K. (1989), 'The three faces of discipline'. In K. Sisson (ed.) *Personnel Management in Britain*, Oxford: Basil Blackwell.
McGregor, D. (1960), *The Human Side of Enterprise*, Maidenhead: McGraw-Hill.
Tietjen, T. (1987), *I'd Like a Word With You*, London: Video Arts Ltd.

PART VII

Pay

32 Strategic aspects of payment

A strange thing about payment is that managers seem to shy away from actually using the word. We hear about 'compensation', 'reward' or 'remuneration', yet the idea of compensation is making amends for something that has caused loss or injury. Do we want to suggest that work necessarily causes loss or injury? Reward suggests a special payment for a special act. Much current management thinking on pay issues is to induce more special effort by employees, but the bulk of the pay bargain for an individual is not affected by performance. Remuneration is a more straightforward word which means exactly the same as payment but has five more letters and is misspelt (as renumeration) more often than most words in the personnel manager's lexicon. Payment seems to us a good, solid, clear word to encompass all that is involved from basic rates to pensions.

Fairness and performance in payment

One basis for deciding who should be paid what is an assessment of fairness – 'a fair day's pay for a fair day's work'. The employer believes that the employee should be paid a fair amount in relation to the skill and effort that has to be exercised, and employees feel there is a reasonable level of payment that can be expected for the contribution made. When both sets of expectations can be satisfied, then we have in place a further dimension of the employment contract described in the first chapter.

The axiom of a fair day's pay for a fair day's work is not necessarily either fair or just. Karl Marx described it as a conservative motto and it undoubtedly impedes change in pay arrangements. What is seen as fair is putting something back to what it used to be: the restoration of a differential or the rectification of an anomaly. Change is almost defined as unfair because it undermines the status quo and reduces standards. By inhibiting change, the fairness principle also impedes restructuring.

Another criticism is that any differences in relative payment are related to the work undertaken, yet that is intrinsically no more logical than the quite different concept of 'from each according to their ability: to each according to their needs'.

Despite these criticisms of the fairness principle, it remains the most useful basis for any discussion of payment because it is the notion used by both employers and employees in considering the acceptability of payment arrangements, actual or proposed, although the other principle of supply and demand is always present.

> Supply and demand have long been held to be at the heart of the wage determination process, at least in the opinion of economists. The supply of manpower should be equated with the organization demand if performance is to be underpinned (Smith 1983, p. 26).

Supply and demand remains only a partial explanation of pay determination, even in the more sophisticated formulae of marginal productivity theory or wages fund theory. Whatever limited validity these economists' explanations may have in explaining national labour market behaviour, the mutual assessment of what is fair remains the most useful starting point for the personnel manager assessing what is to be done within the organisation and for individual employees deciding the acceptability of their level of payment. A group of employees strongly persuaded that they are underpaid will not change their minds if it is explained to them that:

> wages had to be paid out of a fund from the accumulated revenues deriving from past production, and the size of fund, and therefore wages, were determined by the ratio of supply to amounts of revenue set aside for labour (*ibid.* p. 29).

The other basis for deciding relative payment is performance, with above-average performance producing above-average pay and above-average increases in pay. This has certainly been very popular since the late 1980s for payment arrangements related to management posts, and a development of the earlier notion of management by objectives:

> The trend towards performance, rather than merit, assessment is a trend towards rewarding output rather than input. It stems from the concept of performance management – a much wider development than just a change in payment practices. (Fowler 1988).

Neither fairness nor performance are easy principles to implement. Judgements of fairness are typically supported by pay systems based on incremental scales and job evaluation, yet the most widespread reason for industrial action has always been dissatisfaction with relative pay. Performance-related payment arrangements are only relatively easy to run when everyone is doing better. The difficulty of below-average pay for below-average performers is indicated by the fact that schemes typically deliver enhanced pay even when performance by objective criteria such as company profitability declines.

Employee objectives for the contract for payment

Those who are paid, and those who administer payment schemes, have objectives for the payment contract which differ according to whether one is the recipient or the administrator of the payments. The contract for payment will be satisfactory in so far as it meets the objectives of the parties. Therefore we consider the range of objectives, starting with employees.

First objective: purchasing power

The absolute level of weekly or monthly earnings determines the standard of living of the recipient, and will therefore be the most important consideration for most employees. How much can I buy? Employees are rarely satisfied about their purchasing power, and the annual pay adjustment will do little more than reduce dissatisfaction. The two main reasons for this are inflation and rising expectations.

Second objective: felt-fair

We have already discussed the notion of fairness in payment. Here we have the term 'felt-fair', which was devised by Jaques (1962), who averred that every employee had a strong feeling about the level of payment that was fair for the job. Here we move away from the absolute level of earnings to the first of a series of aspects of relative income. In most cases this will be a very rough personalised evaluation of what is seen as appropriate.

The employee who feels underpaid is likely to demonstrate the conventional symptoms of withdrawal from the job: looking for another, carelessness, disgruntlement, lateness, absence, and so on. Perhaps the worst manifestation of this is among those who feel the unfairness but who can not take a clean step of moving elsewhere. They then not only feel dissatisfied with their pay level, they feel another unfairness too: being trapped in a situation they resent. Those who feel they are overpaid (as some do) may simply feel dishonest, or may seek to justify their existence in some way, such as trying to look busy, that is not necessarily productive.

Third objective: rights

A different aspect of relative income is that concerned with the rights of the employee to a particular share of the company's profits or the nation's wealth. The employee is thinking about whether the division of earnings is providing fair shares of the Gross National Product. 'To each according to their needs' is overlaid on 'a fair day's pay...'. This is a strong feature of most trade union arguments and part of the general preoccupation with the rights of the individual. Mainly this is the long-standing debate about who should enjoy the fruits of labour.

Fourth objective: relativities

'How much do I (or we) get relative to … group X?' This is a version of the 'felt-fair' argument. It is not the question of whether the employee feels the remuneration to be reasonable in relation to the job done, but in relation to the jobs other people do.

There are many potential comparators, and the basis of comparison can alter. The Pay Board (1974) pointed out three. First is the definition of pay. Is it basic rates or is it earnings? Over how long is the pay compared? Many groups have a level of payment that varies from one time of the year to another. Second is the method of measuring the changes: absolute amount of money or percentage. £5 is 10 per cent of £50 but 5 per cent of £100. Third is the choice of pay dates. Here we can see a change since the Pay Board report, as not all groups receive annual adjustments to their pay, nor at the same time.

Fifth objective: recognition

Most people have an objective for their payment arrangements of their personal contribution being recognised. This is partly seeking reassurance, but is also a way in which people can mould their behaviour and their career thinking to produce progress and satisfaction. It is doubtful if financial recognition has a significant and sustained impact on performance, but providing a range of other forms of recognition while the pay packet is transmitting a different message is certainly counterproductive.

Sixth objective: composition

How is the pay package made up? The growing complexity and sophistication of payment arrangements raises all sorts of questions about pay composition. Is £200 pay for 60 hours' work better than £140 for 40 hours' work? The arithmetical answer that the rate per hour for the 40-hour arrangement is marginally better than for 60 hours is only part of the answer. Other aspects will relate to the individuals, their circumstances and the conventions of their working group and reference groups. Another question about composition might be: is £140 per week plus a pension better than £160 per week without? Such questions do not produce universally applicable answers because they can be quantified to such a limited extent, but some kernels of conventional wisdom can be suggested as generalisations:

1. Younger employees are more interested in high direct earnings at the expense of indirect benefits, such as pensions, which will be of more interest to older employees.
2. Incentive or performance-related payment arrangements are likely to interest employees who either see a reliable prospect of enhancing earnings through the ability to control their own activities, or who see the incentive scheme as

an opportunity to wrest control of their personal activities (which provide little intrinsic satisfaction) away from management by regulating their earnings.

3. Married women are seldom interested in payment arrangements that depend on overtime: married men frequently are.

4. Overtime is used by many employees to produce an acceptable level of purchasing power, particularly among the lower-paid.

5. Pensions and sickness payment arrangements beyond statutory minima are a *sine qua non* of white-collar employment, and are of growing importance in manual employment.

Employer objectives for the contract for payment

In looking at the other side of the picture, we consider the range of objectives in the thinking of employers, or those representing an employer interest *vis-à-vis* the employee.

First objective: prestige

There is a comfortable and understandable conviction among managers that it is 'a good thing' to be a good payer. This seems to be partly simple pride at doing better than others, but also there is sometimes a feeling that such a policy eliminates a variable from the contractual relationship. In conversation with one of the authors a chief executive expressed it this way:

> I want to find out the highest rates of pay, job-for-job, within a fifty-mile radius of my office. Then I will make sure that all my people are paid 20 per cent over that. Then I know where I am with them as I have taken money out of the equation. If they want to quit they can't hide the real reason by saying they're going elsewhere for more cash: they can't get it. Furthermore, if I do have to fill a job I know that we won't lose a good guy because of the money not being right.

Whether high pay rates succeed in getting someone the reputation of being a good employer is difficult to see. What seems much more likely is that the low-paying employer will have the reputation of being a poor employer.

Second objective: competition

More rational is the objective of paying rates that are sufficiently competitive to sustain the employment of the right numbers of appropriately qualified and experienced employees to staff the organisation. A distinction is drawn here between competition thinking and prestige thinking, as the former is more designed to get a good fit on one of the employment contract dimensions rather than simply overwhelm it. It permits consideration of questions such as: how selective do we need to be for this range of jobs? and: how can we avoid overpaying people and inhibiting them from moving on? Every employer has this sort of objective, even if only in relation to a few key posts in the organisation.

Third objective: control

There may be ways of organising the pay packet that will facilitate control of operations and potentially save money. The conventional approach to this for many years was the use of piecework or similar incentives, but this became difficult due to the unwillingness of most employees to see their payment fluctuate wildly at the employer's behest. Theoretically, overtime is a method of employer control of output through making available or withholding additional payment prospects. In practice, however, employees use overtime for control more extensively than employers. Gradually, other ways in which employers could control their payroll costs are being eliminated or made more difficult by legislation. Redundancy, short-term lay-off and unfair dismissal are all now more expensive, and it is increasingly

---

The case of the AIDS counsellor

The difficulty of determining a fair and satisfactory rate of pay for particular individuals is illustrated in the following example of a nurse employed by a large NHS hospital as a counsellor for haemophilia patients who have contracted AIDS through blood transfusion.

The nurse concerned was employed on a senior sister's grade but was required to work in the community undertaking counselling duties with patients and their families. The nature of the job, however, meant that she was required to work very irregular and unpredictable hours and could not delegate duties to anyone else or share the burden of cases with others. In 1994 she requested a regrading with the full support of her managers who perceived her to be a uniquely good performer. No performance-related scheme had, however, been developed.

Regrading the nurse was not straightforward. The first stumbling block came when her duties were assessed according to grading criteria negotiated by the relevant NHS Whitley Council. Although several attempts were made to try to make the job fit the criteria for the higher grade the task proved impossible. Authorising a regrading on these grounds would have set a precedent leading to large numbers of regrading claims.

The next approach taken was to analyse the nurse's job using the hospital's computerised job evaluation system. This route also failed because the results of the analysis suggested that the job was already graded too highly. To regrade in spite of this would render the decision indefensible were an equal value claim to be brought by a male nurse employed at the same grade.

Finally an attempt was made to justify the proposed regrading by discovering at what level other hospitals paid nurses undertaking similar roles. It was found, however, that other AIDS counsellors were paid on the same or lower grades.

It thus proved impossible to pay the nurse concerned a rate which she and her managers regarded as 'fair' because no decision to regrade could be justified objectively.

---

unreasonable, unlawful and impracticable to regard women as a reservoir of inexpensive, temporary labour.

Fourth objective: motivation and performance

Employers also seek to use the payment contract to motivate employees and thus to improve their work performance. The subject of incentive payment systems is discussed in detail in Chapter 34 but some features of payment and its influence on performance are worth mentioning here.

Prior to the 1980s incentive payment systems were primarily used as part of the payment package for manual workers and sales staff. The design of such schemes is simple with a built-in bias towards rewarding the volume of products manufactured or sold. Wherever the quality of output is a matter of significance such approaches are, therefore, inappropriate. Two extreme examples indicate the weakness of this approach. Someone engaged in manufacture of diamond-tipped drilling bits would serve the employer poorly if payment were linked to output. If it were possible to devise a payment system that contained an incentive element based on high quality of workmanship or on low scrap value that might be more effective. If schoolteachers were paid a 'quantity bonus' it would presumably be based either on the number of children in the class or on some indicator such as the number of examination passes. The first would encourage teachers to take classes as large as possible, with probably adverse results in the quality of teaching. The second might increase the proportion of children succeeding in examinations, but would isolate those who could not produce impressive examination performance.

In recent years a great deal of attention has been paid to the development of incentive payment systems which go beyond rewarding the quantity of output to take account of job performance as a whole. In particular there has been a marked increase in the use of performance-related pay (PRP) for management and professional staff, especially for senior managers; organisations have sought either to re-establish or to introduce for the first time schemes which reinforce the messages required to produce improved performance and increased productivity.

Private sector employers in particular now increasingly believe that they are not providing an appropriate or competitive package for their directors and senior executives unless there is some element of risk money to add on to the basic salary and reward the achievement of company growth, profitability and success. At the same time, companies have been re-examining the use of bonus schemes for more junior employees in order to increase motivation and to reward them for their contribution. The use of PRP is also growing in the public sector following active promotion of its benefits by government ministers.

Fifth objective: cost

Just as employees are interested in purchasing power, the absolute value of their earnings, so employers are interested in the absolute cost of payment, and its bearing on the profitability or cost-effectiveness of their organisation. The importance of this varies with the type of organisation and the relative cost of employees, so that in the refining of petroleum employment costs are modest, in teaching or nursing they are substantial. The employer interest in this objective is long-term as well as short-term. Not only do employees expect their incomes to be maintained and continue to rise, rather than fluctuating with company profitability, but the indirect costs of employing people can also be substantial.

The elements of payment

The payment of an individual will be made up of one or more elements from those shown in Figure 32.1. Fixed elements are those that make up the regular weekly or monthly payment to the individual, and which do not vary other than in exceptional circumstances. Variable elements can be varied either by the employee or the employer.

Basic
The irreducible minimum rate of pay is the basic. In most cases this is also the standard rate, not having any additions made to it. In other cases it is a basis on which earnings are built by the addition of one or more of the other elements in payment. One group of employees – women operatives in footwear – have little more than

Bonus	Profit allocation		Variable elements
	Discretionary sum		
Incentive	Group calculation basis		• Irregular
	Individual calculation basis		• Variable amount
Overtime payment			• Usually discretionary
Premia	Occasional		
	Contractual		
Benefits	Fringe benefits		Fixed elements
	Payments in kind	Other	
		Accommodation	• Regular
		Car	• Rarely variable
	Benefit schemes	Other	• Usually contractual
		Pension	
		Sick pay	
Plussage	'Fudge' payments		
	Special additions		
Basic rate of payment			Basic

Figure 32.1   The potential elements of payment

half of their earnings in basic, while primary and secondary schoolteachers have virtually all their pay in this form.

Plussage

Sometimes the basic has an addition to recognise an aspect of working conditions or employee capability. Payments for educational qualifications and for supervisory responsibilities are quite common. There is also an infinite range of what are sometimes called 'fudge' payments, whereby there is an addition to the basic as a start-up allowance, mask money, dirt money and so forth.

REVIEW TOPIC 32.1

If your employer offered you a 'remuneration package', which could be made up from any of the items in Figure 32.1 provided that the total cost was no more than £x, what proportion of each item would you choose and why? Does your answer suggest ideas for further development of salary policies?

Benefits

Extras to the working conditions that have a cash value are categorised as benefits and can be of great variety. Some have already been mentioned; others include luncheon vouchers, subsidised meals, discount purchase schemes and the range of welfare provisions such as free chiropody and cheap hairdressing.

Premia

Where employees work at inconvenient times, such as shifts or permanent nights, they receive a premium payment as compensation for the inconvenience. This is for inconvenient rather than additional hours of work. Sometimes this is built into the basic rate or is a regular feature of the contract of employment so that the payment is unvarying. In other situations shift-working is occasional and short-lived, making the premium a variable element of payment.

Overtime

It is customary for employees working more hours than are normal for the working week to be paid for those hours at an enhanced rate, usually between 10 and 50 per cent more that the normal rate according to how many hours are involved. Seldom can this element be regarded as fixed. No matter how regularly overtime is worked, there is always the opportunity for the employer to withhold the provision of overtime or for the employee to decline the extra hours.

Incentive

Incentive is described here as an element of payment linked to the working performance of an individual or working group, as a result of prior arrangement. This includes most of the payment by results schemes that have been produced by work study, as well as commission payments to salespeople, skills-based pay schemes and performance-related pay schemes based on the achievement of agreed objectives. The distinguishing feature is that the employee knows what has to be done to earn the payment, though he or she may feel very dependent on other people, or on external circumstances, to receive it.

Bonus

A different type of variable payment is the gratuitous payment by the employer that is not directly earned by the employee: a bonus. The essential difference between this and an incentive is that the employee has no entitlement to the payment as a result of a contract of employment and cannot be assured of receiving it in return for a specific performance. The most common example of this is the Christmas bonus.

We include profit-sharing under this general heading although share ownership confers a clear entitlement. The point is that the level of the benefit cannot be directly linked to the performance of the individual but to the performance of the business. In some cases the two may be synonymous with one dominant individual determining the success of the business, but there are very few instances like this, even in the most feverish imaginings of tycoons. Share ownership or profit-sharing on an agreed basis can greatly increase the interest of the employees in how the business is run and can increase their commitment to its success, but the performance of the individual is not directly rewarded in the same way as in incentive schemes.

The difference between wages and salaries

Since the 1970s the traditional divide in the respective treatment of 'waged' and 'salaried' employees for payment administration purposes has declined. It is clear, however, that there remain a number of differences in emphasis that affect not only the payer of the wages or the salary, but also the attitude of the recipient. This tends both to emphasise and reflect the tendency to identify core and peripheral workforces as we saw in our discussion of labour markets. Some of the most obvious differences between wages and salaries are shown in Table 32.1.

Table 32.1 *Ways in which wage-earning and salary-earning differ*

Salaries	Wages
Annual rate	Hourly rate
Paid monthly	Paid weekly
Paid by bank transfer	Paid in cash
Performance-related pay	Incentive schemes
Occupational pensions	No fringe benefits
Liberal expenses paid	No expenses paid
Company cars	No cars

There are also less tangible differences which reflect the attitudes of the recipients of wages and salaries as perceived by organisation decision-makers. For example, the nature of incentive payments has traditionally been different. Wage-earners are paid tightly measured incentives based on individual or team production levels, whereas salaried staff are rewarded for their performance over a longer timescale with predefined incremental scales.

The last difference to mention is probably the most important, as it is a part of all the others. Those receiving salaries are likely to identify with the management interest in the organisation. This was suggested by the studies by Batstone, Boraston and Frenkel (1977), and Bain (1972) has pointed out that management encouragement is one of the features that needs to be present before white-collar unions expand. Salaried employees are most likely to see themselves doing a piece of the job of management, which has had to be split up because it – and the organisation – have grown too big for top management to handle alone, but unquestionably it is a part of management. Wage-earners see themselves as doing the work that the management would never do and which is independent of management apart from the labour-hiring contract.

REVIEW TOPIC 32.2

Some employers who have moved wage-earners to salaried status have been surprised that the employees do not assume the same attitudes to work as those who are already salaried. Why do you think this is?

Recent survey evidence (IRS 1989, IDS 1992) indicates that in many of the above areas the traditional divide between the way wage-earners and salaried staff are treated has greatly declined. Single-status arrangements are increasingly becoming the norm, especially in respect of access to occupational pensions and in the frequency and in the method of payment. Where a status divide persists it is commonly in the means used to determine basic pay levels and in the design of grading structures. In these organisations manual workers and the lower-graded service staff are now likely to be paid monthly directly into a bank account while the level of their pay continues to be determined through annual negotiations with their representatives. By contrast, individuals in occupations traditionally identified as 'salaried' are more likely to benefit from annual incremental progression or pay rises achieved through promotion along a recognised career ladder. A more detailed analysis of trends in this field can be found in Price and Price, 1994.

Incremental salary structures

A typical organisation will have a salary structure of groups, ladders and steps.

Groups

The first element of the structure is the broad groupings of salaries, each group being administered according to the same set of rules. The questions in making decisions about this are to do with the logical grouping of job-holders, according to their common interests, performance criteria, qualifications and – perhaps – bargaining arrangements and trade union membership. The British Institute of Management study (1973) used a framework of four groups:

1. Senior and middle management: Directors, heads of major functions and their immediate subordinates.
2. Junior management: responsible to the above and including supervisory staff.
3. Technical and specialist: personnel with technical or professional skills and/or qualifications (excluding those working in a managerial capacity), e.g. work study officer, technician, draughtsman/woman.
4. Clerical: all clerical occupations including secretarial staff. (British Institute of Management 1973)

The broad salary ranges are then set against each group, to encompass either the maximum and minimum of the various people who will then be in the group or – in the rare circumstance of starting from scratch – the ideal maximum and minimum levels.

As the grouping has been done on the basis of job similarity the attaching of maximum and minimum salaries can show up peculiarities, with one or two jobs far below a logical minimum and others above a logical maximum. This requires the limits for the group to be put at the 'proper' level, with the exceptions either being identified as exceptions and the incumbents being paid a protected rate or being moved into a more appropriate group.

Salary groups will not stack neatly one on top of another in a salary hierarchy. There will be considerable overlap, recognising that there is an element of salary growth as a result of experience as well as status and responsibility. A typical set of groups could be as illustrated in Figure 32.2.

There are various alternatives to this now rather dated type of arrangement, such as separating senior and middle management; incorporating technical and specialist personnel into appropriate management groups according to seniority; including manual employees as a salaried group. Another alternative is not to have groups at all, but simply a single system of ladders and steps, so that all employees have their payment arrangements administered according to one set of criteria. The argument against such a system is that it applies a common set of assumptions that may be inappropriate for certain groups. In general management, for instance, it will probably be an assumption that all members of the group will be interested in promotion and job change; this will be encouraged by the salary arrangements, which will encourage job-holders to look for opportunities to move around. In contrast, the research chemist will be expected to stick at one type of job for a longer period, and movement into other fields of the company's affairs, such as personnel or marketing, will often be discouraged. For this reason it will be more appropriate

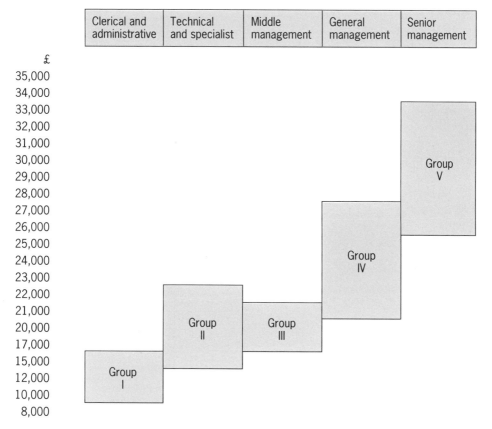

Clerical and administrative	Technical and specialist	Middle management	General management	Senior management

Figure 32.2 Typical salary groups

for the research chemist to be in a salary group with a relatively small number of ladders, each having a large number of steps; while a general management colleague will be more logically set in a context of more ladders, each with fewer steps. It should be noted, however, that employers operating a system of separate occupational pay spines must be able to defend their system against possible equal value claims (see Chapter 33).

Another way of dealing with specialists is to take them out of the corporate salary structure altogether and pay them according to salaries prescribed by an acknowledged outside body. This is done most frequently for nurses working in industry, who are often paid according to scales published by the Royal College of Nursing. A device such as this can solve the problem of one or two specialised employees whose general rank or standing in the organisation is not consistent with the necessary level of payment.

The grouping stage in salary administration has thus identified a number of employees whose remuneration will be organised along similar lines.

Ladders and steps

Because employees are assumed to be career-orientated, salary arrangements are based on that assumption, so each salary group has several ladders within it and each ladder has a number of steps (often referred to as 'scales' and 'points'). As with groups there is considerable overlap, the top rung of one ladder being much higher than the bottom rung of the next. Taking the typical general management group that was mentioned above, we could envisage four ladders, as shown in Figure 32.3. The size of the differential between steps varies from £200 to £600 according to the level of the salary and the overlapping could be used in a number of ways according

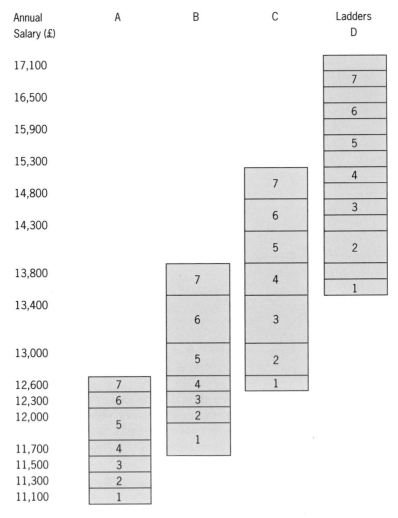

Figure 32.3 Ladders and steps in a salary group

to the differing requirements. Steps 6 and 7 on each ladder would probably be only for those who had reached their particular ceiling and were unlikely to be promoted further, while steps 4 and 5 could be for those who are on their way up and have made sufficient progress up one ladder to contemplate seeking a position with a salary taken from the next-high ladder.

The figures attached to the ladders in this example are round, in the belief that salaries are most meaningful to recipients when they are in round figures. However, ladders are sometimes developed with steps having a more precise arithmetical relationship to their relative position, so that each step represents the same percentage increase. Equally, some ladders have the same cash amount attached to each step.

Some commentators place importance on the relationship of the maximum to the minimum of a ladder, described as the span, and the relationship between the bottom rung of adjacent ladders, referred to as the differential. Bowey (1972) suggests that the most logical arrangement is a 50 per cent span and a 20 per cent differential. There is no inscrutable logic behind those precise figures, so that 49 per cent and 21 per cent would not be 'wrong', but they have a similar value to the use of round figures referred to in the last paragraph. There is a neatness and symmetry about the method, which can commend itself to salary recipients.

The self-financing increment principle

It is generally believed that fixed incremental payment schemes are self-regulating, so that introducing incremental payment schemes does not mean that within a few years everyone is at the maximum. The assumption is that just as some move up, others retire or resign and are replaced by new recruits at the bottom of the ladder. This will clearly not be the case when staff turnover is low.

REVIEW TOPIC 32.3

If incremental scales cease to be self-financing through lack of labour market movement, what advantage is there to the employer in keeping them?

Pay comparisons

Salary structures have to have an internal logic that makes sense to at least the majority of the salary recipients, but they also have to be consistent with what is being paid elsewhere, as was considered in the chapter on labour markets. There are a number of ways in which comparisons can be made. The most reliable is to use salary surveys, which are carried out by consultants. The method is to obtain information from a number of employers and then arrange the anonymous information into a range of categories for comparison, such as size of company by turnover and number of employees. More difficult to define are the jobs for which salaries are being compared, both in terms of the job specialisation and the degree of responsibility and accountability of the post-holder. Incomes Data Services and Industrial Relations Services publish regular reviews of what the surveys are saying.

Salary clubs are informal collections of employers who meet periodically to share information about relative rates of pay for categories of staff they all employ.

A service found especially valuable by its users is the pay comparison information provided by the Hay-MSL management consultancy, where the regular pay reports are based on jobs evaluated by the Hay-MSL system, so there is an unusual degree of reliability in the like-for-like comparisons.

Salary decisions

Who decides where in the salary structure the individual fits? The answer to that question at one extreme is 'job evaluation and fixed increments' and at the other extreme it is the capricious whim of another individual. The first means that decisions are not made about individuals but about systems, and the individual salary emerges from the inexorable process of increments. The second means that decisions on salaries are made without constraint and, perhaps, without logic. Between these two extremes we can list the sequence of decisions that are involved in a typical annual salary review:

1. *How much the salary budget for the next year will be:* decision made by the senior decision-making individual or coalition after submissions of evidence from personnel, finance and other specialists, including an interpretation of labour market indicators and trade union negotiations, if any.

2. *How the additional budget provision is to be divided between general increases (cost-of-living) and individual increases (performance or 'merit'):* this decision is probably made at the same time as the first, but evidence and advice from personnel is given more weight than any other. Possibly a wholly personnel decision.

3. *How performance or 'merit' increases are decided:* recommendation from individual's superior, according to clear-cut rules, vetted by personnel to ensure consistency of approach by all superiors and that no previous undertakings are overlooked.

4. *How individuals hear the news:* face-to-face by line superior, written confirmation from personnel.

A strategic approach to payment administration

Since the late 1980s a number of authorities have expressed the view that the way payment is managed is undergoing a fundamental change. This view has been most eloquently expressed by Armstrong and Murlis in successive editions of their book

Reward Management, where they describe the way they perceive the role of the salary administrator to have changed since the early 1980s:

> Salary administration was very much seen as a back-room function in which numerate specialists worked out details of policies that came from elsewhere – from government, from head office or from general management. There was little obvious link between what happened on the remuneration front and over all business strategy, let alone an organization's human resource strategy – if it had one. There was certainly little line management involvement in, or ownership of, the pay practice that emerged.
> (Armstrong and Murlis 1994, p. 16)

They go on to describe how they perceive practice to have changed. In particular they stress the significance of reward strategies which have led to the replacement of traditional grading structures with less bureaucratic means of determining an individual's pay. As a result it is possible to reward individual contribution to organisational success through payments related to profit, performance or skills acquisition to a far greater extent than was previously the case.

While there has, unquestionably, been a greater interest in incentive payments during the past 10–15 years, it is unclear whether this represents a shift in employer practice of the degree described above. Criticism of this view has been expressed by Smith (1993) who questions the extent to which the various developments in incentive pay have in fact derived from a new-found strategic approach to pay. Rather, he believes, they amount to 'no more than a collection of expedient manoeuvres to deal with the boom conditions of the late 1980s'. According to this view, the continued growth in profit-related pay owes more to government encouragement than to a serious attempt on the part of employers to use pay strategically as a means of improving productivity. The argument that developments in incentive pay are born of short-term considerations on the part of employers is further backed up by evidence of declining labour productivity during the late 1980s and early 1990s.

Attitudes towards payment arrangements vary radically between different countries. In a survey in Singapore 1500 respondents were asked to pick three of the following five factors which they believed would have a significant impact on wage determination: wages in the same industry, wages in a different industry, union representation, government influence and productivity. The proportion of respondents identifying the five factors as significant were:

Productivity	33.5%
Government	29.1%
Wages in the same industry	27.1%
Unions	18.3%
Wages in a different industry	14.8%

The same survey demonstrated that the main cause for differences between individual perspectives was the quality and quantity of information they received from their employer. (Torrington and Tan Chwee Huat, 1994)

32.1 For both parties to the employment contract the main consideration is that the payment arrangement should be 'fair'.

32.2 Employee and employer have different frames of reference that determine their respective views of fairness.

32.3 The main elements of payment are basic rate, plussage, benefits, premia, overtime, incentive and bonus.

32.4 Despite moves towards harmonisation, there remain major differences between wages and salaries.

32.5 The traditional divide between the 'salaried' and 'wage-earning' employee is of increaasingly little importance.

32.6 A typical salary structure has groups, ladders and steps which interconnect to describe and encourage career progression.

32.7 The idea that incremental salary systems keep the total cost of salaries stable around the mid-point of scales is seldom correct when there is little staff turnover.

References

Armstrong, M. and Murlis, H. (1994), *Reward Management: A Handbook of Salary Administration*, London: Kogan Page.

Bain, G. S. (1972), *White Collar Unions: A Review*, London: Institute of Personnel Management.

Batstone, E., Boraston, I. and Frenkel, S. (1977), *Shop Stewards in Action*, Oxford: Basil Blackwell.

Bowey, A. (1972), *Salary Structures for Management Careers*, London: Institute of Personnel Management.

British Institute of Management (1973), *Salary Administration, Survey report no. 16*, London: British Institute of Management.

Fowler, A. (1988), 'New directions in performance pay', *Personnel Management*, November, vol. 20, no. 11.

Incomes Data Services (IDS) (1992), *Integrated Pay. Study no 509*, London: IDS.

Industrial Relations Services (IRS) (1989), *Harmonisation: a Single Status Surge? IRS Employment Trends, 501*. London: IRS.

Jaques, E. (1962), 'Objective measures for pay differentials', *Harvard Business Review*, January/February, pp. 133–7.

Office of Manpower Economics (1973), *Incremental Payment Schemes*, London: HMSO.

Pay Board (1974), *Relativities*, London: HMSO.

Price, L. and Price, R. (1994), 'Change and continuity in the status divide'. In K. Sisson (ed.) *Personnel Management; A comprehensive guide to theory and practice in Britain*, Oxford: Blackwell.

Smith, I. (1983), *The Management of Remuneration: Paying for effectiveness*, London: Institute of Personnel Management.

Smith, I. (1993), 'Reward Management: A Retrospective Assessment', *Employee Relations*, vol. 15.

Torrington, D. P. and Tan Chwee Huat (1994), *Human Resource Management for South East Asia*, Singapore: Simon & Schuster.

33   Job evaluation

One of the main tasks of payment administration is setting the differential gaps. It is always necessary to juggle the three factors of performance, market rate and equity. It is rarely possible or wise to pay people only according to their performance or contribution, and linking payment only to developments in the labour market can make working relationships very difficult. There is always the vexed question of how much more than Y and how much less than Z should X receive? The relative contribution of each individual of the three is difficult to measure, so some acceptable assessment of each job is made. The difficult problem of assessing performance is overlaid with the even more difficult problem of making comparisons.

The standard way of tackling this problem is using a form of job evaluation. In 1993 a major survey was undertaken by Industrial Relations Services (IRS) which examined the use of job evaluation in 164 organisations employing a total of 700,000 people. They found that 75 per cent of the sample used job evaluation in determining the pay of some employees compared to 65 per cent in a similar survey undertaken in 1990. Few organisations abandon it once introduced. It is clear from this survey as well as that carried out by Spencer (1990a) that the chief reason for the introduction of job evaluation is to achieve fairness in pay policy or to increase employees' sense of fairness. It is also commonly used as a tool in organisation restructuring and in harmonising the terms and conditions enjoyed by different groups of employees.

Another important reason for the increased use of job evaluation is the need to comply with the Equal Pay Act, as modified in 1984, which places as central in assessing equal pay claims the question of whether or not a job evaluation scheme is in use. It is significant that the trend towards the introduction of job evaluation in all the major retailing groups in the early 1990s followed threats of legal action to secure equal pay between check-out operators and other groups. Recent judgements in the European Court of Justice have further focused attention on the role of job evaluation in equal value cases.

In this chapter we consider first the background to the problems of getting relative payment right and then the job evaluation methods which are used. Finally, we consider the equal pay aspects.

Relativities and differentials

There are four different types of pay relationship that personnel managers need to understand, as dissatisfaction with relative pay can come from any of these sources.

Differentials

Differentials is the term used to describe pay differences within a single group of people whose jobs are sufficiently similar in content for comparisons to be logical. This will either be by unilateral management decision, by following agreed procedures probably involving members of the group whose jobs are being compared, or by agreement between one set of negotiators representing management interests and one representing employee interests – the simple model of the bargaining relationship. If the management of an organisation negotiates with one bargaining agent on behalf of, for instance, manual employees who are skilled, semi-skilled and unskilled, then any disagreement about different levels of pay between the different categories of employee are for those two parties to resolve. The resolution is normally within their competence, unless the negotiators are so unresponsive to the feelings of their members that one category of employees withdraws its support and seeks separate representation.

Internal relativities

A more difficult type of pay relationship to control is that of internal relativity. Here the employer is constant, but the employees are represented by different agents as a result of being in different bargaining units. The most common internal relativity problem is between manual and non-manual employees, where one union or group of unions represents the manual employees and another represents the non-manuals, although bargaining may be much more fragmented in many organisations – the problem of multi-unionism. Although more difficult to control than differentials, there is at least one common factor, the employer.

External relativities

Employees do not, however, restrict themselves to making comparisons between their own pay and that of others within their organisations, even though this may be the most cogent comparison. They will compare themselves with those in other companies, industries and services. Occasionally there will be a common element in the union, which negotiates better terms with one employer than another for groups of employees who see themselves as being similar.

More often the comparison is with completely different groups of employees. The long-running industrial dispute involving ambulance crews at the end of 1989 centred on the question of external relativity between them and members of the police and fire services.

The difficulty is shown most sharply in public sector bargaining, where there are large numbers of employees doing apparently similar work with pay scales that are broadly the same in all parts of the country. Every recipient of the pay is likely to make comparisons with friends and neighbours who are better off, or who seem to be better off. Public sector employees are extensively unionised and union research departments prepare detailed analyses of comparative pay rates, again picking those comparators that produce comparisons most favourable to their own cause. Any pay claim always has some comparator, as this is what gives it credibility.

A potential problem of external relativity is in the employment of peripheral employees by contractors of consultants, who may be working alongside permanent staff enjoying less attractive (or apparently less attractive) terms and conditions.

External identification

In one specialised category the employee identifies with an external employee grouping for purposes of determining the appropriate pay level. These people are usually taken out of intra-organisational bargaining. The obvious examples are company doctors and nurses, where the appropriate rates of pay are determined by bodies external to the company which proceeds to pay on that basis, unless there is some wish to pay above that rate. Other examples would be such professional groups as solicitors, surveyors and architects, and there will be many others where the number of employees will be so small as well as specialised that some external reference is the most appropriate way of determining the rate. The company employing one or two chemists or actuaries or other specialists would probably accept scales of pay published by the appropriate professional body rather than try to produce a pay structure that accommodated a range of specialists all identifying with an external professional grouping.

> REVIEW TOPIC 33.1
>
> Taking your own job, score from 0 to 5 the relative importance to you of the four types of pay relationship described in the 'Relativities and Differentials' section of this chapter (0 = no importance, 5 = very important). Now do the same exercise with three or four other jobs and job-holders that you know, such as members of your own family. How do you explain any differences?

Limitations on management action

If managers can accept and understand the range of limitations upon their actions in connection with pay comparisons, they can begin to develop a strategy to deal with them. There are five major constraints upon management action.

The product market

The influence of the product market varies according to how important labour costs are in deciding product cost, and in how important product cost is to the customer. In a labour-intensive and low-technology industry such as catering, there will usually be such pressure on labour costs that the pay administrator has little freedom to manipulate pay relationships. In an area such as magazine printing, the need of the publisher to get the product out on time is so great that labour costs, however high, may be of relatively little concern. In this situation the pay negotiators have much more freedom to deal at least with differentials.

In their analysis of the footwear industry, Goodman and his colleagues (1977) found that a major reason why the industry was characterised by peace rather than conflict was the need for employer collaboration on labour matters because of the intensive competition in the product market.

The labour market

We have suggested that external relativity is the most intractable type of pay relationship for personnel specialists because it is so completely beyond their control. It may not be beyond their understanding, and understanding could offer the opportunity at least to pre-empt some problems so as to deal with them before or when they arise rather than being taken by surprise. Accountants and craftworkers, for instance, come very close in our categorisation to those who identify with an external employee grouping, as their assessment of their pay level will be greatly influenced by the 'going rate' in the trade or the district. A similar situation exists with jobs that are clearly understood and where skills are readily transferable, particularly if the employee is to work with a standard piece of equipment. Driving heavy goods vehicles is an obvious example, as the vehicles are common from one employer to another, the roads are the same, and only the loads vary. Other examples are typists, telephone operators, card punchers and computer operators. Jobs that are less sensitive to the labour market are those that are organisationally specific, like most semi-skilled work in manufacturing, general clerical work and nearly all middle-management positions.

Collective bargaining

Perhaps the most obvious constraint for management is the operation of collective bargaining. Employees do not join trade unions in order to comply with managerial wishes, but to question them, and the differential structure that fits in with management requirement will not necessarily fit in with employee expectations. The study by Metcalf (1977) tries to assess the effect of unionisation on relative wages and concludes that it is significant, even if less dramatic than some have argued previously.

Although the influence of trade unions on pay determination has lessened, the extension of collective bargaining to white-collar and managerial groups has reduced the scope for unilateral decisions about differential structures. One of the influences of collective bargaining is in the use of internal relativities as the basis for negotiations. The members of a low-pay group will narrow the gap between themselves and those in a high-pay group; whereupon the higher-paid will seek to widen the gap again by 'restoring the differential'. Before long there will follow more arguments from the lower-paid that the gap has widened – and should be narrowed.

Technology

Technology has an effect on most things, and pay is no exception. As technology changes so there will arise the need for new skills in the organisation and people who are recruited possessing those skills will tend to import a pay level with them. The external identification principle may justify special treatment for one or two such employees, but once the numbers begin to increase, then they must be assimilated into the pay structure, almost certainly upsetting it in the process.

Internal labour market

Just as there is a labour market of which the company is a part, so there is a labour market within the organisation. This is mainly in the constraining influence of custom and practice, so that any substantive and permanent change in the internal relativities needs considerable justification. One pair of commentators, Doeringer and Piore (1971), have classified different types of internal labour market. First is the enterprise market, so-called because the enterprise or organisation defines the boundaries of the market itself. Such will be the situation of manual workers engaged in production processes, for whom the predominant pattern of employment is one in which jobs are formally or informally ranked, with those jobs of the highest pay or prestige usually being filled by promotion from within and those at the bottom of the hierarchy usually being filled only from outside the enterprise. It is, therefore, those at the bottom that are most sensitive to the external labour market. Doeringer and Piore point out that there is a close parallel with managerial jobs, the main ports of entry being from management trainees or supervisors in the organisation, and the number of appointments from outside gradually reducing as jobs become more senior. This *modus operandi* is one of the main causes of the problems that redundant executives face. The second type of market is the craft, where there are rigid rules of entry usually a combination of time-served apprenticeship plus an appropriate union card – but the allocation of jobs to people tends to be much more flexible, emphasising equality of employment experience among the workforce rather than the considerations of seniority and ability which are predominant in enterprise markets.

The situation in internal labour markets may be the most important in attitude formulation on pay relationships:

> Feelings of being inadequately paid usually arise as a result of highly localized anomalies. The macro-system of pay differentials, the argument runs, is generally accepted as just. Therefore, in evaluating their own pay, individuals make the critical comparisons not with levels of earnings throughout society as a whole, but with more restricted 'reference groups'. Individuals compare their earnings against those of people in the same or broadly similar occupations. (Roberts *et al.* 1975, p. 31)

The authors of the article from which this extract is taken go on to question this assumption, on the basis that people are generally ill-informed on what relative pay levels are, but concede that the view expressed represents 'conventional wisdom'. Coates and Silburn (1970) have demonstrated that even the poorest are able to feel satisfaction with their lot if they select appropriate comparators. An opinion, advanced with little supporting argument, suggests that the internal labour market may be the most important influence on attitudes about pay relationships:

> It seems to us at least arguable that most people are little interested in whether other people are better off, or whether they have become better off than others, provided they themselves are treated fairly in relation to most of those with whom they work. No grand design here. (IDS 1977, p. 17)

Management policy decisions and pay relationships

Although there are limitations to managerial freedom of action on pay relationships, there is still a need for managerial initiative in policies to influence differentials and relativities. These are mostly to do with employee groupings or deciding on job families.

The job family is a collection of jobs which have sufficient common features for them to be considered together when differential gaps are being set. What are the management decisions to be made?

Why not one big (happy) family?

The first question is whether there should be sub-groupings within the organisation at all, or whether all employees should be paid in accordance with one overall salary structure. Internal relativities disappear; there is only a differential structure. This arrangement has many attractions, as it emphasises the integration of all employees and may encourage them to identify with the organisation as a whole, it is administratively simple and can stimulate competition for personal advancement. It also allows more flexibility in the pay that is arranged for any individual. Interest in the development of single pay structures has increased in recent years for a number of reasons. It has accompanied a more general interest among employers in taking a company-wide approach to a whole range of personnel initiatives. New technologies often demand a more flexible workforce leading to a blurring of the organisational distinction between groups of workers. Harmonisation of the terms and conditions of employment follows so that all employees work the same number of hours, are given the same training opportunities and enjoy the same entitlement to occupational pensions, sick pay and annual leave. Such practices have also been conspicuously imported into British subsidiaries of Japanese and American companies who typically have longer experience of single-status employment practices.

Interest has also arisen following recent legal judgements in which courts have awarded equal pay to employees who have sought to compare their jobs with those of other individuals in wholly different job families. As a result employers who continue to operate different mechanisms for determining the pay of different groups of employees have had difficulty in defending their practices when faced with equal value claims.

A number of pay-structuring schemes built on the principle of a single pay spine have been developed. Both Paterson (1972) and Jaques (1961) used a single-factor scheme of job evaluation to determine the differentials. Paterson's decision-band method evaluated all jobs in terms of the decisions taken by the employee while Jaques's single factor is the timespan of the discretion that the employee is expected to exercise. Other organisations have developed single pay spines using the computer-assisted multifactor job evaluation schemes which are now available. Useful case histories of the introduction of such schemes have been produced by ACAS (1983) and IDS (1992).

In practice, however, it is very difficult to develop a single pay structure which is acceptable to all parties. The 1993 IRS survey into job evaluation practices found that while over half the organisations in their sample used job evaluation for all their employees only a quarter had a single scheme which applied to the whole workforce. The more diverse the skills, values and union affiliation of the employees, the more difficult is such a single job family. The problems are well illustrated in the National Health Service where there is a diversity of skills that can probably not be matched in any other area of occupational life. While several NHS Trusts have sought to develop single pay structures, to date very few have managed to implement their schemes because they are unable to overcome the difficulty of encompassing doctors, nurses, paramedical cadres, ancillary staff, administrators and technicians in a single scheme. The factors used to compare job with job always tend to favour one grouping at the expense of another; one job at the expense of another. The wider the diversity of jobs that are brought within the purview of a single scheme, the wider will be the potential dissatisfaction, with the result that the payment arrangement is one that at best is tolerated because it is the least offensive rather than being accepted as satisfactory.

The limitations of the single-factor evaluation scheme have been pungently criticised by Fox (1972) on the grounds that it discriminates in favour of those in posts that are traditionally better paid anyway and therefore inhibits change of pay differentials towards a more broadly accepted structure. Other difficulties about a single, integrated system of payment are those of responding to the external labour market and the impact of collective bargaining. If the only variables to control were within the organisation, it would be easier to sustain than in a situation where sectional interests are actively seeking to alter the structure specifically in their favour.

It is also invariably the case that any move towards a single pay structure is costly to the organisation. Whichever job evaluation scheme is used to develop the new pay spine there will always be winners and losers among existing employees as some will now be more highly ranked than others. While those who have hitherto been underpaid can be given pay increases it is not possible to reduce the salaries of those who are overpaid without breaching the contract of employment. This problem is associated with all job evaluation exercises but is especially acute where moves towards a single pay spine are being made.

It is difficult to predict how many organisations will ultimately manage to overcome these problems and develop single pay structures. Spencer (1990a) reports that 35 per cent of new job evaluation schemes cover all the employees in the organisation. IRS (1993), however, found that over the previous five years more employers in their sample had moved away from the single-scheme approach than had adopted it.

REVIEW TOPIC 33.2

In what type of situations do you think a single, integrated job evaluated pay structure would be appropriate? Where would such a pay structure be inappropriate? What are the most likely management problems in each case?

Bargaining units

In our chapter on trade union recognition there was mention of the need to decide the boundaries of bargaining units. A job family and a bargaining unit will normally coincide, as the matter principally being discussed – pay – is common to both concepts. However, job families are created to deal with differential gaps rather than internal relativities even though they influence the internal relativity structure, and it is quite feasible to have bargaining units with more than one job family within them. A company might, for instance, negotiate with a trade union to determine a single salary scale for clerical, computer and administrative staff and then evaluate jobs in two separate families in the bargaining unit to determine the place within the scale for the different jobs. This procedure would be justified by the argument that the skills and requirements of computing staff are specialised, so that differentials are appropriately decided only by comparison with other computing jobs, while the relative position of computing staff is settled by collective bargaining.

In taking this course of action, however, a company would be in danger of losing an equal pay case brought by a clerical officer claiming that her work was of equal value to that of a computer operator. This has been the position since October 1993 when the European Court ruled in the Case of *Enderby* v. *Frenchay Health Authority* that employers could not rely for defence on the operation of separate bargaining arrangements for different groups of staff.

The family structure

Another decision to be made is whether there will be any degree of overlap on the pay scales that relate to each family. There is no right answer to this question although some overlap is usual, as suggested in the last chapter. No overlap at all (a rare arrangement) emphasises the hierarchy, encouraging employees to put their feet on the salary ladder and climb, but the clarity of internal relativities may increase the dissatisfaction of those on the lower rungs and put pressure on the pay system to accommodate the occasional anomaly, especially if climbing is not well supported. Overlapping grades blur the edges of relativities and can reduce dissatisfaction at the bottom, but introduce dissatisfaction higher up.

Another reason why pay scales for different job families usually overlap is to accommodate scales of different length. A family with a flat hierarchy will tend to have a small number of scales with many steps, while the steep hierarchy will tend to have more scales, but each with fewer steps. One of the main drawbacks of overlapping scales is the problem of migration, where an employee regards the job as technical at one time and makes a case for it to be reclassified as administrative at another time, because there is no further scope for progress in the first classification.

Another aspect of migration is the more substantive case of employees seeking transfer to other jobs as a result of changes in the relative pay scales, which reduce rigidity in the internal labour market.

Are executives a special case?

It is usual for executive pay to be discussed and administered differently from the pay of other employees. This is largely because traditional theoretical formulations of economists have no place for executives, who are neither wage-earners in the normal sense nor owners, yet they are both earners and acting on behalf of the owner(s).

A further reason for regarding executives as a special case is the result of a number of investigations that have demonstrated a relationship between executive pay and organisational features such as sales turnover and number of employees. An admirable summary is to be found in Husband (1976) of work by analysts who argue that there is a typical relationship between the number of earners and the number of salaries at different levels.

In recent years the moves towards performance-related pay have been much greater for executives than for other categories of employee and they are rarely included in job evaluation.

Job evaluation methods

Job evaluation is the most common method used to compare the relative values of different jobs in order to provide the basis for a rational pay structure. Among the many definitions is this one from ACAS:

> Job evaluation is concerned with assessing the relative demands of different jobs within an organization. Its usual purpose is to provide a basis for relating differences in rates of pay to different in-job requirements. It is therefore a tool which can be used to help in the determination of a pay structure. (ACAS 1984)

It is a well-established technique, having been developed in all its most common forms by the 1920s. In recent years it has received a series of boosts. First, various types of incomes policy between 1965 and 1974 either encouraged the introduction of job evaluation or specifically permitted expenditure above the prevailing norm by companies wishing to introduce it. More recently the use of job evaluation is the hinge of most equal pay cases. Despite its popularity it is often misunderstood, so the following points have to be made.

1. Job evaluation is concerned with the job and not the performance of the individual job holder. Individual merit is not assessed.
2. The technique is systematic rather than scientific. It depends on the judgement of people with experience, requiring them to decide in a planned and systematic way, but it does not produce results that are infallible.
3. Job evaluation does not eliminate collective bargaining. It determines the differential gaps between incomes; it does not determine pay level.
4. Only a structure of pay rates is produced. Other elements of earnings, such as premia and incentives, are not determined by the method.

There are many methods of job evaluation in use and they are summarised in Smith (1983, pp. 68–106) and in Armstrong and Murlis (1994, pp. 99–110). Where a non-analytical or 'whole job' scheme is used a panel of assessors examines each job as a whole, in terms of its difficulty or value to the organisation, to determine which should be ranked more highly than others. No attempt is made to break each job down into its constituent parts. By contrast, an analytical scheme requires each element or factor of the job to be assessed. Since 1988 it has been the practice of courts only to accept the results of analytical schemes in equal pay cases.

We have already seen the problems connected with those analytical schemes which are built around an analysis of single factors, like those of Jaques and Paterson. The reliability of the outcome can be improved using multifactor schemes but they have the disadvantage of being harder to understand and appear to depend on mechanical decision making rather than on human judgement. This may produce 'better' decisions which are less acceptable.

The most widely used analytical schemes are based on points-rating systems, under which each job is examined in terms of factors such as skill, effort and responsibility. Each factor is given a weighting indicating its value relative to the others and for each factor there are varying degrees. A score is then given depending on how demanding the job is in terms of each factor, with the overall points-value determining the relative worth of each job. Traditionally the analysis has been carried out by a panel of managers and workforce representatives who examine each job description in turn and compare it, factor by factor, with degree definitions. In recent years there has been increased interest in computer-assisted job evaluation systems which award scores to each job on the basis of information gathered from job analysis questionnaires. These developments are described by Murlis and Pritchard (1991) and by Spencer (1990b).

The best-known set of factors, weightings and degrees is that devised for the National Electrical Manufacturers Association of the United States, but the International Labour Organisation has produced a list of the factors used most frequently:

Accountability	Mental fatigue
Accuracy	Physical demands
Analysis and judgement	Physical skills
Complexity	Planning and co-ordination
Contact and diplomacy	Problem-solving
Creativity	Resources control
Decision-making	Responsibility for cash/materials/confidential
Dexterity	information/equipment or process/records
Education	and reports
Effect of errors	Social skills
Effort	Supervision given/received
Initiative	Task completion
Judgement	Training and experience
Know-how	Work conditions
Knowledge and skills	Work pressure
Mental effort	

The points values eventually derived for each job can be plotted on a graph or simply listed from the highest to the lowest to indicate the ranking. Then – and only then – are points ratings matched with cash amounts, as decisions are made on which points ranges equate with various pay levels.

It is virtually inevitable that some jobs will be found to be paid incorrectly after job evaluation has been completed. If the evaluation says that the pay rate should be higher, then the rate duly rises, either immediately or step by step, to the new level. The only problem is finding the money and introducing job evaluation always costs money. More difficult is the situation where evaluation shows the employees to be overpaid. It is not feasible to reduce the pay of the job holder without breaching the contract of employment. There have been two approaches. The first, which was never widespread and appears almost to have disappeared, is buying out. The overpaid employee is offered a large lump sum in consideration of the fact of henceforth being paid at the new, lower rate. The second and more general device used is that of the personal rate or red circling. This is where the rate for the job would be circled in red on the salary administrator's records to show that the employee should continue at the present level while remaining in that post, but a successor would be paid at the lower job-evaluated rate.

The most widely used proprietary scheme is the Hay Guide Chart-Profile Method. IRS (1993) surveyed the use of job evaluation in 120 organisations and found that 77 employed the Hay method for some or all the jobs covered. It is used particularly widely in the evaluation of management jobs. The method is based on an assessment of four factors; expertise, problem-solving, accountability and working conditions. Jobs are assessed by using each of three guide charts, one for each factor. A profile is then developed for the job showing the relationship between the factors, a ranking is eventually produced and the rates of the jobs considered in order to produce a new pay structure. At this stage comes one of the greatest advantages of this system. The proprietors have available a vast amount of comparative pay data on different organizations using their system, so their clients cannot only compare rates of pay within the organisation (differentials and internal relativities); they can also examine their external relativities. The method of operating this system and several other consultants' methods is described by Armstrong and Murlis (1994, pp. 508–31).

Employee participation in job evaluation

The degree of participation by non-managerial employees in job evaluation varies from one organisation to another. In some cases the entire operation is conducted from start to finish without any employee participation at all. Some degree of participation is more common. Apart from negotiating on pay levels and bargaining units, the main opportunities for employee contribution are as follows:

Job families
Employees collectively need to consent to the family structure and they can probably add to the deliberations of managers about what that structure should be, as they will be well aware of the sensitive points of comparison.

Job descriptions
Traditionally job descriptions have been crucial to the evaluation and it is common for job-holders to prepare their own, using a pro-forma outline, or for supervisors

to prepare them for jobs for which they are responsible. Spencer (1990b) reports 88 per cent of his respondents answering that job descriptions were prepared by involving job-holders and 94 per cent involved supervisors. Superficially, this is an attractive method, as there is direct involvement of the employee, who cannot claim to have been misrepresented. Also, it delegates the task of writing job descriptions, enabling it to be completed more quickly. The drawback is similar to that of character references in selection. Some employees write good descriptions and some write bad ones: some overstate while others understate. Inconsistency in job descriptions makes consistency in evaluation difficult.

An alternative is for job descriptions to be compiled by job analysis after questioning employees and their supervisors, who subsequently initial the job description which the analyst produces, attesting to its accuracy.

Panel evaluation

The awarding of points is usually done by a panel of people who represent between them the interests and expertise of management and employee. This is not only being 'democratic', it is acknowledging the need for the experience and perspective of job holders as well as managers in arriving at shrewd judgements of relative worth. Naturally, panel memberships alter so that employees are not asked to evaluate their own jobs. Although there is an understandable general tendency for employee representatives to push ratings up, and for management representatives to try to push them down, this usually smooths out because both parties are deriving differential rankings and not pay levels. The only potential conflict of interest will be if employee representatives and managers have divergent objectives on the shape of the eventual pay structure, with big or small differential gaps.

Job analysis questionnaires

Proprietary, computer-assisted job evaluation methods involve trained analysts putting a series of detailed questions to job holders from a multiple-choice questionnaire. The results are then fed into a computer which generates a score for each job. There is therefore no need for a panel to reach decisions based on written job descriptions. While there is clearly direct employee involvement in providing answers to the Job Analysis Questionnaire, the absence of a panel including workforce representatives can reduce the level of employee influence on the outcome of the exercise. This is particularly the case with those proprietary schemes which are customised to meet the needs of the purchasing organisation.

Equal value

The Equal Pay Act 1970 established that a woman could bring a case to an industrial tribunal claiming entitlement to equal pay with a man working at the same establishment if the claimant and her chosen comparator were engaged in 'like work' or work rated as equivalent under an employer's job evaluation study. A man can equally bring a case comparing his pay to that of a female colleague but this has very rarely occurred in practice. An amendment to the Act, which came into effect in 1984, broadened the definition of 'equal value' so that it became possible for a case to be brought if the claimant believes that her work is equal to that of her comparator in terms of the demands made upon them. This amendment followed a European Court ruling which judged the existing Equal Pay Act to fall short of the standard established by the EEC Equal Pay Directive. Since then other European Court rulings have further extended the scope of equal value law.

Like work

When presented with a claim for equal pay an industrial tribunal will first seek to establish whether the claimant is engaged in 'like work' with the more highly paid man she has named as her comparator. The work does not have to be identical to justify equal pay under this heading, but must either be the same or of a broadly similar nature. In practice this means that the difference in pay can only be justified if there is 'a difference of practical importance' in the work done or if there is 'a genuine material factor' which justifies the higher rate of pay enjoyed by the male comparator.

An example of a difference of practical importance might be the level of responsibility of the man's job when compared to that of the claimant. An employer might, for example, be justified in paying a man more than his female colleague working on a comparable production line if the articles being manufactured by the man were of substantially greater value. Similarly a discriminatory payment could be justified if a man worked under less supervision than a woman engaged in otherwise like work. A common example would be a man working without supervision on night shifts.

Where there is no practical difference of this kind a discriminatory payment can only be justified where there is a 'genuine material factor other than sex' which can explain the difference in pay levels.

Work rated as equivalent

Cases brought under this section of the Act relate to jobs which are different in nature have been rated as equivalent under the employer's job evaluation study. The existence of such a study can also provide the basis of an employer's defence in equal value claims.

A definition of a job evaluation scheme is included in the Act:

> A woman is to be regarded as employed on work rated as equivalent with that of any man if her job and his have been given an equal value, in terms of the demand made on a worker under various headings (for instance, effort, skill, decision), on a study undertaken with a view to evaluating in these terms the jobs done by all or any of the employees in an undertaking. (Equal Pay Act, sect. 15)

Recent case law has further narrowed the definition of acceptable job evaluation schemes. In the case of *Bromley* v. *H&J Quick* (1988) the Court of Appeal ruled that the identification of benchmark jobs and paired comparisons, was 'insufficiently analytical' as this did not involve evaluation under headings as required by the Act. The widely used method of job evaluation whereby only a sample of benchmark jobs are analysed can not, therefore, be relied upon as a basis for an employer's defence. The jobs of the applicants and their chosen comparators must each have been evaluated analytically. In addition a tribunal will look at the means by which scores derived from a job evaluation scheme are used to determine the rate of pay and will take account of a job evaluation study which has been completed but not implemented.

To be acceptable to a tribunal the job evaluation scheme in use must also be free of sex bias. Employers should ensure, therefore, that the factor weightings do not indirectly discriminate by over-emphasising job requirements associated with typical male jobs, like physical effort, at the expense of those associated with jobs predominantly undertaken by women such as manual dexterity or attention to detail.

Work of equal value

A woman who is not engaged in like work, work of a broadly similar nature, or work rated as equivalent is still entitled to bring an equal pay claim if she believes her work to be of equal value. In these cases the claimant names as her chosen comparator a man employed by the same undertaking who may be engaged in work of a wholly different nature. If the tribunal decides that there are grounds to believe that the work is of equal value it will then appoint an independent expert, nominated by ACAS, to carry out a job evaluation study. The report of the independent expert will then be used by the tribunal as a basis of the decision on whether or not to make an award of equal pay to the claimant. A woman may bring an equal value claim in this way even if she has male colleagues engaged in like work and paid at the same rate as her.

A number of significant equal value cases have been brought to tribunals in recent years. In *Hayward* v. *Cammell Laird* (1984) a cook was awarded pay equal to that of men employed as joiners and laggers, but only after an appeal to the House of Lords three years after making the initial complaint. In 1990 the shopworker's union USDAW dropped an equal value case against Sainsbury's when the employer agreed to carry out a job evaluation exercise. The union had claimed that predominantly female check-out operators were engaged in work of equal value to that of predominantly male warehousemen. This led to an 11 per cent rise in Sainsbury's retail wage bill and to a series of similar USDAW settlements with other major retailers during 1990 and 1991.

The Danfoss case

A significant recent development arose in a case brought to the European Court in 1989 with the title *Handels-OG Kontorfunktionaererenes Forbund i Danmark* v. *Dansk Arbejdsgiverforening* (acting for Danfoss), usually referred to as the Danfoss Case. The European Court's judgement greatly extended the basis on which equal value claims can be brought to challenge pay structures by accepting a case built on the assertion that *on average* in the same employment group men were paid more than women. It went on to rule that where this was the case it was for the employer to show that the pay scheme in operation was free from gender bias.

Genuine material factor defences

If it is established, to the satisfaction of an industrial tribunal, that the claimant is engaged in like work, work rated as equivalent, or work of equal value the employer must show that the difference in the respective rates of pay is not due to sex discrimination but to a 'genuine material factor not of sex'.

There are many defences which potentially fall into this category. Among the most significant is the practice of red-circling, whereby an individual's rate of pay is protected for a period following redeployment or a new job evaluation exercise. In most cases, provided it can be clearly shown that the red circle was awarded for reasons other than the individual's sex, this will be an acceptable material factor defence.

Less reliable defences are those based on arguments concerning labour market conditions. A common example would be the situation in which a man is offered a job on a higher rate than an equally well-qualified woman, who is already in a similar post, on the grounds that he asked for a higher salary as his condition for accepting the job. In 1993 the European Court has ruled in the case of *Enderby* v. *Frenchay Health Authority* that a difference in the collective bargaining arrangements under which the pay rates for jobs of equal value are determined is not a sufficient objective justification.

☐ SUMMARY PROPOSITIONS

33.1 The personnel manager needs to understand four types of pay comparison: differentials, internal relativities, external relativities and external identification.

33.2 Management freedom of action in deciding relative pay rates is constrained by the product market, the labour market, collective bargaining, technology and the internal labour market.

33.3 Management policy decisions about organising pay relationships relate mainly to job families, bargaining units, the structure of job families and deciding whether or not executives are a special case.

33.4 Job evaluation schemes are either based on whole job comparisons (non-analytical) or on an assessment of the value of each factor which makes up the job (analytical). The most widely used proprietary scheme is Hay Guide Chart profile method.

33.5 Employees participate in the job evaluation process at any or all of the following stages: job families, job descriptions, evaluation.

33.6 Under the amended Equal Pay Act, women may claim equal pay with that of a man if the work is the same, is broadly similar, has been rated as equal in a job evaluation scheme, or is of equal value in terms of the demands made on them.

References

ACAS (1983), *Integrated Job Evaluation at Continental Can*, London: Advisory Conciliation and Arbitration Services. (This was earlier produced as no. 291 of *Industrial Relations Review and Report*, March 1983.)

ACAS (1984), *Job Evaluation*, London: Advisory, Conciliation and Arbitration Services.

Armstrong, M. and Murlis, H. (1994), *Reward Management: A Handbook of Salary Administration*, London: Kogan Page.

Armstrong, M. and Murlis, H. (1994), *Reward Management*, (3rd edn), London: Kogan Page.

Bromely, V. H. and Quick, J. (1988), IRLR 249.

Coates, K. and Silburn, R. (1970), *Poverty: The Forgotten Englishman*, Harmondsworth: Penguin Books.

Doeringer, P. B. and Piore, M. J. (1971), *Internal Labor Markets and Manpower Analysis*, Lexington: Heath.

Enderby v. *Frenchay Health Authority* [1991] IRLR 44.

Equal Opportunities Commission (1982), *Job Evaluation Schemes Free of Sex Bias*, Manchester: Equal Opportunities Commission.

Fowler, A. (1992), 'How to Choose a Job Evaluation System', *Personnel Management Plus*, October.

Fox, A. (1972), 'Time span of discretion theory: an appraisal'. In T. Lupton, (ed.) *Payment Systems*, Harmondsworth: Penguin Books.

Goodman, J. F. B., Armstrong, E. G. A., Wagner, A. and Davies, J. E. (1977), *Rule-making and Industrial Peace*, Beckenham: Croom Helm.

Hayward v. *Cammell Laird Shipbuilders Ltd* [1984] TLR 52.

Husband, T. M. (1976), *Work Analysis and Pay Structure*, Maidenhead: McGraw-Hill.

Incomes Data Services (IDS) Focus (1977), *The Pay Merry-go-round*, London: Incomes Data Services Ltd.

Incomes Data Services (IDS) Study (1992), *Integrated Pay Structures*, London: Incomes Data Services Ltd.

Industrial Relations Review and Reports (IRS) (1993), 'Job Evaluation in the 1990s', *Industrial Relations Review and Reports*, October.

Jaques, E. (1961), *Equitable Payment*, London: Heinemann.

Metcalf, D. (1977), 'Unions, incomes policy and relative wages in Britain', *British Journal of Industrial Relations*, July, pp. 157–75.

Murlis, H. and Pritchard, D. (1991), 'The Computerised Way to Evaluate Jobs', *Personnel Management*, April.

Paterson, T. T. (1972), *Job Evaluation*, London: Business Books. (This method has now been adopted and developed by the consultants Arthur Young as their own proprietary method.)

Roberts, K., Clark, S. C., Cook, F. G. and Semeonoff, E. (1975), 'Unfair or unfounded pay differentials and incomes policy', *Personnel Management*, August, pp. 29–37.

Smith, I. (1983), *The Management of Remuneration: Paying for Effectiveness*, London: Institute of Personnel Management.

Spencer, S. (1990a), 'Devolving job evaluation', *Personnel Management*, vol. 22, no. 1, pp. 38–42.

Spencer, S. (1990b), 'Job evaluation; a modern day genie for management information?', *Employment Gazette*, May.

34 Incentives, performance pay and fringe benefits

Incentive payments remain one of the ideas that fascinate managers as they search for the magic formula. Somewhere there is a method of linking payment to performance so effectively that their movements will coincide, enabling the manager to leave the workers on automatic pilot, as it were, while attending to more important matters such as strategic planning or going to lunch. This conviction has sustained a continuing search for this elusive formula, which has been hunted with all the fervour of those trying to find the Holy Grail or the crock of gold at the end of the rainbow.

Performance-related pay is the topical version of this idea, with a significant change of emphasis. Incentives are to stimulate performance, while performance pay is to reward it; incentives are for the rank and file, while performance payments were introduced for the managerial elite (although their application has extended). Incentive thinking is preoccupied with the problem of control and avoiding costs getting out of hand, because 'they' will take the management to the cleaners if they are given half a chance. Performance pay thinking is dominated by the need to reward the deserving so that they too can share in the prosperity of the business at the same time as creating it.

Incentives and performance pay are part of a complex arrangement to express and to maintain the working relationship between the employer and the employee. They demonstrate not only what the management is trying to achieve, but also what the managers believe about the relationship. Elaborate incentive systems frequently represent a working relationship in which manager and worker are far apart with considerable mutual mistrust and little common interest. Elaborate systems of fringe benefit often represent a situation in which management is attempting to emphasise the degree of common interest, although they do not always succeed in overcoming mistrust. Schemes of performance pay typically carry the implicit view that those who may receive the payments are loyal, keen and hard-working: the possibility of the scheme being manipulated to achieve levels of payment which are not justified is never mentioned.

The key ideas in understanding the history of incentives are manipulation and luck. Those receiving incentive payment have had a clear, unshakeable conviction that the scheme was a managerial manipulative device to do the worker down.

Those administering payment schemes have developed an equally clear conviction that workers have manipulated payment schemes to frustrate managerial objectives for efficiency and increased productivity in order to optimise employee earnings 'unfairly'. The idea of luck has been used both to explain and to rationalise variations in incentive payment by attributing the variation not to effort but to events not directly under the employee's control, like the level of orders, the share-out of the jobs that can produce high levels of earnings and those that do not, availability of materials, administrative delays, and so on.

Despite the disenchantment, incentive schemes persist, with around one-third of male manual employees and more than 15 per cent of non-manual males receiving incentive payments in 1993. The proportion of earnings that were incentives was usually between 15 and 25 per cent. The proportion of female employees receiving incentive payments is lower, although the proportion of earnings that are accounted for by incentives is often higher. The reasons why they persist include some of the reasons why they have lost favour, such as the way in which managements frequently avoid a problem by buying a way past it through juggling with the incentive arrangement. If there were not an incentive pay scheme in existence it could not be used for that sort of short-circuiting operation. Other reasons are their use to overcome resistance to change, the attractiveness sometimes to employees who feel they are gaining an element of control over their own workplace, the possible help from a supervisory point of view and probably more important than any of these, a deep-seated conviction in the minds of many managers that incentive schemes ought to work as they seem basically sensible.

Managerial expectations of incentive schemes

There is no single managerial view and there is no standard working situation in which managers have to organise payment arrangements. The need for managers to adopt varying opinions is set out by Lupton and Bowey:

> In order to be sure of the outcome of a scheme the manager needs to consider the particular circumstances of his firm. From a contingency perspective we are now able to understand the apparently conflicting prescriptions of people like R.M. Currie who advocated incentive-bonus schemes of various kinds, and Wilfred Brown who recommended that piecework be abandoned. They had each been observing situations in

Table 34.1 *Percentage of workers receiving incentive payments*

	1989	1991	1993
Male manual workers	40.0	35.5	30.9
Male non-manual workers	16.9	16.0	15.6
Female manual workers	31.2	26.2	24.1
Female non-manual workers	12.6	12.0	11.9

Source: *New Earnings Survey* (1989, 1991, 1993).

which the particular system they were proposing had been successful, but were not aware that there was something peculiar about those circumstances which contributed to the success of the scheme. (Lupton and Bowey 1975, p. 79)

Motivational theories

The opinion of managers will first be influenced by the personal theory of motivation they hold. McGregory's Theory X (McGregor 1970), for instance, describes the average human being as having an inherent dislike of work, which will be avoided if at all possible. The manager agreeing with that point of view may well regard incentive schemes as necessary to control workers who will otherwise tend to idle. McGregory's Theory Y, on the other hand, describes the average human being as able to exercise self-control in the pursuit of objectives and to accept responsibility, finding physical and mental effort as natural as play or rest. The manager subscribing to that point of view will be less likely to look for incentives for control and more concerned with clarity, reasonableness and employee involvement. Some managers certainly hold a Theory X point of view about some of the people in the business and a Theory Y point of view about the others, leading to drastically different approaches to payment arrangements.

Control

Control thinking is expressed in the view that the output of individuals has to be measured for incentive payments to be made, and that these measurements provide a useful set of control information for the manager, either to see who is working hard and who is idling, or in order to build up data on how best to distribute tasks among a group of people so that they can all work optimally. This type of information can also demonstrate where there are weaknesses in departmental organisation, and provide some basis for controlling labour costs.

There is much managerial cynicism about control through piecework or Payment by Results schemes because employees, individually or collectively, set out to beat the system. A control system implies rules, and most human beings accept the validity of rules at the same time as they seek to test their flexibility. Especially if the incentive scheme is a management scheme with limited employee involvement in its creation and maintenance, the controlling rules will stimulate a competitive claim for control from employees seeking to optimise their benefits from the scheme rather than those of the management.

The practical logic of piecework is that people want money, and that they will work harder to get more of it. Incentive plans do not, however, take account of several other well-demonstrated characteristics of behaviour in the organisational setting:

Many job descriptions for supervisory positions include reference to responsibility for ensuring that the appropriate health and safety at work regulations are adhered to. Few supervisors, however, left to themselves would see this aspect of their work as a priority. In one organisation known to the authors it was decided to try to raise the profile of health and safety issues by including objectives in this field into managers' annual performance targets. It therefore became clear that the level of performance-related payments in the following year would, in part, be determined by the extent to which the health and safety objectives had been met.

The result was the swift establishment of departmental health and safety committees and schemes whereby staff could bring safety hazards to the attention of supervisors.

1. that most people also want the approval of their fellow workers and that, if necessary, they will forgo increased pay to obtain this approval;
2. that no managerial assurances can persuade workers that incentive rates will remain inviolate regardless of how much they produce; and
3. that the ingenuity of the average worker is sufficient to outwit any system of controls devised by management. (McGregor 1970, p. 71)

Performance-related payment schemes can also be seen as a means by which management control is enhanced. In setting objectives for the employee to achieve over a period of time the manager is identifying those aspects of the employee's job description which he or she judges to require particular emphasis. These work priorities can then be altered year by year as the needs of the organisation change.

Cost

Piecework arrangements are built on the principle that the cost of increasing output through incentive payments will decline with volume, so that the unit costs for each of 100 units of output will be less than the unit cost for each of 99 such units. There can be a situation in which this only appears to happen, as the scheme is manipulated to produce a rather different result. A remark attributed to a Midlands shop steward sums up the reason: 'When we get control of the piecework scheme, management lose control of their labour costs'. All but the most crude methods of payment-by results schemes incorporate an element to compensate employees for an inability to earn an incentive because of delays beyond their control, usually known as waiting time. Few schemes can get round the problem of employees assigning as much output as possible to the productive periods of the day at the same time as recording as much waiting time as possible. There are many other ways in which direct labour costs can increase as a result of incentive arrangements, not least of which is the bargaining of local representatives to increase the cash pay-off. Also the scheme may require high indirect labour costs in clerical and related staff to keep all the records that the scheme requires.

The potential for cost saving is rarely an aim of other forms of incentive pay such as those based on rewarding performance or the acquisition of skills. Such schemes can be expensive to administer and usually result in a general rise in the pay-bill when first introduced. Over the long term they may lead to an increase in productivity but it is extremely difficult to measure this potential effect to any degree of accuracy.

Employee expectations of incentive schemes

Just as there is no single set of managerial expectations, so there is no single set of employee expectations surrounding incentives. The contingency approach is as relevant for them as it is for managers.

Orientation to work

What employees expect from work will influence what they expect of the payment arrangements. If there is a strong instrumental orientation, then there will be a stronger interest in the financial arrangements, although the interest may lead to compliance with management objectives for the scheme or frustration of those objectives, according to whichever provides the best pay-off. Lawler examined a wide range of research studies before producing the conclusion:

> ...pay can be instrumental for the satisfaction of most needs but it is most likely to be seen as instrumental for satisfying esteem and physiological needs, secondarily to be seen as instrumental for satisfying autonomy or security needs and least likely for satisfying social or self-actual needs. (Lawler 1971, p. 121)

Autonomy

Incentive pay programmes can give employees scope for autonomy in providing a satisfactory basis on which to determine a rate and level of application to the job rather than having it determined by others and mediated via close supervision. It may sound contradictory in view of earlier remarks about management control to suggest here that it can be the employees who gain control of their work as well as of the payment scheme, but the reason is that the incentive scheme takes the form of objective setting. The responsibility for exactly when the work is done and how the individual work space is organised is partly transferred from the management to the employee, and supervision is more remote.

Interest

It is not always recognised that an incentive pay structure can be welcome as a source of interest in an otherwise monotonous occupation. Casual conversation with anyone holding a job with a strong element of routine shows how they tend to set up milestones to look forward to. The coffee break is not just a break and a chance to drink coffee; it is also a marker that the morning is half over. Others are such events as the arrival of the post, the bell sounding at the nearby school, the plane from New York flying overhead, the Pullman going past on the way to London, and many more. Financial incentives can build another marker element into the day's routine as people check how close they have come to the target for the day.

Payment by results schemes

Historically the most widely used incentive schemes have been those which reward employees according to the number of items or units of work they produce or the time they take to produce them. This approach is associated with F. W. Taylor and the phase in the development of personnel management described in Chapter 1 under the heading 'The Humane Bureaucrat'. Little attention has been paid to the operation of piecework schemes in recent years and there is clear evidence to show that they are in decline, both in terms of the proportion of total pay which is determined according to payment by results (PBR) principles and in terms of the number of employees paid in this way. The results of a survey carried out by the Institute of Personnel Management (IPM) and National Economic Development Office (NEDO) in 1991, however, show that PBR is still widely used, in some shape or form, by employers of manual workers. One in five of the organisations surveyed operated individual PBR schemes for manual grades and 23 per cent used group PBR, including over half the public sector organisations.

Individual time-saving

It is rare for a scheme to be based on the purest form of piecework, a payment of x pence per piece produced, as this provides no security against external influences which depress output such as machine failure or delays in the delivery of raw materials. The most common type of scheme in use, therefore, is one where the incentive is paid for time saved in performing a specified operation. A standard time is derived for a work sequence and the employee receives an additional payment for the time saved in completing a number of such operations. If it is not possible to work due to shortage of materials or some other reason, the time involved is not counted when the sums are done at the end of the day.

Standard times are derived by the twin techniques of method study and work measurement which are the skills of the work study engineer. By study of the operation, the work study engineer decides what is the most efficient way to carry it out and then times an operator actually doing the job over a period, so as to measure the 'standard time'. Work measured schemes of this kind have, however, been subject to a great deal of criticism and are only effective where people are employed on short-cycle manual operations with the volume of output varying between individuals depending on their skill or application.

The main difficulty, from the employee's point of view, is the fluctuation in earnings that occurs as a consequence of a varying level of demand for the product. If the fluctuations are considerable then the employees will be encouraged to try to stabilise them, either by pressing for the guaranteed element to be increased, or by storing output in the good times to prevent the worst effects of the bad, or by social control of high performing individuals to share out the benefits of the scheme as equally as possible.

Measured daywork

To some people the idea of measured daywork provides the answer to the shortcomings of individual incentive schemes. Instead of employees receiving a variable payment in accordance with the output achieved, they are paid a fixed sum as long as they maintain a predetermined and agreed level of working. Employees thus have far less discretion over the amount of effort they expend. Theoretically, this deals with the key problem of other schemes by providing for both stable earnings and stable output instead of 'as much as you can, if you can'.

The advantage of measured daywork over time-saving schemes, from the management point of view, is the greater level of management control that is exercised. The principal disadvantage is the tendency for the agreed level of working to become a readily achievable norm which can only be increased after negotiation with workforce representatives.

Group incentives

Sometimes the principles of individual time-saving are applied to group rather than individual output to improve group performance and to promote the development of team-working. Cannell and Long (1991) provide evidence to suggest that private sector organisations are increasingly replacing individual PBR schemes with group-based arrangements. Where jobs are interdependent, group incentives can be appropriate, but it may also put great pressure on the group members, aggravating any interpersonal animosity that exists and increasing the likelihood of stoppages for industrial action. Group schemes can also severely reduce the level of management control by allowing the production group to determine output according to the financial needs of individual group members.

Plant-wide schemes

A variant on the group incentive is the plant-wide bonus scheme, under which all employees in a plant or other organisation share in a pool bonus that is linked to the level of output, the value added by the employees collectively or some similar formula. The attraction of these methods lies in the fact that the benefit to the management of the organisation is 'real' because the measurement is made at the end of the system, compared with the measurements most usually made at different points within the system, whereby wages and labour costs can go up while output and profitability both come down. Theoretically, employees are also more likely to identify with the organisation as a whole, they will co-operate more readily with the management and each other, and there is even an element of workers' control.

The difficulties are that there is no tangible link between individual effort and individual reward, so that those who are working hard can have their efforts nullified by others working less hard or by misfortunes elsewhere.

REVIEW TOPIC 34.1

Where manual employees are employed on same form of payment by results, the New Earnings Survey shows that the percentage of average earnings made up by incentive payments is less than 20 per cent for men and more than 30 per cent for women. How would you explain this difference?

Commission

The payment of commission on sales is a widespread practice about which surprisingly little is known as these schemes have not come under the same close scrutiny that has been put on incentive schemes for manual employees. They suffer from most of the same drawbacks as manual incentives, except that they are linked to business won rather than to output achieved.

Tips

The practice of tipping is generally criticised as being undesirable for those receiving tips – it requires them to be deferential and obsequious – and for those giving them – because it is an unwarranted additional charge for a service they have already paid for. It is also often described as an employer device to avoid the need to pay realistic wages. Despite the criticism the practice persists, although it is of varying significance in different countries of the world.

The attraction of tipping is the feeling by employees that they can personally influence the level of their remuneration by the quality of service they give, and the feeling by the tipper of providing personal recognition for service received. This does not answer the criticism that tipping is usually for reasons of convention rather than direct acknowledgement of special service. From the employer's point of view the tipping convention can help ensure application to customers' wishes by employees, but can present problems in coping with known 'bad tippers'.

Disadvantages of PBR arrangements

According to the New Earnings Survey the proportion of manual workers receiving PBR payments has been in steady decline since 1983. This trend can be explained, in part, by changing technologies and working practices. A payment system which puts the greatest emphasis on the number of items produced or on the time taken to produce them is inappropriate in industries where product quality is of greater significance than product quantity. Similarly a manufacturing company operating a just-in-time system will rely too heavily on overall plant performance to benefit from a payment scheme which primarily rewards individual effort.

In addition to the problem of fluctuating earnings, described above, there are a number of further inherent disadvantages which explain the decline of PBR based remuneration arrangements.

Operational inefficiencies

For incentives to work to the mutual satisfaction of both parties, there has to be a smooth operational flow, with materials, job cards, equipment and storage space all readily available exactly when they are needed, and an insatiable demand for the output. Seldom can these conditions be guaranteed and when they do exist they seldom last without snags. Raw materials run out, job cards are not available, tools are faulty, the stores are full, customer demand is fluctuating or there is trouble with the computer. As soon as this sort of thing happens the incentive-paid worker has an incentive to fiddle the scheme for protection against operational vagaries.

Quality of work

The stimulus to increase volume of output can adversely affect the quality of output, as there is an incentive to do things as quickly as possible. If the payment scheme is organised so that only output meeting quality standards is paid for, there may still be the tendency to produce expensive scrap. Operatives filling jars with marmalade may break the jars if they work too hurriedly. This means that the jar is lost and the marmalade as well, for fear of glass splinters.

Renewed emphasis on quality and customer satisfaction mean that employers increasingly need to reward individuals with the most highly developed skills or those who are most readily adaptable to the operation of new methods and technologies. PBR, with its emphasis on the quantity of items produced or sold, may be judged inappropriate for organisations competing in markets in which the quality of production is of greater significance than previously.

Quality of working life

There is also a danger that PBR schemes may demotivate the workforce and so impair the quality of working life for individual employees. In our industrial consciousness payment by results is associated with the worst aspects of rationalised work: routine, tight control, hyper-specialisation and mechanistics. The worker is characterised as an adjunct to the machine, or as an alternative to a machine. Although this may not necessarily be so, it is usually so, and generally expected. Piecework schemes re-enhance the mechanical element in the control of working relationships by failing to reward employee initiative, skills acquisition or flexibility. There is also evidence to suggest that achieving high levels of productivity by requiring individuals to undertake the same repetitive tasks again and again during the working day increases stress levels and can make some employees susceptible to repetitive strain injuries.

The selective nature of incentives

Seldom do incentive arrangements cover all employees. Typically, groups of employees are working on a payment basis which permits their earnings to be geared to their output, while their performance depends on the before or after processes of employees not so rewarded, such as craftsmen making tools and fixtures, labourers bringing materials in and out, fork-lift truck drivers, storekeepers and so forth. This type of problem is illustrated most vividly by Bowey's study of a garment factory, where employees 'on piecework' were set against those who were not, by the selective nature of the payment arrangement (Lupton and Bowey 1975, pp. 76–8).

One conventional way around the problem is to pay the 'others' a bonus linked to the incentive earned by those receiving it. The reasoning for this is that those who expect to earn more (such as the craftsmen) have a favourable differential guaranteed as well as an interest in high levels of output, while that same interest in sustaining output is generated in the other employees (like the labourers and the storekeepers) without whom the incentive-earners cannot maintain their output levels. The drawbacks are obvious. The labour costs are increased by making additional payments to employees on a non-discriminating basis, so that the storekeeper who is a hindrance to output will still derive benefit from the efforts of others, and the employees whose efforts are directly rewarded by incentives feel that the fruits of their labour are being shared by those whose labours are not so directly controlled.

Obscurity of payment arrangements

Because of these difficulties, incentive schemes are constantly modified or refined in an attempt to circumvent fiddling or to get a fresh stimulus to output, or in response to employee demands for some other type of change. This leads to a situation in which the employees find it hard to understand that behaviour by them leads to particular results in payment terms.

Performance-related pay

While the 1980s and 1990s have seen a decline in the use of PBR schemes, such as those described above, there has been considerable growth in the coverage of incentive schemes which reward individual contribution to the organisation on the basis of performance rather than simply on effort. Performance-related pay (PRP), unlike traditional PBR incentives, looks beyond straightforward measures of output and provides a means whereby individual effectiveness, flexibility and work quality can also be rewarded. It has its roots in incentive schemes set up to motivate managers and executives but has increasingly spread downwards through organisations to cover non-manual grades and nowadays some manual grades as well.

In 1991 a survey looking at incentive schemes in 360 organisations was carried out jointly by the IPM and NEDO (Cannell and Wood 1992). The questionnaire responses indicated that 68 per cent of private sector organisations and 43 per cent of public sector organisations had introduced PRP for some or all of their non-manual employes. Twenty-eight per cent of private sector employers used PRP to determine the final pay levels of all employees. The extent of the recent growth in the use of PRP was shown by the fact that 40 per cent of the schemes for non-manual employees had been introduced between 1981 and 1991. Of further interest was the finding that once introduced PRP was hardly ever withdrawn, although modifications to original scheme designs were common. The government has made reference to PRP in its Citizen's Charter initiative and has encouraged the introduction of schemes for several groups of public sector employees, notably teachers and nurses. It is likely, therefore, that the coverage of PRP will continue to grow in the 1990s.

The attraction of PRP

The growth in performance-related pay undoubtedly owes as much to the appearance of fairness as to its supposed incentive effects. In seeking to reward individuals for their personal contribution to organisational success the principles that underlie PRP make it attractive to employers and employees alike. Unlike payment systems which reward everyone on a particular grade equally whatever their contribution or schemes which only reward the quantity of output, PRP appears to accord with widely supported concepts of distributive justice.

In theory, the incentive effect derives from the underlying principle of fairness. Individual employees are encouraged to make a greater contribution because they know they will be financially rewarded for doing so. Performance-related pay, when it works well, also ensures that individual work objectives match organisational goals. This occurs by clearly reflecting the employer's priorities and values in the criteria on which the award of performance-related payments are based.

Furthermore, PRP provides a means whereby individuals can be motivated in an organisational environment with flatter hierarchies and, in consequence, fewer promotion opportunities. It also suits the needs of organisations in an era of relatively low inflation in which annual salary increases are no longer automatic but have to be earned.

Forms of PRP

The most widely used form of PRP is that which relates annual incremental progression to individual performance. An excellent level of performance will thus be rewarded the following year by a substantial increase in the individual's base salary. Conversely, an employee who has been assessed as having performed poorly will only be rewarded with a rise to cover cost of living increases or will receive no pay rise at all. The problem with this form of PRP is its tendency to cause the organisation's pay bill to rise unless there is a high level of staff turnover. An alternative approach is to pay one-off bonuses to reward individual or team performance; sums which are not consolidated into base pay rates.

The schemes also vary considerably in terms of the portion of pay which is performance-related. The question of how much, in percentage terms, a good performer should be rewarded in comparison with a poor one will inevitably depend on the organisation's product market and the culture it wishes to develop. Armstrong and Murlis (1994) provide the following advice:

> As a rule of thumb, those whose performance is outstanding may deserve and expect rewards of at least 10% and more in their earlier period in a job. People whose level of performance and rate of development is well above the average may merit increases of 8–10%, while those who are progressing well at the expected rate towards the fully competent level may warrant an increase of between 5% and 7%. Increases of between 3% and 5% may be justified for those who are still developing steadily. Performance-related increases of less than 3% are hardly worth giving. (Armstrong and Murlis 1994)

Assessing performance

It is feasible to base performance-related pay rises on managerial assessments of each individual's 'whole job' performance. Each supervisor can be asked to assess his or her subordinates' individual contribution over the year on the basis of a set of performance criteria such as; time-keeping, attendance, effort, initiative and customer-care. Such a system, however, while relatively straightforward to operate, is open to charges of unfairness and subjectivity with the awards being judged to be arbitrary.

A more effective method is to link pay to the achievement of preset performance targets. Here each individual agrees performance objectives with their manager at the beginning of the year and is rewarded 12 months later according to the extent to which those objectives have been achieved.

Disadvantages of PRP

The long history of incentive schemes, and particularly of trade union involvement in their development, has been to make them collective and impersonal. The idea of performance pay is usually to make it individual and personal, so that some do better than others – or some do worse than others. Therein lies the problem. If the performance pay arrangement is to be effective, it must have an apparent impact on individual performance, but selective individual reward can be divisive and lead to overall ineffectiveness unless everyone perceives the rules to be fair.

Peter and Patrick are sales consultants for a financial services company and both had business targets for a six-month period. Peter met his target comfortably and received the predetermined bonus of £6000 for reaching on-target earnings. Patrick failed to reach his target because his sales manager boss left the company and poached two of Patrick's prime customers just before they signed agreements with Patrick, whose bonus was therefore £2000 instead of £6250.

Joanne was a sales consultant for the same company as Peter and Patrick. Before the sales manager left, he made over to her several promising clients with whom he had done considerable preparatory work and who were not willing to be 'poached' by his new employer. All of these signed agreements and one of them decided to increase the value of the deal ten-fold without any reference to Joanne until after that decision was made, and without knowing that she was now the appropriate contact. Her bonus for the period was £23400.

Henry is a production manager in a light engineering company with performance pay related to a formula combining output with value-added. Bonus payments were made monthly in anticipation of what they should be. One of Henry's initiatives was to increase the gearing of the payment by results scheme in the factory. Through peculiarities of company accounting his bonus payments were 'justified' according to the formula, but later it was calculated that the production costs had risen by an amount that cancelled out the value added benefits. Also 30 per cent of the year's output had to be recalled due to a design fault.

Peter had his bonus made up to £6250. Joanne had her bonus reduced to £8000, but took legal advice and had the cut restored, whereupon Peter and Patrick both threatened to resign until mollified by *ex gratia* payments of £2000 each. Peter resigned three months later. Henry was dismissed.

The least successful PRP schemes, therefore, are those that cover employees whose performance is most difficult to measure effectively. Recent moves by the government to promote PRP for nurses, doctors and teachers have been widely criticised for this reason. Journalists employed by the BBC went as far as to take industrial action in the summer of 1994 over proposals to relate their pay to performance. All these groups fear that the difficulties associated with measuring their performance will lead to subjective and possibly unfair judgements being made by their assessors.

It is also very difficult to measure performance in many management jobs which, by their very nature, require great flexibility on the part of job holders. The problem here is that as soon as performance objectives and indicators have been agreed the goalposts change, rendering the agreed performance criteria out of date long before the end of the year. As a result the pay award that is finally made does not adequately reflect the individual's actual performance.

When PRP does not work it can easily serve to demotivate employees and can act divisively to damage relationships within a team thus defeating its original purpose. There can be no doubt that organisations have to take great care in its introduction if they are to make it work successfully as an incentive.

The effect of PRP on the paybill

> Individualized pay seems tailor-made for a period of competitive expansion... By all accounts this has had a considerable initial effect on company performance. But at the same time it produced a tremendous inflationary spiral. The systems introduced have generally been highly geared, with a high pay threshold as a carrot to attract employees and secure acceptance of the new arrangements. Awards for below standard performance have often been higher than the general run of increases in other industries. (IDS 1988, p. 5)

When schemes are individualised, it is always difficult to keep pay rises down for the poorer performer. Few managers have the stomach for passing on the bad news and then hoping to get a satisfactory working performance out of the person who has not had a pay rise. If a business is struggling, it cannot afford unfettered performance pay. Sometimes, there is a management justification for performance payments being made only to those in key management posts on the grounds that only they can initiate significant change and improvement in overall business performance. Furthermore, the payments made to this small number of individuals amount to a small proportion of the organisation's total expenditure. The payments are still likely to be inflationary, as the hankering after equity by others in the organisation will put strong pressure on pay levels at every point.

Twenty years ago inflation was sometimes attributed to 'consolidation', as progressively the proportion of pay that was basic as opposed to payment by results was increased, the rewards for the performance gradually being consolidated in the pay that people received regardless of the performance. Currently, this can be seen happening in a very public way in the published accounts of private companies, which include directors' emoluments. There have been several instances of company chairmen having a significant proportion of their income linked to company performance, yet the other directors decide to reward the chairman with a special payment as compensation for the fact that the success of the business has faltered.

The more exuberant schemes are gradually being replaced by arrangements that are better controlled, but the problems remain and it seems as if performance pay still suffers many of the weaknesses that were found in incentive payment schemes during the 1920s and 1930s.

There have been numerous case studies published in recent years examining the introduction of PRP in both the public and private sectors. The most thorough treatment of the problems which have arisen is found in Cannell and Wood (1992) and in Marsden and Richardson (1991).

Skill-based pay

A further kind of incentive payment scheme is one which seeks to reward employees for the skills or competences which they acquire. It is well established in the United States and, according to an IPM survey undertaken in 1991, is becoming more common among British employers. It is particularly prevalent as a means of rewarding technical staff but there is no reason why the principle should not be extended to any group of employees for whom the acquisition of additional skills might benefit the organisation.

There are several potential benefits for an employer introducing a skill-based pay scheme. Its most obvious effect is to encourage multiskilling and flexibility enabling the organisation to respond more effectively and speedily to the needs of customers. A multiskilled workforce may also be slimmer and less expensive. In addition it is argued that, in rewarding skills acquisition, a company will attract and retain staff more effectively than its competitors in the labour market. The operation of a skill-based reward system is proof that the sponsoring employer is genuinely committed to employee development.

Typical schemes

Most skill-based payment systems reward employees with additional increments to their base pay once they have completed defined skill modules. A number of such schemes are described in detail in a study published by Incomes Data Services in 1992. Typical is the scheme operated by Venture Pressings Ltd where staff are employed on four basic grades, each divided into ten increments. Employees progress up the scale by acquiring specific skills and demonstrating proficiency in them to the satisfaction of internal assessors. New starters are also assessed and begin their employment on the incremental point most appropriate to the level of skills they can demonstrate.

In many industries it is now possible to link payment for skills acquisition directly to the attainment of National Vocational Qualifications (NVQs) for which both the setting of standards and the assessment of individual competence are carried out externally.

Disdavantages of skill-based pay

A skill-based pay system will only be cost effective if it results in productivity increases which are sufficient to cover the considerable costs associated with its introduction and maintenance. An organisation can invest a great deal of resources both in training its workforce to attain new skills and in rewarding them once those skills have been acquired only to find that the cost of the scheme outweighs the benefit gained in terms of increased flexibility and efficiency. Furthermore, in assisting employees to become more highly qualified and in many cases to gain NVQs, an employer may actually find it harder to retain its staff in relatively competitive labour markets. Employers seeking to introduce skill-based systems of payment therefore need to consider the implications very carefully and must ensure that they only reward the acquisition of those skills which will clearly contribute to increased productivity.

Profit sharing and profit-related pay

There are a number of different ways in which companies are able to link remuneration directly to profit levels. In recent years the government has sought to encourage the incidence of such schemes and has actively promoted their establishment with advantageous tax arrangements. Underlying their support is the belief that linking pay to profits increases the employee's commitment to his or her company by deepening the level of mutual interest. As a result, it is argued that such schemes act as an incentive encouraging employees to work harder and with greater flexibility in pursuit of higher levels of take-home pay.

Profit sharing

The traditional and most common profit sharing arrangement is simply to pay employees a cash bonus, calculated as a proportion of annual profits, on which the employee incurs both a PAYE and a national insurance liability.

An alternative is the Approved Deferred Share Trust (ADST) which was established under the Finance Act 1978. In this arrangement the company allocates the proportion of profit not in cash to employees, but to a trust fund which purchases company shares on behalf of the employees. The shares are then allocated to eligible employees on some agreed formula. The employee shareholder only pays tax when the shares are sold, and there is no additional national insurance contribution by employee or employer. ADST schemes seldom allow shares to be sold in the first two years after purchase and if they are sold in the following two years the employee pays tax on one of two values – either the price paid originally or the final selling price. If the shares are sold during the fourth year of ownership the tax obligation reduces to three-quarters of what it would have been the year earlier, and after five years of ownership there is no tax obligation at all. Share dividends are received and taxed in the normal way. A variant of this arrangement was made possible by the Finance Act 1980 under which Save As You Earn Schemes can be established enabling employees, if they wish, to purchase company shares through monthly deductions from salary.

The incidence of profit-sharing has increased in recent years and was operated in some shape or form by 55 per cent of the companies participating in the survey undertaken by the IPM and NEDO in 1991 (Cannell and Wood 1992). In the same year Inland Revenue estimated that 1.3 million employees received shares or share options but many more will have benefited from profit-sharing by opting to take cash payments instead of shares.

The level of bonus that employees can expect to receive as a result of profit sharing schemes varies considerably. According to an Incomes Data Services survey of thirty-two companies carried out in 1993 the average level of bonus received by employees covered by profit-sharing schemes was £200–300. Before the recession, however, awards worth over £500 were commonly paid.

Profit-related pay

In a profit-sharing scheme a bonus, either in the form of cash or shares, is paid to employees depending on the level of the company's annual profits. A profit-related pay scheme differs in that it automatically links a portion of an employee's basic pay to profit levels. Tax relief is available up to the point at which the profit-related part of the salary is the lower of either 20 per cent of an employee's total pay or £4000. This allows anyone earning between £8000 and £20,000 an equivalent gross salary increase of around 7 per cent provided the company reaches its stated profit targets.

Tax relief on profit-related pay was first introduced in 1987 but failed to attract many companies. A large proportion of those which did participate were simply converting existing profit sharing arrangements so as to take advantage of the tax relief. Between December 1991 and December 1993, however, the number of schemes rose from 2000 to more than 6400; 1.5 million employees are now covered and the figure continues to rise. The acceleration in the number of applications followed the government's decision to increase the amount of tax relief available and to publish a set of model rules to assist employers in setting up schemes. Interest has undoubtedly also been increased as a result of the recession with employers taking advantage of Inland Revenue rules to give pay increases at no cost to the company.

Disadvantages of profit-related schemes

The obvious disadvantage of the schemes described above from the employee's point of view is the risk that pay levels may decline if the company fails to meet its expected profit levels. If no profit is made it can not be shared. Companies are not permitted to make guarantees about meeting payments and will have their schemes revoked by Inland Revenue if they do so. In any event it is likely that pay levels will vary from year to year.

For these reasons it is questionable to assert that profit-related schemes do in fact act as incentives. Unlike performance-related pay awards they do not relate specifically to the actions of the individual employee. Annual profit levels are clearly influenced by a whole range of factors which are both internal and external to the company. An employee may well develop a community of interest with the company management, shareholders and with other employees but it is unlikely to seriously affect the nature of his or her work. It is also the case that both poor and good performers are rewarded equally in profit-related schemes. The incentive effect will therefore be very slight in most cases and will be restricted to a general increase in employee commitment.

REVIEW TOPIC 34.2

Given the disadvantages of profit-related schemes, what are the relative advantages to the employer of ADST and profit-related pay schemes?

Fringe benefits

Features of payment other than wages or salary have grown steadily in importance since the 1960s, and the United Kingdom has a level of provision that is not found in other western countries. This is especially marked in the executive, management and professional area. Table 34.2 is an example of how the remuneration package can become very elaborate as the employer adds on benefits which are cheaper than actually paying money.

Gill (1989) quotes the exceptional case of a retired company chairman who was made a consultant with a package that included £92 a day for lunch, four centre court tickets for Wimbledon every year and four tickets for each opera season at Covent Garden. A less unusual example is: 'A banker's £35,000 salary typically brings with it a bonus averaging about £9,000 a year, a car and petrol, free health insurance, life insurance cover of £100,000, an interest-free loan of £6,000 and a £60,000 mortgage at 5 per cent interest.'

Table 34.2 *Features of an offer to a 21-year-old graduate joining a graduate training programme in October 1989*

1.	Starting salary of £13,400, to be reviewed after six months
2.	Free private medical insurance
3.	25 days' annual holiday in addition to statutory days
4.	Non-contributory pension scheme
5.	Interest-free season ticket loan
6.	Personal loan facility at reduced rate of interest
7.	Free membership of three London clubs
8.	Participation in annual performance rewards competition
9.	Profits-related bonus scheme, paid monthly in advance

This type of development has been mainly due to taxation advantages either to the employer or the employee, although there is a further refinement, known as the cafeteria approach, whereby the employee can choose between alternatives in putting together a personalised pay and benefits package. This idea has been current for some time without being widely adopted:

> While some UK employers do offer an element of choice over individual elements of the benefits package, very few have adopted a more structured approach where individual choice is seen as a benefit in its own right. Some companies have toyed with the idea of flexible compensation but have not, up to now, regarded the potential advantages as sufficient to outweigh the complexity involved. (Woodley 1990, p. 42).

Over recent years we have all begun to reflect on our payment arrangements in a more calculated way than before with the introduction, for instance, of the option to change from an employer's pension arrangements to a private pension plan, to make additional voluntary contributions, various possibilities of share ownerships, and so forth. Perhaps the cafeteria approach to benefits is an idea whose time has at last come.

Despite their great attraction, fringe benefits can exacerbate status problems, with the have-nots bitterly resenting the privilege of the haves.

Cars

The Automobile Association calculated that in 1992 the cost of owning a car, with an engine capacity of 1500 cc, for the 10,000-mile-a-year driver is £4320 annually. Provision of a car by the employer is clearly a major attraction:

> The company car is a cherished symbol of power, status and prestige. From the most junior commercial traveller to the chairman of a major industrial concern, his metal overcoat says more about him than the cut of his suit, and while that attitude persists,

A few years ago one of the authors was involved in conciliation to find a resolution to a long-running industrial dispute at a small industrial plant where closure was likely with the consequent redundancy of the workforce. The three senior managers at the plant were all geographically mobile, awaiting their next career move to greener pastures. They all also enjoyed the benefit of company cars. In the second week of the dispute all the cars were renewed. In the third week a man from 'Central Personnel', in London, arrived for discussions with the local management team and shopfloor assumptions were that this discussion was to find a solution to the strike. It later transpired that it was to explain why the cars were 1600 cc instead of 2000 cc; the issue being discussed between 12.15 and 2.45 p.m. over lunch in a nearby hotel. In the fifth week outside contractors arrived to lay a strip of tarmacadam from the factory gates across a muddy works yard to the office block in the centre, with a final strip outside the offices wide enough for three cars to be parked.

then so will the poor management of this almost anachronistic device continue. (Blauth 1986)

As that extract demonstrates, the attraction of the benefit is accompanied by significant management problems and the management of their provision is beset with almost as much power, status and prestige as their possession.

The company car is not a free benefit for the user, who pays tax on both the car and on the fuel that it uses. The method of tax collection is a reduction of the personal allowance, depending on the amount of business mileage, the original market value of the car, its age and cubic capcity. Details change with each Budget, but they are set out in booklet IR47, available free of charge from offices of the Inland Revenue. In recent years the government has increased the amount of income tax payable on company cars. As a result organisations are beginning to allow their employees a choice between a car or a cash alternative. Some companies give an option to employees whereby they can choose a smaller car and some cash as well.

An alternative to the company car is a mileage allowance, more widely used in the public sector of employment. This is usually either a standard rate or a rate that varies with engine size. According to an IDS Study published in 1993, allowances vary from 7.8p a mile to more than 70p a mile depending on the car's engine capacity or the length of the journey. Average rates in 1993 were between 25p and 35p a mile.

Other benefits

Employers provide a wide range of other benefits, from free hairdressing in company time to loans to buy season tickets. In 1986 the authors researched practice in 350 organisations providing fringe benefits for their employees. Table 34.3 shows the number of establishments participating in our research which provided any of nineteen different fringe benefits. Answers to other questions showed that more than half provided private medical insurance to management employees (seventy-six provided it for blue-collar employees) and time off for medical and dental appointments was common. One-third of all respondents said that the proportion of employment costs devoted to fringe benefits was increasing, yet the general area of fringe benefits was the one where personnel specialists felt they had least discretion.

A benefit not included in Table 34.3 is the London allowance. According to IDS, in 1974, the typical inner London allowance was £3000–£3500 a year with some companies paying higher salary-related allowances. Some employers also have a lower 'ROSELAND' (rest of south-east England) payment. There is an increasing practice, particularly among retailers, of fitting the allowance to a particular location instead of to a general geographical area. This enables them to target allowances as needed on a store-by-store basis according to prevailing labour market conditions.

Table 34.3 *The range of fringe benefits provided. Number of respondent organisations, out of a total of 350, providing the following fringe benefits for three categories of employee*

	Blue-collar	White-collar	Management
Relocation expenses	124	237	290
Subsidised meals	211	246	245
Long-service awards	228	246	244
Company car	6	54	209
Medical facilities	94	103	180
Car servicing	6	40	152
Subscription to professional bodies	29	87	141
Employee discount on products	18	139	136
Personal loans	56	81	95
Petrol credit card	3	22	83
Share option scheme	64	70	75
Mortgage facilities	30	45	53
Christmas bonus	45	56	47
Company-owned housing	18	42	43
Transport to and from work	42	32	27
Clothing allowance	92	44	24
Service-related shareholding	14	18	19
Subsidised holidays	14	18	19
Share incentive scheme	11	11	15

REVIEW TOPIC 34.3

What are the advantages to the employee and to the employer of payment being weekly in cash rather than monthly by bank giro credit?

Incentives, fringe benefits and personnel management

The very costly aspects of remuneration discussed in this chapter are seldom managed in a positive way with a sense of purpose about why they are provided and what they are to achieve. Usually, an extra is provided because it is a good bargain. Membership of the local health club can be obtained at half price by the employer, so it seems like too good an opportunity to miss. Many benefits are provided simply because it is the accepted practice, such as the company car. Incentive schemes are set up in the belief that they should work, but without any evidence that the method actually proposed will work in that situation. The various schemes are seldom co-ordinated, with different executives responsible for different features. Sometimes the responsibility of the personnel manager is total, sometimes it is nil, yet all these features affect the basic activity of personnel work: matching the expectations of employer with the expectations of employee. Furthermore they form an increasing proportion of employment costs.

Incentives and fringe benefits need to be firmly incorporated within payment policy with the personnel manager reviewing everything that is provided and proposed. What is it? What is it for? Does it achieve its purpose? Is that purpose worth achieving? Does it fit within the overall payment policy? Who administers the feature being considered? Is that the appropriate person? How much does each feature cost? How much trouble does it cause? What benefit does it confer?

Unless incentive and fringe benefit provisions are positively managed, they can become an expensive and ineffective element in the employment relationship.

☐ SUMMARY PROPOSITIONS

34.1 Incentives cannot be understood in isolation from the whole of the working relationship between employer and employee. Incentive arrangements demonstrate what managers believe about that relationship.

34.2 Typical problems with incentive schemes include having to cope with operational inefficiencies, fluctuation in earnings, the effect of incentives on the quality of work produced and on the quality of working life for the producers, as well as the selective nature of incentives and the frequent obscurity of the incentive arrangement itself.

34.3 Performance-related payments tend to be inflationary and present operational problems when overall organisational effectiveness declines.

34.4 Methods of payment by results include individual time-saving, group incentives, measured daywork, plant-wide schemes, productivity schemes, commission and tipping.

34.5 Fringe benefits are not intended to have a direct motivational effect, but are tax-efficient ways of providing additions to the remuneration package and some degree of choice within it. They are more common and diverse for management employees than for others and can cause considerable problems of relative status.

34.6 Fringe benefits include cars, mileage allowance, profit-sharing and many other small perquisites.

34.7 Fringe benefits are an area where personnel managers feel they have little discretion and influence.

34.8 Unless incentive payments and fringe benefits are managed positively, this increasingly costly aspect of the remuneration package can become an expensive and ineffective element in the employment relationship.

References

Armstrong, M. and Murlis, H. (1994), *Reward Management; a Handbook of Remuneration Strategy and Practice*, London: Kogan Page.

Blauth, J. (1986), 'Button up your metal overcoat', *Guardian*, 13 June.

Cannell, M. and Wood, S. (1992), *Incentive Pay: Impact and Evolution*, London: Institute of Personnel Management.

Gill, L. (1989), 'Fitting the perk to the person', *The Times*, 31 October.

Lawler, E. E. Jr (1971), *Pay and Organizational Effectiveness*, New York: McGraw-Hill.

Lupton, T. and Bowey, A. M. (1975), *Wages and Salaries*, Harmondsworth: Penguin Books.

Marsden, D. and Richardson, R. (1991), *Motivation and Performance Related Pay in the Public Sector: A Case Study of the Inland Revenue*, London: Centre for Economic Performance.

McGregor, D. (1970), *The Human Side of Enterprise*, Maidenhead: McGraw-Hill.

New Earnings Survey, Published by Department of Employment, London: HMSO

Woodley, C. (1990), 'The cafeteria route to compensation', *Personnel Management*, May, pp. 42–5.

35 Pensions and sick pay

The provision of pensions and sick pay has been viewed as the mark of a 'good' employer, and yet employees have not, until recently, seen these as benefits which attracted their interest. There is now, however, an increasing public awareness of pension matters, stimulated by governmental actions, the media and the pensions industry. The potential for fraud in occupational pension schemes has been highlighted by the alarming evidence discovered after Robert Maxwell's death, and some serious problems with personal pension schemes have also come to light. Sick pay has also attracted greater attention since statutory sick pay (SSP) was introduced in 1986, and especially since the SSP scheme was revised in 1991 and 1994, each time placing a greater financial burden for sick pay directly on the employer.

This chapter is organised into two major sections. In the first we look at the reasons for increased awareness about pensions provision, various categories of pension schemes, pensions information and the role of the personnel department. In the second part we discuss the role of the personnel department in state and occupational sick pay, and then look at sick pay and absence monitoring and control.

Increased awareness about pensions provision

Pensions are increasingly seen as 'deferred pay' rather than a reward for a lifetime of employment (IDS 1982), and as such are attracting more attention from employees and trade unions, and are seen as more negotiable than in the past. As the state pension scheme is changed and changed again, and its future form becomes more uncertain, greater attention is being paid to company schemes. Concern over the future of the State Earnings Related Pension Scheme (SERPS) has directed attention to other schemes, including both occupational and personal schemes. The nature of work has changed dramatically since the first company pension schemes emerged. There has been a move from lifetime employment with one employer towards greater job mobility for all groups of employees. Sometimes this movement is deliberate; for example, the young executive who joins a new company to further their career; sometimes it is involuntary, as in the case of redundancy. This has prompted an interest in the way that company pension schemes provide for those employees who have had more than one, frequently many, employers. The increasing likelihood of fairly lengthy unemployment between one job and the next, together with increasing attention to the role of women who characteristically have broken records of employment due to family commitments, have highlighted the assumptions on which most company pension schemes are based. The plight of those who, having been made redundant at fifty are never to find work again, has made people more aware of the potential role of pensions schemes.

Our expectations in general have risen, with ideas of early retirement from choice, 'while you're still young enough to enjoy it', and increasing expectations that retirement should not necessarily be a time for 'tightening your belt', but a time to reap the rewards from one's work and to do things that there was never time for before. Retirement is now seen more as a beginning than an end, and consequently the pensions that support this new beginning are seen as more important at an earlier age than before. In addition to this, as information is more generally available, employees expect more information about their pension schemes and about the benefits to which they will eventually become entitled.

REVIEW TOPIC 35.1

Robert Noble-Warren (1986) talks about 'lifetime planning' as a series of 'rest and recuperation' periods throughout life as well as the planning of financial provision. Lifetime planning has to start with a statement of your life's objectives.

What are your life's objectives and what work, rest and financial plans can you make to achieve these?

Types of pension scheme

There are four levels of pension schemes: state schemes, company pension schemes, industry pension schemes and individual schemes.

State schemes

The state runs two schemes: a basic scheme and SERPS. Every employee is obliged to contribute a standard amount to the basic scheme which provides an old age pension on reaching the age of 65 years for men and 60 years for women. By 2020 the pensionable age for both men and women will be 65 years and in the ten years prior to this date there will be a gradual phasing in of the new pensionable age for women.

For those employees who earn over a certain amount (known as the lower earnings limit) a percentage of salary earned between this limit and a higher salary level (known as the upper earnings limit) is also payable. Both these payments are deducted from wages as part of the national insurance contribution. The individual who has paid into SERPS as well as the basic scheme will receive a higher pension from the state on retirement in proportion to the additional amount that they have contributed. The employer also makes a contribution into the state pension scheme in a way similar to the individual employee. The state pension scheme is organised on a pay-as-you-go basis. This means that there is no state pension fund as such, and the money that is paid to today's pensioners comes from today's taxes and national insurance contributions. The money that will be paid to today's contributors, when they become pensioners, will come not from the investment of their and their employers' contributions, but from the contributions of the workforce and their employers in the future. This approach to pension provision is causing great concern, as the number of pensioners is increasing rapidly. Hopegood (1994) notes that at present there are 3.3 people of working age to every pensioner, a figure which reduces to 2.7 by 2030. There has been much criticism of the state pension scheme (see, for example, Butler and Pirie 1983), and the government have in the past put forward proposals for the abolition of SERPS. The 1986 Social Security Act brought in a phased reduction of benefits under SERPS from April 1988. Implications of this and other aspects of the Act are discussed in Amy (1986).

Company schemes

There is a number of advantages to companies in setting up pensions schemes. Nash (1989) gives a good description of these, which include pensions as part of the mechanism to recruit and retain good people, the generation of good will and loyalty, the improvement of industrial relations and a mechanism for managing early retirement and redundancy. In addition to these the provision of such a scheme enhances the employer's image, which can have pay-offs in many areas.

Company schemes vary considerably, and we shall consider their specific arrangements in more depth in the section on 'Varieties of Company Pension Schemes'. They are normally funded by contributions from the employee (for instance, 6 per cent of salary) and a similar contribution from the employer. Sometimes large companies and public sector organisations offer non-contributory pensions, in which case the employee pays nothing. In general, company schemes provide an additional retirement pension as well as the basic state pension, and sometimes as well as SERPS. Most often, however, the company will avoid employee and employer payments into SERPS by means of 'contracting out'. A company can contract out of SERPS only if its pension scheme meets certain requirements. The Occupational Pensions Board (OPB) will decide whether contracting-out will be allowed, and if so they will issue a contracting-out certificate.

Company schemes generally provide better and wider-ranging benefits than the state schemes and they provide some flexibility. They are most often found in large organisations and the public sector, but some smaller organisations also run such schemes. Garlick (1986) reports that more than eleven million employees are members of company pension schemes, but Hayward (1989) records that there are still around ten million employees who are solely dependent on state provision. Men and women have equal access to company schemes, and the Social Security Act 1989 brought further changes which enforced equal treatment of men and women in the schemes. There are still some issues in respect of equality of provision to be clarified and harmonisation with the EC continues (see, for example, Hearn 1992). There is a tendency for a higher proportion of managerial workers than other groups to be in pensions schemes. Blue-collar workers are least likely to be in schemes. Part-time employees are sometimes excluded, as are those on temporary contracts, although this very much depends on the employer.

Company schemes rarely pay their pensioners in the pay-as-you-go manner operated by the state but create a pension fund, which is managed separately from the business. The advantage of this is that should the company become bankrupt, the pension fund cannot be seized to pay debtors because it is not part of the company. The money in the pension fund is invested and held in trust for the employees of the company at the time of their retirement. Very large organisations will self-administer their pension fund, and appoint an investment manager or a fund manager. The manager will plan how to invest the money in the fund to get the best return and to ensure that the money that is needed to pay pensions and other benefits will be available when required. An actuary can provide mortality tables and other statistical information in order to assist planning. Smaller organisations may appoint an insurance company or a bank to administer their pension funds, and so use their expertise. Pension funds can be invested in a variety of different ways, and Garlick comments that: 'They often deploy assets greater than the market capitalization of the companies that sponsor them and have come to dominate investment on the stock market' (Garlick 1986, p.7)

The fund may also be used to purchase property and lend mortgages to others. Government and local govenment stock with specified redemption dates are also useful forms of investment as they may be selected to provide cash when claims are expected. Toulson argues that the investments made by the pension fund should meet the following criteria: 'Wise investment includes at least three criteria. Investments must be safe; they must be profitable; they must also be capable of being realized when cash is required to pay benefits' (Toulson 1982, p. 8). Booth (1986), however, notes that an increasing number of funds are investing in venture capital projects, which is basically investment in new business. This long-term investment is much more risky, and Booth does suggest that only a small proportion of overall funds should be invested in this manner. The structure of some pension schemes and the success of the investments have meant large surpluses of money building up in the scheme. This has enabled both employer and employee to take a contributions holiday, as at Lucas Industries who have taken a two-year contributions holiday (quoted in Garlick 1986).

Another advantage of setting up a pension fund, apart from the protection of the money, is that if the scheme is approved by the Superannuation Funds Office

(SFO) of the Inland Revenue, various tax advantages can be claimed. Both employer and employee can claim tax relief on the contributions that they make to the scheme, and there are also tax advantages for the pensions benefits that are paid out.

In spite of all the advantages of company pension schemes, Hearn cites a range of examples where companies have been guilty of pension fraud. The best-known example of this is the fraud discovered on the death of Robert Maxwell where the company pension funds had been used for other purposes. The Maxwell scandal led to the formation of the Pension Review Committee headed by Professor Goode. This committee reported back in Autumn 1993 and after a period of consultation further pensions legislation is expected. Recommendations include the replacement of the Occupational Pensions Board by a Pensions Regulator with greater powers including, for example, the power to carry out spot checks and investigations. Proposals also would require companies to maintain an asset level which at least equalled 90 per cent of the value of pension entitlements. Further details of recommendations can be found in Allen (1994).

Industry-wide schemes

Sometimes employers and employees will contribute to an 'industry-wide' pension scheme, as an alternative to a company scheme. The reasoning behind these schemes is described very well by Incomes Data Services when they say:

> These schemes are particularly useful in industries where there is a large number of small companies, and employees tend to be mobile within the confines of the industry. The companies would not be large enough to run their own schemes, and the employees would not welcome being tied to a company pension scheme (IDS 1982, p.13)

The operation of such schemes is very similar to company schemes except that a number of different companies contribute to the same scheme.

Personal pensions

Increasing attention is being paid to the possibility of personal pensions. Self-employed people have always needed to be concerned with making their own provisions for retirement, as they are excluded from joing SERPS. More general attention has been focused on this area due to increasing job mobility and the perceived greater portability of personal pensions. A personal pension is arranged, usually through an insurance company, and the individual pays regular amounts into their own 'pension fund' in the same way that they would with a company fund. The employer may or may not also make a contribution to the fund. At present there are very few employers who take part in this arrangement, but in July 1984 the government issued a consultative document on personal pensions (DHSS 1984), suggesting that all employees should have the right to make their own pension arrangements, and from 1988 these recommendations have become operational. There has been a very mixed reaction to the proposals. The Institute of Directors (1986), for example, has been in favour. Moody comments on less favourable responses when he says:

> The concerns seem to be about whether occupational schemes will be damaged, whether there will be administrative chaos, whether individuals will be misled by plausible salesmen and finish up with inadequate pensions, whether personal pensions will prove to be an irrelevance for pension scheme members or even whether they could result in the erosion of the state earnings-related scheme. (Moody 1984b, p. 34)

The IPM working party, in response to the government's consultative document, suggested that a better solution would be to allow members of company pension schemes to make additional pension provision via personal schemes (quoted in Moody 1984b).

More than half a million people have taken out personal pensions since 1988, most transferring when they moved from their current employer, while some have opted out of their employer's scheme. There has been considerable concern over the past year that the pensions advice given to those taking out personal pensions has been inadequate. Of special concern are those who have opted out of well-regarded schemes such as the mineworkers, teachers and nurses. Marsh *et al.* (1994) note that some have clearly lost out by their actions, and compensation is being claimed in many cases. The Securities and Investments Board continues to investigate these type of cases in particular.

Table 35.1 *Pensions provision*

Provider	Type of scheme	Additional benefits
State provision	Basic pension Earnings-related pension SERPS	No facility for additional benefits on tops of SERPS
Company provision	Flat rate scheme Average salary scheme Money purchase scheme Final salary scheme	Sometimes additional benefits provided by 'top hat' scheme or additional voluntary contributions
Industry-wide provision	Flat rate scheme Average salary scheme Money purchase scheme Final salary scheme	Sometimes additional benefits provided by 'top hat' scheme or additional voluntary contributions
Personal provision	Employee-funded money purchase scheme Employee and employer funded money purchase scheme	Sometimes additional benefits provided by further investment in the scheme

Varieties of company pension scheme

We have already looked at the ways that money is paid into the pension fund, and we shall now look at the way that money is paid out in the form of a pension. There is a variety of schemes which each pay out money to pensioners on a different basis. The most common type of scheme is that based on the final salary of the employee, but there are three other forms of well-known scheme. These are a flat rate scheme, an average salary scheme and a money purchase scheme. Table 35.1 shows all these schemes and other forms of pension that are available.

Flat rate schemes

Flat rate schemes take into account the length of service of the employee, but not the wage or salary that they were earning prior to retirement. A fixed rate of money is payable each year on retirement which is determined purely by the employee's length of service.

25-year period
Final salary
(for 4 years)   = £12000

Salary
(for 10 years)   = £10000

Salary
(for 11 years)   = £ 6000

4 years' contribution at £12000 =   1/50 of £12000 × 4 = £ 950
10 years' contribution at £10000 =   1/50 of £10000 × 10 = £2000
11 years' contribution at £ 6000 =   1/50 of £ 6000 × 11 = £1320
                                                                       ‾‾‾‾‾‾
                                           Pension per annum of   £3070

40-year period
Final 25 years as above   = £3070

Salary
(for 8 years)   = £4000

Salary
(for 7 years)   = £2000

8 years' contribution at £4000 =   1/50 of £4000 × 8 = £ 640
7 years' contribution at £2000 =   1/50 of £2000 × 7 = £ 280
                                                                ‾‾‾‾‾‾
                                           Pension per annum of   £3990

Figure 35.1   Average salary schemes: over a 25-year and a 40-year period.

Average salary schemes

Average salary schemes take into account both length of service and salary that the employee has earned in each of those years. The critical figure is the average of all the yearly salaries; they are usually worked out at one-fiftieth of each annual salary the employee has earned. If there was little inflation and the employee had only made a short trip up the promotion ladder, the average salary would be close to the final salary of the employee. In this case a pension that equated to a proportion of the average salary may be quite acceptable. In a case of high inflation and an employee who had started at the bottom and worked their way up to the top, a pension that equated to a proportion of their average salary would be less than acceptable. Some companies will now re-evaluate in line with inflation the contributions made into such a scheme, but many do not, and re-evaluation takes no account of career progression. See Figure 35.1 for an example of an average salary scheme.

Final salary schemes

A final salary scheme, as the name suggests, takes into account the employees' final salary as well as the length of time that they have contributed to the pension fund. For each year of contribution employees earn the right to receive a specified proportion of their final salary as a pension. The better schemes offer one-sixtieth. This means that for each year of contribution to the fund the employee is entitled to receive one-sixtieth of their final salary in the form of a pension. Some worked examples are shown in Figure 35.2. The other commonly used fraction is one-eightieth. Employees in schemes that are based on one-sixtieth would, after forty years of contribution, be able to receive two-thirds of their final salary as a pension, and this is the maximum that is allowable (Toulson 1982). Employees in schemes that are based on one-eightieth would receive half their final salary as a pension after forty years of contributions.

Money purchase schemes

Money purchase schemes are organised in a totally different way from the schemes above, and there are no promises about what the final level of pension will be. Employees and employers contribute to these schemes in much the same way as to the other types of these schemes that is, a certain percentage of current salary. The pension benefits from the scheme are entirely dependent on the money that has been contributed and the way that it has been invested. If investments have been very profitable and there has been little inflation, then the final pension may turn out to be adequate. Money purchase schemes result in a lump sum available at retirement and this is used to buy a pension. However, in times of very high inflation this type of scheme has severe drawbacks, and this accounted for the decline in popularity in the 1970s. Money purchase schemes are, however, seen as more flexible and more

```
1/60 Scheme
Final salary                        = £12000
Contributions for 25 years          = 1/60 of £12000 × 25
                                    = £5000 per annum to be paid as a pension

Final salary                        = £12000
Contributions for 40 years          = 1/60 of £12000 × 40
                                    = £8000 per annum to be paid as a pension

1/80 Scheme
Final salary                        = £12000
Contributions for 25 years          = 1/80 of £12000 × 25
                                    = £3750 per annum to be paid as a pension

Final salary                        = £12000
Contributions for 40 years          = 1/80 of £12000 × 40
                                    = £6000 per annum to be paid as a pension
```

Figure 35.2   Final salary schemes: examples of various contribution periods with a 1/60 scheme and a 1/80 scheme.

easily transferable, and there has been a revival of interest in such schemes (IDS 1982) as the most suitable basis for personal, portable pensions. The 1986 Social Security Act simplified the requirements for opting out of SERPS, which facilitated the use of money purchase and other personal schemes.

In addition to the pension scheme, which forms the major investment for retirement purposes, there are two other types of contribution which may be made for this purpose.

Top-hat schemes

Noble-Warren (1986) notes that top-hat schemes were originally used to top up an individual's pension entitlements with a new employer to ensure that they matched what the individual would have received with the old employer. Top-hat schemes are operated similarly to money purchase schemes, and are particularly flexible because they may be funded by a single or occasional payment and there is no commitment to pay a certain amount each month while in employment.

Additional voluntary contributions

Additional voluntary contributions are a different way of improving retirement benefits. Incomes Data Services points out that although this may well be an efficient form of saving, there are a number of disadvantages:

- There is normally no employer's contribution.
- Once a person starts contributing, he (*sic*) is not usually allowed to stop unless he (*sic*) leaves the company.
- He (*sic*) cannot normally get the money back until retirement age. (IDS 1982, pp. 15–16).

Company pension schemes and the problem of early leavers

We mentioned at the beginning of this chapter that pensions were traditionally seen as a reward for a lifetime's employment, and the way that pensions are structured reflects this. Early leavers may have one or more of three options in making their pension arrangements when they begin work for a new employer. One option can be claiming back the contributions that the individual has made into the pension scheme, and sometimes interest may be paid on these. Deductions are also made in accordance with tax laws and, of course, the employer's contribution is lost. Another alternative may be opting for a preserved pension. With a final salary scheme, if there were no inflation, and if the individual progressed very little up the career ladder, a preserved pension from an old employer plus a pension from the recent employer would equate well with the pension they would have received had they been with the new employer for the whole period. However, if these conditions are not met, which in recent times they have not been, individuals who have had more than one employer lose out in the pension stakes. In some cases it is possible to transfer pension contributions to another scheme, and a transferred pension is often financially the best option. However, transfer value is not necessarily the same as original value, due to the way schemes use different sets of actuarial assumptions.

The disadvantages of leaving one employer's pension scheme and joining a new one have been one of the driving forces behind the recent interest in personal, portable pensions.

Pensions information and the role of the personnel department

Employeees expect more information about their pensions, both in general terms and about their specific circumstances. The personnel department has become increasingly involved in pensions, which until recently have been mainly the province of the finance department or the secretariat. This involvement partly stems from increasing use of the computer and the development of integrated, or at least linked systems, covering personnel, pensions and payroll. It also stems from greater trade union and employee interest in, and awareness of, pensions and the potential of pensions to become another area for negotiation. As information becomes increasingly available, employees expect to know more about the benefits to which they will become entitled at retirement. The computer is ideal to provide up to date statements of contributions and entitlements, and many employers now send these to employees on an annual basis. Pensions modelling also enables employees to be given information about the pension consequences of selecting certain leaving dates. Pensions is increasingly becoming an area where choices have to be made and personnel managers can be in a good position to provide information and advice. The importance of pensions information, and a user-friendly approach to presenting it, is described by Hunt (1988).

Some employers provide an annual report of the pension fund for employees, but many do not. Garlick notes that accountants suggest that there should be four essential components in this annual report:

1. The general activity, history and development of the scheme contained in a trustee's report.
2. The value and transactions of the fund covered by audited accounts.
3. The actuary's report showing the progress of a scheme towards meeting its potential liabilities and obligations to members.
4. A separate report setting out the investment policy of the fund and its performance relative to its stated policy. (Garlick 1986, p. 10)

Pension schemes need to be reviewed frequently to ascertain what benefits they are providing for the company in the light of changing circumstances. Personnel managers can draw on their specialist knowledge of labour markets, the changing nature of employment and the characteristics of the company's manpower to help assess the appropriateness of the pension scheme. Moody (1984a) suggests that a pensions checklist could be used, such as that in Table 35.2.

Sick pay and the role of the personnel department

As with pensions schemes, the provision of sick pay is seen as the mark of a good employer. The personnel manager and the personnel department have a variety of roles to play in relation to sick pay, particularly since the introduction of statutory sick pay in 1983 when state sick pay in additional to occupational sick pay have been administered by the employer.

Advice
The personnel manager is the most appropriate person to advise employees about SSP and the occupational scheme (if there is one) and how these schemes apply in individual circumstances. In particular, managers may need to advise staff who are nearing the end of their sick pay entitlement as to the remainder of their benefit and what special arrangements may be made in their case.

Home visits
Personnel managers or welfare officers may visit employees at home who have been away sick for a considerable period. Such visits are partly intended just to keep in touch with the employee and their progress, but also for the advisory purposes outlined above, and for planning purposes. For example, it might be appropriate to discuss with the employee the possibility of early retirement when sick pay runs out. These visits are sometimes organised on a more regular basis, perhaps every month, and may be included as part of the sick pay procedure. In these circumstances they

Table 35.2 *Pensions checklist*

- Are pensions related to final salary?
- If so, is the fraction used both adequate and competitive?
- Do portions of a year count for benefit?
- Is entry to the scheme monthly, quarterly or must people wait until the scheme anniversary?
- Does the scheme provide immediate cover for lump sum death benefits on joining service (if otherwise eligible)?
- Is the lump sum death benefit payable under discretionary trust thereby avoiding delay or capital transfer tax?
- Can part-time staff join the scheme? If so, is membership compulsory and how are benefits calculated when members change from full to part-time status or vice versa?
- Can life cover continue for a period after leaving service for people made redundant?
- Does the scheme provide for the maximum cash permitted in lieu of pension on retirement?
- Does the scheme give fair value for money to people leaving service before retirement?
- Do the rules contain the requisite transfer-in and -out provisions?
- Are the definitive deed and rules available or, as is often the case, are they still in draft form?
- Is there a simplified and readable explanatory booklet describing the scheme?
- Are members given any form of annual report from the trustees and regular statements of their benefits?
- Are members in any way involved in the running of the pension scheme?
- Is the personnel department closely involved in pensions policy and the running of the scheme?
- Is the scheme used positively as an aid to recruitment and are leavers fully aware of what they may be losing?
- Is there a pre-retirement training scheme?
- Is there any form of post-retirement escalation on pensions in course of payment of pre-retirement escalation for people who have left service?
- Does the scheme contain the flexibility to cope with early retirement problems?
- Are there provisions for pensions to be augmented at the discretion of the trustees?
- Do the rules permit members to make additional voluntary contributions (which attract full tax relief) to augment their benefits in whatever way they choose?

Source: Moody (1984). Reproduced with permission of IPD Publications.

are intended partly as a deterrent to those claiming sick pay under false pretences. Because of this, trade union officials are generally unenthusiastic about home visits.

Dismissal and transfer

The personnel manager will be involved in the dismissal of those employees who are unlikely to be able to return. Dismissal would be on the grounds of incapability. This is a serious step for the personnel manager to consider, and Incomes Data Services suggest that the following aspects are worthy of consideration:

- The nature, length and effect of the illness or disability on the employee's past and likely future service to the company.

- The importance of the job and the possibilities of temporary replacement.
- Whether it is against the employee's, the organisation's or even the public's interest to go on employing the individual.

In many circumstances the personnel manager will be able to investigate a much happier option, that of finding suitable alternative work in the organisation to which the employee may be transferred when sufficiently fit.

Sick pay and absence policy and procedures

Personnel managers are well placed to contribute to or instigate the development of occupational sick pay policy and of the procedures used to administer both occupational sick pay and SSP. Personnel managers also have a part to play in such procedures, apart from the obvious administrative role, as for example they may be involved in interviewing employees with a high level of absence prior to the initiation of disciplinary procedures in cases where there is a lack of evidence of genuine sickness.

Administrative procedures
The personnel manager will be the organisation's expert on SSP, and will normally be responsible for its administration, collating information from line managers and feeding relevant information into the payroll section, unless this is done electronically. There is a number of specialised computer packages available to assist personnel departments with this administrative responsibility, and the introduction of SSP spurred many departments into purchasing a computer. Absence and sick pay recording is particularly important as the DSS may ask to inspect records going back for up to three years. Where possible the records kept for the DSS should be combined with any additional absence and sick pay information so that there is only one sick pay record for each individual, thus avoiding the problems of duplication.

Monitoring of sick pay and absence
The monitoring and analysis of absence and sick pay is an important aspect of personnel work. Based on this information the personnel manager will be able to assist line managers by providing guidelines along which to take action regarding such matters as suspected abuse of the sick pay system.

Disciplinary procedures
The personnel manager will be involved at some stage in disciplinary matters resulting from the abuse of the sick pay scheme, depending on the requirements of the organisation's disciplinary procedure.

State and statutory sick pay

State or statutory sick pay was first administered by employers in April 1983 as a result of the Housing Benefits Act 1982. Since then the administration of the scheme has been amended by the Health and Social Security Act 1984 and the Social Security Act 1985. The changes came into force in April 1986. Under the SSP scheme the employer paid the employee, when sick, an amount equivalent to that which they would in the past have received from the DSS. The employer reclaimed the money that has been paid out from national insurance contributions which would normally have been forwarded to the government. Although low, state sickness benefit does take into account the needs of the person involved, so that a married person with two children would receive more pay than a single person. Since SSP was first administered by employers the scheme has changed more than once. The most recent changes in April 1994 resulted in the employer taking full financial responsibility for SSP for the first four weeks of absence, after which they can reclaim 100 per cent of sick pay paid from the state (see for example IDS 1994). Most employees are entitled to state sickness benefit; however, there are some exceptions which include employees who fall sick outside the EU, employees who are sick during an industrial dispute, employees over pensionable age and employees whose earnings are below the earnings limit. SSP is built around the concepts of qualifying days, waiting days, certification, linked periods, transfer to the DSS and record periods.

Qualifying days

Qualifying days are those days on which the employee would normally have worked, except for the fact that he or she was sick. For many Monday to Friday employees this is very straightforward. However, it is more complex to administer for those on some form of rotating week or shift system. Sick pay is only payable for qualifying days.

Waiting days

Three waiting days have to pass before the employee is entitled to receive sick pay. These three days must be qualifying days, and on the fourth qualifying day the employee is entitled to sickness benefit, should he or she still be away from work due to sickness.

Certification

A doctor's certificate for sickness is required after seven days of sick absence. Prior to this the employee provides self-certification. This involves notifying the employer of absence due to sickness by the first day on which benefit is due – that is, immediately following the three waiting days.

Linked periods

The three waiting days do not always apply. If the employee has had a period of incapacity from work (PIW) within the previous eight weeks, then the two periods are linked and treated as just one period for SSP purposes, and so the three waiting days do not have to pass again.

Transfer to the DSS

The employer does not have to administer SSP for every employee indefinitely. Where the employee has been absent due to sickness for a continuous or linked period of twenty-eight weeks the responsibility for payment passes from the employer to the DSS. A continuous period of twenty-eight weeks' sickness is clearly identifiable. It is not so clear when linked periods are involved. An employee who was sick for five days, back at work for four weeks, sick for one day, at work for seven weeks and then sick for two days would have a linked period of incapacity of eight days. Alternatively, an employee who was sick for four days, back at work for ten weeks and then sick for five days would this time have a period of incapacity of five days.

Record periods

The DSS requires employers to keep SSP records for three years so that these can be inspected. Gill and Chadwick (1986) point out that the new linkage and transfer rules mean that, in theory, an employer could be paying SSP to an individual for almost ten years before twenty-eight weeks' linked PIW came to an end. The DSS, however do not require records for the whole of a linked PIW if this is greater than three years.

Occupational sick pay

Occupational sick pay (OSP) is adminstered in a variety of different ways and the employee's pay while sick can vary between statutory benefit (as above) and full normal pay. Most schemes are individual to the employer and are administered according to different rules from state sick pay. However, with the introduction of SSP, Chadwick argues: 'However, as I hope I have illustrated, two different schemes, OSP and SSP, with totally differing sets of rules and regulations, can only cause confusion for your employees and, perhaps, additional employee relations problems' (Chadwick 1983, p. 29).

The introduction of SSP was an ideal opportunity for employers to review their sick pay arrangements, tighten up procedures and reconsider benefits. A number of employers, however, take the view that occupational sick pay will be abused and either fail to introduce a system or are very cautious about improving it. Employers are understandably concerned about the effects of high absence levels, which increase costs due to temporary cover, overtime or overmanning, and due to delayed or lost production. Additional problems are created by the need for reorganisation when employees are absent. However, some authors argue that this problem is exaggerated or has only a temporary effect: 'A common myth, often elevated into a "fact" by certain employers during negotiations, is that the introduction of, or improvement to an occupational sick-pay scheme will result in increased absenteeism' (Cunningham 1981, p. 55). Incomes Data Services have a slightly different view: 'Any increase in benefit or a reduction of waiting days is normally matched by a marked rise in absenteeism from the date of implementation, but this tends to fall back towards previous levels after a number of months' (IDS 1979, p. 12).

Some industries are better than others in the provision of sick pay, for example shipbuilding, leather and textiles, clothing and footwear are less well provided for than insurance, banking, gas, electricity, water, mining and public administration

(DHSS 1977). Similarly, some grades of employee fare better than others. Higher-paid workers are more likely to be in a scheme (DHSS 1977) and, in particular, white-collar and management staff are still better provided for than most manual workers, with a number of employers running two separate sick pay schemes.

REVIEW TOPIC 35.2

- How would you argue in favour of harmonisation of sick pay provision?
- What objectives may be raised against such a scheme and how would you deal with these?

Occupational sick pay schemes vary according to waiting days, period of service required, amount of benefit available, length of benefit entitlement, the funding of the scheme and administrative procedures.

Waiting days

Many occupational sick pay schemes have no waiting days at all, and the employee is paid from the first day of sickness. This is one area where there is a clear difference between manual and non-manual schemes, and Incomes Data Services comment: 'The manual unions, in particular, see the use of waiting days as the most obvious difference between staff and manual sick-pay schemes' (IDS 1979, p. 57). Many manual schemes still have three waiting days in line with the SSP regulations.

Period of service required

Some employers provide sick pay for sickness absence from the first day of employment. Others require a qualifying period to be served. For some this is a nominal period of four weeks, but the period may be three or six months, or a year or more. There is a major difference here from SSP which is available immediately after employment has begun.

Amount of benefit

Some employers offer a flat rate benefit which is paid in addition to the money provided via SSP. Others, however, link benefits to level of pay. The problem with flat rate schemes is that they quickly become out of date and need to be renegotiated from time to time. The best schemes offer normal pay for a specified period (minus the amount received via SSP). This is very straightforward for those staff who receive a basic salary with no other additions. It is more difficult to define for those whose pay is supplemented by shift allowances or productivity bonuses. Some employers will pay basic pay only with no additions, others may pay basic plus some or all additions, or give an average of the pay that has been earned over the weeks prior to sickness.

The amount of benefit may not be the same throughout the whole period of sickness. Sometimes an employer will pay a period on full pay, and then a period on half-pay, or some other combination.

Length of entitlement

The length of entitlement to sick pay varies considerably and is often dependent on the employee's length of service, so that entitlement to sick pay gradually increases in line with total length of service. Entitlement can vary between a few weeks and a year or more. Very often smaller entitlements will be expressed in terms of the number of weeks payable within any one year. However, unused entitlement can often be carried forward from one year to the next. Public sector employees are often well-off in respect of length of benefit and many employers provide six months' full pay followed by six months' half-pay after three years of service.

Funding of schemes

Most employers run non-contributory sick pay schemes. However, a few do require contributions from their employees. The majority of sick pay schemes are based on the individual employer, but there are some industry-wide schemes. Some employers provide sick pay schemes via insurance companies by paying premiums so that employees claim their sick pay from the insurance company. There is a number of disadvantages with these schemes, including the loss of future entitlement to some state benefits.

Administrative procedures

Each employer will develop administrative procedures which suit their own particular sick pay scheme. However, a number of general points have to be considered when designing procedures, as shown in Table 35.3.

Table 35.3   *Formulating administrative procedures*

- How, to whom and when should employees notify they are sick?
- When is a doctor's certificate required, to whom should it go?
- Any arrangements for return to work interviews?
- How is absence information to be transferred from the line manager to personnel, and from personnel to payroll?
- What should happen if employees are sick while on holiday or on a bank holiday?
- What sickness and absence records are to be kept and who will keep them, in what form?
- How are poor attenders to be identified, and what investigations should be made and action taken?
- What methods should be used to keep in touch with long-term sick employees?
- What arrangements are there to transfer older long-term sick employees on to a retirement pension?
- How do the OSP procedures integrate with the SSP procedures?

Absence and sick pay monitoring and control

The personnel department has a distinct role to play in the monitoring and control of absence levels and sick pay. In addition to the practical problems, high absence is bad for morale and suggests an employer unconcerned about the employees' behaviour. Control begins with formulating administrative procedures, as outlined in Table 35.3.

Procedures, however, are useless unless they are recognised and adhered to. It is, therefore, essential that employees know what is expected of them when they are sick – that they know whom to inform, when they need to do this and what information they need to give. If there is an employee handbook, the rules of the sick pay schemes and absence procedures should be included and this information should be emphasised by line managers. Employees need to be aware of sick pay policy, and what is regarded as acceptable and unacceptable behaviour in relation to the scheme. They need to know how the disciplinary procedure will be implemented with regard to abuse of the sick pay scheme, and the type of information that management will use in order to decide when to invoke the procedure. Sick pay should not, however, be presented in a completely negative way, and the reasons why the organisation provides sick pay and the benefits available should be clearly presented to encourage the employee to take a responsible attitude towards the scheme, so that the use of disciplinary procedures is a rare rather than a frequent event.

Managers also need to be very clear about their role in absence and sick pay procedures, in particular regarding the transfer of information and the interviewing of absentees on their return or after a certain level of absence has been reached. Some form of periodic check needs to be made to ensure that these features are working properly and not being buried under the heavy demands of the production schedule.

A further aspect of control is the monitoring of sick absence and other absence. Information for this monitoring can be used in the development of control procedures. For example, lists may be produced of those employees claiming most sick pay entitlement and managers may be asked to interview these employees in order to provide further information and explanation. Monitoring of sick absence is entirely dependent on the keeping of complete and reliable records. Useful analyses of this information can be produced by comparing different individuals; groups, such as age groups or skill level groups; departments; times of year; or comparing absence over a few years to identify trends. Comparison with the absence levels of other employers may also be illuminating. It is helpful to look at total amount of absence, number of spells of absence and length of each spell of absence. An excellent guide to the monitoring of absence is by Behrend (1978). An example of the type of analysis that Behrend has used with the help of computers is illustrated in Figure 35.3. The computer has also been used quite extensively in absence analysis, and one example of this is by Fell (1983).

Another important factor in absence control is to consider whether sick pay policy and procedures encourage longer spells of absence than necessary due to the use of waiting periods and back-dated payment for waiting periods if they are part of a longer period of absence.

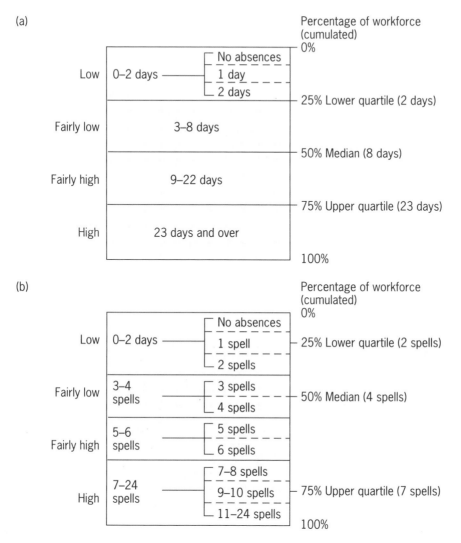

(a)

Percentage of workforce
(cumulated)
0%

Low	0–2 days	No absences
		1 day
		2 days

25% Lower quartile (2 days)

| Fairly low | 3–8 days |

50% Median (8 days)

| Fairly high | 9–22 days |

75% Upper quartile (23 days)

| High | 23 days and over |

100%

(b)

Percentage of workforce
(cumulated)
0%

Low	0–2 days	No absences
		1 spell
		2 spells

25% Lower quartile (2 spells)

| Fairly low | 3–4 spells | 3 spells |
| | | 4 spells |

50% Median (4 spells)

| Fairly high | 5–6 spells | 5 spells |
| | | 6 spells |

High	7–24 spells	7–8 spells
		9–10 spells
		11–24 spells

75% Upper quartile (7 spells)

100%

Figure 35.3 An example of the analysis of absence: (a) classification of employees by number of days lost: (b) classification of employees by number of absence spells (Behrend 1978, p. 13). Reproduced with permission of IPD Publications.

REVIEW TOPIC 35.3

Suggest an absence monitoring and control system for your organisation, describing the role of the line manager and the personnel department.

35.1 The personnel department is becoming increasingly involved in the area of pensions.

35.2 Both the personnel manager and the line manager have a key role to play in absence control.

35.3 Pensions are still seen as the mark of a good employer, and are increasingly seen as deferred pay rather than a reward for long service.

35.4 Many employers feel a moral obligation to provide for employees when they are sick. There are also practical advantages such as a healthier workforce, being seen as a caring employer and being more able to attract new employees.

35.5 Pensions have traditionally been an area where employees have been allowed little choice. The opportunities for choice are gradually increasing.

35.6 Some pension schemes have difficulty in coping with inflation and career progression, and most schemes fail to provide adequately for early leavers.

35.7 Absence control is important, as high absence levels cost money, lower morale and suggest an employer's lack of interest in their employees.

References

Allen, S. (1994), 'Sea-change for the pensions industry', *Personnel Management*, March.

Amy, R. (1986), 'Pensions after 1988: sizing up the options', *Personnel Management*, December.

Behrend, H. (1978), *How to Monitor Absence from Work: From Head-count to Computer*, London: Institute of Personnel Management.

Booth, G. (1986), 'Choosing an investment manager'. In *The Institute of Directors, The Directors' Guide to Pensions*, London: The Director Publications.

Butler, G., and Pirie, M. (1983), *The Future of Pensions*, London: Adam Smith Institute.

Central Statistical Office (1985), *Social Trends, no. 15,* London: HMSO.

Chadwick, K. (1983), 'A prescription for statutory sick pay and the supplementary benefits', *Personnel Management*, March.

Cunningham, M. (1981), *Non-wage Benefits*, London: Pluto Press.

DHSS (1977), *Report on a Survey of Occupational Sick Pay Schemes*, London: HMSO.

DHSS (1984), *Portable Pensions: A consultative document*, London: Department of Health and Social Security.

Fell, A. (1983), 'Putting a price on lost time', *Personnel Management*, April.

Garlick, R. (1986), 'The case for company pensions'. In *The Institute of Directors. The Directors' Guide to Company Pensions*, London: The Director Publications.

Gill, D. and Chadwick, K. (1986), 'The new prescription for SSP', *Personnel Management*, April.

Hayward, S. (1989), 'Coping with pensions changes', *Director*, December.

Hearn, A. (1992), 'All change on the pensions front?', *Personnel Management*, October.

Hopegood, J. (1994), 'Money-go-round: solving the age-old SERPs puzzle – government uncertainty may make it sensible for most people to opt out of earnings related pension schemes', *Daily Telegraph*, 19 March.

Hunt, P. (1988), 'Must pensions always be a turn-off?', *Personnel Management*, November.

Incomes Data Services (IDS) (1979), *IDS Guide to Sick Pay and Absence*, London: Incomes Data Services.

Incomes Data Services (IDS) (1982), *Pensions for Early Leavers: IDS study, no. 274*, London: Incomes Data Services.

Incomes Data Services (IDS) (1994), *Absence and Sick Pay Policies, IDS Study No 556*, June. London: Incomes Data Services.

Institute of Directors (1986), *The Directors' Guide to Pensions*, London: The Director Publications.

Marsh, P., Smith, A., Cohen, N., *et al.* (1994), 'The personal pensions time bomb; thousands pay dearly for company agents' poor advice', *Financial Times*, 28 February.

Moody, C. (1984a), 'Pensions and other forms of non-cash remuneration'. In D. Guest and T. Kenny (eds) *A Textbook of Techniques and Strategies in Personnel Management*, London: Institute of Personnel Management.

Moody, C. (1984b), 'The perils of portable pensions', *Personnel Management*, December.

Nash, T. (1989), 'Know your own pension', *Director*, January.

Noble-Warren, R. (1986), 'Lifetime planning'. In *The Institute of Directors, The Directors' Guide to Pensions*, London: The Director Publications.

Toulson, N. (1982), *Modern Pensions*, Hemel Hempstead: Woodhead-Faulkner.

36 Interactive skill: negotiation

Negotiation is a longstanding art, which has developed into a major mode of decision-making in all aspects of social, political and business life, even though there is always a feeling that it is no more than a substitute for direct, decisive action. Henry Kissinger was US Secretary of State when protracted negotations eventually brought to an end the war in Vietnam. He commented:

> A lasting peace could come about only if neither side sought to achieve everything that it had wanted; indeed, that stability depended on the relative satisfaction, and therefore the relative dissatisfaction, of all the parties concerned. (Kissinger 1973)

In employment we have acquired the institutions of collective bargaining as a means of regulating some parts of the employment relationship between employer and organised employees. To some this is the cornerstone of industrial democracy and the effective running of a business, but to others it is seen as impairing efficiency, inhibiting change and producing the lowest, rather than the highest, common factor of co-operation between management and employees.

Is negotiation rightly viewed as an activity that is only second best to unilateral decision-making? If the outcome is no more than compromise, the choice seems to be between negotiation and capitulation. Some would argue that capitulation by one side would be a better outcome for both than a compromise that ignores the difficulties and dissatisfies both. There is, however, an alternative to splitting the diffrence in negotiation and that is where the differences in view and objective of the parties are accommodated to such an extent that the outcome for both is better than could have been achieved by the unilateral executive action of either.

Any negotiation is brought about by the existence of some goals that are common to both parties and some goals that conflict. Between employer and employees the desire to keep the business in operation is one of the goals they usually have in common, but there may be many that conflict, and the two parties negotiate a settlement because the attempt by one to force a solution on the other would either fail because of the other's strength or would not be as satisfactory a settlement without the approval of the other party. Both parties acknowledge that they will move from their opening position and that sacrifices in one area may produce compensating benefits in another. Many years ago G. C. Homans expressed the situation thus:

The more the items at stake can be divided into goods valued more by one party than they cost to the other and goods valued more by the other party than they cost to the first, the greater the chances of a successful outcome. (Homans 1961, p. 62)

The nature of conflict in the employment relationship

The approach outlined later in this chapter depends on the view that conflict of interests is inevitable between employer and employee because there is an authority relationship in which the aims of the two parties will at least sometimes conflict. A further assumption is that such conflict does not necessarily damage that relationship.

This has led a number of commentators to discuss negotiation in terms of equally matched protagonists. The power of the two parties may not actually be equal, but they are both willing to behave as if it were. The negotiation situation thus has the appearance of power equalisation, which can be real or illusory, due to the search for a solution to a problem. When both sides set out to reach an agreement that is satisfactory to themselves and acceptable to the other, then their power is equalised by that desire. Where the concern for acceptance by the other is lacking, there comes the use of power play of the forcing type described later in this chapter:

> ...negotiators seek to increase common interest and expand cooperation in order to broaden the area of agreement to cover the item under dispute. On the other hand, each seeks to maximize his own interest and prevail in conflict, in order to make the agreement more valuable to himself. No matter what angle analysis takes, it cannot eliminate the basic tension between cooperation and conflict that provides the dynamic of negotiation. (Zartman 1976, p. 41)

The relative power of the parties is likely to fluctuate from one situation to the next; this is recognised by the ritual and face-saving elements of negotiation, where a power imbalance is not fully used, both to make agreement possible and in the knowledge that the power imbalance may be reversed on the next issue to be resolved.

The classic work of Douglas (1962) produced a formulation of the negotiating encounter that has been little modified by those coming after her. Walton (1969) has written a most helpful book, too little known in the United Kingdom, about the application of this thinking to the interpersonal relationships between equals in the management hierarchy. However, this needs further thought if it is to be applied to the negotiations that take place between representatives of management and representatives of employees about terms and conditions of employment. Cooper and Barlett point out the difficulty:

> If equality is available to all...conflicting groups can meet. All they need to shed are their misperceptions and their prejudices. Any differences are psychological rather than economic. The truth of the matter is, of course, that...there are glaring inequalities of

wealth and power. Each society contains its own contradictions which arise from the distribution of money, of status and control. So conflict resolution is not just a matter of clearing away mistrust and misunderstanding, replacing them with communication. It is also concerned with political matters such as the re-allocation of power. (Cooper and Bartlett 1976, p. 167)

Sources of conflict in the collective employment relationship

Many texts on organisational behaviour include sections on reducing conflict and management talk is full of the need for teamworking, corporate culture and collaboration, so why do we find one area of working life where conflict is readily accepted, even emphasised?

Those who have charted the evolution of the human race, such as Konrad Lorenz (1966) and Robert Ardrey (1967), demonstrate for us the innate aggressiveness of man. Although the processes of civilisation tend to constrain it there is a natural impulse to behave aggressively to some degree at some time. It has a number of outlets; for example, watching football, wrestling or boxing. Another outlet for aggression is in negotiations within the employing organisation, which is a splendid arena for the expression of aggressiveness and bravura without actually incurring the phsyical risks that would be involved in violent combat. Dr Johnson summed up the attractions of vigorous disagreement when he said, 'I dogmatise and am contradicted, and in this conflict of opinions I find delight'.

Divergence of interests
Probably the main source of industrial relations conflict is divergence of interests between those who are classified as managers and those who are seen as non-managers. One group is seeking principally such things as efficiency, economy, productivity and the obedience of others to their own authority. The members of the other group are interested in these things, but are more interested in features such as high pay, freedom of action, independence of supervision, scope for the individual and leisure. To some extent these invariably conflict.

Potential benefits of such conflict
It is widely believed that conflict of the type described here – and described frequently and more luridly in the press – is counter-productive, and that all should make strenuous efforts to eliminate it. There are, however, some advantages.

Clearing the air
Many people feel that a conflict situation is improved by getting bad feelings 'off their chests' and bringing the matter into the open. Sometimes combatants feel closer as a result.

Introducing new rules

Employment is governed by a number of rules – formal rules that define unfair dismissal and the rate of pay for various jobs, as well as informal rules like modes of address. Management/union conflict is usually about a disagreement over the rules and the bargain that is struck produces a new rule: a new rate of pay, a new employment practice, or whatever. It may be the only way of achieving that particular change, and it is a very authoritative source of rulemaking because of the participation in its creation.

Modifying the goals

The goals that management set can be modified as a result of conflict with others. Ways in which their goals will be unpopular or difficult to implement may be seen for the first time and modifications made early instead of too late. A greater range and diversity of views are brought to bear on a particular matter so that the capacity for innovation is enhanced.

Clash of values

Most fundamental is the possible clash of values, usually about how people should behave. These may be variations of allegiance to the positions of different political parties on questions such as 'What is production for?', or differences of social class attitude to what constitutes courtesy. Most frequently the clash is about the issues of managerial prerogative. Managers are likely to believe and proclaim that management is their inalienable right, so that those who question the way their work is done are ignorant or impertinent. Non-managers may regard management as a job that should be done properly by people who are responsive to questioning and criticism.

Competitiveness

One of the most likely sources is the urge to compete for a share of limited resources. Much of the drive behind differential pay claims is that of competing with other groups at a similar level, but there may also be competition for finance, materials, security, survival, power, recognition or status.

Organisational tradition

If the tradition of an organisation is to be conflict-prone, then it may retain that mode obdurately, while other organisations in which conflict has not been a prominent feature may continue without it. It is axiomatic that certain industries in the United Kingdom are much more likely to display the manifestations of extreme conflict in industrial relations than others. Indicators such as the number of working days lost through strikes show a pattern of distribution which varies little between different industries year by year. The nature of the conflict can range between the extremes of pettiness, secrecy, fear and insecurity on one hand, to vigorous, open and productive debate on the other, with many organisations exhibiting neither.

Understanding or respective positions

Combatants will come to a better understanding of their position on the issue being debated because of their need to articulate it, set it forth, develop supporting arguments and then defend those arguments against criticism. This enables them to see more clearly what they want, why they want it and how justifiable it is. In challenging the position of the other party, they will come to a clearer understanding of where they stand, and why.

Potential drawbacks of such conflict

These advantages may not be sufficient to balance the potential drawbacks.

Waste of time and energy
Conflict and the ensuing negotiations take a great deal of time and energy. Conflict can become attritive when over-personalised, and individuals become obsessed with the conflict itself rather than what it is about. Negotiation takes a lot longer than simple management decree.

Emotional stress for participants
People vary in the type of organisational stress to which they are prone. The need to be involved in negotiation is a source of stress which some poeple find very taxing, while others find it stimulating.

Organisational stress
Accommodating conflict often causes some inefficiency through the paraphernalia that can accompany it: striking, working to rule, working without enthusiasm, withdrawing co-operation or the simple delay caused by protracted negotiation.

Risks
Engaging in negotiation may be necessary as the only way to cope with a conflictual situation, but there is the risk of stirring up a hornets' nest. When conflict is brought to the surface it may be resolved or accommodated, or if the situation is handled badly it may get worse.

Worsening communications
The quality and amount of communication is impaired. Those involved are concerned more to confirm their own viewpoint than to convey understanding, and there are perceptual distortions such as stereotyping and cognitive dissonance. The attitudes behind the communications may also become inappropriate as there are greater feelings of hostility and attempts to score off others.

Bargaining strategies
A reading of Schmidt and Tannenbaum (1960) and Lawrence and Lorsch (1972) helps us to identify various strategies that are adopted to cope with conflict and some of the likely effects.

Avoidance

To some extent conflict can be 'handled' by ignoring it. For a time this will prevent it surfacing so that it remains latent rather than manifest: the danger being that it is harder to deal with when it eventually does erupt. Opposing views cannot be heard unless there is apparatus for their expression. The management of an organisation can fail to provide such apparatus by, for instance, not having personnel specialists, not recognising trade unions and not recognising employee representatives. If the management organise the establishment as if conflict of opinion did not exist, any such difference will be less apparent and its expression stifled. This is a strategy that is becoming harder and harder to sustain due to the developing legal support for employee representation.

Smoothing

A familiar strategy is to seek the resolution of conflict by honeyed words in exhortation or discussion where the emphasis is on the value of teamwork, the assurance that 'we all agree really' and an overt, honest attempt to get past the divergence of opinion, which is regarded as a temporary and unfortunate aberration. This is often an accurate diagnosis of the situation and represents an approach that would have broad employee support in a particular employment context, but there is always the risk that the smoothing ignores the real problem, like giving a massage to someone who has suffered a heart attack.

Forcing

The opposite to smoothing is to attack expressions of dissent and deal with conflict by stamping it out. This is not easy and has innumerable, unfortunate precedents in both the political and industrial areas.

Compromise

Where divergence of views is acknowledged and confronted, one possibility is to split the difference. If employees claim a pay increase of £10 and the management say they can afford nothing, a settlement of £5 saves the face of both parties but satisfies neither. However common this strategy may be – and sometimes there is no alternative – it has this major drawback: that both parties fail to win.

Confrontation

The fifth strategy is to confront the issue on which the parties differ. This involves accepting that there is a conflict of opinions or interests, exploring the scale and nature of the conflict and then working towards an accommodation of the differences which will provide a greater degree of satisfaction of the objectives of both parties than can be achieved by simple compromise. We suggest that this is the most productive strategy in many cases and offers the opportunity of both parties winning. It is this fifth strategy which we consider in the remainder of this chapter.

Bargaining tactics

In preparing for negotiation there are a number of things which bargainers must set in their minds before they begin.

Resolution or accommodation

Conflict can be resolved so that the original feelings of antagonism or opposition vanish, at least over the issues that has brought the conflict to a head. The schoolboy story of how two boys 'put on the gloves in the gym' after a long feud and thereafter shook hands and became firm friends is a theoretical example of a conflict resolved. This type of outcome has a romantic appeal and will frequently be sought in industrial relations issues, because so many people feel acutely uncomfortable when involved in relationships of overt antagonism.

Alternatively the conflict may be accommodated, so that the differences of view persist, but some *modus vivendi*, some form of living with the situation, is discovered. In view of the inevitability of the conflict that is endemic in the employment relationship, accommodation may be a more common prospect than resolution, but it is an interesting question for a negotiator to ponder when approaching the bargaining table: which is it – resolution or accommodation?

Tension level

Most negotiators feel that they have no chance to determine the timing of encounters. This is partly due to reluctance; managers in particular tend to resort to negotiation only when necessary, and the necessity is usually a crisis. A more proactive (instead of reactive) approach is to initiate encounters, to some extent at least trying to push them into favourable timings.

A feature of timing is the tension level. Too much and the negotiators get the jitters, unable to see things straight and indulging in excessive interpersonal vituperation: too little tension, and there is no real will to reach a settlement. Ideal timing is to get a point when both sides have a balanced desire to reach a settlement.

Power balance

Effective negotiation is rarely limited to the sheer exploitation of power advantage. The best settlement is one in which both sides can recognize their own and mutual advantages (Fowler 1990, pp. 11–16). The background to any negotiation includes the relative power of the disputants. Power parity is the most conducive to success:

> Perceptions of power inequality undermine trust, inhibit dialogue, and decrease the likelihood of a constructive outcome from an attempted confrontation. Inequality tends to undermine trust on both ends of the imbalanced relationship, directly affecting both the person with the perceived power inferiority and the one with perceived superiority. (Walton 1969, p. 98)

The greater the power differential, the more negative the attitudes.

Synchronising

The approaches and reciprocations of the two parties need a degree of synchronising to ensure that an approach is made at a time when the other party is ready to deal with it. Management interpretation of managerial prerogative often causes managers to move quickly in the search of a solution, virtually pre-empting negotiation. When what they see as a positive overture is not reciprocated, then they are likely to feel frustrated, discouraged and cross; making themselves in turn unready for overtures from the other side.

Openness

Conflict handling is more effective if the participants can be open with each other about the facts of the situation and their feelings about it. The Americans place

---

John Dunlop is known as one of the great theorists of industrial relations and the processes in collective bargaining. David Farnham summarises the ten points of Dunlop's (1984) framework for analysing the negotiating process:

1. It takes agreement within each negotiating group to reach a settlement between them.
2. Initial proposals are typically large, compared with eventual settlements.
3. Both sides need to make concessions in order to move towards an agreement.
4. A deadline is an essential feature of most negotiating.
5. The end stages of negotiating are particularly delicate, with private discussions often being used to close the gap between the parties.
6. Negotiating is influenced by whether it involves the final, intermediate or first stages of the conflict resolution process.
7. Negotiating and overt conflict may take place simultaneously, with the conflict serving as a tool for getting agreement.
8. Getting agreement does not flourish in public.
9. Negotiated settlements need procedures to administer or interpret the final agreement.
10. Personalities and their interactions can affect negotiating outcomes.

(Farnham 1993, p. 337)

great emphasis on this and we must appreciate that openness is more culturally acceptable in the United States than in the United Kingdom, but we note their concern that negotiators should own up to feelings of resentment and anger, rather than masking their feelings behind role assumptions of self-importance.

The negotiation sequence

Having reviewed the background to bargaining and negotiation we now consider the various stages of the negotiating encounter in which aspects of ritual are especially important, making perhaps for formality and awkwardness rather than relaxed informality. However, the ritual steps are not time-wasting prevarication, but an inescapable feature of the process.

Preparation
In Figure 36.1 there is a summary of the various stages in the negotiating process itself.

Agenda
The meeting needs an agenda or at least some form of agreement about what is to be discussed. In some quarters a naive conviction persists that there is some benefit in concealing the topic from the other party until the encounter begins, presumably because there is something to be gained from surprise. In fact this only achieves a deferment of discussion until the other party have had a chance to consider their position. The nature of the agenda can have an effect on both the conduct and outcome of the negotiations. It affects the conduct of the encounter by revealing and defining the matters that each side wants to deal with. It is unlikely that other matters will be added to the agenda, particularly if negotiations take place regularly between the parties, so that the negotiators can begin to see, before the meeting, what areas the discussions will cover.

The agenda will influence the outcome of negotiations as a result of the sequence of items on it as the possibilities of accommodation between the two positions emerge from the discussions. If, for instance, all the items of the employees' claim come first and all the management's points come later, the possibilities do not turn into probabilities until the discussions are well advanced. An agenda that juxtaposes management and employee 'points' in a logical fashion can enable the shape of a settlement to develop in the minds of the negotiators earlier, even though there would be no commitment until all the pieces of the jigsaw were available. Many negotiations take place without an agenda at all, sometimes because there is a crisis, sometimes because neither party is sufficiently well organised to prepare one. Morley and Stephenson (1977, pp. 74–8) review a number of studies to draw the conclusion that agreement between negotiators is facilitated when there is the opportunity for them to experience 'orientation' – considering on what to stand firm and on what to contemplate yielding – or where there is an understanding of the issues involved. An agenda is a prerequisite of orientation.

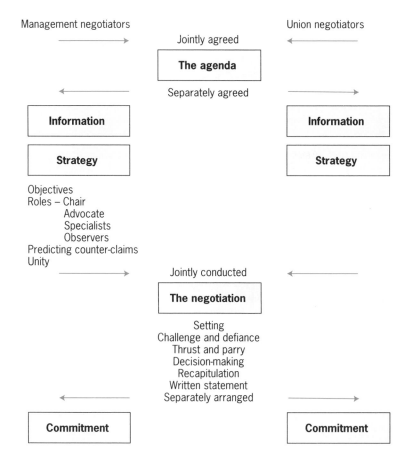

Management negotiators   Union negotiators

Jointly agreed

The agenda

Separately agreed

Information   **Information**

Strategy   **Strategy**

Objectives
Roles – Chair
       Advocate
       Specialists
       Observers
Predicting counter-claims
Unity

Jointly conducted

The negotiation

Setting
Challenge and defiance
Thrust and parry
Decision-making
Recapitulation
Written statement
Separately arranged

Commitment   **Commitment**

Figure 36.1   The negotiating process.

Information

Both parties will need facts to support their argument in negotiation. Some information will be provided to employee representatives for the purposes of collective bargaining and both sets of negotiators have to collect what they need, analyse it so that they understand it, and confirm that the interpretation is shared by each member of their team.

Strategy

The main feature of preparation is the determination of strategy by each set of negotiators. Probably the most helpful work on negotiation strategy has been done by Fowler (1990), with his careful analysis of bargaining conventions and possibilities. In this chapter we limit our considerations to four aspects of strategy.

Objectives

What do the negotiators seek to achieve? Here one would ask them to produce clear and helpful objectives. When the question has been put to management negotiators entering either real or contrived negotiations in recent years the following have been some of the statements of objectives:

> 'Get the best deal we possibly can.'
> 'Maintain factory discipline at all costs.'
> 'Remain dignified at all times.'
> 'Look for an opening and exploit it to the full.'

Apart from their general feebleness, all these declarations have a common, negative quality. The initiative is with the other party and the only management strategy is to resist for as long as possible and to concede as little as possible. If this is the best management negotiators can contrive, then their prospects are indeed bleak. They are bound to lose; the only unresolved question is how much. They cannot gain anything because they do not appear to want anything.

More positive objectives are those that envisage improvements, which could flow from a changing of the employment rules – changes in efficiency, working practices, manning levels, shiftwork patterns, administrative procedures, flexibility, cost control, and so forth. Unless both parties to the negotiations want something out of the meeting there is little scope for anything but attrition.

Roles

Who will do what in the negotiations? A popular fallacy is that negotiation is best conducted by 'everyone chipping in when they have something to say' and 'playing it by ear'. This is the style for a brainstorming, problem-solving group discussion, and negotiation is quite different. Problem-solving implies common interests; negotiation implies conflicting interests between groups who are opposed in debate. Negotiators need a specific role, that they stay in. The roles are:

1. *Chair:* in the majority of cases the management provides this function, and one of the management team will chair the discussion and control the meeting.
2. *Advocate:* each party requires one person who will be the principal advocate to articulate the case and to examine the opposing case. This provides focus to the discussion and control of the argument. Although it is common for the roles of chair and advocate to be combined in one person for status reasons, this can put a great strain on the individual, who is bowling and keeping wicket at the same time.
3. *Specialist:* the third role is that of specialist. One person who fully understands the details of the management proposal or arrangement that is being questioned, another to provide expert comment on any legal points, and so forth. The important emphasis is on what the specialist does *not* do. One would not expect this particular negotiator to become involved in the general debate, as this is confusing and moves control from the advocate. The specialist's role is to provide advice when required, rather like the civil servants who regularly pass notes to Ministers appearing before House of Commons Committees. Negotiating does not benefit from free-for-all, unstructured discussion.

4. *Observers:* there is no need for all those attending to speak in order to justify their presence. There is an important part to be played by those who do no more than observe the discussions. They are less emotionally involved in the interplay and point-scoring, and are able to evaluate the situation as it develops. When there are adjournments the observers often initiate discussions within their team as strategy is redefined and further tactics considered.

Predicting counter-claims

No strategy survives intact the first encounter with the opposition, but its chances are improved if the negotiators have tried to predict what they will hear from the opposition. In this way they will be prepared not only to advance their own arguments, but also to respond to arguments put to them.

Unity

Because negotiations are the confrontation of different sets of interests, each team works out a united position before negotiations begin and expresses that unity in negotiation. If the position is to be modified, then they will agree the modification. This is another aspect of the vital difference between this activity and problem-solving. It is the differences between the parties that have to be handled; differences within the parties are simply a nuisance.

The negotiations

Setting

The number of people representing each side will influence the conduct of negotiations. The larger the number the greater the degree of formality that is needed to manage the meeting; this is an argument in favour of negotiations between very small teams. On the other hand, meetings between two or three people in 'smoked-filled rooms' give rise to allegations of manipulation and are difficult for members of trade unions to countenance in view of their dependence on democratic support. Another problem is that different phases of negotiation call for different arrangements. Relatively large numbers can be an advantage at the beginning, but are often a hindrance in the later stags:

> it is not uncommon for the trade union side to field a sizeable team – a union official, perhaps, supported by a shop stewards' committee. It is unwise for a single manager to attempt to negotiate alone with such a team. Negotiation demands a high level of concentration and quick thinking and it is difficult for one person to maintain full attention to everything that is said, and to detect every nuance in the discussion. This does not mean that the management team must equal the trade union team in size. Indeed, to go beyond a fairly small number runs the risk of poor coordination between team members and the possibility that differing views will emerge within the team as negotiations proceed. (Fowler 1990, p. 35)

When asked to suggest an appropriate number, most experienced negotiators opt for three or four on each side.

The nature of the seating arrangements needs to reflect the nature of the meeting, and that means that the sides face each other, with the boundaries between the two being clear. The importance of the physical arrangements were demonstrated by the Paris peace talks, which were intended to bring an end to the Vietnam war. The start of talks was delayed for some weeks due to the delegations not being able to agree about the shape of the table.

Challenge and defiance

The somewhat melodramatic term 'challenge and defiance' is used to describe the opening stage of the negotiations, for the deliberate reason that there is a deal of theatricality about the various processes.

Negotiators begin by making it clear that they are representing the interests of people whose will and desire transcends that of the representatives themselves. They also emphasise the strength of their case and its righteousness as well as the impossibility of any movement from the position they are declaring. The theatricality lies in the realisation by both sides that there will be movement from the relative positions that they are busy declaring to be immovable. The displays of strength are necessary for the negotiators to convince themselves that they are right and to convince the opposition.

The substantive element of this phase is to clarify what the differences are. By the time it draws to a close the negotiators should be quite clear on the matters that divide them, where and how. This, of course, is an important part of the process, differentiation precedes integration.

It is important for the participants to keep the level of interpersonal animosity down. This is a part of the emphasis on their representative role that has already been mentioned. Different behaviours are needed later that depend on an open, trusting relationship between the negotiators, so this must not be impaired by personal acrimony at the opening. It is similar to the ritual whereby a lawyer may refer to a legal adversary as 'my learned friend'.

Thrust and parry

After the differences have been explored there is an almost instinctive move to a second, integrative stage of the encounter. Here negotiators are looking for possibilities of movement and mutual accommodation:

> Douglas distinguishes between the public role-playing activities of the first stage and the 'psychological' (individual) activities of the second stage as being concerned, respectively, with inter-party and interpersonal exchange. Behaviourally the inter-party exchange is characterized by official statements of position, ostensibly committing the

party or parties to some future action congruent with that position. The interpersonal exchange, on the other hand, is characterized by unofficial behaviours which do not so commit the parties in question. (Morley and Stephenson 1970, p. 19)

Thus the statements made by negotiators are of a much more tentative nature than earlier, as they sound out possibilities, float ideas, ask questions, make suggestions and generally change style towards a problem-solving mode. This has to be done without any commitment of the party that is being represented, so the thrusts are couched in very non-committal terms, specifically exonerating the party from any responsibility. Gradually, the opportunities for mutual accommodation can be perceived in the background of the discussion. We can now incorporate the idea of target points and resistance points advanced by Walton and McKersie (1965).

The target point of a negotiation team is the declared objective – what they would really like to achieve. It will be spelled out in challenge and defiance. The resistance point is where they would rather break off negotiations than settle. This point is never declared and is usually not known, either. Although negotiators frequently begin negotiations with a feeling of 'not a penny more than…,' the point at which they would actually resist is seldom the same as that at which they think they would resist. Normally the resistance points for both parties slide constantly back and forth during negotiations.

Decision-making

Through thrust and parry all the variations of integration will have been considered and explored, even though negotiators will have veered away from making firm commitments. The third phase of their encounter is when they reach an agreement, and it is interesting to pause here with the comment that agreement is inevitable in all but a small minority of situations, because the bargainers need each other and they have no one else with whom to negotiate. The employees want to continue working for the organisation. Even if they take strike action, they will eventually return to work. The management need the employees to work for them. Employees collectively cannot choose a different management with whom to negotiate and managers can seldom choose a replacement workforce with whom to bargain. They have to reach agreement, no matter how long it takes.

After an adjournment the management will make an offer. The decision about what to offer is the most difficult and important task in the whole process, because the offer can affect the resistance point of the other party. The way in which the other's resistance point will be affected cannot be predetermined. A very low offer could move the other's resistance point further away or bring it nearer; we cannot be sure until the negotiations actually take place.

The offer may be revised, but eventually an offer will be accepted and the negotiations – not the full process – is over.

Negotiations on the contract for collective consent are thus significantly different from those other types of bargaining in which people engage. The negotiations to purchase a second-hand car or a house may seem at first sight to be similar, but in both those situations either party can opt out at any stage and cease to deal any further. The possibility of losing the other is always present, just as is the possibility of negotiating with a different 'opponent'. For this reason the political analogies are more helpful. A peace treaty has to be agreed between the nations that have been at war, and no one else.

Recapitulation

Once a bargain has been struck the tension of negotiation is released and the natural inclination of the negotiators is to break up and spread the news of the agreement that has been reached. It is suggested that they should resist this temptation and first recapitulate all the points on which they have agreed and, if necessary, make arrangements on any minor matters still outstanding that everyone had forgotten.

In the wake of a settlement there is usually a number of such minor matters. If they are dealt with there and then they should be dealt with speedily because of the overriding feeling for agreement that has been established. If discussion of them is deferred because they are difficult, then agreement may be hard to reach later as the issues stand on their own, instead of in the context of a larger settlement.

Written statement

If it is possible to produce the brief written statement before the meeting is ended, both parties to the negotiations will be greatly helped. The emphasis here is on producing a brief written statement before the meeting ends, not as soon as possible afterwards. This will help all the negotiators to take away the same interpretation of what they have done and make them less dependent on recollection. In most circumstances it can also be used to advise non-participants: retyped as a memorandum to supervisors, put up on notice-boards, read out at union meetings, and so on. This will reduce the distortion that can stem from rumour. Until the agreement is in writing it rests on an understanding, and understanding can easily change.

Commitment of the parties

So far agreement has been reached between negotiators only, and it is of no value unless the parties represented by those negotiators accept it and make it work. This requires acceptance at two levels: first in words and then in deeds.

Employee representatives have to report back to their membership and persuade them to accept the agreement. To some extent management representatives

> Lemuel Boulware, Vice-Presidence for Employee Relations in the General Electric Company of the United States, tried to side-step the ritual dance described above by developing a strategy which he called 'truth in bargaining'. The essence was that his first offer was also his last. He claimed that in conventional bargaining everyone knew that the first offer would be improved, so it was articially low. He intended to be direct and truthful, making one offer that would not be varied so as to save time and speculation about the final outcome.
>
> This policy had short-run success, but trade unions objected to Boulwarism on the grounds that it eliminated the constructive interchange of normal bargaining and diminished the importance of union representatives in negotiation. Eventually they challenged the policy successfully in the US courts on the grounds that it was not bargaining in good faith.

may have to do the same thing, but they customarily carry more personal authority to make decisions than do employee representatives.

Although this is a difficult and uncertain process, it is no more important than the final level of acceptance, which is where people make the agreement work. Benefits to the employees are likely to be of the type that are simple to administer – such as an increase in the rates of pay – but benefits to the business, such as changes in working practices and the variation of demarcation boundaries, are much more difficult. They may quickly be glossed over and forgotten unless the changes are painstakingly secured after the terms have been agreed.

REVIEW TOPIC 36.2

1. What was Lemuel Boulware's mistake?
2. Why is the process (as well as the result) of negotiating important to both management representatives and employee representatives?
3. Is the process of negotiation important to the members of management and to the employees who are represented, but not participating in the negotiations; or are they only interested in the result?
4. In view of the assertive, take-it-leave-it approach of some managements during the 1980s is Boulware just a historical footnote, or is there still a lesson to be learned from his experience?

References

Ardrey, R. (1967), *The Territorial Imperative*, London: Collins.

Cooper, B. M., and Bartlett, A. F. (1976), *Industrial Relations: A Study in Conflict*, London: Heinemann.

Douglas, A. (1962), *Industrial Peacemaking*, New York: Columbia University Press.

Dunlop, J. T. (1984), *Dispute Resolution*, London: Auburn.

Farnham, D. (1993), *Employee Relations*, London: Institute of Personnel Management.

Fowler, A. (1990), *Negotiation Skills and Strategies*, London: Institute of Personnel Management.

Homans, G. C. (1961), *Social Behaviour: Its Elementary Forms*, London: Routledge & Kegan Paul.

Kissinger, H. (1973), in *New York Times*, 25 January.

Lawrence, P. R. and Lorsche, J. W. (1972), *Managing Group and Intergroup Relations*, Homewood, Ill.: Dorsey.

Lorenz, K. (1966), *On Aggression*, London: Methuen.

Morley, I. and Stephenson, G. M. (1970), 'Strength of case, communication systems and the outcomes of simulated negotiations', *Industrial Relations Journal*, Summer.

Morley, I. and Stephenson, G. M. (1977), *The Social Psychology of Bargaining*, London: George Allen & Unwin.

Schmidt, W. and Tannenbaum, R. (1960), 'Management of differences', *Harvard Business Review*, November/December, pp. 107–15.

Walton, R. E. (1969), *Interpersonal Peacemaking: Confrontations and Third Party Consultation*, Reading, Mass: Addison-Wesley.

Walton, R. E. and McKersie, R. B. (1965), *Towards a Behavioural Theory of Labour Negotiations*, London: McGraw-Hill.

Zartman, I. W. (1976), *The 50% Solution*, New York: Anchor Press/Doubleday.

PART VIII

Finale

37 The international dimension

Throughout this book we have referred to strategy and have chosen to separate out strategic aspects in each of the six central parts. At the beginning we made the familiar comments that human resouce management was generally regarded as being more strategic than personnel management, with the rider that much of the value of personnel management was lost if one *only* looked at strategically: operational personnel management was crucial to organisational success, quite as much as strategic initiatives. We can open this chapter by stating unequivocally that the international dimension is exclusively strategic. This is summed up in the idea, 'think globally; act locally'.

> Successful international managers, whether mobile or non-mobile, must be able to act locally, but to plan and think strategically and globally. (Barham and Rassam 1989, p. 149)

There is a strict limitation on the extent to which employment practices can be harmonised between different countries and cultures. The Germans have a system of works councils that operate in a way that is quite different from the United Kingdom or Ireland. The French use graphology as a selection method much more extensively than any other western country. Methods of performance appraisal have to be modified to suit local conditions, as Ling Sing Chee reports in describing the processes of Singapore International Airlines:

> The Thai office reported difficulty with the performance appraisal process, namely in writing negative comments (because of religious beliefs about reincarnation) and have adapted the system to accommodate cultural differences. (Ling Sing Chee 1994, p. 154)

Actual personnel and employment practice will always need to be appropriate to the local cultural and legal situation. This will be set within a much wider strategic framework of international human resource management.

Working internationally is now more extensive and varied than ten years ago. Then the phrase conjured up visions of expatriates acting as technological or managerial missionaries in developing countries, overseas sales representatives doing deals in cosmopolitan hotels, or the foreign predator buying up your business cheaply and making everyone redundant. Although each of those images is still apt, they do not constitute the whole. The patterns of international management are diverse and few companies work in the same way. There is a great deal more collaboration and working together across national boundaries between organisations with common interests (see, for example, Caulkin 1993), and international working is no longer the preoccupation of a small elite group of managers.

There is a great management challenge at the close of the millennium for managers to place their local actions in a framework of global thought and strategy. This is particularly demanding because of the persisting variations in practice, despite international initiatives like that of the European Community.

> Systems which in most countries have evolved incrementally over the course of many decades – even centuries – have each acquired a distinctive coloration, adapted to the idiosyncrasies of national socio-economic structure, national political regimes, and perhaps also national temperaments. (Ferner and Hyman 1992, p. xvii)

At the same time there is the ever-increasing significance of the multinational company as the means whereby individual economies are integrated into a global economy, with a small number of very large companies accounting for a disproportionately large number of people in employment.

Management implications of international activities

International business involves both *decentralisation* and *expansion of management*. As an organisation increases its international activities it steps up the degree of decentralisation, but it would be an oversimplification to suggest that internationalisation is merely a form of decentralisation. It is the most complex form of decentralising operations and involves types of difference – language, culture, economic and political systems, legislative frameworks, management styles and conventions – that are not found in organisational growth and diversification that stays within national boundaries.

In a detailed analysis of what they see as necessary for companies to survive in the global marketplace, Bartlett and Ghoshal (1989) argue that international businesses need to both fragment and integrate. The fragmentation is the decentralisation that is needed to empower the subsidiaries, so that they become autonomous units within a corporate family instead of being overseas subsidiaries of a parent company. Some features, such as recruitment and industrial relations negotiations, are almost entirely fragmented, so that there is little need for a co-ordinated, centrally driven policy. Indeed a centrally driven policy could destroy the viability of the operation. One of the attractions of setting up manufacturing operations in eastern countries such as Korea or Sri Lanka was that employment costs were relatively lower. If they had been harmonised with those of the Californian or British parent company, the benefit of the relocation would have been lost.

Integration is the expansion and intensification of management activities in increased co-ordination to ensure that the business remains whole. New features are added, such as advanced schemes of remuneration for cosmopolitan employees, new forms of communication to ensure the necessary 'corporate glue'. Although nearly all recruitment and selection is decentralised a new activity is developing in the recruitment, selection and training for an elite corps of international managers.

The inflexibility of cultural patterns in employment practice can be illustrated by the example of Japan, which shares with Britain the situation of being geographically and culturally on the margin of a large continent. This has led them to feel a sense of isolation that persists despite the extraordinary growth of their economy in the second half of the twentieth century and their consequent involvement in virtually every country of the world.

There is a strong emphasis on human efficiency and group conformity. As well as a strong male dominance in the culture. The idea of individual autonomy is a relatively recent development of European/American influences and an even more recent development was a change in attitude regarding the role of women. Takako Doi was the female leader of the Socialist Party, known as the Iron Butterfly, and the American entertainer Madonna was a powerful role model for Japanese women. The durability of this change may be in question as the 1992 recession led to redundancies in which women suffered disproportionately. Richard Mead quotes from an article in the *Bangkok Post*:

> Toyota Motors will reduce its intake this year of young male high school graduates by 7.4 per cent to 1,580, while the number of women graduates is to fall by 25.6 per cent to 570. Nomura Securities will halve its annual intake of women from last year's (1991) 800 and the total number of women workers is likely to fall to 3,000 in 1997 from the present 5,000. (Mead 1994, p. 435)

Effective international management is also concerned with *managing cultural diversity*. It is not simply transferring complete operational practices from one country with its set of cultural assumptions to another where the cultural assumptions are different – no matter how slight the difference may be. Technically, operationally and financially that may be appropriate, but not in that subtle essence of management – the organisation of the people – that makes the difference between failure and success. We have already reviewed, in Chapter 6, the work of Hofstede (1980 and 1991), who has identified clear differences for country groupings.

Management methods do not necessarily transfer from one culture to another, but international management is not a process of all managers learning the cultures of every country in which they have to deal and suitably modifying their behaviour when dealing with those nationals. This is simply too difficult. Cultures are robust and subtle and we have great difficulty in achieving more than a modest level of behaviour adaptation. International management requires the understanding and managing of cultural diversity. It is not a process of becoming polycultural.

In many ways international management is simply national management on a larger scale; the strategic considerations are more complex and the operational units more varied, needing co-ordination across more barriers. It is possible, however, to identify some aspects of human resource management activities that are different in nature when a business is international and we review three of these in this chapter.

People working internationally

International management involves the employment of people who spend part of their time in another country. There are four broad categories of such employees and we consider the different management implications of their working.

The cosmopolitan

A very small number can be described as cosmopolitans. Constantly on the move and having their main working area away from their home base, these managers develop their own culture and ways of working together in a separate cultural world, inhabiting identical international hotels.

Cosmopolitans will be mobile and experienced in a number of overseas locations. Van Houten describes the Philips job rotation approach:

> The job rotation practice leads to a rich exchange of perspectives. When you send a Norwegian to Brazil, a Pakistani to Singapore, or an American to the Netherlands, the cultural influences that are traded are bound to result in an international point of view in the company as a whole. (van Houten, 1989, p. 110)

Managing the cosmopolitan requires careful selection, so that those who move into these demanding roles are emotionally and physically equipped for the challenges involved. It requires extensive and specialised preparation – probably through a well-chosen MBA – to acquire international competence and expertise. It requires people with language proficiency and the intercultural self-confidence that such proficiency develops. This is, however, a small group in any business:

> The number of executives falling into this category is extremely small, with each firm counting them in tens rather than hundreds, and even in the largest firm in our study, this group was said to number about 200. It is therefore as numerically insignificant as it is qualitatively vital. (Atkinson 1992, p. 74)

The expatriate

Cosmopolitans touch down in foreign countries; expatriates go and live in them, probably taking a family and staying for two or three years. This requires thorough management of the process before they go, while they are away and – crucially – when they come back:

> UK multinationals are becoming increasingly conscious of the importance of a successful repatriation process...preparing for expatriation and developing an adequate support system for expatriates while overseas...are now well established and are generally well done. Attention must increasingly turn to repatriation as the third element in the process. (Johnston 1991, p. 108)

Although many western countries have long experience of expatriates, this has been mainly in the colonial mode, with companies assigning young managers to manage local workforces. Expatriation is no longer one-way, there are fewer people who spend their whole career overseas and more who include one or two overseas assignments in acquiring the necessary breadth of experience and vision to operate at senior level in an international organisation.

The effect of expatriation on the expatriate and on the expatriate's family is likely to be considerable. The great majority of expatriates are married men, whose wives are nearly always placed in a position of total or partial dependency by corporate expatriation: one career is subordinated to another. For the increasing proportion of expatriate wives with a professional career in suspension, this can require considerable ingenuity to adapt.

The question of expatriation or not is the major question in selecting people for this type of assignment, but the particular location is the next most important determinant in matching the person to the job. Among the most important issues are the following.

Culture

How different from home is the culture of the country – religion, the social position of women, the degree of political stability/instability, personal security and petty crime, local press and television, cable television, availability of foreign newspapers, health hazards.

Economic development

How well developed is the economy of the country – standard/cost of living, availability of familiar foods and domestic equipment, transport, post and telephone, local poverty, health and education facilities, availability of international schools.

Geographical location

How far away is it and where is it – climate, in a cosmopolitan city or more remote, the importance/ unimportance of language proficiency, the size of the local expatriate community, employment prospects of spouse.

The job

What has to be done and what is the situation – nature of the organisation, proportion of expatriates, technical, commercial and managerial demands of the job, staffing and support, the extent of role in managing local nationals. Many expatriates are simply moving to exercise their company expertise in a different location, but the situation will always be different, no matter how similar the conventions and procedures, especially when managing local nationals.

Coming back from an overseas assignment seldom receives the attention it needs. Why should there be problems about coming home? There is first the issue of what the overseas experience was like. If it has been thoroughly satisfactory for all members of the family there may not be much enthusiasm for returning. On the other hand, the overseas experience may have been difficult, so that the prospect of returning home produces a great build-up of anticipation that leads to some letdown on actually getting back.

Second is the career situation of the returning expatriate. Johnston (1991) found that virtually all repatriated personnel had problems in reintegrating on return to the UK organisation, loss of status, loss of autonomy, lack of career direction and lack of recognition of the value of overseas experience (Johnston 1990, p. 103).

> ...little appears to be done at a personal level for the returning managers who are expected in the main to work things out for themselves. No companies within the Chemicals, Manufacturing and Services sectors sample had a formal company reorientation for repatriates to aid their social and professional integration into what will inevitably be a substantially different organisation from that which they left. (Johnston 1991, p. 106)

REVIEW TOPIC 37.2

Can a manager be an effective cosmopolitan without first being an expatriate?

The engineer

The term 'engineer' is used here broadly to cover all those technical specialists who spend spells of a few weeks or months at a time in an overseas location to carry out a particular job, such as commissioning new plant or training local personnel in its use. The overseas spell is not as long and the role more specific than that of the expatriate. It is similar to seafarers, airline crew, travel couriers and the increasing number of western academics who spend a few weeks or months abroad. They are not living abroad: simply away from home for a spell.

The engineer needs complete technical expertise and the personal resourcefulness to cope with unforeseen technical problems and a wide variety of social situations. Compared with cosmopolitans and expatriates engineers are more likely to be assigned to remote locations, even though they are usually accommodated in an international hotel. It can be a monotonous life, with little scope for social activity apart from the hotel bar and pool. Regular health checks are essential and efficient administrative arrangements for travel, accommodation and contact with base during assignment. Some engineers find it very difficult to settle back into the more routine tasks that often await them when the days of travelling are over.

The occasional parachutist

Occasional parachutists are those people who 'drop in' occasionally for a few days to deal with some very specific question that has cropped up, such as a problem with the computer system, or an input to a training course, or technical assistance

---

Some of the issues in expense claims are:

Class of travel. On long haul flights it is usual for personnel to travel in business class, but the practice varies on shorter journeys, so that economy class will usually be booked for journeys of two to three hours or less. In companies where only employees of a certain specified rank travel business class and others travel economy, a group will all travel in the class of person with the highest status. If someone entitled to a business class ticket wants to trade it for two economy tickets to allow a wife or husband to travel as well, this is not often allowed within the policy rules if the visit is a short one. If the period abroad is to be longer then exchanging one business class for two economy tickets is more likely.

Cash or credit cards. Although the airline ticket (and possibly hotel accommodation) will be purchased by the company before departure, travellers incur considerable expenditure while away. The normal travellers' arrangements of cash and travellers' cheques are one way of dealing with these charges, but of growing popularity is the company credit card, issued to the employee on departure and recovered on return. This avoids the problems of carrying large amounts of cash or cheques and provides a convenient way of identifying the actual items of expenditure on return.

Car hire. When a hired car is to be used while abroad there will obviously need to be the appropriate checks on the status of the licence, the possible need for an international licence, adequate insurance and so forth. If the arrangement can be made in advance the cost will probably be less than if booked on the spot.

Insurance. With the possible addition of car insurance, what is required is insurance cover similar to that taken out by most holidaymakers: insurance against sickness and related expenses, including the possibility of emergency travel home, and insurance of baggage and personal belongings.

---

with a round of commercial negotiations. Like the engineer, they are representatives of the company and can form invaluable network connections for formal and informal communication. Many employees move between countries only in this mode and the exchanges can be vital in developing mutual understanding between nationalities and compatibility of the systems and procedures in different parts of the business.

They can also do harm. Someone visiting for only a few days has little incentive to learn about the country and the people, and may therefore carry stereotyped assumptions that could be damaging to relationships within the company. It can be helpful if novices travel together with an experienced person and talk before travelling with an expatriate or someone else familiar with the culture.

Each of these four categories of personnel require specific HRM initiatives and procedures. Not the least of these is the different arrangements for payment. The cost of expatriate assignments can be considerable and the number of arguments about appropriate levels of expenses for engineers and occasional parachutists can be even greater.

Organisational co-ordination

> To operate as an effective strategic whole, the transnational must be able to reconcile the diversity of perspectives and interests it deliberately fosters, integrate the widespread assets and resources it deliberately disperses, and coordinate the roles and responsibilities it deliberately differentiates. (Bartlett & Ghoshal 1989, p. 166)

We saw at the beginning of this chapter that international companies have to pursue both fragmentation and integration simultaneously. The above quotation shows how managers give themselves major problems of co-ordination by adopting the measures that they see as necessary for business success. Approaches to co-ordination must increasingly move to a more intercultural style, as the dominance of the parent company nationality declines in favour of the multinationality of the global business. Co-ordination is the way to synergy, so that the global business does more and better together than it could possibly achieve as a number of independent units.

Frequently in management matters theory moves ahead, and independently, of practice. In this matter practice is moving rapidly, and independently of theory. There appear to be different methods of co-ordinating the fragments.

Evangelisation

Evangelisation works through *shared belief*, relatively simple doctrines to which members of the organisation subscribe and through which they are energised. It is now commonplace for companies to have mission statements, which come close to being unifying articles of faith.

At the top is the mission statement, a broad goal based on the organization's planning premises, basic assumptions about the organization's purpose, its values, its distinctive competencies, and its place in the world. A mission statement is a relatively permanent part of an organization's identity and can do much to unify and motivate its members. (Stoner & Freeman 1992, p. 188)

They can also be seen as wish lists, with all the associated difficulties of unrealised aspirations.

Evangelisation also works through *parables*. Ed Schein (1985, pp. 237–42) identified 'stories and legends' as one of the key mechanisms for articulating and reinforcing the organisation's culture. The company house magazine can help to circulate the good news about heroic deeds in all parts of the company network. Word of mouth exchanges and accounts of personal experience are better. Those who visit another country have stories to tell to all members of the company when they return, not just to the senior managers conducting the de-briefing.

REVIEW TOPIC 37.3

Think of examples where you have felt a greater degree of understanding about what your organisation is doing, and what its activities mean through listening to parables about it.

Evangelisation can work through *apostles*, ambassadors sent out to preach the faith. These are the cosmopolitans described above. Because of their frequent movement they know the worldwide organisation well and can describe one component to another, explaining company policy, justifying particular decisions and countering parochial thinking. They can also move ideas around ('In Seoul they are wondering about . . . what do you think?') and help in the development of individual networks ('Try getting in touch with Oscar Jennings in Pittsburgh . . . he had similar problems a few weeks ago.')

Apostles are likely to be especially busy at times of crisis, strengthening resolve and cooling anxiety. It may be important that they come from headquarters and have personally met, and can tell stories about, the founder. Anita Roddick's Body Shop grew rapidly by working in a way that was markedly different from the conventions of the cosmetics industry that it was challenging. People in all parts of the business identified closely with the vision and personality of the founder:

The inductresses' eyes seem to light up whenever Anita's name is mentioned. We are told, in semi-joyous terms, the great tale concerning that first humble little shop in Brighton. And . . . one of our inductresses uses the phrase, 'And Anita saw what she had done, and it was good.' (Keily 1991, p. 3)

Standards and Norms

Co-ordination can be improved by the development and promulgation of shared standards and norms, and they do not necessarily have to be developed at the centre. Decentralised standard formulation can enable different parts of the global business to take a lead as a preliminary to universal adoption of the standard they have formulated: an excellent method of integration.

Few businesses will be able to develop universally applicable standards in all aspects of management. Many manufacturing developments in Asia have been for the explicit reason of being able to enjoy the benefits of low labour costs. It is most unlikely that the American/European/Japanese parent company would develop a company-wide standard on the level of pay rates in manufacturing. In contrast a company-wide standard set of terms and conditions for expatriate assignment would be much more feasible. The Institute of Personnel and Development Library in London has just such a document from IBM in the form of a sample letter of 24 pages!

Systems and procedures

Many global businesses are dominated by a single system, which reaches every part of the business. An airline has a ticketing and booking system which links thousands of computer terminals. At a booking desk in Moscow you can book a seat on an aircraft travelling from Hong Kong to Manchester. Hotel chains have central reservation systems to book rooms throughout the world. These systems are only useful if they provide the global link, and providing the systems link constantly reinforces with all personnel the interrelationship of the company's activities. All businesses have systems and they provide a useful management opportunity for integration. In one country, for example, a team might develop a spare part retrieval system that is quickly adopted for use throughout the business, while in another country they concentrate on an aspect of accounting procedures or systematic advice on training opportunities. In this way there is co-ordination through interdependence, as well as avoiding of duplication.

Capability

Another possibility is the concentration of *capability* by encouraging the development of particular expertise in different locations, but for groupwide application. Bartlett and Ghoshal (1989, p. 106–7) describe how Teletext was developed by Philips. Because of an interest from the BBC, the British Philips subsidiary began work on the possibility of transmitting text and simple diagrams through a domestic television set. Within Philips generally it was regarded as 'a typical British toy – quite fancy but not very useful'. The British persisted and ten years later there were three million Teletext receivers in use in Britain. Philips had established a world lead in a product for which there was initially only a British market.

Philips have pioneered this type of development, settling activities in places where the culture suits the activity.

> ... their centre for long-range technology development was recently moved from the United States to the Far East, where the time orientation was seen as more conducive to innovation than the 'quick fix' mentality of North America. Some major research departments are located in Italy, which is seen by other firms as an impossible country for important facilities. Yet their Italian research laboratories are highly successful, as are the important R & D facilities of IBM and DEC in the same region. All of them run in a uniquely Italian way, and are left to do so since this appears to lead to their success. Manufacturing plants are likely to be located elsewhere – Germany, for example. (Evans, Lank and Farquhar 1989, p. 116)

REVIEW TOPIC 37.4

Are there activities in your business that would be better located in a different part of the world because the culture of that country would be more suitable for the activity?

International communication

The dissemination of information throughout the organisation helps managers to think globally before taking local action, so that members of the different units in the business understand why a company has been acquired in South America, even though it seems to threaten the livelihood of some parts of the parent organisation. Foulds and Mallet (1989, p. 78) suggest the following as purposes of international communication:

- to reinforce group culture so as to improve the speed and effectiveness of decision-taking;
- to encourage information exchange in internationally related activities and prevent the 'reinvention of the wheel';
- to form the background to the succession planning activity – certain cultures demand certain types of people;
- to establish in people's minds what is expected of them by the parent company;
- to facilitate change in a way acceptable to the parent company;
- to undermine the 'not invented here' attitudes and thereby encourage changes;
- to improve the attractiveness of the company in the recruitment field – particularly where the subsidiary is small and far from base; and
- to encourage small activities, which may be tomorrow's 'cream', and give such activities a perspective within the international activities.

There is an assumption in that list that the company is a parent with subsidiaries, and this is not always true, but it remains a useful summary. There is a need for constant communication throughout the organisation to disseminate information and to sustain changing values. The organisation must operate holistically. It is not the sum of its parts: the whole exists in every part. Customers have a holistic view of the organisation. If your motor car breaks down you are dissatisfied with the manufacturer or the supplier and you are not mollified to be told that the problem was caused by a component manufactured in the Korean subsidiary. Managers cannot work effectively in their part of the business without understanding its simultaneous relationship to the whole. Businesses function holistically and holism is a function of constant, efficient communication, as do the bloodstream and the central nervous system.

Communication in any organisation mainly follows the workflow, as members communicate with each other in connection with their work, first within a particular work group, then between one work group and another which is adjacent in the workflow, and then between departments. When a company is operating internationally the workflow pattern may provide the logical main channel for communication. If a washing machine is produced by manufacturing electronic components in California, sub-assemblies and wiring harnesses in Korea and final assembly in Scotland, there is an easy sequence to follow. Among the most effective international communicators are airlines, as their entire business is moving not only customers but also staff constantly across national boundaries to different organisational outposts of the business: the business activity creates the communications.

When the company is operating not serially but in parallel, organisational communication becomes much more difficult. Using the analogy of a hotel chain, the hotel in Manila is a complete operation in just the same way as the hotel in Copehagen that is part of the same group: guests are not bedded in one and passed on to another to be fed. The workflow communications link is missing. All international businesses require centralised, co-ordinated communications to create common purpose and to share ideas and benefits, but those that do not have a natural workflow link across national boundaries will have this need more highly developed.

The international HRM specialists

If the international dimension is exclusively strategic, as has been suggested in this chapter, the skills and attributes of the International HRM specialist are quite different from those of the typical personnel specialist. The competencies identified by the Personnel Standards Lead Body are of only marginal relevance.

> Human resource managers can expect to participate more fully in top management decision-making. As the business environment evolves, so greater value will be placed on the capacity to identify environmental shifts and to interpret these in terms of

labour supply and demand. The human resouce manager will take on functions of developing new models of transnational roles and responsibilities. (Mead 1994, p. 375)

Mead goes on to suggest the need to recruit HRM specialists who possess:

(a) Wide professional skills and an understanding of the other functional areas represented across the worldwide organisation;
(b) a capacity to develop good personal relationships across the organisation;
(c) excellent communication skills;
(d) a capacity to think flexibly in terms of inter-unit linkages across the organisation;
(e) a capacity to learn from and apply experiences;
(f) a sensitivity to cultural differences; and
(g) a reputation for integrity.

The interesting thing about that list (apart from the strange omission of an ability to walk on water) is that only two of those qualities – (a) and (f) – are to do specifically with an international business. The tasks and specific challenges may be different, but the skills and aptitudes are similar to those of any major personnel role.

☐ SUMMARY PROPOSITIONS

37.1 Managing an international organisation requires management to fragment by spreading some responsibility to be carried as near as possible to the local action, and to integrate by having some features of organisation that are closely followed throughout the component units.
37.2 Employees who work internationally can be classified as either cosmopolitans, expatriates, engineers or occasional parachutists.
37.3 Expatriates need thorough preparation for both expatriation and repatriation; the problems of repatriation are frequently overlooked.
37.4 Among the means of co-ordination in a fragmented international business are evangelisation, sharing standards and norms, systems and procedures, and distributing activity according to local cultural capability.
37.5 Communication in an international business confirms the holistic nature of the enterprise.

References

Atkinson, J. (1992), 'Corporate employment policies, women and 1992'. In R. M. Lindley (ed.), *Women's Employment: Britain in the Single European Market*, London: HMSO.
Barham, K. and Rassam, C. (1989), *Shaping the Corporate Future*, London: Unwin Hyman.
Bartlett, C. A. and Ghoshal, S. (1989), *Managing Across Borders*, London: Random House.
Caulkin, S. (1993), 'British firms resurrected by courtesy of Japan', *Guardian*, 8 May, p. 38.

Evans, P., Lank, E. and Farquhar, E. (1989), 'Managing human resources in the international firm: lessons from practice'. In *Human Resource Management in International Firms*, London: Macmillan.

Ferner, A. and Hyman, R. (1992), *Industrial Relations in the New Europe*, Oxford: Blackwell.

Foulds, J. and Mallet, L. (1989), 'The European and international dimension'. In T. Wilkinson (ed.) *The Communications Challenge*, London: Institute of Personnel Management.

Hofstede, G. (1980), *Culture's Consequences: International Differences in Work-Related Values*. Beverly Hills, California: Sage Publications.

Hofstede, G. (1991), *Cultures and Organizations: Software of the Mind*, London: McGraw-Hill.

Johnston, J. (1991), 'An empirical study of the repatriation of managers in UK multinationals', *Human Resource Management Journal*, vol. 4, no. 1. Summer, pp. 102–9.

Keily, D. (1991), 'Body Shop Blues', *The Sunday Times*, 8 December, p. 3.

Ling Sing Chee, (1994), 'Singapore Airlines: strategic human resource initiatives'. In D. P. Torrington (ed.) *International Human Resource Management*, pp. 143–59. Hemel Hempstead: Prentice Hall International.

Mead, R. (1994), *International Management: Cross Cultural Dimensions*, Cambridge, Mass: Blackwell.

Pages, M., Bonnetti, M., de Gaulejac, V. and Descendre, D. (1979), *L'Emprise de l'Organisation*, Presses Universitaires de France.

Schein, E. H. (1985), *Organizational Culture and Leadership*, San Francisco: Jossey-Bass.

Stoner, J. A. F. and Freeman, R. E. (1992), *Management*, 5th edition. Englewood Cliffs, New Jersey: Prentice Hall Inc.

van Houten, G. (1989), 'The implications of globalism: new management realities at Philips'. In P. Evans, Y. Doz and A. Laurent (eds) *Human Resource Management in International Firms*, London: Macmillan.

38 Personnel management and the future

For as long as either of us can remember the imminent demise of personnel management has been confidently predicted. Academic commentators have always criticised personnel managers, who have been held accountable for management failures in the employment field and have been derided as powerless because of their apparent inability to carry out simple tasks like introducing genuine equality of opportunity and humanising the workplace. Thirty years ago Flanders criticised them, and their managerial colleagues, for getting the balance wrong between who did what in management:

> Confusion over the role of personnel management can produce a compromise that gets the worst of all worlds. In major areas of industrial relations policy – such as employment, negotiations, communications and training – line management may shed all the details of administration, while retaining ultimate authority and an illusion of responsibility. (Flanders, 1964, p. 254)

A similar argument featured strongly in the Donovan analysis that was referred to in Chapters 27 and 28. As interest in HRM intensified during the 1980s, other inadequacies were reported. Daniel (1986) found that personnel specialists were normally excluded from decisions about reorganisation resulting from new technology; Purcell and Gray (1986) reported personnel departments being run down; Guest (1987) said that personnel managers lacked a necessary strategic view

---

One of the most telling caricatures of the personnel manager comes not from academia but from a Tyneside shopfloor.

> Joe, an old labourer, is trudging through the shipyard carrying a heavy load on his shoulders. It is a filthy, wet day and the sole of his shoe is flapping open. The personnel manager, passing at the time, stops him, saying 'Hey Joe, you can't go round with your shoe in that state on a wet day like this' and reaching into his back pocket takes out a bundle of bank notes. Joe beams in anticipation. 'Here,' says the personnel manager, slipping the elastic band off the bundle of notes, 'put this round your shoe, it will help keep the wet out.' (Murray 1972, p. 279)

and Armstrong (1989) claimed that the future of the personnel profession was doomed without a better understanding of accountancy. These are simply examples of the continuing, conventional wisdom that personnel specialists are ineffectual.

Other management specialists do not receive these criticisms, either because their activities are more limited in their social implications or because their academic commentators are more interested in the technical rather than social aspects of what they are doing. The unfavourable view of personnel managers persists, and is duly passed on to personnel students, despite contrary evidence. The Institute of Personnel Management continues to attract large numbers into membership:

> The membership of the Institute of Personnel Management exceeds the combined membership of the Institutes of Marketing, Administrative Management, Industrial Managers, and Purchasing and Supply, despite having appreciably higher entry standards. (Torrington 1989, p. 64)

At 1 September 1993, Institute membership had risen to 52,000. The professional qualification of personnel specialists is more securely rooted in institutions of higher education than most other specialisms, so that they are well aware of the generally disaparaging conclusions of academics.

Personnel management continues despite its criticism and at the moment its demise seems as likely as the end of the world, which is foretold even more regularly. We shall undoubtedly see changes, many of which have been mentioned in the preceding pages, the most significant of which will probably be the continuing decline of organisation as entity with which we opened our first chapter. Personnel management as an activity and preoccupation of managers will continue – at least until the end of the world – but to round off this book we offer some other thoughts about how things may be in the future.

IPM, IPD and PSLB

In 1994 the Institute of Personnel Management merged with the Institute of Training and Development to create the Institute of Personnel and Development. This should overcome the peculiarity of having a training qualification that is apart from a personnel qualification. It consolidates the wholeness of the personnel function and strengthens its lobbying potential, as well as giving it greater authority. It could be under threat as a qualifying association because of the NCVQ mission to provide vocational qualifications that are not exclusive and controlled by professional, or quasi-professional bodies. At first sight that sounds like a welcome move. After all, why should people have to join and pay a membership subscription to IPD in order to become qualified to practice?

Further consideration shows how valuable IPD will continue to be. An NVQ in personnel will aim to do no more than attest to a person's competence in personnel work, as construed from a managerial perspective. The Personnel Standards Lead Body, as referred to in Chapter 23, has the objective of setting vocational standards and qualifications in the area. The purpose of personnel management is defined by this body as:

> Enable management to enhance the individual and collective contributions to the short and long term success of the enterprise. (PSLB 1993)

This definition says nothing about ideas or values. In contrast the 1993 IPM mission statement read:

> The mission of the Institute of Personnel Management is to be the professional body for all those responsible for the optimum use of human resources to the mutual benefit of the enterprise, each person and the community at large. (IPM, 1993)

REVIEW TOPIC 38.1

What are the essential differences between these two definitions and what are their implications for the work that personnel specialists do?

IPD may be a useful Aunt Sally for academics, but it does provide a network of people working in the field, a headquarters staff who commission research and publish journals, as well as codes of professional conduct. There are very few sanctions, but there is a constituency and a reference group. All of this is largely sustained by the qualifying process; at any one time one third of IPD members are students. The professional education scheme of the Institute is largely conducted through the institutions of higher education and is therefore in touch with research and forward thinking on social as well as managerial issues. IPD involvement with higher education, including those with the strongest research orientation, is probably greater than for any other specialist management body. Throughout their period of qualifying students are in touch with the ideas and values that fellow members of IPD share and they take into that arena the ideas and values of management education.

If IPD were ever to lose its influence among personnel specialists through the diversifying attempts of NCVQ, then the practice of personnel management will be no more than the exercise of competence – amoral and antisocial. PSLB have realised the crucial importance to their work of collaborating with IPD rather than competing with it. The competence route to effectiveness will run alongside the existing qualification route and IPD will continue to provide the much wider role in personnel affairs that has been their unique contribution.

Organisational decentralisation and autonomy

The decline of organisation as entity will be accompanied by a trend towards decentralisation of organisations; operational units will be smaller and more manageable by having more scope delegated to them from the centre and less emphasis on conformity to a single pattern. This is not always consistent with meeting customer preference. Retail banks cannot vary their operational patterns much, as their interconnection is a major feature of their working, but gradually operational units of all types are gaining more independence for their operations. This provides more managers with more scope as accountability, responsibility and autonomy are made more feasible through managers being required to conform to organisation-wide norms on only a relatively narrow range of activities while having considerable scope to run the undertaking in their own way.

The decentralisation trend could lead to more people having senior management responsibilities and opportunities. This type of professional autonomy makes the idea of the *empowered* manager with skills suitable for a number of different situations, a more feasible proposition for the future than it has been in the past. Empowerment in practice varies widely and sometimes is no more than exposing people to blame in situations they can not handle. Increasingly, however, empowerment practice involves both giving people responsibility and enabling them to exercise that responsibility without close supervision. Those who have acquired a degree of poise and confidence in dealing with people, and have reasonable scope to decide how to handle situations, normally value those twin aspects of their work because it enhances their ability to deal with so many other aspects of their lives. The role of the personnel specialist is always altered when this happens and it requires a creative response from them, as there is always a need for personnel expertise and a personnel perspective that is wider than that of the individual unit or departmental manager. Individual managerial autonomy always has to be balanced with reasonable consistency with practice elsewhere, as well as expert monitoring, advice, information and support.

There is a cautionary note to be sounded about the attractions of decentralisation, what Keith Sisson has called 'the tyranny of the strategic business unit'. The delegation of authority can be so narrowly prescribed that the strategic business unit is only an operational unit, with closely defined, short-term objectives and lacking any scope for strategic decision and action. In this situation the strategic control of the business is in the hands of a small number of head office strategists and those in the operational units have relatively little range to their activities. This is a part of the management style whereby strategy is conceived as acquisition and divestment rather than investment.

Managing the managers

It has already been suggested that one feature of the HRM phase in the development of the personnel function has been the concentration on 'managing the managers'. Legge (1989) and Storey (1992) have pointed out that HRM is directed more towards managing the employment of managers than the employment of anyone else, who are dealt with at arm's length.

Bob Ramsey was Personnel Director of Ford when he made the comment at an IPM National Conference that employees expected a better service from management. Ford is not know as a soft, namby-pamby type of business and Bob

Ramsey was making a basic, 'bottom-line' point. Those who get good service from management will produce an efficient operation, and good service includes more than the right strategic decisions so that the company stays in business. Much of the service lies in the operational features of personnel management and that comes from the personnel function as well as from the line. It has been suggested above that empowerment is one of the benefits of HRM, but an empowered line is not enough of a management service for the rank-and-file. Indications from current research about performance management suggest, for instance, that performance management needs not only empowered line managers but also a skilled personnel function to provide additional expertise and an alternative perspective, to avoid individual employees feeling remote and uncommitted.

The point has already been made that one of the advantages of HRM is that training expenditure has been sustained. Most of this expenditure, however, has been in management development. Will personnel managers continue readily paying the huge sums of money that are involved in management development, even when the rewards are dubious, yet fail to invest in technological training when it is axiomatic that we are short of technical skills?

Information technology

The personnel manager's love/hate relationship with the computer is set to continue. We have plenty of predictions and mostly these are prophecies of what the computer and the microprocessor can do and then logically developed to produce a picture of what will happen; manufacturing will progressively be taken over by robots, rapid transfer and manipulation of data, the paperless office, people working from home instead of coming into a centre, and so forth: the golden age of the post-industrial society and the information super-highway. Our questions about this are first, the extent to which the possible will become reality and secondly, to wonder what will be done to make up what the computer will take from us.

Managers have long had the opportunity to spend more of their time, and make more of their decisions, by rational planning and operational research methods than in fact they do. The strange thing is that managers seem to spend increasing amounts of time working, especially with the emphasis on the culture of enthusiastic commitment, which is typically construed as trying to go home later than anyone else.

There continues to be a preference among managers in general and personnel managers in particualr to spend their time talking with people and to make their decisions as a result of discussion and shrewd judgement. Will managers now begin to eschew face-to-face discussion in favour of face-to-terminal decision-making, or will they continue to confer and keep busy while others feed to them an ever-increasing flow of processed information requiring interpretation, evaluation and further discussion? Research findings suggest that managers work the way they do at least partly because they like it that way.

> The manager actually seems to prefer brevity and interruption in his work. Superficiality is an occupational hazard of the manager's job. Very current information (gossip, hearsay, speculation) is favoured; routine reports are not. The manager clearly favours the...verbal media, spending most of his time in verbal contact. (Mintzberg 1973, p. 51–2)

The date and male gender of that quotation may be significant. Most of the studies of managerial work have been of men and of men and women working in a male-dominated culture. It may be that the increasing proportion of managerial jobs done by women will alter the stereotype. How significantly will managers allow this pattern of working to change and how great will the influence of the computer on personnel management work actually become?

Apart from the specific question about what personnel managers will do, there is the more general question about how everyone else will make up for what the computer takes away. If there is a general tendency for people to work at home, taking their terminal with them, how popular will that turn out to be? It is more than a century since the household ceased to be the central productive unit and the men, and later the women, began to spend a large part of their waking hours at a different social centre – the factory, shop or office. To be housebound has become a blight. We can see how it used to be:

> In 1810 the common productive unit in New England was still the rural household. Processing and preserving of food, candlemaking, soap-making, spinning, weaving, shoemaking, quilting, rug-making, the keeping of small animals and gardens, all took place on domestic premises.
>
> Although money income might be obtained by the household through the sale of produce, and additional money be earned through occasional wages to its members, the United States household was overwhelmingly self-sufficient ... Women were as active in the creation of domestic self-sufficiency as were men. (Illich 1981, pp. 111–12)

Since that time we have dismantled, or allowed to wither, all the social mechanisms that supported that self-sufficiency, and developed the social institution of the workplace as the arena for many of our human needs, such as affiliation, interaction, teamworking and competition. It really seems most unlikely that the move away from working in the household will be reversed. In every country of the world roads and railways are jammed with people at the beginning of the day going to work or returning, despite the tendency for organisational entity to decline.

The information super-highway may not turn everyone into a homeworker, but it is still having a significant impact. There is the slightly isolating nature of the work that computerisation produces. The individual employee is not one of many in a crowded workshop, but one of a few scattered around a mass of busy machines. The clerical employee spends more time gazing at a computer terminal and less talking to colleagues. What employee behaviour will this engender and what attitudes will be associated with that behaviour? As more people become able to use the computer, especially for word processing, there will be a net loss of jobs. This has been seen in its most dramatic form in the publishing of newspapers, where typesetting has been eliminated through journalists typing their copy directly at a computer terminal. Early editions of this book were composed initially in a series of hand-written and manually typed drafts, which were then cut, edited and pasted up for a professional secretary to produce the final typescript, which was then typeset all over again by the publisher. This book has been composed, edited and a final type-script produced by the authors using two word-processors and the computer disks will be used by the publisher to produce the printed version. That is a single example of the changes that the computer has brought.

REVIEW TOPIC 38.2

What difference has the computer made to your working life so far? What further effect do you expect it to have in the next five years? How readily would you be (or are you) a homeworker?

Worldwide regional management?

We have considered in Chapter 37 some of the international developments that are likely, and the challenge of the global business. There may be an intermediate stage between national management and global management, and that is a form of management that is generally applicable in one of the main regions of the world. Most international companies are originally either North American, West European or Japanese. In 1985 Ohmae described this as the Triad, three regions with 600 million residents:

> …whose academic backgrounds, income levels, life style, use of leisure time and aspirations are quite similar. In these democratic countries, the national infrastructure, in terms of highways, telephone systems, sewage disposal, power transmission, and governmental systems, is also very similar. (Ohmae 1985, p. 37).

Despite the similarities, we have seen how markedly different management methods often are. Also the decade since the remarks were made has seen the inexorable rise of the South East Asian countries.

Canada, Mexico and the United States are making moves to harmonise the nature of their employment legislation, there are moves towards harmonisation among the Association of South East Asian Nations (ASEAN) countries and the development of the European Community is slowly continuing.

In Britain most of the writing about *international* management is in fact about management across Europe and the evolution of Community legislation is gradually bringing together the legal framework within which employment is managed. In the ASEAN countries there is a similar degree of common features, despite the marked difference in economic health of the constituent countries. These common features derive from the legacy of nineteenth–twentieth century colonialism, the high level of unemployment and illegal migration between member countries, the prominent role of trade unions in achieving political independence, and the fact that many of the workers are illiterate and therefore require a great degree of protection from unscrupulous employers (Torrington and Tan Chwee Huat 1993, Ch. 21).

With this type of economic and social co-operation, there may be a stage at which it is possible to recognise regional management as a stage between national and international, with national gradually being superseded by its regional version. That will change the international dimension of personnel work, and might make more operational personnel work possible on an international level, rather than simply the strategic HRM type of work as was suggested in the previous chapter.

By the 1960s trade unions had become a feature of almost every industrial country of the world and personnel managers always had the industrial relations portfolio as a key part of their role. Trade unions, however, varied greatly between different countries in their ways of operating. In some they were the vehicle of fundamental political change, especially in the overthrow of colonial rule. In some they were the vehicle for the intended achievement of a Communist government; in others they became a part of the mainstream political movements. They grew in power and influence, but then the tide turned against them in the West.

Unions in the United States lost popularity because of allegations of corruption and a disenchantment with their methods. The elected leaders of the new post colonial powers felt that unions were useful when in opposition, but an encumbrance when in government. The Communist Party failed to achieve government in the countries of Western Europe and one of the most popular stories in the United Kingdom of the decline of Communism in Eastern Europe was the rise of Lech Walesa and the trade union Solidarity to bring about the collapse of a Communist government under the inspiration of the Roman Catholic Church. By 1985 the percentage of employees who were trade union members had sunk to 17 per cent in both France and the United States, 29 per cent in Japan and 52 per cent in the United Kingdom (Dowling and Schuler 1990, p. 142).

In the age of human resource management, industrial relations and trade union negotiation has nothing like the prominence it had, and practice is extremely varied:

> ...industrial relations phenomena are a very faithful expression of the society in which they operate, of its characteristic features and of the power relations between different interest groups. Industrial relations can not be understood without an understanding ...of the society concerned. (Schregle 1981, p. 27)

These variations are often solidified in a legal framework that was elaborately constructed at a time when governments saw unions as a threat to social stability. This diversity means that there is little scope for a co-ordinated global industrial relations strategy for any business. There may be a strong case for a regional strategy.

Ethics and social responsibility

The 1980s saw the rise in interest in business ethics. Like many developments it was rooted in the United States, but has been echoed at various volume levels in other countries. As was shown by the 1993 mission statement of the IPM, personnel people have long held a strong interest in ethics, although it was usually caricatured as welfare. Many of the academic critics mentioned at the opening of this chapter argue that personnel managers should remain aloof from management hurly-burly so that 'professional values will be paramount and prevail over other interests' (Hart 1993, p. 30). The problem with that simplistic argument is that personnel managers do not have a separate professional existence from the management of which they are a part. Personnel management is a management activity or it is nothing.

The company doctor and the company legal adviser are bound by codes of professional ethics different from those of managers, but they are employed for their specialist, technical expertise and they are members of long-established, powerful professional groupings with their own normal places of work. When they leave their surgeries or the courtrooms to align themselves with managers in companies, they are in a specialised role. They can maintain a non-managerial, professional detachment, giving advice that is highly-regarded, even when it is highly unpopular. Personnel specialists do not have separate places and conventions of work which they leave in order to advise managements. They are employed in no other capacity than to participate closely in the *management* process of the business. They do not even have the limited degree of independence that company accountants have, as their activities are not subject to external audit, and it is ludicrous to expect of them a fully-fledged independent, professional stance.

The change in general management orientation during the 1980s towards the idea of the leaner and fitter, flexible organisations, down-sizing, de-layering, out-placement and all the other ideas that eventually lead to fewer people in jobs and fewer still with any sort of employment security have usually been implemented by personnel people. Personnel managers cannot behave like Banquo's ghost and be silently disapproving. What they can do is to argue vigorously in favour of what they see as the best combination of efficiency and justice, but they can only argue vigorously if they are present when decisions are made. If they are not generally 'on side', they don't get to the decision-making and they probably don't keep their jobs. They are either a part of management, valued by their colleagues, despite their funny ideas, or they are powerless. There are no ivory towers for personnel managers to occupy, and no more employment security for them than for any other member of the business, so the voice of a personnel manager crying in the wilderness is one that no one wants to hear, let alone pay a salary to and provide a company car for.

In the different era of the 1970s Legge (1978) propounded her formulation of the conformist and deviant innovator as alternative strategies for the personnel manager to pursue. The conventions of employment security then, especially of managers, were such that personnel specialists could perhaps pursue a deviant path with impunity. Now it is more difficult.

The 'deviant innovator' bolt hole based on a plea to consider the merits of social values and to ponder the value of an independent 'professional stance' appeared to be offering a less secure refuge. (Storey 1992, p. 275)

They can still do it, if they are valued by their managerial colleagues for the wholeness of their contribution, and if they accept the fact that they will often lose the argument: they can not do it by masquerading as an unrepresentative shop steward. They have no monopoly of either wisdom or righteousness, and other members of the management team are just as likely as they are to be concerned about social values. What is impressive is the strength of feeling on these issues that is found in so many personnel managers and the courage with which many advocate their policies.

Personnel managers have not abandoned their interest in welfare; they have moved away from an approach to welfare that was trivial, anachronistic and paternalist. In the personnel manager's vocabulary the term 'welfare' is code for middle-class do-gooders placing flowers in the works canteen. Personnel managers increasingly shun the traditional approach to welfare not for its softness, but because it is ineffectual. It steers clear of the work that people are doing and concentrates on the surroundings in which the work is carried out. It does not satisfy personnel managers in their obsession with getting progress in the employment of people, and it certainly does not do enough to satisfy the people who are employed. In many undertakings personnel specialists are taking their management colleagues along with them in an enthusiastic and convinced attempt to give jobs more meaning and to humanise the workplace. Their reasoning is that the business can only maintain its competitive edge if the people who work there are committed to its success, and that commitment is volitional: you need hearts and minds as well as hands and muscle. Investment in training and the dismantling of elaborate, alienating organisation structures do more for employee well-being than paternalistic welfare programmes ever did.

The international dimension of the social responsibility question has still to be developed. During the last half of 1992 several powerful western countries suffered serious economic problems because of speculation against their currencies and much of this was at the hands of major banks. Logging operations in South America are ravaging the rain forests, which are essential to life continuing on the planet. Error, or neglect, in the management of manufacturing processes can produce a tragedy like that of Bhopal in India, Chernobyl in Russia or the various discharges of crude oil that have occurred all over the world. Since the first formal warning by the American Surgeon General about the risks of smoking, tobacco consumption has been falling in western countries, so the tobacco companies have increased their marketing in less developed countries.

Ethical standards vary. The 'Recruit affair' was a major Japanese scandal involving allegations of corruption among the country's most senior politicians. In the aftermath there was much American criticism of Japanese business practices and a flurry of righteous indignation in western newspapers about the need to use 'slush funds' in various countries to obtain business. Becker and Fritzsche (1987) carried out a study of different ethical perceptions between American, French and German executives; 39 per cent of the Americans said that paying money for business favours was unethical. Only 12 per cent of the French and none of the Germans agreed. In the United States Japanese companies have been accused of avoiding the employment of ethnic minority groups by the careful location of their factories (Cole and Deskins 1988, pp. 17–19). On the other hand Japanese standards on employee health and safety are as high as anywhere in the world (Wokutch 1990). In South East Asia the contrast in prosperity between countries such as Malaysia and Singapore on one hand and Indonesia and the Philippines on the other means that there are ethical questions about the employment of illegal immigrants that are superficially similarly to those of Cubans and Mexicans in the United States, but which do not occur in other parts of the world (Torrington and Tan Chwee Huat 1993, Ch 3). There are very low wages and long working hours in China and in Europe, Britain refuses to accept the social chapter of the Maastricht Treaty harmonising employment conditions across the European Community.

The disparate nature of ethical standards between countries will be one of the key issues to be addressed by personnel managers operating in the international arena in the future. There will gradually be a growing together of national practice on working hours, but it will take a great deal longer for rates of pay to harmonise. One can visualise common standards on health and safety developing much more quickly than equality of opportunity between the sexes and across ethnic divisions.

There seem to be games being played between governments and multinational companies:

> Corporations in the international arena…have no real desire to seek international rules and regulations…that would erode the differential competitive advantage which accrues as a consequence of astute locational decisions. Indeed the strategies are centred on endless negotiations, or the ability to play off the offer from one nation against that of another…Examples of this strategy can be found in the recent negotiations over CFC restrictions, ozone depletion and the preservation of the Amazon rain forest. (McGowan and Mahon 1992, p. 172)

Balance

This chapter closes with a reiteration of the comment made at several different points in this book about the need for balance in personnel work. There is an over-preoccupation with strategic issues, which is one of the main planks of HRM and which has also become an obsession with managers generally through the 1980s. For personnel managers it could be undermining their claim to some sort of quasi-professional, specific set of skills, as well as making employees' experience of management more remote and impersonal.

While it is clearly important for managers to avoid an over-preoccupation with procedural trivial, which reinforces the status quo and inhibits change,

> British Foreign Secretary Douglas Hurd recently made a neat comment about the European Community. Disparaging some of the grand ideas of certain other European statesmen, he said that Britain adopted the role of craftsman rather than visionary in all the discussions, asking the difficult questions and forcing other people to face up to the implications of their grand designs.
>
> That seems in many ways to be the essence of the personnel role in any commercial organisation: reacting positively and with constructive criticism to strategic plans about the direction of the business, so as to modify the plans and shape their implementation. Personnel people can only react, you can hardly devise a personnel strategy and then ask the marketing people to develop a marketing strategy to fit.

management is not all about strategy and personnel management has only a modest strategic element.

It is the operational or technical aspects of personnel management that require the skill and confer the status. Is there anything harder for a manager to do well than carry out a successful appraisal interview? Are there many more important jobs to be done than *explaining* strategy, or making the absolutely right appointment of someone to a key role? This is operational management for personnel specialists, yet so often we find that the personnel manager has retreated to the strategy bunker to think great thoughts and discuss the shape of the world with like-minded people consuming endless cups of coffee, while the appraisal and the selection and the communication is left to 'the line'. If you leave all the operational aspects to other people, there is precious little of personnel management left. This is not a plea to ignore strategy, but to put it into a perspective and recover the operational imperatives. One afternoon a week is ample for strategy.

In this concluding chapter we have suggested a few possibilities for the future. Personnel managers progressively need to develop a personal survival kit that will enable them to be effective in a wide variety of situations, becoming less organisationally dependent and more self-sufficient.

Future personnel managers will need a shrewd strategic sense and a set of operational managerial skills of the type that we have described in these pages. They will also need an ethical sense, able to set management action in its context, understanding the implications (as IPM put it) 'for the enterprise, each person and the community at large'. Many aspects of management work can be developed into a science: successful personnel management is an art.

☐ SUMMARY PROPOSITIONS

38.1 Personnel management will continue to thrive as a management specialism, despite constant criticism and untimely obituaries.

38.2 Much of the criticism is because of the social significance of personnel work and the interest commentators have in that, rather that in the technical aspects of the role.

38.3 In the United Kingdom the 1994 amalgamation of the Institute of Personnel Management and the Institute of Training and Development establishes a professional grouping of considerable significance and confirms the logical place of training and development as a feature of human resource management.

38.4 The importance of the new Institute of Personnel and Development is its network and codes of conduct. This prevents the practice of personnel management being no more than an exercise of competence: amoral and anti-social.

38.5 The practice of personnel management will increasingly run alongside the empowering of individual managers to provide expert monitoring, advice, information and support.

38.6 The substantial current investment in management training may need to be more evenly distributed across other types of training as well.

38.7 Personnel managers have particular challenges from information, both in dealing with how it alters personnel practice and in dealing with its implications for employment generally.

38.8 At the international level personnel managers will need to develop a human resource strategy that is both regional and global. Questions of different ethical standards will be a major challenge.

38.9 Although many aspect of management will be developed as a 'science', successful personnel management will continue to be an art.

References

Armstrong, P. (1989), 'Limits and possibilities for HRM in an age of management accountancy'. In J. Storey (ed.) *New Perspectives on Human Resource Management*, London: Routledge.

Becker, H. and Fritzsche, D. J. (1987), 'A comparison of the ethical behaviour of American, French and German managers', *Columbia Journal of World Business*, Winter, pp. 87–95.

Cole, R. E. and Deskins, D. R. (1988), 'Racial factors in site location and employment patterns of Japanese auto firms in America', *California Management Review*, Fall, p. 11.

Daniel, W. W. (1986), 'Four years of change for personnel', *Personnel Management*, vol. 18, no. 12, December, pp. 40–5.

Dowling, P. J. and Schuler, R. S. (1990), *International Dimensions of Human Resource Management*, Boston, Massachussets: PWS-Kent.

Flanders, A. (1964), *The Fawley Productivity Agreements*, p. 254. London: Faber & Faber.

Guest, D. E. (1987), 'Human resource management and industrial relations', in *Journal of Management Studies*, vol. 24, no. 5, pp. 505–12.

Guest, D. (1989), 'Personnel and HRM: can you tell the difference?', *Personnel Management*, January, vol. 21, no. 1. pp. 48–51.

Hart, T. J. (1993), 'Human Resource Management; time to exorcise the militant tendency', *Employee Relations*, vol. 15, no. 3, pp. 29–36.

Illich, I. (1981), *Shadow Work*, London: Marion Boyars.

Institute of Personnel Management (1993), *Annual Report*, London: Institute of Personnel Management.

Legge, K. (1978), *Power, Innovation and Problem-solving in Personnel Management*, Maidenhead: McGraw-Hill.

Legge, K. (1989), 'Human Resource Management: A critical analysis'. In J. Storey (ed.) *New Perspectives on Human Resource Management*, pp. 19–40. London: Routledge.

McGowan, R. A. and Mahon, J. F. (1992), 'Multiple games, multiple levels: gamesmanship and strategic corporate responses to environmental issues', *Business and the Contemporary World*, vol. 14, no. 4, pp. 162–77.

Murray, J. (1972), 'The role of the shop steward in industry'. In D. P. Torrington (ed.) *Handbook of Industrial Relations*, Epping, Essex: Gower.

Ohmae, K. (1985), *Triad Power, The Coming Shape of Global Competition*, London: Macmillan.

Personnel Standards Lead Body (PSLB) (1993), *An Occupational Survey of Those Working in Personnel*. London: PSLB.

Purcell, J. and Gray, A. (1986), 'Corporate personnel departments and the management of industrial relations', *Journal of Management Studies*, vol. 23, no. 2, pp. 205–23.

Schregle, J. (1981), 'Comparative industrial relations: pitfalls and potential', *International Labour Review*, vol. 120, no. 1, pp. 15–30.

Storey, J. (1992), *Developments in the Management of Human Resources*, Oxford: Blackwell.

Torrington, D. P. (1989), 'Human Resource Management and the personnel function'. In J. Storey (ed.) *New Perspectives on Human Resource Management*, p. 64. London: Routledge.

Torrington, D. P. and Tan Chwee Huat (1993), *Human Resource Management for South East Asia*. Singapore: Simon & Schuster.

Wokutch, R. E. (1990), 'Corporate social responsibility, Japanese style', *Academy of Management Executive*, May, pp. 56–72.

Index

absence 148–50, 631–7
ACAS *see* Advisory, Conciliation and Arbitration
    Service
Ackers, P. 136
administration manager 21
ADST *see* Approved Deferred Share Trust
advertising 217–20, 222–224, 357, 362
Advisory, Conciliation and Arbitration Service 9,
    251, 252, 264, 480, 539
job evaluation 585, 588, 593
trade unions 489, 493, 494
age 182, 369–70
AIDS counselling 566
Aikin, O. 226
*Al-Tikriti v. South Western Regional Health
    Authority* 256
Allan, J. 237
Allen, S. 623
Amar-Ojok v. Surrey 254
analysis 90–1, 150–1
Anderson, G.C. 382, 384
Anderson, N. 235
Ansoff, I. 30
Anstey, E. 284
Anthony 115
appeals *see* Employment Appeal Tribunal
    application forms 234–7
    appraisal 93, 377–88
    appraisers 380–1
    contrasted approaches 378–80
    effectiveness 387–8
    interview 381–7
    management development 433
    systems 319–28
        assessment centres 323
        behavioural scales 324–6
        by peers 322
        by subordinates 322–3
        contributors 320–1
        criteria development 327
        customers 323
        effectiveness 327–8

objectives 326–7
performance against job competencies 327
performance against job description 327
personality measures, avoidance of 324
purposes 319–20
self-appraisal 321–2
Approved Deferred Share Trust 611
aptitude tests 242
Ardrey, R. 642
Argyle, M. 172
Argyris, C. 295
Arkin, A. 360
Armstrong, M. 510, 576–7, 588, 590, 607
Armstrong, P. 672
Arthurs, A. 143–4
asbestos 516
assessment centres 244–5, 323, 367–8, 452–3
Athanasion, T. 458
Atkinson, J. 183–4, 185, 195, 663
attainment tests 242
attitude development 456
Atwater, L. 295
Austin, N. 292
Australia 118
Austria 119
autonomy 443, 600

Bacon, F. 404
Baird, L. 44
Banner, D.K. 339, 342
bargaining, collective 583
bargaining units 492–500, 586–7
Barham, K. 659
Barnes, R. 301
Barnett, J.G. 384
Barocci, T.A. 46
Barratt, A. 118
Barrett, B. 508, 512
Barron, H. 240–1
BARS *see* behaviour scales
Bartlett, A.F. 641–2
Bartlett, C.A. 660, 666–7

Harbour, T. 365
Hargreaves, L. 252, 265
Harlan, A. 446
Harris, M. 246
Harrison, R.G. 105, 242, 394, 461
Hart, T.J. 12, 497
Hartley, J. 294
Harvard model 54–5
Hawes, W.R. 496
Hawkins, P. 311, 312
Hay Guide Chart-Profile Method 590
Hayward, S. 622
Hayward v. Cammell Laird 593
Health and Safety at Work Act 495, 502, 504,
    507, 508, 509–16
Control of Substances Hazardous to Health
    Regulations 507, 513–14
Health and Safety Commission 505, 508, 509,
    510, 512
Health and Safety (Display Screen Equipment)
    Regulations 515
Health and Safety Executive 509, 513
Health and Safety Signs Directive 516
health, safety and welfare 20, 502–21
    definitions 502–3
    development and importance 503–6
    employee 156, 511
    legislation 506–9
    management 516–21
    occupational 519–20
    personnel department activities 505
    programmes 521
Health and Social Security Act 632
Hearn, A. 622
Heavy Loads Directive 515
Heim 242
Hendry, C. 44, 55–6, 67, 394, 401
Henley, J.S. 511
Hepple, B.A. 254
Herriot, P. 231
Hickson, D.J. 119
Hilton International Hotels Ltd v. Prototapa 263
Hitt, M. 293
Hodge, L. 393
Hodgson, V.E. 429, 430
Hoerr, J. 336
Hofer, C.W. 27
Hofstede, G. 118, 119, 120, 121, 662
Holden, L. 482
Holden, N.J. 70
Holding, D.H. 467
Hollis, W.P. 242
Hollister v. The National Farmer's Union 261
Homans, G.C. 640–1
Honey, P. 424–5, 431
Honeycutt, A. 301, 302
Hong Kong 119, 120
Hopegood, J. 621
Hopfl, H. 74

horns effect 132
Housing Benefits Act 631
Howells, R. 508
HRM *see* human resource management
Huczynski, A.A. 148
Hulbert, J.M. 72
human attribute classifications systems 232
human resource 20, 54, 82, 92
    management 10–14, 671, 674–5, 681
        business strategy 29
        Butler's unified model 50
        Harvard framework 55
        internationalisation 666, 669
        involvement 483
        performance 293, 294–5
        policies 45, 46
        regional management 678
        and strategic change 56
    strategy 44–61, 306
        definition 44–7
        and development 398–9
        formal models 53–7
        learning and change 59–61
        organisational strategy, interaction with 47–9
        personnel function role 49–52
        themes 58–9
        visioning 76
Hungary 73
Hunt, D.M. 427, 428
Hunt, P. 629
Hurd, D. 682
Hurley, B. 136
Husband, T.M. 588
Hussey, D. 77
Hutchinson, S. 186
Hyman, R. 660

identity 117, 443
IDS 200, 585, 615, 619
IIP *see* Investors in People
Iles, P. 245, 247, 294, 396
Illich, I. 676
ILO *see* Internal Labour Organisation
improvement notices 512
incapacity from work 632, 633
incentives 569–70, 596–617
    control 598–9
    cost 599–600
    employee expectations 600–6
    managerial expectations 597–8
    motivational theories 598
    payment systems 567
    see also benefits; performance-related pay
income 478
Incomes Data Services 610, 612, 623, 627, 630,
    633
independence 109, 111, 112, 443
individualism 118–19
Indonesia 119

induction 536
Industrial Democracy, Committee of Inquiry on 479
industrial relations 136, 488
Industrial Relations Act 251, 252, 479, 493
Industrial Relations Commission 496, 498, 499–500
Industrial Relations Review and Report 136, 137
Industrial Relations Services 579, 585, 586, 590
Industrial Society 136, 402
Industry Act 495
inefficiencies, operational 604
information 143–60, 144–6
  aggregate employee 148–54
  computers 73, 143–4, 146, 159
  confidentiality 158
  exchange 273
  grievance and discipline 536, 541
  individual employee 146–7
  organisation and strategy 71–4
  personnel 144–6, 154–6, 157
  privacy 158
  security 160
  technology 111, 112, 308–9, 432, 675–7
Inland Revenue 612, 615, 622–3
INSEAD 119
Institute of Directors 624
Institute of Personnel Management 50–1, 606, 610, 612, 624, 672–7, 682
  appraisal 377
  communication 130
  competencies 409
  ethics and social responsibility 679
  and gender equality 359
  grievance and discipline 535
  incentives 601
  members 370
  organisational performance 302, 304, 306
  resourcing 186
  selection 239
Internal Labour Organisation 589
internal movements analysis 89–91
International Sports Co. Ltd v. Thomson 257
internationalisation 659–69
  communication 667–9
  cosmopolitans 662–3
  culture 663
  economic development 663
  engineer 664–5
  expatriates 663
  geographical location 664
  human resource management 669
  job 664
  management implications 660–2
  organisational co–ordination 666–7
interview
  appraisal 380, 381–3
  disciplinary 554–7
  factual 385–6
  and gender equality 358

grievance 551–4
  racial equality 363
  sequence 383–4
  structure 384–7
  see also selection
Investors in People 72, 483–4
involvement 303, 475–86
  employee 476–81
  investors in people 483–4
  strategy 484–5
  team briefing 481–2
  Total Quality Management 482–3
IPD 357, 507, 514
IPM see Institute of Personnel Management
Ireland 659
Ireland, D. 293
IRS see Industrial Relations Services
Irwin 345
Isabella, L.A. 428, 429, 430
IT see information technology
Italy 667
Itzin, C. 370
Ive, T. 144

Jackson, B.W. 370
Jackson, D.L. 77
Jackson, J.H. 530
Jackson, S.E. 45, 46
Jacobs, R. 413
James, P. 502
Japan 405
  ethics and social responsibility 680–1
  information and communication 72
  internationalisation 661
  involvement 483
  job evaluation 585
  organisational performance 301
  performance 292
  regional management 678
  structure and culture 117, 118, 120
Jaques, E. 563, 585
jargon 132
Jarman, J. 353
Jeffery, J.R. 303
Jenkins, J.F. 223, 230
Jenkins, R. 364
Jenks, J.M. 276
Jessel, D. 115
JIT see just in time
job
  analysis questionnaires 591
  competencies 327
  criteria, individual 232–3
  definition 103
  description 215, 221, 224, 327, 328, 519, 591
  duties 221
  evaluation 358, 579–94
    bargaining units 586–7
    differentials 580
    employee participation 590–4

Stewart, A. 321, 326, 327
Stewart, R. 420
Stewart, V. 321, 326, 327
Stoner, J.A.F. 24, 69, 483
Storey, J. 29, 44, 49, 225, 306, 481, 674, 680
strategy 28–30, 45, 50, 190, 306, 484–5
    see also human resource; organisation/
        organisational
Strauss, G. 131
strengths *see* SWOT
structure and culture 101–24
    alternative forms 105–9, 111
    corporate 114–15
    development 121–4
    differentiated 110–13
    international context 117–21
    national context 116
    organisation/organisational 102–5, 114, 120
Stumpf, S.A. 428
style 533–4
sub-contracting 202–3, 214
succession planning 90
Super, D.E. 438
suspension 537
Swallow, P. 394, 401
Sweden 333, 481
Sweetland, R.C. 242
Swinburne, P. 242–3
SWOT (strengths, weaknesses, opportunities,
    threats) 33–4

Taiwan 120
Takako Doi 661
Tan Chwee Huat 577, 678, 681
Tannenbaum, R. 644
Tanton, M. 401
Tarpey, T. 245
task identity 103
Tatsuoka, M.M. 243
Taylor, D.S. 386
Taylor, F.W. 8, 601
Taylor, G.S. 322
teaching 455–71
    job instruction 464–71
    learner types 458–63
    learning, approaches to 455–7
Teague, P. 476
team briefing 135–8, 481–2
team performance 333–47
    effectiveness 342–6
    interchangeability 335
    personnel function implications 346–7
    task and functional range 335–6
    time span 334–5
    types 336–42
technology 583
    see also information
tele-cottaging 111–12
telephone screening 237–8
teleworking 111

Temporary Workers Directive 514
testing 238–43
Thomason, G. 11
Thompson 373
Thompson, L. 157
Thompson, M. 328, 330
threats *see* SWOT
Thurley, K. 292
Thurstone, L.L. 242
Tichy, N.M. 48, 53–4, 112
Tiger, L. 115
time-saving, individual 601–2
Timperley, S.R. 87
tips 603–4
Tomlinson committee 367
top-hat schemes 627
Torrington, D.P. 12, 15, 21, 130, 143, 207, 320,
    383, 413, 421, 456, 475, 481, 504, 577,
    672, 678, 681
Total Quality Management 72
    communication 128
    involvement 482–3
    organisational performance 300–7, 309, 311
    performance 295, 297
Toulson, N. 622
Townley, B. 136
TQM *see* Total Quality Management
Trade Union and Employment Rights Act 356–7
Trade Union and Labour Relations Act 495
Trade Union and Labour Relations
    (Consolidation) Act 262
trade union recognition 488–500
    bargaining units 492–500
        contract 499–500
        eligibility 493
        legislation 494–5
        management 495–8
        organisation, communication and
            responsibility 499
        organisational strategy 497
        preparation 498–9
        reasons 492–3
    collective consent 490–2
Trade Union Reform and Employment Rights Act
    493
Trades Union Congress 488
trainability tests 242
training 303, 345
    activities 155–6
    courses 422–4
    and development 20, 399, 401–2
    grievance and discipline 536
    and management development plans 93
    programme 613
Training Commission 402
    see also Manpower Services Commission
transfer 630–1
Transfer of Undertakings Regulations 262, 495
Trevithick, B. 279
Truelove, S. 455